Joey Adams'
Encyclopedia
of Humor

BONANZA BOOKS • NEW YORK

Contents

Books by
Joey Adams

GAGS TO RICHES

THE CURTAIN NEVER FALLS

JOEY ADAMS JOKE BOOK

STRICTLY FOR LAUGHS

IT TAKES ONE TO KNOW ONE

JOEY ADAMS JOKE DICTIONARY

CINDY AND I

ON THE ROAD FOR UNCLE SAM

JOEY ADAMS' ROUND THE WORLD JOKE BOOK

L.B.J. TEXAS LAUGHS

HOW TO MAKE AND TELL JOKES FOR ALL OCCASIONS

THE BORSCHT BELT

YOU COULD DIE LAUGHING

Part One ☞

Choose Your Weapons

WIT, HUMORIST, STORYTELLER, SATIRIST, OR CLOWN?

No matter what you are trying to peddle, the first thing you must do is sell yourself. It's the same thing in comedy. But in order to sell yourself, you must make sure you know just what it is you are.

You must decide what kind of comic you want to be. Are you a wit, a humorist, storyteller, satirist, or clown? These are the basic types. But there are other categories, such as Ed Sullivan, who was described by the great wit Fred Allen as a "pointer." He doesn't do anything except "point" to the actor to go into his act. Arthur Godfrey calls himself a "personality" who gets a few laughs. There is still another species we could come up with if we were to cross an Arthur Godfrey with, say, a Fred Allen . . . the result would be Steve Allen, or Jack Paar, or Johnny Carson, or Mike Douglas, or Merv Griffin—a personality with a wit. Of course, there are also spin-offs, like the double-talker or the punster.

In this era of specialists, you must choose your specialty carefully if you want to be a hit with the public. Nowadays they have doctors who specialize only in right-handed thumbs or palmists who read only knuckles.

The parlor or table comic who wears his wife's hat could find himself in enemy territory if he tries to use the same old wheezes in the outside world. You can't always depend on the reaction of your family. But even there you should know your subject as well as your subjects. Tell Mamma a sexy joke and she may throw you out of the house, but the same fireball at a stag may bring down the house.

The guys at the office may scream at you when you deliberately take that pratfall or the pie in the face, even if your maiden aunt doesn't find it amusing. On the other hand, the gang at the house may howl at your family barbs even if the boys at the club don't get it.

In other words, you've got to find out first what is funny and second what is funny for you—they do not necessarily go together. Ed Wynn used to prove it in his act. In his funniest sketch, his straightman came out in the middle of the stage and told three of Ed's favorite stories while Ed watched from the proscenium. All the man got with the stories were polite snickers.

3

Then he turned to Ed and asked, "What's wrong? When you tell these same stories they get big laughs."

"Oh," Ed said, "maybe the audience doesn't think you're funny—*or* the joke."

"Well," he asked, "what *is* funny?"

"Darned if I know," Ed said. Then he walked over and, taking the new straw hat off the man's head, admired it and asked him if he liked it.

"Sure," he said, "it's expensive. . . ."

And as Ed was talking he took out a huge knife and cut the hat to pieces, leaving only the crown, which he gravely put back on the man's head.

Then Ed asked him, "Do you think that's funny?" The reply could be heard in the next town: "No!" Ed pointed to the audience, which had greeted each slice of the hat with a roar—"Look, *they* think it's funny."

And while the poor man was still protesting, Ed cut off his tie and dropped it on stage. Then he cut off all his coat buttons, and as the unhappy soul grabbed his coat, Ed cut his suspenders. Then, while the man was trying to hold up his pants and the audience was falling out of their seats laughing, the Perfect Fool asked: "Do you think *that's* funny?"

"No! No!" howled the man.

Then Ed pointed to the audience as he walked off and said, "Look—*they* do!"

The point of all this is, firstly, what's funny for one may not be funny for another, and secondly, maybe you should stick to being a straightman or a storyteller instead of a clown—or vice versa.

Choose your style and choose it well if you want to be the hit of the party. Are you a wit, a humorist, storyteller, satirist, or clown? Perhaps, like the man who went to the Turkish Baths, this book will help you find yourself.

THE WIT

Wit is the most respected form of comedy. A brilliant wit has always been regarded by his less endowed fellows as an uncrowned king. He is quoted even by his rivals, and posterity continues to repeat his sayings like the Proverbs from the Bible.

The influence of such men has been great—for both good and evil. To be able to seize the words of friend or foe and twist them around to turn the laugh in one's own favor—that's wit.

Any character, given time and topic, can, by hard work and research, come up with something that can pass as humor. But only the most brilliant minds can come up against an opponent who has taken basic training in the joke files and is ready to kill, and eliminate him with one cutting line.

Of course, it's very easy to be witty tomorrow, after you get a chance to do some research and rehearse your ad libs. If only the attacker could be induced to wait a day or two!

The wit thinks while he's talking, or, even worse, while you're talking. At one party for Elizabeth Taylor, the toastmaster opened the ceremonies by toasting, "Tonight we present the lives and loves of Elizabeth Taylor." Jack E. Leonard interrupted, "Relax, folks—we're gonna be here a long time."

Groucho Marx was sitting in a hotel lobby when an attractive woman approached and asked, "Are you Harpo Marx?" Groucho sizzled, "No, are you?"

When Winston Churchill was a young man he was growing a mustache. The young lady who was to be his dinner companion didn't seem to appreciate the future Prime Minister. "Mr. Churchill," she remarked, "I care for neither your politics nor your mustache."

"Don't distress yourself," Churchill replied. "You are not likely to come in contact with either."

A true wit transforms experience into humor. He doesn't tell jokes—just spins a humorous web of life and expression. But when he catches someone in this web the laugh is at the other's expense. Some people call Oscar Levant a "sick wit." He spares nobody, including himself. "They asked me to be on 'This is your life,' " he remarked, "but they couldn't find one friend." Levant had a typical Oscar for the sweet Dinah Shore. "I can't watch her," he said. "I have diabetes."

Henry (acid wouldn't melt in his mouth) Morgan explains Levant away by saying, "People who watch Oscar are like people who stand on street corners waiting for an accident to happen."

A wit's bite can be far worse than a snake's, but he must have people around to watch him needle. Without an audience he is like a bandmaster whose band didn't show up. What's he going to do with the baton?

Fred Allen waited until everybody turned on his radio before he got angry: "If the United States can get along with one Vice-President, I don't know why NBC needs twenty-six."

Will Rogers turned his wit on the entire government: "We are a nation that runs in spite of and not on account of our government—yep, the U.S. never lost a war or won a conference."

President John F. Kennedy used his great wit on all—including family, friends, foes, press, and himself. Barry Goldwater is an excellent photographer. The former Presidential candidate took a good picture of Kennedy and sent it to him for an autograph. Then Kennedy inscribed it, "For Barry Goldwater, whom I urge to follow the career for which he has shown so much talent—photography. From his friend, John Kennedy."

At one point when Kennedy was asked to comment on the press treatment of his Administration, he replied: "Well, I'm reading more and enjoying it less."

Like the true wit he was, nobody escaped his bite—not even his family: "I see nothing wrong with giving Bobby some legal experience as Attorney General before he goes out to practice law."

LITTLE BOY: "Mr. President, how did you become a war hero?"
KENNEDY: "It was absolutely involuntary. They sunk my boat."

There is no weapon more feared by man than ridicule, and no wounds take longer to heal than those caused by the tongue. Will Rogers, singlehandedly, scared more people in Washington than all the house detectives put together—with nothing more than his caustic wit. Voltaire was feared more than any other man in Europe because of his cutting tongue. Fred Allen has made many an opponent quake when he was ready to attack: "Jack Benny is the only fiddler who makes you feel that the strings would sound better back in the cat."

You don't have to be a college graduate to be a wit. It doesn't matter if you're prince or pauper—rich man, poor man, beggar man, comic. If you are capable of that one-punch knockout under attack, you have a brilliant mind and, naturally, a brilliant wit. Now would you call yourself a wit? Are you the type who gets bugged when the headwaiter sees you standing with just your girl friend and asks, "How many?" Do you get the urge to purr, "Seventy-eight, please"?

Are you the kind of character who crouches in a theatre and when a friend approaches and asks, "What are you doing here?" you answer, "I'm hunting tigers"? Or when the switchboard operator sings, "May I ask who is calling?" do you jab back with, "No, you may not!"

Well, if you get a kick out of things like that, you have the makings of a wit . . . maybe.

THE HUMORIST

The humorist is a storyteller who doesn't let you take yourself too seriously. The world is better because these fellows laugh at it on every front.

While the wit is more aggressive and destroying, a humorist just pokes fun at the daily happenings as they unfold. The wit does it with a sword, but the humorist uses a pen—caricaturing the world as he sees it, for fun rather than abuse. Humorist Herb Shriner comments about his Indiana home town: "Well, usually it's pretty slow weekdays, but on Saturday we go down and watch 'em give haircuts." Herb likes to talk about his travels. "Of course I've been to Europe. I was there during the War; you know about World War II, don't you? It was in all the papers."

One of the great humorists of all time was the legendary Mark Twain. He was able to put the world on just by writing the story as he saw it, and we have been laughing ever since. Of course, like all stars, he was never a hero in his own neighborhood. One old crony discounted the glory and fame of his

6

erstwhile school chum: "Shucks," he said, "I knew as many stories as Sam Clemens; he jist writ 'em down."

In his reporting days, Mark Twain was instructed by an editor never to state anything as a fact that he could not verify from personal knowledge. Sent out to cover an important social event some time later, he turned in this story: "A woman giving the name of Mrs. James Jones, who is reported to be one of the society leaders of the city, is said to have given what purported to be a party yesterday to a number of alleged ladies. The hostess claims to be the wife of a reputed attorney."

Twain could be as biting as the sharpest wit. About an alleged friend he said: "I admire him, I frankly confess it; and when his time comes I shall buy a piece of the rope for a keepsake."

The humorist doesn't care too much if he doesn't get big laughs—just big money. He'll settle for a smile or a chuckle or even a pat on the head, depending on what's in your fist when you're patting him. He is not as bitchy as the wit and he makes use of longer comments rather than the short hard-hitting stabs.

Another thing: the humorist comes prepared with categories of jokes or stories, whereas the wit relies on quick thinking to capitalize on the immediate situation. You might be able to spot the humorist as the guy who leaves the room—to dig up remarks he can ad-lib later. Then again, he might just be going to the john—or both.

Let me make this clear. A good wit *should* have his material or routines ready when he is called on. Then his extemporaneous wit will be the plus-factor that makes him stand out from the others. The humorist *must* be prepared. Of course, like Mark Twain and Will Rogers, the wit and humorist are often entwined. Nobody was faster than Rogers as a wit, but he could also paint with words a picture that was always an amusing and often a hysterical caricature of life.

"I must tell you about Venice," he said after a trip to Europe. "Say, what a fine swamp that Venice, Italy, turned out to be. I stepped out of the wrong side of a Venice taxicab and . . . they were three minutes fishing me out. . . . I got seasick crossing an alley."

Sam Levenson is the happiest humorist in America. He is the first to laugh at his own comic observation of life. You must join him in laughter when he talks about the mountains—and I don't mean the Himalayas:

"Comes July 4th, the Jewish population of New York declares its independence and goes off to the Catskill mountains. There's a long, long trail a-winding along Route 17 on a straight white line made of pure sour cream, heading north in search of oxygen, pickled herring, pinochle under the elms, or romance among the radish blossoms.

"The young element knocks itself out on the athletic field and the old folks rock and groan and sigh and exchange diets and Sal Hepatica and recommend doctors and boast about their children and complain about the bedbugs and lack of fellers for their 'heiresses.' "

JOKE TELLER

The most common form of comedian is the joke teller and his first cousin the gag man. They specialize in retailing humor that they bought wholesale—or stole retail.

The long-winded joke teller or storyteller follows a slightly different set of rules. Myron Cohen, Lou Holtz, Harry Hershfield, Georgie Jessel, and Sam Levenson are all masters of the long story or anecdote. With them it's not so much the success of the punch line but the build-up that keeps them healthy and working. It's the way they tell the joke that counts.

The storytellers are masters of vivid description, perfect dialect, and detailed character sketches, and present a joke as clear as a technicolor cinemascope movie. Storytellers like Lou Holtz with his Sam Lapidus, Sam Levenson with his family anecdotes, and Myron Cohen with his garment center tales, have always relied heavily on dialect as their strongest technique.

Myron kills people with the story of the happy couple celebrating their 25th wedding anniversary at their sumptuous home on Long Island. Everybody was happy—that is everybody but the husband. He was glum. When his lawyer came in to congratulate him on his silver anniversary, the husband screamed, "You louze! You doidy dug! You bum! Remember when I waz married only five years to dot doidy skunk, end I esked you waht would heppen if I stick a knife in her—and you said I would get twenty years in jail? Vell, tonight I would have been a free man!"

Who cares about punch lines when Myron uses dialogue like: "Nu Sadie, I got to go now, if I live I'll see you Wednesday. If not, Thursday." Or, "You so crooked, dat de wool you're pulling over mine eyes is 50 per cent cotton."

THE GAG MAN

The gag man is a different breed entirely. He throws lines from any angle and it doesn't matter whose they are or where they came from or where they're going. Henny Youngman starts with a line like, "My wife has a nice even disposition—miserable all the time!" and then continues for no reason at all, "Which reminds me: I love Christmas—I receive a lot of wonderful presents I can't wait to exchange." He could use these jokes at a dinner for Cardinal Spellman, a roast for Governor Rockefeller, or a Bar Mitzvah in the Bronx.

Now, don't take Henny's success as the example to follow—he is the mistake that proves the rule. You should be able to throw gags from any angle, but you must have a direction—the right jokes for the right situation and the right time.

Modern gag men like Joey Bishop, Alan King, Buddy Hackett, and Jackie Kannon are pretty good wits as well, but they are always ready with their studied monologues:

"The new Israeli air line is great!" Alan King says in his prepared routine. "They don't have stewardesses as we know them. They have little old ladies giving out fruit.

"Then you hear the voice on the loudspeaker say, 'Your stewardesses are Mrs. Rose Goldberg and Mrs. Fannie Schwartz and of course, my son the pilot.'"

Joey Bishop is great if he is challenged, but until then he is set with his bag of gags:

"My family was so poor we couldn't give my sister a Sweet Sixteen party until she was twenty-eight.

"When I performed in Washington for the President, I didn't stay at the White House. My mother wasn't crazy about the neighborhood."

Buddy Hackett writes most of his material and it's usually from his own experiences. Even though he is one of the truly talented wits, he does not take any chances and is ready with his routines:

"I remember I was driving and I hit a motorcycle cop. He walked over to me with a big grin on his face—ear to ear. He had the handle bars stuck in his mouth."

Jackie Kannon is like the proverbial bride. He always has "something old, something new, something borrowed, something blue":

"Russians will never land in New York," he starts from a borrowed routine, "they'll never get a parking place."

You can always depend on Milton Berle to dig up the old ones. Like antiques—in his hands they are more valuable:

"I just got back from Lindy's—I always go there for a cup of coffee and an overcoat.

"My girl is so skinny—she swallowed an olive and four men left town.

"What is this, an audience or a jury?—I know you're out there—I hear breathing.

"I was an old newspaperman—but I found there was no money in old newspapers."

Bob Hope is the smoothest gag man in town—but it takes a dozen writers to get him ready for those ad libs as he says:

"Think of it—it took the wagon trains six months to get across the country. Today they send rockets millions of miles into space and back in fifteen minutes. But nobody is watching. They're all home watching 'Wagon Train' on television."

A good gag man must be a good gag collector. Joe Miller, the proverbial whipping boy of jokes, actually lived, but not as good as the comics who have lived off him since. Actually, Joe Miller was neither a comic nor the originator of a single comedy line—he was strictly a collector. Yet he is known as the father of the most popular joke book ever published, and the alleged author of every jest in this past generation.

Thievery is a matter of degree; if you steal one joke, it's called plagiarism; if you borrow hundreds of them, and compile them in a book—it's called research. Milton Berle became a professor of research. He often billed himself as the "Thief of Bad Gags."

"Unlike myself," Milton says, "Youngman never stole from the top comedians—he stole from the unknowns, a word which later became synonymous with his career. The greatest form of flattery is imitation, and one of Henny's unusual talents is that he is flattered by the fact that for many years he has been an imitation of a comedian."

The fact is that Henny is an original in a sea of carbons—hailed as the King of the One-Liners—although I wouldn't exactly compare them to the ones Moses carried on the Tablet.

So, be a gag collector—listen to your friends, the salesman that comes calling, the comics on radio and television. Get the joke book collections that come out every day, get yourself a scissors and paste and clip the jokes out of the Broadway columns. Study them. Learn how to use them. Then store them away for the right time and the right home.

When you become a professional, you can buy your gags from the gag writers who get them the same way.

DOUBLE-TALK

One of the rare forms of comedy storytelling is double-talk. I can best explain it by saying—it's like reading an eye chart. If you should meet a fugitive from the English language who says, "I am Charley Imglick and I'd like javlin with my liebst. Can you get me a rabinald or a flang?" don't get hysterical and run to the nearest ear doctor or blame the acoustics or figure you've lost your mind—you have just been introduced to double-talk.

Except for a handful of double-talk artists like Cliff Nazarro, Sid Gary, and of course Al Kelly, most of this art was used for play or rib, rather than professionally. Sid Gary loves to put the town on—to the amusement of his pals. Sid dropped into a one-armed restaurant with a couple of Friars. "We'll have three filbers and coffee," he said to the counter man. The latter repeated the order to the chef exactly as he heard it: "Three filbers and coffee." He figured let the chef worry. Four minutes later the chef stuck his head out of the hole and said, "We're all outta filbers—how about crullers?"

The most common forms of double-talk are:

1. Fade-Away Double: the voice of the speaker keeps getting softer and softer until your ears are practically in his mouth.

2. Fractured English: the right words put in the wrong places. The speaker sounds like he's breaking in a new set of teeth. "I like the with all the should not if he comes or not—and that goes whether he is Republican or Democrat!"

3. Drowned English: the speaker says nothing—but with expression! "Together we shall crant—and nothing—nothing can make us roist the pranit of all the millions—wherever they are—and that goes for the Mides *or* the Zermans!"

Try it on your friends before you try it on stage—and if your friends understand you—believe me, you better change friends.

THE CLOWN

The clown, even with his mouth closed, can overwhelm an audience with his antics. He sees life as though it were reflected in a fun-house mirror, with all its weird and exaggerated effects. A clown will take things out of life and distort them, twist them, blow them up, or mold them in any way to achieve his goal. Charlie Chaplin reversed a real-life situation when he once sat down next to an elderly woman. He glanced at her and she immediately gave him a contemptuous look, whereupon Chaplin slapped *her*. There was nothing too sacred back in the days of Chaplin and W. C. Fields, when they would reverse life situations by kicking dogs, children and old ladies. Today a comedian would never dare attempt this before an audience. Most of them wait till they get home to do these things.

Another technique of the clown was to start with a small incident and build it until it approaches huge proportions. Laurel and Hardy were famous for this. In one of their pictures they were caught in a traffic jam on the highway, with cars lined up bumper to bumper. Laurel and Hardy accidentally bumped the car ahead of them, which touched off a chain reaction resulting in complete chaos: people fighting, ripping off fenders, breaking windows, throwing fruit, smashing cars, until the entire scene looked like an auto junk yard. These guys were capable of starting a world war by merely stopping to tie their shoes.

W. C. Fields used a similar building technique in his famous golf game, where for eighteen minutes he prepared to strike the ball—and never did get around to hitting it.

Chaplin employed a still different type of build in his role as a waiter. In going from the kitchen to the customer's table Chaplin had to cross a large dance floor with a roast duck. As Chaplin stepped out onto the dance floor the orchestra struck up and the floor suddenly became crowded with people, engulfing Chaplin, so that all we could see was the tray of roast duck, held high in the air, bouncing all around the floor. Some college letter men show up and eventually the whole thing turns into a football game, with Chaplin carrying the roast duck tucked neatly under his arm.

You might have noticed that in all of these examples each clown created a certain amount of tension, leaving the audience in an anxious state of mind. That is, would Chaplin ever reach his customer with the roast duck? Or would W. C. ever hit the golf ball? Through the antics of the comic this tension is relieved, and the result is laughter.

When the clown goes into his act, he invariably uses a prop, whether it be a hat or a bobby pin. Very often a clown will speak little or no dialogue, so the prop aids him in conveying thoughts, ideas, etc. Chaplin used his cane as part of his character, showing that he is a little man who needs "a cane to lean on." However, he also would find broader uses, like poking people with it, hooking it on a railing, tripping someone with it, etc. A clown will find a million and one uses for his prop, depending on his character and his immediate surroundings.

Another characteristic of the clown is that he will go to any extreme to get that laugh. Jerry Lewis has walked into a swimming pool with all his clothes on, just for a laugh. In the movie "Casablanca," Harpo Marx was leaning against a building when Groucho came up and asked him if he was holding it up. Harpo smiled, walked away—and the entire building collapsed. Charlie Chaplin in one of his films was on the job at a shipyard when the foreman told him to find a small piece of wood. Chaplin looked all over but couldn't find one, until he spotted the piece he was looking for under some pilings. Chaplin proceeded to pry loose the piece of wood. He finally yanked it out from beneath the pilings and then to his horror looked up and discovered he had launched a huge ship, as it went sailing down the launching platform.

From Emmett Kelly to Olson and Johnson to Red Skelton we've roared from the first bust in the mouth to the last pratfall. If we were to take a situation, for example, just setting a door on the stage, and put to work all our great clowns, here's what might happen:

Charlie Chaplin would approach the door and before he could open it, a large fat lady would come through from the other side. She would become wedged in the threshold as Chaplin stood watching her struggle to get through the narrow opening of the doorway. He would attempt to help by trying to pry her loose with his cane and soon become entangled with her, pinned between her and the doorway. Unable to move and almost suffocating, he'd then try to push her out, but find a tough time locating a spot at which he could apply pressure.

Abbott would open the door in Costello's face and then Costello, holding his nose, would proceed to walk right into the wall next to the door.

A closed door for Olson and Johnson is a simple feat. They would merely have three midgets, two giants, and a two-headed monster take a battering ram and knock the door down.

Laurel would go to open the door, but Hardy would stop him, insisting that he go through first. Hardy would then open the door first, only to have a bucket of water fall on his head.

Red Skelton, in his drunken stupor, would stagger up to the door and start pulling frantically on the knob. He'd pull and pull until a sweet little old lady would appear. Skelton would tip his hat as she opened the door inward, to Red's dismay.

Jacques Tati, the great French clown, would walk up to the door, begin to turn the knob, only to have it come off in his hand.

PUNS

"The pun is the lowest form of humor," says Oscar Levant, "when you don't think of it first."

Many comics use it in their act. Even now when Jessel reminisces in his act, which is always, he says, "I remember the old days—they were more romantic. I remember when Fanny was a girl's name, when a Pansy was a beautiful little flower, when they had fine restaurants like Churchills and Resienwebers—now they got One Lung Huey, Two Lung Fooey. . . ."

The pun is a definite form of wit—bravely defended by those who use it, even though they duck when they pun-ish you with it—and violently opposed by those who find it "punfull."

Oddly enough the master pun-lover is a civilian called Frank Berend who makes pro and amateur alike cringe with his jests—jest to keep them baited.

"This girl is so dumb," Frank says, "I told her something with two meanings and she didn't understand either."

Frank and I were having a drink at a bar in Copenhagen. I raised my glass in a toast. "Skoal," I said. "It should be!" he answered. "There's ice in it."

When a doctor at the March of Dimes was talking to my pun-pal, he was told that there were definite hormones around. What a chance for his art. "Do you want to hear a hormone?—don't pay her."

Nobody kicks harder than these punsters. A diplomat met an American woman at a reception. She did not know him and asked sweetly, "What nese are you—Japanese, Chinese, or Javanese?"

"I'm Japanese, madam. What kee are you?—Monkee, Donkee, or Yankee?"

The punsters have infiltrated the highest places. Why, some of my pest friends are ready to jump u-pun me if I give them the slightest o-pun-ing.

Somebody from his embassy was looking all over town for Syngman

Rhee. When he finally found him at a local restaurant he chanted in relief, "Ah, sweet Mr. Rhee of life, at last I've found you."

The renowned song writer Richard Rodgers loved to challenge friends that they couldn't list four islands whose names are complete questions. The answer—are you ready?—Hawaii, Jamaica, Samoa, and Staten Island.

SATIRE

There is an uprising in the comedy world instigated by the angry young men of show business. Some of them are angry old men, but the one thing they have in common is that they are all steamed. Like any volcano that's ready to burst, they've got to open their mouths to let the hot air out.

These angry comics don't bother with the American humorists' surface irritations, like women drivers, parking, mothers-in-law, or nagging wives. These so-called sick comics have been packing night spots and theatres with customers who come to read their fever charts in public. They find humor in such taboos as religion, politics, homosexuality, dope addiction and matricide.

This satire stuff isn't exactly new. Men like Henry Morgan were picking on the world before some of our angry young comics were in it. Many claim that the perturbed, social-critic funnymen trace hunks of their material and attitudes back to the old Henry Morgan diatribes against society in the early days of radio.

The sound and fuming of Mort Sahl have reached into the highest places. His mental processes have been defined as irreverent with an extra dose of social satire:

"I am against analysis, along with the Church and the Communist Party, because it turns you against your folks. On the other hand, I always enjoy Arthur Miller because before the second act is over, I get a chance to hit my father. The best thing about analysis is that if you don't make it with 'em, they'll refer you to another analyst. They call it rehabilitation-referral-motivation therapy. We call it fee-splitting."

Dick Gregory is more than angry—he's furious. His impact is derived from satire based on the racial situation:

"I understand there are a good many Southerners in the room tonight. I know the South well. I spent twenty years there one night. It's dangerous for me to go back—I don't even like to work the southern part of this room. You see, when I drink, I think I'm Polish. One night I got so drunk I moved out of my *own* neighborhood! The last time I was down South I went to visit my brother in Biloxi. But I got there too late.

"I walked into a restaurant and this white waitress said: 'We don't serve colored people in here!' 'That's all right,' I said, 'I don't eat 'em—bring me a whole fried chicken.' About that time three 'cousins' came up to me and said,

14

'Boy, we're warning you: anything you do to that chicken—we will do to you!' 'Okay,' I said, putting down my knife and fork, 'y'all line up,' and I kissed it on the last part that goes over the fence."

One of the comic proponents of social significance was "The Rebel With a Caustic Cause," Lenny Bruce. He went out of this world only recently fighting every step of the way:

"By any moralistic yardstick, Jimmy Walker was certainly a more heinous figure than some poor schlub I read about that breaks into a warehouse and steals a couple of tires. So, the public raises its eyebrows at this handcuffed, unshaven villain, and Hollywood eulogizes Walker by making a picture of his life. It's the old cliche: there's no such thing as a little pregnant." Lenny admitted, "We're all hustlers—we're all as honest as we can afford to be."

Another member of the satiric society is a very literate comedian called Shelley Berman who says he is angry at nobody—it just turns out that way. Shelley picks on everything from buttermilk to flying:

"I don't like buttermilk—it's not the buttermilk that bothers me—it's the way the glass looks when you're through that makes me sick."

"Air lines are always bragging about their safety records: 'Flying is the safest way to travel.' I don't know how much consideration they have given to walking.

"Propaganda efforts on the part of the commercial air lines are terribly confusing. I haven't the slightest doubts about my safety in a plane, until I walk into an airport terminal and realize there is a thriving industry in this building selling life insurance policies—good for one flight—which is very cautious. They have booths selling them—even slot machines. I may be confident about landing safely but there is a serious doubt in somebody's mind that I can make it."

Phil Leeds is an old veteran of the angry society—his satire is devastating:

"It's easy to get work nowadays if you work cleaner, better, and cheaper than anybody else.

"I come from a neighborhood where the only sound you hear is an occasional call for help. When I was a kid, my living room was decorated as a swamp.

"I started in show business by working in a small trio—it was so small there were only two of us."

Phil's stories are way-out. Like the one about the eight-year-old boy who came home from school and put on a dress, lipstick, make-up and high-heeled shoes. When his mother caught him, she screamed, "If I told you once I told you a thousand times—don't play with Daddy's things."

Another one of the "way-out" boys is Ronny Graham. He was sour on society before it was sweet to do it. As one of the original angry young men, Ronny was dropping barbs on the "squares" way before it became the famous national pastime. Graham likes to aim his sights at the behavior pattern of America's middle class.

Professor Graham's favorite lecture platform is "The Downstairs at the Upstairs," where his class of beatniks and hipsters worship at his shrine. They come to cheer his marksmanship as he slings his intellectually guided missiles at the world around him. Ronny suggested a new dance called Doing the Psycho-neuro-tic:

"You dream while you're dancing,
And if you dance with Henry Luce's wife,
That means that you're in love with Time and Life.

"My little boy could have his choice of girls every night,
But my little boy says nay.
Yes, my little boy is crazy, he's not right;
Or could it be he's gay?"

Jonathan Winters complains: "Man, I don't dig society and they don't dig me."

Once he ambled into a Manhattan bank, whipped out a sketch pad and began to diagram the interior. A guard sidled up, not knowing quite what to do. Winters drew on, humming cheerfully. Then he said, "Tell me, my good man, do you have a television set in here?" "Why no," said the guard, "this is a bank." "Quite so," Winters replied, noting the fact on the pad in large block letters. "And what are the hours?" "They're printed right over there, mister," the guard said nervously, "nine to three." "Fine," Winters said, "I just wanted to hear your voice again. How loud can you holler?"

Stan Freberg is one of the few comic figures who are strictly satire. Stan honestly hated Las Vegas and it showed in his bitter satire:

"It all started," his story begins, "with the notorious rivalry between the two famous night clubs in Las Voroces; one is called the El Sodom and the other the Rancho Gomorrah. Thus when the El Sodom staged a lush extravaganza called 'Rock Around Romeo and Juliet,' the Rancho Gomorrah countered by engaging the World Orchestra, featuring Harry Truman on piano. When the El Sodom built the world's largest swimming pool, so immense that a long-distance swimmer lost her life while attempting to cross it (there were rumors that the opposition had tampered with her hot nourishing broth), the boys at the Rancho Gomorrah presented—twice a night—'The Presidential Inauguration of 1960.'

"Now the El Sodom went all out. 'Flash!' rasped the voice of a celebrated radio commentator. 'Sam Mohammed, Nevada gambling biggy, has booked an international incident into his plush nitery, El Sodom. He is flying in, by continuous airlift, a half-mile of the Suez area, complete with soldiers and implements of war.' And just in case the incident should be rained out,

16

Mohammed had lined up some insurance. In the lounge, a rare record of Adolf Hitler singing 'I Didn't Raise My Boy to Be a Soldier.' And in the garage, the Saint Valentine's Day Massacre, with the original cast."

Well, what's your decision? Are you a satirist by instinct? Are you angry? A little peeved maybe? Or, do you have the makings of a clown? Don't pick your style off a rack. Be custom-made. Select the material and niche in comedy that suits *you*. Don't pattern Bob Hope when you're a natural clown. Don't make with the one-liners if you have the flair to do dialect stories.

Whatever you decide to do, don't rush it. Study the comedians on television—and then do plenty of research in the portable gag file I have in this book. If you think you have the talent of a wit, look under Adlai Stevenson or Will Rogers or John F. Kennedy. If it's a gag man you are suited for, look under Bishop and Youngman and Berle and dozens of other comics. Your gag file has jokes, stories, anecdotes, routines, and monologues on every subject and every style—choose your ammunition and enjoy!

Prepared for Battle

Laughter has eased the tensions of a troubled world ever since the days of the court jesters, through the age of the wandering minstrels, the burlesque bananas, and on through the era of the sick comedians and the sicker audiences that laugh at them.

That's why I am writing this book. To give you the tools to sustain that laughter. And to show you how, when and where to use them—for fun and profit.

I'll give you the jokes to fit every occasion and pick out the setting. I'll tell you how to tell them and how to switch them to fit that setting. I'll rehearse you and give you your own portable gag file.

I'll show you how to adapt the humor to suit you, and how to personalize your stories. I'll even set you up with "savers" in case the joke dies. In other words, I'll get you ready for everything but failure.

Now if you're called on to "say a few words" at the dinner table, your lodge, the party, the Roast for the Mayor or the stag for the star, the convention or the sales meeting—you should be prepared for battle.

These notes do not distinguish between amateur and professional. When you are on your feet and the spotlight is on you—*you* are the star—whether you are Georgie Jessel or the local bartender. It doesn't matter if the audience is twenty thousand at Madison Square Garden or two Jews in a kibbutz—you've got to live or die by yourself.

I hope to show you in ten easy steps—or twenty hard ones—how to be the life of the party when you're asked to "say a few words":

1. Be funny. Leave the preaching to the rabbi, priest, or minister. Win your argument with a funny story instead of a sad one.

2. Be prepared—don't be caught with your gags down and your mouth open without anything to say.

3. Use the joke or the gag that fits and fits you.

4. Practice. Every day—on the butcher, the baker, or the candlestick maker's wife.

5. Personalize your stories—name the characters and the place.

6. Be brief—the mind cannot accept what the seat cannot endure.

7. Laugh at yourself—use yourself or your family as the butt.

8. Use the gag file to find the subject or the jokes you want and then apply it to your target.

9. Switch the gag if necessary to give it a custom fit.

10. Memorize the "savers"—they may save you from sure death.

Laugh and the world laughs with you, even if you're not a Sam Levenson—if the joke is good and appropriate. So, if you're going into battle on stage, at a stag dinner, a Roast, or a TV show, you've got to be prepared.

BE PREPARED

A plumber can't work without his tools. What is Liberace without his teeth, or Brigitte Bardot without her towel? Bob Hope is lost without his passport, or take the case of Sophia Loren. . . .

You sometimes hear a person say that he will speak "off the cuff," by which he means that his remarks will be impromptu. But the term "off the cuff" originally meant that the speaker had prepared himself, at least to some extent. He had made notes on his shirt cuff: notes which he could easily read without seeming to have any because there were no notes on paper or cards in evidence.

I used to write my notes on my shirt cuff myself. However, I stopped when I heard my laundryman on the Merv Griffin show one night doing my whole act—and was a big hit, too. No matter what your handicaps are as a speaker, they will be increased a hundred-fold if you are not thoroughly prepared. And if you are, many of these supposed handicaps will disappear. Don't rely on inspiration—ever. Be prepared—or prepare to run.

I once introduced Bob Hope at a Boy Scout luncheon with a glowing eulogy that even he didn't believe. "After such an introduction," he said modestly, "I can hardly wait to hear what I have to say."

But even the itinerant Hope wouldn't be so cockily confident if he weren't prepared for battle. All I'm trying to tell you is that you've got to do your homework—if you want to pass the exam.

A GAG MUST FIT—AND FIT YOU

The most important thing is to get the gag that fits—and fits you. First, you must decide what kind of comic you are. Are you a wit, a humorist, a satirist, or a clown? Then you must pick the appropriate story, gag, or bit. Appropriateness is more important than the story. All humor must have a purpose.

To paraphrase old Sam again: Laugh and the world laughs with you—cry and it means you used the wrong joke. There is no such thing as a bad audience—if you give them the humor they want or that fits or that they understand.

So, if you want life in your party, you naturally can't tell undertaker jokes at a doctor's convention or a drug banquet. Conversely, you wouldn't tell drug or doctor jokes at a Christian Science gathering.

Take a page out of the joke file of the old pro Harry Hershfield. Harry is ready with the appropriate story for every occasion. If he is to speak at a banquet to stop juvenile delinquency, he is prepared with a story like: "Strike your child every day. If you don't know why—he does!"

If the subject is art, Harry is ready with the story of the marriage broker who introduced an ugly girl to a young man. The victim protested that the lady had misplaced eyes, a broken nose, and a deformed face. "Ah," said the marriage broker, "it is apparent that you do not like Picasso."

Is divorce in the headlines? Harry tells of the wife who was a wonderful housekeeper. Every time she divorced she kept the house.

When he is introduced as the oldest living humorist—he's eighty-two as of this writing—he is ready with the story of the two octogenarians sitting in their club; one cracked: "Do you think there's as much lovemaking going on as there used to be?"

"Yes, but it's another bunch doing it," wheezed the other.

Harry also might report his favorite line about the three stages of man: "Youth, Middle Age, and—You're Looking Fine."

If he was asked to speak at a union affair he would dig up the right stories for the situation. Harry tells the one about the woman who calls the owner of a store and says, "Please call my husband, Mr. Traum, to the phone."

"We have no Mr. Traum working here," the owner replies.

"I know," says the woman, "he is outside picketing your store."

He makes them scream when he tells the story of Bernard Baruch going to a fine restaurant with two men dressed in overalls. When the owner protests Mr. Baruch says, "I can't help it—I bought a hearing aid and the union makes me carry two electricians."

Is Harry addressing an Irish audience? He suggests: "The Irish always fight amongst themselves—to be sure of having worthy adversaries."

PERSONALIZE

It's always funnier when you use a name and a place that fit the situation. Instead of just saying "a drunk breathed on my suit—it was the best cleaning job ever," use a famous name or the local drunk who is a famous drinker. For example, "Dean Martin just remodeled his home. His wife wanted a game room in the basement and Dean wanted a wine cellar!—They compromised and the first time I played ping-pong there, I kept losing. I'm not used to volleying with a champagne cork!"

Joe E. Lewis' line wouldn't be as funny about just a guy in a sweater as when he says: "Mort Sahl is the hottest thing in a sweater since Marie Dressler!" Or take Jack E. Leonard's personal attack: "I hear Joey Adams has been in Indonesia for the past eight weeks—I can't wait till he stays there."

Both these lines could be used on your local sweater boy or the town celebrity or pest who is on safari.

Doing a line about a guy who is cheap is not as funny as when you say:

"Jack Benny is so cheap that the only time he'll pick up a check is when it's made out to him." Change the name to fit the crime.

Instead of telling the story about some kid, tell it about your own, or your own wife—or yourself: "My son looked at his mother's fur coat and remarked 'How that poor beast must have suffered so that you might have that coat.' His mother answered, 'Shut up, you shouldn't talk about your father that way.' "

If given a "handle" or a name these lines take on a much funnier look:

"My brother-in-law embarrassed us—he drank his soup and six couples got up and danced."

"My boss's wife is very proper—she won't even look at things with a naked eye."

"My wife says she only asked for pin money. But the first pin she wanted had twelve stones in it!"

"My wife called her mother and cried that she wanted to come to her house. 'How will that punish *him*?' my mother-in-law asked. '*I'll* come to *your* house.' "

Phyllis Diller became famous because she uses herself as the target. "I spent seven hours in a beauty shop—and that was for the estimate. I said, 'Make me look like Elke Sommer.' He said, 'You already look like an elk in summer—would you like to try for a walrus in winter?' "

This gave Garry Moore the right signal to say about his favorite sex siren, "She couldn't lure you out of a burning building."

Totie Fields, the brilliant young 200-pound comedienne, says about Phyllis Diller, "I make sexier looking things out of pipe cleaners!" Of course, Totie took the cue from her friend who set the pace by making herself the butt. In addition, Totie does the same thing about herself, "I really have an 18-inch waist—through the center."

It's much funnier if you use Zsa Zsa Gabor's name when you say, "The best years of her life are figured in man hours." Or use Elizabeth Taylor if you want to use the joke, "The only thing that can make her blush is the corner drug store." Of course, you can also use the same line about any girl that your listeners know or recognize—if it applies.

Monique Van Vooren, the Belgian Bulge, loves to play up her sex: "Fellows don't whistle at a girl's brains," she says. She's happy when I say to her, "That's a lovely fur coat—how much did you play for it?" Nobody laughs louder than Monique when I say about this famous sex-symbol: "Her theory is: Girls who do right—get left."

These jokes could be just as good if applied to a Gina Lollobrigida or a Brigitte Bardot or a Zsa Zsa Gabor—but definitely not to a Katherine Hepburn or her brother Audrey. And that goes for your local siren as compared to the Mayor's wife.

Regional Jokes

Don't burden your listeners with regional jokes unless they apply to that particular audience. For instance, Philadelphia is not interested in the smog troubles of L. A., or the traffic problems of New York. On the other hand, if you're working to a New York audience, any traffic joke must get a laugh. Mayor John Lindsay took Allen and Rossi's joke and switched it to kid Fun City. "I found out how to solve the traffic problem: one-way streets all going north—then it would be Connecticut's problem."

The audience howled when the Mayor pulled that at a recent dinner. "And while you're laughing," he said to the crowd, "my police are now towing away your cars."

You can't do smog jokes in Arizona, but Californians are always good for a laugh when you say: "I came here during the smog—felt the sights, and went home."

When New York had some smog headlines recently, it became the proper setting for this bulletin which read: "Mayor Lindsay is doing something constructive about the N.Y.C. smog—he's putting up street signs in Braille."

POLITICS

"I'd rather be right than President," Richard Nixon was telling some pals. "Don't worry," said a fellow Republican. "You'll never be either." This is a funny joke—but not at a Republican convention.

Stay away from political jokes if you can, but if you must, make sure you're the life of the right party. Georgie Jessel annihilated a Republican Presidential candidate with one line—but he was safe in the arms of 20,000 Democratic fans at the time.

"Ladies and gentlemen," he began, "most of my eloquent colleagues have this evening taken up much of their time in expounding the weaknesses and vices of President Roosevelt's opponent, Thomas E. Dewey. I shall not and I could not do this. I know Governor Thomas E. Dewey is a fine man." Then there was a hush that might have been followed by bedlam, and he quickly followed it up with, "Yes, Dewey is a fine man—so is my Uncle

Morris. My Uncle Morris shouldn't be President—neither snould Dewey. Good night."

If you want to take sides it's okay with me—just make sure you know which side you're buttering. "I've decided to become a Democrat," the man wearing the three hats said. "Why the three hats?" his friend asked. "A Democrat has one hat to cover his head, another he tosses in the ring, and one hat he talks through."

Funny! But make sure you switch the joke to Republican—if you bump into an audience of Democrats and vice versa.

If you ever hit a Socialist gang you'll be safe with the one about the two senators—one a Democrat and the other a Republican—who had been fighting for twenty years. Finally, a mutual friend insisted they have a drink together and bury the hatchet—but not in each other.

Raising his glass the Democrat said: "Here's wishing you what you're wishing me."

"Oh, now you're starting in again," yelled the Republican.

PRACTICE

Confidence banishes stage fright and practice assures you of your ability. Whatever material you do, do it with authority. Some have it—others must acquire it. If you are prepared and then practice, practice, practice, that's your authority.

Pick out the joke, anecdote or story you like—the one that fits and fits you—and then tell it to anybody who will listen—even to your dog, if that's the only friend available. Most men use their wives to try their material. In some cases that's helped them win an audience—but lose a wife. Which could have been their intention in the first place.

George Bernard Shaw always used his wife to rehearse his stories. One friend who was visiting the famous wit noticed Mrs. Shaw knitting while her famous husband kept telling stories. The friend asked her: "What are you knitting?" Mrs. Shaw replied: "Oh, nothing in particular. It's just that I've heard these stories of his a thousand times, and if I didn't do something with my hands, I'd choke him!"

So if you want to make good as a comedian as well as a husband—buy the wife a knitting needle and give her your yarns and practice, practice, practice. . . .

Of course, you can't expect to be a Bob Hope the first time out—but then, neither is Hope. Our goodwill ambassador tries his gags around the world before he brings them back here. I try mine on taxi drivers. I figure the wheel is *their* knitting needle.

Practice on your friends, wife, and/or sweetheart as the case may be—and particularly your mother-in-law. Why wait for a paid critic to annihilate you? And if your mother-in-law likes your act, let me know and you can pick out *my* material.

Try your stories out at your dinner table, your lodge or your office—any stories that you like. Don't worry if it's a new joke or an old joke—if they didn't hear it, it's new. And if it fits—it's new. Just keep telling them. A hundred years from now no one will remember an old joke—unless Milton Berle is still telling it.

Sam Levenson was a teacher who loved to plant his routines on his pupils: "When I need your opinion—I'll give it to you." He did so much homework on his gags, he was demoted to a professional comedian.

Myron Cohen was a silk salesman who told jokes with every order he took. He loved to tell the story about Mr. Cohen who came home and found his wife in bed with his best friend: "Max," he scolded him, "I *must*—but you?" Every time he told it, it got funnier and so did Myron. He kept adding stories and gags. When he found he was getting more orders for his jokes than his silks, he got himself an agent who started to sell *him*.

Phyllis Diller rehearsed on her neighbors and the guys at the supermarket: "My neighbor is built like a truck. The other day she was standing beside a parking meter and somebody stole her kneecaps."

Phyllis used to kid herself for fun way before she did it for profit: "My skin is so dry they declared it a fire hazard. And my hair! Are you ready for this? The girl at the beauty parlor said 'Mind if I tease it?' I said 'Sweetie—you can drive it to drink for all I care!' "

When her gags got funnier than her outfits, she knew it was time to go pro.

Phyllis found the dialogue that suited her and then kept using it. After you select a line and make it your own, the next thing is to figure out how to tell it and how to sell it. This matter of delivery is strictly assurance, knowing your material and knowing it well. Tell it like you just made it up. The real skill will come with constant practice and growing assurance. For the art of humor, like every other art, requires constant exercise.

TIMING

Before you tell a story, figure out where to pause or how to strike the punch line. Most comedians or professional storytellers have a trick giggle or clear their throats before or after the punch. Some waggle cigars or flick the ashes off their cigarettes. One stamps his foot, another slaps his thigh or claps his hands. Some just pause for the slightest moment—to let the audience know the punch line is coming or gone.

As an example, here's a funny story: "A ninety-five-year-old man married a ninety-three-year-old lady. They spent the first three days of their honeymoon trying to get out of the car."

To get the biggest results with this gag—time it your own way. You must use the least amount of words, and you can't separate "honeymoon" from "trying to get out of the car."

Thus, you might do it this way. "A ninety-five-year-old man married a ninety-three-year-old lady—(pause, or scratch your head or clear your throat), they spent the first three days of their honeymoon (this is to be said matter of fact); pause, and bang this out: *trying to get out of the car!*" After the punch line you use your own personality. You can laugh like Sam Levenson does; or just stare, the way Bob Hope does; or turn your head from side to side the way Henny Youngman does; slap your knee like Berle, or raise your eyebrows like Groucho.

George Jessel learned his best trick from George M. Cohan, "who taught me how to pause while talking to an audience so as to make them believe that I was thinking of something important, or some new line that had just come to mind—when it was actually something tried and true that I knew would get a laugh."

Everything needs practice. You can't just look at a recipe and memorize it—you've got to make the cake if you want to be a good baker. Rembrandt's first painting wasn't his best—neither was Wright's first plane. When I first saw Henny Youngman, who was always telling the same jokes to anyone who would listen, I said he was going to make it. And I still say he's going to make it.

Timing is a feel that comes with experience at throwing the punch line. Confidence comes after your first snicker. The more laughs you get, the stronger your delivery. If you don't believe in yourself and use your own personality, nobody else will. Of course, many great storytellers are great technicians—but couldn't create a belch after a Hungarian dinner. These characters need a little more practice in timing. But Thomas Edison wasn't born with a light bulb in his mouth. Even Groucho Marx didn't have a great delivery when he was born, no matter what his doctor says.

Timing is important in getting attention or starting the joke. Don't get into it until you have set up your audience in advance, whether the audience is one or one thousand. That's why comedians started with "A funny thing happened to me on the way to the theatre—a bum stopped me and said, 'Boss, will you give me a quarter for a sandwich?' I said, 'Let's see the sandwich!'" The first part has nothing to do with the story, but it's just there to get you set for the story to come.

Timing also depends on the right joke in the right place and that depends a little on your brain file of gags or your gag file of brains. Pick out the gems you like, tell them over and over in your own style and then file them away in your funnybone for future use.

For instance, if you're at a Chamber of Commerce meeting and the speaker before you brings up the traffic problem, you've got to be a hit if you can dig out of your memory an opening line like: "Three out of every four automobiles in the world are in the USA (pause or whatever), and two of them will get to the parking space before you do." Now that's telling a story that you've told before and that fits now. If your homework is good you might add: "The only way to get to the other side of Main Street is to be born there." If you want to prove you're a real pro, you follow it up with, "The California police are the politest—when a lady driver sticks out her hand to make a turn—they kiss it." Now, that's timing. The right joke in the right place at the right time.

If you throw the right jokes, you can even make the losers laugh in Las Vegas: "Nobody forces you to gamble; nobody forces you to have sex either—but it's more sociable." Now, no matter how funny the gag is in this case, you can't tell it to the poor sucker when he is standing at the crap table losing his next year's salary—that would be bad timing.

After he's had a chance to dry his tears a little and you meet him in the restaurant or the night club, then you've got to get a laugh if you attack yourself: "I come here every year to visit my money and leave a little interest." If your timing is right, they will love it should you kid the gambling business: "Even the parsons here flip a coin—double or nothing. The Justices of the Peace are the biggest gamble of all; from the picture 'When your hair has turned to silver (pause)—put it in the slot machines!' "

You can always tell a star by his timing. The champ is always ready to take advantage of every situation. If he's following a long line of dull talkers, he's got to get a laugh with his opening remark. "I was a young fellow when these speeches started," or if he's following a big smash act, he sets himself up when he says, "I wouldn't give such a spot to a leopard." Either way, he's protected.

Talking about timing, and knowing what to do at the right time or the wrong time—here is one of the great classics. I was at a Friars dinner where Adlai Stevenson was a guest speaker, but he had to follow Fred Allen, who was in great form that night. When Fred finished to thunderous applause, Stevenson weakly rose to his feet. "Gentlemen," he said, "before the meeting I was out in the lobby talking to Mr. Allen and he confessed to me that he didn't have a speech for tonight's occasion. I graciously gave him my speech. So you have just heard it." And he sat down.

One more timing tip. Never give yourself away. Don't set up your story with, "Here's a joke." After that, it's like trying to follow a world war with a popgun.

BE BRIEF

In this modern stepped-up world of ours, we don't have time for anything but the punch line. Instant coffee, powdered eggs, and quick-frozen foods are our speed. In other words, you've got to be brief to be recognized— as Brigitte Bardot will testify.

Ed Sullivan might even manage a full smile if you would do five funny minutes for him on his TV show. The best after-dinner speakers have learned that they must stand up to be seen, speak up to be heard, and shut up to be appreciated.

Fred Allen found himself in great discomfort listening to a long-playing bore at a banquet. After an hour of saying nothing, the speaker said: "Well, to make a long story short—"

"It's too late now," bellowed Allen.

One time, Willie Collier Sr., one of the top speakers of his time, had to follow fifteen long-winded orators. When the toastmaster said: "Mister Collier will now give his address," Collier got up and announced: "My address is the Lambs Club, 130 West 44th Street," and sat down.

Collier's memorable one-line speech following a long list of lengthy army and navy speakers: "Now you know what they mean when they say 'The army and navy forever.' "

Don't get the reputation of that famous Chinese comic "On Too Long." All good things come in small packages. Don't get me wrong, I'm not knocking Elizabeth Taylor.

Today everything is in capsule form. Science has brought all things down to their smallest, most minute degree. Everything is concentrated. You can take one tablet which represents a whole meal.

Today, comedy too is in capsule form. Years ago comedians would have twenty-minute sketches—just for one big laugh at the end. Now the comic tells the whole laugh picture in one line: "There's a new perfume in Europe that's guaranteed to drive Europeans crazy—it smells like American money." Or "A mistress is like a wife only you don't have to do the dishes." Or "I don't know if we'll ever cure poverty, but the way taxes and prices are going up—we're sure to cure wealth."

SAVERS

No comedian, storyteller or public speaker should be without "savers." They are the gags that could save your life when you're dying. Even the finest and newest ships afloat have lifesavers, no matter how impossible it is for the boat to go down.

On the other hand, Babe Ruth, the greatest ball player of all time, didn't hit a home run every time at bat. I know you are not going to believe this—but even I have laid an egg or three here and there in my long career in show business. When things are going a little rough for me—which is very rare, it says here—my saver usually is "Are you sure Milton Berle started this way?" Of course, if you're a writer you can substitute the name Bennett Cerf. Or if you're a businessman, use the boss's name or the big shot in your field. If you're a musician you might use Lawrence Welk or if you're a singer Nelson Eddy.

When the laughs aren't coming, you might save your life by kidding yourself: "I left my home town to set the world on fire—I think I better go back for some more matches." "I started at the bottom—and after this show I'll stay there." "My mother said I would come out on top. She was right—I'm getting bald." "This could be worse—I could be here in person!" "Before I came out here I was a comer—now I'm a goner!" "I want to thank all of you for coming to my funeral." "Ever get the feeling you're in the wrong business?"

My favorite saver, the one that never fails, is the sympathy line. "I have a little boy at home who is all alone. I'm the only one he has in the whole world. And when I come home at night, he rushes up to me and says 'Daddy, were you a big hit tonight—did they laugh, Daddy, were you a big hit tonight, did they laugh, Daddy, did they, huh?' And if I have to tell him I was a flop—it would break his heart. So your laughs and your applause are not for me really, they're for that poor little kid who is sitting home alone—just waiting to hear how I did tonight."

Like the man has been saying, it's difficult to think on your feet, unless you've done some thinking before you get on your feet. If you're asked to "say a few words"— make sure you got the words.

If not, it might be better to do as Willie's father did on a sea voyage. The sea was rough enough to make Willie's father deathly ill but it didn't bother Willie at all. In fact, he was more energetic and annoying than usual.

Willie's mother noticed he was bothering everybody on deck. She said to the dying and greenish-blue soul lying in the deck chair next to her, "Father, speak to Willie."

The poor man, with what seemed to be his last effort, turned his head toward the brat and in a weak voice said, "Hello, Willie."

So, if you're called upon to say something and do not have something to say, just say "Hello, Folks," and sit down.

But, if you listen to me, I can make you the talker of the town. You know Milton Berle? Big star? He listened to me! George Burns? Great monologist? He listened to me! Bob Hope listened to me! Liberace? He didn't listen!

How to Create a Joke

All gags have a formula that can be applied to any subject. Let's take a look and see how formula gags can be made to fit our needs.

Suppose our comedian wants do a monologue about being invited to a society affair. How do we go about dreaming up "society" gags?

The first thing I do is write down a list of associations that come to mind when I think of the word society. Okay, let's try some free-association and see how it works out:

Society . . . hostess . . . estate . . . money . . . lots of money . . . snobs . . . Rolls Royce . . . high taxes . . . Republicans . . . servants . . . gold . . . inheritance . . . will . . . diamonds . . . mink . . . happiness . . . travel . . . the four hundred . . . butlers . . . rich . . . rich Texan. . . .

Make your list as long as you like. All the things that you conjure up in your mind when you think of society. Each list will be a little different and naturally your gags a little different.

Since the comic might start the monologue by saying he was invited to a swanky society affair, it might be a good idea to make the first gag about the estate—where it was held. If the comic is playing it strictly for laughs, this description must be ludicrous or the height of exaggeration.

Exaggeration is the perfect comedy formula to use here. "The place was so swanky that—even the owners had to use the servants' entrance." In this case, it is exaggeration and caricature that work out for useful formula laughs.

"The hostess was such a big snob that when she died and arrived at the gate of Heaven and St. Peter welcomed her and said 'Come right in,' she sneered, 'I will not—any place where a perfect stranger can get in without a reservation is not my idea of Heaven.' "

Now think of some of the other thoughts you wrote down at the beginning: rich, Rolls Royce, diamonds, mink, etc.

"I saw people in minks, diamonds, and chinchillas come out of their Rolls Royces. Do you think they are happy? You're damn right they are!" "I saw one Rolls Royce pull up and a Cadillac got out."

Think of rich: "She was so rich that the finance company owed *her* money." "She was so wealthy that she had platinum walls and mink garbage." "She was so rich that when they served green salad—it was shredded tens and twenties."

You wrote down money—think of what money does. Okay, money talks! Now for the exaggeration and/or caricature: "Money talks—but it's hard of hearing when I call it." "Money can't buy happiness—but it gets you a better class of enemies."

Go a step further. Money makes you cheap or mercenary or rich or miserable or successful or happy. Lack of money, or money you save. Pick the theme and then apply the exaggeration: "Be sure to *save* your money— you never know when it will be valuable again some day." "You don't have to make a lot of money to amount to something in this world—you can always inherit it." "Remember, the most important thing in life is happiness, and you can't buy it with money—of course, it can make you pretty comfortable while unhappy." "Money doesn't always buy you happiness. A man with 2 million can be just as happy as a man with 3 million." "What good is money? Can money buy you love, or happiness, or friendship? I'm talking about Confederate money."

Here's a combination of pun, caricature, exaggeration and description, starting with my favorite word which is the perfect bridge: THAT.

"He's so rich *that* he bathed in a solid gold bathtub and left 14-carat rings. He's tall, dark and has some 10 million bucks. It's easy to spot him at a football game—he's the one with the electric blanket. He complains that he owns a gold mine which is no good—oil keeps coming out."

Society, rich, money; the thing that follows is Republican. Will Rogers once said, "Anybody can be a Republican when the market is up; but when stocks are selling for no more than they're worth—I tell you, being a Republican is a sacrifice."

Talking about Republicans and money, of course, you must think of Rockefeller and elections. "So what if Rockefeller loses New York State? He can always buy New Jersey!"

And when you think of rich, you must think of Texas: "One rich Texan (is there any other kind?) claims that he had a bankroll so big *that* he had to have it put on microfilm before he could stuff it in his pocket."

We've come a long way from the society party—but the route has been interesting if we found some laughs along the way.

Let's try one more game. Now pretend that you need a routine for automobiles. That should be a good subject for exaggeration and caricature.

Now let's see: automobiles . . . new automobiles . . . power brakes . . . power windows . . . power steering. How about, "The power steering is so sensitive *that* it turns even if you burp?" No, we can do better. How about sneezing? Sensitive power steering and sneezing. Something like, "I got a new car. The power steering is so sensitive *that,* I'm driving down the road—I sneezed—and whoops I'm in the other lane." Fair, but needs a little more exaggeration. Let's see, maybe sneezing attack . . . let's go wild: "My new car has power steering so sensitive *that* I'm driving along—I sneeze and whoops I'm on the shoulder. Once while I'm driving from New York to Chicago I got a hay fever attack and wound up in Florida."

Now you can try it with any subject. All you need is the word *that,* a little imagination and a lot of exaggeration:

She was so fat *that* she had to put on a girdle to get into her kimono.

He was so poor that the churchmouse was his landlord.

They were so poor that they couldn't afford shoes, so they laced up their feet.

He was so nearsighted that he kissed the cat good night and put his wife out.

The nurse was so pretty that when she took his temperature she took off 10 per cent for personality.

They came from such a large family that when they got together in the backyard, it looked like recess.

He was such a heavy drinker that when he took a blood test, the doctor offered him sixty dollars a case.

She had such bony legs that when she sat down, her knees made a fist.

The plane was so fast that it took off from Los Angeles with two rabbits and landed in New York with two rabbits.

He was so bigheaded that he couldn't get an aspirin to fit him.

His legs were so short that he put his feet in his pocket and walked on his hands.

He had such a big stomach that if he put a golf ball where he could see it, he couldn't hit it, and if he put it where he could hit it, he couldn't see it.

He was so unlucky that he drowned from a hot-water bottle breaking.

She was so ugly that when she walked into a room, the mice jumped on a chair.

He was so bald that when you looked at him from ten feet away, it seemed like his neck was blowing bubble gum.

He was so nervous that he kept coffee awake.

He was so crooked that he could stand in the shadow of a corkscrew.

He was so cheap that he squeezed a penny so hard, Lincoln's face was black and blue.

It was so hot that we had to feed the hens ice cream to keep them from laying hard-boiled eggs.

She had such a turned-up nose that every time she sneezed she blew her hat off.

He had such big feet that they used him to stamp out forest fires.

He had such big feet that he could walk through the house one room at a time.

He had such a big nose that he could smoke a cigar under a shower.

The brothers were so round-shouldered that when they stood together they looked like parentheses.

She had such buck teeth that every time she kissed her fella she combed his moustache at the same time.

Her hair is so long it grows all the way down her back. Too bad it doesn't grow on her head.

She is so dumb that when she rented a furnished room, the landlady left the VACANT sign up.

He is so hep that when he saw the Statue of Liberty, he said, "Man, dig that crazy lighter."

She is so hep that when she saw the sun setting, she said, "Man, dig that crazy stop sign."

He is so square that he thinks a bebopper is someone who bops bees.

She is so square that she won't read Webster's Dictionary until they make it into a movie.

She is so rich that she has mink ulcers.

He is so lazy that he gets in a revolving door and waits.

She is such a prude that she blushes when somebody says intersection.

He has such a big mouth that he can eat a banana sideways.

It was so cold that the hens were laying eggs from a standing position.

He was so old that he remembers white toothpaste.

He was so tired that he made Ovaltine sleepy.

He was carrying a torch so long that he joined the plumbers' union.

She had such bad eyes that she wore contact lenses to see her glasses.

He was so small that he could go ice skating on an ice cube.

He was so unpopular that he tried to get B.O. to attract attention.

He was so polite that he wouldn't open an oyster without knocking on the shell.

She was so ritzy that even her husband had to use the servants' entrance.

It was so dry that a seagull followed him for three blocks, because it heard he had water on the knee.

The climate is so healthy in that town that they had to kill a man to get a cemetery started.

It was so cold that he had to part his hair with an axe.

She was so short that when she wore a miniskirt the hem got dirty.

The Big Switch

There is no such thing as an old joke—if you dress it up with new clothes. The seven original jokes (puns, insults, sex, domestic, underdog, incongruity, topical) that form the basic pattern of humor have been transformed into the fifty thousand-odd jokes you hear on radio and TV yearly.

This simple process is called "switching" by the professional gag writer or comedian. It takes the comparatively few formula gags and readies them for the laugh that fits the occasion.

Like a jewel, a joke is always more important in the proper setting. A good storyteller or writer will switch the gag to make the punishment fit the crime or in this case the gag fit the laugh.

When Rockefeller's wife Happy had the new baby, every alert comic or comedy writer used the line, "The first word Rocky's baby spoke was 'Money!' " This joke could be switched to every rich man's son, or you can give it a double switch: "The dress manufacturer had a baby boy and the first word the kid said was 'Returns!' "

To continue the switch: "When Rockefeller was a kid his father gave him blocks to play with: 49th Street, 50th Street, 51st Street," and "The Hollywood producer gave his son dolls to play with—real live blonde dolls." "The rich Texan (is there any other kind?) gave his kid a cowboy outfit—a thousand-acre ranch outside of Houston."

Somebody used the line about the boast of China, which hasn't taken over a country in a while: "Long time no seize." This could be switched very easily to Zsa Zsa Gabor. When Zsa Zsa was working on her fifth husband, I cracked, "It's about time she got married again—long time no seize."

It's not tough to make the switch. "Baseball is our national pastime," somebody said. "Now go and convince Elizabeth Taylor." Of course, this could be switched to Sukarno or the ever-popular Zsa Zsa.

Any comedian worth his weight in laughs has his own flying jokes when he opens in a town. Henny Youngman quips: "I don't fly on account of my religion—I'm a devout coward." Milton Berle's prepared ad lib is: "I just flew in from California and my arms are tired." Jonathan Winters' switch is "I just flew in from Chicago. No plane—I had 200 pigeons Scotch-taped to my arms."

If a man is rich and plays tennis your zinger might be, "He has cashmere tennis balls." Or if he's a baseball nut, "He's got a mink baseball bat." Or in ιne case of the millionaire who married the girl fifty years younger, "For a wedding present, he gave his wife a set of platinum jacks." This joke is perfect for anybody from Sinatra to Justice Douglas. Or for the real switch, about a wealthy character who was a little off, "For a Christmas present we gave him a solid gold yo-yo."

There are many kinds of switching. The first type comes under the heading of substitutions. Thus, "I call my girl 'appendix' because she's so expensive to take out."

By merely substituting a few words but leaving the basic structure we get, "I call my girl friend 'United Nations'; all the parts are there—they just can't get together."

Another kind of switch is the one that follows the same thought.
"Tough luck, boss, I just took your favorite horse to the glue factory."
Well?"
"They refused him!"

Switch that to "I just took your underwear to the laundry."
"Well?"
"They refused it."

Or, "I sent my mother-in-law to the country—they refused her."

Switching the insult is the easiest. I once said about Ed Sullivan, "As a wit he is second only to Arthur Murray." This is easily switched to "As a singer he is second only to Andy Devine," or to spin off this subject, "If you want to remember his voice—tear a rag." Or, "if you want to remember his singing—flush the toilet."

About somebody who is dressed badly you might switch the stale line to read, "He leaves a bad taste in my eyes." Or a bad voice, "She leaves a bad taste in my ears" or "nose."

Another form of switching is done by juxtaposing one word in a phrase or even the whole phrase. There are many famous sayings, proverbs, and cliches that can be upside-downed and turned into laughter with the twist of a word:

"I got a frog in my throat."
One frog said to another, "I got a man in my throat."

"I'm so sick I couldn't eat a thing."
One cannibal said to another: "I'm so sick I couldn't eat a person."

"A wolf in sheep's clothing."
"I went out with a sailor—he was a wolf in ship's clothing," or, "A wolf is a guy who's always in there pinching."

36

"This is still a free country where a man can do—as his wife pleases."

" 'Four years of college,' said the girl grad, 'and whom has it gotten me?' "

"One alligator said to the other, 'I'm gonna make me a man bag.' "

"I think it happened while she was under the influence of mink."

"One sardine said to the other—'Man, we're packed in here like commuters.' "

"He's the kind of guy who likes to eat his cake and have yours too."

"She's a good girl, but she got mixed up in the wrong company—me!"

All the Jayne Mansfield and Brigitte Bardot gags started way back with Mae West, then switched to Jane Russell and Lana Turner—then Marilyn Monroe and finally this year's bosom.

"She makes my wife look like a boy," or Henny Youngman's switch, "Take away her bust, her beautiful hair, her lovely face and her gorgeous figure and what have you got?—my wife."

"She is a Mia Farrow that kept growing," or the reverse switch, "Mia is a Brigitte Bardot that was deflated."

The comic leers at Gina and says, "If I told you you had a beautiful body—would you hold it against me?" Or the obvious switch, "I'm not afraid—they can put me up against you any day."

"The way she's built—it takes her ten minutes to get her feet wet under a shower," or "She could never drown—she has her own set of built-in water wings."

For those who would rather switch than fight with the oldies, the surprise ending is the best formula. You start with the same first line and then switch to the incongruous or unexpected.

"It is better to have loved and lost—much better."

"A friend in need—is a pest."

"If you ever need a friend—buy a dog."

"A fool and his money—are some party."

All you need is the saying, and to follow my own advice, "If the switch fits—use it."

Another form of switching is to think of the punch line first—and then make the story fit the wound. For instance, "He's crazy," or "He became a comedian because he lost his marbles." It's easy to build a story to make the

37

insult more palatable: "When he was a kid he used to exercise by filling his mouth full of marbles. Every day he dropped one marble, and when he lost all his marbles—he became a comedian."

This is easily switchable to a bus driver or a psychiatrist. Like the story about the young man who loved the rocking chair his father gave him. He used it day and night; one day the rocking chair broke, and when they discovered he was off his rocker—they made him a theatrical agent.

The old legend says that when you eat a Chinese meal—an hour later you are hungry again. This is a field day for the switch comics:

"Never rob a Chinese bank—an hour later you want to rob another one." Or,

"They should not allow Red China in the UN. You know the Chinese; once they vote—an hour later they want to vote again."

"Never marry a Chinese wife—an hour later you want to marry another one." Or "Never eat a Chinese fortune cookie—an hour later you want to know 'What's new?' " and so on.

Switching is also accomplished conversely by changing the punch line but leaving the build-up as is.

"Why are you so stingy? Don't you know you can't take it with you?"
"No? Then I'm not going!"

Consider the switch: "Why are you so stingy? Don't you know you can't take it with you?"
"All right, then—I'll have it sent ahead."

The location switch is another prime example of dressing up a gag. The kid was bothering everybody. "Why don't you go play in the traffic," is the standard heckle. Or to change the scene, the pest was annoying everybody on the plane. Finally one of the hostesses suggested, "Why don't you play outside?"

"Formula" is one of the most important bases of switching. Like Jack Benny's cheapness, Bob Hope's traveling, Bing Crosby's money, or Dean Martin's drinking.

All the W. C. Fields or Joe E. Lewis gags are perfect settings for Dean Martin drunk lines with a slight twist. "Dean sees a psychiatrist once a week to make him stop drinking—and it's working. Every Wednesday between five and six he doesn't touch a drop."

Or the natural switch: "I'm afraid Dean will break his New Year's resolution, which is not to drink while he's sleeping."

To go even further, "I never saw Dean with a glass in his hand—a bottle yes!"

The farthest-out switch of all is an old Joe E. Lewis line, "They gave him a hot foot—and he burned for four days."

The switch must be a custom fit to be big time. When Joe E. Lewis had an operation that lasted three hours he cracked when he came to: "I'm responsible for a new surgical technique—instead of stitches they used corks."

The occupation switch is easy. The comic's wife was having a baby and his pal heckled, "I hope she has a better delivery than you." This is interchangeable with a letter carrier, Western Union boy, or United Parcel.

Gambling and Las Vegas are perfect targets for switching—they go with the extreme bit. "Vegas is one place where money isn't everything; if you stay there long enough—it's nothing." It's easy to switch to "I lost my money in Nevada and told the hotel owner 'Hope you have more luck with my money than I did' or 'I'm going back to Vegas to visit my money.' "

The way-out switch is, "I wouldn't say the roulette table was crooked but how come the table says 'tilt'?"

The best is still Joey Bishop's crack switch, "The only way to beat the tables in Las Vegas—when you get off the plane—walk into the propeller."

Repetition is another perfect formula for the big switch.

"Old Generals never die—they just fade away" became the subject for hundreds of switches to fit the occasion or the target:

"Old comics never die—they just gag a little."

"Old judges never die—they just lose their appeal."

"Old strippers never die—they just peel away."

"Old doctors never die—they just cut out."

Praise switched to poison is one of the best recipes used by the switch artist.

"I've got the finest wife in the country—I only hope she stays there."

"I regret that I have but one wife to send to the country."

"Two can live as cheaply as one—if one doesn't eat."
With the knife of the switcher it becomes: "If two can live as cheaply as one—why don't they?"

The perfect example of love turned sour is to switch it this way: "I love him—I have no taste but I love him." Or, "I love him—but what the hell do I know?" or "You have my vote—but I also voted for Barry Goldwater and Wendell Willkie."

39

Mother-in-law jokes have been switched for years to fit the in-law or outlaw as the case may come up. The first mother-in-law joke recorded was in Asia about twelve hundred years ago by Nasreddin Hoca. Nasreddin's mother-in-law was drowned while crossing a river, and although all the villagers went downstream in seach of the body, Hoca insisted on going upstream. "If you knew her as well as I did, you'd know what a contrary woman she was."

This has been switched down through the years to, "I hear you're taking your mother-in-law to Los Angeles. Won't the weather disagree with her?"

"It wouldn't dare."

Or to switch it further, his mother-in-law was missing. The kidnappers sent a note saying, "If you don't send $25,000—we will send her back."

But like the switch boys point out, mother-in-law jokes go back to when the world started: "Only Adam didn't have a mother-in-law. That's how we know he lived in Paradise."

The switch-hitters had a field day during the recent rash of older men marrying young girls. Henny Youngman cracked, "Frankie married a girl thirty years younger; Cary Grant's wife is thirty-five years younger. Xavier Cugat's bride is forty years younger, and Justice Douglas married a girl forty-five years his junior—I can't wait till I get old!"

One comic switched, "Sinatra couldn't be here tonight—he had to take his wife to an orthodontist."

Dean Martin cracked, "I've got Scotch older than she is." Jack E. Leonard switched it, "I want to know how Frankie can kiss a girl while she's teething."

One writer quip-switched, "Cugat expected to meet his bride here—but her mother wouldn't let her cross the streets by herself."

Definitions are always good for a laugh or a switch. "The definition of a diplomat—he talks interestingly for an hour and doesn't say anything." Or switch it this way: "It's the art of skating on thin ice without getting into deep water."

"A diplomat is a person who can be disarming even though his country isn't."

"When a diplomat isn't straddling an issue—he's usually dodging one."

And for the all-out switch, "A diplomat is a guy who can convince his wife she looks fat in a mink coat."

Descriptions of people are always good for a switch—especially if you let your exaggeration run away with you.

"Is she bowlegged!"
"Lots of girls are bowlegged!"
"All the way up to her shoulders?"

Or the wild switch, "She's so bowlegged—I hung her over the door for good luck."

Or to go all the way, "She's bowlegged and he's knock-kneed—when they stand together they spell the word OX."

Have another switch: "She's so ugly, when elephants get drunk—they see her." Or, "When a mouse sees her—the mouse jumps on the chair."

This should make you switch-happy:
"She's so ugly—she has her face done up in curlers."

Or to switch the switch bit: "She was too ugly to have her face lifted—so they lowered her body instead."

To press on: "He has enough wrinkles in his face to hold a two-day rain." The switch: "He has so many wrinkles in his forehead—he has to screw his hat on."

"She has so many double chins they have to have a bookmark to find her pearls." The switch: "She had so many double chins when she drove over a bump—they applauded."

To continue the exaggeration bit or to do caricature:

"He was so nervous that he kept coffee awake."

"He was so unpopular that he tried to get bad breath to attract attention."

"She was so rich that she bathed in a solid gold bathtub and left 14-carat rings."

"He was so bald that when you looked at him from ten feet away—it seemed like his neck was blowing bubble gum."

"He had such big feet—they used him to stamp out forest fires." And so on.

Exaggeration is the greatest form of flattening. "The room you gave me is so small that when I lie down—the doorknob gets in bed with me." To switch it to the positive: "The room is so small when a girl visits me she's got to lie down."

To go the exaggeration bit one switch further: "My uncle just had a terrible accident—he fell in a barrel of cold cream and softened to death."

41

It's worth the switch: "My uncle got so loaded—he fell in the ice and got stiff as hell."

Switching a religious or an ethnic joke is the most sensitive. You've got to be sure you place it in the right pew.

"They broke up on account of religious differences—she worships money and he doesn't have any."

The sensitive switch is the story of the little Jewish boy who wanted to play with the gentile kid next door who said, "My father won't let me play with you because you're Jewish." The boy answered, "That's all right—we won't play for money."

Or the switch of the Catholic kid who bragged to the Jewish kid: "My priest knows more than your rabbi!" The Jewish kid answered: "Sure— why not?—you tell him everything."

Will Rogers was one of the greatest phrase-turners who ever lived. Once after a long confinement he cracked: "People couldn't have been nicer to me if I had died."

Naturally, Georgie Jessel stole it—I mean switched it. When he received a particularly glowing introduction he quipped: "After that introduction—I thought I was dead."

Every speaker worth his weight in gags has lived through a bad audience or a lack of one. You've got to be able to laugh at the story of the speaker who saw one remaining man in the audience. "Thank you for staying," he said. "I won't be long now." "That's okay," said the lone spectator, "I'm the next speaker." Or to switch the punch line, "I'm the janitor waiting to clean up." Or, "Here's the keys—lock up." Or, "Don't worry when they walk out on you—it's when they walk toward you that you have to worry."

I could go on switching all day, but like my wife said, "Don't you ever come to a period?"—or the big switch—"Even a train stops."

The Monologue

After you create or choose the gags or jokes you like, the next step is to put them together in one setting—if you want to be a monologist.

The important thing is the set-up. If you don't think so—try romancing a girl in a noisy cafeteria.

The dictionary defines a joke as something said or done to evoke laughter or amusement—a thing or person laughed at rather than taken seriously. Don't misunderstand, I wouldn't give a Funk or a Wagnall for all the jokes in the world if they weren't packaged right.

The first thing is to get the theme you want. Sex, Alaska, Texas—or anything that is popular or that you want to talk about. Next, beg, borrow, or steal any gag or joke on the subject. You'll never be overweight from too much material. Get the gags from the portable gag file in this book, from the papers, from friends, from gag writers, and walk around with your eyes open and your ear to the ground. And if you don't end up a good comic—at least you'll be a hell of an acrobat.

When you have collected all the material you want—get it in working order by trying to tell a story. Then by a process of trial and error you will eliminate the lines that don't go and you will embellish the ones that do.

I have tried to lump together some topics that have often been rehashed for good comedy fare. You can use these and enlarge on them with different gags, or you can start your own theme and fill in the jokes from any source you can.

ALASKA

Nobody was happier than I when Alaska became our 49th state. Only I don't intend to go there again until it melts. I love God's frozen people but I get a chill when I open the refrigerator. Our new state is so cold even the janitors are complaining.

The first and last time I was there it was so subzero the hens laid eggs from a standing position and penguins were bringing babies instead of the stork. The only way my Cindy could part her hair was with an ax. One Eskimo advertised in the local snow-sheet that he was looking for a man with a high fever for a roommate.

Alaska is very proud of her statehood. The first day our new flag was born with a 49th star on it, the stores in Anchorage were flooded with orders. One little old lady, after waiting in line for hours, finally reached the counter to purchase her flag. After looking it over she said admiringly, "It's beautiful. What other colors do you have them in?"

Since Alaska has become a state, the Eskimo population is rapidly becoming Americanized. In fact, some of them have even hacked holes atop their igloos in order to stand up when they hear "The Star-Spangled Banner."

TEXAS

I'm tired of Texans bragging about the size of their state. Just the mention of the Lone Star State and everybody from Texas stands at attention. Just hum, "The Eyes of Texas Are Upon You," and any of its drunks will yell themselves sober.

Trouble with those Texas millionaires is that all that money is going to their pockets. Some of those oillionaires are real cowboys—every spring they saddle up and round up the banks. The biggest spenders aren't Texas oilmen—they are the wives of Texas oilmen.

One Texas oilman I know has a bankroll so big, he has to have it put on microfilm before he can stuff it in his pocket.

There is a movement afoot to teach Texas school children how to spell the word "small."

One rich Dallas kid wanted a new playpen, so his father bought him Alcatraz. Another oilman from Houston is dickering to buy Hollywood because his kid would like to study the stars.

In Texas everything but a Caddy is considered a foreign car. On one highway between Galveston and Corpus Christi stands a sign with this legend: "Keep Our Highways Clean: No Chevrolets, Fords, or Plymouths Allowed."

A 14-carat Texan strode into a Cadillac showroom and told the salesman: "My wife has a touch of flu—what do you have in the way of a get-well car?"

A Texan was dictating his will to his lawyer: "To my son I leave three million dollars—and he's lucky I didn't cut him off entirely."

SEX

Sex makes the world go 'round. If Queen Isabella didn't dig Chris this world would still be square and that goes for its inhabitants.

Down through the centuries, the subject of sex has always been good for a laugh. That's not so surprising since sex itself is pretty entertaining. Ever since Adam and Eve started the whole mess, there have been stories about it. I'm sure the gang that hung around with Romeo and Juliet, Tristan and Isolde, Napoleon and Josie, and Brigitte Bardot and anybody, have made jokes about the Boy and Girl problems.

Times have changed but the jokes linger on. In ye olden days when French kids studied anatomy, they went to college. Nowadays they enroll at Brigitte Bardot movies.

There are two periods in a man's life when he doesn't know anything about women—before marriage and after marriage.

Sex, according to old man Webster, is the difference between man and woman, and as long as there is man and woman, they will have their differences.

One woman told her lawyer she wanted a divorce:

"On what grounds?"

"My husband isn't faithful," she said.

"What makes you think so?" the lawyer asked.

"Well," she said, "I don't think he's the father of my child."

HOLLYWOOD

I am an Academy Award loser.

The best acting in Hollywood is done by the stars congratulating the Academy Award winners. A good friend of mine won top honors last year. He's not an actor or director—he makes popcorn.

I made a picture called "Ringside" which took seven days to make—with retakes. I posed longer for my graduation pictures. I don't want to say it was a cheap picture, but I did get a little nervous when my big technicolor scene was photographed with a Brownie No. 2. I don't want to louse up my own picture; I can only tell you it was the only new picture ever shown on TV.

We ran a sneak preview—and after the first reel, everybody sneaked out. When the critics reviewed it, they all saw eye-to-eye—they couldn't look at the screen. When it opened around the country—even the popcorn was panned. At one theatre, thirty-two people had their names taken off the free list.

WESTERNS

I have seen so many Western movies that I sit at the dinner table side-saddle. I've even tried running my Cadillac on oats. My wife calls me Drag-along Adams. A Western is my favorite sandwich. I can never make a pass at a crap table because I'm a six-shooter. I hate Indians so much that when

I go to a hotel, I refuse to make a reservation. I can't even stand the song "Sweet Sioux."

I changed from 7-Up to Stick 'em Up. I went broke ordering "Drinks on the House" in every saloon I entered. Even my tuxedo has buckskin lapels. I want to teach dramatics just so I can be a stagecoach. I wouldn't want to be found dead without my guitar.

My favorite Western hero is Gene Autry. He can rope a steer, set fire to 1,200 Indians, hold 30 outlaws at bay, save a kid on a runaway horse, make love to the heroine, save a pal from a lynching, and with his other hand play a crazy guitar.

THE MAD DOC

Dr. Brandywine was in his office mixing a prescription—three parts gin, one part vermouth. The mad doc never did anything in halves—only in fifths. In medical school, they nicknamed him "Half-pint." Little did they realize he'd grow up to be a full quart. His face had a gin grin. As he sipped his drink, he said, "How brightly does the moon shine."

The doctor was born in London in a little town called Calvert-on-the-Breath, which is just an olive's throw from Rye-on-the-Sly near Nottingham, which is a suburb of Nottingcheese!! There was a rumor that the doc wasn't born—he was mixed!

He was half Scotch and half shot all the time. Brandywine was a specialist. With him there was no guesswork. Whatever he treated you for, you died from. One patient said he was the best doctor who ever lived—those were his last words.

Brandywine was a throat specialist . . . too bad he never specialized in medicine. I wouldn't say he was a quack, but his favorite actor was Donald Duck. Ever since he was a boy, he's been in medicine and hot water. He may not be a good doctor, but he's the cleanest surgeon in town!

He was sitting in his office, running his fingers through his hair—which is very difficult because he doesn't have any hair—when the door opened and so did his mouth. A beautiful patient walked in. She was in pretty good shape for the shape she was in. He greeted her at the door with open arms. He was wearing a jacket without sleeves. He motioned her to the chair and said, "Lie down."

At the autopsy, they discovered the patient had two holes in her head. "I shot her," the doctor confessed. "I didn't realize I was loaded."

THE TV COP AND THE PRIVATE EYEBALL

My name is Saturday. It was Friday, but I hate fish. This is New York. I'm a cop. Badge number 162785437193. In New Jersey, it's Bigelow 8-8200. The story you are about to hear is untrue, only the names have been changed to protect the guilty. . . . I was off duty sitting in my office, picking initials out of hotel towels, when the captain called me. What he called me is unimportant. He told me to send out a bulletin to warn housewives about a new burglar operating in the Bronx apartment houses. He is a notorious second-story man, so all of you who live on the second story, move in with someone on the third story. Because of his sneaky methods, the burglar is called the Cat Man. He answers to the name of "Here, Kitty, Kitty." This Cat Man is a notorious criminal . . . the only man who ever served nine life imprisonments. Don't let him cross your path. If a tall, dark man with whiskers rings your doorbell, before you open it, question him as to what he wants. If he answers, "Meow, meow," lock your door and bark as loudly as you can.

The case that threw me off the force was 90 proof. I was seated in my inner office when I heard the phone ring in my outer office—I knew it was a trick—I don't have an outer office; what's more—I don't have an inner office. I decided to answer the phone, which is rather difficult—because I don't have a phone. The big blonde who entered my office was a tall brunette with a short build. She was clean shaven with a long mustache.

When I pinned her down, she began screaming—one of the pins stuck her. She finally admitted she shot him with a bow and arrow because she didn't want to wake the neighbors.

The judge sentenced her to the electric chair with the ceremonies to be filmed on the Ed Sullivan show. She became The Toast of the Town.

OPERA

I go to the opera—whether I need the sleep or not. To me opera is Italian vaudeville. It's where a man gets stabbed and instead of bleeding he sings.

I knew Madame Butterfly when she was a cocoon but when my friend woke me up to ask if I like Madame's fiery cadenza, I said, "Yes, but if she wears a long kimono it won't show."

I don't care how big her vibrato is or what she does with her tremolo—personally I dig Ella Fitzgerald.

GEORGIE JESSEL ON THE TELEPHONE

"Hello, Mamma? This is George. Isn't it nice to have your own phone? What? Nobody calls you? Even before you had the phone nobody called you either? I see.

"Look, Mamma, maybe you'd like a new French dial phone better? . . . You're what? . . . You're too old to learn to speak French? Skip it, Mamma! How do you feel? You're hot and the flies are bothering you? Why don't you put the screens up? . . . You're not going to put the screens up this summer? . . . They're a nuisance. Why? . . . Last summer the flies that were in the house couldn't get out? I see. . . . What's new otherwise, Mamma? Who? . . . Mr. Finebaum? Yes, Mr. Finebaum who belonged to Pappa's lodge? . . . He passed away? I'm sorry to hear it—what from? . . . You can't remember, but it was nothing serious . . . I see. . . . Tell me, Mamma, are your eyes better? . . . You still see spots in front of them? Put on your glasses. . . . You have them on? How is it now? . . . You see the spots much clearer. I see. . . . Well good-bye, Mamma, I'll call soon."

THE MOVIES

I love movies.

I see anything. I even go when I can't get passes.

However, certain cinematic idiosyncrasies give me a stiff pain in my loge. F'rinstance, the cowboy stars who have knockdown, drag-out fights. They're whipped, tripped, raced, chased, smashed, and bashed. They lose their cattle, their ranches, their guns, their girls . . . but never their hats! Must be when a cowpoke gets Bar-Mitzvah'd he goes through a ritual; they nail a five-gallon hat onto him which gains one gallon every birthday until the kid owns a ten-gallon hat at eighteen. From then on he and the hat are together for richer for poorer, in sickness and health, until a bullet do 'em part.

I am also a despiser of the He-Man type who singlehandedly sabotages forty Nazi supply dumps—or was it forty dumpy sloppy Nazis? Anyway, this hero what in real life couldn't handle a sauerbraten alone is shot and beaten. The enemy uses his head as a bowling ball, stuffs an atom bomb up his nostril, kicks him, stabs him, and plays mumblety-peg with his features until his face looks like chopped liver—next scene he's wearing one skinny Band-Aid on his temple.

I further hate, abhor, and am not fond of the heroine who before saying nighty-night swallows eighty Nytols, some instant opium and a vat of gin. She's so dead asleep she's getting messages from the spirit world. Next morning when the hero awakens her she flashes more warpaint than Geronimo when he's cranky. Her eyelashes are out to here, her coiffure's coifed to there, and the lipstick is perfect. Either she's a slob who doesn't wash before retiring or she walks in her sleep!

KIDS

I never met a parent yet who didn't pull his kid's picture out at the drop of a "hello." If you should just politely ask, "What's new," this guy is gonna tell you! Forty-five minutes' worth on the exploits of the Star of the Family: "My kid said 'Dada' three times today—and he's only fifteen years old."

"Not because he's my kid," is the usual opener, "but my junior sneezed today—and he doesn't even have a head."

Just because your kid says "Dada" doesn't mean he belongs on a quiz program—or that you're his Dada.

TRAFFIC

I first got interested in traffic when I became a hit-and-run driver. It all started when a policeman arrested me for running over a button—it was on his coat.

I've been in traffic twenty-five years—I couldn't find a place to park. The average New Yorker is someone who's never seen the Statue of Liberty, Grant's Tomb—or a parking space.

The main reason for traffic congestion in New York City is—automobiles. There are more cars in New York City than in all of Germany. There are more cars in California than in England and France put together. There is only one solution—we will have to park overseas.

I have another great solution. There are 9 million people in New York City. My idea is to take 5 million and move them to Hoboken. That will cause a traffic congestion in Hoboken—but that's *their* problem.

And finally—I would make every two-way street—a dead end.

The Adams Daily Dozen

Thinking funny is a twenty-four-hour-seven-day-a-week job and you can't strike for shorter hours. Who ever heard of a comedian who's only funny on Thursday? As Dick Shawn says, "Comedy is most difficult to do because your option comes up after every joke."

That's why you have to think funny at all times, whether you feel it or not. If you're sad, think of sad jokes: "If you want to forget all your troubles —wear tight shoes." If you're ill, think of sick jokes: "I took a four-way cold tablet but it didn't know which way to go!" Did you have a bad night? Make a joke about it—"My insomnia is so bad, I can't even sleep when it's time to get up."

You've got to keep thinking funny from the moment you get up to the time your head hits the pillow at night. If your wife is annoying, laugh it off: "You promised to love, honor and obey—right now I'd settle for any one of them." If she is overdrawn at the bank, don't let it bug you—use it to find a new gag: "The joint checking account is a device that permits the woman to beat you to the draw."

For "thinking-funny" exercises, take your average day and pick out things, any things, and try and make jokes about them. Just regard your brain as a thinking man's filter that sifts the humor out of life. Here's a typical exercise for the laugh muscles in your skull—Adams' Daily Dozen:

You sit down at the breakfast table and your mother-in-law is there staring at you—you must protect yourself by thinking of a good line. "Behind every successful man stands an astonished mother-in-law."

The young maid is not there—laugh it off: "It's not whom you know that matters—it's how your wife found out." Instead, your dear wife is serving you. "My wife had to let the maid go—'cause I wouldn't."

Think of something to brighten up your morning and the breakfast table: "My mother-in-law can help Lady Bird's 'Beautify America' campaign by leaving the country."

You open your papers and find that your city is now putting in a city income tax, in addition to your state and federal tax. Think of a joke fast: "Help Mayor Lindsay stamp out take-home pay."

Only your wife can louse up corn flakes—save yourself by gagging: "The only thing my wife knows about good food is which restaurants serve it."

Your brother-in-law drives you to the train. He's an accountant (most of them are). Tell him a joke that will keep him amused and you sharp: "You can't win when you make out your income tax. If you're wrong, you go to jail—if you're right, you go to the poorhouse."

Traffic is terrible and you may be late for your train—think of a laugh quickly: "The shortest distance between two points is always under construction." You're standing still and a woman hits you with her 1950 Hupmobile: You've got to think, "The lady driver said, 'Why didn't you signal you were parked?' "

You get on the train and tell the conductor how late you are. You ask him if he could run any faster. "Yeah," he says, "but I gotta stay on the train." You just can't let him clobber you like that without one punch line: "Just because my socks are guaranteed not to run—that doesn't mean I can't get around in a hurry." All right, so think of a better line yourself.

You are going into your office building and you bump into an old schoolmate who looks twenty years older than you and greets you with "What happened to you, Joey, you got old." Grab for a gag fast: "There are three signs of old age—the first is your loss of memory—the other two I forget."

Your manager is giving you a hard time from the moment you get in the office—reach for a joke instead of a pink slip: "A good executive is a man who will share the credit with the man who did all the work."

If he threatens you with a computer taking your place—laugh yourself out of it with a good story: "The man in front of the computer that matches couples said, 'I am six-four, considered very handsome; I have oil wells and am a millionaire'—so the machine mugged him."

The pretty girl in your office with the lovely figure is wearing a long dress but the ugg is wearing a skirt just below her navel. To save your sanity, think of a laugh: "The only thing a mini-skirt does for her is to give her cold knees."

It's very hot and the air-conditioning is off. Think of a cool line: "It was so hot in Miami Beach—the women didn't carry minks—just the appraisals."

Your favorite restaurant is crowded for lunch and you have your best client with you. If the waiter gives you a hard time laugh it off: "I impressed my friends—I ordered the whole meal in French, which shook up the waiter —it was a Chinese restaurant."

It's pretty drunk out and you can't get a drink for yourself *or* your client—reach out for a laugh: "Everybody was drinking so much, they had to put a sign on the menu. It said, 'Please don't tip the waiters—they can hardly stand up as it is.' "

The lunch tab is on the expense account but even then you don't want to pay the owner's rent for the year—grab for a joke instead of the check:

"What's this five dollars for on my bill?"

"The chopped liver sandwich."

"Whose liver was it—Rockefeller's?"

You stop off at your stockbroker before you go back to the office and find the bears have eaten up the bull market. Instead of selling short or crying long, invest a joke: "Do you know what's the latest dope on Wall Street? —My son!"

Don't blame the government for the tight money—just laugh at it: "They may not cure poverty, but the way they are raising taxes—they sure will cure wealth."

Back at the office, you find a letter canceling a big order. The boss has you on the carpet—come up with a joke: "Business is so bad, even the people who never pay have stopped buying."

If the boss cries poverty, laugh him out of it: "Running into debt isn't bad—it's running into creditors that hurts."

The boss calls in an efficiency expert to bug the whole office—hit back with a joke:

"One ambitious executive who is strictly with the efficiency kick hung up a sign in his office which read 'DO IT NOW.'

"Within twenty-four hours, the cashier scrammed with the money in the safe, the secretary eloped with the boss's son, the office boy threw the ink bottle into the electric fan, and the entire office force took the day off."

You get into a taxi to go to the station and you ask the cabbie, who just sits there: "Are you engaged?" And he answers, "No, but I'm going steady." Then he wants to know where you're going as he's just pulling in or going to lunch or his tires can only go west or something. In other words, you've got to go where *he* wants to go. Now you get out the real laugh artillery: "You're nobody's fool—but see if you can get somebody to adopt you." Or, "If they ever put a price on your head—take it."

If he hollers: "Why should I go out of my way for you—what kind of dope do you think I am?" you must tell him: "I don't know—are there other kinds?"

The one night you are loaded with packages, your wife doesn't meet you at the train. In fact, your wife doesn't meet you the other nights either. Amuse yourself with a story that's appropriate while you look for a taxi: "One commuter was bragging that 'I've got a wife who meets my train every night—and we've been married ten years.' The second one said, 'I've got a wife who's been doing the same thing every night and we've been married twenty years.'

'I can beat that,' said the third, 'I've got a wife who meets me every night and I'm not even married.' "

When you get home and your wife spots the powder on your lapel, divert her with a line: "A wife is a woman who can't see a garage door thirty feet wide but can spot a blonde hair on her husband's lapel from across the street."

If her charge accounts are really too much this month, show your teeth in a smile instead of a sneer: "You'd make a hell of a Congressman—you're always introducing new bills in the house."

When she nags you about doing some work around the house—think of the poor shnook in any of the henpecked gags: "He thinks his marriage is breaking up because she never helps him with the dishes anymore."

Many married men insist they are on speaking terms with their wives when all they do is listen. If you happen to be in that category, you can always have the last word—without saying a thing. If you want to drive your wife crazy—don't talk in your sleep—*just grin*.

The Roast of the Town

In this era of masochistic comedy, our most famous personalities have accepted testimonials just to be carved to pieces by their murderous confreres, the comedians. The Friars, AGVA, Saints and Sinners, and dozens of other organizations pride themselves on the massacre of their honored guests.

These murderers don't get the chair unless it's the center one on some dais to trigger the slaughter of a poor unsuspecting guest. This honored guest is sworn to take it. It's laugh and the world laughs with you—cry and you're a poor sport.

In May, 1966, at the Annual March of Dimes Man of the Year Dinner, Ed Sullivan was the roast of the town. A couple of thousand pounds' worth of comedians showed up to make sure the roast was well done. The only reason Smiley graciously submitted to this vivisection in front of 1,500 people in the Grand Ballroom of the New York Hilton was to raise $100,000 for the March of Dimes.

As toastmaster, I fired first shots. "You can sum up Ed Sullivan's succes in one word—lucky."

I followed that with, "Ed has done everything from sportswriter to Broadway columnist to TV star and motion picture actor. Now his friends want him to do what Ronald Reagan and George Murphy did—get the hell out of the business."

"Everybody says Ed has a dull personality," Morey Amsterdam started. "That's not true—he has no personality at all."

Then Morey added, "Ed knows a lot—he just can't think of it." "They keep sending Sullivan to Europe to find new talent but the trouble is they keep sending him back."

Jack Carter was sweet: "I was going to bring you a present—but what do you give a man who has nothing?"

Jan Murray hollered: "He takes stars and makes unknowns out of them."

Ed laughed the loudest when Johnny Carson elaborated on his theory that Sullivan has ruined as many careers as he has helped. "Take Harry Harlow, the hypnotist. The man with the magic vision. In 1957 he made his first

54

TV appearance. Ed was in rare form that Sunday. He was pointing extra well. Suddenly he turned quickly and said, 'There he is!' Got Harlow right in the eye."

Carson's parting shot was, "The ear, nose, and throat hospitals are full of ex-sword swallowers from Sullivan's shows."

The only consolation the target has is that they never give you a dinner until you can afford to buy your own. As Georgie Jessel reminded Ed: "I have never known anyone who was the recipient of a dinner who didn't have something that was pretty good. No one ever gave a dinner to Willie Sutton, Leftie Louie, or Sitting Bull."

Then he said: "Ed is a great man. He belongs on Mt. Rushmore with Washington and Jefferson and Lincoln. In fact, you don't have to chisel him out of stone—he's ready right now."

Sylvia Sullivan, Ed's beautiful wife, his daughter Betty, and his producer son-in-law Robert Precht made up the laughing section when thespian Paul Ford sauntered up to the mike to say, "I first met Mr. Sullivan at the Actor's Studio. He was their first dropout. Later on he learned how to mumble by himself."

"The real reason the circus came to town was to see Ed Sullivan," claimed Soupy Sales.

Peter Lind Hayes said softly, "He's the only golfer who falls asleep in his own backswing."

The murderers were in good shape as each one stood up to thrust the knife for charity:

"It was Vincent Lopez who predicted Ed would be a big star on television—Vincent also predicted Elizabeth Taylor would become a nun."

"Ed has been on CBS for eighteen years. You want to know why? It's because no other network wanted him."

Chairman Earl Wilson closed the inquisition. "Ed knows what the public likes. And one of these days he's going to give it to them."

A sense of humor is what makes you laugh at something that would make you mad if it happened to you. But given the choice, show people would rather be rapped than ignored. You can always pick out actors by the glazed look that comes into their eyes when the conversation wanders away from themselves.

Allen and Rossi were never happier than when the American Guild of Variety Artists Youth Fund saluted them as the Men of the Year in show business and invited the hatchet men to carry out the honors.

"Allen and Rossi," I started, "are the greatest team since Leopold and Loeb."

"When their first film was seen at Paramount, the president said, 'Get that Italian organ grinder out of my studio and tell him to take the monkey with him.' "

Mayor Lindsay took note of Marty Allen's mau-mau mop, a coiffure the Barbers' Union of Zululand had invented, and announced he was appointing him his "Commissioner of Hair Pollution."

Bandleader Lionel Hampton promised he was going all out to promote a television series for Marty and Steve because, "You are good for big bands. When you are on TV—more people go out dancing."

Virginia Graham said her friendship for Marty Allen goes back a long way, "Ever since we first met under a drier."

"It's right that we honor them for the Youth Fund," Henny Youngman said lovingly; "they are an inspiration to the youth of America. The kids love them. They figure if they can make it—anybody can."

Tom Poston wondered how in the world Marty Allen had ever gone so far. "After all, what does he have except a pretty face?"

Soupy Sales said, "His was the only face that looked better with a pie in it."

William B. Williams said, "They're testing that great lover Steve Rossi to play the old Clark Gable parts. The only thing is—they found his old parts don't work as good as Gable's did."

At this dinner, a few other heads rolled as well. After Judge Di Falco's speech, Soupy Sales shouted: "Hey, Judge, you're funny! Not tonight! In court yesterday."

"You remember Joey Adams who was so popular years ago?" Robert Alda blasted.

Somebody introduced Eddie Fisher as "The most successful loser in show business."

"At least," Eddie answered, "I've been there!"

It was a great night for the two boys who were compared to St. Jo and St. Paul: "Two of the dullest towns in America."

As I said to the boys at the end of the evening: "You have my vote— but I also voted for Barry Goldwater, Richard Nixon and William Buckley, Jr."

There's an old Japanese proverb which says: "The tongue is only three inches long—yet it could kill a man six feet high." That's why it takes a good comic surgeon to get so close to the cuticle without cutting.

These roasts are verbal cartoons that are only planned to do good. Certainly they are not meant for evil. In effect, they are oral caricatures that are set up to be amusing and at the same time help some charity raise some money.

The master surgeon is George Jessel, who was tabbed "Toastmaster General of the United States" by Earl Wilson and adopted by four Presidents of the United States.

At a dinner for Joey Bishop he started: "Our fall from grace is self-explanatory on this occasion tonight. This evening had been planned as a dinner for Chief Justice Earl Warren and *look what we got!* Last year we wanted Hubert Humphrey and we got B. S. Pully."

56

George introduced Danny Thomas as one of the real great geniuses of our time. "Although he is not an Israelite, he is a native of a Semitic country —as a matter of fact, he is the George Washington of his country. This is not such a big compliment, because in the whole country there are twenty-four people and a zebra."

He said Danny Kaye was "The current favorite of Great Britain during the fog."

Of course, Jessel's victims have had many opportunities to return the compliments. Georgie has had more dinners thrown at him that any other public figure since Henry the Eighth. "I have been honored by every type of worthy charity," Georgie says proudly. "Catholic, Jewish, and Protestant. Of course, the Moslems I'm not so close to at the moment."

At any Jessel dinner the wine and the barbs flow freely. "Georgie Jessel is one of the great humanitarians of all time," I introduced him at one banquet; "this year alone he supported 1 million Jews in Israel and 325 chorus girls in the USA."

Jack Benny said, "Mr. Jessel has the unique distinction of being the only American mentioned in *Who's Who* and the *Kinsey Report*."

Bob Hope appeared at a dinner for Jessel when the famous toastmaster was working as a producer at 20th Century-Fox under Darryl Zanuck. "George is a key man at Fox," Bob started. "Every time Zanuck goes to the washroom, Jessel hands him the key."

Bob continued, "This kosher Errol Flynn was always destined for greatness. It was obvious nothing could stop him—not even his talent.

"Everybody connects him with women. I know him pretty well, and I know he doesn't give a second thought to women—his first thought covers everything.

"He's a very loyal fellow and crazy about his boss, Zanuck. The other night at the Academy Awards when Darryl bent over to kiss the Oscar, Jessel bent over to kiss Zanuck. It was a pretty sight. I can't tell you what he does to keep his job, but it is banned in Boston."

But go fool around with Gene Autry. Jessel always has the last word: "This has been a most trying evening for me, listening to many great gentlemen, highly successful in their own vocations, attempting to be after-dinner speakers. Considering this great fund of inexperience, they have done remarkably well and I compliment them as I would compliment a sixty-year-old baseball umpire who had crocheted a fine lace tablecloth."

Jessel has the most beautiful trick in speaking. He starts with a tear and winds up with a laugh. "I'm not a rich man," he said after he was honored at one function, "but whatever I have is profit. All this—all this is profit. I began with nothing—not only that, after I was a few days old they took yet something away from me."

Another dinner brought out his great sentiment: "I feel like Will Rogers, 'I never met a man I didn't like.' I have something in common with

Mr. Rogers, for I had a girl, once, who felt the same way—she never met a man she couldn't like!"

Personally, I enjoy the world more because we are able to satirize each other with every squeeze of the grapefruit.

If you were to take a bunch of different type comedians and shove them into one room, you'd probably go nuts—which would give you a head start in becoming a comedian.

That's what happened to me recently when the March of Dimes voted me "The Man of the Year," and gave me a testimonial dinner at the Waldorf-Astoria Hotel. All the comics showed up, and the target for the evening was me!

Earl Wilson said in his opening remarks as toastmaster, "Broadway has the strange custom of publicly razzing somebody it likes and tonight's victim is Joey Adams." Looking at me he said, "It's tough for me to rib you. I think you're funny—not your gags—the way you dress."

Morey Amsterdam kicked it off with, "It's fitting we give Joey Adams a dinner—everybody does—he hasn't picked up a check in twenty-four years —but that's on account of his religion—he's a devout cheapskate. Don't misunderstand—I like him. I have no taste—but I like him."

Jack Carter, an old friend, naturally swatted me with some new lines. "The things he does for his friends," he said with his arms around me, "can be counted on his little finger." Jack got sentimental: "This dinner for Joey has me all choked up—with jealousy. Joey works for every charity committee. The other day he joined an organization so small, they didn't have a disease yet."

Henny Youngman was loving: "Joey lights up a room—by leaving it."

Red Buttons heaped his praise on my philanthropic work: "Fooling around with charity," was the way he put it, "has made Joey a very rich man."

Horace McMahon talked about my childhood. "We tried to dig up somebody who knew Joey when he was young—and we'd probably have to." He said, "Everybody knows that the late and great Fiorello, Mayor of New York, raised Joey, but what they don't know is that La Guardia was a parole officer at the time."

Harry Hershfield related the saga of when I was dating a beautiful young lady whose father objected. "No actor will ever be a son of mine," he warned. "After seeing Joey's act," Harry explained, "the father told the girl not to worry—she could marry him—he's no actor."

Earl then introduced Lou Holtz. "I'm glad to be here tonight," the great dialectician announced, "because there is only one Joey Adams—I found that out by looking in the telephone directory." He continued affectionately, "This boy has a lot of talent—but it's in his wife's name."

Jack E. Leonard took care of me in very short order. "Joey," he sliced, "has a great sense of humor. He doesn't care whose it is. Some day you'll go too far," he said to me, "and I hope you stay there."

Myron Cohen said that I'm the man about whom President Johnson once said "Who's he?" and he added, "Joey is one of the most sought after people in the country today—for income tax evasion."

Henry Morgan said, "I don't know what I'm doing here—I'm pretty unique—nobody even invited me to this thing."

The next executioner was Steve Allen, who opened with "Maybe nobody invited Henry Morgan but I'm even more unique—Henry invited me." Steve talked about my literary career. "Joey always felt he could write. One day, in one of those cheap magazines, he spied an ad that said, 'How do you know you can't write?' Seeing that ad fired Joey to send his jokes, anecdotes and other masterpieces. One month later he received a telegram which said, 'Now you know you can't write!' "

George De Witt was short and to the point:

"I'd love to say something nice about my friend Joey Adams, but I just can't think of it."

Jan Murray swept on furious. "I don't understand this whole bit," he fumed. "Who the hell elected him Man of the Year? We started together. I'm better looking than him. I have a daily TV show. He's made Man of the Year and I can't even get chosen Jew of the block! Don't you think it's a little incongruous?" By now he was screaming. "They give this little jerk a big dinner at the Waldorf-Astoria—and Bernard Baruch sat on a park bench by himself. Don't you think it's blasphemous when Joey gets a plaque and Albert Schweitzer's trophy room was empty? Don't you people notice anything wrong? Here Joey is being honored by the March of Dimes and Dr. Jonas Salk can't get an interview on a local radio show."

I knew my dear wife Cindy would save me—and she did—for the knockout. "We've been wed a long time and I think married life is wonderful," she began. "It's just Joey I can't stand. Of course, many people thought our marriage wouldn't last because my husband is so much older than I. I don't think he's so old, although recently he did receive a brochure from an old age home—and it was marked URGENT.

"I find it hard to forget that Joey Adams is the world's foremost authority on humor today—and so would you if you had to write it on the blackboard 500 times before you got your first mink coat."

To me, those were the sweetest sounds I ever heard—it meant she loved me. Comedy, in order to be effective, must be at somebody's expense. In this case I'm glad it was mine—it showed they were all my friends. I'd worry if they said something nice at a dinner like this.

Roasting is a comic's way of kissing. Jack E. Leonard, born with a silver scalpel in his mouth, spares nobody, not even himself. Jack claims his homicidal barbs are a defense mechanism. "I was so fat I couldn't fight and

59

I couldn't run, so I used my brain and my tongue." Jack salves his bleeding targets by announcing that he only needles people he likes.

Julius La Rosa asked Jack the other day why he was angry at him. "I'm not," Jack said. "Why do you say that?"

"I dunno," he answered, "you just passed and didn't insult me."

I have been invited to be toastmaster or guest speaker at some of the most famous roasts in town. I'm always prepared for battle with the right stabs in the right backs—but the punishment must fit the crime without killing. Remember, you came to roast him, not electrocute him.

Only, watch out for the sensitive spots. You can't rib your neighbor about his wife's drinking, or the boss about his bald spot, or your partner about not being able to see but refusing to wear glasses because he's vain.

You can't murder the guest of honor about his delinquent son—no matter how funny the joke is. You can't kid the man about his weight or height—unless, of course, he uses it as a gimmick—as part of his personality. Bob Hope jokes about his ski nose, Myron Cohen about his bald head. Then it's okay to take aim in that direction.

For instance, Jack E. Leonard kids about his weight. "I won't tell you how much I weigh, but don't get in an elevator with me—unless you're going down." In that case, it's okay to say about him, "He went on a three-week diet and lost twenty-one days."

In introducing another fat boy who loves to make jokes about his size I said, "Jackie Gleason loves food; until he can find a dog who can cook—this man's best friend is a chef."

In introducing Milton Berle I said, "He started comedy on TV twenty years ago—and this year he finished it." Presenting Joe E. Lewis I said: "He is the only man with an honorary liquor license. Everybody says Joe E. is a heavy drinker—that's not so—he only weighs 130. It was Joe E. who invented the slogan, 'If you drink, don't drive—you might hit a bump and spill some.' "

What I am trying to tell you is that you can't do drunk jokes about Berle or TV jokes about Joe E.: Milton doesn't drink nor does he have that reputation. ("I get drunk on rye bread or scotch tissue," he says.)

On the other hand, you can apply any drinking gags to Joe E. or his fellow bar-mates Dean Martin, Phil Harris, or Jackie Gleason. Jackie admits that's not tea that puts him in his cups. I mean, that he puts in his cups. "I drink for the sole purpose of getting bagged," says the Great One. "Drinking removes warts and pimples. Not from me—but from those I have to look at."

Conversely, you can't do TV jokes about Joe E., who is seldom on the air—or in it, for that matter.

When Oscar Levant cracked that "Zsa Zsa does social work among the rich," everybody laughed, including Zsa Zsa. Nobody enjoys it more than Zsa Zsa when I say about her: "Zsa says a good girl should get married for love—and keep on getting married till she finds it." Or, "Zsa Zsa says when a girl breaks her engagement she should return the ring—but she should keep the stone, of course."

Zsa Zsa, who admits she loves everything about America—the people of America, the songs of America, the Bank of Amercia—will never resent any gags about her sex life or her interest in jewels or money. That's all romantic to her. But just do one joke that takes away her glamor and she'll hate you forever. Once the Las Vegas *Sun* printed a line about her dunking doughnuts with me and she threatened to sue the paper for a million dollars for making her sound like the common people.

Henny Youngman loved it when Johnny Carson said about him, "Every joke that comes out of Henny's mouth is lying in state." But he made the crack after he booked him on the show.

Martha Raye and Joe E. Brown do gags about their big mouths, so naturally Martha didn't resent it when I said: "I kissed her and lost my head completely."

Ed Sullivan doesn't claim to be a comedian or a Master of Ceremonies. Actually he is an editor or a producer who knows how to put a great show together. Consequently, he enjoyed it when I said: "There's a new Ed Sullivan doll on the market—you wind it up and for one hour it does nothing." He laughed the loudest when I jabbed, "People say he has a dull personality on TV. That's not true—he has no personality at all."

At a party for the dean of the after-dinner speakers, Harry Hershfield, I said: "He's been speaking at dinners since food was invented. In fact, if you take a close-up of the last supper—he's the third from the right."

I introduced Soupy Sales as "The only teen-ager eligible for Medicare," and Dagmar, "Who has all her talent in her bra." Mayor Lindsay added, "It's my ambition to see Dag play an accordion."

In each case, we were caricaturizing what each was noted for.

However, it is dangerous to pick on your superiors unless you can handle it and you know they can. It's okay to say about your fellow worker, "He's always around when he needs you," or "He picks his friends—to pieces." But the same kind of jokes about your boss, "If you kicked him in the heart, you'd break your toe," or "He's so stingy he won't even tip his hat," could get you a nice pink slip and I don't mean underwear.

And don't pick on your inferiors—they got enough trouble now. It's okay for a fellow comedian to introduce Milton Berle as "The Thief of Bad Gags." He makes jokes about that himself. Or that "Milton knows the secret of making people laugh—and he sure knows how to keep a secret." Berle has been getting laughs for a bunch of years so it could only be funny. But the same jokes about Sam Schnitzer or any unknown comic could only hurt him —and your gag.

I introduced Red Buttons by saying: "I always knew he'd make it in

61

pictures. I remember the exact words I said. I said, 'Red—you got about as much chance in Hollywood as I have.' " This wouldn't be funny if Red didn't win an Oscar or at least an Irving.

At a party for Jack Benny I said, "Any man who needs so many character witnesses shouldn't be a guest of honor." If Jack weren't important and the dais guests weren't—the line wouldn't be either. In comparison, you can do the same thing at your local Y.M.C.A. or Rotary Club if they are on your level.

In other words, be kind unless you know how to hit and run without leaving scars. Which is just what this book is about. To paraphrase the Bard's bit, "The joke's the thing." But only if it's at the right hams. And we hope you'll be cured by the time you finish this book.

The Hecklers

The show business fraternity has left longer-lasting scars on hecklers than Zoro—but still the lampshade wearers and the table comics keep coming. When are they going to learn that a professional can make a jerk out of them in one line? And that would improve their status.

Every circle has a square who is "funnier than the guy on stage"—until the "guy on stage" puts him back in the woodwork where he belongs. Professional comedians play their own version of pin the tail on the donkey. Point out the jackass and they pin the joke on him: "You have a nice personality—but not for a human being."

Professional comics are weaned on insults. If they don't have hecklers, they work on each other to keep in trim.

Don Rickles blasted Harry James: "Your lip is gone—why don't you hum?"

Jack E. Leonard tortured Sinatra: "You have a nice voice—one of these days it will reach up to your throat."

"Why, ya crumbum," Toots Shor said to Jackie Gleason, "I'll put you in my back pocket."

"Then," the Fat One answered, "you'll have more brains in your pocket than you have in your head."

Jonathan Winters attacked a fellow-comic: "I've got just the thing for you, friend, a do-it-yourself Ox-Bow Incident."

Henny Youngman to a pal: "I think the world of you—and you know what I think of the world."

Jack Zero was asked to contribute five dollars to bury an agent. "Sure," said Jack. "Here's ten dollars—bury two agents."

Milton Berle was challenged by a small-timer at the Stage Delicatessen. "You want to have a battle of wits?" asked Milton. "I'll check my brains and we'll start even."

Joe E. Lewis said to comedian Gene Baylos, who had lifted some of his material: "You have very witty ears."

Gene said to one well-known star: "I saw your show—when are you gonna make a comeback?"

All I'm trying to tell you is—don't fool around with Gene Autry—or the professional comic. This is their business and they are prepared to give it to you any time you ask for it. Like Baylos says, "A lotta guys say I don't have to do this for a living, but I got news for you—*this is it.*"

Don't misunderstand, you don't have to be a professional to handle a heckler. Mr. and Mrs. Civilian can do it pretty well in their everyday lives. It's just that a pro is better trained and equipped for all occasions. The civilians can miss but the pro must bat 100 per cent at all times.

I hope that these lines will help your batting average when you come up against that party pest, the caustic cab driver, your mother-in-law, or your favorite bus driver. Don't misunderstand, I'm not planting these bombs to create more hecklers for my fellow comedians or myself. I just hope you take this ammunition at farce value and only use it to defend yourself.

Here are my favorite answers, with muscles, guaranteed to flatten the toughest opponent. Don't get upset if they walk out on you—it's when they walk toward you that you have to worry.

"It's all right to drink like a fish—if you drink what a fish drinks."

"In your case, brain surgery would be only a minor operation."

"One good way to save face—is to keep the lower half shut."

"Next time you give your old clothes away—stay in them!"

"There's a bus leaving in five minutes—get under it."

"Find yourself a home in a wastebasket."

"I don't know what I'd do without you—but I'm willing to try."

"If you had your life to live over again—don't do it."

"Do you have a chip on your shoulder—or is that your head?"

"I hear they just redecorated your home—put new padding on the walls."

"Say—you're a regular C.P.A.—a constant pain in the neck."

Of course, the insult didn't begin with the comics. Stars like Oscar Wilde and George Bernard Shaw were on the warpath way before Milton Berle encountered his first heckler.

Oscar Wilde said: "Bernard Shaw hasn't an enemy in the world—and none of his friends like him."

Gertrude Stein taunted Hemingway: "Ernest, remarks are not literature."

Shakespeare boasted that as a country schoolmaster he had never blotted out a line. To which Ben Jonson remarked: "I wish he'd blotted out a thousand."

Alice Roosevelt Longworth heckled: "Calvin Coolidge looks as if he had been weaned on a pickle."

Gypsy Rose Lee was annoyed at a snooty chorine: "She is descended from a long line that her mother listened to."

The art of insult has replaced the art of self-defense. Only make sure you're a David when you sling mud at a Goliath. An insult is like a married man coming home with lipstick on his collar—it's hard to laugh off. In the wrong hands, it could be the sincerest form of flattening.

The noisy diner was banging on the table with his cutlery. "The service here is lousy," he bellowed. "Look at my glass, it's empty. What've I got to do to get some water?"

The quiet waiter leaned over and whispered, "Why don't you set fire to yourself?"

The elevator operator was tired of the same old cliche. The stranger began, "Say, Cutie, you sure have your ups and downs, don't you?"

"It's not the ups and downs that bother me," she snapped, "it's the jerks."

The bar was unusually noisy one convention night. Joe E. Lewis looked up and drawled, "They redecorated the bar—they put new drunks around it."

A lush blonde turned blonde lush was annoying Jan Murray one night. Looking down her plunging neckline, he remarked, "Be careful, honey, or you'll spill that dress all over your drink."

Singing star Sonny King was interrupted all through his favorite ballad by a coughing and sneezing drunk. "No wonder this guy has a cold," he sneered. "He's got a hole in his head!"

The woman in the movies had chronic palpitation of the tongue. She wouldn't stop talking until the man in front of her tapped her on the shoulder and hissed, "Lady, you should be wired for silence."

Georgie Jessel insulted a whole country. "France," he said, "is like a country run by the Marx Brothers."

The customer complained to the tailor that his pants weren't ready on time. "It only took God six days to make the whole world," he beefed.

"Yeah, but look at the shape of the world, and look at the shape of my pants."

Morey Amsterdam to a pest: "You should have been born in the Dark Ages—you certainly look awful in the light."

Henny Youngman to a bore: "When you were born something terrible happened—you lived."

Max Asnas of the Stage Delicatessen was bothered by a woman who complained, "Your food gives me heartburn."

"What did you expect—sunburn?"

"Do you mind if I have you X-rayed?" Joey Bishop said to an alleged celeb who was a bore, "I want to see what they see in you."

Mickey Manners described a certain Broadwayite "who has so little personality that he worked a color TV show—and came out in black and white."

FEMALE HECKLERS

Handling a female is a little more delicate, although they get rougher, and if you want to win, sometimes you have to counterpunch pretty hard.

65

"I hear you're getting a divorce—who's the lucky man?"

"Get a load of those legs—I've seen better looking bones in soup."

"She's the kind of girl to take to the movies—when you want to see the picture."

"There goes a girl with polish—on her fingernails."

"There you have the greatest single argument for twin beds."

"She spends most of her time outside the draft board waiting for rejects."

"She looks like a kept woman—like she's been kept under a rock."

"She's just sore because I can read her like a book—and I like to read in bed."

MALE HECKLERS

"He says he's a self-made man—I think it's nice of him to take the blame."

"If they ever put a price on your head—take it."

"He must have a sixth sense—there's no sign of the other five."

"He's not himself today—and it's a great improvement."

"If you need me—hesitate to call."

"Please don't talk when I'm interrupting."

"With the cost of living so high—why do you bother?"

"Will you please follow the example of your head and come to a point?"

CRITICS

If I've been warning you that the comic's cut can be deeper than the surgeon's, in comparison, the critic makes him look like a minister. Alexander Woollcott had the reputation of being not only the most merciless and meanest of critics; he also was the fattest. He very often attempted a well-advertised but short-lived diet. During such a period one playwright was overheard telling another, "I hear Woollcott has dropped forty pounds."

"On whom?" inquired the other.

Kelcey Allen's review of a show heckled it out of existence. "The cast was well balanced—they were all rotten."

One of the shortest musical criticisms on record appeared in a Detroit paper: "An amateur string quartet played Brahms here last evening—Brahms lost."

Another pithy review lasted much longer than the play called, "Dreadful Night." The account: "Dreadful night: PRECISELY!"

And you think comics are bad boys? After an ambitious performance of *Hamlet* in a small city, the local critic scalded: "There has long been a controversy over who wrote Shakespeare's plays—Shakespeare or Bacon. I propose to settle it today by opening their graves. Whoever turned over wrote *Hamlet*."

Percy Hammond demolished one show. In closing he said: "I have knocked everything except the knees of the chorus girls—and God anticipated me there!"

Dorothy Parker said about Katherine Hepburn: "She runs the gamut of emotion from A to B."

Carl Sandburg kept his promise to appear at the dress rehearsal of a young playwright's show—but he slept during most of the performance. His young friend was distraught later: "How could you sleep when you know how much I wanted your opinion?"
"Sleep," Sandburg reminded him, "*is* an opinion."

John Mason Brown was at his meanest best when he scratched: "Tallulah Bankhead barged down the Nile last night as Cleopatra—and sank."

Heywood Broun was once sued by some actor called Stein for calling his performance "atrocious." The next time Mr. Broun reviewed Stein, he brushed him with "Mr. Stein's performance was not up to his usual standard."

"He played King Lear as though someone had led the ace."

The murderers don't have to be actors, comics or critics. They could be doctors or lawyers—like Clarence Darrow, the famous criminal attorney, who met a childhood pal who had become a doctor.
"If you had listened to me," said the friend, "you would be a doctor too."
"What's wrong with being a lawyer?" Darrow asked.
"Well, I don't say lawyers are crooks," answered the doctor, "but you must admit that the profession doesn't exactly make angels of men."
"No," answered Darrow, "you doctors have the better of us there."

One ham was bragging to the guys at the Lambs' Club: "When I'm on stage you can hear them laughing across the street."
"Why?" asked a listener. "What's playing there?"

George Bernard Shaw was invited to a party in London. After a boring hour the hostess asked, "Mister Shaw, are you enjoying yourself?"
"Yes—and that's all I'm enjoying!"

Only Mrs. Shaw could top the Bearded One. Once when he asked his wife to agree that "Male judgment is superior to female judgment," she answered, "Of course, dear; after all, you married me and I you!"

Talking about handling hecklers of every description, Scottish playwright Sir James Barrie held the shortest interview on record. An enterprising newspaperman gained entrance to the author's flat and began, "Sir James Barrie, I presume?"

"You do!" replied Barrie, closing the door immediately.

One actor had the guts and the joke to hit back at newspapermen. "I've been fortunate," he stated, "that newspapermen have always written nice things about me. So they're 'A' in my book. In fact, I think most of them are A. A."

"I'm very proud to be a friend of his—and it's not easy to be a man's only friend."

Will Rogers heckled the entire Congress when he intoned: "I might have gone to West Point—but I was too proud to talk to a Congressman."

When the Stage Delicatessen burned down, almost every comic in town, including myself, wired owner Max Asnas: "First time the food has been hot in your place in years."

Henny Youngman's special target for heckling is his patient ever-loving wife: "My wife," he croons, "has a slight impediment in her speech—every once in a while she stops to breathe. Her hair color is changed so often, she has a convertible top; and when she goes to sleep at night, she packs so much mud on her face, I say, 'Good night, Swamp!' "

My all-time favorite squelch is the one about the famous Shakespearean actor who is accosted by a bum who pleads, "Sir, can you spare me a quarter for something to eat?"

The actor pulled himself to his 6-foot-2 and emoted in his best Bard manner, "Young man—'neither a borrower nor a lender be'—William Shakespeare."

The bum looked at him for a second and answered: 'Screw you'— Tennessee Williams."

I will try to get you ready for any emergency. Like if you run into a bad audience: "Don't move—I want to forget you just the way you are." Or if you find yourself a sloppy drunk: "He's suffering from bottle fatigue." Or a sleeping beauty at ringside: "I don't mind your falling asleep on me— but the least you could do is say good night!"

Each heckler should have his own burial. If you're bothered by a newspaperman: "He has what in newspaper circles is called know-how. He knows how the leading columnists do it—and he copies them."

ELDERLY HECKLER: "Most people nowadays have more respect for old age— if it is bottled."

DOCTOR: "He's the kind of doctor who feels your purse." "Are you a bone specialist?—You sure have the head for it!"

LAWYER: "He's a trial lawyer—only *he's* the one who should be on trial."

INDIAN CHIEF: "He's one of Chief Running Water's three sons—there was Cold, Luke Warm, and he's Not-So-Hot."

RICH MAN: "Wealth has made him eccentric instead of impolite, and witty instead of rude. To me, his great wealth hasn't changed him—he's still a bum."

POOR MAN: "He's so flat—they could play him on the Victrola."

BEGGAR MAN: "He's a jack of all trades—and out of work in all of them."

THIEF: "He's a man of convictions—and he's served time for every one of them."

TO LAVENDER HECKLER: "You'd rather swish than fight."

BULLY: "I'd like to run into you again sometime—when you're walking and I'm driving."

DUMB: "He's so stupid—he once took a clock to bed with him because he heard it was fast."

COUPLE: "Aren't they a lovely couple—she's from Boston and he's from Hunger." Or, "They make an ideal couple. He's eligible and she's desperate."

SKINNY HECKLER: "Send his picture to the underprivileged countries—and they'll send *us* food." Or, "He went to the blood bank and forgot to say when!"

EGOTIST: "He's so conceited—he has his X rays retouched."

BORE: "He never opens his mouth unless he has nothing to say."

BIG MOUTH: "Her tongue is so long—she can seal an envelope after she puts it in the mailbox." "He could talk his head off—and never miss it." "When all is said and done—she keeps on talking."

CHEAPSKATE: "When it comes to picking up a check—he has a slight impediment of the reach." "He talks through his nose to save wear and tear on his teeth." "He's the first to put his hand in his pocket—and keep it there." "He tosses quarter tips around like manhole covers." "He finds lost golf balls—before they stop rolling."

CRANK: "He had three phones installed—so he could hang up on more people."
"He has an even disposition—always nasty."
"Whatever is eating him—must be suffering from indigestion."

SMART ASS: "He always goes through the revolving door on somebody else's push."

"Well, it takes all kinds of people to make up a world—too bad you're not one of them."

"He may talk like an idiot, he may look like an idiot, but don't let that fool you—he *is* an idiot!"

"He picks up a girl on your whistle."

SCREWBALL: "The psychiatrist told him he doesn't have an inferiority complex—he's just inferior."

POLITICIAN: "He approaches every question with an open mouth."

"We knew he had to be a politician. Even as a kid he said more things that sounded well and meant nothing than any kid on the block."

"He claims he's self-made—but he's really machine-made."

"His slogan is, 'They have been stealing for years—now give me a chance!' "

LIAR: "You can always tell if he's telling the truth or not. If his lips are moving—he's lying."

"The only thing that keeps him from becoming a bare-faced liar—is his mustache."

ACTOR: "On stage he is natural and simple—it's off stage that he is acting."

JUVENILE DELINQUENT: "The delinquents of today are the same as the delinquents of fifty years ago—only they have better weapons."

"He's a lovable kid; instead of a sandbox—they should have filled it with quicksand."

When he goes to school—the teacher plays hookey."

LAZY: "Automation could never replace him—they still haven't found a machine that does absolutely nothing."

DUMB: "She's so dumb—she takes off her sweater to count to two."

BALD-HEADED PEST: "First time I ever saw a part with ears."

TALL MAN: "I wish you'd fall down—so you'd be out of town."

SHORT MAN: "He sits down and stands up—he's the same size."

TABLE COMIC: "Let's give him a big hand—right across the mouth."

PHOTOGRAPHER: "His mind is like his pictures—never quite developed."

PHARMACIST: "Calling All Drug Stores—Calling All Drug Stores—one of your pills is missing!"

DUMB: "She was fired from the 5 & 10—she couldn't remember the prices."

"He's so dumb. He lost his job as an elevator operator—he couldn't remember the route."

ENTERTAINERS: "He wasn't hissed, because the audience couldn't yawn and hiss at the same time."

"The entire audience hissed him—except one man. He was applauding the hissing."

"What a ventriloquist—his dummy is quitting him to find a new partner."

"He has no talent and he knows it; but he can't quit—he's a star."

"There's an act that should go far—and soon."

"I wish I were the leader of the band—I'd lead them right into the river."

"He'd dance better—if he would take the shoe trees out."

"He's so funny—I can hardly keep from laughing."

"He's going to live to be unknown."

UGLY: "A Peeping Tom reached in and pulled down her window shade."

"She had her face lifted so many times—it's out of focus."

"She looks like a professional blind date."

"She has the most beautiful, long black hair—on her face."

"She's so ugly—they hung her and kissed the mistletoe."

"She has everything a man desires—muscles and a beard."

CHILD HECKLER: "Isn't he adorable? You know what I love most about him? The fact that he isn't mine!"

PEST WITH GLASSES: "He had his reading glasses changed six times, and he still can't read. It wasn't until his last change that the doctor discovered the reason—he's illiterate."

I've tried to give you ammunition to hit any target. Just make sure you use it in good health. Don't say to a heckler, "You have thirty-two teeth, would you like to try for none?" if you don't think you can handle him. It's okay to say, "The best way to keep your youth—is not to introduce him to anybody," if you're sure the youth won't try to introduce you to a right cross.

Of course, you don't have to worry how big or tough they are. Even if you're Casper Milquetoast, you can deliver a punch line—but in that case just make sure you deliver it on the phone and hang up.

I think it was Johnny Weissmuller who said, "Do not insult the mother alligator until after you have crossed the river." Or was it Henny Youngman? No, I think it was Three-Finger Jones.

One very special warning. Make sure that you *do not*, under any circumstances, use these lines to *start* an argument—only to *finish* one.

Censorship and Ethnic Humor

Remember the old boxing bit in burlesque? The referee says to the fighter, "Remember, *this* you can't do" (rubbing his thumb in his eye), "and *this* is out" (hitting him below the belt), "and *this* is not allowed" (kicking him in the shin), "and definitely not *this*" (biting him on the ear), "and by all means you can't do *this*" (pulling his hair).

"Hey," says the fighter, "you've taken away all my best punches."

"That's what's happened to TV," say the comics. "They've taken away all our best punch lines."

Almost every picture that comes to town has five four-letter words and three girls having children without being wed and at least one abortion—but just do one sexy line on TV and you're a dead comic.

You know the joke about "The women on Mars are built different—they have their bust in the back—it doesn't make them more attractive—but it's better for dancing"?—That's out.

And you can't do a joke like:

PHYLLIS DILLER: "Is this MGM? Do you have a handsome actor—who has been under the hot lights all day?"
PRODUCER: "Yes."
PHYLLIS: "Well, send him over before he cools off."

Of course, you can't do bathroom jokes. Remember the uproar Jack Paar caused with his harmless W.C. story?

You know the one about the comic telling his straightman, "I had the most expensive drawing room on the train to California."

"Was it comfortable?"

"Yes, but every time we got to a station the conductor locked the door." —That's out.

And definitely no reference to homosexuality. Do you like the story of the boy who complained that a man asked him to dance? "I got so mad," the boy said, "I hit him with my purse." Well, you can't even think of doing it on TV.

Anatomy gags are definitely out. This kind of joke will never make it:

"I'm going to the ballet tonight—I have a box seat."
"Wear a long coat—it won't show."

Now, don't misunderstand, I'm not complaining—just explaining—so that you'll know what to do or rather what not to do, if you're called to do the Ed Sullivan Show or your local TV. Smiley guards his home audiences like they were his own family. Jackie Mason was almost given a life sentence just for giving our Man Sunday the finger on television.

Censorship plays an important part on the air. The mildest joke is deleted if some V.P. figures it will offend one kid on a farm someplace in Omaha.

You can't do jokes on milady's chapeaux, or the millinery association will jump on you, or worse still, on your sponsor. Jokes against butchers, bakers, or even candlestick makers invariably bring local protests, as do gags kidding Brooklyn, Harlem, or Staten Island.

Stations cut out gags that refer to suicide or robbery, etc. Needless to say, swear words are out or even words that have a double meaning—like "fanny" or "bust."

Of course, this is not new. Even in the days of radio, when Jack Benny and Fred Allen were calling each other "anemic," they had to stop when irate anemic listeners besieged the stations with letters saying they could see nothing funny in anemia.

Even before that, during the days of vaudeville, many of the theatres had big signs posted backstage for the comics to see: "No blue material—no jokes lousing up the town—or the trolley or the railroad—and no foul punch lines in songs—*or you will be canceled!*"

Like I've been saying all along, you have to know what material to do where. Television is a particularly sensitive area because it goes right into the living room or bedroom and anybody from the President of the United States to the newborn baby could be watching. So TV has set itself up as the Big Daddy. Everybody who does jokes is censored. Only a Bob Hope, who is known as the Sacred Cow of Joke Tellers, gets away with almost any type of line. In talking about Bishop Sheen, Bob said, "The Bishop is making a Western—the title is going to be 'Sheriff of Vatican City.' " When the Bishop was opposite Milton Berle on TV and started to beat the comic's rating, Hope cracked, "Well natch, the Bishop has a better writer than Berle."

The thing that bothers me the most is that censorship has practically eliminated the dialectician. Only a few years ago, a dialectician was an honorable profession. It ranked number one among storytellers. Today, because of the touchy age we live in, everybody has become super-sensitive and ready to fight at the drop of an accent that might offend their race or religion.

Do a Jewish dialect story and the anti-defamation league is down on you. Reference to a Negro sics the NAACP after you. The Italian, Irish, and Germans have their own American societies waiting and ready to challenge anybody who satirizes their people.

The late and great Bill Robinson, the foremost Negro star of his time, used to get howls with the one about a little colored soldier who tried to break out of camp and was stopped by the guard. Our hero challenged the guard with, "I've got a mother in Heaven, a father in Hell, and a girl in Harlem—and I'm gonna see *one* of them tonight!" You do that kind of gag now—you're in trouble.

Sammy Davis tells the story of the Negro lad who comes to Heaven and St. Peter stops him at the gate:

"We only have heroes in here," says St. Peter.

"But I'm a hero."

"What heroic thing did you do?"

"I was married to a white girl on the steps of Biloxi Mississippi City Hall at twelve noon!"

"When did this happen?" St. Peter asks.

"Two minutes ago!"

Sure it's a funny story. But only a Sammy Davis could get away with it—*maybe*.

Comedians today are often self-censored to avoid any repercussions. Joey Bishop used to tell this story for a lot of laughs: A little Jewish boy went to his neighbor and asked the youngster to come out and play. The little Christian boy said, "My father says I can't play with you because you're Jewish." And the little Jewish boys said, "That's all right, we're not going to play for money!"

When the religion situation got sticky, Joey took it out so there would be no chance of misunderstanding.

Of course, in the hands of a real pro, dialect is still a fine art. Only experts like Myron Cohen have survived. But even Myron is careful with the stories he tells today. Who could be hurt when he teases his own mother, who never quite captured the English language or its idioms, but tried to keep up with the modern jargon? She heard her children use the expression, "out of this world." One day while enthusing over something she had cooked for her family, she exclaimed, "This soup is out of town."

Myron feels he is hurting nobody when he tells the story of the two women who met and one said:

"I was in Majorca on my vacation."

"Where's Majorca?" asked her friend.

"I don't know—we flew."

And yet, even Myron gets complaints for giving accents to the people in his stories.

I have appeared at dozens of benefits for Boys Town of Italy, and Italian-American organizations all over the country. But when I cracked in a newspaper interview, "When I was in Rome I saw a very unusual Italian movie—the heroine was flat-chested," I was severely reprimanded by some Italian pals.

74

Once I did a joke with Horace McMahon on TV. Horace says, "I hear you come from a tough family."

I said, "Are you kidding? My kid brother, Tony, once slapped Al Capone right in the kisser."

"I'd like to shake hands with your kid brother."

"Are you kidding—do you think we're gonna dig him up just for that?"

The next day an Italian-American newspaper in New Jersey did an editorial against me for making all Italians gangsters—just because I used the name Tony in the gag.

You can't picture an Irishman as a drunk, or even a Scotsman as being tight, in spite of the fact that they were the first to tell those stories themselves. But now everybody is too sensitive—even the Irish and the Scots.

One Irish comedian said on radio the other day, "Pat read so much about the evils of drinking that he gave up reading." Next day, dozens of letters from members of the Irish Society demanding an apology.

The Scots have always been the most liberal when it came to jokes about their being thrifty. But the other day I did the joke about the Scotsman, the Welshman, and the Englishman who were left legacies by a friend on condition that each should put five pounds in his coffin.

The Englishman put in a five-pound note. The Welshman put in a five-pound note which he borrowed from the Englishman. The Scotsman took out the two five-pound notes and put in a check for fifteen pounds, payable to bearer.

Three days later he was astonished to learn that the check had been presented and cashed. The undertaker was an Irishman.

I was insulted by several Scotsman who said, "Enough is enough."

Personally, I think we're all a little too sensitive. I admit there are certain areas that we have abused, but mostly a dialect story is strictly for fun and warm fellowship. Where do we stop? Pretty soon a man with a legitimate accent will be stopped from talking altogether.

It all reminds me of my favorite story of the two pals having a gab session and one says: "Did you hear about the two Jews that got off a bus and one says to the other—"

"What is wrong with you?" interrupted his buddy. "Why must it always be two Jews?—two Jews—always we tell stories to abuse the Jews—they have had enough trouble—why don't you pick on some other nationality for a change?"

"Okay," said his friend, "if that's how you feel about it. Two Chinamen got off the bus and one said to the other—are you coming to my son's Bar Mitzvah?"

The Comedians

by Joey Adams

Mothers attempting to discover what makes an ordinary, happy, care-free boy become a comedian ask, "Where did he go wrong?" Is it because they as parents have failed? How can they detect the early signs?

If in infancy he grabs for the nurse instead of the rattle, and if in kindergarten his favorite story is about the traveling salesman instead of Little Red Riding Hood, and if in public school he's reading joke books instead of history books, and if in high school while other kiddies are cutting out paper dolls he is cutting up real live people, and if when he's growing up he is stealing gags as well as the spotlight—these are the danger signals.

It is said that all comedians are insecure and this makes them neurotic. This is a lie. I know many clowns who are completely secure—and are neurotic.

The average big-time comedian is a hardworking gent who is on your radio once a day, on your TV channel four times a month and on his analyst's couch five times a week. He is like any other nice, normal, crazy mixed-up kid of fifty-three who retired at the age of sixteen without ever having worked.

Take any comedian from A to Z—from Adams to Zero, Mostel that is—and you will find that he lives and breathes on laughter. He has one-liners where his veins should be; he has a joke file where his brain should be. And if you look closely you'll see something in him that makes him stand out from all other people—you'll see that he is a little nuts.

But we're not all the same kind of nuts. Comics are rugged individualists and each of us is wacked in his own way. Red Skelton, for instance, won't talk on the phone and has a bed that is half desk, half bed. Buddy Hackett is always on a diet and has three sets of clothes: fat, fatter, and jumbo. Jackie Gleason has diabetes so he doesn't eat sweets, but he can drink twenty-five Scotch doubles in one evening. "If I'm going to go I want to go boozing, not eating." As the Great One says, "Drinking removes warts and pimples. Not from me. It's the people I have to look at."

Groucho Marx is an insomniac. He's tried everything from pills to showers in the middle of the night to an electric vibrator to yoga but he still can't sleep. Jimmy Durante is a hypochondriac. Take for instance, if he should hurt his little finger. Instead of a simple bandage he'll have it covered with splints and keep rushing off to the doctor. He'll flap his arms and race around wildly, hollering, "Dis is a catastastroke."

Now take the case of Morey Amsterdam. His bug is that he loves everybody. And that could get to be a bit annoying. I mean you just can't get choked up when you think of a Hitler or a Nasser. "All right," I said to Morey, "let's hear you say something nice about Nasser—I dare you."

"Well," he said happily, "I admit he's a bit of a louse—but you must admit he's the best in his line." He says about Castro, "Anybody with a firing squad who shoots only twenty people every day can't be all bad."

Morey could be called an oddball in another respect too. He's always happy. The bouncy little comic who's sort of shaped like a beach ball doesn't fit any of the tailor-made patterns for the average comic. Nor for the average human, either.

For one, his wife is part Indian, his children are Catholic and he's Jewish. Besides that, his dog is named "Pussycat." Discussing his show business beginning he grins, "When I started at fourteen I was only the size of a kid of ten. By twenty, though, I'd shot up to the size of a kid eleven."

Morey, who grew up in San Francisco, made history as the youngest student at the University of California up to his time. He enrolled at twenty-four. He quit at fifteen. Mamma, who was practical, wanted him to be a lawyer. Poppa, who was a musician, wanted him to be a cellist. Baby wanted to be an actor—he had started as an amateur at the age of ten.

Years later, when he appeared on the Ed Sullivan Show playing his cello and making jokes, he became the comedy sensation of the air. Poppa, however, still sulked because sonny boy hadn't become a musician. After Morey's smashing performance Poppa wired merely, "Your cello is out of tune." Comments Morey, "I was the black sheep of the family. I was the one who made money."

By sixteen Morey Amsterdam was M.C. at Colosimo's, the toughest saloon in Chicago. It was owned by big Jim Colosimo, who made even Al Capone look shy and retiring.

"Capone loved me," Morey likes to reminisce. "He'd pick me up and drive me to his house, which was behind a night club in Cicero. There I'd play Italian songs for him and he'd cook spaghetti for me. One night Charles G. Dawes, Vice-President of the United States, came in and requested I join his table. Later Capone picked me up as usual. That was the night in my life that I had dinner with both the Vice-President and the President of Vice."

Morey is a push-button comedy machine. Drop any subject and a joke comes out. Beverly Hills? "It's so exclusive even the police have an unlisted number." Yell "Fat" and the Amsterdam computer says, "My uncle is so fat when he sits around the house, he sits around the house."

Morey is reputed to have the largest joke repertoire in the business, and he probably does, but it's in his head rather than in any card file. "It's quicker for me to create new jokes than to look up oldies anyway," he says. But during the filming of a movie in 1959 he almost lost the file. He fell on the set and injured his head, and for three weeks, although he could remember his name and other familiar details, he could not recall any of his old jokes. He was about to sue on the grounds that he had lost his main stock-in-trade when his mental stock of jokes suddenly returned.

Jackie Gleason has his own hang-up. He has those special individual characteristics that make him stand out—besides his belly. His shtick is that he's a sybarite.

Gleason is an enjoyer. An appreciator. He's a sampler of the finer things in life. For instance, the Great One digs music. But he doesn't want to be encumbered by a transistor radio. So, instead, he does what any other intelligent, well-adjusted czar would do—he carries an eighteen-piece jazz band with him wherever he goes.

Jackie is a throwback. He should have been born a Roman Emperor. Even in the old days when he was 180 pounds and beautiful and was a flop as a night club comic, he acted and lived like he was a millionaire. His top salary was seventy-five dollars a week and he would often borrow fifty dollars from me and then take me out on the town until all the money was gone.

When he was broke and in the hospital, he wired me for all the money I had, $1,000, so he could have a suite at the hospital and a bar open to all his friends who came to visit. He paid me back the thousand many years later and then, for interest, every benefit I appeared at for the next year, he sent a thousand-dollar check in my name.

Even when he died in night clubs he acted like he was Joe Star. Once, in the old days when he was slaving over a hot microphone and a cold audience in some shlock night club in Jersey, he noticed Tony Galento, the heavyweight champ, sitting ringside. The Great Gleason approached him with his fancy footwork and ad-libbed, "Okay, you crum-bum, stand up and meet your master, put up your hands."

Tony had no sense of humor. He did as he was told. He stood up and flattened the Great One with one punch. And that ended Jackie's career as a night club comedian.

Georgie Jessel is one of my favorite comedians of all time, on stage and off. He is equally at home on the dais as well as the stage or at a table at the Friars. At seventy he is the dean of the storytellers and has been called "The Toastmaster General" by four Presidents. He has served as a writer, actor, producer, director, and comedian. But his Achilles heel is young girls.

Somebody once introduced Jessel, I think it was me, as the man who this year personally supported 1,250,000 Jews in Israel and 325 chorus girls in the United States. Georgie is the first to laugh and admit I was telling the truth when I cracked, "Jessel is getting married again this summer but he doesn't know whether he should take his bride on a honeymoon to Europe —or send her to camp."

Jessel has raised hundreds of millions for the State of Israel, the City of Hope, and every type of charity, Catholic, Jewish, and Protestant. But he get his biggest jollies delivering a eulogy.

Jack Benny likes to tell about the time George delivered the eulogy for James Mason's cat. "When Jessel finished eulogizing the cat there wasn't a dry eye. I never knew that cats did so much for Israel and the Democrats."

Jessel has very often doubled at two eulogies or more in one day. He is proud that he is known as the greatest master at these funerals. Once, at a particularly tender moment during his eulogy, he accidentally glanced down on the deceased in the coffin. "My God," Jessel gasped, "*I know* this man."

Jessel's biggest bug is name-dropping. At the age of eleven he was reminiscing about "the halcyon days of George M. Cohan and David Belasco."

Once George was signed to do a tour with Eddie Cantor. When they arrived in Bridgeport, Jessel noticed the billing: "Eddie Cantor with George Jessel." "What the hell kind of a conjunction is that Eddie Cantor with George Jessel," he complained to manager Irving Mansfield. Irving promised to change the conjunction. The next day the marquee read, "Eddie Cantor *but* George Jessel."

George and I were flying in from Cleveland after a benefit. What else? Jessel, who will never use one name if three will do, was talking about one of my books. "When George Jessel tells you something, Joey Adams"—he was making sure everybody in the plane knew who we were—"I keep my word. Darryl Zanuck and Joe Levine want the Joey Adams book *On the Road for Uncle Sam* and when George Jessel tells you—" Just as we reached Kennedy we were held in the air for over an hour. Jessel's voice and names grew weaker and weaker as it looked like we might never land. George got nervous and quiet. "My luck," I said. "We'll get killed and you'll get top billing." Jessel didn't even seem to hear me. When we finally landed on the ground Georgie said to me, "Hey, that's very funny what you said up there about me getting top billing—give it to the columns."

Wagnall and his pal Funk tell you a comedian is "A very amusing person"—but as anybody who has ever been to a Turkish bath will tell you— all men are not created equal. With some guys their shtick works overtime when things go wrong. If he loses his job or blows his contract. If he can't find his agent. If his wife walks out on him and he can't get his mistress on the phone. That's when the tick in his nervous system starts beating double time.

But with a comic like Red Buttons, the whole thing is in reverse. Red is a great guy but he's greater when he's on his behind. When everything is coming up roses he admits that's when he worries the most.

His pal comedian Phil Foster tells about Red: "After he became a big hit on television, Buttons gave all his old Lindy's pals, like myself, the brush. Then followed a period when he wasn't doing too good, and he returned to the old gang contrite.

"Not too long after the reunion, Red scored again. This time in movies. He was up for an Academy Award for 'Sayonara' and the night he was to get it I sent him a telegram which read: 'Congratulations and good-bye again.' "

Jack Carter is a professional handwringer. It's been said of Jack that "he doesn't worry about what's happening to him today because he's still busy worrying about what happened to him twenty years ago."

Jack Carter is so nervous he keeps coffee awake. Jack Benny built himself up as a devout cheapskate. When he played Las Vegas recently he had them put in penny slot machines just for him. George Burns' mania is singing old songs to young broads.

Alan King makes millions as a comic and spends it as a producer. Bob Hope is a traveler. He can't sleep unless somebody stays up all night and hollers, "Fasten your seat belts."

Jack E. Leonard and Don Rickles regard their subjects as targets. Don's soft spot is his mom. That's where he brings his opponents for chicken soup after he has cut them to pieces.

Joey Bishop is quiet, serious, even sad off stage, while Jerry Lewis is always "on." And you better laugh at his shtick or he'll lie down and sulk all day. He could walk into a shower with all his clothes on just to get a laugh from a stranger or a friend. But you better laugh or you'll have a sick boy on your hands.

Dick Gregory, the angry young comic, has been furious lately. His bugaboo is politics and civil rights. Only now he's serious about his laughs. "If it weren't for bad luck, I wouldn't have no luck at all."

"You know why Madison Avenue advertising has never done well in Harlem? We're the only ones who know what it means to *be* Brand X."

Phyllis Diller has only been in show business for about thirteen years. The gal about whom Bob Hope says, "She has that rare beauty that drives men sane," used to kid herself for fun way before she did it for profit. "My skin is so dry they declared it a fire hazard. And my hair! Are you ready for this? The girl at the beauty parlor said, 'Mind if I tease it?' I said, 'Sweetie, you can drive it to drink for all I care.' "

When her gags got funnier than her outfits, she knew it was time to go pro.

Milton Berle's trauma is his gag stealing. Which he's been doing since he found out he liked playing with jokes rather than toys. And he's proud of his title as, "The Thief of Bad Gags." He loved to brag, "I saw that Hope. He was so funny I almost dropped my pencil."

When he became Mr. Television he paid dozens of writers to sweat over a hot gag file. But he still continued to do the same old gags which he does to this very day. But, like real antiques, when he handles them they are worth a fortune.

Milton, who is not only one of the best comics but the best liked, keeps his gag files open to any new comedians who want them. I guess he figures easy come—easy go.

Henny Youngman is one of the all time great original comedians. This is not only my opinion. It's Henny's.

Milton Berle, who has known Henny, man and joke file, for thirty-five years, says, "Unlike myself, Henny did not steal jokes from the top comedians of that era. Youngman stole from the unknowns, a word which later became synonymous with his career."

Youngman is a wonderful father, grandfather, and husband—but that doesn't stop him from using them as material for his gags. Especially his wife Sadie: "My wife went to a beauty parlor. Every woman who comes out of a beauty parlor looks like Jacqueline Kennedy. Not my wife—she looks like Lyndon Johnson."

Henny's special gimmick is his violin. He started as a bandleader in the Catskills and still thinks he can play. Believe me, Heifetz has nothing to worry about. Even Jack Benny won't lose any sleep over him. To tell the truth, Venus De Milo could have played better.

Everybody knows that Joe E. Lewis has a drink now and then. As he says, "I only drink to quiet my nerves." Nobody's nerves are that noisy. "I once quit drinking," Joe E. admits; "it was the most boring ten minutes of my life."

What you don't know is that Lewis is an old-fashioned guy. He doesn't believe in zippers and still has buttons on his pants. And he's a sucker for a guy with his hand out. In fact, he looks for beggars.

One casual race track acquaintance asked to borrow ten bucks. Joe took the chance, and at the end of the day received his ten-spot back. The next day, the same character made another request—this time for twenty dollars, and after the seventh race, refunded the loan. On the third day when he asked for thirty dollars, Joe waved him away, "Nothin' doin'," said Joe. "you fooled me twice."

Some of the clan are sticklers for the natural bit. Danny Thomas has refused to shorten his nose: "If you're going to have a schnoz, have a good one." Myron Cohen won't wear a toupee, "How will it look for a silk salesman to put on a rug?" Menasha Skulnik kept his name even after he left the Jewish theatre for the English stage. Sam Levenson never left Brooklyn even when he changed from schoolteacher to super star.

From A to Z we are all a little wacked up someplace. And when you get to Z there is Zero Mostel, the biggest nut of us all. I admit he is the most versatile comedian of the lot. He's an accomplished painter, writer, night club star, actor and lecturer—and also the biggest slob.

There are many who say that Zero is the funniest comic in the business.

But he's also the sloppiest. He keeps all his shoes in a cardboard carton under his bed. "That way nobody will steal them." He puts his suits on a nail next to his bed. "I believe in functional living." He encouraged his children to write on the walls of his home. "Self expression is important for kids growing up." He travels with matched luggage. Two shopping bags from the corner grocery store.

But you ain't heard nothing yet until you spend the night with him. A few years ago, Zero and I were working in Detroit at different night clubs. I was writing a book called *From Gags to Riches,* and I thought it would be a good idea to have him do the illustrations for it. Zero consented but he insisted on staying at my hotel with me.

He hates tidiness, so he started by taking all my suits off the hangers and stuffing them in the hamper. Then he rumpled up my shirts and underwear and knotted them together with my ties. This didn't upset me too much. It was worth it to get those great Mostel caricatures. But what sent me to the nearest nuthouse was his sleeping habits. Every time I opened my eyes during the night I found him in a different position. The first time was about four o'clock in the morning. I felt something staring at me while I was sleeping. When I opened my baby blues there was Zero sitting squat on the dresser in the nude, with a ribbon tied on him, a lampshade on his head and a bulb in his mouth—made up like a live lamp.

Me? I'm told I'm the only normal comedian in the country. As my mother-in-law said, "Joey, you have my vote as the best adjusted person in show business." But she also voted for Barry Goldwater, Alf Landon, and Wendell Willkie.

Opening Lines

The most important thing for any comedian or storyteller is to put his best laugh forward. Once you get that first yock over with—you got it licked.

Of course, opening impressions are the most important, whether you're a comic, a singer, a speaker, a toastmaster, or just a guy looking for a job. It's all got to do with what you're trying to sell.

Naturally, a singer should be impeccably groomed (the mods and the beatniks will be thrilled with this news). A businessman can hide a multitude of fears by sporting a vest. A comic needs that opening laugh.

Red Skelton used to come out in front of the curtain, do any opening line: "I'm back by request—request hell—I begged them." Then two unseen hands would grab his ankles—pull—and he'd fall flat on his face.

One vaudevillian walked out on stage, fired a gun in the air and shouted, "Nobody sleeps during *my* act."

Jack Durant throws his opening line as he reaches the mike, "I heard what you said as I walked out, lady—'I wish he were mine!' All right, so I'm no Rock Hudson—but can Rock Hudson do this?" And he does a somersault and falls flat on his back. In the days of vaudeville he used to fall right into the pit.

Everything is designed to get that first belly. Now, I'm not suggesting you fall on your face or shoot up the place—I do intend, however, to suggest some good opening lines that could take the place of a pratfall.

A funny thing happened to me on the way to this show—if it didn't I wouldn't have an opening line. A kid walked over to me and said, "Hey, Joey, I saw you on the Ed Sullivan Show—you'd be a big hit on color television"—so he hit me till I was black and blue.

As I walked in the club tonight, some character gave me a bang on the back—almost knocked me on my face—he said, "Hello, Berle." I said, "Wait a minute, my name is not Berle—it's Joey Adams! And even if it were Berle—is that any reason for you to hit me so hard on the back?" He said, "What do you care what I do to Berle?"

On my way into the studio some lady approached me and said, "Mr. Merv Griffin—I'm a big fan of yours—would you please give me your autograph for my five-year-old daughter?" I said, "Lady, I'm not Merv Griffin—I'm Joey Adams." She said, "What's the difference?—my kid can't read anyway."

You must remember to tear yourself down. The humility bit is always a welcome laugh-getter. Tennessee Ernie Ford's opening sets him up pretty good: "I'm as nervous as a tomcat in a roomful of rocking chairs."

Will Rogers very often would start his act ungrammatically and then add, "Maybe 'ain't' ain't so correct—but I notice a lot of folks who ain't usin' ain't—ain't eatin'."

Fat Jack Leonard starts right out drawing his own blood first: "I'm not exactly bald—I simply have an exceptionally wide part." He admits, "Sinatra is the voice—Durante the nose—I'm Leonard the Lump! You've heard of the streetcar named Desire—I'm the freight car named Leonard."

Kidding yourself or your family is always a good beginning. The audience is the first to recognize your plight—"better you than me," they laugh.

"My wife gave me a choice—of a new fur coat or a nervous breakdown."

Wrecking yourself brings out the sympathy and the laughs. When I returned to one television show after being away awhile, I announced: "There was a big sign to greet me when I entered the studio. It said, 'Welcome Home Joey Adams.' But they can't even spell! They spelled home—H-A-M."

This program comes to you live from New York. At least, *it starts out live*—it sometimes dies in twenty minutes.

There's been talk of putting our show on film—if they can find anyone with nerve enough to develop it.

This is Joey Adams—the only comedian recommended by dieticians— I am No-Cal. Many people turn me on before eating to build *down* their appetites.

I'm a low pressure comedian. But I'll straighten *that* out as soon as I find the leak.

There was a big sign in front of the theatre which says "Welcome to Joey Adams, the greatest comedian in America today." It really embarrassed me—they caught me putting up the sign!

I'm here on a percentage deal—I get 10 per cent of everything over 150 thousand.

I'm here on a percentage deal—I get 10 per cent of the gross—Irving Gross—he's a waiter here.

I get letters. "Dear Joey Adams—I've been watching you man and boy for over twenty years and I want to tell you—I don't like you any more as a man than I did as a boy!"

I get letters. "Dear Mr. A.—I really enjoyed your show last night. My girl's parents went to see it and left us alone for the whole evening— I really enjoyed your show last night."

It's great to be back here in this studio—this is home to me—they won't let me back in my apartment.

This is a return engagement for me—I was here twenty-three years ago.

I get letters; here's a nice one. "You are the worse comedian on the air—you're from hunger—when I see you, I'll knock your block off—you stink—signed Sal Demaye. P. S. Please excuse the pencil."

I suppose you're wondering why I called this meeting?

Thank you for that wonderful hand of indifference.

Thank you for that big hand—I could never live up to it—so good-night.

You're going to have a great time tonight. Bob Hope gets $30,000 a show, Red Skelton $35,000, Milton Berle $25,000—I do the same jokes.

I want to thank you for all the fan mail I received—thousands of letters saying "We want Adams." There was only one trouble—they were all from collection agencies.

I almost didn't get here tonight. I was driving down 5th Avenue and I didn't see the light. Anybody wanna buy a brand new Cadillac with a Chevrolet sticking out of the side?

I had a blind date with a sweater girl and she showed up. My luck! I always get the ones that knit them—not the ones that wear them.

Thank you for that swell reception. It brings me a lot of happiness—but what good is happiness—you can't buy money with it.

Before we go on with the show, I have something to say to all the fans who have written me—I can only say in all sincerity—*the same* to you!

Today is a very important anniversary. William Tell was born 900 years ago. When I was a kid, William Tell was my idol. I remember I used to go in the backyard with my best friend. He would put an apple on his head and I'd shoot it off. He would have been thirty-four tomorrow.

Before I went on the air I was handed this note: "Will the man who found a fur coat here in the studio last week—please return the blonde that was in it?"

This is an easy, relaxed-type show. Make yourself comfortable. Fellows, open your tie and shirts; ladies do the best you can. Everybody, take off your shoes—I'm serious—take off your shoes—I'm not going to continue until everybody takes off his shoes—(pause)—okay? Now will the ushers go through the aisles and collect the shoes? This is one show *nobody* walks out on.

We get letters—here's a beauty—it starts—"Dear Friend, of all the television shows I have ever seen, yours is undoubtedly the best. You are clever, charming, witty, genuine, and wholesome.

"This is the only time I have ever written a fan letter, but I had to tell you this. You have the best show on the air. Sincerely yours, Sylvia Potkin." (Looks up) Isn't that nice of Sylvia? I'm not quite sure of her sincerity, though. This letter is mimeographed.

Of course, topical jokes are great for openers. *If it's snowing hard:* I came here with my girl—by dog sled—she was hollering mush—I was hollering mush—and while we were mushing—somebody stole the sled.

If it's very cold: I'm sorry I'm late—I couldn't get out of bed. My house is so cold these nights—every time I open the apartment door—the lights go on.

If it's very hot: It was so hot today—we fed the chickens cracked ice to keep them from laying hard-boiled eggs.

Election Day: If one more actor gets elected in California that will be the only state in the union with their own marquee.

Politics: Well, I hope you're satisfied with the results. Now they want Ronald Reagan to run for President. At least if he wins, things will be different. For one thing, we'd be six months ahead of Russia in cowboy movies·

Closing Lines, or Leave 'em — Laughing

Most entertainers, like most civilians, are tough leavers. Some of our greatest comedians don't know when to get off—or how.

These lines are designed to get you off—and leave 'em laughing:

Well, I gotta go now—it's the children's night off and I have to go home and take care of the maid.

And when you go home tonight—please drive carefully—the life you save may be mine—I'm walking.

Well, good night, folks—I got to be going now. I took my girl to the movies last night and I'm going back tonight to see the picture.

I've got to be going now. If I'm not home by midnight—my wife rents out my room.

Well, I gotta go now. I'm double-parked—a fifteen dollar fine and I'm losing money on this show.

Well, good night—and remember, if there's anything about the food, drinks, service, or show you didn't like—the manager wants you to keep it to yourself—he's tired of hearing it.

I leave you with this thought: America is the only place where it takes more brains to make out the income tax—than it does to make the income.

May I leave you with this thought: People who live in glass houses—should use their neighbor's bathroom.

If you liked the show tonight—send me a postcard—I'm all out of them.

Before I leave—I have a note from a man who offers a reward for his wallet. If you find it—please bring it backstage. It's a genuine Moroccan leather wallet. He says he doesn't mind losing the wallet—but the money has a sentimental value to him.

Well, good night, folks—I just thought you'd like to know that money or fans mean nothing to me. Applause is my food—I live on it—so far I haven't had breakfast yet—so—good night, folks.

You've really been a wonderful audience—you showed up. No, you've really been fair and square—mostly square—good night, folks.

I've worked to great audiences in my time—but not tonight. Good night, folks.

Before I leave—I have a special message to the gardeners in the audience: Plant pistachios this season—they're nuts—but then again, aren't we all?—Good night.

And now—if you want to dance—there's a bus leaving for Roseland.

I leave you with this message for tonight: I once worked at Luxor Baths. I was head masseur—I also massaged the rest of the body—and I've learned one thing—all men are not created equal.

Before I leave—one word of precaution—when you're out driving tonight—please be careful of our children—they're terrible drivers.

I leave you with this thought: Remember, you're not drunk as long as you can lie on the floor without holding on.

Before I go, I want to remind you about my new album—it's only just out and already sold 500,000 copies. If you can't get a copy—call me—I got 500,000 of them.

Get a copy of my new book. It's a book of the month selection—and I can't make money selling one book a month. All the royalties go for a very worthy cause—a mink coat for my wife.

Remember the words of that great philosopher who said—I can't remember his name—I can't even remember what he said—oh yes, he said: "Show me a man who has no money—and I'll show you a bum!" Good night all.

Before I go, I leave you with this thought: Keep your words soft and sweet—you never know when you might have to eat them some day.

Before I go, I'd like to leave all the men out there with one thought: Stay single!

Ladies and Gentlemen, in closing, I leave you with this thought: Whether you're rich or you're poor—it's good to have money.

Before I go, I'd like to leave you with this thought: A healthy home is a happy home—so send your home to the doctor twice a year.

Remember, if you send in a self-addressed envelope, I will send you a picture of myself to sit on your dresser. If you enclose a dime I will autograph it for you. If you enclose a quarter—I'll come and sit on your dresser myself.

Before I go, I'd like to leave you with two nice words: Brigitte Bardot.

Well, it's time to say good-bye for another week; my cast, my crew, and I are leaving you now—my studio audience left twenty minutes ago.

Well, it's good-bye for today but we'll see you next week. Remember, if you like fun; if you like laughs, and singing and dancing—throw a party and invite *me*!

I leave you with this thought: Remember, nothing is ever lost by being polite—except your seat on a bus.

Just a final thought before I leave: Never hit a man when he's down—he might get up again.

Here's a handy hint for our female listeners before I leave. Your latex rubber girdles will slip on much easier if you chill them overnight in the refrigerator.

Naturally, though, you have to put them on quickly or they'll stick—

like a popsicle wrapper. Also, be sure you're entirely thawed out before leaving for the office—or you'll leave quite a puddle in the bus.

Well, I hate to bring this to your attention—but my act is over.

Now, when I leave—give me a tremendous hand—not for me—but all the acts backstage are waiting to hear the reaction to my act—and if you give me a terrific hand they will say, "What a great audience"—and they will knock their brains out to give you the greatest show of their lives—so—when you're applauding for me—it's really those acts backstage—who are waiting to give you the show of a lifetime. Okay, folks—*now*—Good night.

Introductions

Ever since I saw my first elephant, I've been listening to spielers tell me I was going to see "The Greatest Show on Earth." Burlesque used to advertise, "You'll see something you never expected to see." I did too: the first time I went to Minsky's, I saw my father sitting in the front row.

Even as a youngster I thought the M.C. was exaggerating when he said: "Here she is, the greatest body in the world!" I was sure of it when she took off her clothes and I heard one voice in the rear shout, "Put it on."

Over-selling has long been the art of the M.C. and toastmaster. Nobody could live up to those introductions of "The greatest of all time." Our President is introduced just simply "Ladies and gentlemen—the President of the United States." Does the comic from Brooklyn deserve more?

In the first place, you're lousing yourself up with the audience, because he could never be as good as you say. And secondly, you're lousing yourself up with the act, because you could never say as good as he thinks he is.

You're better off giving him a gag introduction: this way, if he lives down to it, at least you didn't lie. And if he does great, you're both heroes.

Here are some of my favorite intros—be my guest.

If you saw the pictures "Dr. Zhivago" and "Sound of Music"—this man—saw both pictures too.

Here is the man about whom President Johnson once said: "Who's he?"

In his last appearance at a theatre he drew a line three blocks long—until they took his chalk away.

I never saw this man before tonight—if he's good, let's hear him—if he's not, let's get it over with.

When he was young he was determined to climb the ladder of success. He's not so successful—but boy—can he climb ladders!

He has risen from obscurity and is definitely headed for oblivion.

Years ago he was an unknown failure—now he's a known failure.

NBC and CBS are fighting over him. NBC wants him to go with CBS, and CBS wants him to go with NBC.

He's ALWAYS kept his nose to the grindstone and today he's famous —he's the only person in America who can cut a steak with his nose.

We have here tonight a man who has made quite a name for himself— but I'm too much of a gentleman to tell you what that name is.

And so—I bring you tonight the world's greatest author, comedian, storyteller, producer, and the man who wrote this introduction—Charley Latke.

Another thing to remember, steer clear of cliche-ridden intros like: "And now without further ado . . . " or, "And now here is a person who needs no introduction . . ." or, "Here's a great guy you all know . . ." or, "I've had the pleasure of working with this performer many times . . ."

You can easily louse up a whole act with a stale introduction. Of course, you can also louse up a good introduction with a crummy act.

However, if you take these stale intros and turn them into laughs—you've got something going.

You've heard many M.C.'s say: "This act needs no introduction." Well, I've seen his act, and he needs plenty of introduction.

Now here's a very famous personality you all know—his name is a household word—he's on the tip of every tongue—er, ah—what's your name again?

I've had the pleasure of working with this next act many times—at the post office during the Christmas rush.

BUSINESSMAN: Here is a genuine millionaire. You wouldn't believe this—but when he first came to this country he only had ten cents in his jacket pocket. But in the lining he had a million in cash.

or

When he first came to this city—he was broke—now—he owes over $200,000.

INTRODUCING FAT GOLFER—like Jack E. Leonard or Jackie Gleason: He's a miracle golfer—I still don't know how he does it. When he puts the ball where he can hit it—he can't see it. And when he puts the ball where he can see it—he can't hit it!

COMIC: Bob Hope and our next guest used to pack them in back in L.A. Hope was in a theatre—and *he* drove a bus.

or

If Hope had his material—*he'd* be working here too.

STRIPPER: She does a very unusual dance. The only thing on her is the spotlight.

BAND: The finest band in the country—in the city they're not too good.

or

A great band—for five pieces. They sound like four.

ACTOR: And now I introduce the world's greatest actor. And don't think that's just my opinion—it's his too.

COMEDIAN: To date he's been responsible for the sale of more television sets than any performer on TV. I know I sold mine—my father sold his. . . .

LAWYER: I'd like to introduce a very talented lawyer. I know he's good—you should see him trying to break his girl's will.
He's a criminal lawyer—but we can't prove it.

DOCTOR: I'd like to present one of the finest doctors in the country—I'd like to—but right now he's operating at Mt. Sinai.
He's a very famous doctor—a bone specialist—carries his own dice.

POLITICIAN: One of the finest politicians money can buy.
I'd like you to meet one politician that's honest and sincere—but I'm not going to dig him up just for you.

JUDGE: One of the finest judges on the bench—the park bench.

BUSINESSMAN: I've known him for twenty-five years—I'm not bragging—I'm complaining.
Never knew the meaning of the word defeat—besides hundreds of other words he never knew the meaning of.

COMEDIAN: He's back by request—well, it was more than request—he *begged* us to bring him back.

BUSINESSMAN: One of the most successful in the business world—he attributes his millions to five things: honesty, integrity, kindness, patience, and his uncle who died and left him millions.

VAUDEVILLE ACT: Due to conditions beyond my control—we present the act originally scheduled for this show. He's been hailed by millions—he was a taxi driver at the time.

GIRL SINGER: She comes to us tonight direct from a sensational run—around my apartment.
She's in her third month—here in New York City.

BOY SINGER: And now I really take great pleasure in introducing a singer who has been breaking records wherever he goes—Frank Sinatra's records—he's very jealous.

CHORUS: Here they are—a line of thirty-two—some are older.

Here's a young lady who stopped the show at Carnegie Hall last week—she turned out the lights.
Here's a young lady who recently made her mark in show business and is now learning to write her full name.
Here is a young lady who at the Strand Theatre recently had the customers standing in the aisles—she was an usherette.
Here is a young lady who only a few short years ago was unknown in show business, and today, after years of hard work—she is unknown in *every* business.

92

Here is a young man who recently appeared at the Policeman's Ball, where he sang for the cops—here's that dirty stool pigeon now.

Here is a singer who as a little boy took lessons from the great Caruso himself—and today that little boy is Mark Plant—who can make the best spaghetti in town.

And now—a man who has been acclaimed by millions—his tailor has a claim—his bookie has a claim—his wife has a claim.

This man was in the dress business and failed—the shoe business and failed—the fur business and failed—and then he went into show business and tonight—he makes his farewell appearance before he goes back in the dress business.

And now, I'd like you to meet a former champion—as a fighter, he was a credit to the ring—and today—he can't get a ring on credit.

Next we have an act that I'm sure you're going to love. He's just the greatest—sings, dances, tells stories—a voice that's only wonderful—now for my first song.

Double Act

Some of the most ordinary performers in show business have doubled up to become the sensations of the era. Jerry Lewis was just a small-time mime act and Dean Martin a standard club singer when they teamed up to make history in the entertainment world.

George Burns was ready to open a candy store and Gracie Allen was going back to typing school when they met and started their "dumb" act.

Who knows what would have happened if Amos had never met Andy, or Charlie Dale didn't annex Joe Smith, or Buck never teamed up with Bubbles? Who could say if Bud Abbott and Lou Costello would have reached those heights if they had never met while working the same burlesque theatre? Could Laurel and Hardy have made it without each other? I only know that they clicked because they were the perfect marriage on stage. They fed each other right and played each other's best talent. Once they found the right formula they stuck to it all the way.

Almost every star has used a "crutch," in the guise of a stooge, to help his act. Jack Benny has worked with Rochester for years. Bob Hope's faithful was Jerry Colonna. Jackie Gleason's partners were Art Carney and Frank Fontaine. Milton Berle, Eddie Cantor, Jack Pearl, Phil Baker, Ted Healy, and almost every big star have used stooges or straightmen to lean on for better results.

The stars used each other if the formula was right. Hope and Crosby, Fred Allen and Jack Benny, Walter Winchell and Ben Bernie teamed up because they found they could bounce off each other pretty good.

It takes a good comic with a good sense of humor to be a straightman. Jack Benny is strictly playing straight for Rochester's comedy. Same goes for Gleason with Fontaine and Hope with Colonna.

George Burns was always a funny man, but he became a star by playing straight for Gracie. Dean proved before and after that he could be a good comic but with Jerry he only played it straight.

Smith and Dale, Amos and Andy, and Buck and Bubbles played straight for each other. All double comedy is action, reaction, and counteraction. It's formula all the way, and these boys were the scientists who figured it out.

I have been doing comedy all my life. Even as a child, my neighbors thought I should have a gag in my mouth. Yet I found great success in my comedy life working as an alleged straightman with everybody from Jane Russell to Tony Canzoneri, and Mark Plant to Al Kelly, to Zsa Zsa Gabor and Peter Lawford.

The most important thing in doing an act with anybody is to find the specific formula and stick to it—and make each joke a "formula" joke.

Let's start with the dumb formula, which is the most common and the most successful.

COMIC: "I had some job filling the salt shaker. It took me all morning."
STRAIGHTMAN: "It took you all morning to fill one salt shaker?"
COMIC: "Sure. It's hard to get the salt in through those little holes on top."

The greatest proponents of this art were Burns and Allen. They never deviated from the formula.

GEORGE: "Me, I'm a pauper."
GRACIE: "Congratulations. Boy or girl?"

GRACIE: "My sister had a baby."
GEORGE: "Boy or girl?"
GRACIE: "I don't know, and I can't wait to find out if I'm an aunt or an uncle."

GRACIE: "My brother has a suit like that. It's just the same."
GEORGE: "Is that so?"
GRACIE: "Yes, only it hasn't any stripes. His is brown. It's more like a blue black, sort of yellow."
GEORGE: "More like white!"
GRACIE: "That's it. A white suit, only yours is double-breasted and his is single-breasted and his has no pockets, and a bow on the side."
GEORGE: "A bow on the side?"
GRACIE: "My sister wore it to a dance last night."
GEORGE: "Your sister wore your brother's suit to a dance?"
GRACIE: "I haven't got a brother."
GEORGE: "You haven't got a brother but your sister has?"
GRACIE: "It's a long story—pull up a chair. You see, when my sister and I were children, we were left orphans, and he was one of them."

You see, the insanity was established fairly early and never was cured. They stayed with this formula through several million dollars.

GEORGE: "This family of yours—did they all live together?"
GRACIE: "Yes, my father, my uncle, my cousin, my brother, and my nephew used to sleep in one bed and my—"
GEORGE: "I'm surprised your grandfather didn't sleep with them."
GRACIE: "He did. But he died, and they made him get up."

Another popular formula is the "smart ass" or wise guy, topping the stooge or comic.

95

COMIC: "Have you seen the evening paper?"
STOOGE: "No, what's in it?"
COMIC: "My lunch—and I'm getting hungry."
COMIC: "Stick with me and you'll have the pleasures of life."
STOOGE: "You mean girls?"
COMIC: "I said pleasures—not necessities."
STOOGE: "Don't worry about me. I do okay with the girls. You shoulda seen me yesterday walking down Broadway with a blonde on one arm and a brunette on the other."
COMIC: "Really? Who does your tattooing?"
"You're an old wolf. I saw you on the corner winking at girls."
STOOGE: "I wasn't winking—that's a windy corner—something got in my eyes . . . "
COMIC: "She got in your car, too!"

I used this formula with singing star Mark Plant. He played straight, while I heckled, wise guy style—in the business it's called *the topper*.

MARK: "I will now sing a song that's sweeping the country."
ME: "That's what *you* should be doing."

MARK: "I recently completed an album which was three years in the making."
ME: "A stamp album."

MARK: "Just three years ago the critics said I had very little chance of becoming a star."
ME: "Tonight, here at the Copa, he will prove the critics were wrong—he has *no chance at all* of becoming a star!"

MARK: "And now a song which I helped make popular."
ME: "By never singing before."

MARK: "This tune has a haunting melody."
ME: "It should have—you murdered it!"

MARK: "I want you to know there is a lot of music inside of me."

ME: "There should be. I never hear any of it come out."

And on and on and on, always formula. He is the big, tall, good looking, talented singing star and I am the fresh little comic who has the wise guy lines. Now, the same lines switched wouldn't be funny. Audiences don't like to see the little guy abused. Even if he is the "dope," they enjoy his getting the laugh.

Tony Canzoneri, former champ turned comic, played the "dumb" fighter, with me doing straight, but I always set him up with the punch line.

96

JOEY: "What's the matter with your finger?"
TONY: "I sawed it off."
JOEY: "You sawed your finger off—why?"
TONY: "I couldn't find any wood!"
TONY: "And you better laugh at my jokes—okay—why does a faucet drip?"
JOEY: "I don't know—why does a faucet drip?"
TONY: "Because it can't sniff."
JOEY: "That was the worst, stinkiest joke I ever heard in my life!"
     (Tony grabs me by the collar.)
JOEY: "But it was funny. It sure was funny." (If I got fresh—it was always
     Tony with the topper.)

ME: "You're not smart enough to talk to an idiot."
TONY: "Okay—then I'll send you a letter."
ME: "You're next door to an idiot."
TONY: "Okay—then I'll move away from you."

One of the happiest combinations is the exaggeration and funny picture formula combined with the wild or zany attitude. This is actually a caricature of life.

COMIC: "I was hunting and I came across a big black bear. He grabbed the
     rifle out of my hands and pointed it at me!"
STRAIGHTMAN: "What happened?"
COMIC: "What could happen? I married his daughter."

This formula was used well by many of our great teams.

BUBBLES: "I saw you running down that dark cellar today. What were
     you hiding from?"
BUCK: "It was lightning out and I wanted to get away from it."
BUBBLES: "Don't you know if lightning is gonna get you—it's gonna get
     you?"
BUCK: "If lightning is gonna get me—let him look for me!"

They were the perfect example of exaggeration of life.

BUBBLES: "Why you laying down—you tired?"
BUCK: "No."
BUBBLES: "Then why you laying down?"
BUCK: "I'm laying down so I don't *get* tired."

Another perfect example of the wild exaggeration of caricature formula was Smith and Dale. Take their Dr. Kronkite act.

DR. CHARLIE DALE: "What is wrong with you?"
PATIENT JOE SMITH: "I can't move my hand. See? It's stiff. I used to be
     able to raise it this high—but I can't do it anymore. What is it?"

97

DR.: "Did you ever have it before?"
PATIENT: "Yes."
DR.: "Well, you got it again!"

A sure fire spin-off to the exaggeration formula is the play on words or malaprop formula.

DR. CHARLIE DALE: "When you eat dishes—what kind of dishes you eat—when you eat dishes?"
PATIENT JOE SMITH: "Dishes I'm eating?—what am I, a crocodile?"

I did the play-on-words bit with Mark Plant.

MARK: "A little respect—I'm an important singer."
ME: "You're a singer?"
MARK: "Yes, I'm a singer."
ME: "Hey, singer!"
MARK: "Yes?"
ME: "Show me your sewing machine!"

Then there is the build-up or three-way gag:

STRAIGHTMAN: "I fell for her the first moment I saw her. My *eyes* said, 'she's beautiful'—my *heart* said, 'this is it'—"
COMIC: "What do you hear from your liver?"

I used this formula often with Zsa Zsa and Jane Russell.

ME: "I'll talk to Earl Wilson—he'll give you a good write-up."
JANE: "Oh, Joey—thank you" (she kisses me).
ME: "I'll talk to Bob Sylvester—he'll put your picture in his column."
JANE: "Thank you, darling!" (Now she hugs me and kisses me.)
ME: "I'll tell Charles McHarry and Leonard Lyons to write that you are the greatest actress."
JANE: "Joey, how can I ever thank you?" (Now she is practically on top of me.)
ME: "If I could only think of one more writer."

ZSA ZSA: "I only go with continental men."
ME: "What's a continental?"
ZSA ZSA: "He picks you up in a long, shiny, black car."
ME: "So does an undertaker."
ZSA ZSA: "He wines and dines you in the best places. Orders the best champagne—caviar—pheasant under glass—near your plate there is a diamond bracelet—the bigger the diamonds the better the continental —he brings you orchids, mink, sables, and then he takes you home, walks you to the door and says good night."
ME: "That's a continental? We got the same thing in New York. Here we call them suckers."

98

Martin and Lewis used the three-way build-up successfully whenever they had a guest on their show.

GIRL: "Ah, Mr. Martin, you are more my type. I wish you could be with me some time in gay Paree—the city of wine, women, and song."

DEAN: "That's for me—I like wine."

GIRL: "And I like song."

JERRY: "That leaves me with what I like."

Again the three-way build-up:

GIRL: "Those artists. They see feminine beauty in everything they paint— to an artist, a chair is a woman, an umbrella is a woman, a hat rack is a woman—"

JERRY: "They must go out on some awfully funny dates."

It never fails.

JERRY: "When I was in gay Paree, I ordered everything in French. The waiter brought me one dish and I said "Très bon." Then he brought me another dish and I said, "Très bon.""

DEAN: "What did the waiter finally serve you?"

JERRY: "A tray of bones."

Truth is another comedy formula:

COMIC: "I've been taking wedding pictures for years."

STRAIGHTMAN: "Tell me. At a wedding—who would you say smiles the most—the bride or the groom?"

COMIC: "The bride's father."

A gag I used to do with Jane Russell:

JANE: "I must ask you to stop walking into my dressing room without knocking. After all, you might walk in sometime and I might not be dressed."

ME: "That's silly—you know I'm too much of a gentleman to do that—I always peek through the keyhole first—and if you don't have any clothes on—I don't walk in."

Another switch on the truth bit:

COMIC: "You're handsome—you're talented—you're witty—that's all admitted."

STRAIGHTMAN: "You mean you admit it?"

COMIC: "No—but you do."

COMIC: "You look like a million."

STRAIGHTMAN: "You never saw a million."

COMIC: "Yeah! You look like something I never saw."

The sex formula is the comic's favorite. The boy and girl gags with this theme are as different from Burns and Allen's style as Gracie was from Mae West.

The comic working with "the body" throws a dozen opening lines as his foil walks out: "She makes my wife look like a boy."—"If I told you you had a beautiful body, would you hold it against me?"—"Honey, I love every little thing about you, only I can't find any little things about you."

The gags are all about sex:

COMIC: "You know I had a dream about you last night."
GIRL: "Did you?"
COMIC: "No, you wouldn't let me!"

GIRL: "I heard about your lovemaking."
COMIC: "Oh, it's nothing."
GIRL: "Yeah—that's what I heard."

COMIC: "How about going for a drive with me?"
GIRL: "Oh no, I heard when you drive you only use one hand."
COMIC: "That's not true. I use both hands and drive with my feet."

GIRL: "I want a man that makes me warm, then he makes me cold—then he makes me warm—then me makes me cold again."
COMIC: "You don't want a man—you want a janitor."

The sophisticated sex formula was the one I used with Zsa Zsa Gabor—and it's the one she uses successfully in life:

JOEY: "How about dinner Friday night?"
ZSA ZSA: "Sorry, I'd love to dine with you—but I'm getting married Friday night."
JOEY: "Oh well, my luck."
ZSA ZSA: "But Saturday is all right."

JOEY: "Zsa Zsa, do you have a pin-up picture of yourself?"
ZSA ZSA: "There's nothing about me that needs pinning up."

JOEY: "Do you believe in large families?"
ZSA ZSA: "I believe every woman should have at least three husbands."

JOEY: "Do you think a girl should get married for love?"
ZSA ZSA: "I do, and I think she should keep getting married until she finds it."

JOEY: "By the way, how many proposals have you had since you have been in Washington?"
ZSA ZSA: "About fifty—two of them were for marriage."

JOEY: "Zsa Zsa, do you think every woman should have a mink coat?"

ZSA ZSA: "Why not? Every mink has one."

JOEY: "But suppose your husband can't afford a mink coat?"

ZSA ZSA: "Then let him wear a trench coat."

JOEY: "When a girl breaks off her engagement—do you think it proper to return the ring?"

ZSA ZSA: "Definitely—but she should keep the stone."

JOEY: "When do you think is the right time for a girl to marry?"

ZSA ZSA: "Whenever she's single."

JOEY: "Speaking of marriage—I heard your mother got married—do you approve of her getting married?"

ZSA ZSA: "Of course. I think all mothers should be married."

JOEY: "Was your mother a good teacher?"

ZSA ZSA: "Yes, she taught me I should always sleep in a king-size bed."

JOEY: "A king-size bed?"

ZSA ZSA: "With a real king in it."

JOEY: "What are your plans when you leave here?"

ZSA ZSA: "I am not quite sure. Last night I had dinner with a big producer and he wants me desperately."

JOEY: "For a movie?"

ZSA ZSA: "He didn't say."

Okay—I've tried to give you every example and formula for a double act. Did you find your style? Are you a Zsa Zsa or just a sexpot? Are you the "dumb" type or the wise guy? Do you need somebody to play with or would you rather work alone? Have you found the type you'd like to play with?

If you know—get to work on that style. If you click with your partner in temperament and talent, if you bounce off each other naturally, and if you find that rapport—get the formula and the formula gags and stick to them—and good luck!

Here now are some tried and truly funny double acts that have made them laugh down through the years:

"DOES-DO ROUTINE"

STRAIGHTMAN: "What took you so long to get here?"

COMIC: "I couldn't help it. I was standing in the subway minding my own business—I had my hand in my pocket—"

STRAIGHTMAN: "Yes?"

COMIC: "And my pocket got off at Ninety-sixth Street!"

STRAIGHTMAN: "Do you always ride the subway?"

COMIC: "I always does."

STRAIGHTMAN: "Always does??? You mean you always do. You see, 'do' is only used in the first person singular—and 'does' is used in the third person singular. For instance, you do ride the subway—I do ride the subway . . . he does ride the subway . . . she does ride the subway . . . they do ride the subway."

COMIC: "No wonder it's so crowded!"

STRAIGHTMAN: "No, you don't understand . . . do is the first person singular and does is the third person singular . . . now do you know where to use 'does'?"

COMIC: "Sure, when I wash my undies!"

STRAIGHTMAN: "No, your grammar—your grammar—I'm talking about your grammar!"

COMIC: "Oh, she uses Lux!"

STRAIGHTMAN: "You're just hopeless . . . I'll give you one more chance: I'm your boss. For instance, I can't say—your boss do pay you a big salary."

COMIC: "Brother, you can't say my boss *does* pay me a big salary!"

STRAIGHTMAN: "Remember, I'm you're boss and you're nothing."

COMIC: "BIG DEAL. BOSS OVER NOTHING!"

"SUE-SAW"

STRAIGHTMAN: "Do you mind if I tell a joke? After all I'm a comedian. I know the secret of comedy."

COMIC: "I know, and that's what I like about you."

STRAIGHTMAN: "That I know my comedy?"

COMIC: "No, that you know how to keep a secret!
Look, let me tell a joke first."

STRAIGHTMAN: "All right, go ahead. But remember we're on the air—be careful what you say. After all, there are a lot of women, children, and sailors in the audience."

COMIC: "Don't worry about me. I'm very careful about my jokes."

STRAIGHTMAN: "Stop stalling—tell the joke!"

COMIC: "All right. Here's a simple little joke about two old ladies who go out to buy a girdle."

STRAIGHTMAN: "I'm sorry—you can't say girdle!"

COMIC: "I'm sorry—I pulled a bloomer!"

STRAIGHTMAN: "Ah, ah, watch out . . . be careful what you say."

COMIC: "Well, these two old ladies walk over to this store.
They're just about to step in . . ."

STRAIGHTMAN: "Wait a minute! You can't say step-in. It's a personal garment."

COMIC: "I'm sorry—it was just a slip!"

STRAIGHTMAN: "Ah, ah, you can't say slip! They're all taboo under the censorship rules."

COMIC: "Under where?"

STRAIGHTMAN: "And you can't say underwear!"

COMIC: "That one crept up on me!"

STRAIGHTMAN: "All right, stop stalling—let me hear the joke."

COMIC: "Well, these two old ladies—"

STRAIGHTMAN: "What's their names?"

COMIC: "It doesn't matter."

STRAIGHTMAN: "It does to me!"

COMIC: "All right, if it means so much to you—one lady's name is Mrs. Dunn—and the other lady's name is Sue. . . . Well, just as these two old ladies are about to enter the store—do you know what Sue saw?"

STRAIGHTMAN: "Sue saw?????"

COMIC: "Sue saw? . . . I think I got a homogenized infinitive in there somewhere!"

STRAIGHTMAN: "You should watch your syntax."

COMIC: "My what?"

STRAIGHTMAN: "Syntax! Syntax!"

COMIC: "Don't tell me they got a tax on that too!"

STRAIGHTMAN: "Never mind. What did Sue see?"

COMIC: "Sue see???? That's worse than Sue saw!"

STRAIGHTMAN: "No, you don't understand—when I say it, it's Sue see—and when you say it—it's Sue saw—see?"

COMIC: "When you say it, it's Sue see—and when I say it, it's Sue saw—see!"

STRAIGHTMAN: "That's right!"

COMIC: "Shall we dance?" (They start to dance.)

STRAIGHTMAN: "Oh, cut it. . . . Now tell me, what had Sue seen?"

COMIC: "Sue seen???? . . . I think you got a blowout in your subjunctives! Sue saw Mrs. Dunn's husband with another woman . . . and do you know what Dunn did?"

STRAIGHTMAN: "Dunn did????"

COMIC: "I think I got a dangling participle in there!"

STRAIGHTMAN: "What did Dunn do?"

COMIC: "Did Dunn do???"

STRAIGHTMAN: "What is it that Dunn's done?"

COMIC: "Dunn's Dunn??? . . . Look, let's go back to Sue saw—I liked that much better!"

STRAIGHTMAN: "Never mind . . . who told you this joke anyway?"

COMIC: Shostovorkapitch—now let's see you fool around with that!"

STRAIGHTMAN: "This is your life!"

COMIC: "Why not—I might have lived. The first forty years of my life I was very poor."

STRAIGHTMAN: "And after that?"

COMIC: "I got used to it."

STRAIGHTMAN: "You came into this world as a bundle from heaven."

COMIC: "And every few minutes the bundle needed a new wrapper."

STRAIGHTMAN: "As a baby—you had many trials and tribulations—as a matter of fact, you didn't see daylight for the first six months."

COMIC: "That was my mother's fault. She was so nearsighted that she kept diapering the wrong end."

STRAIGHTMAN: "But your father was very devoted to you. He made your formula, which consisted of orange juice, cereal and cream, with sliced bananas, bacon and eggs, buttered toast and a large glass of chocolate milk. But in spite of all this nourishing food, you never seemed to gain any weight—can you tell me why?"

COMIC: "Sure—the food looked so good that my father ate it himself—this I didn't mind—but three times a day he used to feed me milk."

STRAIGHTMAN: "Well—that's not so bad—all children get milk three times a day."

COMIC: "From a saucer—under the sink?"

STRAIGHTMAN: "Oh, I guess your father must have had some fondness for you. Surely he loved his own flesh and blood."

COMIC: "His own flesh and blood he loved—mine he didn't."

STRAIGHTMAN: "Anything unusual happen to you when you were a kid?"

COMIC: "I swallowed a small watch."

STRAIGHTMAN: "Does it bother you?"

COMIC: "Only when I wind it!"

JOE SMITH AND CHARLIE DALE

Just a bit of their famous Dr. Kronkite act that is a primer for double acts.

DOCTOR CHARLIE DALE: "What kind of dishes you eating?"

PATIENT JOE SMITH: "Dishes I'm eating?—what am I, a crocodile?"

DOCTOR: "Now, when you're drinking drinks, what kind of beverage drinks are you drinking?"

PATIENT: "You mean like coffee, milk or chocolate?"

DOCTOR: "Yes."

PATIENT: "I drink tea."

DOCTOR: "What's troubling you?"
PATIENT: "Bursitis and it's on the back of my neck and that's a bad place!"
DOCTOR: "Where would you want a better place than the back of your neck?"
PATIENT: "On the back of *your* neck!"
DOCTOR: "What is your big complaint?"
PATIENT: "I can't move my arm above my head—see? It's stiff."
DOCTOR: "Have you had this before?"
PATIENT: "Yes."
DOCTOR: "Well, you got it again. Now, regarding your bursitis—you should go to Mount Clemmons."
PATIENT: "Is that a good place for bursitis?"
DOCTOR: "The best place in the country."
PATIENT: "How do you know?"
DOCTOR: "That's where I got mine!"

A thumbnail sketch of
SMITH AND DALE'S "SHNAPPS AND SHTRUDEL"

Shnapps sees a familiar figure, slaps him on the back.

SHNAPPS: "Well, if it ain't my old friend Jake."
SHTRUDEL: "Hey! My name ain't Jake, and if it would be Jake do you have to give me such a crack on the back?"
SHNAPPS: "Well, if your name ain't Jake, what do you care how I hit Jake?"
SHTRUDEL: "But you hit me. Say, who are you?"
SHNAPPS: "Don't you remember your old friend Bernard?"
SHTRUDEL: "There are all kinds of Bernards. Gimbel you ain't and Baruch you can't be, so you must be Saint Bernard."
SHNAPPS: "I'm Bernard Shnapps."
SHTRUDEL: "I'm pleased to meet you, good-bye."
SHNAPPS: "Wait a minute . . . you're Jake Strudel!"
SHTRUDEL: "My name is not now Jake. It's Stonewall."
SHNAPPS: "From Jake to Stonewall?"
SHTRUDEL: "Yes. Jake is Jack and Jack is Stonewall and Stonewall is Jackson. It's well known that's the name of a park."
SHNAPPS: "And do you own it?"
SHTRUDEL: "No, but I got other properties."
SHNAPPS: "I didn't see you for years."
SHTRUDEL: "I followed the advice of that great man Morris Levy who said, 'Go West, Young Man.' So I went to Florida."
SHNAPPS: "Wait a minute. In the first place Horace Greeley said 'Go West Young Man' and in the second place, is Florida West?"
SHTRUDEL: "Key West. And there I made good and plenty. And how's things with you?"

SHNAPPS: "How should it be?"

SHTRUDEL: "I'm glad to hear it, and you're making plenty money?"

SHNAPPS: "How much can I make?"

SHTRUDEL: "So much? And what business are you in?"

SHNAPPS: "I'm in every business that begins with an A."

SHTRUDEL: "What do you mean, begins with an A?"

SHNAPPS: "Well, I'm A match maker, A jewelry salesman, A real estate agent, A furniture salesman. . . ."

SHTRUDEL: "Whose furniture are you selling?"

SHNAPPS: "So far I'm selling my own. To get a lot of business one has got to succeed."

SHTRUDEL: "Why don't you stick better to one trade?"

SHNAPPS: "I don't like to work for a boss, so this way I'm my own boss so if I'm not here, I'm there and if I'm not there, where am I? I'm here, and there you are."

SHTRUDEL: "It was nice meeting you and if you ever get down to Florida, look me up."

SHNAPPS: "Where will you be?"

STRUDEL: "I'll be in California!"

MAGICIANS

Magicians don't start out as comedians—but most of them wind up that way. That is, if they want to keep eating—and I don't mean their rabbits.

TV and night clubs have ended the careers of most magic acts—unless they can make the laughs appear.

Today, the more tricks that fail—the more laughs and the more bookings. Flop sweat has been replaced by flop gags: "This trick was given to me by a great magician—and he was glad to get rid of it."

Now it's rehearsed failure—with the "savers" set up to produce the laughs instead of the rabbit: "I don't have to do this for a living—I could always starve."

Magicians have found they can make more money and get more bookings by using their magic as a gimmick instead of the main attraction. Victor Borge learned a long time ago that he could get to the top quicker by using the piano only as a prop to accent his gags. Jack Benny does the same thing with his violin. So does Henny Youngman. Morey Amsterdam uses a cello as his crutch. Will Rogers started telling gags while spinning a rope. Fred Allen and W. C. Fields were jugglers who stepped into comedy and used their clubs just as a plant to get the laughs that put them into the biggest time.

In the case of the magician—the funnier the patter, the less the audience cares about how you do the trick: "Notice—at no time do my fingers leave my hand." "If you think this is sad—you should see my pay envelope."

Your material does not have to have any relationship to the tricks you are doing. Sometimes it's even funnier if they have no connection: Eve said to Adam—"Who do you love?" Adam answered—"Who else?" Or, did you hear about the two Hollywood kids who were talking and one said to the other—"My father can lick your father!" and the other kid said, "Jerk, your father *is* my father." Or, two alligators were talking and one said to the other—"I think I'll go out and buy a man bag today."

In other words, which should be funny, good comedy material, gags, jokes or stories can be used by the bright magician for the best results.

In the heyday of vaudeville, straightman magicians headlined everywhere. Almost every show on the two-a-day had a man of magic who sawed a woman in half. That's all a thing of the past. The era of the great Houdini is gone, if not forgotten. Although the lady he cut in half is still alive and living in New York and San Francisco.

It's always a good laugh policy to make fun of yourself as well as your magic:

I come from a family of magicians—my mother-in-law is a great magician—you should see the daughter she palmed off on me.

My wife is a magician—nobody makes money disappear like her.

My brother-in-law is a magician—you should see him turn into a saloon.

My brother is a comedy magician—the funniest thing he pulls from his hat is his head.

The "savers" are the biggest laugh-getters. They change disaster into victory, when a trick goes wrong.

I bet when I came out you thought I was going to be lousy.

My next trick is even worse.

Just give me a ten yard head start.

We will now pause for thirty seconds of silence for that trick that just died.

In this age of capsule comedy, hyped-up teenagers and nervous listeners, manipulating cards, clubs, or razor blades, or producing doves can be as dull as a date with your spinster aunt, during the dead quiet of the trick. You have got to entertain the funnybone as well as the eye if you want to contribute to the unemployment insurance instead of collecting it.

Two bunnies were watching as I pulled a rabbit out of my hat. One finally said to the other: "I don't know how you feel about this—but I like the old fashioned way better."

Not only have magicians become comics, but many comics have "borrowed" some tricks to make their gags funnier. Milton Berle, who is a very good card manipulator, offers you a card and then asks you, "Is it the ace of spades?" when you say "No" he throws the deck in the audience and hollers "Then the hell with the trick."

Another comic, imitating the magician who tears a newspaper by cutting out little pieces behind his back or without looking and turns it into a fancy design, keeps tearing the paper as the music plays louder and louder and winds up with a fistful of confetti.

Still another funny trick is bringing a "plant" up from the audience and putting two eggs in his hat and promising to make them disappear after breaking them. Of course, there is always the continual patter. "These cards are so thoroughly shuffled—you can't tell an ace from a hole in the ground."

I'm a crackerjack magician—I work for peanuts.

I've got magic in my veins—I wish I had blood instead.

I walked off with a medal for that trick—but the manager made me put it back.

I paid ten cents for that trick—it was either that or go to the bathroom.

This could drive normal men crazy—imagine what it does to me!

I did this trick before President Johnson—was in office.

I did this trick before the President—of my lodge.

My magic act has put more people to sleep than Sanka—my act is a sure cure for insomnia.

I'm what's called a magician—I know—I read it in my contract.

You're looking at me like I started income tax.

Everybody makes mistakes—that's why a lot of us are here.

I always say—what's a show without a magician? And the answer comes back—much better!

Ventriloquy

The big difference between the amateur and the pro ventriloquist is his material. Your routines must be good enough to hold the audience after the first few minutes, when they are marveling at your mimicry, voice-throwing and dead lips.

After that, you must have something interesting and funny to say. Your dummy must be believable and a definite character. So that now you're selling a double act that must be entertaining. Except that you have a large advantage. A dummy can get away with saying and doing things you wouldn't dare do. Somehow, people never consider it's *you* doing it. They will take it from the dummy whereas they would never take it from you.

VENTRILOQUIST: "Nice audience tonight."
DUMMY: "Yeah—my teacher is out there."
VENTRILOQUIST: "Your teacher? Which one is she?"
DUMMY: "Well, see that girl with the beautiful blonde hair in the second row?—"
VENTRILOQUIST: "Yes."
DUMMY: "And the gorgeous blue eyes and the luscious lips and sexy figure?"
VENTRILOQUIST: "That's your teacher?"
DUMMY: "No, my teacher's the ugly one sitting next to her."

Anybody can be a ventriloquist. You don't need a special voice box or a solid gold larynx—all you need is practice—and a dummy.

You must give your "figure" or "dummy" a personality. You can make him dumb, arrogant, sophisticated, wise guy, or smart, but once you create him, you must go all the way. That goes for clothes, facial expression, body movement, and of course, dialogue. Only *you* can give him the character or personality you want and make him so real that *even you* will believe him.

A good idea is to write a biography on him to make him come to life: when and where he was born, habits, schooling, parents, work, etc. Now you have a true live partner with a full life of his own—and more important—a voice to match.

You can make your dummy a braggart, a sissy, a moron, a cry-baby, a monster—anything you choose or want for your partner—or the kind of playmate you could have the most fun with. Of course, you must make him likeable or amusing—if the audience doesn't like your dummy, they ain't gonna like you.

I can't tell you how to physically build a dummy to fit your character or how to throw your voice—but my good friend Paul Winchell, TV's top ventriloquist, has written a book called *Ventriloquism for Fun and Profit* that gets you ready for everything but failure—in the dummy business.

Paul shows you how to use your voice and how to build the dummy and how to manipulate him according to his personality. Swagger if tough— drop eyes if shy—head on rakish angle if brash or wisecracking, etc.

The successful practitioner of the art of ventriloquism must avoid voice strain through mastering of breath control and use of abdominal muscles. In his book, Winchell tells you how to throw your voice through your figure or dummy without upsetting your larynx. I can't tell you how to push your voice through a prop phone or sing while drinking a glass of water or recite with a handkerchief in your mouth or dozens of other tricks that Winchell has in his book, but I can supply you with the material to fit your partner or at least put you on the right road for laughs.

The basic elements in ventriloquism are things like creating a dummy voice, lip control, manipulation, character and most of all practice.

Illusion is the basic magic of all ventriloquists. Since it's a physical impossibility for anybody to *throw* his voice from one place to another—the ventriloquist does it by creating an illusion at the moment by giving action to the dummy. And since hearing is the least reliable of our five senses, you are easily deceived.

Thus, when the ventriloquist talks in the ventriloquial voice without moving his own lips, and a dummy some distance away from him opens and closes his mouth, the illusion is created that the dummy has talked or that the ventriloquist has "thrown" his voice. This illusion, of course, is naturally the basic magic of all ventriloquists.

Now you come to the thing that separates the men from the boys or the big money from the amateur—material. And even more important, the material that fits you—or rather, your dummy.

Here's a typical Winchell gag with his Jerry Mahoney—strictly a wise guy:

JERRY: "Look, Winchell, I don't think I can go on tonight."
WINCHELL: "What's the matter, Jerry?"
JERRY: "My uncle is very sick."
WINCHELL: "Oh?"
JERRY: "Yeah—he thinks he's a chicken."
WINCHELL: "Thinks he's a chicken??? Jerry, you ought to put him in the hospital!"
JERRY: "We would—but we need the eggs."

110

Another smart-ass line has Winchell asking:

WINCHELL: "How do you like the suit?"
JERRY: "I like it. It makes you look real doggy."
WINCHELL: "Do you really think so?"
JERRY: "Yes, indeed—your face looks like a cocker spaniel."

Paul Winchell can tell you how to build a dummy—but it's your material that will help you hold an audience. Here's a good exercise of short one-liners for beginners:

VENTRILOQUIST: "I have a job for you."
DUMMY: "Doin' what?"
VENTRILOQUIST: "Ventriloquist."
DUMMY: "Ventrick-o-what's that?"
VENTRILOQUIST: "Really want to know?"
DUMMY: "Yes."
VENTRILOQUIST: "Well, there are two people."
DUMMY: "Yeah."
VENTRILOQUIST: "One is a ventriloquist."
DUMMY: "Yeah."
VENTRILOQUIST: "And one is a dummy."
DUMMY: "Which one are you?"

Always remember, of course, that the dummy is the comic and you are the straightman. Don't get jealous when you hear who's getting the laughs. And remember, make the routines fit the character. If you choose a tough guy as your partner:

DUMMY: "My kid brother slapped Capone in the kisser."
VENTRILOQUIST: "I'd like to shake hands with your kid brother."
DUMMY: "We ain't gonna dig him up just for you."

VENTRILOQUIST: "What big jobs did you pull?"
DUMMY: "I held up the foist National Bank—I held up the toid National Bank!"
VENTRILOQUIST: "How about the Second National Bank?"
DUMMY: I got *my* money in there!"

The brash or wise guy is the popular one because he can get away with so much that most of us can't:

VENTRILOQUIST: "I'm mad. I want to take a bath, and my mother-in-law has been in the bathtub for hours."
DUMMY: "Well, look on the bright side—maybe she drowned."

Another favorite is the dumb dummy. It makes us happy because we feel a superiority over him:

111

VENTRILOQUIST: "Did you know that Abraham Lincoln did his homework on a shovel?"

DUMMY: "That's impossible—how could he get a shovel in the typewriter?"

Ventriloquism was not always used by performers in the theatre to amuse. In the ancient times, it was used as a sort of witchcraft. Various priests and medicine men used it to make a rock talk or a tree sing to prove they had performed a miracle. The modern counterpart of this deceit is the phony medium who claims you are hearing the voice of "Dear departed Uncle Charlie," when it's nothing more than the medium using a ventriloquial voice.

There is much discussion about who started the whole thing. Some say it was Louis Brabant in the household of King Francis of France in the 1500s. Others claim it was a Viennese named Baron Menger who lived about 1770. Still others bestow the distinction on Le Sieur Thiemet who they say amused Napoleon and Josephine with his ventriloquial tricks.

But most show business chroniclers agree that the person who first aroused the public's attention to ventriloquism was a Frenchman named Nicholas Marie Alexander.

However, none of these used a dummy. They created the illusion of people talking offstage—or the chair or piece of sculpture speaking, etc.

There is also some dispute about when the first dummy made its appearance. Some say a Spanish count created a doll with a moving mouth so he could amuse his friends.

Of course, Mr. Punch and his wife Judy became famous in England with their "Punch and Judy" shows. However, while they were in a sense dummy characters, ventriloquism wasn't used for the voices in the act.

It was an Englishman named Arthur Prince who at the turn of the last century made ventriloquism a big time act in show business. He toured Europe and the U.S. with his dummy named Sailor Jim.

About 1903 Harry (The Great) Lester began to appear on the stages of our leading vaudeville theatres, and for twenty-five years or more Lester and his dummy George Byron Jr. were considered the top ventriloquist act in the business. When he retired to Hollywood he continued to teach ventriloquism to the show business fraternity and the pros in the picture business.

Ventriloquists were the first to disappear when vaudeville hit the skids, until the 1930s, when Edgar Bergen brought his Charlie McCarthy to radio. Charlie McCarthy is a perfect lesson in the sophisticated dummy. Here is a perfect scene for students of the man-about-town figure. It was presented on the radio in 1952 by Edgar Bergen and Charlie McCarthy—with their guest star Zsa Zsa Gabor.

BERGEN: "And now, ladies and gentlemen, it is my pleasure to introduce our guest of the evening . . . one of the world's most beautiful women . . . the fabulous Zsa Zsa Gabor."

GABOR: *"Thank you,* everyone . . . thank you, Edgar."

CHARLIE: "Wow! And I thought the Hungarian national dish was goulash."

GABOR: "Oh, so you are Sharlie?"

CHARLIE: "Sharlie?"

GABOR: "You must excuse my accent, but as you know I am very short in this country."

CHARLIE: "Short of what? . . . heh, heh! . . . oh, Zsa Zsa, my little lily cup, let me drink from the fountain of your beauty. . . . Hic . . . strong stuff!"

GABOR: "Charlie, I have been looking forward to meeting you."

CHARLIE: "Oh, puttee, puttee . . . so you've really been anxious to meet me?"

GABOR: "Mais oui!"

CHARLIE: "We may, we may . . . but first there's a show to do."

GABOR: (Laughs) "Oh, Charlie, why do you make me laugh so much?"

CHARLIE: "That way, it's more fun for everybody . . . oh, that dress you're wearing . . . it's so beautiful, so gorgeous."

GABOR: "Oh, it isn't much."

CHARLIE: "You're so right . . . Zsa Zsa, how about going for a drive with me?"

GABOR: "Well, maybe."

CHARLIE: "I think you'll just fit in my wire basket."

GABOR: "A bicycle! . . . Charlie, I go out with men of the world."

CHARLIE: "I'm a man of the world."

GABOR: "I mean this one."

CHARLIE: "She's got all that . . . and jokes, too."

GABOR: "The men I go out with give me expensive gifts . . . you know, right now, I don't have a diamond necklace."

CHARLIE: "That's all right . . . I don't have one either."

GABOR: "But a girl likes little trinkets like a diamond necklace or a mink coat. They give her a feeling of being . . . wanted."

CHARLIE: "If I got you those, I'd be wanted, too!"

Paul Winchell was the first to combine puppetry and ventriloquism—thus taking the dummy off the ventriloquist's lap—which had been the standard arrangement.

His technique has produced dummies that move their arms and legs and function as separate entities as the ventriloquist moves around freely—throwing his voice while not manipulating the dummies.

Now, you could do scenes with them and practically treat them as humans.

Ventriloquists, unlike magicians, should have routines on related subjects. Like this dialogue that Winchell suggests to new students of the art. Of course, as you go along, you will steal—I mean borrow—that is, do research on television—and find new gags to fit the character of your partner and add to the scenes that you are doing now. Here's a school routine that you can use and add to as you go along.

VENTRILOQUIST: "Just look at your report card! C in Arithmetic, D in Geog‚raphy, E in History, and what's this—L in Behavior?"

DUMMY: "Maybe I behaved like L."

VENTRILOQUIST: "Tell me, how long can a man live without brains?"

DUMMY: "I don't know, how old are you?"

VENTRILOQUIST: "Have you been playing hooky?"

DUMMY: "Excuse me—I think I'm sick."

VENTRILOQUIST: "Now look at me when I'm talking to you!"

DUMMY: "That makes me even sicker!"

VENTRILOQUIST: "Now quit stalling. Did you play hooky? I want the truth."

DUMMY: "Oh, well, that'll take a little longer."

VENTRILOQUIST: "For the last time, did you play hooky?"

DUMMY: "Yes I did."

VENTRILOQUIST: "You didn't! You didn't! You didn't!"

DUMMY: "I tell him I did—he tells me I didn't."

VENTRILOQUIST: "If you didn't go to school—where did you go?"

DUMMY: "I went swimming."

VENTRILOQUIST: "Don't be ridiculous. It's too cold to go swimming this time of the year."

DUMMY: "No it ain't. There were lots of kids in swimming."

VENTRILOQUIST: "Really—boys or girls?"

DUMMY: "I couldn't tell—they didn't have no clothes on."

As a pro, you are in competition with the highest priced comedy acts in the business, who pay fortunes to writers for material to keep feeding these hungry TV machines.

The amateur ventriloquist entertaining at school or for some local charity or organization is not under the same pressure as the pro. Sure, he wants his dummy to be funny—but somehow the audience understands that he is not getting paid.

But your first job as a pro must have material that is up there with the giants—and since you are in competition for that comedy spot on TV, you must have routines that are fresh and bright. You can put together some very funny skits from the gags in my joke dictionary; you can dig down in your own funnybone, and then you can go to a writer who will help put the routine into shape. As you go along, you will be able to afford better writers. That is, writers who understand your partner and you.

Here are some routines that could be the basis of an act. You can add to them by looking up the subject in the back of this book or following the Broadway columnists and their latest jokes, or looking in all the joke books and watching television, especially the late night shows, and then try to find yourself a bright young writer who is trying to make it just like you—maybe you could grow and get funny and lucky together.

VENTRILOQUIST: "I introduce my partner, who is ubiquitous, pristine, and didactic. I say that without reservation."
DUMMY: "And without knowing what you're talking about."

VENTRILOQUIST: "You know, you're not smart enough to talk to an idiot!"
DUMMY: "Okay, I'll write you a letter."
VENTRILOQUIST: "Now, speak clearly and watch your diction—say 'how now brown cow.' "
DUMMY: "How now brown cow."
VENTRILOQUIST: "No, no! It's BR-R-R-OWN COW—BR-R-OWN COW. Now what do you say?"
DUMMY: "MOOOOO!"

Here's a funny standard routine that you can use as an encore or an opening bit:

VENTRILOQUIST: "I forgot to ask—how's your family?"
DUMMY: "Not so good—you know my two brothers, Izzy and Wuzzy?"
VENTRILOQUIST: "Izzy and Wuzzy—sure, I know them very well."
DUMMY: "Well, Wuzzy's sick."
VENTRILOQUIST: "Is he?"
DUMMY: "No, not Izzy—Wuzzy's sick!"
VENTRILOQUIST: "Is he?"
DUMMY: "Look—don't start making trouble. I told you it's not Izzy—it's Wuzzy that's sick."
VENTRILOQUIST: "Look, you don't understand. When I say is he, I don't mean Izzy—I mean is he?"
DUMMY: "When you say Izzy—you don't mean Izzy—you mean Izzy?"
VENTRILOQUIST: "That's right!"
DUMMY: "Are you sure Jerry Mahoney started this way? Look, maybe if I explain it like this. Wuzzy is sick, Izzy is fine. He's in good health—except that he's in jail—he was caught stealing."
VENTRILOQUIST: "Was he?"
DUMMY: "No, not Wuzzy! Izzy's in jail—Wuzzy's too sick to steal."
VENTRILOQUIST: "Is he?"
DUMMY: "No, not Izzy—Wuzzy! Wuzzy's in jail—I mean Izzy—oh, forget it!"

Here's a funny routine that will give you a chance to expand and do takes and tricks with your partner.

Singing Routine

VENTRILOQUIST: "Sing a song for the people."
DUMMY: (In a whisper) "I can't."
VENTRILOQUIST: "What's the matter with your voice? It sounds terrible."

115

DUMMY: "Don't blame me—that's your job."

VENTRILOQUIST: "Wait a minute—I'll bet it was that bottle of soda you drank. What was that stuff?"

DUMMY: (Whispers) "I was drinking 'UP DOCK.' "

VENTRILOQUIST: "UP DOCK?—what's UP DOCK?"

DUMMY: "Nothing much—what's up with you?"

VENTRILOQUIST: "I'd like to sing 'In my sweet little Alice blue gown.' "

DUMMY: "I don't care if you sing in your B.V.D.'s."

VENTRILOQUIST: "I'd like to sing a song that's sweeping the country."

DUMMY: "And that's what you should be doing!"

VENTRILOQUIST: "All right—what would you like to hear?"

DUMMY: "Frank Sinatra—but I guess we're stuck with you."

VENTRILOQUIST: "The trouble with you is you don't know anything about music. You don't know the great masters like Beethoven."

DUMMY: "Is that so—I used to know Beethoven very well."

VENTRILOQUIST: "Oh you did, huh?"

DUMMY: "Yes!"

VENTRILOQUIST: "It so happens that Beethoven lived in 1572."

DUMMY: "Well, we lived next door in 1574."

VENTRILOQUIST: "You are mighty close to an idiot."

DUMMY: "Keep your mouth shut and nobody'll notice it."

VENTRILOQUIST: "Now listen, you—I'm getting tired of all this—I want to sing!"

DUMMY: "Can you really sing? Do you have a good voice?"

VENTRILOQUIST: "Do I? Listen to this! (Sings) Yes sir, singers run in my family!"

DUMMY: "They should."

VENTRILOQUIST: "It happens that I was with the Metropolitan."

DUMMY: "Did you sell a lot of policies?"

VENTRILOQUIST: "I want you to know—I was a musician on the other side."

DUMMY: "Well—turn over."

VENTRILOQUIST: "This tune has a haunting melody."

DUMMY: "It should have—you murdered it."

VENTRILOQUIST: "Okay, wise guy—you sing—do you know Shostakovitch's Fifth?"

DUMMY: "I don't know—was it a boy or girl? I'm kidding—everybody knows Shostakovitch's Fifth is a bottle of booze!"

VENTRILOQUIST: "Okay now—what are you gonna sing?"

DUMMY: "A song entitled—

"A hero unsung is Mr. Lum Fung, he fed his chicken a rice cake—and it laid an egg foo young,

116

or

"There is no R in my mother-in-law's name—but she looks like an oyster just the same,

or

"Hello young lovers wherever you are—watch out for the house detective."

VENTRILOQUIST: "All right—let's hear the song."

DUMMY: "Okay—I'll sing a song I have just rotten."

VENTRILOQUIST: "No, no, it's written—not rotten!"

DUMMY: "You ain't heard this song yet."

DUMMY: (Sings to tune of "Home on the Range")

> "Oh, gimme a home—where the buffalo roam,
> And the cowboys all work till they drop.
> Where the cows all relax,
> And lie flat on their backs,
> And this brings the cream to the top."

Jimmy Nelson and Danny O'Day

"The Girl Friend Routine"

JIMMY: "I'd like you to be on your best behavior because we have a wonderful audience and this will be a very informal show."

DANNY: "That's a good idea. The more informal the better."

JIMMY: "Good. What are you gonna do?"

DANNY: "Nothing—that's as informal as I get. Besides, tonight I'm in love!"

JIMMY: "You're in love?"

DANNY: "Yes—what's that on your neck?"

JIMMY: "It's a freckle."

DANNY: "Well, it's moving!"

JIMMY: "No, it's not moving."

DANNY: "I'm not kidding about being in love."

JIMMY: "Love?"

DANNY: "Yes—oh, there's nothing like turning the lights down low."

JIMMY: "I know."

DANNY: "Smooching a little."

JIMMY: "Smooching?"

DANNY: "Then you sit in the loving room."

JIMMY: "Loving room? That's living."

DANNY: "You said it—that's living!"

JIMMY: "Look, I want to know a little about . . . what's the matter?"

DANNY: "Your freckle has a friend."

JIMMY: "Never mind . . . I want to know a little about your girl friend."

DANNY: "What girl?"

JIMMY: "You said you were in love."

DANNY: "So?"

JIMMY: "I just naturally assumed you had a girl."

DANNY: "Good thinking, Nelson! Oh Gad, this boy's a regular Univac—spelled backwards, that's cavein—what do you want to know?"

JIMMY: "Some simple little thing."

DANNY: "That's her—that's my girl!"

JIMMY: "I don't mean that."

DANNY: "No?"

JIMMY: "I mean some peculiar characteristic."

DANNY: "She bites her nails."

JIMMY: "Lots of girls bite their nails."

DANNY: "Toenails?"

JIMMY: "Look, is that the silliest thing you're gonna say here tonight?"

DANNY: "No, but that's the funniest—well, that's the act, ladies and gentlemen—good night!"

Greeting Card Humor

Old jokes never die. They wind up in greeting cards. When vaudeville passed on it came back to this world in the form of the Ed Sullivan Show. The old comedy writers now send their messages through 7 billion greeting cards a year.

Instead of writing for one comedian, the gag writers are now writing for thousands of would-be comics who send out 700 million dollars' worth of cards annually.

The studio card writer must be more than a humorist. His ideas and gags not only must entertain but they must have some personal identification for the customer. A buyer should be able to go into any store and find a card that he can apply to himself as if he thought of it. That means each card should have a personal application for at least a couple of hundred thousand individuals to be effective or profitable.

Instead of stealing gags—the customer buys one for twenty-five cents or more—in the form of a greeting card which should give him the sense of humor he wishes he had or thinks he has.

The first humorous cards were valentines which were printed in violent color on foolscap and were called "Penny Dreadfuls" or "Vinegar Valentines." They started as early as 1850 and were most popular at the end of the nineteenth century:

> If I had plenty of dough,
> I'd loaf around with you.

They also did funny cards in rhyme:

> You shouldn't hold your head so high,
> You are not such a funny guy,
> You only think of pride and self,
> And ought to go and drown yourself.

Immediately after World War II, the greeting card industry exploded into a giant business, partly because of the availability of paper, which had been curtailed during the war, but mostly because now we were in an era of celebration and gaiety. It wasn't a business now only for Christmas, birthdays and valentines.

Everytning and anything was a reason for a card—sickness, health, alimony—the day your mother-in-law left—the day the butcher's son's face cleared up—when you won at cards—or lost at golf—anything called for a card or gag.

During 1949-50 the studio card emerged—so called because they were designed by and printed by small artists in their studios which were usually their kitchen tables. The first ones were amusing captions and simple art work on long slim cards.

Then they became violent with insulting messages like, "Do me a Big Favor (over) DROP DEAD" or "May the Bluebird of Happiness (over) Crap all over your birthday cake."

The cards became so sick, you needed a prescription to buy them. "The day you were born something terrible happened—(over)—You LIVED."

On the front of the card there was always the happy start of the message: "PLEASE DON'T EVER CHANGE—Stay just as your are— (then you turn card over)—Rotten, stupid, cheap, evil, dirty, vicious, foul and diseased."

These were lovely valentines: "You Really Have Everything—(Over) —Diarrhea, Pyorrhea, Beri-Beri, and a Double Hernia."

"You've got everything a man wants—(over)—A mustache, a beard, and muscles."

"You're really cooking with gas—(over)—Now how about inhaling some?"

"I'd like to know you better—(over)—If I can keep my stomach from turning."

"You're real swell—(over)—Especially around the head."

"I like your looks—(over)—It's your personality and bad breath I can't stand."

"You're okay in my book—(over)—I wish I knew you when you were alive."

"You must be older than you look—(over)—You couldn't get so dumb so fast."

These cards, written with a scalpel, stayed popular until about 1963 when the more sophisticated and subtle message took over. The humor became more topical and clever than deadly. Harry Hershfield received this card from a friend on his eighty-first birthday:

"You are a nobleman. You are a credit to mankind—a joy to the people around you—(over)—That's only the sentiment of the guy who printed the card—not mine."

Today, dozens of free-lance writers can make a pretty good living using their talents, rather than their hammers, to inject a sense of humor in the card sender.

Somebody must be doing something right. The American Greetings Corporation—one of the biggest in the world—takes in 78 million dollars a year with these cockamamie cards.

So, if you want to write for greeting cards, here's your chance. They employ hundreds on a free-lance basis. Or, you can use some of these gags that fit your funnybone to send cards or messages to your friends or relatives. These messages fit every and any occasion. Choose your weapons to fit your sense of humor and fire away:

"I think you're the greatest—(over)—But what the hell do I know?"

"I think you're wonderful—(over)—But what's my opinion against millions of others?"

"Why don't you come over for dinner—(over)—If you don't mind imposing."

"You should go to Hollywood—(over)—The walk will do you good."

"If I gave you a going away present—(over)—Would you go away?"

"Our love is eternal—(over)—But will it last?"

"I must decline your invitation—(over)—Due to a subsequent engagement."

"I don't know what I'd do without you—(over)—But it's fun thinking about it."

"You haven't been yourself lately—(over)—And I notice the improvement."

"You must have a sixth sense—(over)—There's no sign of the other five."

Christmas cards are the biggest sellers—valentines come second—but any holiday brings out the cards and gag men.

ST. PATRICK'S DAY

"If anyone insults you on St. Patrick's Day by offering you a shot of Scotch—(over)—Just swallow the insult and have a happy St. Patrick's day!"

"Sure, 'n' if you're wearing any green on St. Pat's day, don't wear it near your nose—(over)—Red and green are Christmas colors!"

EASTER

"I'll bet the Easter Bunny will leave a little something on your doorstep this year—(over)—But don't worry, a good stiff brush and a strong detergent should take care of it."

"Don't expect the Easter Bunny at your house this year—(over)—They got him on a morals charge."

BIRTHDAY

"At your age—(over)—The candles cost more than the cake."

"Life is a funny game. Just about the time you learn the rules—(over)—You're too old for the team."

"Happy Birthday. You ain't as good as you once was—(over)—But you're as good once as you ever were."

"I was tempted to buy an expensive present for your birthday—(over)—Congratulate me on my will power."

"I'd give you a birthday present—(over)—But how do you wrap up a saloon?"

"If I had a million dollars, do you know what I'd send you on your birthday?—(over)—A card from Paris."

"Happy Birthday from my heart—(over)—Or would you prefer another part?"

ANNIVERSARY

"Happy Anniversary. Live and learn.—(over)—Of course, by the time you learn—it's too late to live."

"Happy Anniversary. It's no wonder that you two are so happy. You have a lot in common—(over)—and you both are."

"Happy Anniversary. Why don't you two celebrate by going out to a good movie. I saw a love scene at Loew's Theatre the other night that lasted nearly an hour—(over)—It probably would have lasted longer, but the usher broke it up."

GET WELL CARDS

"To keep everything sanitary—Use Dutch Cleanser—(over)—That's what they call Ex-Lax in Holland—Get Well."

"You're just what the doctor ordered—(over)—A patient with a good credit rating."

"The gang at work all wish you'd get well and come back to work—(over)—It's your turn to clean out the john."

"We thought you were only faking just to get out of work—(over)—But when you didn't show up on PAYDAY, we knew you must *really* be sick!"

122

"Modern medicine has made tremendous studies in all areas save one—(over)—Hospital food! Get out of there quick."

FRIENDSHIP

"We have so much in common—(over)—We both are."

"Hold Me! Squeeze Me! Kiss Me!—(over)—Not the card, stoopid—me!"

"A FRIEND IN NEED—(over)—Is a PEST!"

TRAVEL

"If you want to come back with a man on your arm—(over)—I'll give you the name of my tattoo parlor."

"Let me hear from you—(over)—Even if it's only a check."

"Have a good trip and come back soon—Not too fast and not too slow—(over)—Sort of half fast."

VALENTINE

"You have an hourglass figure—(over)—But time is running out."

"You're so charming. Every time men look at you—(over)—The young wish you were willing and the old wish they were able."

"You're dark and handsome—(over)—When it's dark—you're handsome."

"You look like a million—(over)—Every year of it."

"You look like a dream—(over)—A nightmare."

"You are a vision—(over)—A real sight."

"You have a winning smile—(over)—And a losing face."

"I love you—(over)—I have no taste—But I love you."

Teenage Humor

Statisticians say that by 1970 half the population of the United States will be under twenty-one. Parents say: "HELP."

You just can't brush it all off as a "teenage problem" any longer. It's now become a "parents problem," according to the youngsters. They figure if Sinatra thought enough of them to take one for his bride—even for a few minutes—they must be pretty important. And wasn't it the teeners who got the Queen to knight their Beatles?

The teenagers' revolt against grownups in general and parents in particular has manifested itself as a private world of their own with their own language, their own music, their own dances, and their own humor. Their rebelling against the squares is flaunted in the twist, the frug, the monkey, the jerk, and all the other dances that helped them shed their inhibitions and supplied them with a personality of their own. And where can you find a better way to let off steam?

If the music is loud, "it's a gas." If the dance is crazy, "you're in." If you dig the sex bit, "you're a swinger," and if your jokes are sick, you're "way out." In other words, if you want to have a ball, you gotta dig the scene, baby. You gotta get with it or you're in "outsville." Cousin Brucie doesn't just play a record, he "lays one on you," and Murry the K doesn't spin a disc—he will "hit you with a scorcher." *IT'S WHAT'S HAPPENIN', BABY.*

The teenager is always fighting for recognition and is ready to defend his stand at the drop of a gag. "Sure our parents didn't have gang wars—they had world wars."

When the modern teenager busted out all over with a humor of his own, it hit back at all the bosses—especially in the home. As one kid put it, "Laugh and the world laughs with you—cry and you're a parent."

The spokesman for the youth of America is a bright, handsome young comedian called London Lee who bills himself as the Teenage Defender. Youngsters pack the clubs with their parents wherever their champion appears just to hear him lash out at boss rule in the form of parental supervision.

In the summer, says London, every parent says, "I work hard and want my kid to have what I never had"—so in summer they send you to camp to have what they never had—poison ivy.

124

They send you to camp for $800 in order for you to learn to make an ash tray for fifteen cents.

When you start to date, parents say, "If you're happy—we're happy. But remember—it's just as easy to marry a rich one as a poor one."

Then mother fixes you up with a date. When you ask, "Is she pretty?" she gets evasive. "Well, she's got a wonderful personality." That means forget it—she's a loser.

If a kid does something wrong, mother curses: "I hope when you grow up you have children like you." In order for him to have children like "you" —first he must become a parent like you.

If mother sees a messy room she screams: "Look at this room. It's a pigsty. I'm not the maid." Father says: "Right, she's not the maid. If she was I would have fired her years ago."

The big beef from the old man when you are supposed to be in by midnight and you show up at 2 A.M. is always: "What could you possibly do till 2 A.M.?" If my father, after all these years, doesn't know, why should I tell him?

When one mother kept hollering, her daughter talked back: "Don't yell at me—I'm not your husband."

When mother threatened her with "Just wait till your father comes home!" she waited and waited. By the time her father came home she was forty-three years old.

Mother complains her daughter is on the telephone too much. I know a progressive father who got his daughter her own telephone. That night he came home and found his daughter on *his* telephone. "Are you crazy?" he screamed. "Why are you using my phone? I just got you your own phone." She said: "I can't use my phone—that's for incoming calls."

Father complains about his son's haircut—meanwhile good old dad stands in front of the mirror with three strands of hair, trying to cover eight inches of scalp.

If the son comes in looking like a Beatle, the father says "cut your hair." Let's face it—that's not good advice—that's jealousy.

"I'll break it all down," says the teen hero. "Teenagers are blamed for everything. Every day the papers say we did this wrong, we did that wrong. If one is caught committing a crime—all the teenagers are blamed. This is not fair—there are plenty of teenagers who *don't* get caught."

These are the jokes youngsters laugh at to forget the "parents problem."

I overheard a teenager telling his barber, "Just take a little off around the hips."

I think we ought to let teenagers vote as well as drink. We're getting married earlier than ever. I recently threw a party for a bunch of Cub Scouts —and they all brought their wives.

MOTHER: "Why did you spank junior?"
FATHER: "He gets his report card tomorrow and I'll be out of town."

Like the man says, in order to be a teenager today, you got to suffer—*you*—not them. They love the sick jokes. It's their way of thumbing their noses at society and laughing at the world through rose-colored glasses.

The tailor called Toulouse Lautrec and left a message with his valet: "Tell Mr. Lautrec his tailor called—his Bermuda shorts are ready."

"Do you have rat poison?"
"Yes, shall I wrap it up?"
"No, I'll eat it right here."

The kid yelled to his mother, who was taking a bath: "Mom, the steam roller just ran over brother!"—"Well, I can't come out—just slip him under the door."

LITTLE CINDY: "Grandma, can you eat nuts?"
GRANDMA: "No, my dear, I have no teeth!"
LITTLE CINDY: "Good. Then you can mind the pecans till I get back."

"And how much would you care to contribute to the Indian relief fund, Mrs. Custer?"

"Mom, Dad's been hit by a car!"
"Don't make me laugh, son. You know my lips are chapped."

"Daddy, why can't I play with other kids?"
"Shut up and deal!"

"I don't care who you are, Fatso. Get them reindeer off my roof."

"Mommy, where are the marshmallows? Marvin's on fire."

"Your aunt fell into the fireplace!"
"Well, poke her up, it's chilly in here."

Then there was the model who sat on a broken bottle and cut a good figure.

"You made a mistake in that prescription you gave my wife. Instead of quinine you used strychnine!"
"You don't say. You owe me twenty cents more."

"That's enough out of you," said the surgeon as he sewed up his patient.

Most teenagers identify themselves with certain comics. Like Jerry Lewis, for instance, in his act as the lovable delinquent. The kids love him cause he's "kooky" and gets away with things that other kids get punished for. He's always in trouble—always in a situation any kid can get into. And then he lets go and all hell breaks loose—especially for the grownups.

126

They love Jerry's special kind of talk, even when he answers their fan mail. "Dear Dandy Darbs—Luv ya madli—Your letters are Peachy Keen—Groovy—Jer." They scream at Jer's favorite: "Did you hear about the near-sighted snake that fell in love with his other end?"

Anyone who rebels against discipline, management and direction wins teen sympathy and there is no greater rebel than Soupy Sales. Our boy defies all custom and lives strictly on bedlam and slapstick—where the pratfall and the pie-in-the face are the law of his land. "Soupy for President," say the kids. "Anybody who can fall on his face—can't be all bad." If London Lee is the Teenage Defender, Soupy is the Teenage Insulter. Soupy's sayings are the Bible for thousands of teeners:

Don't play in the street—you may get that run down feeling.

If your wife wants to learn how to drive—don't stand in her way.

Show me a prison break—and I'll show you a con-go.

Show me a fat bed—and I'll show you a chunky-bunky.

Show me a tadpole in a rainstorm—and I'll show you a soggy froggy.

Don't drop out of school—especially if you're on the third floor.

Don't kiss a girl under the mistletoe—it's more fun under the nose.

Blood is thicker than water—so is toothpaste.

Girls who eat sweets—take up two seats.

Show me a baby with a fever and I'll show you a hotsy-totsy.

Show me an angry teacher grading papers—and I'll show you a Grouchy Marx.

Show me a nation with all pink cars and I'll show you a pink carnation.

Show me the first pair of false teeth and I'll show you the George Washington Bridge.

The youngsters love Soupy most when his defiance is showing. Like in the song parodies he does on his show:

> You better not cry—you better not shout,
> You better not pout—I'm telling you why,
> Santa Claus is dead.

The biggest word in a teener's dictionary is self-expression. As a matter of fact, any good rebellious youngster has his own dictionary. Only now they are called Daffynitions:

BATHING BEAUTY: A girl worth wading for.

TV: Watching machine.

OLD MAID: A woman who's been good for nothing.

VOLCANO: A mountain that blew its top.

CARGO: What gasoline makes.

MISER: A doughnut.

HUG: A roundabout way of making love.

COLLEGE BRED: A four year loaf with father's dough.

CHAPERONE: An old maid who never made the first team—but she's still intercepting passes.

The modern teener is happier and brasher with the kid jokes and the school gags:

One kid asked his old man to tell him a bedtime story and Pop began, "Fuzzy Wuzzy wuz a bear, Fuzzy Wuzzy had no hair—Fuzzy Wuzzy wuzn't fuzzy—wuz he?" And the kid hollered: "Mom, come and get Pop, he's loaded again."

"Parents say the subway system is not safe in New York," one kid says. "So they put 800 cops in the subways. I was on the subway on my way to school and I got up to give my seat to a woman—and a cop grabbed it."

All the old animal jokes have been changed by the kids to strictly elephant jokes:

"How can you tell if there's been an elephant in your refrigerator?" "If you see his footprints in the cottage cheese."

Two elephants were talking and one said: "Don't care what people say—I can't remember a thing!"

"How do you know if an elephant is standing near you in an elevator?" "By the smell of the peanuts on his breath."

"How do you make an elephant float?" "You take a scoop of ice cream, soda water, and an elephant."

"Why do elephants lie on their back with their feet in the air?" "So they can trip birds."

"Bobby, can you tell me where the elephant is found?"
"Well, teacher, the elephant is such a large animal it hardly ever is lost."

The one thing that several generations of teeners did have in common are the riddles—although this generation is slightly more hep.

Grandma's gang was pretty mild:

128

"How did Jonah feel when the whale swallowed him?"
"Down in the mouth."

"What is the difference between an elephant and a flea?"
"An elephant can have fleas but a flea can't have elephants."

"Which is more valuable, a paper dollar or a silver dollar?"
"The paper one because when you put it in your pocket you double it and when you take it out you see it in-creases."

"What has eighteen legs and catches flies?"
"A baseball team."

Mom's bunch was just as sweet:

"When is a dress like a secret?"
"When it is let out."

"Why are balloons like beggars?"
"Because they have no visible means of support."

"Why does a fireman wear red suspenders?"
"To keep his pants up."

"What gives milk and has one horn?"
"A milk truck."

Now The Kids have swinging riddles:

"What's red and goes Ding-Dong?"
"A red Ding-Dong."

"What's blue and goes Ding-Dong?"
"A blue Ding-Dong?"
"No, they only come in red!"

"What's got four legs and lies on its back?"
"A dead bug."

"How can you tell the bridegroom at a Polish wedding?"
"He's the guy with the purple bowling shirt."

"Did you hear about the accident with the red Cadillac and the Pepsi-cost?"
"What's a Pepsicost?"
"Ten cents."

The modern teener believes that laughter is a vaccine for the ills of the world. I guess that's what made the Beatles so popular. They never took themselves too seriously. With each new triumph they added more laughs and their popularity kept growing. Their last record sold something like

600,000 copies the first week, and I think the kid next door has them all. But what can you do? You've got to laugh at it all. So far the Beatles have laughed me out of three nights' sleep.

But if the Beatles can laugh at themselves, why can't we?

Paul says of George, who is the most sensitive about his hairdo, "He only goes to the barber when he finds himself knotting his hair instead of his tie."

A reporter wanted to know, "What's the greatest threat to your career? Nuclear warfare or dandruff?" Ringo Starr said, "We've already *got* dandruff."

When asked why he wore so many rings on his fingers, Ringo answered, "Because I can't fit them all through my nose."

One girl wrote to Paul and confessed that she loved him a little more than the others and wanted to know if he minded. He replied, "I love me a little more than the others, so I don't see why you shouldn't too!"

One reporter told the boys that a "stamp-out-the-Beatles" movement had sprung up in Detroit. "We're going to start a campaign to stamp out Detroit," John responded.

At a Command Performance in London John told an audience composed mainly of wealthy nobility, "People in the cheaper seats, clap. The rest of you just rattle your jewels."

They laugh at the critics who don't think they are any good. "We're not," said Paul. John says, "We're kidding you, we're kidding ourselves, we're kidding everybody. We don't take anything seriously, except the money."

A modern teenager's jokes tell the story of the times. When beatniks were popular a few minutes ago they were gagging, "Did you hear about the beatnik who starved to death rather than have a square meal?"

A combination of delinquency and the Martians brought out the teeners best artillery. "Did you hear about the Martian that landed in Central Park and was mugged?"

Everyone had an astronaut joke. "Big deal! Our astronaut went into space and back in fifteen minutes. I'd like to see him go crosstown in that time." One astronaut asked the first for advice. He said: "The whole secret is—don't look down!"

To sum it all up, here are the jokes-a-go-go that are the most popular with the teeners:

SON: "Dad, may I borrow the car tonight?"
FATHER: "No—what have you got two feet for?"
SON: "One is for the gas pedal—the other for the brake."

The six-year-old boy asked his mother: "Mom, where do I come from?"
The mother said: "The stork brought you."
"Where do you come from?"
"The stork brought me too!"
"And Granma?"
"The stork brought her too!"
"That's funny," said the kid, "we haven't had a normal birth in our family in three generations."

The pedestrian screamed at the reckless driver: "Whatsa matter with you—are you blind?" And the driver answered: "What do you mean blind —I hit you, didn't I?"

The lady asked: "Do you have any wallpaper with flowers in it?"
"Sure," said the clerk. "Lots of it."
"Can I put it on myself?" the lady wanted to know.
"Of course you can," the clerk replied, "but it looks better on the wall."

A freshman at Wellesley came home one Christmas and announced to her dad who met her at the train: "Paw, there's something you might as well know right off—I ain't a good girl anymore."
The old man cried out, "Eighteen years Maw and I made sacrifices so you could go to a smart Eastern college and what happens? You come home after three months there and you're still saying ain't!"

JACK: "I'm homesick."
JILL: "But don't you live at home?"
JACK: "Yes, and I'm sick of it!"

OFFICER: "Do you know you were doing seventy miles an hour?"
LADY DRIVER: "Gee, and I only learned how to drive yesterday!"

What did one wall say to the other?
Meet you at the corner.

DOCTOR: "I'm sorry to tell you that your wife's mind is completely gone."
HUSBAND: "I'm not surprised. She's been giving me a piece of it every day for twenty years."

RONALD: "Mother, please change my name."
MOTHER: "But why should I do that?"
RONALD: "Because Dad says he's going to spank me as sure as my name's Ronald."

FARM BOY: "My pop can't decide whether to get a new cow or a tractor for his farm."

131

CITY BOY: "He'd certainly look silly riding around on a cow."
FARM BOY: "Yes, but he'd look a lot sillier milking a tractor."

FATHER: "How do you stand in school?"
JIMMY: "Right in the corner as usual."

DAD: "Do you like math, son?"
SON: "It's wonderful, Dad. I'm stuck on every problem."

HOST: "If you stay overnight you'll have to make your own bed."
GUEST: "That's okay with me."
HOST: "Here's a hammer and saw."

WAITER: "I have boiled tongue, fried liver, and pig's feet."
MAN: "Don't tell me your troubles, sir. Just give me a cheese sandwich and a glass of milk."

JOAN: "I haven't slept for days."
ANNE: "Aren't you tired?"
JOAN: "No, I slept nights."

TED: "Gosh! This story is about a man who lives on onions alone!"
NED: "Well, anyone who lives on onions ought to live alone."

MOTHER: "How could you be so rude as to tell your sister she's stupid? Tell her you're sorry."
GEORGE: "Please, Sis, I'm sorry you're stupid."

PETE: "That girl in the red dress doesn't seem very intelligent."
BILL: "I know, she hasn't paid any attention to me, either."

DICK: "We've got an animal family."
NICK: "How's that?"
DICK: "Mother's a dear, Sister's the lamb, I'm a kid, and Dad's the goat."

PAPA KANGAROO: "Susie, where's the baby?"
MAMA KANGAROO: "Oh, dear! I've had my pocket picked!"

A peanut sat on a railroad track;
His heart was all a-flutter;
A train came speeding down the track,
Toot! Toot! Peanut butter.

Father to teenager: "What kind of in crowd do you travel with—in doubt, in debt or in trouble?"

Limericks

Here are some of the printable limericks. Most of the better ones decorate the choicer men's room walls around the country.

Nobody seems to know where this five-line nonsense verse got its name. Limerick, the happy little Irish town on the banks of the Shannon River, vehemently denies any association.

Most of these comic verses do not have an author who is proud to call them his own. Even Edward Lear, who popularized the limerick in the middle of the nineteenth century in *The Book of Nonsense,* got the hell out of England when he realized what he had started.

The origin of the limerick is to be found in the old nursery rhymes like "Hickory, Dickory, Dock" and "The Old Man of Tobago," which was the inspiration of Edward Lear:

> There was an old man of Tobago,
> Who lived on rice, gruel, and sago;
> Till much to his bliss,
> His physician said this:
> "To a leg, sir, of mutton you may go."

Since the best of the limericks are unprintable, they are more often heard and repeated than read. And although there are some popular verses by the acknowledged masters, most are anonymous because the authors have forgotten they wrote them or are in hiding.

SMART ASS

> There was a young lady of Kent,
> Who said that she knew what it meant,
> When men asked her to dine,
> Gave her cocktails and wine,
> She knew what it meant—but she went.

PEEPING TOM

> There was a young lady so thin,
> In the nude she resembled a pin;

Don't think that I'd creep,
To her window and peep,
I was told by a friend who looked in.

LOVE

There was a young lady of Lynn,
Who was deep in original sin,
When they said, "Do be good!"
She said, "Would if I could."
And straightway went at it again.

SHAME

There once was a sculptor named Phidias,
Whose statues by some were thought hideous,
He made Aphrodite,
Without any nightie,
Which shocked all the ultra-fastidious.

The most common of limericks is the place-name type where you reveal the city, country, town or place in the first line. This determines the primary rhyme of the verse:

There was a young man from the city,
Who met what he thought was a kitty,
He gave it a pat,
Saying, "Nice little cat."
They buried his clothes, what a pity!

TOUGH LUCK

There was a young man from the West,
Who loved a young lady with zest,
So hard did he press her,
To make her say, "Yes, sir,"
He broke three cigars in his vest.

FAITH

There was a faith healer called Neal,
Who said, "Although pain is not real,
When I sit on a pin,
And it punctures my skin,
I dislike what I fancy I feel."

The second most-used verse is the personal-name category:

GAMBLER

A certain young lady called Snookie,
At betting was quite a smart cookie,
Before every race,
She went home to her place,
And curled up with a very good bookie.

SKATING

There was a young lady, a Swiss
Who said, "I think skating is bliss."
But no more will she state,
For a wheel on her skate,
¡sᴉɥʇ ǝʞᴉl ƃuᴉɥʇǝɯos dn ɥsᴉuᴉɟ ɹǝɥ ǝpɐW

DIET

There was a young lady called Maud,
Who was really a terrible fraud;
To eat at a table,
She never was able,
But out in the kitchen—oh, Gawd.

There is no limit to the variety of nonsense that goes into making up a limerick. They include everything from low puns to high vulgarity—from pure wit to unfiltered dirt.

FUNERAL

A silly young fellow named Hyde,
In a funeral procession was spied,
When asked "Who is dead?"
He giggled and said,
"I don't know; I just came for the ride."

COLD

Two eager and dashing young beaux,
Were held up and robbed of their clothes,
While the weather is hot,
They won't miss a lot,
But what will they do when it snows?

BAD BOY

A naughty old colonel from Butte,
Had a habit his friends thought was cute,
He'd slip off to Spokane,
And proceed from the train,
To a house of distinct ill-repute.

SILLY ASS

A dashing young fellow of Leeds,
Rashly swallowed six packets of seeds,
In a month, silly ass,
He was covered with grass,
And he couldn't sit down for the weeds.

FANNY

Young Fanny, a doll from Bryn Mawr,
Was given a long foreign car,
Her control was superb,
Till she parked at the curb,
Then Fanny stuck out too darn far.

Now, be my guest and try your hand at these five-line verses. Almost everybody commits at least one limerick in his career, even though he can't repeat it publicly or won't admit it privately. The late Heywood Broun was the fearless one who admitted he perpetrated this verse:

There was a young man with a hernia,
Who said to his surgeon, "Gol dernia,
When improving my middle,
Be sure you don't fiddle,
With matters that do not concernia."

Now to show you that I'm not a high brow,
I'll try it myself so you'll know how,
And if this doesn't work,
You can say I'm a jerk,
But the fact is that I gotta go now.

136

The Life of the Party

Not everybody wants to develop the art of humor so that they can make $10,000 a week and replace Garry Moore or Danny Kaye. Not all of us want the jokes to jolly the boss for that raise we really don't deserve.

Some don't want to speak at dinners or get laughs at the stag or heckle the bus driver. Some of us may want the humor just to get joy out of life—like having a fun party, for instance. Meanwhile, by following this formula, who knows, maybe you can become another Elsa Maxwell, or a Perle Mesta.

Nothing is more annoying than not being invited to a party you wouldn't be caught dead in—except, maybe, being the host. That's the reason most people don't like to give parties. If it gets boring—they can't leave. You can always tell the host at these gatherings—he's the one watching the clock.

No matter how crowded the affair, there's always room for one bore who takes the life out of your party, and regardless of how much the host makes you feel at home—that's where you wish you were.

If you run a party, whether it's to impress the boss or win a client or make a friend or lose a relative—you have an obligation to all your guests. Including the bore who tries to take over, the poor soul lying in the corner, your husband's relative who came to sneer, or the friend you really care about.

Planning the fun is just as important as the food, the service, and the guest list. Kids have the most wonderful time at parties, because, besides the ice cream, they get a chance to play games like "Pin the Tail on the Donkey," "Spin the Bottle," "Post Office," and others, according to their age group. Many grownups still play these games, but of course, it's a stepped-up version. The bottle they spin is gin, and the way they play "Pin the Tail on the Donkey," it's not a kid's game any more.

So, if you want to be a good host and put life in your party, don't let your guests play Christmas Tree—where everybody stands in the corner and tries to get lit up.

Play these games that have been tried and true friends for the host and hostess for years. Like good wine and good jokes, they have put life in many a party.

THE SAFETY PIN GAME

Everybody is given a safety pin when he enters. After dinner, the host announces that the game is on. For forty-five minutes, you are not allowed to say the word "No." Naturally, everyone tries to bait the others into answering "No." When you say the forbidden word, you must give up your safety pin—to the person who tricked you into saying it. At the end of the forty-five minutes, the person who has the most pins wins.

Prizes could be anything from a three-pound box of cement to a 1968 Cadillac windshield wiper.

WHO AM I?

The host makes a series of cards with the name of a famous person on each. It could be anybody from the President of the United States to Willie Sutton to the Talking Mule. Then he pins one of these cards on each player's back. The participants can look at each other's cards but can't see their own.

Each player is allowed three questions, answerable only by yes or no. The first player to guess who he is—wins.

As in most games of this type, the smart player starts by asking general questions, to establish himself quickly: "Am I alive now?" "Am I an American?" "Am I a man?"

By the time it comes your turn again—you have a good chance to find out who you are in the next round.

ALPHABET GAME

Arrange your guests in a circle which should include the host. Start the game by saying: "Yesterday I had dinner at Charlie's house and they served artichokes."

The person sitting next to you now repeats what you just said and adds some other edible beginning with B. For example:

"Yesterday I had dinner at Charlie's house and they served artichokes and bacon."

The next person now repeats this, adding an edible beginning with C which becomes: "Yesterday I had dinner at Charlie's house and they served artichokes, bacon and coleslaw."

Each person in turn repeats what the previous person has said and adds the name of some edible beginning with the next letter in the alphabet. The player who misses any of the names on the list, or hesitates more than the allotted time, is declared out of the game. The one remaining the longest —wins.

BALONEY

Arrange guests in a circle, and starting with number 1, tell them to count—each one saying the next highest number, but instead of saying the number 7 or any multiple of 7 like 14, 21, 28, etc., the word "Baloney" must be substituted. The counting must proceed as quickly as is possible, and anyone failing to say "Baloney" in place of 7 or its multiples is out of the game.

THE ENDLESS STORY CHAIN

Arrange guests in a circle, including the host, and start by telling a story—any story at all. You continue for as long as a minute but do not end the story—very unexpectedly you stop abruptly and touch the person on your right, who must continue the story in his, or her, own style and thought. Some pretty queer themes can result from this, and the story must be kept going until everyone in the circle has had a chance to have his say.

WRONG IS RIGHT

Form two lines—boys and girls or single men and married men or mixed couples. Have them stand up or sit and face each other. The object of the game is to answer questions *incorrectly,* and anyone giving the correct answer is out.

The man at the head of the line starts by asking the lady opposite him a question. She must answer immediately. And if she answers it correctly she is declared out of the game. If she gives the wrong answer, she must ask the next boy in line another question and he, after answering it wrong, asks the girl opposite him another question—and so on down the line and back again. The winner is the one who remains standing the longest—or the biggest dope on purpose. The answers to all questions must be immediate —any hesitation puts a player out of the game.

OCCUPATION CHARADES

When each person comes to the party—give him or her an occupation different from his own and as wild as possible. Then have each one act it out in the old-fashioned charade manner. The person who guesses his or her occupation first—wins.

ORANGE UNDER THE CHIN

This is a sure warmer-upper. The idea is to place an orange under the chin of the gentleman. As he holds his partner with both arms and dances with her, he has to maneuver the orange from under his chin and place it under her chin without either one using the hands.

The trick is to pair the tallest boys with the shortest girls or vice versa. Of course, an added refinement is to select females with the largest bosoms and the smallest chins. Watching the oranges plop into the undercovered and overdeveloped bosoms can be bedlam.

IMITATIONS

Each guest picks a paper out of a hat with the name of a famous actor or actress. The contestant is obliged to do an imitation of the star designated, to the best of his or her ability, while the other guests try to guess who it is. The first person to guess—wins. A running count is kept, so that the one with the highest score wins the game.

MUSICAL CHAIRS

In the middle of the floor, set up a row of ten chairs with every other one facing the opposite way. Invite ten men to sit in the chairs and eleven girls to march around them. When the whistle blows, each girl is supposed to dive for the nearest lap and settle in it. When you eliminate the girl without a lap to sit in, simultaneously remove one man and one chair. This game is played through to the end and the last girl with the last lap—gets the prize.

SIMON SAYS

The host, or somebody he selects, acts as the master of ceremonies or the dictator, who tells everybody what to do: "Simon says—take one step forward"—"Sit down"—"Slap the man next to you," or anything you want. The cue is "Simon says." The participants must not do what the M.C. says unless it follows, "Simon says"—"Simon says stand up," etc. If he says "Stand up" and you do it without his saying "Simon says" first, you are out of the game. The last one remaining is the winner.

NAME THE MUSIC

Here is a good use for your old records—at the same time you can play a very enjoyable game. The host plays about eight bars or a little more of a record and the first to guess the title or the band or the vocalist wins that round. Scores may be kept and a prize given.

OBSERVATION

Arrange about twenty-five objects on the coffee table—apple, scissors, nail file, shoe horn, etc. Let each guest walk in and look at the table for about thirty seconds to one minute or whatever you designate as fair. Then, equipped with a pad and pencil, each participant writes down every article he can remember. The one who lists the most objects correctly—wins.

THE GAME OF CITIES

Start the game off with the name of a city. Suppose you choose Cleveland. The person on your right must continue and name a city which begins with D—the last letter in Cleveland. He says Dallas, and the player on his right must name a city beginning with S—the last letter of Dallas. He says Scranton, and the player on his right must name a city beginning with N. This keeps going until someone fails, or hesitates too long, and is eliminated. Naturally, the last one in the game is the winner.

THE JOKE BOX

This is my favorite game of all. If it's played by amateurs it can be very entertaining, even hysterically. If it's played by pros, it can be challenging as well.

Put a dozen or more subjects on as many pieces of paper and put them in a box—then let each contestant pick a subject and tell a joke or anecdote or gag about it.

For instance, if they pick "Porcupine" the joke could be: "How do porcupines make love?—Very carefully—very carefully."

Now, if the contestant can't think of a joke on the subject, give him a joke you have prepared or have the joke inside the folded paper that he picks.

This way, even if he misses on the gag, he still has a story to tell. You can have as many jokes in the box as you wish and continue the game as long as somebody keeps remembering the jokes.

Of course, you can pick any subject, and the jokes that go with them, in the Portable Gag File in this book, or go to any source you choose.

RIDDLES AND CONUNDRUMS

During the childhood of the human race, the riddle was the highest form of humor. Although its chief appeal today is juvenile, the best way to have fun at a party is to be a kid again.

Use the riddle to play a game for a lot of fun. Pick a quizmaster and two teams. The team that answers the most questions correctly—wins.

Here are some of my all-time favorite riddles you can use for the quiz:

What men are the most above board?
    —Chessmen.

Why should fish be well educated?
    —Because they are found in schools.

What table has no legs?
    —A time table.

How do you make a slow horse fast?
    —Don't give him anything to eat for a while.

When is a shaggy dog most likely to enter a house?
    —When the door is open.

In what month do women talk the least?
    —February—it's the shortest month.

What is the difference between an old penny and a new dime?
    —Nine cents.

What is it that dogs have and nothing else has?
    —Puppies.

Can you mention eight different kinds of paper? Must have the word paper in it.
    —Tissue paper, newspaper, flypaper, carbon paper, toilet paper, typing paper, paper towels, wax paper, papier mache, paper bags.

Can you name eight different kinds of fly? Must have word fly in it.
    —Fly on a baseball field, fly in a theatre, tsetse fly, house fly, fly in a plane, fly on trousers, fly in the ointment, butterfly.

What kind of hen lays the longest?
    —A dead one.

Which is correct—the whites of the egg are yellow or the whites of the egg is yellow?
    —Neither—white is never yellow.

What would a cannibal be who ate his mother's sister?
    —An aunt-eater.

What is worse than finding a worm in an apple?
    —Finding half a worm.

What is full of holes—yet holds water?
—A sponge.

How much dirt is in a hole six by six feet?
—There is no dirt in a hole.

How long is a piece of string?
—Twice the distance from the center to either end.

What two coins equal 55¢—if one of the coins is not a nickel?
—The answer is—a half-dollar and a nickel. One is not a nickel—but the other is.

What do you sit on, sleep on and brush your teeth with?
—A chair—a bed—and a toothbrush.

What did the porcupine say to the cactus plant?
—Is that you, Mamma?

Before you start the game, it might be a good idea to ask the contestants to look for the wild, the silly, the ridiculous or the nutty for the answer.

Now, let's include the conundrum—which is the first cousin of the riddle. A conundrum is a riddle based on wordplay. Have some good ones on me to add to the game:

Why does a donkey eat thistles?
—Because he's an ass.

Why would Samson have been a good actor?
—He brought down the house.

What has four legs and flies?
—A dead horse.

What is the best way to keep a fish from smelling?
—Cut off his nose.

Who is it marries many a wife and yet lives a single life?
—A priest.

Who wears the biggest hat in the army?
—The man with the biggest head.

What is it that never asks any questions and yet requires many answers?
—The doorbell.

What's all over the house?
—A roof.

What is a pig doing when he's eating?
—Making a hog of himself.

Why is a lucky gambler an agreeable guy?
—Because he has such winning ways.

What musical instrument should we never believe?
—A lyre.

Where was Peter when the lights went out?
—In the dark.

What is it that is put on a table, cut, but is never eaten?
—A deck of cards.

Should a man stir his coffee with his left hand or his right hand?
—Neither. He should use a spoon.

What is the difference between an umbrella and a woman?
—You can shut up an unbrella.

When is a queen like a piece of wood?
—When she becomes a ruler.

So, if you want to make sure you don't have a "fete" worse than death, play the game. You can have a masquerade party, or a come-as-you-are party (each one come in the outfit he or she was wearing when he was invited), or a vice-versa party (the men dress as women and the women as men), or a native party (each one comes in the native dress of some country), etc., etc., etc. But no matter what the costume, the guest list or the setting, if you play the game for laughs—you can't lose.

International Humor

Some of my best friends are jokes that I have picked up around the world. I have translated them from French, German, Indonesian, Asian, and even English. I have switched them, cleaned them up, and made them fit—only to prove that there is no such thing as a new joke—only an old joke with a new setting and new characters.

I imagine if Joe Miller came back to earth, the only thing he would recognize are the new jokes.

Humor, more than any other expression, reminds you that, "The more it changes—the more it is the same."

A long time ago, before Bob Hope took his first trip around the world, there was a lovable character in Afghanistan called Mullah Nazardin. In Iran he is called Mullan Nasir-Ud-Din. In Turkey, this Moslem Will Rogers is called Nasreddin Hoca, and in Cairo his name is Goho. In Syria and Mesopotamia he is known as Abu Nawwas. Some say he has survived twelve hundred years and is still going strong. Most Persians say he was a legendary character. Many Arabs are convinced he was a real person. All the children of these ancient lands are familiar with his simple wit, and the adults with the shrewdness of his wisdom. But his adventures and sayings all prove that wit is the source and preserver of health and happiness.

Hoca's wit is eternal and will never grow stale. His stories are as fresh and appropriate today as they were when first told centuries ago. I should know because I'm still telling them.

Nasreddin may be responsible for the first mother-in-law joke. The way he told it, his mother-in-law was drowned while crossing a river, and although all the villagers went downstream in search of a body, Hoca insisted on going upstream. "If you knew her as well as I did," he said, "you would know what a contrary woman she was."

Way before Henny Youngman said, "Now take my wife—PLEASE," Hoca was doing wife jokes. When his donkey died his grief was great. His neighbors kidded him, "Hoca, it's not nice you should grieve more for your donkey than your wife who died last summer."

"When my wife died," Hoca answered, "you all consoled me by saying that you would find me a younger and prettier wife, but so far no one has suggested finding me another donkey."

145

So like I said, I don't claim these jokes that I found around the world are original or spanking new. All I want to do is give you a touch of home laughs that might come in handy wherever you come from or wherever you are going.

Each country has something special to laugh at. Even Russians find humor in their everyday life, and I don't have to tell you that modern Russia is certainly laughable.

Russia's biggest joke is China. It all began in 1960, the current Soviet jest says, when Mao Tse-tung cabled to Khrushchev: "Starving. Send grain."

Khrushchev replied: "Short of grain ourselves. Can't send any. Tighten your belts."

Whereupon Mao Tse-tung came back: "Send belts."

Although all humor is basically the same, each country has some special kind of laugh formula that is sure-fire. The Jews are known to be tardy when it comes to meetings and functions, so their humor often reflects it. I heard one radio announcer in Haifa announce: "When you hear the chimes it will be exactly 5 P.M.—or a few minutes later."

The English are supposed to have a backward sense of humor. There is an old fable that an Englishman laughs at a joke three times: once when he hears it, once when it's explained to him, and once when he understands it. This is strictly a legend and untrue. They have a great sense of humor.

It's true that English humor could be droller and perhaps more subtle; some say more stuffy. "I hear they buried your wife," one lord said to the other. "Had to; dead, you know," he answered.

Comedy, in order to be funny, must be devastating. Somebody must be hurt in order for a gag to be funny, even if it's only yourself. There's no such thing as gentle humor.

That's why the Oriental is not known for his sense of humor. How can you do mother-in-law jokes if you have been trained since childhood to revere your parents? How can you make fun of human relations when you are too busy bowing to show your respect?

Of course, the *modern* Orientals are as hip as a hunk of Sinatra dialogue. Their language is strictly from modernsville and they let their quips fall where they may hurt—they spare nobody.

"God, he make the universe and then he rested. He then make man and then he rested again. He next make woman—and nobody have rested ever since."

I will try to bring you the stories, wit, wisdom, humor and laughs that tickle the funnybones of the people of the world. From the halls of Montezuma to the shores of Katmandu, you can hear their voices raised in laughter if you can find the material or joke to bring out the jest in them.

In Nepal, for instance, they are proudest of their fighting Gurkhas.

146

These are the same Gurkhas whom the world remembers as the toughest guerrilla fighters of all in World War II. A Nepalese soldier in Patan told me this story:

One division that had just joined the paratroopers was instructed to jump when they reached 5,000 feet in the air. The hardiest of the Gurkhas refused, saying, "We don't mind jumping 500 feet, but 5,000 feet is too much even for us—"

"But," said the captain, "if you jump five hundred feet you won't have time to open the parachute."

"Oh," grinned the Gurkhan leader, "if we have parachutes we don't mind jumping 5,000 feet."

I hope to show you here the wit of the Irish and the humor of Asian justice, the laughter of Italy and the sexy jokes of France (if sex can be funny). I will try to bring you the Australian 'umor in its simple, unsophisticated and easygoing manner.

PASSERBY: "That drainpipe's a bit hard for a pillow, isn't it?"
SWAGMAN: "It's all right. I've stuffed it full of straw."

Throughout the centuries, the crises, tragedies, fables, poverty and wars have needed humor as a leveler to keep mankind fairly warm and happy. The ability to laugh at ourselves and our troubles has made it possible for the survival of so many down through the ages. Wit and humor have no favorites: they attack the rich as well as the poor, the sick as well as the healthy, the weak as well as the strong—but from them come a healthier existence.

Laughter and a sense of humor know no boundaries—language or religion. Of course, whether you come from Afghanistan or Pittsburgh, Cambodia or the Bronx, humor in the hands of a fool can be a dud; in the hands of the expert, it can be the sharp instrument for self-defense needed down through the years to make life more like an enjoyable game than a struggle for survival.

Humor is catching—laughter is contagious. In all the years I have been traveling for my country on good will missions, I never put out my hand that somebody didn't shake it. I never saw a sign "Yankee go home" when I came to bring cheer. If the waves you send out are funny, they must come back to you as waves of laughter. A dose of joy is a spiritual cure. Everybody is susceptible—rich man, poor man, dictator too; Russian, Asian, European Jew.

Good jokes like good wine can mellow with age. If they can hold up all through the years, they must only get better, like fine antiques. The trick is to know when to use them, where and to whom.

So, here are my favorite stories that are making people laugh around the world—set down in alphabetical order according to countries—to help you laugh your troubles away.

AFGHANISTAN

When I made a good will tour of the world for our President, my first stop on the road for Uncle Sam was Afghanistan. That's about as far away as you can get from the Stage Delicatessen and still be in this world. That's off-Broadway even to the Arabs. Still, their humor was as bright and fresh as anything we do. In fact, in many instances, they did it way before us.

As Judge of his village, Mullah Nazardin was trying a case. Listening to the plaintiff, he said: "You are right." Listening to the defendant, he said, "You are right." The clerk of the court bent down and whispered to the judge, "But Mullah, they can't both be right." To which Nazardin replied, "You are right, too."

Now, that story is over 1,200 years old. The other day I heard Harry Hershfield tell it to a gathering of lawyers, and he used a certain judge's name. Like it just happened. It was the laugh of the night.

The Afghans have their own humor. Sort of a shaggy-camel type story. A favorite that's killing 'em in Kabul right now is: Mullah Nazardin had a donkey who had a voracious appetite. Mullah wondered whether by gradually decreasing the animal's food every day it would not be possible to condition the beast to get along without any food at all. This interesting experiment was continued for several weeks, but a few days after all food had been stopped, the donkey toppled over and died, to the chagrin of Mullah Nazardin, who sadly murmured, "What a pity that he should have died just when he was getting accustomed to hunger!"

Mullah was attending the funeral services of the richest man in the village. Because he was weeping bitterly, a man inquired sadly, "Was the deceased one of your dear relatives?"

"No," said Mullah sorrowfully.

"Then why are you crying?" asked the stranger.

"Because I'm *not* one of the relatives," answered Mullah.

Another popular story about Mullah Nazardin: in this story Mullah is a tailor. He was brought before the holy man for committing murder. It seems our hero made a low-cut dress for a Moslem girl, and as she was passing a painter on a scaffold, the painter got so interested in her figure that he fell off the scaffold and was killed. The holy man passed the death sentence. But when they took Mullah to hang him, they found the gallows was not high enough; his feet touched the ground. So, to show there is nothing wrong with Middle Eastern justice—they sent for a shorter tailor and they hanged *him*.

AFRICA

"That's a beautiful stuffed lion you got there. Where did you get him?"
"I was on that hunting expedition with an American."

"What's he stuffed with?"
"The American."

ASIA

On being asked his age, Nasreddin Hoca said, "Forty."
"But, Hoca—that is what you said last year."
"I am a man of my word. I always stick to what I say."

This is one of the many jokes that had its origin somewhere around the thirteenth century and is still going strong on radio and TV shows in the U.S.A. Another one is about Goha, the Turkish great, great, great grandfather of Joe Miller. His wife woke him up in the middle of the night, telling him in a terrified whisper that there was a burglar downstairs.

"Go to sleep," Goha answered. "Before a burglar could steal anything from our house, he would have to bring something in."

Abu Nawwas was approached by a neighbor. "I understand you have vinegar that is forty years old. Could you give me some?"

"I'm sorry," Abu replied, "it wouldn't be forty years old if I kept giving it away."

Goha took his eight-year-old son to the market to buy a sheep. Everybody knows that the value of a sheep depends upon the amount of fat which it stores in its tail. Goha proceeded to massage and weigh in his hands the tail of one sheep after another until his son asked: "Father, why do you do that?"

Goha replied, "I must do so before I decide what sheep to buy."

"Father," said the boy, "our neighbor was in our house yesterday. I think he wants to buy Mother."

AUSTRALIA (Orstrayelian 'umor)

The general impression of Australia is a nation which largely lives outdoors with kangaroos and boomerangs under a hot sun. Their pleasures are simple: a glass of beer, a day at the races, an afternoon surfing in the ocean. The men of the outback (the inland) often live 500 miles from the nearest town, looking after vast herds of sheep and cattle, spending much of their lives in the saddle.

Consequently, Orstrayelian 'umor is mostly unsophisticated, stoic: a yarn told in a pub or a story exchanged on a country road. It's a humor heavily spiced with exaggeration, with gentle leg pulling:

"It was so cold in our town that the candle light froze and we couldn't blow it out."

"That's nothing," his mate replied, "where we were the words came out of our mouths in pieces of ice, and we had to fry them to see what we were talking about."

JOE: "What's the idea of that double layer of wire on the fly door?"
JACK: "They're two different meshes. A course mesh with big holes and a fine mesh with little holes."
JOE: "I know. But how come?"
JACK: "Simple. The big holes to keep out the big flies and the little holes to keep out the little flies."

The big cities of Australia are modern and industrialized. Swaggies no longer travel the breadth of the country looking for odd jobs. Yet the mainstream of humor remains tough, sardonic, humane, born of the days when there were no radios or TV sets in the country's vast inland.

FARMER: "So there's one of them city blokes down on the river—what's he getting—rabbits?"
BOY: "No."
FARMER: "Is he getting fish?"

BOY: "No."
FARMER: "Well, what is he getting?"
BOY: "Drowned."

The very nature of the Australian makes him grin at the story of the wounded soldier being carried across no man's land (between his own men and the enemy) on the back of a perspiring buddy. Rifle and machine gun fire was heavy.

" 'Ere," the wounded one suddenly burst out, "what about turnin' 'round and walkin' backwards for a spell? You're gettin' the V. C. but I'm gettin' all the bloomin' bullets!"

The Australian loves to tell jokes perpetuating the myth that he's the laziest man alive. A swagman was lying in the sun by a country road when a passerby saw a deadly snake dangerously close to his feet. "Mind out there, mate," he yelled, "there's a snake near your foot." The swagman slowly looked up. "Which foot, mate?" he yawned.

SWAGMAN: "How did you like the bottle of wine I gave you?"
ABORIGINE: "It was just right, boss."
SWAGMAN: "What do you mean it was just right?"
ABORIGINE: "Well, if it had been any better, you wouldn't have given it to me—and if it had been any worse, I couldn't have drunk it at all—so, it was just right."

There seems to be a good deal of jealousy in the various districts of South Australia about the size of their mosquitoes. A group of countrymen were discussing it one day. "Yes," said a husky Northerner, "I ain't seen no skeeters to equal them we 'ave above. Now, look 'ere; there's an old stagnant dam on my farm, and at night yer ken hear the skeeters splashin' about in the water like birds. In fact, a new hand I got last week shot a couple of 'em just afore dark one night, thinkin' they was ducks."

"That's nothing," observed a thin, sunburnt little man. "Over 'round Lake Wangary, on the West Coast, yer can 'ear 'em goin' to roost on the fences at night. They make the wires twang like banjos."

"Well," said a lanky individual, "yer wanter go along the Murray for them insects; on that strip of wetness you get 'em big and good. 'T'ain't nothin' jest 'fore sundown to see a mosquito dive into the Murray and come up and fly away with a twenty-pound cod."

The last man now chipped in: "Sorry to hear you've got sech small mosquitoes in your districts. Now if yer want real sizable mosquiters, jest go across to Yorke peninsula. They seem to fatten up wonderful on Cornishmen. I was campin' over there in a tent last week, and about midnight I was woke up by a hummin' voice, like a motor car doin' a record, and next minute a small mosquiter settled on my chest. ' 'Ere,' I yelled to me mate, 'give us a hand; there's a mosquiter dropped on me!' 'Well, knock 'im off,' 'e says. ' 'Ow ken I,' sez I, 'when 'e's got both me 'ands pinned down!' "
The meeting adjourned.

AUSTRIA

An Austrian pianist was engaged as accompanist to a singer whose voice was always out of tune. At last the Austrian threw up his hands in despair.

"Madam," he said, "I giff up der chob. I play der black notes—I play der white notes—and always you sing in der cracks."

BELGIUM (Antwerp)

A: "I know an artist that painted a cobweb so real—that a maid spent an hour trying to get it down."
B: "Sorry—but I don't believe you."
A: "Why not, artists have been known to do such things—"
B: "Yes—but not maids."

BELGRADE

"I hear Mrs. Van Voren is down with blood-poisoning."
"That old gossip—she must have bit her tongue."

BERLIN

"My wife disappeared yesterday and I asked you to try and find her. Don't trouble any more."
"Has she returned?"
"No. I have thought it over."

BONN

Always be tolerant of a person who disagrees with you. After all, he has a right to his stupid opinion.

BRAZIL

POLICEMAN: "Didn't you hear me tell you to stop?"
DRIVER: "I didn't know it was you. I thought it was someone I ran over."

BUCHAREST

A girl answered the doorbell to find a tax collector. "Ma, the tax collector is here," she shouted to her mother upstairs. "I'll be right down," the mother called down. "Give him a chair."
The girl shouted back, "A chair won't do—he wants all the furniture."

BUENOS AIRES

It is often very true you can see more through a keyhole than on a 21-inch screen.

CAMBODIA

Cambodia has been having its own internal and external battles. At one point they even tore up U.S. aid. Now that's what I call real trouble. But her humor goes on. Their jokes, like most of this area, are mostly blue. One of the clean favorites is about the visitor to the zoo who noticed one of the keepers sobbing quietly in the corner. On inquiry he was told that the elephant had died.
"Fond of him, was he?" the visitor asked.

"It's not that," was the reply. "He's the chap who has to dig the grave."

In the time of the Lord Ben, one could have ten virgins for a bar of silver and 5 widows for half a bar; today it takes five bars to have a virgin—and the widows demand as much as the young girls.

CANADA

"What is the name of that selection your daughter played?" asked the guest.
"That wasn't a selection," replied Mr. Johnson, "it was forced on us."

CHILE

"Yes, but has the dog a pedigree?"
"Señora," said the street seller, "if that dog were to speak it wouldn't talk to either one of us."

CHINA

The original Chinese humor is the most basic of all. It goes right down to the essentials—life, death, sickness, accidents, and toilet habits.
Their humor is direct—and how! If you wanted me to tell them all to you—the only place I could print it would be on the walls of the men's room in your local subway.

Humor, as distinct from wit, arises among the common people with a special comic wisdom:
"Wherever there is a stone, a lame foot will find it."
"If you have no door, why have a doorman?"

They kid the fact that we all welcome calamities that are profitable to ourselves: "The carpenter desires cracks—the doctor wants broken bones to cure."

A man went riding on a donkey and happened to meet a man on a fine horse. He dismounted suddenly, bowed, and said, "Wouldn't you like to change your mount for mine?"
The other said: "Are you a fool?"
"No," said the man, "but I thought you might be."

A certain man, beaten by his wife, crawled under the bed.

"Come out of there at once!" screamed the wife.

"I am a man too! If I say I won't come out, I simply won't."

Chinese are taught early to have the humor to laugh at sickness, old age and death—most of all the last: "To know one's fate, yet be heedless of it, is to overcome the world."

A deaf man visited his friend and the dog barked at him like mad. Being unable to hear anything, he said to his friend after they had exchanged greetings, "Your dog didn't sleep well last night."

"Why do you say that?"

"He looked at me and kept yawning."

A man was seized and carried off by a tiger. His son ran after it and was going to shoot it, when from the mouth of the tiger the father shouted "Aim at the feet! Don't injure the fur."

The Chinese can scream with laughter at a broken leg or a horrible accident or a toilet story but there is nobody more moral. Their humor is a contradiction to their poetry and art.

A woman went to court and sued a man. She said, "I went to the well to draw water, and this man came from behind and assaulted me."

The judge asked, "Then why did you not run away?"

"I was afraid that if I stood up and went away it wouldn't be finished."

A maidservant happened to belch in front of her master, who became angry and was going to strike her, but, seeing her wide hips, his anger suddenly abated, and he took his pleasure with her. The next day, when he was in his study, there was a knock on the door. It was the maidservant. "What is it? What do you want?"

"Please, sir, I belched again a little while ago."

There was a banquet at a certain house and two men were sitting there in the principal seats. One had no left eye and the other no right eye. A shortsighted man came into the chamber and looked around at the guests. He whispered to the man next to him, "Who is that broad-faced man in the chief seat?"

The modern Chinese have gone instant western but with a rush. They have abandoned the abacus for Diners' Cards and are twisting, frugging and monkeying in their cheongsams like any of our maniacs back home.

They have taken the great Confucius and brought him into the twentieth century with a bang. A new star has reared his funnybone as the new idol of the swingers in Hong Kong. His name is Ah Too and he really takes off.

My friend Ah Sum, he say he really not want to marry his rich wife for her money—but there was no other way to get it.

Psychiatrist, he is person who when pretty girl she enter room—he watch everybody else.

You can learn plenty about romance at movie—that is, if you not let picture disturb you.

Everybody he not love fat man—or flat woman.

Married men, he have two ages: when they want to be faithful and are not, and when they want to be unfaithful and cannot.

Well-balanced girl, she is one who have empty head and full sweater.

My friend Ah Wong he say he would like to drown his troubles—but he say he not can get wife to go swimming.

One way for husbands to get last word is to apologize.

Never start argument with woman when she is tired—or when she is rested.

Opportunity she knock—but last night knock spoil opportunity.

Kindness one thing you cannot give away—it come back to you.

DENMARK

The summer night was dark and peaceful. Olaf and Gretal sat a good distance apart, on the park bench.

OLAF: "May I kiss you?"

A long silence.

OLAF: (impatient) "Gretal, are you deaf?"

GRETAL: "Olaf, are you lame?"

He fell in love with a pair of big blue eyes—then made the mistake of marrying the whole girl.

When I was in a restaurant in Copenhagen, they asked me what I'd like. I said: "A hunk of Danish." Two waitresses ran over and gave me their telephone numbers.

ENGLAND

If anybody tells you the English have no sense of humor, hit him—with some of the great English jokes: "She gave birth to twins—one at two and the other at seven—in England everything stops for tea." Or, "He's so dumb, he thinks the English Channel is one in which you view the British movies."

Although the English admit there is a university in England "so conservative, it refuses to teach liberal art courses," they were making fun before Berle stole his first joke. The great poet Milton, and I don't mean Berle, once was asked if he would teach his daughter several languages. "No, sir," he replied bitterly, "one tongue is enough for any woman."

They not only originated our language but a good part of our humor as well. One Englishman was inspecting Washington's home in Mt. Vernon. An American was being very condescending: "That house comes from your country. George got it from Merry Old England."

The Britisher smiled, "I don't doubt it—he got his whole blooming country from England."

The English are not averse to laughing at themselves. "It gets foggy here in London; in fact, I've been in one city that was more foggy, but it was so foggy at the time, I couldn't see what city it was."

The English have been answering hecklers way before Churchill lit his first cigar. When the distinguished Prime Minister was a youth, he was making a speech in a market square and was suddenly hit by a large cabbage. Brushing away the debris he said, "I asked for the gentleman's ears—not his head."

A young barrister was a candidate from a Lancashire town. "I'm very pleased to address a working class constituency," he started. "It may interest you to know that I am a working man myself. In fact, I often work when you are asleep."

"You must be a blooming burglar," said a voice in the rear.

Nobody laughs at the stuffy, absent-minded, boring English gentleman more than the English. There was a beastly smash-up on the Devonshire-to-London train and two English professors were aboard. One, fatally injured, was gasping his last breath and he whispered to his friend, "Good-bye, Adru, I'm done for."

"I say, don't talk like that, Bwan," pleaded the other professor in fright, "for the love of God—don't end your sentence with a preposition!"

Two Britishers were crossing on the Queen Mary. After a few short ones and a couple of longer ones they left the bar and went topside looking for dates. A while later one of them was back in the bar with a "live one" when the other staggered up. "Beg pardon, old bean," he mumbled, "but would you mind awfully changing ladies? Due to the whiskey and the fog, I seem to have gotten hold of an old aunt of mine."

An English wit's bite can be far worse than a black widow's. Someone once asked Disraeli to define the difference between a misfortune and a calamity. The reply was typically Disraeli: "Well, if Gladstone fell into the Thames it would be a misfortune. But if anyone dragged him out it would be a calamity."

The slender George Bernard Shaw was once the butt of a few jokes by the bulky G. K. Chesterton. "Why, look at you, one would think there was a famine in England."

156

"And to look at you," Shaw retorted, "one would think you were the cause of it."

Scratch a Welshman or a Scotsman or an Englishman and you'll find a betting man. This is that kind of a story. In a little mining town in England, a pit explosion injured several men and killed Samuel Brown. His three closest friends conferred on who would break the news to his wife.

After a long discussion, they decided Albert would be the most tactful. So he set out for Samuel Brown's house and the two friends went along to lend moral support. Up the bleak hillside they filed. Albert knocked on the door and Mrs. Brown opened it.

"Are you the Widow Brown?" he asked.

"No," she replied.

"You want to bet?" he asked.

After being injured in a cricket match, the English sportsman went to a doctor who put three stitches in his wound. "That will be five pounds," the doctor told him.

"Five pounds?" howled the injured one. "For three stitches?"

"That's right," smiled the doctor.

"I'm glad you're not my blooming tailor."

FLORENCE

Sign in a window: "Be mistaken for an American tourist—wear Italian made clothes."

FRANCE

Ever since Madame Pompadour used her derriere for a calling card, France has been known for its sex. Down through the centuries the subject of sex has always been good for a laugh. That's not too surprising since sex itself is pretty entertaining, and France is one of the most entertaining places in the world.

It was Will Rogers who was traveling through Europe and sent this letter to a friend: "It's pronounced Neece—not nice—they have no word for nice in French."

Don't misunderstand, I'm not knocking France or sex. Sex makes the world go 'round and France caught the gold ring. All I want to do is sell you the French postcards and the jokes that go with them, and since sex is the biggest industry in France, that's the kind of jokes we must do. Like the Frenchman always reasons when he kisses a woman's hand first—"I have to start somewhere—"

An American and a French bride were discussing love. "A Frenchman is very subtle when it comes to love," the French bride explained. "He begins by kissing the fingertips, then he kisses the shoulder, then back to the neck—"

"Boy," the American bride interrupted, "by that time an American husband is back from his honeymoon."

BABETTE: "I'll never forget the night my husband discovered my great love."
FIFI: "What happened?"
BABETTE: "He beat the hell out of him."

To get the real humor of France, you must get to the core of the people. Take Place Pigalle, for instance. Here the peddlers sell live French postcards that you can't get in the post office. "In France, the postman isn't the only working person who has to walk the streets to pick up the male." In the average Parisian night club the strippers peel to their birthmarks. "I saw a girl in the nude and never gave it a second thought—I was too busy with the first thought."

The local traffic in sin makes Sing-Sing look like a choir sing—but to the French it is a song and nobody likes to laugh about it more than the French: "Things must be getting tough in France. I just got a postcard from Paris and there was writing on it."

I think the French have a great idea, but if you can't take part in it, you might as well laugh at it. My wife has been laughing at it for years.

Henri, whose fiancée had been seen kissing his friend Louis, sent Louis a letter asking him to appear for a duel so that he could avenge his honor.

Louis replied with a note saying, "Dear Henri, I have received a copy of your circular letter, and will be present at the gathering."

Maman LaPlace noticed that her four-year-old son was very wary about showing affection to the young governess she had just engaged to take care of him. One day she asked, "Pierre, why do you not hug and kiss your pretty nurse as the other children do?"

"But Maman," he answered, "when Papa kisses her she slaps his face."

CLAUDE: "I would gladlee pay you ten francs for one kees. Oops, I beg zee pardon, did I offend you?"
YVONNE: "No, I was thinking about the fortune I gave away for nothing last night."

In France the men like to stay out until the "oui" hours of the morning.

NANETTE: "That fresh taxi driver offered me 100 francs for a kiss."
CECILLE: "What are you looking in your pocketbook for?"
NANETTE: "I thought I'd lost the 100 francs."

FIRST GIRL: "So in Paris I met this masseur—"
SECOND GIRL: "Not masseur, but Monsieur. A masseur is a guy who rubs you, pinches you, squeezes you, and massages you all over."
FIRST GIRL: "Like I said—I met this masseur—"

The ardent honeymooning of her eighty-year-old groom was exhausting the young bride. During a momentary lull, while he was shaving, she sneaked out and staggered into the hotel coffee shop downstairs.

"I don't get it," her friend the waitress exclaimed. "Here you are, a teenage bride with an ancient husband, and you look a wreck! What happened?"

Yelled the young bride: "The old goat double-crossed me! He told me he saved up for sixty years—and I thought he was talking about money."

SIMONE: "What a beautiful coat. It probably cost you a fortune."
GINETTE: "No, it only cost one kiss."
SIMONE: "One that you gave your husband?"
GINETTE: "No, one that he gave to the maid."

A Parisian genius invented a new version of Russian roulette. It's called shower roulette. Six men have to take showers, and then are handed towels. In one of the towels is wrapped Brigitte Bardot. Now, if we could only get her to play.

Suzette thinks that it may not only be old age that makes men sensible but the lack of strength to do otherwise.

Nanette is a girl of few words—and those words are francs—dollars—and pounds.

"I'm returning your candy and books," Babette wrote to her fiancé, "but I am keeping the jewelry for sentimental reasons."

The woman ran over to the officer yelling: "There's a man following me! I think he must be drunk."
The officer scrutinized the woman and answered, "Yes, he must be!"

GEORGETTE: "I hear you're getting a divorce because you haven't any children!"
BABETTE: "Oh, yes, we've spent many a sleepless night over it!"

A well-known citizen of Paris met his ex-wife at a cocktail party, and, warmed by the libations, suggested they have another go at connubial bliss.

"Over my dead body," said the lady haughtily.

"My error," said the erstwhile spouse. "I see you haven't changed a bit."

FIFI: "If you want to hold your shape you should take swimming lessons."
MIMI: "I tried one last night but the swimming instructor seemed to derive all the benefits."

French artist Jean Gabriel Domergue wrote about women with despair: "The world belongs to women. When a man is born, people ask how his mother is. When he gets married, people exclaim, 'Isn't the bride sweet?' When he is dead, people ask 'How much did he leave her?' "

For years Marie suspected that her husband Claude was playing house elsewhere—she just couldn't catch him.

One day, as this sexy story goes, they received two tickets to a costume ball, which gave Marie the idea to trap her husband once and for all. She picked out her costume without telling Claude and on the evening of the ball she said she was ill but insisted that her husband go without her. As soon as he left, she donned her costume and mask that Claude had never seen and followed him to the ball.

During the evening, the couple made many visits to the garden and Marie was satisfied she had her husband cold—or was it hot?

Marie left the ball before it broke up and rushed home to accost her husband with her accusations. She removed her costume and waited for Claude for the payoff.

Much later, when the unsuspecting Claude returned, he was amazed to find his wife awake and asked about her health. She said, "Fine, and did you enjoy the ball?"

To her amazement he answered, "No, I must confess I did not attend the ball. My dear friend Pierre was without something to do tonight and since I was sure that I would not enjoy myself without your company, I lent him my costume and he went in my stead. I spent the night at the club. As I was leaving the club I met Pierre and he told me he had the greatest time of his life, he met the sexiest girl . . ." Marie fainted.

Never again did Marie have her husband followed, but had Claude the same suspicions and had her followed—he could have found that a good many of Marie's afternoons were spent with his friend Pierre.

GERMANY

A German and a Russian were on a river in Germany. The German was fishing on the West Zone, and was catching fish right and left—well, not left—but the Russian in the Red Zone wasn't having any luck at all. He yelled to the German, "How come you manage to catch so many fish?" and the answer came back, "Over here the fish aren't afraid to open their mouths."

160

GREECE

An American tourist was gazing into the crater of a Greek volcano. "It looks like hell," was the only comment.

"Oh, you Americans," said his guide, "you've been everywhere."

INDIA

India is the chief origin of world humor. It was refined by the Persians, unrefined by China, switched a little by the Koreans, and cleaned up a lot by the Japanese.

The old Indian mind did not strike me as particularly humorous:

> "The blind one found the jewel;
> The one without fingers picked it up;
> The one with no neck put it on;
> And the one with no voice gave it praise."

Yet, their fairy tales and myths are the origin of all fables. To this very day, Indian families and gatherings sit around the table and tell these after-dinner stories—keeping them alive down through the ages.

"Fate decrees everything: none can resist fate," declared a fatalist one day to his friend, who was no believer in it. The friend, with a view to teach him a lesson, gave a blow to the fatalist, who returned it with three-fold ferocity.

"Why beat me for what fate did?" asked the friend.

"Why ask me for what fate did?" returned the fatalist. "Fate decreed that you should beat me first, that I should return the blow with threefold ferocity, and that we should talk as we do now. Fate decrees everything. None can resist fate."

"Goats eat up forests and for this men eat goats, agreeably to the law of Karma," proclaimed an enthusiastic advocate of the conservation of forests to an admiring audience. The next speaker went one better. He said, "Goats eat up forests and for that are eaten by men. For this, these men are eaten up by hellfire. For this, hell is plunged in darkness by God. For this, God has, as his eternal enemy, the devil. For this, all religions hate the devil. For this, the devil plays perpetual mischief in this world. How can we prevent all this? Stop the goats from entering the forests and eating them up!"

There was a brave king. He lived carefree and happy, though enemy princes surrounded him on all sides. One day, a friend and admirer said to him, "I wonder how you can sleep so well, with so many enemies about."

"The tongue sleeps peacefully, though surrounded by thirty-two teeth," was the reply.

No people have suffered more than the people of India, yet they have always managed to laugh through it. Even though they have fallen behind almost everyplace else, their humor has kept pace because they can laugh at themselves.

MERCHANT: "I pity your lame condition; but it is better than being blind."
BEGGAR: "You are right, sir. When I was blind, people used to give me bad coins."

Begging used to be an honorable profession in India. Children used to borrow other deformed children at a fee—the better to beg with. Although now they have beggars' homes and laws against it, it is still going on—but certainly their sense of humor has not been banned.

A man threw a rupee to a blind beggar, who expertly retrieved it. The man was astonished. "I thought you were blind!"

"No, sir, I am not that blind beggar who sits here usually. Today he has gone to see the cinema."

LADY AMERICAN TOURIST: "Here's a penny, my poor man. How did you become so destitute?"
BEGGAR: "I was like you, mam, giving away vast sums to the poor and needy."

TOURIST: "Are you content to spend your life walking around the country begging?"
BEGGAR: "No, lady. Many's the time I've wished for a car."

"And do you admit," asked the judge, "that, in addition to the money, you stole jewelry and furs?"

"Yes, your honor," replied the prisoner. "I was taught that money alone does not bring happiness."

"I shot this tiger here in India. It was a case of me or the tiger."
"Well, the tiger certainly makes the better rug."

TEACHER: "You can't sleep in my class."
HAMID: "If you didn't talk so loud, I could!"

INDONESIA

The fun-loving former President Sukarno of Indonesia is one of the best storytellers of our time and gets screams with his traveling-salesman type stories that you have to clean up before you tell them at a stag or smoker. His favorite that I can tell is the story of the man who is about to check into the hotel and meets a lovely girl in the lobby. After a moment's conversation, he signs the register. "Mr. and Mrs. Sartono." The next morning when he checks out the clerk hands him a bill for 3 million rupees. "For one night?" he screamed at the cashier.

"*You* have been here one night," the cashier answered, "but your wife has been here for eight months."

A pest met a cabinet member at the Indonesia Hotel in Djakarta and gushed, "You know, I passed your house this morning."

"That was kind of you," said the minister, "thank you."

In less than twenty years the Indonesians went from 6 per cent literacy to over 75 per cent. But their humor is 100 per cent. One new student, a married man, was intrigued with a new humor book and asked the bookseller Ganung Agung for the price.

"Only fifty rupees," he said, "and it will make you die laughing."

"Good," said the student, "give me two. It's just the book for my mother-in-law."

IRELAND

Ireland must be heaven 'cause the best jokes come from there—especially the ones about the fighting, drinking Irishmen. "In the part of Dublin where I come from, it's no disgrace to get drunk—it's an achievement."

As the laureate of the drinkers said: "Each man kills the things he loves" —and with that he opened another fifth of Irish whiskey.

The Irish are the warmest, dearest, softest people in the whole world. However, they love a good fight. They love to drink. And they love to love. Mostly, they don't like to worry. "Even if the pound should decline still further in value, you can always take the optimistic view that you haven't many of them."

Every time you see a picture of John Wayne as the fighting Irishman, you can bet he is taken from real life.

"I love these places with sawdust on the floor," said the visitor in the little bar. "Sawdust my eye," said the bartender, "that's yesterday's furniture."

Pat walked into a bar in Dublin, his face beaten to a pulp. "And who did that to you?" asked the bartender.

"I had a fight with Mike Shannon!"

"What?" asked the bartender. "You let a little guy like that beat you up? You ought to be ashamed of yourself, a little good-for-nothing runt like Mike!"

"Hold on there," said Pat, "don't be talking disrespectfully of the dead."

The Irish have the greatest sense of humor. According to the stories, nine out of ten Irishmen love drunks. Of course, that's far from the truth. They just love to tell these jokes on themselves. I never met an Irishman without having to listen to one of his favorite drinking stories.

"Flowers are grateful for watering—whiskey is not."

"The doctor warned me against drinking—he said I'd have to limit my drinking to one a day—right now I'm up to January 6, 1987."

Two drunks were riding on a bridge and one said, "When you come to the end of the bridge, turn left." And the other said, "What're you tellin' me for?—you're driving!"

"Things were so bad that sometimes I had to live for days on nothing but food and water."

"Whiskey has killed more men than bullets."
"Yeah, but wouldn't you rather be filled with whiskey than bullets?"

The wife was furious at her husband. "Every time I see you, you have a bottle in your pocket."
"You don't expect me to keep it in my mouth all the time, do you?"

"They say drinking shortens a man's life."
"Yes, but he sees twice as much in the same length of time."

The judge was reprimanding the prisoner: "You have been brought here for drinking."
"Okay, lesh get started."

"Women get drunk faster than men."
"That's because they're littler and fill up faster."

Nurse: "I think he's regaining consciousness, doctor, he tried to blow the foam off his medicine."

The heading of the *Irish Times* said, "New home sought for liquor museum." An old army colonel sent a letter asking, "Where is the said museum? I got a home for it."

The judge looked sternly down at the defendant. "Young man, it's alcohol and alcohol alone that's responsible for your present sorry state."
"I'm glad to hear you say that, your honor," the man replied with a sigh of relief. "Everybody else says it's all my fault."

ISRAEL

Modern Israel was born in battle, anguish, and privation. Although it is a humor of people schooled in suffering, its laughter is without self-pity or bitterness: "Don't give up the ship—sell it." In fact, you might say it is wholesome and spontaneous. Like the story of the American tourist who came to Jerusalem and asked the taxi driver to take him to the Wailing Wall, and he immediately drove him direct to the income tax office.

Ever since Moses made his trek across the desert, the Jews have had the ability to change adversity into joy and laugh at themselves and their troubles. David Ben-Gurion's wife Paula told a visitor to Israel, "Why don't you get married, so you can have troubles of your own?"

In the case of a sensitive people like the Jews, its humor will not only stimulate laughter, but will give the mind a pretty good workout as well.

A Yemenite, seeing an elevator for the first time, watched an elderly lady go up in it, and when the car came down—a beautiful young girl skipped out. "It's magic!" he exclaimed, and rushed home to get his wife and put her into it.

My wife Cindy admired a paratrooper in Haifa and asked, "How many successful jumps have you made?"

"Oh," said our modest hero, "every one of the jumps must be successful."

Although Israel is a new country, its folklore is as abundant as its experiences are varied. In these last few years, the people of Israel have crowded several centuries of progress, tragedy, happiness, and torture into their turbulent years.

A recent kibbutz (cooperative farm) advertisement read: "Dov, 28, wishes to meet girl, about 25, with tractor. Please enclose picture of tractor."

An Arab officer, harassed by an Israeli sharpshooter on a steep hill, sent his entire platoon to knock off the Jew. Shortly, the platoon returned minus several men. The sharpshooter was still in action.

"Why have you come back?" the officer demanded.

"We are sorry, Effendi," spoke up an Arab noncom, "but there were two Jews."

On a bench in Jerusalem two elderly gentlemen were discussing the war. "How long do you think this will last?" asked one of them. "Two months," came the reply. "My son has just joined the army—and he's never held a job more than two months in his life."

When an air-raid siren went off in Tel Aviv a woman was annoyed that her husband was slow in leaving the apartment, so from the stairs she shouted, "Come on, Harry!"

"I'm coming," replied her husband, a denture wearer. "I've just got to get my teeth."

"Never mind your teeth," shouted back his wife. "What do you think they're dropping—pastrami sandwiches?"

The Arabs planted a spy by the name of Rabinovitz in Jerusalem. When they got no communication from him for some time, they sent a second spy to get the word. The passwords were "Camels are thirsty." The agent maneuvered his way through the many lines, past soldiers and police, and finally found himself in Jerusalem at the apartment house where he was told he would find Rabinovitz—but alas, there were four Rabinovitzes in the apartment house, and he did not know what the man looked like. He decided to start at the top, the likeliest place for a spy. The woman who answered the door looked him over suspiciously. "I'd like to see Rabinovitz, it's very personal." When he was ushered into the room he insisted on seeing Rabinovitz alone. The master of the house dismissed the woman and said, "Yes, what can I do for you?" The Arab secret agent said "Camels are thirsty."

"Oh," said Rabinovitz, "you want Rabinovitz the spy. He's on the first floor."

Making fun of the slowness of the railroads is still popular. On a certain line, one story goes, a woman gave birth to a baby. When the ordeal was over and the mother and child were resting comfortably in one of the carriages the conductor gave expression to his annoyance. "Young lady," he scolded, "you never should have boarded the train, knowing you were in that condition."

The young mother retorted, "When my husband and I boarded this train, I was not in that condition."

Israel, they brag, is the greatest place for millionaires—why?—No millionaire has died there yet.

A man went to see the head of a government department about a job. "What experience?" he asked. "What can you do?"

"Not a thing," replied the applicant.

"Good," said the civil servant, "then we won't have to break you in!"

The Tel Aviv buses are the most crowded in the world. Sometimes you wait for hours while dozens of buses pass you by—so packed they can't take a single passenger. One old man struggled aboard a crowded bus and handed the surprised conductor one of the reduced fare tickets issued to children of school age. "That's how long I've been waiting," he explained as he reached for the strap.

A boy came late to school and his excuse was they had a family situation that had to be taken care of. He went on to explain that his father had to take the bull to the cow. The teacher asked, "Couldn't your father do it himself?" "I guess he could," the boy replied, "but the bull would do it better."

A Tel Aviv businessman was interviewing an applicant for an opening in his small plant. "Are you married?" he asked. The applicant, a young veteran, responded with a question: "Do you prefer to have married men working for you, sir?"

"Well, yes," said the boss. "They don't seem to mind so much when I shout at them."

While the Israelis have made a name for themselves with outstanding feats of bravery, they love to kid themselves. They tell the story about the young Israeli soldier who was sent on reconnaissance to investigate the possibility of crossing a bridge. He came back tattered and bleeding and said, "To the right there are tanks and artillery and infantry in great numbers. To the left there are numerous atomic weapons and machine guns. I am sure we can go either to the right or left, but I'm afraid we cannot cross the bridge."

"Why not?" his commander asked.

"They got a big black dog at the other end."

During the time of the War of Liberation, there were not enough guns and ammunition to go around, let alone uniforms. An American volunteer tried to join the Israeli army. He passed his medical but when he asked for a uniform they told him, "We are a poor country, we cannot afford uniforms." He tried the air force. Again he was told no uniforms. So he decided to join the navy, where a uniform is not important on a ship. When he was interviewed he was asked if he could swim. He shrieked, "My God—don't you even have ships here?"

ITALY

The Italians are the happiest. They admit they are lovers, not fighters. If you are traveling through any part of Italy you will find the best welcome of any country in the world. They certainly are the friendliest.

A plane was flying over Italy, then over the Bay of Naples, when the Italian pilot turned to his passenger and said, "Pardon me, but have you ever heard of the expression 'See Naples and die'?"

The passenger answered, "Yes, I have, why?"

The pilot said, "Take a good look, the propeller just came off!"

JAPAN

Down through the years the Japanese have been proud of the fact that they have no sense of humor. In fact, there is no word in Japanese for humor. They say they have too much respect for their family, friends, and neighbors to laugh at them: "Confess your sins to God, he will forgive you—confess them to man and you will be laughed at."

167

For a long time Japan took itself too seriously. Even when Japanese ladies smile or giggle, they hide it behind their fans or behind their palms—like it was naughty.

Oh, the Japanese have a sense of humor, of sorts. It's just that there is no spitefulness or rudeness or personal animosity in it.

"The Sumare picks his teeth—even though he has not broken his fast."

"Rich men and spitoons—the more they collect—the filthier they are."

Japanese humor is perhaps more subtle, more poetical than Chinese. Certainly it avoids the vulgar and obscene.

"Pockmarks seem dimples to lovers."

"We have no power over a crying child or a magistrate."

"Money makes strangers."

A stingy old man visited a temple with a boy servant. He wanted to offer a three-sen coin, but when he searched his purse he found only four-sen coins, so he offered one very unwillingly and said to the boy, "You'll have to pray, too!"

Humor is a criticism of life. Japanese do not wish to dwell on the painful truth of things—or live with it. For humor must make it come alive—and stay alive, and Japanese like to live with wisdom, not with folly.

A stingy man sent a servant to borrow the next door neighbor's hammer, but was told, "Ever so sorry, but we don't happen to have one." "Stingy brutes," the stingy man said. "Well, it can't be helped, use ours."

A thief climbed up a watchtower in order to steal the bell. The watchman woke up and challenged him. The thief pretended innocence, and said, "I want to ask you, how can I get to Honcho Street?" "Ah, Honcho Street! You come down the ladder, and . . . "

If Japan was subtle and tender before, it is just the opposite now. "The kimono is perhaps the most beautiful but impractical form of native dress of any country in the world, especially when you're trying to get her out of one."

If they didn't laugh before, now they'll laugh at anything, anywhere, even if it's only a tragedy. "We went bankrupt last week, Mr. Goldfarb, but as soon as we get our new stationery, we'll be ready to serve you like before."

Japan, and especially Tokyo, is really swinging right now—and that goes for the twist, too. "We finally got something over here in Japan that's made in America!"

Where the Japanese had reverence for home, family, and human relations, and never would dare laugh at such things, now nothing is sacred to a laugh: "Japanese homes are about as comfortable as a sidewalk in Alaska."

168

"Japanese business establishments for tourists fleece you just like in Europe, but they bow so damn low as they take your money, you just can't help but smile—you sucker!"

And brother, if they are hip—they are hip. A diplomat was in America and met an American woman at a reception. She did not know him and asked sweetly, "What 'nese are you—Japanese, Chinese or Japanese?"

"I'm Japanese, madam; what 'kee are you? Monkee, donkee or Yankee?"

A tourist, after a meal in a Japanese restaurant, hollered, "No wonder they make you take your shoes off—after you eat this stuff you really wanna kick the hell out of them."

The biggest laugh, especially if you're not riding with them, are the kamikaze taxi drivers. Even stunt riders refuse to ride with them. They put their lights on at night, not to find their way, but to look for you—then they aim right at you. One driver hit some little old tourist from the States and hollered after he struck him, "Look out!"

"What'sa matter," asked the tourist, lying in the gutter, "coming back?"

Once upon a time there lived a happily married couple. One day the wife quietly got behind her husband, who was smoking a cigarette, and kissed him. This very much annoyed him, and he complained that a Japanese wife must not trespass on the legitimate bounds of propriety.

The wife replied: "I did not know that it was you."

MILAN

"Marry for money and you'll probably earn it."

NEPAL

The only defense against poverty and austerity is a good sense of humor. Nepal, which is rushing into the sixteenth century, is practically naked of roads or sanitation or plumbing. But the people do have a genuine 14-carat sense of humor, and a people who can laugh at themselves have it made.

When I did some shows in Katmandu on a cultural exchange for Uncle Sam, one performance was in an open field of swamp and mud. Before I walked on stage, I asked one of the eager helpers, a local lad, to get me a rag to clean my shoes. "I'm sorry," he laughed, "here we don't have rags— we wear them."

The kind of joke that makes the Nepalese laugh is the one about the Nepali who went to his friend's house and remarked, "How come your chairs are so dirty?" and the host answered, "Because nobody sat on them today."

KRISHNA: "Why do you refuse to let me marry your daughter?"
RAMA: "Because you have no money."
KRISHNA: "But I have intelligence."
RAMA: "I doubt it."
KRISHNA: "Why?"
RAMA: "Because you want to marry my daughter."

MR. RAM: "My wife comes from a very large family—did yours?"
MR. SHYAM: "No, she brought it with her."

SERVANT: "Excuse me, sir, I happened to give you a dose of ink instead of your medicine."
MASTER: "Then give me a blotter to swallow."

PEON: (at the post office) "Sir, my master asked me to get letters from you if there are any for him."
POSTAL CLERK: "Well, what is your master's name?"
PEON: "Why do you ask me, sir? It must be written on the letter."

PALERMO

Giovanni met a friend who had contracted a wonderful marriage, but whose wife, although very rich, was the ugliest woman in the world. After they spoke a few minutes and were separating, the friend said, "And remember to embrace your wife for me." "As you wish," said the married man, "but only because it is for you!"

POLAND

In Warsaw, two strangers were admiring a new car. One exclaimed enthusiastically, "A handsome machine, no? Another triumphant exhibit of Soviet ingenuity and initiative." The other man said, "That's an American car. Can't you tell one when you see it? Didn't you know that?" The other said, "Yes, I know it—but I don't know you!"

ROME

Josephine to her girl friend: "Do you think thirty years is too great a difference in age between a woman and a man if he is a director of a bank?"

RUSSIA

Laughter is one commodity that hasn't been exported from Russia—unless you call Khrushchev a big joke. When Bob Hope was in Russia he saw Brezhnev on TV. "Of course," he said, "it's easy for him to be a hit on television—all his critics are in Siberia." Bob says, "In a hotel room in Russia you don't watch TV—TV watches *you*."

The only gags in Russia are the ones on the people. Russia has so much censorship—you can't even sneak out caviar. Over there, even the fish are afraid to open their mouths. The only jokes they make are about China.

"Miaou," says the first cat on the roof.

"Maooo," says the second.

"What's the matter with you?"

"Quiet—don't breathe a word—I'm learning Chinese."

"A Chinese is like a thermos. It is impossible to tell from the outside whether the contents are hot or cold."

"Have you heard the Chinese launched a sputnik of their own? Yes they did, and you've got to give them credit. True, it took 6 million coolies to pull the sling shot, but they did it."

Lately our great American stars and entertainers have been going to Russia on cultural exchange. Ed Sullivan, Benny Goodman, Louis Armstrong, and Ringling Circus are only a few who brought a little cheer to the U.S.S.R. Maybe our sense of humor and laughter will rub off on them.

One thing we did bring them is the twist. Only over there the boy and girl don't face each other—they follow.

I'll tell you one thing. Russia surprised me. I was treated like a czar—and you know how they treated the Czar.

As far as I'm concerned, the greatest laughs don't come out of Russia, but because of Russia. Some of our comics think the U.S.S.R. is pretty funny.

"Kosygin was sick; something he agreed with was eating him," or "That astronaut Titov is a very intelligent man—twice in one year he got out of Russia."

The newspaper *Pravda* recently ran a contest for the best political joke—first prize, twenty years.

A Russian who lived in Germany many years accepted an offer to return to his native land. He decided to go alone and then have his wife and two-year-old daughter Anna join him after he got settled. Three months later, his wife received his first letter. He wrote, "It's wonderful here. Even more so than I expected. I'm so anxious to have you here with me. However, I would suggest that you postpone your trip till Anna gets married."

There is the story about a fellow who shunned American ships to Europe. Against the pleadings of his friends, he took a Russian boat. When told he would regret it, he announced sardonically, "Do me something—what can you do me?"

When he was halfway across the ocean, they sent him a radiogram to the ship reading: "If you can't knock off Kosygin—get Brezhnev."

One sober day when Kosygin was reviewing the troops, he beckoned to one little soldier and asked, "How's everything?"

"Oh, I can't complain," the boy answered.

"You bet your life you can't," answered Kosygin.

A Moscow University professor told his class that interplanetary junketing was distinctly in the cards. "We will be able to travel to Mars, Pluto, and Venus," the savant said. "Are there any questions?"

A student in the rear raised his hand. "When," he asked, "can we travel to Vienna?"

One Russian was found to be physically equipped to survive the first rocket to the moon but he refused to make the trip. "Don't you like to travel?" the commissar insisted.

"Sure," said the comrade, "but not to the moon."

The commissar asked, "Then where would you like to travel?"

"To America," he answered.

Said the commissar, "If we could send you to America, I'd go myself."

SCOTLAND

Scotland is proud of its bonnie lassies and it's canny laddies—and they enjoy being called thrifty—and I should know: some of my closest friends are Scotsmen.

I loved Scotland and the Scots. All that talk about their being tight was probably started by them. They really don't mind it—they feel it's free publicity. I know a fine man who lived there, and he was the biggest-hearted man I ever knew. It was his pleasure to sit by the window and throw pennies to the children in the streets. One day he died of heart failure—the string broke.

The Scots love the thrifty jokes credited to them: "In Scottish restaurants, we heat the knives so you can't use so much butter."

It's all great for a laugh, and the Scot laughs hardest of all when they say, "They stopped the crime wave in Scotland by putting up a sign over the jail saying: 'Anyone caught and put in jail will have to pay his board and lodging.'"

172

Who cares if it's true, but it sure is funny: In Scotland they had to take the "pay-as-you-leave" cars off the streets; they found two Scotsmen starved in one of them.

They start the thrift kick pretty early in the land of the bagpipes. One father was worried about his wee laddie. "Look," he offered magnanimously, "here's a penny for you, if you'll stop yer crying."

"Oh, Pop," said the wee one. "I've cried at least three pence worth."

Little Angus, given five dollars for his birthday, had the druggist change the bill into pennies, nickels and dimes. Then he went to another store and got a five-dollar bill for the change, then to a third store for change again. Asked by his father to explain, Angus replied, "Sooner or later somebody will make a mistake in the change—and it sure won't be me."

TRAVELER: "May I see the chief?"
YOUNG LAD: "He is not disposed to travelers."
TRAVELER: "How about if I give you a pound?"
YOUNG LAD: "Thanks, mon, fire away, I'm the chief."

A Scotsman decided to celebrate New Year's Eve. He got himself a pip of a drunk by going around in a revolving door all night.

The Scotsman asked the bank for a loan of a dollar and was told that he would have to pay 4 per cent interest at the end of the year.
"That's four cents, eh?" asked the Scotsman.
"What do you have for security?" asked the banker.
"Fifty thousand dollars in U. S. bonds."
The bank accepted the bonds and gave him the dollar. At the end of the year the Scotsman was back with a dollar and four cents to clear up his debt, and asked for the return of his fifty thousand in bonds.
As he returned the bonds, the banker asked, "I don't want to get personal, but if you have all these bonds, why did you have to borrow a dollar?"
"Well," said the Scot, "do you know any other way I can get a safety deposit vault for four cents a year?"

The Scotsman was so tight he wouldn't even tip his hat. After sixty years his wife talked him into taking a vacation—an ocean voyage to America.
He complained on the entire trip about the expense and was still grumbling as he was walking down the gangplank. Suddenly, he noticed a deep-sea diver emerge. "If I had an outfit like that," said the Scotsman, "I'd have walked over, too."

SICILY

In the courtroom, he continued to maintain his innocence although seven eyewitnesses saw him rob the automobile.

"It does not mean a thing, your honor," the prisoner answered. "If you wish, I will show you seven thousand who did not see me."

SOUTH AMERICA (Including Mexico)

In the vastness of South America, with its thirteen countries and millions upon millions of people of Spanish, Indian, Negro, Portuguese and European descent, humor is like a giant patchwork quilt: there are many different colors and styles, but common threads run through it all. Jokes and stories vary from country to country, depending on local traditions and environment. The simple tale that makes an Argentine gaucho (cowboy) laugh so hard that he nearly falls off his horse, leaves a sophisticated Chilean totally unsmiling. A subtle story poking holes in Mexican bragging is way over the head of a Peruvian Indian. But every country loves to hear about the ways of women and the way they make trouble for men. And everyone laughs at religion, at government, at the mysterious ways of foreigners.

"Do you like flowers?" a Mexican asks a friend who has double-crossed him.

"Yes."

"Well, then, tomorrow you shall have them," says the Mexican—and shoots his friend down.

This is the kind of story the Mexican Indian likes—simple and to the point. Mexican humor also illustrates some other facets of the Latin temperament; for example, the men are very much concerned with how strong and masculine they are.

"Here in Mexico," boasts a Mexican to a Chilean, "we are all very machos (virile)."

"Well, in Chile," says the Chilean, "some of us are machos (male), and some are hembras (female), and we like it just fine!"

Peru has a large and colorful variety of Indians. One day a Peruvian dandy rides a bicycle to a hill town where such machines are unknown. The Indians gather around it admiringly. "How much is it?" asks one.

"Forty dollars," says the owner proudly.

"What? For forty dollars I can buy a cow."

"Perhaps," says the owner, "but you'd look pretty silly riding a cow into town."

"I'd look even sillier," replies the Indian scornfully, "trying to milk a bicycle!"

In Chile, which has a great deal of German in its background, the people are very conscious of their heritage, and proud of being Chilean. A German immigrant has an argument with a native one day. He claims his children, though born in Chile, are German because their parents are German. The Chilean says no, they were born in Chile, and so must be Chilean. And the German replies: "So if a cat has kittens in the oven, they are cookies?"

SPAIN

A Spaniard was once wrecked on the South American coast. As soon as he opened his eyes, he asked his rescuer: "Is there a government in this country?"

"Yes."

"Well, then," he shouted, "I am against it!"

The Fans

by Joey Adams

"I go to bed with you every night," the lady gushed to Johnny Carson. "Really?" Johnny answered. "I hope you enjoy it."

A fan will get so flustered when she sees her TV hero come to life, she'll say or do anything that comes to her mind. Morey and Kay Amsterdam were having dinner at Danny's Hideaway. When the woman spotted the comedian and his wife, she dropped her napkin and her husband and rushed over to coo: "Mrs. Amsterdam, I hope you don't mind, but I enjoy your husband so much—he gives me such pleasure."

"I wish," Kay mumbled to Morey, "I could say the same."

Nobody escapes a fan's bite—once he gets a bead on you. A few weeks ago, I was going backstage for rehearsal on the Ed Sullivan Show. I was just about to open the door when I received a bang on the back that almost knocked my head off. "Well," said the two-fisted fan, "Ed Sullivan— as I live and breathe."

"In the first place," I growled, "my name is not Ed Sullivan—it's Joey Adams—and even if it were Ed Sullivan, is that any reason for you to bang me so hard on the back?"

"What do you care what I do to Ed Sullivan?" was her answer.

One lady attacked me in front of the Merv Griffin theatre and pleaded, "Please Mr. Griffin—I must have your autograph for my daughter—she's six years old and she just loves you—if I don't bring your autograph back— she'll die."

"But," I pleaded, "I'm not Merv Griffin—I'm Joey Adams."

"What's the difference?" she said. "The kid can't read anyway."

They never want the autograph for themselves. It's always for their niece or kids. Except the little boy of twelve who encountered Liberace and asked for his signature. "It's for my mother," he mumbled. "Personally I don't dig you—but the old lady thinks you're a gasser."

If I wasn't sitting with Tony Martin I wouldn't believe it either. A middle-aged woman approached Tony and drooled, "Mr. Martin, I must tell you, I personally enjoy your act as well as my husband."

A very well-dressed lady saw my wife Cindy at a theatre opening and greeted her effusively. "What's the name of the show you do again?" she asked.

"The six-thirty news," my wife answered pleasantly.

"What time does it go on?" the lady wanted to know.

Nobody can hit harder and hurt more than a well-meaning fan. They never see themselves getting old, but one wrinkle or one gray hair and you become a target that they can see from across a crowded street.—"My God, you've gotten old—and fat—what happened to you, Joey?" the fat old lady asked. "I used to see you when I was a kid."

"That was my father," I barked, running home to look in the mirror and start my diet again.

Once when I was getting a haircut and shave at the Waldorf barber shop, an old man who looked like 130 hobbled over to my chair and squeaked, "Don't remember me, eh?—big man, eh? Well, you'll be surprised when I tell you—you entertained at my Bar Mitzvah."

I had to kill him. I would have, too, if the manicurist, the barber and the shoe shine boy didn't tie me down.

An admirer met Vicki Baum for the first time. "Why, Miss Baum," she gushed, "it's so nice to find you so blonde and young—I had pictured you much older and a brunette."

"My dear," replied the author, "I am."

And the customers always write—and believe me, their pens can be mightier than their tongues. One fan of mine wrote to me with undying love: "Dear Joey Adams," he started affectionately, "you are the worst comedian on TV—you stink—if I ever meet you I must kick you in the head—you are from hunger.

Sincerely, Sam Schmoe
P. S. Please excuse the pencil."

Sinclair Lewis received a fan letter from a girl who asked for a job as his secretary—just to be around him. "I am willing to do anything for you," she wrote, "and when I say anything—I mean anything."

Mrs. Lewis, who handled the famous author's mail, answered the girl: "Thank you for your letter and offer but Mr. Lewis has a good secretary and I do everything else—and when I say everything—I mean everything."

"Dear Milton," one fan wrote to Milton Berle, "I really enjoyed your show last night. My girl's parents went to see it and left us alone for the entire evening—I really enjoyed your show last night."

Dean Martin received this letter from a follower: "Dear Dean, I saw your show last week—here's hoping you have a successful comeback."

Henny Youngman proudly displays this card that was sent to him from a TV listener: "Dear Mr. Youngman, I've been watching you, man and boy, for over 30 years and I want to take this opportunity to say—I don't like you any more as a man than I did as a boy."

One enthusiastic viewer wrote to Mike Douglas: "I love you on TV —you belong in pictures. Hollywood is always looking for new faces—why don't you send yours in?"

Tex Antoine, the weather man on TV, is one of the most popular commentators on the air. One fan wrote: "Dear Tex Antoine, I never miss your show whenever you are on—you are the complete dope on the weather."

"I watch you every time you're on TV," one fan wrote to Jackie Gleason, "and I'm gonna keep watching you till I like you."

It's when they meet you in person that they really send you to your Bible. One girl got so excited when she met me, she got all choked up as I left. "I'm terribly sorry to have met you," she stammered.

"I saw you on the Gleason show," one fan said to Morey Amsterdam. "The way you played that 'Home on the Range' on your cello, I cried like a baby."
"Are you a Westerner?" Morey asked sweetly.
"No—a musician."

"I never miss your show," the man said to Arthur Godfrey. "I never see it—so I never miss it."

The late President Kennedy was approached by a little boy who asked, "Mr. President, how did you become a war hero?"
"It was absolutely involuntary," J.F.K. answered. "They sank my boat."

"I hope you won't be insulted," one woman asked the comedian, "but are you Jack Carter?"

"I just saw your show," the Texan banged Bob Hope on the back. "What a great audience."

This one fan was so mixed up and excited seeing all the stars at the premiere that when the party broke up he kept shaking hands with everybody. "You already said good-bye to me twice," I reminded him.
"It's always a pleasure," he said, "to say good-bye to *you*."

One old dowager insisted on talking to Herbert Hoover at a party. "What do retired Presidents do?" she asked to try and engage him in conversation.
"Madam," he answered, "we spend our time taking pills and dedicating libraries."

Robert Benchley was enjoying his solitude drinking his gin at the bar when a bore tried to be his friend. "That stuff is slow poison," the intruder started.

"That's all right," said Benchley without looking up. "I'm in no hurry."

The civilian will think of any excuse to talk to the star just so he can go back home and tell the gang, "I was with Jack Paar last night!" And he's got the autograph to prove it. "Sign it to Charlie boy," they plead. Or, "Say something special for my wife—she loves you on CBS." The fact that you are on NBC has nothing to do with it. Sign you must.

Jack Paar was sitting with his lovely daughter Randi at a roadside restaurant in Maine enjoying a quiet lunch when the traveling salesman spotted him. What an opportunity. He had the great Jack Paar to himself. What's the best way to approach him?

"I just came over to offer my condolences," he started. Jack didn't know if he meant that he was off the Tonight Show or because of the special he just did for NBC. But being a gentleman, he decided to just say thanks. And anyway, it was the easiest way to get rid of him.

"Can I help in any way?" the man asked.

"No thanks," Jack said, still trying to be nice.

"I know how much he meant to you," the man continued. "I just wanted you to know that I'm with you."

It suddenly hit Jack that he was talking about an actor who was on his show once in a while and who had passed away a couple of weeks before.

"My deepest sympathy." The man wouldn't leave. "If there is anything I can do—"

"No, thanks," Jack said quietly.

"I'd like to express my feelings," he insisted. "Where can I send it?"

Paar figured the easiest way to get rid of him was to give him the address of his television station in Maine, and anyway, perhaps the widow of the actor would like to receive this thoughtful message.

The next day Jack received a big box from the salesman. It was gift-wrapped and carried the legend, "My deepest sympathy." Inside the box was the product the salesman was pushing—a carton of Saran Wrap.

The golf nut approached L.B.J. at the Democratic dinner and naturally tried to bring up his favorite subject. "What's your golf handicap, Mr. President?" he asked.

"I don't have any," the President answered. "I'm all handicap."

The lady was so excited when she bumped into Jack Carter and his wife Paula who was about to have her first baby. "I hope," she cooed, "you will have a better delivery than your husband."

Groucho Marx was sitting in the lobby of the hotel when the little lady spied him. "I beg your pardon," she giggled, "I've seen you in pictures so many times—are you Harpo Marx?"

"No!" he barked. "Are you?"

W. C. Fields never catered to fans or family. One unidentified youth put in an appearance at the gate of the famous comedian's home claiming to be his son.

Fields decided to see him. "Hello, father," the youngster greeted him. "How are you?"

"Have a drink?" asked Fields.

"Oh, fine, father—I'll have a Coke."

Fields screamed for his butler. "Coke?" he hollered. "Throw the bum out—he's no son of mine."

Please don't read me wrong. If this turns out to be a rib of the kind of fans we have today—I thank you. Stars like Cary Grant refuse to sign autographs—others charge twenty-five cents per signature and give the money to charity. Me? I seem to attract the characters.

The "Who am I?" or "Remember me?" approach is the killer. This type begins his onslaught by first blocking out your line of vision. He plants his body directly in front of yours and bellows, "Well?—where do you know me from?"

It's usually somebody you met in an elevator going up five floors about twenty years ago. Or like the clown who turned me around and challenged, "So you don't remember me? When I tell you—you'll fall through the floor. You're a friend of Jackie Gleason, right? Do you know his manager? Well, his cousin and my best friend are engaged."

The friendly murderer spends his off-hours doing research. His idea of a perfect evening is to spy a celebrity and call him by his real name. He blows his top when he can yell Aaron Chwatt to Red Buttons. Or, "Well, if it isn't Eugene Klass," to Gene Barry. Or, "Hey, Milton Berlinger—say hello to David Kaminsky for me." He wants him to know that he knows it's Milton Berle and Danny Kaye.

The biggest pain in my fans is the guy who tries to be your pal while he buries you. "Hey, Adams," he greets you, "I don't care what they say— I like you—I still like the old stuff no matter how many times I hear it."

The character to watch is the fellow who greets you after the best show of your life. "Don't worry," he comforts you, "everybody is entitled to an off-day."

But the one that drives me to count my money is the joker who rushes up to me and leers, "I saw your show last night—" And that's all he says. No good, bad, or go to hell.

Of course, you do get letters from fans that bring you much comfort and joy. Like the one I received recently from an admirer in Philadelphia. "To my favorite star," was the greeting, "you are number one in my book—

nobody comes near you as an entertainer or a personality. Please send me a picture so I can worship you—you are the greatest."

Do you think he was sincere? The letter was mimeographed.

Virginia Graham of "Girl Talk" is the glibbest and brightest lady in television. She calls herself the Menopausal Coty Girl because she won stardom at a later age.

Consequently, she is the hope of millions who figure, as one fan of eighty said to her, "Miss Graham, after seeing you, thank God, we can still find employment."

Nobody enjoys it more than the gracious Graham and nobody has a better sense of humor. And there are times she really needs it. As one fat lady fan said, "I can't get over how much thinner you look on my television set." Another complimented her, "You should thank God how TV flatters you."

So often they know her face, but can't place the name. "You're uh— what's-her-name?" one lady asked. "Virginia Graham." the star of "Girl Talk" tried to be helpful. "No," the woman said, "it can't be."

Another lady approached her. "Where do you know me from?" she asked.

One elderly woman waited to see Miss Graham after her show, just to tell her, "You're my greatest fan."

The only fan-atic that drives her to the beauty parlor is the old, fat, bedraggled, sloppy woman between sixty and ninety who invariably walks over to Virginia when she is dressed in her finest and looking her best and says, "Huh?—I wanted to see you—everybody says we look so much alike we could be twins."

The obsequious fan kept interrupting Joe E. Lewis' drinking. For the first ten minutes he was only a pest—but after that he became annoying. Finally, he said, "I think you're the greatest—what else can I say?"

"You can say good-bye," Joe E. suggested.

Will Rogers was approached by a woman as he walked out the stage door where he was appearing in the Ziegfeld Follies. "Why aren't you in the army?" she asked.

"For the same reason that you aren't in the Follies, madam—physical disabilities."

Michigan State's football coach Duffy Daugherty actually got a letter addressed to "Duffy the Dope."

"It really didn't annoy me," he said. "What really bothered me was the fact that the post office knew exactly where to deliver it."

The one thing that always burned Fred Allen the most was the fan who saw the star after a performance and merely said, "Not bad."

Fred always countered with, "It wasn't supposed to be."

181

Perry Como received a letter from one little boy who said, "I'll send you my picture if you'll send me yours."

One fan wrote to Perry offering, "If you'll give me a haircut—I'll pay you double."

Harry Hershfield shared the elevator with the little lady and her big dog. "You're Harry Hershfield—right?" she asked.

"Everybody takes me for him," Harry said pleasantly.

"Now that I'm looking good on you," she said, "you ain't him."

One lady ran over to Hershfield after his speech on civil rights. "I'm with you, Mr. Hershfield," she embraced him. "Look at me—I'm from the South—and I'm not anti-Semitic to the colored people."

The greatest and kookiest fans are the ones that follow the Beatles. Even the Queen of England is one. Didn't she have them decorated? Their last record sold 600,000 copies the first week—and I think the kid next door has all of them. But what can you do—you've got to laugh at it all. So far the Beatles have laughed me out of three nights' sleep.

One little girl fan wrote to Paul and confessed that she loved him a little more than the others and wanted to know if he minded. He replied: "I love me a little more than the others, so I don't see why you shouldn't too."

One fan asked Ringo why he wore so many rings on his fingers. "Because," he answered, "I can't fit them all through my nose."

"My darling, beautiful, wonderful George," one conservative little fan wrote, "on account of you I lost 20 pounds and my mother says you can have it. I just stare at your picture all day—and I can't eat." Does she mean he spoils her appetite? If that's so, who needs pills—what a cheap way to diet!

"Dear John," one girl wrote, "please marry me and I'll never bother you again."

Second only to the Beatles are the fan letters that the Mets get. The fact that they are always in the cellar doesn't stop their fans from writing and even asking for help. "Dear Team," one seven-year-old wrote, "please send me all the information you have on hitting home runs. That is all the information I need."

Bill Adler has put some of these love letters to the Mets into a book. One of the funniest is:

"To my pals the New York Mets,

You should ask for Alvin Newsome to be the official scorer for the Mets. Alvin is in the fourth grade and he is the official scorer for our league in Flushing. Only Alvin can't add so good and sometimes when he adds up the runs from the innings, he has the wrong team winning.

If Alvin was the official scorer at Shea, you would win lots of games. You better call for Alvin right away before he gets into the fifth grade and learns to add."

Your pal,
Alvin's brother, Herbie

This must be the all-time record for FANERVE. One little Italian girl in Rome was having a baby. She wasn't too sure which soldier was the father. When her family pressed her, she looked through the fan magazines and hit upon her idol, Robert Alda, who had spent a lot of time making pictures and starring in Italian musical comedies.

"Dear Mr. Alda," she wrote, "we never met—but would you please be the father of my child? He should be born in about 2 months and my mother and father insist my child have a father. I already told them you were the father—do you mind?

"You don't have to marry me or anything—unless you want to—but how would it look for a big star like you being a father without being married? If you do this for me—I'll never ask you for anything again.

Very truly yours."

Harry Hershfield received a telegram from his biggest fan, Joe E. Lewis, when Harry was made Abbott of the Lambs. "I am thrilled beyond words," he said in his wire, "but not more than 10."

Hershfield received this card from a fan on his eighty-first birthday: "You are one of nature's noblemen—you are a credit to mankind—a joy to the public you serve."

Underneath that the fan wrote: "That's only the sentiment of the guy who printed the card—not me."

The kids love to receive fan mail from Jerry Lewis because he talks their language and they figure he's a delinquent just like them. "Dear Dandy Darbs—Luv ya madli," he writes, "your letters are peachy keen—groovy—Jer."

However, Jerry's older fans can get a little annoyed when they don't get the answers they like—like money, for instance. One insistent follower wrote: "In your letter your representative informed me that you are adopting a silly policy of contributing only to organizations that are authorized to help the needy. Since I am not attached to any organization, I want from you only a loan of $50,000 which will be payable within a limited period—100 monthly installments.

"This is strictly business. Hence, I request that my case may please be considered as special and given an exemption from your policy.

"Since I am a very old fan of yours and see all your pictures and since I have sent many letters for this small loan, I think it only fair that you take care of this matter immediately.

"I know you will reply favorably please."

Jayne Mansfield received this letter:

"Dear Jayne: Brigitte Bardot has nothing on you. I like you best when you have nothing on you. I have been loving you for years and you must admit that I never tried to get fresh or attack you when you signed my autograph—but I'm much older now and I'm very anxious too. My friends say I sing better than Eddie Fisher and if he had Debbie and Liz—why can't I have you? Your fan—"

Dave Clark of the Dave Clark Five received this proposal in the mail. "Dear Dave: I love you. I'm 14 and pregnant. Will you marry me? Very sincerely. P. S. My measurements are 30-20-30, but right now it's 30-50-30."

One thirteen-year-old wrote to the Animals' singing star Eric Burdon: "I need a picture of you very badly, or a lock of your hair or your car or something of yours because I am crazy about you and can't sleep. Please help me in my hour of need."

Herman's Hermits have a fan club that collects one dollar for dues. One kid sent an application to join the club and enclosed a book of green stamps.

One youngster wrote to Soupy Sales: "I have never seen you—I don't know you—and I don't know who you are—so please send me an autographed picture so I can know you—Thank you."

Soupy Sales was fresh from his triumph on the "Tonight Show." One kid rushed up to him, "Hey, Soupy—how about an autograph," "Sure," Soupy said graciously. And the kid pulled a paper and pencil out, signed his name and handed it to Soupy.

One boy of fifteen approached Jerry Lewis as he was having a sandwich at the Stage Delicatessen. "I hate to bother you while you're eating," the youngster said politely. "That's all right," Jerry said graciously with his fingers akimbo ready to sign the autograph. "Can I have your pickle?" the kid asked. "You don't seem to be eating it anyway and I love pickles."

Rex Harrison got very unhappy when one young lady asked if he could get his son Noel's autograph for her.

"Can I impose on you for an autograph?" one boy of fourteen asked Danny Thomas. "Sure," Danny said. "Who shall I address it to?" The boy gave him his name and address. "I don't have to write you," Danny said, "I'll give it to you now."

"Oh," the kid said, "I don't want yours, thanks anyway—but can you please ask your daughter Marlo to send me hers?"

184

Most of the stars get requests for anything from a used cigarette to the money to pay their mortgage. Perry Como gets requests for the stool he sits on or "the tranquilizers you must use." He also receives many pleas for his ties, "since you never use them anyway."

Perry's requests come from all over the world. Like this one from Africa:

Dear Sir:

I am glad to write you this letter and I hope you will be confirm to reply me. Please I have been hearing of you in my country Ghana but I don't no you and I was writing to you for you to give me your picture so that I will no you. "Please" last one of my friends told me that Perry Como is friendly to many people in Ghana and I don't know who are you, that is why I was giving you this letter for you to give me your picture. And I tink you will post me some note books and world map of America. Greeting to you and your wife, friends and children. I hope you will give me your wife picture and chldren. Look "Good" and do it for me. Thank you for what is going on.

Your son,
/signed/ A. H.O.
Tamale, W. Africa

The sweetest fan story ever told actually happened to Burt Bacharach, the renowned composer, when he was eight years old. He saw a picture in the paper of the President of the United States with the New York Yankees, throwing out the first ball. "Gee," he said to his father, "I'd love to be President of the United States."

"That's quite an ambition," his dad said. "Why do you want to be President?"

"Well," he answered, looking at all the ball players in the picture with the President, "then I could get all those autographs."

Part Two ☞ ☞
The Joey Adams
Portable Gag File

The Joey Adams Portable Gag File

Anybody can get laughs if he has the tools. This joke file should be able to get you ready for any emergency—like in case you bump into an audience or a roomful of hecklers or a traveling salesman.

We have gags on any subject from the astronauts to the zoo, and jokes from any type comic from Adams to Zero, and I do mean Mostel. If you want to say, "A funny thing happened to me on the way to the office ... " look under A for automobiles, T for traffic, or O for office, and you're bound to find something appropriate.

If you're on your way to Houston and you want to do a joke about it, look under T for Texas or M for money. If you're looking to rap your mother-in-law look under M for mother-in-law. If you're looking to praise your mother-in-law, look under P for psychiatrist.

We're loaded with gags, stories, and anecdotes on the Borscht Belt as well as religious humor. There are funny song titles and daffynitions, limericks and witty sayings—all in place and ready for you to pick up.

If you admire a certain comic and want to study his style and gags, we have everybody from Amsterdam (Morey) to Burns (George) to Jessel (George) to Youngman (Henny) of the old school—and anybody of the new school from Lee (London) to Winters (Jonathan)—even if most of them never went to school.

Every comedian is know for his "shtick" (piece of business or style), and bearing this in mind, you'll find it more valuable to look under "Angry Young Man" for anybody from Mort Sahl to Lenny Bruce. Of course, you could look under G for Gregory (Dick) or L for Leonard (Jack E.) or R for Rickles (Don).

If you're looking for jokes about the suburbs look under S for suburbs or K for King (Alan). If you want ethnic humor look under E for ethnic or N for Negro, J for Jewish, I for Italian, S for Scotsman or C for Cohen (Myron).

We have stories, jokes, gags, and anecdotes on any country in the world. Just look up A for Afghanistan, N for Nepal, or Y for Yugoslovia. We have Russian jokes and Chinese jokes, from the old country and the new; we got laughs from India and Indonesia, South America and Cambodia —they are just sitting here waiting for a home.

There are jokes here for every occasion, laugh lines for every emergency. If you're making a speech at a drug convention, you can find doctor jokes, sick jokes, pill jokes, and accident jokes. If you want to impress the boys at the club or office, there are jokes on every category from booze to broads to boozed-up broads. If you want to be the clown prince of your country club, we list all sports from golf to swimming to fishing to lying.

We have gags on every subject to fill in your monologue, switch around your routines, or hype-up your act.

You will find there the wit of anybody from Lincoln (Abe) to Zero (Jack), from J. F. K. to L. B. J., from Churchill (Winston), Stevenson (Adlai), Twain (Mark), and Philip (Prince), to Joey Bishop, Will Rogers, and Fred Allen.

Anybody can use this book. All you have to know is the alphabet. If you get in the habit of consulting this gag file any time you're going to make a speech, or do a TV show, or go to a party or write to a friend, or con your boss, or sell the buyer, or weasel your wife, you'll not only have the funniest bone in town, but you'll get to know the alphabet better. Take a tip from me—I've been doing this for years and one thing about me— I may not be the greatest comedian in the whole world—but I sure know how to spel goode.

So if you're on the dais at a political rally, look under P for politics, R for Republicans, D for Democrats—or C for crooks. You'll find jokes that will even make you the life of the Socialist Party.

There are Boy Scout jokes and Hollywood jokes. There are sex jokes and lavender jokes. We got jokes about juvenile delinquency and parent jokes. We got jokes about every business and every holiday. We got train jokes, plane jokes, boat jokes, and travel jokes. We give you jokes on anything from the mini-skirt to Phyllis Diller. We give you jokes on wholesale, retail, or a fire sale, and the humor of anyone from Hope to Hershfield.

Laughter is a vaccine for the ills of the world. A dose of joy is a spiritual cure. So use this gag file to choose a joke instead of a sword. Say something funny instead of something nasty. Throw a punch line instead of a punch. Laugh and the world laughs with you—especially if it's a good joke.

In the following pages I've alphabetized every type of joke, gag, story or anecdote according to subject, person, or place. I have put a lifetime of experience into the selection of these laugh lines and I am proud to say I have helped many youngsters on the road to stardom. It was I and I alone who single-handedly discovered such a great talent as Bella Magdovitz. It was one of my joke books that was the springboard for that international funnyman John J. Potkin. My jokes have helped make such famous stars as Sylvia Fardenharber, Paul Finekuchen, and Charley Mustache.

Now, if you take the advice I have given you in this book, and pick out the jokes to match from the gag file, I personally guarantee you will be an overwhelming success as a comedian, public speaker, or personality— and if it really works, please let me know and I'll try it myself.

Absent-Mindedness

"What's that string tied to your finger?"
"To remind me to mail a letter."
"Did you mail it?"
"I forgot to write it."

BETTY: "My husband is so forgetful."
ALICE: "So I've noticed; at the party last night I had to keep reminding him he's married to you and not to me."

AL: "My wife has the worst memory in the world."
JACK: "Forgets everything?"
AL: "No—she remembers everything."

HUSBAND: "I saw the doctor today about my loss of memory."
WIFE: "What did he do?"
HUSBAND: "Made me pay him in advance."

HE: "I know I proposed to you last night but I can't remember whether you accepted or not."
SHE: "I knew I said 'No' to somebody last night but couldn't remember to whom."

"That Charlie is really getting absent-minded. Last night he kissed a woman by mistake."
"You mean he thought it was his wife?"
"I mean it *was* his wife."

DROWNING MAN: "Help, help! I can't swim."
ABSENT-MINDED MAN: "That's nothing —I can't play the French horn!"

He was so absent-minded that he poured catsup on his shoelaces and tied knots in his spaghetti.

NURSE: "The doctor's here."
PATIENT: "Tell him I can't see him— I'm sick."

The absent-minded waitress kissed her boy friend good night and said, "Will that be all, sir?"

The poor soul fell in the water and was drowned—he forgot he was a good swimmer.

This absent-minded professor dictated to his dog—then tried to give his stenographer a bath.

An absent-minded girl fiddler kissed her violin good night and took her beau to bed with her.

He's so absent-minded that he complained to his wife that his secretary doesn't understand him.

An absent-minded idiot stopped his girl and went too far with his car.

In the middle of the picture the wife let out a shriek, "Geez—I forgot to turn off the iron."
"Pipe down," the husband calmed her, "it can't burn too long—I forgot to turn off the faucet in the bathtub."

Accidents
(*see Cars, Automobiles, Driving, etc.*)

He fell out of the window, feet first. His widow collected the insurance, as well as the federal, state, and Social Security benefits. But then came the lawyers, relatives, government deductions, bills, inheritance tax, etc. When the doctor came to see her, she was a wreck. "Sometimes," she cried, "I almost wish my husband hadn't fallen out of the window."

The woman driver hit the little man, He was knocked twelve feet in the air —then the cop arrested him for leaving the scene of the crime.

191

The two assassins were hiding in wait for their "hit" who they knew passed that way every day at that time. When he didn't show after two hours, gun in hand, one said to the other: "I can't understand what happened to him—I hope he didn't have an accident."

"Ma'm, your husband has just been run over by a steam roller!"
"I'm in the tub. Slip him under the door."

DOCTOR TO ACCIDENT VICTIM: "What's your name so we can notify your family?"
ACCIDENT VICTIM: "My family knows my name."

WIFE: "How did you happen to hit that telephone pole?"
DRUNK: "I only hit it in self-defense."

"In New York there's a man run over every five minutes."
"Somebody ought to tell him—he'll get killed."

I don't believe in that junk about breaking mirrors and having seven years of bad luck. My uncle broke a mirror last week and he was killed in an accident that very same day.

"What happened to you?"
"I threw a horseshoe over my shoulder."
"So?"
"There was a horse nailed to it!"

My brother fell down the stairs with two pints of gin and didn't spill a drop —he kept his mouth closed.

The car hit her, and a hundred yards away he stopped and looked back. "Watch out," he shouted. The woman raised herself on her elbow and screamed, "What's the matter—coming back?"

I had a bad accident. I tried to turn the corner—and I was in the middle of the block.

He was injured in the football game —he fell off the bench.

Actors
(see Show Business, Hollywood, Theatres, etc.)

"How could you stand up in court and say you're the greatest living actor of all time?" the agent asked his client.
The ham pulled himself up to his full five-foot-two: "I was under oath—I didn't want to commit perjury."

"The actor's style would have been great in 1923. Unfortunately he wasn't able to get a 1923 audience."—Garson Kanin.

The bum approached the Shakespearian actor and pleaded for a quarter for something to eat. The disciple of the Bard looked down at him and in his full Shakespearian manner said, "Young man, 'neither a lender nor a borrower be'—William Shakespeare."
The bum looked up and said: "'Screw you'—Tennessee Williams."

The actor was talking about his home being filled with his wife's relatives: "My house looks so much like a hotel —last night I caught myself stealing my own towels."

When I was a kid I was in love with a girl and asked her father for permission to marry her. "Never," he said, "would we let our daughter marry an actor."
"At least see my show," I pleaded.
"Okay," he promised, "but we would never, ever, let our daughter marry an actor."
After the performance I ran to the

old man. "Son," he said, "don't worry about a thing. You can marry my daughter—you're not an actor."

"Please, doctor," the ham actor pleaded with the psychiatrist, "I'm developing a terrible inferiority complex —I'm beginning to think that there are other people as good as me."

"I can't leave the theatre," the actor preached, "I'm married to it!"
"Then," his wife asked, "why don't you sue it for non-support?"

He's always me-deep in conversation.

The first film made by Alfred Lunt and Lynn Fontanne, titled "The Guardsman," was good, but they, perfectionists that they are, were unsatisfied. Miss Fontanne was the first to view the film's rushes, and she sped back to their suite where her husband was waiting and burst into tears.
"Alfred, Alfred!" she cried. "We're ruined! I've seen the rushes. You photograph without lips and I come out old and haggard and ugly and my tongue is thick and I lisp and I stumble around ungracefully. I look like I forgot my lines and my feet are big and my clothes look like a sack on me!" Just then her tears overcame her voice and she faltered.
In the silence that ensued, Lunt muttered, "No lips, eh?"

The great actor was known for his many romances coast-to-coast. He was faced with many claimants to his paternity down through the years.
Once while in his dressing room, a young man gained entrance and introduced himself, "I'm your son."
The Great One looked intently at the youth for a moment. "So you are!" he said, and turning to his valet he said, "Give the boy a pass."

Did you hear about the ham actor who died and was buried in a curved casket so it would look like he was taking a bow?

An unemployed actor applied for a Santa Claus job at a large midtown department store. He told the interviewer that he had experience working two winters in the largest department store in Brooklyn. The interviewer said, "Well, that would be fine for an off-Broadway store, but we want Broadway experience."

The famous star entertained many young ladies in his dressing room. After one matinee—and there was no show on stage that day—the matinee idol handed the girl a pass for his performance that night.
"But," she pleaded, "I'm hungry— I need bread!"
"If you want bread," he emoted, "make love to a baker—I'm an actor— I give passes."

"What's with the ten bouquets of flowers?" the actress screamed on her opening night.
"That's wonderful!" the manager said gleefully.
"What's wonderful?" she yelled—"I paid for fifteen!"

"I'm not conceited—although God knows I have every reason to be."

"An actor is a guy who if you ain't talking about him—ain't listening."— Marlon Brando.

What Is An Actor?
by Hy Gardner

Actors aren't people. Though there are plenty of people who are actors.

I love 'em for their illusions just as much as I love them for their talents, their exaggerations, their persistency, their guts, their faith and belief in God and themselves. And I hope they forgive me for giving God top billing!

Actors don't like to get up in the morning. But they'll stay up all night and all day if they can help some person they've never met to live an extra day by their devoted deeds.

Actors like to laugh a lot and cry a lot and sleep a lot and make a lot of money so they can pay a lot of taxes and brag about it.

Actors were the originators of the credo of blood, sweat, and tears. They give blood to the Red Cross. They sweat to make the Big Time. They shed tears when one performance out of a thousand dies a dud.

Actors are belligerent, gentle, cranky, jolly, silly, canny, phony, funny, sad, glad, drunk, sober, healthy, sick, stupid, slick, temperamental, sentimental. . . . Actors wear toupees but not spectacles, elevated heels under flat feet, dress suits with torn shorts and holey socks.

Actors love to play death scenes, and at a crony's funeral try to upstage the corpse and steal the final bow. . . . Actors would rather have a front chaise longue at Danny's or Toots Shor's than a seat in the Stock Exchange. . . . An actor'd rather have his caricature hanging above the pantry wagon in Sardi's than have a portrait hanging in the Metropolitan Museum.

The only thing an actor fears more than losing his mind is regaining it. . . . An actor prefers his name in electric lights rather than on bank books. His scrapbook is a dramatic demonstration of the power of a free press . . . to bulk it up he even pastes in the sour notices.

The actor had a miracle drug long before miracle drugs were ever heard of—he called it flattery.

An actor is always on the go. He likes to sign up for a Broadway play, hoping it's a hit so he can complain he's weary of working in the city. An actor likes to go on the road so he can complain he misses Broadway. . . . An actor likes to make a movie so he can complain about Hollywood. . . . An actor likes any job where he can make a buck or make a pass at a pretty lass.

An actor falls in love at first sight, marries at second sight, and then falls out of sight forever. An actor is a motor gypsy. He can be led and bled, used and abused, kicked and caressed and always comes up smiling . . . if anybody's watching.

An actor was the first to sign a loyalty oath—to himself.

I love actors. And most of all I love the kind of humor that runs in their funny bones. An odd kind, a philosophical kind, a wonderful kind, an exclusive kind of humor that proves with every studied ad lib that there's no business like show business, no people like show people. . . . It's a tradition that will survive A-bombs, H-bombs, and Z-bombs. The only bomb an actor worries about is the one he may drop at the theatre.

Advertising
(*see Business, Offices, etc.*)

AD IN THEATRICAL PAPER: "Wanted—Human Cannonball — must be able to travel."

The stenographer put an ad in the want ad section of the paper: "Secretary wants job—no bad habits—willing to learn."

Advertising sure brings quick results—last week I advertised for a night watchman—the same night my safe was robbed.

The manufacturer decided to stop his advertising to save money. "You might as well stop your watch to save time," his salesman added.

Wire your Congressman now! Demand they stop defacing our billboards with highways.

"Girl needs job—is willing to struggle if given opportunity."

Doing business without advertising is like winking in the dark at a pretty girl —you know what you are doing but nobody else does.

AD IN LOCAL PAPER: "We do not tear your laundry with machinery—we do it carefully by hand."

Talk about progressive advertising: This department store ad offered in a local New York paper, "Maternity dresses—for the modern miss."

"Small boat for sale by widow—with a wide bottom."

Sign in the window of a health food store:—"Closed on account of sickness."

WANTED: "A salesgirl—must be respectable—until after Xmas."

FOR SALE: "Large crystal vase—by lady slightly cracked."

The man who writes the bank ads is not the man who makes the loans.

I saw an ad for a loan company. It said: "Don't borrow from your friends —borrow from us. You'll lose your friends. You'll never lose us."

Before advertising—a virus used to be known as the flu.

CLASSIFIED AD IN NEWSPAPER: "For sale—complete set of encyclopedias. Never used. Wife knows everything."

A serious ad in *Mines Magazine*: "Wanted: Man to work on Nuclear Fissionable Isotope Molecular Reactive Counters and Three-Phase Cyclotronic Uranium Photosynthesizers. *No experience necessary.*"

One sandwich man was walking down Madison Avenue with a blank sign. When I asked him what he was advertising he said. "Sh—I'm on a secret mission."

Advice
(*see Sayings, Proverbs, Quotations, etc.*)

Be kind to your mother-in-law— baby sitters are expensive.

I'd like to help you out—which way did you come in?

Next time you pass my house—pass my house.

If you're driving—make sure you have a car.

The average bride gets enough advice to last for several husbands.

The widow told bachelors, "Take it from me—don't get married."

Never let a fool kiss you—or a kiss fool you.

195

DEAR LONELY HEARTS ADVISER: "I'm in love with a beautiful girl but she's poor—and there's an ugg with lots of loot in love with me—shall I marry the rich girl or the poor girl?"
DEAR SIR: "Marry the rich girl and be good to the poor."

Don't marry for money — you can borrow it cheaper.

People aren't going to take your advice unless you are a lawyer or a doctor and charge them for it.

Affairs
(*see Sex, Playgirls, Playboys, etc.*)

"You look great!"
"Sure, why not, I'm having a wonderful affair!"
"Really? Who's the caterer?"

"Marta," Mrs. Davis said to her maid, "my husband is having an affair with his secretary."
"I don't believe it," Marta answered. "You're just saying that to make me jealous."

Mr. and Mrs. Max Katz were married thirty-two years. As they were sitting in the restaurant celebrating, he said, "You might as well hear it from me—see that blonde?—she's my mistress."
"You doidy dog—after all these years, you bum—you got a mistress?"
"Wait a minute—see that redhead with the bangs?—she's Pincus' mistress."
"That little shrimp got a mistress—why—"
"And see that brunette with the hair on top of her head? That's Levine's mistress."
"Levine—that fat slob—he got a mistress? You know something, Max? I like ours the best."

Africa
(*see "International Humor" chapter*)

A is for Africa. I was rather disappointed with the pictures I took in Africa of the native women . . . they weren't very well developed.

They've educated the Ubangis in Africa to work. Some of them work for the post office sealing envelopes after they're dropped in the mailbox.

In Africa, the savage tribes pay no taxes. Then what makes them savage?

Age
(*see also Old Age, Teenagers, Juvenile Delinquents, Kids, Children*)

Some women are very loyal. When they reach an age they like—they stick to it.

The three stages of man are: Youth—Middle Age—and "You're Looking Fine."

Two women were meowing one lunch time. "Time separates the best of friends," purred one.
"How true," clawed the other. "Twenty-five years ago we were both fourteen and now I'm thirty-nine and you're twenty-three."

Every woman knows that if she wants to keep her youth—she shouldn't let him go out at night.

Middle age is when the narrow waist and the broad mind begin to change places.

You're getting old when you don't care where your wife goes—just so you don't have to go along.

Most every woman's age is like the speedometer on a used car—you know it's set back but you don't know how far.

The father was reprimanding his son who didn't want to do his homework: "When Abraham Lincoln was your age he walked ten miles to school every day and studied by the light of the fire in his log cabin."

"So what?" the kid answered. "When John F. Kennedy was your age he was President."

The youngster asked the old gentleman who was quite a romantic figure in his day: "Are these days as romantic as the old days; I mean was sex and lovemaking bigger in those days?"

"No," said the old gentleman, "it's still going on—but there's a new bunch doing it now."

Nowadays they only have respect for old age—if it is bottled.

It's easy to find out how old a woman is—just ask her sister-in-law.

The best way to tell a woman's age is not to.

Mae West is ageless—but not the men in her life. She is still saying "Come up and see me sometime," but those guys she first told that to would now have to be carried up.

"How long have you known her?"
"Why, I've known her ever since we were the same age."

"I hope I look as good as you do when I'm your age."
"You did."

Her family didn't approve of her marrying me. Mostly because of the difference in our ages. She was nineteen and I was poor.

Even though Mr. Goldberg was sixty-five, he still loved to chase after young girls. A neighbor brought this to Mrs. Goldberg's attention and asked her what she was doing about it. "Who cares? Let him chase girls," she said. "Dogs chase cars, but when they catch them, they can't drive."

Middle age is that time of life when you can feel bad in the morning without having had fun the night before.

"I don't intend to be married until I'm thirty."
"I don't intend to be thirty until I'm married!"

He had been reading about Sinatra, Cugat, Grant, Justice Douglas, et al., marrying all the pretty young girls, so the seventy-five-year-old bachelor married a girl of twenty. After the third day of his honeymoon he collapsed and they called the doctor.

"Overweight?" he asked the doc.
"No—overmatched."

She never forgets her age — once she's decided what it's to be.

He's still a gentleman—but at his age the most he could do is pick up her handkerchief—certainly not the woman.

Walter Cronkite's mother, a divorced lady in her seventies, was invited to go to the movies in Washington the other evening by a gentleman considerably older than she. When she got home that night, she was asked whether she and her escort had had a good time.

"Oh yes," she said brightly, "but you know, I had to slap his face three times."

197

"Because he was . . . ah . . . fresh?"
"No," said Mrs. Cronkite. "To wake him up."

You're only as old as the girls you feel.

The best way to cure your wife of anything is to tell her it's caused by advancing age.

If you want to get a youthful figure —ask a woman her age.

She was born in the Year Of Our Lord only knows.

How well she keeps her age — to herself.

He's so old he doesn't learn history —he remembers it.

She claims she just turned twenty-three—before she turned it she was thirty-two.

A woman has reached middle age when her girdle pinches and the men don't.

A woman is getting old when she buys her shoes for comfort and her sweaters for warmth.

I'm at the age now where I only chase girls if it's downhill.

She's at the age where any man who looks back—looks good.

He doesn't have an enemy in the world—he's outlived them all.

He just got a letter from an old age home and it was marked urgent.

Nothing makes a woman feel older than meeting a bald-headed man who was two grades back of her in school.

Agents
(*see Actors, Show Business, Theatres, Hollywood, etc.*)

An agent watched an act where a guy was shot out of a cannon one hundred feet in the air and, as he came down, played a violin solo in mid-air. When he finished, he approached the agent. "Well?" he said proudly. "Well," the agent commented, "a Heifetz you're not."

When an agent died, they approached all the people in show business to contribute to his funeral. One actor approached comic Jack Zero who hated all 10-per-centers: "Will you give me five dollars to bury this agent?" Jack scowled, "Here's ten dollars, bury two agents."

A tired-looking actor marched into a vaudeville house with a kangaroo and asked for a job.
BOOKER: "A job? What does the kangaroo do? Can he sing, dance, tell funny stories?"
ACTOR: "He doesn't do anything."
BOOKER: "Then why did you bring him here?"
ACTOR: "I had to . . . he's my agent."

A small-time night club act was in a plane crash and found himself in a strange place. "Where am I?" he asked a man standing near him.
"You're in hell!"
"That's my agent for you," sighed the comic, "still booking me in these crap joints."

I give my agent 10 per cent of my unemployment checks: after all, this is one situation he is responsible for.

I got a great agent—he books me in Miami during the summer, Boston during Holy Week, Alaska during the winter and Vegas during the atom bomb tests.

PRODUCER: "The girl we're looking for must be five-foot-one—your client is at least five-foot-nine."
AGENT: "Have you seen her lately?"

The agency is only picking young agents now. Mine is so young, he can't come and see me in night clubs. His mother won't let him out after dark.

The actor pleaded with the agent to at least see his act. "My act is different—look—I fly." Then he lifted his arms and flew around the room and landed on the desk.
"Okay," said the agent, "so you can imitate birds—what else can you do?"

AGENT: "If you carry out my instructions to the letter—I'll make a big star out of you."
ACTOR: "What's the first thing I got to do?"
AGENT: "The first thing is to get an extra cot put in your room — so I can move in with you."

An actor showed up at a party with a deep tan.
"What a wonderful sunburn," his hostess greeted him. "Such a bronze—how did you get it?"
"I have a lousy agent," the actor growled.

"Kid," the agent said, "I want to book you when the time is right—not before."
"When is that?"
"When I get an offer for you."

AGENT: "Some actor called me a pig—and with the price of pork today, that's a compliment."

When the small-time actor came home, his wife grabbed him hysterically and cried, "Darling, your agent was here and he tried to make love to me and forced me to kiss him and ripped off my clothes and beat me."

"Hmmmm," mused the actor, "my agent was here, huh? I wonder what he wanted."

Her agent went along on her honeymoon—he insisted on 10 per cent of everything.

The agent listened to the talking dog recite scene after scene from Shakespeare, Truman Capote, and Arthur Miller. Finally the dog's manager asked the agent, "Well—what do you say?"
"Oh," said the agent, "I'm not sure—let's see her legs."

Air Conditioning

They got air conditioning everywhere now—even in the steam rooms. And with the new buildings without windows, they now have the air conditioning going all year round. Now you don't have to wait for the winter to get a cold.

The car was unbearably hot, and it was one hundred degrees outside but the windows were closed.
"Will you please open the windows?" the husband pleaded.
"Are you nuts?" she screamed. "And let our neighbors know our car isn't air-conditioned?"

Air Force
(*see War, Army, Airplanes, Flying, etc.*)

My brother was in the Air Force. He brought down five planes. All his own.

A sweet young thing gushed to the young captain: "How many successful parachute jumps have you made?"
"Oh," said the captain, "they all must be successful."

The pretty little doll was so impressed with the Major: "It must be wonderful to be a parachute jumper. I imagine you have had some terrible experiences."

"Yes, Miss," the Major agreed. "Why, once I came down where there was a sign, 'Keep off the grass.' "

Congressman flying an Air Force plane: "How will I know if anything goes wrong?"

"Oh," said the Captain, "you'll know immediately; our co-pilot will become hysterical."

Airplanes

The passengers seated in the plane in flight heard this over the intercom system: "Sit back and relax. This plane is entirely automatic. Automatic pilot, automatic food servers, and automatic landing devices. You are perfectly safe. Enjoy your ride. Nothing can go wrong . . . nothing can go wrong . . . nothing can go wrong. . . ."

During my plane trip, we lost one engine and everyone got excited and scared. The man next to me said, "Everybody's panicking. Quick, do something religious." So I took up a collection.

Jet planes can already travel faster than sound—but not if you tell a secret to my neighbor.

"Does anyone on this plane know how to pray?"

"I do."

"Good. Start praying. The rest of us will use parachutes—we're short one."

Those plane schedules are very important — otherwise how would we know how late we are?

The passenger list on one flight across the Atlantic included people of many different nationalities. During the course of the flight, a storm blew up and forced the pilot to lighten the weight of the plane. He asked for volunteers to bail out.

A Frenchman arose and yelled, "Vive la France," and jumped out the door. Then an Englishman got up and yelled, "Long live the Queen," and leaped out. Finally, a Texan arose and shouted, "Remember the Alamo," and pushed a Mexican out the door.

Before her first plane ride a little old lady was told that chewing gum would keep her ears from popping during the flight. After finally landing, she turned to her seat companion and said, "The chewing gum worked fine, but how do I get it out of my ear?"

One major trouble with jet planes is that they've put us all in an awful spot —we no longer have any distant relatives.

The French air line doesn't show movies—just postcards.

PEPPER DAVIS: "I'm going to California by train."

TONY REESE: "Why don't you fly?"

DAVIS: "I think planes are unsafe."

REESE: "Statistics prove planes are the safest way to travel."

DAVIS: "I still prefer the train."

REESE: "Did you hear about the train wreck yesterday?"

DAVIS: "What train wreck?"

REESE: "A train was going down the track eighty miles an hour when all of a sudden—*CRASH!*"

DAVIS: "What happened?"

REESE: "A plane fell on it!"

I was going to fly to California— but I canceled it—I saw the picture.

I think it's a little dangerous with those big pictures on planes. When intermission rolls around, somebody has got to step outside for a smoke.

Air Pollution
(*see Fog, Smog, etc.*)

Everybody talks about air pollution —but they'll do nothing about it until it starts to interfere with TV reception.

Pat Henry says he didn't realize how bad New York's air pollution was until the other night when he was held up— and all they took were his cough drops.

So much air pollution—I don't water the flowers—I dust them.

Stalin's daughter predicts there'll be no World War III. Probably the Russians read about our air pollution, and figure all they have to do is wait.

"On a clear day you can breathe forever."

These gloomy reports on New York's air pollution are enough to take your breath away.

Alaska
(*see Cold, also "Monologue" chapter*)

She was hollering mush—I was hollering mush—and while we were mushing—somebody stole our sled.

Even the rich still ride sleds—but they're not pulled by dogs—six Volkswagens.

Alaska is so cold—even the janitors are complaining.

So what if I didn't go to Florida this winter. I came back from Alaska with a color—blue.

As the bop musician put it: "This country is cool."

I couldn't buy a thing there — my assets were frozen.

Many young couples are shoving off to Alaska on their honeymoons—they want to have a long first night—and six months is a long night.

If there's one thing tougher than selling a Ford to a Texan, it's selling a refrigerator to an Alaskan.

If they don't have blankets they cover themselves with ice to keep warm. Four picnickers found themselves away from home with only enough ice for three—the fourth one froze to death.

Alaskan women aren't frigid — they're just *cold*.

TEXAN: "Just tell me one thing that Alaska has that Texas doesn't have more of."
ALASKAN: "Modesty."

It's not that the bus system in Fairbanks is old-fashioned—but it's the first time I ever heard a cross-town bus bark.

A snowman was stationed in front of my hotel—and all night long he kept knocking on the door and asking for a hot water bottle.

Alimony
(*see Wives, Husbands, Divorce, Judges, Court Rooms, etc.*)

ALIMONY: A system by which when two people make a mistake—one of them continues to pay for it.

"My first husband wants to marry me again—but I suspect he's after the money I married him for."

Alimony is like paying off the installments on the car after the wreck.

Alimony is a man's cash surrender value.

Alimony is something that enables a woman to profit by her mistakes.

I don't beieve it either—but one Texan was so rich—he was *ahead* in his alimony payments.

When a woman sues for divorce—there's only one thing she wants—*everything*.

He got custody of the kids—she got custody of the money.

She's been married five times and gets richer by decrees.

Even a bad marriage has its compensations—like alimony, for instance.

There are only two ways to avoid alimony—stay single or stay married.

You never realize how short a month is until you pay alimony.

Fred Allen
(*see "Wit" chapter*)

An advertising agency is 85 per cent confusion and 15 per cent commission.

A vice-president in an advertising agency is a "Molehill Man"—that's an executive who comes to work at 9 A.M. and finds a molehill on his desk —and by 5 P.M. he makes it into a mountain.

California is great—if you happen to be an orange.

Our great country has one Vice-President. I can't understand why NBC needs twenty-six.

He's so anemic—when a mosquito lands on him—all he gets is practice.

On his fun-feud with Benny:
Jack Benny ought to pluck the horsehairs out of his bow and return them to the tail of the stallions from which they were taken.

He has a ramrod in the back of his vest to keep his spine from drooping.

He has to starch his legs—so they won't wobble.

Muscles?—His arm looks like a buggy whip—with fingers.

I've seen better looking legs on a bridge table.

The first time I saw Jack Benny he was doing a monologue on stage at a vaudeville theatre in Ohio. He had a pig on stage with him—the pig was there to eat up the stuff the audience threw at him.

An actor has three salaries: the one he thinks he ought to get; the one he really gets; and the one he tells the income tax collector he gets.

The reason some chorus boys wear flowers in their lapels is because they can't wear them in their hair.

SONG TITLE: "I walked her down to the meadow and she listened to my bull."

If Noah had forgotten to put two herrings in the Ark, half of Far Rockaway would have starved to death years ago.

Things are so tough in Chicago that at Easter time, for bunnies, the little kids use porcupines.

I was so sick — the insurance companies wanted me to give back their free blotters.

Woody Allen
(*see "Comedians" chapter*)

I went to a psychoanalyst for years—and it helped—now I get rejected by a much better class of girls.

I don't dig ballet—the last time I went with friends—there was a lot of money bet on the swan to live.

My parents didn't want me—they put a live teddy bear in my crib.

Woman's husband ran to the drug store screaming, "My husband took poison by mistake—he's turning blue at home—an antidote—hurry!" The druggist was Allen Funt—he kept her there a half hour.

They kidnapped me when I was a kid —soon as my father got the ransom note—he sprung into action—he rented out my room.

My education was dismal. I went to a series of schools for mentally disturbed teachers.

I have a lovely gold watch—a family heirloom. My grandfather, on his deathbed, sold it to me.

My apartment has been robbed so many times that finally, in desperation, I pasted a blue and white sticker on the door that said: "WE GAVE."

I was married once, but my wife was very immature. Whenever I was in the bathtub taking a bath, she would come in and sink all my boats.

The only reason I wear glasses is for little things—like driving my car—or finding it.

I seldom drink—once I sipped a martini—and I wanted to hijack an elevator and fly it to Cuba.

My luck is getting worse and worse. The other night, for instance, I was mugged by a Quaker.

Morey Amsterdam

A chestnut is a guy who's crazy about chests.

"Honey, wake up, there are burglars in the kitchen! I think they're eating the biscuits I baked this morning!"
"What do we care, as long as they don't die in the house!"

She said, "Kiss me, kiss me!"
He said, "What, are you crazy? I'm a married man. I shouldn't even be doing this!"

I was a Boy Scout till I was sixteen . . . then I became a Girl Scout.

Nothing is all wrong. Even a clock that stops is right twice a day.

People who live in glass houses might as well answer the doorbell.

Pet lovers, save money—feed peanuts to your cats. Instead of milk, they'll drink water.

You wanna lose ten pounds of ugly fat? Cut off your head.

Guy went in a drugstore and said, "Gimme some roach powder."
Clerk said, "Should I wrap it up?"
Guy said, "No, I'll send the roaches down here to eat it."

"I fell downstairs with two pints of rye."
"Did you spill any?"
"No, I kept my mouth closed."

203

"That's a beautiful stuffed lion you've got there. Where did you get him?"

"In Africa, when I was on a hunting expedition with my uncle."

"What's he stuffed with?"

"My uncle."

"How do porcupines make love?"
"Very carefully."

Analysis
(*see Psychiatrists, Doctors*)

I realized after four years and $10,000 worth of analysis that if I'd had the $10.000 in the first place. I wouldn't have needed the analysis.

"I went to a psychoanalyst for years —and it helped—now I get rejected by a much better class of girls."—Woody Allen

Sam Levenson says his first visit to an analyst was a big let-down. "I was paying him fifty dollars for a ten-minute visit and all he did was ask me the same question my father used to ask —'Who do you think you are anyway?' "

The analyst was annoyed with her patient who said she didn't dream the night before. "Look," she warned her, "if you don't do your homework—I can't help you."

I've just heard my husband wants a divorce. I don't know what to think— my analyst is out of town.

"Yes," she explained to the analyst, "I'm a virgin—but I'm not a fanatic about it."

1ST ANALYST: "A man came to see me last week who thinks he's a taxicab."

2ND ANALYST: "Are you helping him?"
1ST ANALYST: "Why should I? He drives me home every night."

Animal Stories

They crossed a parrot with a boa constrictor. They don't know what they've got, but believe me, when it talks—*they listen*.

How to tell the difference between male and female worms: the female doesn't signal when she turns.

The mother turkey was reprimanding her children. "You bad kids," said the gobbler, "if your father could see you now, he'd turn over in his gravy."

An impresario was interested in a dancing fly for his new show. A carnival man promised to deliver one that he had in mind. Later he apologized: "I couldn't train that fly to dance— he's got two left wings."

When the bottle of Scotch broke on the floor, the three little mice lapped it all up. Now they were really blind: "I'm going to find Cassius Clay and knock his brains out," said the first one. The second said, "Just let me at that Mao Tse-tung, I'll annihilate him." The third mouse had his own plans: "You boys do what you want. I'm going upstairs and make love to the cat."

So, big deal — an elephant never forgets — so what has he got to remember?

Two camels were taking a stroll in Cairo. One said to the other, "I don't care what people say—I'm thirsty."

George Gobel complained that he was having trouble with his prize boxer Irving, who likes to chase automobiles.

"Every boxer chases cars," a dog expert explained. "I know," George said, "but Irving catches them."

Did you hear about the whale who fell in love with a submarine? The whale followed the submarine all around the ocean, and every time the submarine shot off a torpedo, the whale gave out cigars.

FIRST SHARK: "What's that funny two-legged thing that just fell in the water?"
SECOND SHARK: "I dunno, but I'll bite."

Three dogs—an English bull, a French poodle, and a Russian wolfhound—were talking. The English bull and the French poodle agreed that they loved their respective countries and were content to stay there. The Russian wolfhound said, "I have the best of everything to eat and drink in Russia, but I sure would like to go to America." "How come?" the other two dogs asked. "Well," said the wolfhound, "I'd like to bark once in a while."

A very rich lady had a dog who had his own little doghouse complete with little furniture. A neighbor was looking at it one day and asked, "How does he keep it so clean?"
The owner said haughtily, "Oh, he has a French poodle come in once a week."

A tiger walked into the bar and the bartender gave him a funny look. "That's okay," said the tiger, "I'm over 21."

The goat was in the dumps and picked up a can of film. After he ate it all up, his friend asked him, "How was it?"
"To tell the truth," he answered, "the book was better."

The two monkeys were arguing and one was putting the other down pretty good. "Don't fool with him," said the third monkey, "he'll make a man out of you."

The gambler rode into the dusty little Western town. His poker chums were standing in front of the saloon. One of them asked, "Care for a little stud?" The horse looked down at him and said, "Don't mind if I do!"

One cow said to the other: "Here comes that louse with the icy fingers again."

Two fleas were talking. One said, "I'm saving up to buy my own dog."

Mamma cat was scolding one of her kittens for coming home late and kitty said, "Can't I lead one of my own lives?"

Two leopards were having dinner and one sat back and sighed contentedly, "Mmmmmm, just hit the right spots!"

The mother mouse said to her daughter, "Go ahead and marry that rat if you wanna live in a hole the rest of your life."

A trout stopped a herring one day and asked pleasantly, "Where's your brother?" and received this rude response: "What am I? My brother's kipper?"

The elephant and the lion were talking. "I fill my trunk with peanuts," the elephant bragged. "Really?" the lion said. "Where do you keep your clothes?"

One worm proposed to the other and the answer came, "Are you kidding—I'm your other end!"

205

CIRCUS ELEPHANT: "I'm getting sick and tired of working for peanuts."

The leopard complained to the eye doctor, "Every time I look at my wife I see spots in front of my eyes."
"What do you expect?" the doctor asked. "You're a leopard, aren't you?"
"Yes—but my wife is a zebra."

A tiger was prowling through the jungle when he happened to run into a gorgeous hunk of female tigress. "How about a little kiss, baby?" he purred.
"Scram," she answered, "you smell from gasoline."

One firefly to another: "Give me a push—my battery is dead."

So the girl octopus married the boy octopus and they walked down the aisle hand-in-hand, hand-in-hand, hand-in-hand, hand-in-hand, hand-in-hand, etc., etc., etc.

Anniversaries
(see Birthdays, Holidays)

He was very sentimental. "Today is a very important anniversary," he mused. "William Tell was born 900 years ago. When I was a kid, William Tell was my idol. I remember I used to go in the backyard with my best friend. He would put an apple on his head and I would shoot it off. He would have been thirty-four years old tomorrow. . . . "

Last week my wife and I celebrated our tin anniversary—ten years eating out of cans.

She's celebrating the tenth anniversary of her thirty-second birthday.

Every anniversary her husband takes a day off—and she takes a year off.

Antiques

When the wife came home with her arms loaded with antiques the husband commented: "I'm amazed to see all the things you would rather have than money."

One way to get rich is to be able to determine when a piece of junk becomes an antique.

If you really want trouble — walk into an antique shop and ask: "What's new?"

The man in the antique business—to make sure the stuff is authentic—makes it all himself.

They found themselves in a museum ogling a mummy. On the bottom was marked: "1268 B.C."
"What does that number mean?" asked the first one.
The second, all-knowing, said, "That must be the number of the car that hit him."

One man's junk is another man's antique.

In an antique shop on 3rd Avenue, the owner was "selling" the pair of early American portraits. "They're really old," he enthused, "they're ancestors."
"Whose?"
"Be my guest," he answered.

Apartment Houses

It was so cold in my apartment house —even the janitor was complaining. In fact, he came up and banged on the radiator with me.

This apartment house was so particular when I was looking for an apartment, they quizzed me longer than the C.I.A. "Do you have any children?—Do you have any dogs?" When I said no to both he continued, "We insist on quiet here—do you have any canaries or any other pets?"

"No," I said, "but I do have a fountain pen that scratches a little."

LANDLORD: "The rent control is out—we will have to raise your rent."
"Fine—because *I* can't raise it!"

"How much are they asking for your apartment right now?"
"About twice a day."

TENANT: "My roof is leaking and the rain keeps coming through the broken window—and my floors are flooded—how long is this going to continue?"
LANDLORD: "What the hell are you asking me for—what am I, a weatherman?"

The landlord insisted he could not carry him any longer. He was six months behind in his rent. "I'll give you just three more days and out you go."
"Good," said the tenant. "I'll take July 4th, Labor Day, and Christmas."

"I wish I were living back in the stone age—ask me why."
"Okay—why?"
"Because they used rocks for money—and would I like to pay off my landlord."

"Darling," he announced to his wife excitedly, "now we don't have to move to a more expensive apartment—the landlord just raised our rent."

Most of the new swank apartment houses don't allow children—and they're very strict, too. In one apart-

ment building on 3rd Avenue, there's a woman who's so afraid of being evicted —she's in her fifteenth month.

The best way to make the landlord paint the apartment is to move out.

The landlord ignored all the restrictions, rent laws, and frozen rents and tried to evict the tenant illegally anyway. But the tenant knew the law and answered in writing—short and to the point: "Sir, I remain. Yours truly."

The walls of the apartment are so thin—I asked my wife a question and I got four different answers.

The only time we'll get enough heat is when the house burns down.

APARTMENT HOUSE: Where the tenant and the landlord are both trying to raise the rent.

I tried to get into one of those low-priced housing projects—but the rent is too much.

Molly Picon says: "My grandmother raised eleven children in four rooms."
"How did she manage?" she was asked.
"Easy—she took in boarders."

The walls in the apartment were so thin—when my wife peeled onions—the guy next door cried.

Army
(*see War, Draft, Air Force, etc.*)

I don't know why they call them privates—they eat with 500 other guys —they sleep with 500 other guys—they can't even go to the can-teen alone.

The Declaration of Independence says "All men are created equal." Those guys who made that up never saw a bunch of draftees taking their physical.

Harvey Stone was the Will Rogers of World War II. He received the Bronze Star, the Purple Heart, and, adds Harvey, "The Purple Head — for scheming how to get out."

I loved the Army. Where else can you lie around in bed until four o'clock in the morning? The sergeant used to come around every morning and pat us on the head and say, "Good morning, little man from Army-land. Time to get up, up, up!" Everyone got up, too. Why not? He had a bayonet in his hand! I had the largest vaccination in the Army.

The food was great. My favorite dish was Filet of Sand. Another is Borscht and Alka Seltzer—then you belch in technicolor.

They had signs all over the Mess Hall, "Food is Ammunition." Why shoot 'em? Get 'em to eat it! Invite 'em to dinner and get 'em all.

One of the best things I liked about the Army were the sex films to show you what not to do while on pass. Then why go?

She had a lot of private affairs—until she married the colonel.

The general was wounded during a battle—his barber cut him.

I wonder what Private Adams did before he joined the Army. Every time he fires a shot—he wipes his finger prints off the gun.

The soldier was asked what kind of cook his wife was. "Figure out for yourself," he answered. "I'm the only soldier on the base who packs a lunch to go home."

PRIVATE SMITH: "Do you like it at this base?"
PRIVATE BROWN: "Yes—it's great."
PRIVATE SMITH: "You must have a lousy home life."

That French broad has been contributing to the delinquency of a major.

"My uncle has twelve medals—he won them during the war."
"He must have been a great sharpshooter."
"No—a great crapshooter!"

When I was in the Army they used to wake us at four o'clock in the morning. The first thing I used to do is run out and shake a tree. I figured if I'm awake why should the birds sleep.

I was the only guy in the Army who was awarded the yellow heart.

The chef noticed that the soldier wasn't eating his food. "You shouldn't waste food like that," he scolded. "Don't you know the old saying, 'Food will win the war'?"
"It sure would," the private agreed. "Now how do we get the enemy to eat here?"

If you believe the old saying old soldiers fade away—try getting into your old Army uniform.

The private told his buddies: "This has got to be love at first sight—I've only got an eight-hour pass."

Art
(see Artists)

CRITIC: "How do you get such a modernistic, wild effect?"
ARTIST: "I use a model with hiccups."

A woman in Greenwich Village looked at a sidewalk painter's wild modern painting and remarked, "How frightful!"

"I only paint what I see," the artist said haughtily.

"You shouldn't paint when you're in that condition," she replied.

Two five-year-old kids were looking at the abstract painting in the Guggenheim Museum. "Let's get out of here," one said, "before they say we did it."

"You're the first model I ever made love to," he lied tenderly.

"Really?" she glowed. "How many models have you had?"

"Five: a tree, an apple, a violin, and two swords."

After posing all day she asked the artist, "Well, does it look like me?"

"Hours ago, lady—I'm now improving it."

AT THE ART MUSEUM: "Look, mamma," the kid said to his mother. "This painting—they copied it from the calendar we got in our kitchen."

While touring France a couple from Texas decided to send some gifts to three friends at home. Sauntering into an art gallery, they picked out a Van Gogh, a Rembrandt, and a Picasso. "That'll be $600,000 in American money," the dealer told them. The husband paid him in cash and then turned to his wife. "Now that we've got the cards—let's go get the presents."

Mrs. Newly-Rich was told to get some culture. She walked into a famous Madison Avenue art shop. The first painting she saw was by one of the masters. It was a beautiful oil of a bum in ragged clothes sitting on a park bench.

"Sure," she remarked, "I'll never give those beggars a cent again. He's too broke to buy a decent suit but he's got money enough to get his picture painted."

Trying to figure out abstract art is like trying to follow the plot in a plate of alphabet soup.

ABSTRACT ART: Things are not as bad as they are painted.

He who claims things aren't as bad as they're painted has never seen pop art.

Artists
(*see Art*)

As soon as the pretty model comes in —the first thing he draws is the venetian blinds.

"Do you draw pictures in the nude?"
"No, I always wear a smock."

It's easy to recognize a modern painting—it's the one you can't recognize.

Many a time he had to paint on an empty stomach—he couldn't afford a canvas.

A modern artist is one who throws paint at the canvas, wipes it off with a cloth—and sells the cloth.

I hung the picture — because I couldn't find the artist.

ABSTRACT ART: The proof that things aren't as bad as they are painted.

There's only one way you can tell when a modern painting is completed: "If the paint is dry—it's finished."

A pop artist fell in love with one of his models—a can of soup.

I won't have any of those abstract paintings around my house. I have a teenage daughter and you never know for sure whether or not those paintings are decent.

209

A holdup man robbed Picasso and stole some of his paintings. When the police questioned the famous abstract artist, he drew a picture of the thief. "Now," he said, "you'll have no trouble capturing him." With the picture the gendarmes went out and arrested a one-eyed ballet dancer, the Eiffel Tower, and a wheelbarrow.

Astronauts
(*also see Martians*)

The astronaut is the second highest man has been—Dean Martin holds the record.

In Russia they let me visit a launching site. I met the astronaut. Through an interpreter I said, "He looks worried —what's he concerned about?" The interpreter said, "The landing—if he makes a mistake, he might come back here."

Two Jewish astronauts were talking. One said: "Forget the moon—everybody is going to the moon—we go direct to the sun."
"But we can't go to the sun—if we get within 13 million miles of the sun —we'll melt."
"Okay—then we'll go at night."

"Did the astronaut come down yet?"
"I don't know—I didn't see him go up—I live in the back."

Did you hear about the sporty astronaut? When the weather is nice— he wants to ride with the top down.

We'll really be in trouble if the astronauts form a union—like the taxi drivers. Imagine having to pay them by the mile?

Our astronauts have the latest equipment. Inside the space capsule, they have oxygen masks, pressurized space suits, automatic controls, safety ejector, and, in front of the seat, a little paper bag.

One astronaut's space suit costs 30,-000 dollars. And it only comes with one pair of pants.

When our first astronaut returned safely from his trip, the other astronauts asked him if he could give them any advice. He said, "The whole secret is—don't look down."

Trouble with being an astronaut— it's too seasonal.

We send the first girl astronaut to Mars and she returns a year later— pregnant.

What's so new about the way the astronauts count down—10-9-8-7; my wife has been counting her birthdays like that for years.

WIFE TO ASTRONAUT: "Just when we're beginning to get along with our neighbors—you want to go to the moon."

HE: "Isn't that great the way the two astronauts went around the world sixty-two times?"
SHE: "Big deal—you got money—you can travel."

Atomic Energy
(*see Science, etc.*)

With atom bombs, H-bombs, ballistic missiles, I'm moving into the Harmon Theatre—it hasn't had a hit in years.

With all these new-fangled bombs that can destroy worlds, my mother-in-law's only worry is: "Wherever they send you—I'm going with you."

Don't worry about the bombs—you want to be safe—just go to your friend at Chase Manhattan. He'll give you a 10,000-dollar loan. Then forget about it. He'll see to it that nothing happens to you.

"Our planes *now* travel faster than sound."
"Yeah? Try telling a secret to my mother-in-law."

A couple of scientists were watching their colleagues at the crap tables in Vegas between experiments.
"Say," said one of them, "that Anderson is gambling like there's no tomorrow."
"Maybe," said the other, "he knows something."

With all the new bombs that everybody claims they have and threatens to use — it doesn't pay to save Green Stamps or Raleigh coupons.

Auctions

The scene is an auction. Bidding for various objects is going furiously when the auctioneer suddenly slams down his hammer and announces: "A gentleman in this room has lost a wallet containing $1,000. If it's returned, he will pay a reward of $200." There's a moment's silence and then from the back of the room comes the cry, "$210."

Automation
(*see Computers, Office, etc.*)

Automation could never replace my brother-in-law. They still haven't found a machine that does absolutely nothing.

I'll be for it when they can find a machine to replace my mother-in-law.

"I know," the secretary said, "it's supposed to replace twelve men—but I'd rather have the men."

I really loused up the machine—I stepped on my card with my golf shoes. Do you know I'm now worth a million? If only my machine will tell it to my bank.

"Replacing you with automation," the boss said, "is going to be a tough job—I've never been able to figure out just what you do."

The only thing people do with their hands any more is scratch themselves.

I had a tough day at the office—the electronic brain broke down and I had to think all afternoon.

Automation is a $75-a-week clerk replaced by a $250,000 machine.

Automobiles
(*see Cars, Traffic, Accidents, Parking, etc.*)

Automobile manufacturers have a new safety test—they crush new cars with dummies in them as a test to study accidents and injuries. The truth is—they have made cars safer—for dummies. But that's great—considering all the dummies that are driving cars these days.

Talking about treacherous driving—did you ever own one of those really low sports cars and be surrounded by a dozen tall dogs?

It's not so easy to get parking tickets these days—first you got to find a place to park.

I got a friend that figured out a way to beat the parking tickets—he removed his windshield wipers.

A woman driver wouldn't have as much trouble squeezing into a parking space if she would imagine it was a girdle or a pair of shoes.

The traffic was so terrible the cars were bumper-to-bumper. Some were even closer than that. What traffic! One guy bought a car from a used car lot, and after two hours, he had to sell it back to the dealer—he couldn't get it out on the highway.

A friend of mine who was out driving that day was hit by another automobile. He wound up with eight holes in his hood and it wasn't a Buick. The top was down, and it wasn't a convertible! My friend looked like he had just finished ten rounds with Cassius Clay. From out of nowhere, a lawyer came. "Look here, man, I can get you some damages!"
The fellow said, "Nothing doing. I've got plenty of damages already. What I need are some repairs!"

He had to push his automobile two miles to a garage. And the way those garages take advantage of you! They made him push it back again two miles so they could send out a tow car for it!

One last word of advice: If you're out driving, just make sure you have a car.

The English sports car has a monocle instead of a windshield.

Babies
(*see Children, Juvenile Delinquents, Jokes for Children, Kids*)

I was a war baby—my parents took one look at me and started fighting.

I was such a big baby—when I was born the doctor was afraid to slap me.

I was offered a job as a baby-sitter. But who wants to sit on babies?

They said the baby looked like me—then they turned him rightside up.

The neighbors think the baby is spoiled—but all babies smell like that.

We feed our baby onions—so we'll find it in the dark.

Getting the baby to sleep is hardest—when she's about eighteen years old.

We spent three weeks poking a broom into the baby's face to get him used to kissing grandpa.

The best way to keep this baby quiet is to let him suck on a bottle of glue.

Many a woman's mistakes are covered by a baby blanket.

I was a premature baby—my father wasn't expecting me.

I read somewhere that in the world today a woman gives birth to a child every tenth of a second. Somebody better stop this lady before she falls down altogether.

"Doctor," the young married screamed over the phone, "my baby just swallowed a bullet—what should I do?"
"The first thing is—don't point him at anybody."

A woman in London gave birth to twins—one at 2 P.M. and the other at 8—you know the English—everything stops for tea.

I was born at home—but when my mother saw me she went to the hospital.

212

The six-year-old looked at the new wrinkled baby and remarked, "So that's why mother hid him under her coat for so long."

Joan Rivers says she was an ugly baby: "When my parents left me on a doorstep they were arrested. Not for abandonment—for littering."

Bachelors
(*see Men, Girls, Playboys, Playgirls, etc.*)

A bachelor is a guy who comes to work every morning from a different direction.

A bachelor wouldn't make the same mistake once.

A bachelor has nobody to share his troubles with—but then, why should a bachelor have troubles?

BACHELOR: "Come up to my apartment —we'll toast in the New Year with some beautiful imported champagne."
GIRL: "But the New Year is three months away."
BACHELOR: "What's our hurry?"

The only thing worse than being a bachelor is being a bachelor's son.

The widow advised the bachelor— "Take it from me—don't get married."

A bachelor is a man who is lucky in love.

A bachelor would rather have a woman on his mind than one on his neck.

A man calls himself a bachelor until he gets married—then you should hear what he calls himself.

A man who refused to fight used to be called a coward—today they call him a bachelor.

Not all men are fools—some are bachelors.

Bald
(*see Faces, Head, Barbers, etc.*)

He looks like somebody I shot into the side pocket this afternoon.

He has a beautiful head of skin.

His head looks like a landing field.

I wouldn't say he was bald—but he has the widest part I have ever seen.

He looks like his neck is blowing bubble gum.

I look into his head to tell the future.

Ballet
(*see Opera*)

"I don't dig ballet—the last time I went with friends there was a lot of money bet on the swan to live."— Woody Allen

Why do they have to dance on their toes? Why don't they just get taller dancers?

Bankruptcy
(*see Business, Offices, Bosses, etc.*)

Many a going business is going the wrong way.

Business was so bad that even people who didn't pay had stopped buying.

Things got so bad I asked the boss: "What goes? and he said: 'You!' "

213

Business is so quiet you can hear the overhead piling up.

This year business has gone directly from the summer slump to the fall recessional.

Business is really slow right now. A fellow walked into a place to change a twenty-dollar bill and they made him a partner.

A store which went bankrupt after only a few weeks displayed this sign: "Opened by mistake."

Banks
(see Money, Inflation, etc.)

I brought a one-cent check to the teller at the bank and asked him to cash it. "How do you want it," he asked, "heads or tails?"

Getting a loan from a bank is tough these days because of the tight-money situation. A senior loan officer was standing by the desk of a junior loan officer when the telephone rang. The junior officer answered, saying, "No . . . no . . . no . . . no . . . yes . . . no," and hung up. The senior officer questioned him immediately. What had he said "yes" to?

"Don't worry," said the junior officer reassuringly. "I said yes only when he asked me if I was still listening."

HUSBAND: "The bank has returned your check."
WIFE: "Splendid—what can we buy with it this time?"

A woman went into the bank and noticed there was a new face behind the window. "Has the cashier gone away to take a rest?" she inquired. "No," replied the new man, "he's gone away to avoid it."

A banker is a man who lends you an umbrella when the sun is shining and wants it back when the rains come.

A man asked for a $100,000 loan from the bank. The bank president remarked that it was a lot of money and asked the man for a statement. "Yes," said the man, "I'm optimistic."

A bank is a place where you keep the government's money until the tax man asks for it.

A bank robber opened the safe with his toes just so he could drive the fingerprint experts crazy.

The captured bank robber was told that the bank's hidden camera had taken pictures of him, and it was this that led to his capture. The bank robber replied, "Gee, do you think I could get some wallet-size for my wife?"

MISS GOTROCKS: "You! You want to marry me?"
YOUNG MAN: "Yes!"
MISS GOTROCKS: "But, my dear boy, you've only known me three days."
YOUNG MAN: "Oh, much longer than that, really! I've been two years in the bank where your father has his account."

A: "Where are you going to get your check cashed?"
B: "I don't know—I can't think of a single place where I'm unknown."

The Texan received his check back from the bank marked "insufficient funds." Then added—"ours—not yours."

The man who writes the bank advertising is not the man who makes the loans.

The bank is so big—they have a special window for hold-ups.

My wife had an accident at the bank —she got in the wrong line and made a deposit.

WIFE: "I can't be overdrawn—I still have five checks left."

"Why this bank?" the efficiency expert asked the new depositor.
"I'm in love with your teller," he answered.

Barbers
(*see Hair, Faces, Bald, etc.*)

A Times Square barber shop advertises: "Six barbers—*continuous discussion.*"

CUSTOMER: "Why did you drop that hot towel on my face?"
BARBER: "Do you think I was going to burn my fingers!"

"May I shave him, daddy?" the barber's son asked. "I need the practice."
"Okay—but be careful—don't cut yourself."

He spent twenty minutes combing his hair—and then forgot to bring it with him.

The barber was cutting me with every stroke of the razor. After half a dozen nicks, I sat up. "Will you give me a razor?" I asked.
"Why, do you want to shave yourself?" the barber asked.
"No—defend myself!"

BARBER: "Did you have catsup for lunch?"
CUSTOMER: "No."
BARBER: "Then I've cut your throat."

The way hair styles are today—you can't tell from the back if it's a man who needs a haircut or a woman who just had one.

"Just a shave, please—I haven't time to listen to a haircut."

"Do you want your hair cut?—or just change the oil?"

SIGN IN WINDOW: "4 barbers in attendance—Panel discussion."

The man told the barber he wanted the kind of haircut Tony Curtis has. "Can you give me exactly the same haircut?"
"Sure," the barber assured him. With that the customer sat back in the chair and dozed off.
Fifteen minutes later he woke up and looked in the mirror. Much to his horror, his head was completely shaved. He jumped out of the chair and screamed at the barber. "Tony Curtis. I told you I wanted a haircut like Tony Curtis."
"Sure," said the barber, "and that's what I gave you. I know what Tony Curtis' haircut looks like. Why, only last week I saw him on TV in 'The King and I.' "

Barber shop in hippie neighborhood has a window sign: "One barber—no waiting."

Bars
(*see Drinking, Restaurants, etc.*)

"I hate to see young girls like you hanging around in bars—why don't you come up to my apartment?"

"Do you serve women at the bar?"
"No, you have to bring your own."

215

Whiskey is a drink that takes away the taste of water.

SIGN IN BAR: "We don't have TV—but we have fights every night."

I asked the bartender for something tall and cold with plenty of gin in it— and he called his wife over.

The bartender put two cherries in my Manhattan—my doctor told me I should eat more fruit.

When men drink at bars—it means they have no wife to go home to—or they have.

I'm for safety belts on bar stools.

Beatnik and Bop Humor
(*see Hippies, etc.*)

DEFINITION OF A BEATNIK: A man on the bottom—looking down.

BEATNIK: Santa Claus—the day after Christmas.

"Sorry," the waitress explained, "the pie is gone."
"Oh that crazy pie," said the bopper. "I'll take two pieces."

Swimming in Florida waters a hipster yells, "An alligator just bit my leg!"
"Which one?" his pal asked.
"How do I know, man, all these alligators look the same."

"Who was that beatup baggage I saw you with? Where are all those mellow broads you usually dabble with?"
"What's the matter—don't you dig distortion?"

"Take me to Brooklyn, man, Bensonhurst," the man told the cab driver.
"I don't know how to get there," he answered.
"Fake it, man."

This beatnik came to the party incognito—he took a bath.

A beatnik home is one in which, no matter what time of day it is, you can always use the shower.

His place was such a mess—the phone rang—and he couldn't find it.

Two beatniks were walking down a street, and a man in front of them fell into a manhole. The man looked up and said, "Hey, fellow, give me a hand."
So, the two beatniks applauded.

Two bopsters were attending a concert when a fire broke out. All the musicians cleared the stage, and the audience began heading for the exits. "Come on, man, let's beat it," said one. "You go ahead, man," replied the pal. "I want to dig this crazy finale."

Two bopsters visited the Swiss Alps. A skier whizzed down the chute, then up into the sky. "We're in luck, man," grooved one bopster. "Somebody here sells our brand of cigarettes."

"What's a beatnik?"
"Those characters with dirty pants, filthy sneakers, long shaggy hair, and dirty sweat shirts."
"Oh I know them—we call 'em slobs."

The beatnik maid comes in every day and dirties up a little.

The headwaiter stopped the two beatniks at the door. "You can't come

216

in here without a tie," he insisted. They returned fifteen minutes later. Only one was wearing a tie.

"What about him?" the headwaiter demanded of the one without a tie.

"Him?" replied the beatnik. "That's my wife!"

I went to a beatnik wedding in Greenwich Village—and they gave the bride a shower just before the wedding.

Beauty Contests

When I worked in the Catskills, I was the social director at a hotel where the girls were so ugly—we had a beauty contest—and nobody won.

A raving beauty—is a girl who comes out last in a beauty contest.

A beauty contest is like a candy store—everything looks good—but you can't touch.

She won a beauty contest in England. It was a very foggy day in London town.

When she was twenty-one she was chosen Miss America—in those days there were very few Americans.

Beggars
(see Bum)

The nice old lady answered the door to the beggar who wanted something to eat. "Do you mind eating yesterday's soup?" she asked.

"No ma'm."

"Then come back tomorrow."

The boss was sitting at his desk unhappily when his assistant came in unannounced and announced, "There's a man outside who says he hasn't eaten in four days." "Bring him in," said the boss. "If he tells us how he does it, we can stay in business another month."

The beggar stood at the street corner and asked a passing gentleman for money.

"Not now," said the gentleman, "but I'll give you something on my way back."

"Nope, that won't do," said the beggar. "Why, you'd be surprised how much money I've lost giving credit that way."

The beggar approached the rich man for a dime. The millionaire refused but he offered to buy him a meal in the best restaurant in town. "I've already eaten," the bum said. "I need a dime for the parking meter."

My wife offered a suit to a beggar and said, "It'll only need a little alteration."

The bum said, "OK, no rush. I'll be back in a few days when you've had it fixed for me."

Robert Benchley
(see chapter on "Humorists")

Mr. Benchley was quietly drinking his martini in the corner when a lady approached him. "Don't you know," she said, "that stuff you're drinking is slow poison?"

"That's all right—I'm in no hurry."

"It took me fifteen years to discover I had no talent for writing—but I couldn't give it up because by that time I was too famous."

Mr. Benchley once sent a foreign check to his bank in New York with this legend on the back: "Having a wonderful time—wish you would cover!"

Benchley told any new listener about the clown in the circus who got himself shot out of a cannon—it was a great new act. When the new listener asked how he stood the shock, he answered, "I don't really know—we haven't found him yet."

"In America there are two classes of travel—first class and with children."

Benchley was spending the weekend at the estate of a very boring elderly maiden aunt. She had planned to go walking with him one morning but he excused himself because of bad weather. Later on she saw him sneaking out of the house alone. "Oh Robert," she cried, "has it cleared up?"
"Just partly—enough for me—but not enough for two."

Mr. Benchley was annoyed at all the hands out when he was leaving the fashionable hotel. When the doorman stuck his hand out and said, "I hope you won't forget me, sir!" Benchley grasped his hand and said warmly, "I should say not—I'll write you every week."

Jack Benny

"Give me my golf clubs, the fresh air and a beautiful woman as a partner—and you can have the golf clubs and the fresh air."

All through the years Jack and Fred Allen had their phony feud. Once, after Allen had massacred Benny with gags, Benny cried, "You wouldn't call me that if I had my writers with me."

Bob Hope says he remembers that during World War II Jack Benny was a dollar-a-year man. "You mean that's all he got?" he was asked. "Oh, no," Hope replied. "That was all he spent."

The honeymoon is really over when he phones to say he'll be late for dinner—and she's already left a note saying his TV dinner is in the freezer.

I like the one about the Englishman who says to the waiter, "Didn't you hear me say, 'Well done'?" The waiter, ignoring the rare steak, absent-mindedly answers, "Yes, sir. Thank you sir. It's seldom we get any thanks."

The captain of the cruise ship invited the rich couple to sit at the table with him.
"We spent a fortune to get the best of everything on this ship," the husband shouted, "and now they want us to sit with the help."

Fred Allen in his fun-feud with Jack Benny said, "There is a saying—you can't take it with you—but if you see a funeral procession with a Brink's armored car behind the hearse, you'll know Jack is having a try at it."

Remember the total eclipse of the sun? Jack Benny ran over to the Western Union office to send a night letter.

Milton Berle

What is this—an audience or an oil painting?

I know a three-fingered pickpocket—he steals bowling balls.

I was an old newspaperman—but I found out there was no money in old newspapers.

I never file my nails—I just cut them off and throw them away.

My girl was so skinny—she swallowed an olive and four men left town.

I lost my TV show. I knew I was in trouble when I found 50 per cent of the studio audience wasn't listening.

I have a lovely room and bath—it's a little inconvenient, though. They're in two different buildings.

My room is so small—I closed the door and the doorknob got in bed with me. I put the key in the keyhole—and broke the window.

I learned dancing with Arthur Murray—later I found it was more fun with a girl.

There's something about him—but he won't spend it.

The way she's built—it takes her twenty minutes to get her feet wet under a shower.

My brother is very superstitious—he won't work any week that has a Friday in it.

Guy called the doctor and said, "My kid just swallowed my pen—what should I do?" Doc said, "Use a pencil."

I said to my mother-in-law—make like this is your home—so she sold it.

I gave my wife a new watch for her birthday—waterproof, shockproof, unbreakable, and anti-magnetic. Absolutely nothing could happen to it—she lost it.

Bible Humor
(*see Religion, Ethnic Humor, Churches, etc.*)

"What's another name for God?" the little boy was asked.
"Harold," the child answered.
"How do you get that?"

"Well, when I say the prayers at night I say, 'Our Father which art in heaven, Harold be thy name.' "

The man hoeing in the field asked the farmer if he could stop to get a drink of water. "No," said the farmer. "Remember, it says in the Bible: 'Ho! Everyone that thirsteth'!"

Peter the fisherman was stopped by a bunch of hoodlums on the corner. "Is it true that your Master tells you to turn the other cheek? Is that in the Bible?" the head of the riffraff asked.
"Yes," said Peter quietly.
"Well—here's a slap on the kisser—now how about the other cheek?" When he slapped Peter the second time, on the other cheek, he smirked, "And here's another." As he lifted his hand for the third time Peter picked him up and threw him over the fence.
"It also says in the Bible," Peter reminded them, " 'Thou shalt not tempt the Lord.' "

As the waters of the Red Sea were parted Moses said, "Why do I always have to go first?"

"I'll be glad to turn the water into wine—but the first one that gets drunk is out of the game."

The song was first written by Cain for his brother Abel: "I'm walking behind you—"

The two lavender boys said to Noah, "You said two of every kind."

The youngster listened attentively as the Rabbi read the Bible. "May I ask a question?" the boy wanted to know.
"Sure."
"The Bible says the children of Israel built the Temple—the children of Israel crossed the Red Sea—the children of

219

Israel did this and that—didn't the grown-ups ever do anything?"

The Three Wise Men were on their way to Bethlehem. All of a sudden, one of them ground his camel to a halt. "Now listen, fellows," he said to the other two, "remember, no mentioning how much we paid for the gifts."

Two refugees were working on the Negev. They were tired and weary trying to make the desert bloom. "Who needed it?" said one with perspiration running down his body. "So we were persecuted a little in Russia, but who worked so hard?"
"You jerk," said the other, "don't you realize Moses walked forty years, day and night, just to get here? This is the Promised Land."
"You know something," the first refugee said, "if Moses walked one more day and night, we'd be on the Riviera right now."

As one of the boys said after the Last Supper, "Talk about miracles—Judas says he's buying tonight."

The kid said to his father, "The Rabbi told us a fantastic story about the Jews that were chased out of Israel—and they came to the Red Sea. The Jews are so smart, they saw the Egyptians following them—so they built a bridge over the Red Sea and went over in safety. But when the Egyptians kept coming—the Jews are so smart, they put dynamite under the bridge and when all the Egyptians came on top of the bridge the Jews blew up the bridge and the Egyptians fell in the Red Sea and were drowned."
"The Rabbi told you this story?" father wanted to know.
"No," said the boy, "but if I told you what the Rabbi told me—you'd never believe it."

Moses was addressing his audience after his chat on Mt. Sinai. Pointing to his Tablet, he said, "And now—a word from my sponsor."

As Pontius Pilate said to his prisoner, "This has nothing to do with the fact that you happen to be Jewish."

"Father—weren't the Apostles Jews?"
"Yes."
"So how come the Jews let go of a good thing like the Catholic Church and let the Italians grab it?"

I wish I were Adam. If I pulled a joke—no one could say, "I heard that one before."

"Why did you hit your sister?"
"We were playing Adam and Eve, and instead of tempting me with the apple—she ate it herself."

It happened in the Garden of Eden. "Do you really and truly love me?" Eve asked Adam.
"Who else?" he answered.

This lady wanted to mail a Bible to her son at college. The post office clerk wanted to know if the package contained anything breakable.
"Only the Ten Commandments."

Bills

She couldn't pay the grocer—she had given all she had to the butcher.

"Mama—the bill collector is here. Have you got the money—or do you want me to go out and play for a while?"

"Daddy, I saw mommy kissing the TV repairman this morning."
"My God! She wastes time with him and we owe the furniture man $300!"

220

WIFE: "I bought this dress for a song."
HUSBAND: "Okay—send a bill collector and I'll sing to him."

My wife should run for Congress—nobody brings so many bills to the house.

"You owe me this bill for a year. I tell you what I'll do—I'll meet you halfway. I'm ready to forget half what you owe me."
"Great—I'll meet you. I'll forget the other half."

There's something much bigger than money—bills.

I don't have any trouble meeting my obligations. My trouble is ducking them.

He got a bill from his dentist with this notation in red: "This bill is one year old." His answer came back quickly: "Happy Birthday."

Running into debt isn't so bad—it's running into creditors that hurts.

"Madam," the butcher said, "I can't give you any more credit—your bill is bigger now than it should be."
"I know that—make it out for what it should be and I'll pay it."

"If you didn't intend to pay the bill anyway, why the hell did you haggle on price with your tailor?"
"I didn't want him to lose so much."

"PLEASE pay the bills immediately. After all, we've done more for you than your mother—we've carried you for twelve months."

"How come you haven't hounded me to pay my bill?"
"I never ask a gentleman for money."

"But suppose he doesn't pay?"
"After a certain time if he doesn't pay, I know he's not a gentleman—and then I ask him."

Birthdays
(*see Anniversaries, Holidays, Age, Old Age, etc.*)

There's the story about the fellow who each day walked to work and passed a window where he saw a lady hitting a boy over the head with a loaf of bread. The fellow decided it was none of his business and walked on. He saw this same thing happen every morning for five months—each day, the lady hitting the boy with a loaf of bread. Then one morning he saw the woman toss an entire chocolate cake into the boy's face. Astounded, he peered into the open window and asked why. "Oh," the lady said, "it's his birthday."

It was the lavender lad's twenty-first birthday. A friend, unaware of this, called and suggested they get together. "I can't see you today," said the first lavender lad. "Why not?" asked the other. "Because today I am a man . . . I'll see you tomorrow, sweet."

"I'm looking forward to my twenty-third birthday."
"You're facing the wrong direction."

"Today is my wife's birthday."
"What are you getting for her?"
"Make me an offer!"

Her thirtieth birthday isn't far away —only eight years ago.

My wife is so economical—she had only twenty-six candles on her fortieth birthday cake.

221

At her birthday party, I tried to count the candles on the cake—but the heat drove me back.

WIFE: "For weeks I've been telling you not to buy me anything for my birthday and still you forgot to bring me something."

He always remembers your age—but forgets your birthday.

She never forgets her age — once she's decided what it's to be.

She's very loyal—years ago she reached an age she liked—and she's stuck to it.

She has a twin brother who is an identical twin except for one minor detail—he's forty-five and she's thirty-five.

She's celebrating the twenty-fifth anniversary of her thirty-fifth birthday.

At last she admitted she was forty—but she didn't say when.

She could add years to her life—just by telling the truth.

A well-adjusted woman is one who not only knows now what she wants for her birthday, but what she's going to exchange it for.

Birthstones

For Maid: The Soapstone
For Builder: The Cornerstone
For Politicians: The Blarneystone
For Executives: The Grindstone
For Stock Brokers: The Curbstone
For Motorists: The Milestone
For Pedestrians: The Tombstone
For Borrowers: The Touchstone

For Policemen: The Pavingstone
For Burglars: The Keystone
For Wit: The Headstone

Dean Martin and Phil Harris don't need any special birthstones—they are stoned all year 'round.

Joey Bishop

Last week I gave Dean Martin a cigarette lighter. He finished it in one gulp.

The other day I drove home filled with pride and a sense of achievement. I entered the house and there was my mother. "Ma," I said proudly, "I have a new Corvette outside."
Mamma shook her head sadly and said, "Please, Joey, don't bring her in the house."

I once called my mother during a hurricane. She got on the phone and said, "I can't talk to you now, the lines are down."

A salesman called on my wife and tried to sell her a freezer. "You'll save a fortune on your food bills," he promised.
"I'm sure you're right," said my wife, "but we're already saving a fortune with our new car by not taking a bus. We're saving a fortune with our new washing machine by not sending out laundry. We're saving a fortune with our new dishwasher by giving up the maid. The plain truth is that right now we just can't afford to save any more."

Art Linkletter has interviewed so many children he can't talk to you unless he bends down.

When I performed in Washington for the President, I didn't stay at the White House. My mother wasn't too crazy about the neighborhood.

The traffic was so heavy yesterday I drove fifteen miles in neutral.

I don't want to be a star overnight. I got a lot of things to do tomorrow.

My family was so poor we couldn't give my sister a Sweet Sixteen party till she·was twenty-eight.

American TV shows are very big in Europe. Lloyd Bridges is a natural in Venice.

Boats

"Do boats like this sink often?"
"Only once."

I was so seasick—I looked like my passport photo.

He is so rich—he bought a new yacht. The old one got wet.

MESSAGE TO SEA-DIVER: "Come up quick—the boat's sinking."

And you think you have trouble? What about the deep sea diver coming up—who passed his ship going down?

SAILOR: "They've just dropped their anchor."
LADY: "I was afraid they would—it's been dangling outside all day."

Her family is so exclusive—they didn't come over on the Mayflower—they had their own boat.

Bob and Ray
(*Bob Elliott and Ray Goulding*)

Kids, send in for your do-it-yourself hydrogen bomb kit. Be the first on your block to rule the world.

They're going fast, folks, so send in soon for your "get rich quick" burglary kit.

Buy Bob and Ray coffee. It's packed in a vacuum as clean as you'll find in your own vacuum cleaner.

We're now offering a special April sale on used Christmas cards.

And now to our on-the-spot reporter, Wally Ballu, and his wife Hulla . . .

And now it's time for Our Gal Saturday who asks the question, "Can a girl from a small mining town out West find love and happiness in a small mining town out East?"

And now our story asks the question, "Can a nice run-of-the-mill girl find happiness running a mill?"

There's been a crisis here at CBS. They had an emergency case in Studio 25 when young Dr. Malone dropped his pince-nez during a delicate operation. They tried to reach Doctor Stanton but he was on a house call.

Bookmakers
(*see Horse Racing and Sports*)

Definition of a Bookmaker:
That's a pickpocket who lets you use your own hands.

There's so much heat on the bookies —you can't even find one that won't pay off.

223

I don't bet with bookmakers any more—I give my money directly to the cops.

I bet fifty dollars on the horse to win—the next day I found out they sold her for twenty-five.

As one cop said to another, "My life is an open bookie."

The cops are really going after the bookies now. The bookies claim race prejudice.

Books

Your book is going like wildfire—everybody is burning it.

I'm a comparative unknown as a writer—and when you compare me to other writers, you'll know why I'm unknown.

My first book was so funny, one fellow fell out of his chair laughing—but I'm all right now.

My book is in the fifth printing—the first four were blurred.

It's a book-of-the-month selection—but how can you make money selling one book a month?

A book is like TV—it can reach millions of people who fortunately can't reach you.

Your book is selling like mad—whoever reads it goes away mad.

Your book is attracting big crowds—to television.

Your book is fine. The only trouble is the covers are too far apart.

Your book packs a wallop—as soon as I read it, I fell asleep.

"Have you read my last book?"
"I hope so."

Your book has a happy ending—I was so glad when it was over.

My latest book has sold 500,000 copies. If you can't get a copy—call me—I got 500,000 copies.

Who needs a dictionary? If you read one—you've read them all.

It's a little silly to spend six months writing a novel—when you can buy one for $3.98.

There are so few books in my house—when the TV set is busted—we have to talk to each other.

Bob Orben dedicates his book to his wife, "Without whose aid I never could have been able to spend the money my last book made."

The dedication in one book I wrote was to my wife Cindy, "Who spent her days writing this book with me—and spent the royalties before I received them."

Earl Wilson's dedication was, "To the wonderful little woman who cooks my meals, darns my socks, and rears my son—my mother-in-law."

Another warm dedication, "To my wife, without whose constant companionship on my trips—I'd have met a hell of a lot more girls."

I gladly dedicate this book to the one I shall always owe a great deal as long as I live—the Collector of Internal Revenue.

"When I want to read a book—I write one."—DISRAELI

My book is in its twentieth printing —we printed them one at a time.

Shakespeare's plays are nothing but famous quotations—strung together.

I read the dictionary but I don't care for it—it changes the subject too often.

Oh, I don't like the telephone book —a lot of names but no plot.

Larry Gore dedicates his book *Blintzkrieg '67* about the Israeli-Arab war:—"To my wife Selma—who always puts up a better fight than the Egyptians."

Book Titles

Brain Surgery—Self Taught.

How to Build a Swamp.

How to Retire at the Age of Eight.

Love Letters from King Faisal to Phyllis Diller.

Musical Favorites of Dr. Sam Sheppard.

Will the Pressure Cooker Replace the Atomic Bomb?

How to Cheat at Badminton

How to Stop Raising Rabbits

Bores

When there's nothing more to be said—he's still saying it.

He lights up a room—by leaving it.

He says everything but "Good-bye."

He never opens his mouth unless he has nothing to say.

He's very cultured—he can bore you on any subject.

No matter how crowded the party is —there's always room for one bore— who approaches every question with an open mouth—and a head to match.

Borscht Belt Laughs

My father received this letter in answer to a request for accommodations at a hotel in Monticello:
Dear sir:
We regret to inform you that all the worthwhile accommodations are already taken. We have nothing left but "Luxury Lodge."

Today, the Borscht Belt is so big— one hotel is thinking of air-conditioning the forest. Another is planning an indoor mountain. A third will have tiger hunting under glass.

At one luxury hotel a rich manufacturer fell in the pool and would have drowned if the lifeguard hadn't pulled him out. He asked a friend: "What do you tip for a thing like that?"

The lifeguards were working over a young lady they had just fished out of the water. "What are you doing?" her father asked. "We're giving her artificial respiration," one answered.
"I can afford it," he said, "give her the real thing."

I regret that I have but one wife to send to the country.

Vacations are easy to plan—your boss tells you when, and your wife tells you where.

A resort in the Catskills is going to make a fortune—no more actors—they're going to book only unmarried doctors and lawyers.

The hotel had so many "dogs" that one July 4th they had a beauty contest —and nobody won.

"Will I get a sin for playing golf on the Sabbath?"
"The way you play—it's a sin to play any day."

This fellow was crazy about the chambermaid, but she kept running away from him. One day he finally grabbed her and whispered his dishonorable intentions in her ear. To his amazement, she readily consented. "If that's the way you felt, Olga," he panted, "why have you been running away from me all this time?"
"Well," she said, "all time I tink ya vant extra towel!"

Grossinger's, the Catskill Mountains resort, observes dietary laws adhered to by the Jewish people, and accordingly has two kitchens: one where milk or dairy products are prepared and the other for meats. Strictly separate.
One night I drove up to emcee an all-star show and found that due to alterations the theatre was closed and the performance was scheduled to go in the dining room. A stage, spotlights, etc., had been set up and a thousand persons jammed the huge hall. After the overture, I took over with greetings and opening jokes.
As I began to introduce the first act, "Tip, Tap and Toe," two of the hoofing trio hissed from the side near the kitchen door: "Stall, stall . . . Toe just got here and he's changing clothes."
So I announced, "The boys need another minute. One of them is changing clothes."

Paul Grossinger, sitting out front, yelled, "Where?"
I pointed and said, "Right through that door."
"Oh, my God," he wailed, "in the dairy kitchen?!"

L.B.J. was in the Catskills last summer for the first time. They have a sign at the Nevele in Ellenville where the President spent his time: "L.B.J. shlept here."

The people on the Borscht Belt have their own way of speaking. They answer a question with a question: "How do you feel?"—"How should I feel?"
"What's new?" — "What could be new?"
After the President's visit to the Borscht Belt, I asked him: "Did you enjoy it?" "Why not?" he answered.

My room has a beautiful view—if you look straight up.

My room is so small—when a girl comes in she *must* lie down.

BELLHOP: "You're not going to forget me, Mr. Traum?"
MR. TRAUM: "No, I'll write you regularly."

Sign in bathroom: "Watch your children—don't throw anything in the bowl."

Sam Levenson recalls: "The Catskills have everything: girls, bedbugs, handball, chicken (for ten straight weeks one summer), milk from a hot cow, swimming in a pool about the same size as in the picture postcard, and nature —manure at my window."

Max was standing in front of the hotel in Fallsburgh when the farmer passed. "Good morning," the city man greeted him.
"Mornin'," answered the farmer.

"Where are you going?"

"'T' town."

"What have you in the wagon?"

"Manure."

"What do you do with the manure?"

"Spread it over the strawberries."

"Why don't you come over to our place? *We get sour cream!*"

Bosses
(*also look for Office, Business, Executives, Work, Employment*)

EMPLOYEE: "Boss, could I have Monday off? It's my twenty-fifth wedding anniversary."

ANGRY BOSS: "Do I have to put up with this every twenty-five years?"

He'll raise the roof before he raises your salary.

"You can't help liking him," one of his employees said to another. "If you don't he fires you."

"You look worried, boss."

"Listen, I have so many worries that if something happened today, I wouldn't have time to worry about it for another two weeks."

Ability is what will get you to the top—if the boss has no daughter.

"I don't like yes-men," the boss told his new clerk. "I want you to tell me what you really think—even if it costs you your job."

"What's this I hear about your going to church and praying for a raise? Don't you know I never stand for anybody going over my head?"

1ST SECRETARY: "So you thought I was going to marry the boss, huh? Well, I just broke our engagement."

2ND SECRETARY: "That's too bad. What happened?"

1ST SECRETARY: "Well I saw him in his swimsuit and he looked so different without his wallet."

Boy Scouts

The eleven-year-old Cub Scout went on a hunting trip with his troop. He sent his mother a post card. "Yesterday our scoutmaster took us on a mountain climbing expedition. I wasn't too good so I broke a leg—but don't worry—it wasn't one of mine."

Two Boy Scouts whose younger brother had fallen into a pond rushed home to mother with tears in their eyes. "We're trying to give him artificial respiration," one of them cried. "But he keeps getting up and walking away."

During a first-aid course for Boy Scouts, the question was asked, "What would you do if you swallowed a house key?" One boy answered: "I'd climb in through the window."

Brides
(*see Marriage*)

The bride didn't look happy—she looked triumphant.

Telling that bride what she should know on her wedding night—is like giving a fish a bath.

The only time you see a blushing bride these days—is when the groom doesn't show up.

BRIDE'S FATHER TO GROOM: "My boy, you are the second happiest man in the world."

Did you hear about the sleepy bride who couldn't stay awake for a second?

The bride was so ugly—everybody kissed the bridesmaid.

The bride was so ugly—everybody kissed the groom.

British Humor
(*see chapter, "International Humor"*)

A woman in a court in London was charged with shoplifting. The magistrate asked if she had anything to say in her own behalf.

"Yes, your honor," she said proudly, "I only take British goods."

"I think it's disgusting that some of our comedians earn more than cabinet ministers."

"Well, it's only fair: on the whole, they're funnier."

PEDDLER: "Any pens, pencils, plates, pots, teapots, or baskets today?"
LADY OF THE HOUSE: "If you don't go 'way I'll call the police."
PEDDLER: " 'Ere you are, mum—whistles, sixpence each."

DOCTOR: "Now what about this ear?"
COCKNEY PATIENT: "This 'ere wot?"

I was visiting an English friend and his wife for the weekend, and one morning I accidentally walked in on the wife in her bath. I immediately rushed to the husband and apologized. He looked up and said nonchalantly, "Skinny old thing, isn't she?"

"I'll give you fifty shillings for that pup."

"Oh, sir, that's impossible. That pup belongs to me wife, and she'd sob 'er 'eart out—but I tell yer wat—give me another twenty bob an' we'll let 'er sob a little!"

BUTLER: "The post, m'lady."
THE LADY: "Oh—Christmas cards, I imagine. Well, Jeeves, examine them carefully—and if you consider any of them too familiar—just destroy them!"

"What's all the commotion at Percy's 'ouse?"
"Nothin' much—they're takin' 'im away in the ambulance for beatin' 'is missus."

POLICEMAN: "Beg pardon, sir, if you're the dog-faced gentleman with the bald head, the green teeth, the vegetable nose, and ears like taxi doors —I am to tell you that your wife couldn't wait for you any longer and she'll see you at home."

Jenkins and Diggs had a big fight but the bartender insisted they make up.

"I hold no anger in me," Diggs said, "and to prove it I'll drink to yer—'ere's lookin' at yer—and 'eaven knows that's a real heffort!"

Brooklyn
(*see Phil Foster*)

If we didn't have Brooklyn, where would the other end of the bridge rest?

"How could a guy almost blind himself drinking coffee?"
"He left the spoon in the cup!"

He was aping one of his Brooklyn heroes . . . from Murder, Incorporated. He was shot and stabbed coming out of a candy store with the halvah still in his teeth. He was bleeding from head to foot and it was three blocks to his home. He crawled painfully on his hands and knees all the way. He was losing blood rapidly and was near collapse as he inched his way up the steps to the door of his home. He knocked on it weakly and his mother opened the door. He crawled into the room and fell at her feet. "Dolling," she soothed, "first you'll have a bite to eat—then we'll talk."

How about the tough neighborhood he hailed from. "It was so tough that a cat with a tail was considered a tourist, and we used to play games like spin the cop."

Bums
(*see Beggars*)

This bum approached the fat lady and begged: "Lady, I haven't eaten in four days."
"I wish I had your will power."

LADY: "Do you think it proper to go from door to door begging for food?"
BUM: "No—but they refuse to bring it to me."

He's not afraid of work—he's fought it for years—and won.

He doesn't drink coffee in the morning because it keeps him awake all day.

He's the idol of the family—he's been idle for years.

A guy tossed a nickel in the beggar's cup but didn't take a pencil. The beggar advised him, "Whether you take one or not—pencils cost ten cents each now."

Burlesque
(*see Strippers, Vaudeville*)

The first time I went to a burlesque show I saw something I never expected to see—my father sitting in the first row.

George Burns Monologue
(*see "Double Act" for Burns and Allen act*)

GEORGE

You know today it costs a young fellow ten dollars to take a girl to lunch. When I was a boy, if you asked your father for ten dollars it meant you were going to get married, and have enough money left over to open a business. . . . In those days money went a long way. For a dollar you could take a girl to dinner and to a movie and have sodas afterwards. My only problem was to find a girl who had a dollar. . . . I remember when I was seventeen I had a real big date, and my father gave me a dollar. I told him I'd be home at twelve, but I didn't get in till four in the morning. There was my father, sitting up. He wasn't worried about me, he was waiting for his change. My father didn't believe in spoiling his sons. He made us work for our money. And he started us out pretty early. Once at dinner he suddenly pointed at me and said, "Look at that big boy, sits around and does nothing but eat!" I really wasn't that big, but the high chair I was sitting in made me look that way. . . . And when I was a kid, it wasn't always girls. If I had a few nickels saved, I'd go to a ball game. They let you in for fifty cents if you wore long pants, and twenty-five cents if you wore short pants. One day I figured out a way to get in for nothing, but I caught cold before I even left the house. . . .

I remember some of the tricks I used to save money. When a girl suggested dinner, I always said, "Fine," and then I'd go to her house and have it. . . . And I'd sit around her parlor and eat some fruit and candy and smoke a good cigar. I wouldn't go out with a girl unless her father smoked good cigars. . . . And if she said, "How about going

229

to a movie," I'd give her a kiss, and ask her if any boy had ever given her a better one. By the time she'd named the boys, it was too late for the movie. . . . But if she insisted on going out somewhere, I was a good sport about it. And when she got back, I was still there smoking her father's good cigars. After a while my reputation got around. You know how fathers sit in the parlor and watch their daughters. The fathers I knew used to sit in theirs to watch their cigars.

Business
(*see Office, Bosses, Percentage, Employment, Work, Executives, etc.*)

Sign on closed Broadway store: *"We undersold everybody."*

I wanted my son to share in the business—but the government beat me to it.

A feller called his partner from Miami and said, "Sam, this is Max, how's everything in New York?"
SAM: "Very good."
MAX: "How's the weather up there?"
SAM: "The weather's how it should be."
MAX: "How's business in the shop?"
SAM: "Very good, but I got bad news for you."
MAX: "What's the matter?"
SAM: "We've been robbed."
MAX: "Don't be silly, put it back!"

Two partners decided to take a trip to Florida. Just as they got on the train and were seated comfortably, one of them jumped up and screamed, "My God! I left the safe open!" The other partner shrugged his shoulders and replied, "What are you worried about? We're both here, ain't we?"

1ST SALESMAN: "I'd like to learn the secret of your success as a house-to-house salesman."

2ND SALESMAN: "Oh, it's easy. The minute a woman opens the door I say, 'Miss, is your mother in?' "

Whenever the American businessman comes up with a new idea—a month later the Russians invent it—and two months later the Japanese copy it and sell it to us cheaper.

"Business is so bad—this last year I've been losing at least $500 a week—week after week."
"Then why don't you give up the business?"
"Then how am I going to make a living?"

"I can't understand it," he cried to his partner, "here we are bankrupt—through—kaput—and only yesterday the President said business was booming."
"Maybe the President has a better location."

The preacher was lecturing to his flock: "Remember, my good friends, there will be no buying and selling in heaven—"
"That's not where business has gone," a salesman in the rear mumbled.

Business is so bad that even people who don't intend to pay aren't buying.

The young business executive gave an interview to the *Wall Street Journal* and bragged: "Those early days were tough—but I put my shoulder to the wheel, rolled up my sleeves, gritted my teeth—and borrowed another 100,000 dollars from my father."

We're a non-profit organization—we don't mean to be—but we are.

An efficiency expert died and was being carried to his grave by six pallbearers. As they approached their destination the lid popped open and the efficiency expert sat up and shouted, "If you'd put this thing on wheels, you could lay off four men."

A big business tycoon died and went to his eternal resting place. When he arrived in the other world, he was greeted by a salesman who used to visit him on earth. The salesman greeted him with a big hello. "Max, old boy, I'm here for the appointment." "What appointment?" asked the businessman. "Don't you remember?" asked the salesman. "Every time I used to try to see you at your office, you'd tell me you'd see me here."

"How can you make money selling watches so cheap?"
"Easy—we make our profit repairing them."

If at first you do succeed—it's probably your father's business.

BUSINESSMAN: He talks golf at the office and business on the golf course.

Then there's the absent-minded businessman who took his wife to dinner instead of his secretary.

Cads
(*see Mean*)

His parents never struck him—except in self-defense.

They're speaking well of him lately —he must be dead.

Someday he'll go too far—and I hope he stays there.

What good is asking him to act like a human being—he doesn't do imitations.

He and I have a lot in common—we both think he's wonderful.

I owe everything I have to him— ulcers, headaches, nausea. . . .

Godfrey Cambridge

Block busting is when one of our colored brothers moves into an all-white neighborhood and the white people are supposed to panic and start throwing bricks and bombs and burning crosses. Now the Negro who's living there is not afraid of bricks and bombs and burning crosses—he's afraid of another Negro moving into the neighborhood.

Now I remember we were the first one in our block and my mother came running in one day and shouted, "Look, they're moving in," and I said, "Ma, do you know *they* are *us?*"

I got off the bus in Scarsdale by accident and in the fifteen minutes it took me to get another bus, property values dropped 50 per cent. I remember when I just got out of college and was looking for a job and I walked into this office building and there I saw my soul brother in the lobby of this building sweeping and mopping the floor, and I asked him where the personnel office was and he said, "We don't hire colored help," and I said, "I'm hip. . . ."

I ran into this cat on the train and there he was in his overalls and his attaché case and he sat down next to a white bejeweled Scarsdale dowager and she said, "Hmph—colored people," and he said, "Where—where?"

When this man goes to the store to buy a watermelon he's so ashamed he says, "Wrap it up and put handles on it." You meet him on the street and ask him what he's got there. He says, "My bowling ball!"—Did you ever see an oblong bowling ball?—And he takes it home and he won't eat it in the dining room, 'cause he's afraid someone would see him through that big picture window, so he takes it into the closet and eats it, seeds, rind, and all, and when he drives from Scarsdale and reaches a Negro neighborhood, he acts just like the white people do, he says, "Lock your doors, colored people live here!" He ought to remember he used to be colored.

I keep telling all my white actor friends, "Go on, fool, keep tanning yourself, you'll be tanning yourself out of a job." And I have a whole lot of experience to prove it.

Cannibals

The chief asked the U. S. State Department to send him a comic, in cultural exchange, who tells dirty stories—he wanted to have some spiced ham for dinner.

CANNIBAL: "I'm very hungry."
WAITER: "Would you like to see the menu?"
CANNIBAL: "No, the passenger list."

Oh, believe it or not, the cannibal ate his mother-in-law—then found she still disagreed with him.

This young cannibal chief noticed a particularly beautiful young lady about to be placed in the burning kettle. "Wait," he shouted to the chef, "I'll have my breakfast in bed."

The chief's wife sent a message to another tribal chief in the neighborhood, "Please come and visit Saturday night—we're having the Browns for dinner."

232

As one teenage cannibal said to his date: "Let's take a stroll down to the old campfire and see who's cooking."

Johnny Carson

We spared the rod—and got a beat generation anyway.

Adam may have had his troubles, but he never had to listen to Eve talk about the other men she could have married.

There are some people who ask if an astronaut has the qualifications to run for Congress. I don't know why not. After all, he's already been around the world three times at government expense!

Benjamin Franklin may have discovered electricity, but the man who invented the meter made all the money

Before a man is married, he lies awake all night long thinking of what she said; after marriage, he falls asleep before she has finished saying it.

A Hollywood producer received a story entitled, *The Optimist*. He called his staff together and said, "Gentlemen, this story is great, but the title must go. It's got to be switched to something simple. We're intelligent and know what an optimist is, but how many of the morons who will see the picture—will know he's an eye doctor?"

If you want a thing done well—don't do it yourself.

Caution

Caution is the fellow who makes a dinner reservation at an umbrella-topped hot-dog stand.

Cemeteries
(*see Tombstones, Death*)

The man was crying as he knelt in front of the three tombstones lined up next to each other.

"Relatives of yours?" a passerby asked, just to be friendly.

"This one is my first wife," he offered. "She died from eating poisoned mushrooms. The second is my second wife—she also died from eating poisoned mushrooms!"

"What about the third?" the man asked.

"Fractured skull."

"How come?"

"She wouldn't eat the poisoned mushrooms."

The town is so healthy that they had to shoot a traveling salesman to start the cemetery.

He was accused of stealing a car. He pleaded guilty with an explanation. "The car was parked outside the cemetery—so I thought the owner was dead."

Charity

The jeweler was approached by a fund raiser "for a very worthy cause." "Can I ask you something?" asked the jeweler. "I have a brother who has six children to support, and he's not working. Would you call that a worthy cause? I have an elderly, unmarried sister who hasn't worked in thirty years. Would you call that a worthy cause? I got an uncle who's on relief. Would you call that a worthy cause? My father hasn't got food to eat. Would you call that a worthy cause?" "Of course," nodded the other man. "Well," said the jeweler, "I don't do a damn thing for these people. Why should I do something for you?"

The big game hunter was lost in the jungle. He was missing for weeks. He built a little shelter and tried to stay alive. They sent a searching party who got to the shelter just as he was ready to collapse from hunger and fever. The rescuers knocked on the door. "Who is it?" he asked weakly. "The Red Cross," came the brisk answer. "I gave at the office," the dying man said.

He announced his donation every year at the charity dinner: "Ten thousand." And he made out the check—but it always bounced. This year they insisted—"No checks. We don't tell you what to give—but it must be cash or keep your mouth shut." When it came donation time, he stood up and hollered, "200 dollars in cash and here it is—but don't deposit it until a week from Thursday."

I know one charity that collected 5 million dollars and doesn't even have a disease yet.

At every one of the charity dinners, everybody gets a chance to take bows, tell jokes and make speeches before he makes his donation. As one toastmaster said, "I'm not going to stand up here and tell you a lot of old jokes—but I'll introduce speakers who will."

At a certain affair recently, one member announced that he was making a donation of $1,000. Another announced, "I'll give $5,000!" A third brought the auditorium down when he cried, "I'm giving $10,000!"

The pledges are always followed by an officer of the organization, making a plea for a little extra dough. Always saying: "Now who'll give more money, in the name of something they hold near and dear to them?" With that, the big donor got up and cried, "I now give $500 more for something I hold near and dear to me—$10,000 I just gave you!"

233

The investigator for the Internal Revenue phoned the head man of a charitable organization. "Did Mr. Frank Fump give you a $10,000 donation last year like he says?"

"Not yet," he answered gleefully— *"but he will!"*

"I'm sorry," the secretary told the man collecting for the hospital fund, "but Mr. Adams can't see you today— he has a sprained back."

"Well, tell Mr. Adams I didn't come here to wrestle him—I just want to talk to him."

I went to a very odd kind of charity auction. Everybody was told to bring something they didn't have any use for—68 women brought their husbands!

The shady lady visited the local community chest and offered, "Honey, I'd like to donate 5,000 grand to the chest."

"Madam," said the chairman, "and I don't use the word loosely, we don't need that kind of money."

The co-chairman poked him and said, "Take it, jerk—it's our money anyway."

Cheapskates

(see Scotland in "International Humor" chapter, also Scotland)

He's so cheap that the only time he'll pick up a check is when it's made out to him.

When the check comes—he gets a slight impediment of the reach.

I'm sure you know about the cheap Texan who still has the first million he ever made.

They were trying to decide who was the stingiest man in town when someone told about Jones.

"One day Jones was walking down the street and he found a package of cough drops. That night he made his wife sleep out in the rain to catch a cold."

He's so stingy he heats the knives so his wife won't use too much butter.

SUE: "Are you saving any money since you started your budget system?"

HELEN: "Sure. By the time we have balanced it up every night, it's too late to go anywhere."

Sign on a Scotch golf course: "MEMBERS WILL KINDLY REFRAIN FROM PICKING UP LOST GOLF BALLS UNTIL THEY HAVE STOPPED ROLLING."

He's so cheap that he gets angry because gum machines won't take credit cards.

They stopped the crime wave in Scotland by putting up a sign over the jailhouse saying: "ANYONE CAUGHT AND PUT IN JAIL WILL HAVE TO PAY HIS BOARD AND LODGING."

In Scotland they had to take the "Pay-as-you-leave" cars off the streets when they found two Scotsmen starving in one of them.

"Stand behind your lover," said the Scotsman to his unfaithful wife. "I'm going to shoot you both."

"Goodbye," said McIntosh, "and don't forget to take little Donald's glasses off when he isn't looking at anything."

"My Scotch boy friend sent me his picture."

"How does it look?"

"I don't know, I haven't had it developed yet."

A Scot was engaged in an argument with a conductor as to whether the fare was five or ten cents. Finally the disgusted conductor picked up the Scotsman's suitcase and tossed it off the train, just as they passed over a bridge. It landed with a splash.

"Mon," screamed Sandy, "isn't it enough to try to overcharge me, but now you try to drown my little boy?"

HUSBAND: "I suppose you won't go to the opening without a new gown?"
WIFE: "I should say not."
HUSBAND: "I thought so—so I only got one ticket."

She's so cheap that she tells the Chinese waiter to wrap up the Chinese food that's left—says she has a Chinese dog at home.

Cheap is cheap—but she uses a substitute for margarine.

Somebody suggested he give his daughter cash as a wedding gift. "Oh, no," he said, "you can't get cash wholesale."

He even found a way to save money on his honeymoon—he went alone.

He's saving all his toys for his second childhood.

He tries to make every dollar go as far as possible—and every girl too.

You get in five minutes late and he docks your pay. You get in five minutes early and he charges you rent.

When he pays his own check—he's treating.

He's always the first to put his hand in his pocket and the last to bring it out again.

Cheap—but who walks in a drug store and orders one Kleenex?

If he were at the Last Supper he would ask for separate checks.

You've paid for dinner the last eight times—let's flip for this one.

Cheating

All the world loves a lover—except the husband.

Sitting in a restaurant, Mr. Klein said to his wife, "It's about time you knew it—I want to tell you before you find out from somebody else. See that blonde sitting there? She's my mistress."

"You bum! After thirty-five years I've been faithful—you got a mistress?" she cried.

"Not only that," he continued, "we all do it. See that brunette with the bangs? That's Pincus' mistress."

"That little runt got a mistress? That dirty—"

"And see that redhead with the hair up on her head? That's Rubin's mistress!"

"How do you like that. That fat nothing got a mistress," she squealed. "You know something, Max, I like ours the best."

The wife found her husband with her girl friend. The argument was hot and heavy. "Let's play gin for him," the girl suggested when they couldn't find a solution. "If I lose, I give him up— if you lose you give him up."

"Well," the wife answered, "to make it more interesting—let's play for a penny a point."

235

He never goes back on his word— without consulting his lawyer.

"Did you sleep with my wife?" threatened the husband.
"Not a wink," he replied.

Comic Morty Gunty now laughs at his old trick of making a person-to-person call to himself at home so he could tell his family where he was without paying the toll charges. After arriving in New York, he put in a call to himself in Chicago so his mother would know he arrived safely. When the phone rang, his mother answered the phone. The operator asked if Morty Gunty was there. "No, he's not," his mother said, "and tell him to be sure to wear his sweater."

I wouldn't say he doesn't trust his wife—but she is the only lady in town who has a combination lock on her zippers.

The husband saw his wife going into the movies with a strange man but he didn't follow them—he had already seen the picture.

Imagine that cheating sweetheart of mine? I've been going with her two years and I never knew she was married —until my wife told me.

For years I wondered where my husband spent his evenings. One night I came home early—and there he was.

Mr. and Mrs. Davis met his girl friend accidentally. The wife acknowledged the introduction and said, "My husband has told me so little about you."

"I know a guy who's been wearing a girdle for three months—ever since his wife found it in the glove compartment of his car."—Henny Youngman

Children
(*see Kids, Babies, Parents, Jokes for Children, and Juvenile Delinquents*)

Uncle asked the eight-year-old if his two-year-old brother had started talking yet.
"Why should he talk?" the kid groaned. "He gets everything he wants by yelling."

Their little baby was very quiet. It never spoke. They were pleased while he was a baby, but as he grew up he was also quiet and never once spoke. Finally, when the kid was eight years old and had never uttered a sound, all of a sudden he said, "Pass the salt." Shocked, the father said, "How come in eight years you never spoke?" The kid replied, "Well, up to now everything was all right."

The mother reprimanded her son for using a four-letter word.
"But, mother," the boy explained, "Tennessee Williams uses that word all the time."
"So don't play with him no more."

Five-year-old: "Why does it rain, daddy?"
"To make the flowers grow—and the grass and the trees."
"So why does it rain on the sidewalk?"

The three-year-old bragged to her mom that she learned to write in school today.
"What did you learn to write?" mom asked.
"I don't know—I can't read."

My child is very sensitive. If he does something wrong, beat the child NEXT to him and that will be punishment enough for him.

Last week I told my son about the birds and bees. Now he wants to know about Brigitte Bardot.

The kids almost wrecked the house. When their parents arrived home, mother wanted to know who started it.

"It all started," one kid said, "when Charlie hit me back."

Kids rarely misquote you—especially when they repeat what you shouldn't have said.

Granpa was doing some carpentry at home and asked his grandson to bring him a screwdriver.

The kid came back a few minutes later and announced, "I have the vodka, but I can't find an orange."

Jokes for Children

JANE: "Peanuts are fattening."
JUNE: "How do you know?"
JANE: "Did you ever see a skinny elephant?"

PASSENGER: "What good is your timetable? The trains never keep time."
CONDUCTOR: "Well, how would you know they were late if it weren't for the timetable?"

PASSENGER: "Does this train stop at San Francisco?"
CONDUCTOR: "Well, if it doesn't, there will be a big splash."

"Give me a round trip ticket, please."
"Where to?"
"Back here."

"How long can a man live without brains?"
"I don't know—how old are you?"

"How did you enjoy the movie?"
"Awful. I could hardly sit through it a second time."

"Do you understand why Robin Hood robbed only the rich?"
"Sure—because the poor had no money."

There is a pupil in our class who is so thin that when he stands sideways the teacher marks him absent.

An autobiography is a history of motor cars.

"Did you buy any Christmas Seals?"
"No, I wouldn't know how to feed them."

"Do you like codfish balls?"
"I don't know. I've never been to one."

"This goulash is terrible."
"That's funny—I put a brand new pair of goulashes in it."

"How do foreign dishes compare to American dishes?"
"They break just as easily."

"Which hand do you use to stir your tea?"
"My right hand."
"Funny—I use a spoon!"

"Do you believe in free speech?"
"Sure!"
"Good—mind if I use your telephone?"

Churches
(*see Religion, Restricted, Ethnic Humor, etc.*)

A clergyman was telling a very interesting story when his little girl interrupted, "Now, daddy, is that really true—or is it just preaching?"

The old maid was telling her friend who was visiting from a different city, "Our church is so small—when the minister says, 'Dearly beloved,' I blush all over."

The preacher was telling his clan that there are over 700 different kinds of sin. He was besieged with mail and phone calls the next day from people who wanted the list—to make sure they weren't missing anything.

Coming out of church, Mrs. Peterson asked her husband, "Do you think that Johnson girl is tinting her hair?"
"I didn't even see her," admitted Mr. Peterson.
"And that dress Mrs. Hansen was wearing," continued Mrs. Peterson. "Really, don't tell me you think that's the proper costume for a mother of two."
"I'm afraid I didn't notice that either," said Mr. Peterson.
"Oh, for heaven's sake," snapped Mrs. Peterson. "A lot of good it does you to go to church."

Sign on a church in Portland, Oregon:
"COME THIS SUNDAY, AVOID THE EASTER RUSH."

A wealthy jazz musician decided to go to church one Sunday. After services, he approached the preacher with much enthusiasm. "Reverend," he said, "that was a swinging sermon, man. I flipped my lid—that was the grooviest."
"I'm happy you liked it," said the Reverend, "but I wish you wouldn't use those terms in expressing yourself."
"I'm like, sorry, man, Reverend, but I dug that sermon so much," said the cat. "In fact, it sent me so much I flipped a C-note in the collection pot."
The Reverend replied, "Crazy, man, crazy."

"I hear you went to the ball game last Sunday instead of to church."
"That's a lie, and I've got a fish to prove it."

A small town is where people go to church on Sunday to see who didn't.

The drunken commuter collapsed in the subway. A clergyman rushed to his aid. Seeing the man's condition, he started to lecture him: "You're either going to heaven or the other place according to the life you intend to live."
"I don't care where I go," gurgled the drunken commuter, "just so long as I don't have to change in Jamaica."

The minister was leaving the church to go to a different parish. "I'm so sorry you're going," the little old lady cried as she said good-bye, "I never knew what sin was until you came here."

She sang in church—and fifty people changed their religion.

"I advertised that the poor would be welcome in this church," said the minister, "and after inspecting the collection, I see that they have come."

He has some kind of religion—at least he knows what church he is staying away from.

GIRL PRAYING: "Oh, Lord, I ask nothing for myself—but will you please send dear mother a son-in-law."

The minister asked the congregation to raise their hands if they wanted to go to heaven. All did so except one. Then he asked who wanted to go to hell. Nobody raised their hands. "Where do you want to go?" the minister asked the man who didn't vote for either side. "No place," he answered, "I like it here."

The impatient teenager was bothered because she had to wait in line so long for Confession. "They should be more efficient," she beefed. "They ought to have a fast line for those with three sins or less."

The pastor at a church was asked how many persons could sleep in the church building in case of an attack.

"I don't know," replied the pastor, "but we sleep four hundred every Sunday morning."

Winston Churchill

A lady member of the House of Commons snarled at Mr. Churchill one night when they were in session: "Winston—you're drunk." Churchill answered her like any good comic would reply to a heckler: "Bessie, you're ugly, and tomorrow morning I'll be sober, but you'll still be ugly."

The Prime Minister said it: "A fanatic is one who can't change his mind and won't change the subject."

Churchill about Clement Attlee, of the Labor Party: "Attlee is a very modest man—and with reason."

Referring to Sir Stafford Cripps: "He has all the virtues I dislike and none of the vices I admire."

Lady Astor once said to Churchill: "If you were my husband, I'd poison your coffee."

Churchill answered: "If you were my wife I'd drink it."

Churchill was asked how he liked New York City during his visit here. This was his instant critique: "Newspapers too thick—lavatory papers too thin."

Too often the strong silent man is silent because he does not know what to say.

About a Socialist in the House of Commons: "He spoke without a note and without a point."

George Bernard Shaw had a running feud going with Churchill. He sent the Prime Minister a note saying: "I am reserving two tickets for you for my premiere. Come and bring a friend—if you have one."

Churchill replied immediately: "Impossible to be present for the first performance. Will attend the second—if there is one."

About Prime Minister Ramsay MacDonald's speech: "He has the gift of compressing the largest number of words into the smallest amount of thought."

He was against peace at any price: "Look at the Swiss! They have enjoyed peace for centuries. And what have they produced? The cuckoo clock!"

Churchill was always fighting to get more and more protection for England—just to make sure. He used to accentuate his demands with the story of "the man whose mother-in-law had died in Brazil and when asked how the remains should be disposed of replied, 'Embalm—cremate—and bury. Take no risks.' "

Cigarettes
(*see Smoking*)

Winston cigarettes and Christine Jorgensen have the same claim to fame: "It's what's up front that counts."

239

A well-bred man steps on the cigarette so it won't burn the rug.

The cigar store Indian is now smoking cigarettes.

Filter-tipped cigarettes have stopped coughing and other things, but they have caused more hernias by dragging on them.

If those Winston cigarettes get any longer—only trombone players will be able to light them.

He's such a hypochondriac—he only smokes filter-tipped marijuana.

"How many cigarettes do you smoke a day?"
"Oh, any given amount."

Circus

Did you hear the story about the man on the flying trapeze who caught his wife in the act?

ELEPHANT: "I'm getting sick and tired of working for peanuts."

I get shot from a cannon—I get ten cents a mile and traveling expenses.

When I was ten I ran away with a circus—but the police made me bring it back.

The lions were so fierce that when the tamer went into the cage with the chair—he didn't get a chance to sit down.

Clothes
(*see Fashions*)

With today's prices—clothes break the man.

"I would like a new mink coat," the wife demanded.
Said the husband: "But you've only worn the one I gave you two years."
"You forget," reminded the wife, "the eight years the mink wore it."

If the shoe fits—it's out of style.

Clothes don't make the man—but a good suit has made many a lawyer.

His pants are tighter than his skin. He can sit down in his skin—but he can't sit down in his pants.

His pants are so tight—they wear out on the inside.

He is making suits out of awning material—only trouble is when the sun goes down—his pants roll up.

She wanted new clothes in spite of the fact that her closets were bulging with the best gowns in town. "Darling," she tried to explain to her husband, "I just must have some new clothes—all the neighborhood has seen everything I own."
"Well," the husband growled, "it's cheaper to move to a new neighborhood."

A dress shop received this note from a woman: "Dear sir, you have not delivered the maternity dress I ordered. Please cancel the order. My delivery was faster than yours."

The man put his high silk hat down on the seat next to him in the theatre. When the fat lady came in, she just sat down on the hat without looking. She jumped up immediately and they both surveyed the black silk pancake. "Madam," he said to her icily, "I could have told you my hat wouldn't fit before you tried it on."

240

She is middle-aged when she chooses her shoes for comfort and her sweater for warmth.

His suit is so shiny—if he ever fell down—he'd have seven years hard luck.

He got a very expensive suit for a ridiculous figure—*his.*

SIGN IN LINGERIE SHOP: "Destiny may shape your end—but if it doesn't we have the best girdles in town."

A girdle is the difference between facts and figures.

There's nothing so cold as a woman who's been refused a fur coat.

She doesn't have the legs for miniskirts—only the nerve.

If the skirts go any higher—my wife has a couple of blouses that will be just about the right length.

Clothes make the man—poor—if he's married.

"What would go best with that tie?"
"A long beard."

He's really in trouble—he told his wife her stockings were wrinkled—and she wasn't wearing any.

It was so hot in Miami—the women weren't wearing their mink stoles—just the appraisals.

HUSBAND: "Another new dress? When am I going to get the money to pay for it all?"
WIFE: "I may be a lot of things—but inquisitive, I'm not."

She dresses to be seen in the best places.

The girls on the beach were wearing their baiting suits.

She looks like an unmade bed.

The way the women's dresses are getting shorter and shorter—you never know what they'll be up to next.

The little boy got lost in the crowd. "Why didn't you hold on to your mother's skirt?"
"I couldn't reach it," the kid bawled.

"Of course you can buy that hat," the husband said. "It gives you that mature look."

The honeymoon's over when the groom stops praising his wife's clothes and starts pricing them.

Those short skirts are keeping us ignorant about what's going on in the world—I haven't read a newspaper or magazine on a subway in months.

Her Easter hat had so many flowers on it—two funerals followed her home.

Girls, here's a tip for a big buy on dresses—Milton Berle is having a sale on his old clothes.

Myron Cohen

The drunk was walking along 5th Avenue at 4 A.M. in a state of panic. A cop approached him and growled, "Do you have an explanation?"
The poor soul answered, "If I had an explanation, I would be home with my wife."

The Italian immigrant entered the bank and asked, "Pardon mia—I'd like to talk with the fella that arranges loans."
"I'm sorry," the guard replied, "the loan arranger is out to lunch."
"In data case—I talk to Tonto."

Two men met on 7th Avenue and one said, "Lend me twenty dollars until I come back from Chicago." The second one asked, "When are you coming back?" And the first answered, "Who's going?"

The drunk suddenly stumbled down the subway stairs and reeled up to another entrance, still loaded. "Where you been?" asked his friend who was sitting on the street. "In the basement of a friend's house," hicc'd the drunk, "and boy has he got a set of trains."

The little five-year-old boy said to his little boy friend, "My daddy can beat your daddy." The other answered, "Big deal—so can my mother."

Cold
(*see Alaska, Weather*)

Winter is officially here in New York. The Italian pizzerias have changed to winter-weight olive oil.

I just arrived from Canada—I came in by dogsled.
We had a woman driver. She hollered, "Mush!" I hollered, "Mush," and while we were mushing, somebody stole my sled.

It was so cold in Winnipeg that the hens were laying eggs from a standing position.

It was so windy that one chicken had her back to the wind and laid the same egg twenty-seven times.

When I got home, my wife said, "Why don't you take off that purple sweater you're wearing?" I said, "What purple sweater? It's me—boy, was I cold!"

It was so cold in Florida, they were selling frozen orange juice right off the trees.

It was so cold that the farmers had to milk their cows with ice picks.

When I received the contract to play Anchorage, I grabbed my tux and snowshoes, and off I skidded. North Pole nights are six months long. I arrived half-past January. The daytime is also six months and everybody stays up—that's why they have those Arctic circles under their eyes. But I wasn't disappointed about not playing Florida that winter because I came back from Alaska with a color—blue. Oh, I was a big hit. The only trouble is the audience is a little cold. I talked to one guy for an hour before I found out he was a snowman. I had a high-class opening at the club I worked. Everybody came to the premiere formal, sporting tuxedos with built-in parkas and patent leather snowshoes. The center ringside was reserved for eight —the mayor, his missus, and six huskies.

Colleges
(*see Universities*)

"He's a perfect student. He is studying reading, writing and rioting."

"My cousin is in medical school."
"What's he studying?"
"Nothing. They're studying him."

You can lead a girl to Vassar but you can't make her think.

My nephew sent me a note from college. "Dear Uncle . . . I'm doing well in everything except school."

INTERVIEWER: "Tell me, Professor, you've taught for ten years at Yale,

fifteen years at Oxford, nine years at the Sorbonne . . . tell me, what has been your biggest problem?"
PROFESSOR: "Spitballs."

1ST STUDENT: "Congratulations! I hear you won a scholarship to Harvard Medical School."
2ND STUDENT: "Yes—but they don't want me while I'm alive."

How would I know the name of the school—I'm only a football player here.

If I'm studying when you come in—please wake me up.

I don't like to brag, but I'm putting a kid through college. He belongs to the guy who fixes my TV set.

CO-ED TO GIRL FRIEND: "I have a horrible feeling we are not being followed."

I saw six college kids stagger out of a bar and park themselves into the little car. One of them said, "Charley, you drive, you're too drunk to sing."

CO-ED TO HER ROOMMATE: "Frank is a perfect gentleman—but it's better than having no boy friend at all."

He went through school by writing short stories—he wrote them to his father.

Sending a kid through college is very educational—it teaches his parents to do without a lot of things.

Comedians
(see individual names and chapters in Part I)

How do you become a comedian? You take a mouthful of marbles and one by one you drop them. And when you've lost all your marbles—you're a comedian.

I became a comedian when my father gave me a rocking chair—I loved that rocking chair—I used it day and night—one day it broke—and when they discovered I was off my rocker, they knew I was a comedian.

People say I have a wonderful delivery. Ten days for shirts and two weeks for sheets.

The last time he played a night club he was such a hit, the manager jacked up the price of sandwiches to twenty cents apiece.

When I was at the Palace, I drew a line two blocks long—but they made me erase it.

His jokes are original. But the people who originated them died years ago.

I wouldn't say his jokes are bad, but after every show he gives his writers a loyalty test.

He's got a lot of funny lines—too bad they're all in his face.

The comedians are so young these days—the make-up men don't know which end to put the powder.

Ed Wynn died. At his grave somebody said, "This is the first time you ever made us sad."

As a comedian, I feel I'm not getting the money I deserve—but I'm keeping quiet about it because at the present time I can't afford to take a cut.

Henny Youngman says, "If you want to get the real dope about comedy—come to the real dope."

The big things lately have been the sick comics—some of them are really sick—they're stretcher cases.

His act is so sick—he could collect in full from Blue Cross.

One sick comic went to a psychiatrist and was cured after six visits—but now the comic is out of work and the psychiatrist is making a fortune with his act.

They say great comedians are born —well, I was born—wasn't I?

It was such a religious audience. After each joke they said, "Oh God."

When I finished my act they sat open-mouthed—I never saw so many people yawning at the same time.

A comedian is a guy who knows a good gag when he steals one.

He is the hottest act in town—every part of it is stolen.

"A comic is a guy who says funny things—a comedian is a guy who says things funny."—Ed Wynn

The Comedians

Many "civilian" friends (those who aren't in show business) have made it through my joke books, thereby gaining me a lot of rivals and losing me a lot of things wholesale! Many of these pals have sprung from the ranks of the healthy, normal citizen and been converted into successful, neurotic, rank comedians. There are humans in every walk of life who run to their gag file at the drop of a joke. Myron Cohen used to be a silk salesman on the road. Now look at his "route": The Copa, Latin Quarter, Las Vegas, etc. Or take a gander at Sam Levenson, the Brooklyn schoolteacher, whose class today numbers in the millions. Could be this book will fire up other raw talent and show them the art of do-it-yourself comedy.

Now, leave us take f'instance the case of Irving. Irving, to quote his own modest words, is a highly famous comedian. He's on your radio station once a day, on your TV channel four times a month and on his analyst's couch five times a week. He's like any other nice, normal, crazy mixed-up kid of fifty-three.

Irving was born of ordinary parents. His mamma was a bearded lady and so was his papa. He was the only child of three brothers and sisters. He was a shy, retiring lad, the only kid who ever retired at sixteen without ever having worked. His mamma coddled him because she saw something in him that nobody else saw. She saw that he was nuts. Whilst other kiddies were cutting out paper dolls Irving was cutting up real live comedians.

When he was twelve years old and in the seventh grade his favorite pastime was marbles. A bully began copping a couple from him every day, and when he'd lost all his marbles, he decided to go into show business. He figured anything's better than working. He scraped together all the money he could rob and bought a Joey Adams Joke Book. Then he bought another. And another. And another. And when he had eight, he traded them in for one Joe Miller book.

When he was fourteen years old in the seventh grade, the teacher caught this poor but dishonest boy stealing answers off another kid's test paper—a definite symptom of humorosis borrowiasis—otherwise known as joke-lifting. When the principal begged him to explain, he said, "Well, a funny thing happened to me on the way to the cloakroom. . . . "

Years passed but he didn't. Here he was seventeen years old and he'd moved to the sixth grade. When he married the principal, his mamma suggested he quit school to earn enough money to keep him in joke books. Then he had a baby, which upset him because it was he who had it, not his wife. However, when the doctor commented that the baby had a better delivery than he did, he decided to forget his theatrical aspirations and invade the business world. He became a carpenter. One day he nailed together some nuts and bolts and screws and they all fell apart. "Goodly gracious," his mamma shouted, "the boy's got a screw loose!" So back he went into show business.

His family complained he wasn't bringing any bread into the house. Corn, yes, but bread no! But did that bother a staunch, fearless, talented, great show-must-go-on trouper like Irving? Yes! However, he laughed at them (which was the only laughs he ever got), and grabbed a little joke book and a lotta friends and began comeding. Nothing happened. Then he collared an audience of his daddy's employees who'd laugh him up if he recited his income tax return. And he did. And they did.

Immediately he made up what little mind he had left and, upon hearing his mamma say to his papa, "That Irving's a big joke," he announced, "Daddy dear and mummy dear, I are going to be a comedian." "Better you should be a bum or something steady like a dope peddler," cried the family.

Irving wanted very badly to be a successful M.C. He tried and tried but he couldn't make it. Finally he divorced his old hag wife, grabbed himself a sexy chorine and—y'know what? He made it! But he found that it didn't help his career any.

Somebody suggested he go to school so he could understand what the audience was talking about when they weren't listening to him. For years he went to school at night, though he never learned anything because that particular school closed at 3 P.M. It was while he was going to school that he first got his break. The surgeon placed his arm in a plaster and in a few months he was as bad as new.

Poor Irving. He burrowed his pointed scalp deeper into his joke book until he began telling funny stories even in the morning. Got so he couldn't crawl out of bed until he'd done three minutes of material. He actually began punning when he was alone. He was no longer a social-joker. Eventually, in serious condition, he enrolled in G. A.: Gagsters Anonymous. They told him not to think about never making jests again, but just to promise himself that he wouldn't tell them for that day. They told him if he ever woke up at three in the morning with an uncontrollable urge to throw a punch line, he should call a certain number and they'd send Milton Berle over to sit with him until the spell was gone. One night after doing this he fell into a stupor, talked in his sleep, and Berle wrote all his routines down and did his act in Miami.

Irving became a has-been who never was. He became a neurotic. He did odd things like tell other comics they were good and he said kind words about his confreres. When this occurred, well-meaning friends took him away.

'Tis said all comedians are neurotic because they have insecurity complexes. This is a lie. I know many clowns who are completely secure— and are neurotic. However, I do resent people saying we are abnormal, poorly adjusted individuals who require psychiatry. And I am not alone in my resentment. My psychiatrist feels the same way.

245

Irving eventually recovered from this experience because he had faith that someday someone would recognize him. Several months later when he was walking down the street with his yo-yo, his kindergarten teacher stopped him and said, "Say, aren't you Irving?" and knowing he'd been recognized gave him confidence, and he grew and grew. When he'd started in show business he was only five feet, three inches, but soon his ego was six feet two.

Today, dear, sweet, stupid Irving has gone the way of all other successes. He has a Cadillac with a built-in Rolls. He is at home in country houses, winter houses, and a coupla houses that aren't exactly homes. He is a sports enthusiast and plays all games. Friends say he even likes the outdoor athletics. He makes a grand ten grand a week. His hunting lodge in the Virgin Islands is so big he has to take a taxi to the bathroom. His faucets pour only champagne—domestic, of course, since he's always been chintzy with a buck. He has solid-gold silverware, diamond inlays, and takes weekly "humble lessons."

But, you ask, is he happy? Would he do it all over again? Was it all worth it? Do I think comedians can laff happily ever after? Yes, he would, it was, and I do. . . .

Commercials
(*see Television, Advertising*)

They televised the entire ceremony at Sing Sing. Just as the murderer was about to sit down in the electric chair, the commercial came on, "You can be sure—if it's Westinghouse."

If not completely satisfied—return the unused portion of the can—and we will return the unused portion of your money.

If you have indigestion, do as thousands do—belch.

Use Jack Carter's big liver pills. One man I know used them all his life and finally died at the age of 103—and three days later they had to beat his liver to death with a club.

I don't know why they advertise bad breath—nobody wants it.

Ladies—live alone and like it—remember—Duz does everything.

Our bras will support you in the manner to which you are not accustomed.

Girls—are you putting up a good front? Use our bras. The living bra for those who have been dead for years.

Don't kill your wife with washing. Let our product do it. Our product is never touched by human hands—just kick it into the washing machine.

Look, ma, no cavities—but all my gums are gone.

Look, ma—no teeth. .

Do you have teeth like the Ten Commandments? All broken? Use Adams' tooth powder and get a good paste in the mouth.

"Look, ma—no cavities!"
"Wonderful!"
"Yeah—but I'm pregnant."

Communism
(*see Russia; also Russia in
"International Humor"*)

A Communist is a man who minds his own business at the top of his voice.

When they have each other as friends —they don't need any enemies.

Three prisoners in a Soviet prison were letting their secrets down: "I was put here for coming to work late," said the first.

The sceond said: "I came to work too early. They said this proved I was an imperialistic spy."

"I'm here," the third confessed, "because I arrived exactly on time. This meant I owned an American watch."

When the Red arrived in hell the devil asked him which section he preferred—Communist or capitalist. "Are you joshing?" he asked. "Communist, naturally; I know the heating won't work!"

A Communist is a person who wants to share his nothing with everybody.

COMMUNIST: One who borrows your pot to cook your goose.

The Moscow resident was sent to jail for five years for shouting "Down with Khrushchev." Anxious to make amends, when he got out, he went around shouting, "Hooray for Khrushchev." He was sent back to jail for another five years.

Computers
(*see Office and Automation*)

There will be fewer office parties this year—who wants to kiss a computer?

Some people just like to brag. A guy boasted about being fired and being replaced by a $250,000 computer.

The mating computer at Grossinger's hotel was very active that day. A tall handsome six-footer stood in front of it. "I'm a millionaire—I have twenty oil wells and a gold mine and I run five banks in Texas." So the computer mugged him.

Computers are getting wiser every day. A couple of college kids put cards into the machine to see if they were well matched — and the computer wound up with the girl.

A bachelor said he'd visited a computer dating office and listed specifications. He wanted "someone on the small side; one who likes water sports; is gregarious; likes formal dress and says little." "So," he sighed, "I drew a penguin."

Confucius Confused
(*see "International Humor" chapter under Chinese, and Sayings, Proverbs, Quotations, etc.*)

Chun King say smart man his views always same like yours.

Cooing he stop with honeymoon— but billing he go on forever.

Golf he is game in which small ball he is chased by man who too old to chase anything else.

City she full of teenage girls who have reached the dangerous age when their voices are change from "no" to "yes."

Reckless driver he is person who pass you on road in spite of all you can do.

When women they kiss—she always remind me of prize fighter who shake hands.

Chasing pretty girl never hurt anybody—trouble she come after catch them.

Platonic love he all same, like be invited to cellar for drink of ginger ale.

If you want proof that girls she are dynamite—just try to drop one.

If at first you not succeed—your father he own business.

An optimist he is man who marry his secretary and think he will continue dictating to her.

Chun King say smart lady she never let fool kiss her—or kiss fool her.

Every man he like to see broad smile—especially if broad she smile at him.

If any person he disagree with you, forget same—after all—he have right to stick to his ridiculous opinion.

Chun King say when hostess she not have enough chair for everyone—she give buffet dinner.

God he make universe and then he rested. He then make man and then he rested once more. Next he make woman—and nobody have rested ever since.

Fun he all same like life insurance—older you get more he cost.

Chun King say husband he living proof that woman can take joke.

Many husband he kiss with eyes open—he want make sure his wife she not around to catch him.

Mermaid she not so good after all—she not enough fish to fry and not enough woman to love.

Old maid she is girl who do not have mush experience.

Tactless man is one who voice what everybody else is thinking.

Chun King say wolf he is man with lot of pet theories.

Person who buy second hand car—he know how hard it is to drive bargain.

Spinster she woman who know all answers—but nobody ask her questions.

When man he bring wife flowers for no reason—there usually reason.

Pedestrian he man who have two motorcar, one wife and one son.

Chun King say flirt she is girl who believe it is every man for herself.

Conventions

When your wife goes along on a convention—you have twice the expenses and half the fun.

Cooking
(*see Marriage, Food, Restaurants*)

I got a wife that dresses to kill—and cooks the same way.

She runs the only kitchen in the world where flies come to commit suicide.

She got along fine in her cooking school until one day she finally burned something—her cooking school.

These days when you go into a restaurant and order a five-dollar dinner, the waiter wants to know "On rye or white?"

The husband told his wife he wanted to be surprised for dinner—so she took all the labels off the cans.

248

His wife will put on anything for dinner—except an apron.

It takes her an hour to cook minute rice.

It took her the first three months of their married life to discover you can't open an egg with a can opener.

The only thing she knows about good cooking is which restaurants to go to.

Bill Cosby

When I was a kid I never went to school—I said I was sick—but I always managed to get better by 3:30—I'd run into the kitchen—"Look, ma—a miracle happened! I'm well! A little angel came and sat on my bed—she touched me with a wand and said 'Go out and play.' "

We had a Philco radio about 6 feet tall—it had about 287 knobs—of which only 2 worked—off/on volume and the station selector.

We had a teacher in school who hated kids—he caught me reading a comic book in class and snatched it away from me. "You'll get this back at the end of the semester." "Why, is it gonna take you that long to read it?"

I never liked doctors—they always keep their stethoscopes in the freezer.

Counterfeiters
(*see Money, Banks*)

This counterfeiter is chicken—still has the first dollar he ever made.

He made big money—about a quarter of an inch too big—that's why he's in Sing Sing.

Number 32146, whom we'll call Blinky for short, was only recently taken from the mental ward of a prison and assigned a regular cell.

It all dates back to the reason for his incarceration. Blinky was known as the Grandpa Moses of counterfeiters. He was so meticulous copying a bill, it took the eagle eye of a trained professional to detect his funny money from the real McCoy.

For many months, Blinky worked on what he thought was a foolproof set of engraving for a ten-dollar bill. His chore completed, he wrinkled his work of art, compared it with the original through a powerful magnifying glass, and decided to test-pass it before going into volume production.

Within two hours Blinky was arrested. "I defy you," he raged at the Treasury agent, placing the original and the spurious bill side by side, "to tell me the difference between these two ten-spots."

"There is no difference, Blinky," the T-man agreed, "and that's the trouble. Seems you only made one mistake. You copied your counterfeit from a counterfeit!"

This counterfeiter was going out of the business. So, in a last big fling, he made a fifteen-dollar bill. He went into a candy store, bought a couple of fifty-cent stogies, and handed over the bill. The clerk looked at it for a moment, went into the back of his establishment, and gave him two seven-dollar bills in change.

Court
(*see also Judges, Lawyers, etc.*)

JUDGE: "Haven't I seen you before?"
TAILOR ON TRIAL: "Maybe—so many men owe me money—I can't remember their faces."

249

JUDGE: "Can't this dispute be settled out of court?"

DEFENDANT: "Sure—that's what we were trying to do when the police interfered."

"The court will give you three lawyers because of the importance of this case," the judge said.

"If it's all the same to you, your honor," the criminal said, "just get me one good witness."

This is the only country in the world where they lock up the jury and let the prisoner go home every night.

As a judge, when Goha hailed a husband before him for killing his wife, the husband in self-defense stated that he caught his wife in the act of adultery. "Why did you not kill the man, the stranger who wronged you, instead of killing your wife?" asked Goha.

"Because," the man answered, "if I had spared her I would have had to kill a man a day; by killing her, I put an end to her adultery with only one murder."

A jury consists of twelve people who determine which side has the best lawyer.

She asked the judge for a divorce because her husband only talked to her three times in their five years of marriage and she wanted custody of her three children.

The jury foreman stood up when the judge asked him if they had come to a decision. "We're all of one mind—temporarily insane."

In a little town in the West, a middle-aged woman was found guilty of killing her husband. But the judge suspended the sentence—he had compassion for her because she was a widow.

The racket guy paid off the juror to hold out for a verdict of manslaughter. After two days and nights, the jury returned with the verdict he paid for.

"I'll never forget you," said the hood. "You must have had a bottle of trouble —I mean two days and nights."

"I had plenty of trouble," the juror answered. "Everybody else on the jury wanted an acquittal."

"I always had his best interest at heart," the wife told the judge.

"So how come she married me?" the husband asked.

"Is it true," the judge asked, "that you haven't spoken a word to your wife in five years of married life?"

"Yes."

"Explain yourself."

"I didn't want to interrupt her."

"Honest, judge—I didn't desert my wife—I'm just a coward."

"You've been acquitted on the charge of bigamy," the judge said. "You can go home now."

"Oh, ah, your honor, sir—which home?"

The foreman of the jury announced, "Your honor, we find that the man who stole the money is not guilty."

Crazy

"It is an irrefutable fact," said the woman lecturer, "that throughout the world there are three men to one woman in every asylum."

"True," a man in the rear shouted, "but who put them there?"

Crazy Laughs
(*see Off-Beat Humor*)

DENTIST: "Your teeth are fine—but your gums will have to come out."

Man on phone to bank teller: "This is a stick-up—send me fifty thousand dollars."

Youngster to mounted policeman: "Why can't you ride in a patrol car like the other policemen?"
"I could—only there isn't room for my horse!"

PROFESSOR: "Does the question bother you?"
STUDENT: "Not at all—the question is quite clear—it's the answer that troubles me."

MOTHER: "If you don't stop playing that saxophone, I'll go crazy!"
SON: "Too late, ma, I stopped an hour ago."

"How did your backside get so cut up?"
"The guy next door was hanging pictures in his flat. The wall is thin—the nails are long—and the guy is a midget."

The doctor never saw such a fat patient. When she sat down on the chairs, the doc said, "Open your mouth and say moo."

The shy man jumped off the bus backwards when he heard a man say: "Let's grab his seat when he gets off."

The doctor called the police. "Listen—a crazy man escaped. He weighs three hundred pounds and is three feet, four inches tall."
The cop said, "Are you kidding?"
Doctor said, "I told you he was crazy!"

Crazy Mixed-Up Humor
(*see Crazy Laughs and Off-Beat Humor*)

His latest invention was crossing a rabbit with a piece of lead—he hopes to get a repeating pencil.

"Who are you writing this letter to?" the attendant asked the patient.
"To myself."
"What does it say?"
"How should I know? I haven't received it yet."

"Carrots are good for your eyes."
"I don't believe that baloney!"
"Did you ever see a rabbit with glasses?"

The stripper awoke after a high night and found herself with her clothes on and yelled: "Ye gads — I've been draped!"

The girls around here are crazy about me. In fact, one girl has been trying to break my door down all day—I got her locked in my room.

"All week long before the baby was born he brought his wife roses. A rose in the morning—a rose at night. Guess what they named the baby."
"Rose?"
"No, Max. It was a boy."

The reporter knocked on the door of the circus midget who was to be interviewed. He was astonished when a man six feet tall answered the door.
"Is this the residence of Tom Thumb?" the reporter asked.
"I'm Tom Thumb the midget—but this is my day off."

Never slap a guy in the face when he's chewing tobacco.

251

I can't understand it—no matter where a service station puts up a pump—they find gas.

Credit

You have to give most American families a lot of credit—they can't get along without it.

Credit Cards

Today you need credit cards even if you want to pay cash.

He's steamed because the gum machine won't take credit cards.

A credit card is a printed I.O.U.

"Do you live within your income?"
"Are you kidding? I can't even live within my credit cards."

A customer phoned a restaurant in New York to ask if they honored credit cards. "Not only honor, but also love and obey them," the manager answered.

Wife: "Why can't we pay our Diner's Club bill with our American Express card?"

A little old lady walked into the credit department at Diner's Club and demanded, "I don't care to bandy words with underlings about my overdrawn account. Take me to your computer."

Most department stores are willing to give a woman credit for what her husband earns.

Today's moneyless society won't seem really complete to us until we find a panhandler who accepts credit cards.

Crimes
(*see Court, Judges, Lawyers, etc.*)

It's getting so bad in New York—that even the muggers travel in pairs.

The bandit walked into a Chinese restaurant—walked over to the cashier and said quietly: "Give me all the cash you got in small bills—to go."

I know a burglar that is so hep—if his clients don't have cash—he'll accept credit cards.

This snooty shoplifter always insists that his loot be gift-wrapped.

He's a police reporter—once a week he reports to the police.

He was locked up for something he didn't do—he didn't wipe the fingerprints off the safe.

The crook's mother assured him, "I left everything in your room the way I found it—your gun—knife—blackjack."

The laws are strictly for the crooks. They lock up the witness and the jury—and they let the prisoner out on bail.

Under the laws of this country, a man is innocent until proven guilty. Then, if he isn't crazy, he is pardoned.

"We hang the petty thieves and appoint the great ones to public office."—Aesop.

One guy walked over to me in front of my house and ordered, "Stick 'em down!" I asked, "Don't you mean, stick 'em up?" He answered, "No wonder I'm not making any money."

He's a modern Robin Hood—he steals from the rich and from the poor.

He spent three months forging a check—only to have it come back from the bank stamped, "Insufficient Funds."

Critics
(see Theatres, Actors, Show People, etc.)

MONTY WOOLLEY: "For the first time I envied my feet—they were asleep."

"A critic is a legless man who teaches running."—Channing Pollock

A critic is a man who writes about things he doesn't like.

"I never read a book before reviewing it—it prejudices me so."—Sidney Smith

The show got divided notices—we liked it—but the critics didn't.

Go to any public square—and see if you can find one statue erected to a critic.

The producer came to his wife and gleefully announced, "I think I got a hit."
"How do you know?"
"I met three of the critics and they each told me if I change one of the acts —I'll have a hit."
"That's wonderful," she said.
"Yeah, but each picked a different act."

Two shipwrecked critics were drifting for weeks on a raft. The more frightened of the two started seeking forgiveness for his sins.
"I've been a louse all my life," he said. "I've been cruel to actors. Too often I went out of my way to hurt them. If I'm spared, I promise . . . "
"Just a moment," shouted the other critic, "don't go too far. I think I see smoke from a ship!"

"I saw the show at a disadvantage— the curtain was up."—Groucho Marx

Irving Hoffman critikilled a play, The producer went to his publisher and complained that Mr. Hoffman has very bad eyesight. "I may not see very well," Irving answered later, "but there is nothing wrong with my nose."

Milton Berle was his own critic when his show "Spring in Brazil" was a 300,-000-dollar flop. "The trouble with the show is," Milton suggested, "the theatre is constructed wrong—the seats face the stage."

John Chapman said about a Mae West show, "Miss West has one more bust than she needs."

Dorothy Parker about Katharine Hepburn in "The Lake": "Hepburn ran the gamut of emotion from A to B."

"The picture was so bad," one critic said, "two people called up to be taken off the free list."

The picture is so bad, it should be retaken and then put on the shelf.

George S. Kaufman buried an alleged comedy with his review: "Judging by the laughter in the rear of the theatre—someone must have been telling jokes back there."

A sneak preview critic wrote on his criticard, "When you cut this picture— cut it into little pieces."

It is easier to pull down than build up.

"Critics! Those cut-throat bandits in the path of fame."—Robert Burns

George S. Kaufman about a movie that had gotten a big build-up: "Frankly—I was underwhelmed."

253

If there is a hero in this book—he should kill the author.

CAPSULE CRITICISM: "The show had a cast of ten—buried in one plot."

Critic: One who finds a little bad in the best of things.

A critic on the *San Francisco Chronicle* brought back memories of the old Alexander Woollcott days with his neat scalping of a recent performance of the Royal Ballet in that city. The thrust went: "Nureyev danced as though he very much needed a vacation. I've seen better leaps from a popcorn machine."

Crossword Puzzles

"My uncle loved crossword puzzles so much that on the day he died he asked to be buried six down and three across."

Daffynitions
(*see Definitions*)

A GOOD STORYTELLER: A person who has a good memory and hopes you haven't.

ALIMONY: The high cost of leaving.

The fee a woman charges for name-dropping.

AMBASSADOR: Best way he could serve his country is by leaving it.

ANTIQUE SHOP: Where the stock is old but the prices are brand new.

ASHTRAY: Where you put butts if the room doesn't have a floor.

ATHEIST: A teenager who doesn't believe in Rock 'n Roll.

BACHELOR: A man who comes to work from a different direction every morning.

A man who never makes the same mistake once.

A man who has no children to speak of.

A man who can tell the doctor his symptoms without having his wife interrupt.

BAGEL: A doughnut dipped in cement.

BARBER: A man you've got to take your hat off to.

BIGAMIST: A guy who has taken one too many.

A man who leads two wives.

BORE: A person who has nothing to say—and says it.

BUDGET: A family quarrel.

CLOSET: Where a girl puts all her clothes when she's dressed for the evening.

DELEGATE-AT-LARGE: A government official who travels without his wife.

DIPLOMAT: Who can talk interestingly for one hour and say nothing.

Is a man who can convince his wife she looks fat in a fur coat.

EGGHEAD: A schmoe who has found something more interesting than a woman.

EGOTIST: "I" strain.

ETIQUETTE: Learning to yawn with your mouth closed.

FAN CLUB: A group of people who tell an actor he's not alone in the way he feels about himself.

254

FATHER: The kin you love to touch.

FIREPROOF: The boss's son-in-law.

FLIRT: A woman who believes it's every man for herself.

GAG WRITER: He has a good memory and hopes you haven't.

GIGOLOS: Hired hands.

IDEAL HUSBAND: The guy next door.

I. O. U.: A paper wait.

JUDGE: Part of the familiar saying, "Never judge a book by its movie."

LIBERAL: A person who makes enemies left and right.

MADAM: For whom the belles toil.

MAL DE MER: French for "You can't take it with you."

MEAT PACKER: Girdle manufacturer.

METEOROLOGIST: A man who can look into a girl's eyes and tell whether.

MIDDLE AGE: When a man is warned to slow down by a doctor instead of a policeman.

MINK: What's used to keep a woman —quiet.

MINOR OPERATION: One performed on somebody else.

MISTRESS: Like a wife only she don't have to do the dishes.

NUDISTS: Folks who grin and bare it.

OLD MAID: A woman who's been good for nothing.

OLD TIMER: Who can remember he used to dream of salaries—that he can't live on today.

PHONY: A cross between nothing.

POLITICIAN: A man who divides his time running for office and running for cover.

RAVING BEAUTY: One who came out last in a beauty contest.

RICH WOMAN: She isn't afraid to ask the clerk to show her something cheaper.

SADIST: Is a guy who does nice things to a masochist.

SAILOR: A wolf in ship's clothing.

SOCIETY PLAYBOY: In small towns they are known as the town drunk.

STRIPTEASER: A busy body.

TACT: The ability to describe others as they see themselves.

TOTALITARIAN: A machine for keeping track of bets at horse races.

TOMBSTONE: Something that covers pedestrians who didn't make the grade.

UNDERTAKER: The last guy to let you down.

WHOLESALE: Anything you buy for only twice what it's worth.

WHISKEY: The stuff that takes away the taste of water.

WOLF: A guy who is always in there pinching.

zoo: A place where animals look at silly people.

Dais
(*see Speakers—also chapter on Roast of the Town, etc.*)

He speaks straight from the shoulder —too bad his words don't start from higher up.

"They never give you a dinner— until you don't need one."
—Will Rogers

I finally found out why talk is cheap —there's more supply than demand.

You'll never live to be as old as the jokes you hear at banquets.

If you are the guest of honor and you are called upon to speak and you don't know what to speak about—take my advice—speak about a minute.

They discovered a new pill at banquets. You put it in your food and it gives you heartburn immediately instead of four o'clock in the morning.

speaker: One who talks in other people's sleep.

Did you ever wonder why we don't have any women speakers on a dais? It's because no woman can wait until after dinner to say what she has to say.

You've got to be brief to be recognized—as Brigitte Bardot will tell you.

A speech is like a love affair. Any fool can start it, but to end it requires considerable skill.

The female of the speeches is more deadly than the male.

A toastmaster is a man who eats a meal he doesn't want so he can get up and tell a lot of stories he doesn't remember to people who've already heard them.

When Richard Nixon was hospitalized with an injured knee, Adlai E. Stevenson turned up at the American Bar Association dinner as a replacement for Nixon. He began his talk by kidding about his substitute role: "It reminds me of the vicar out in a remote corner of England. One Friday he telegraphed his bishop: 'My wife just passed away. Please dispatch a substitute for the weekend.'"

Gene Buck: "I am," he liked to say, when presiding at a banquet, "merely the toastmaster—the punk that sets off the fireworks."

When Johnny Carson was the guest of honor for the March of Dimes, I was the toastmaster and naturally aimed first: "It's been said that Carson is the greatest wit in America—and tonight we're honoring the man who said it.
"The Governor of Nebraska is here tonight to honor his native son Johnny Carson, a man who did so much for the State of Nebraska—he moved the hell out of it.
"He owes his success to 'know-how.' He knows how Jack Paar did it—and copies him.
"People want to know has this multi-million-dollar deal with NBC changed him any. That's only people who don't know him. People who know him say nothing could change him—he's still the same arrogant guy he always was.
"Johnny has a percentage deal with NBC. He gives them 10 per cent of what they make.
"I won't say all this success has gone to his head or anything—but I heard the President of NBC talking to one of

the Vice-Presidents and he said 'What a deal we are giving Carson—*My God!*' "And Johnny said, 'Yes?' "

Dates
(see Romance, Girls, Men, Women, Playgirls, Playboys, etc.)

She likes going out with the chiropractor—'cause he always has a new twist.

Lots of men fought for her hand—but they quit when they saw the rest of her.

Love at first sight—is a labor-saving device.

She looked just like Monroe and he was a great President.

What a date! I had more fun on a rainy day on the beach.

She is the kind of a girl you take to the movie when you want to see the picture.

Once I dated a girl whose father was so rich that he had Swiss money in American banks.

Daughters

She was only a Communist's daughter—but everyone got his share.

She was only a baggage man's daughter—but she knew all the grips.

She was only a credit man's daughter—but she allowed anyone advances.

She was only a stagehand's daughter—but she had the loveliest props.

She was only a parson's daughter—but she'll never go to heaven.

She was only a florist's daughter—but she was potted all the time.

She was only a convict's daughter—but she never was caught.

She was only a governor's daughter—but what a state she was in.

She was only a lawyer's daughter—but anyone could break her will.

She was only a plumber's daughter—but oh what beautiful fixtures.

She was only a railroader's daughter—but oh what a caboose.

She was only a politician's daughter—but she said yes on every proposition.

She was only an air raid warden's daughter—but was she good in a blackout.

She was only an artist's daughter—but she never drew the line.

She was only a pitcher's daughter—but you ought to see her curves.

She was only a farmer's daughter—but all the traveling salesmen sold her.

She was only an innkeeper's daughter—but they couldn't keep her in.

She was only a sculptor's daughter—but her bust was the biggest in town.

She was only a salesman's daughter—but she gave out plenty of samples.

She was only a jockey's daughter—but she never did say nay.

She was only a grass-widow's daughter—but she certainly wasn't green.

She was only a violinist's daughter—but she liked to fiddle around.

She was only a builder's daughter—but what a terrific build.

She was only a bricklayer's daughter—but she sure was well-stacked.

She was only a wrestler's daughter—but she sure knew all the holds.

She was only a boxer's daughter—but she knew what to do in the clinches.

She was only a musician's daughter—but she had a few tricks of her own.

She was only a car dealer's daughter—but she had the best chassis in town.

She was only a pirate's daughter—but she had a sunken chest.

She was only a pirate's daughter—but she had a treasure chest.

She was only a schoolteacher's daughter—but she certainly taught me a lesson.

She was only a film censor's daughter—but she knew when to cut it out.

Death

(see Tombstones, Cemeteries)

The waiter dies and his wife is distraught. One day she meets someone who assures her that she can speak to her beloved husband through a medium. An appointment is made, the wife visits the medium and the seance begins. She presses both hands on the table and calls out, "Sam—Sam, speak to me!" A haunting, whistling noise follows and then a faint voice cries, "I can't—it's not my table!"

The society snob died and was greeted by St. Peter: "Welcome—glad to have you," he said.
"Thanks—but no," she said haughtily. "What's the big deal if you let anyone in here—this is not my idea of Heaven."

The actor died and played to standing room only at his funeral. "If he knew he would have an audience like this," his agent remarked, "he would have died years ago."

St. Peter said to the newcomer, "I don't see your name on my register." When he looked further he said, "Oh yes, here it is. You're not due for twenty years—who's your doctor?"

FAN: "Why don't you write your life story?"
STAR: "Not right now—my life story will be written posthumously."
FAN: "Good—make it soon."

"Dad, can my new boy friend replace your partner that died this morning?"
"It's okay with me—if you can arrange it with the undertaker."

There are two things we are sure of: death and taxes. Now if we could only get them in that order!

The son was sitting at the bedside of the elderly gentleman who was dying. "Where do you want to be buried," the kid asked, "in Forest Lawn or New York?"
The old man creaked up on his elbow and answered, "Surprise me!"

Decorating

(see Apartment Houses, Homes, Antiques, Suburbs, etc.)

My wife got rid of me because I clash with the drapes.

Bessie was the one in the sisterhood who was the world traveler. "What do you think of Red China?" Sylvia asked her.

"Please," Bessie said, "not with your yellow tablecloths."

"What do you think of the Colosseum?"

"It's nice—but I like modern."

The interior decorator advised the rich Texan to paper his walls with thousand-dollar bills. "Nobody has anything like it."

"Yeah," drawled the Texan, "but won't it clash with my solid gold floors?"

Definitions
(*see Daffynitions*)

ACQUAINTANCE: Someone we know well enough to borrow from—but not well enough to lend to.

ALIMONY: Like pumping gas in another man's car.
The high cost of loving.
The pay-as-you-burn plan.
Fly now—pay later.

APOLOGY: Only way for a husband to get the last word.

BACHELOR DOCTOR: The answer to a mother's prayer for her daughter.

BANK: Where you can borrow money, if you can prove that you don't need it.

BANKER: A gent who lends you an umbrella when the sun is shining and wants it back when it starts to rain like hell.

BARGAIN: What happens to all that money your wife has been saving you for years?

BEST MAN: The one who isn't getting married.

BOOKMAKER: That's a pickpocket who lets you use your own hands.

BRISS (circumcision): A surgical operation that has become a catered affair.

CHARACTER: A jerk with personality.

COMEDIAN: A person who knows a good gag when he steals one.

CONFERENCE: A group of men who, individually, can do nothing, but as a group, can meet and decide that nothing can be done.

COURTSHIP: An entertaining introduction to a dull book.

EFFICIENCY EXPERT: If a wife did it— they'd call it nagging.

EGOTIST: A man who always talks about himself—when you want to talk about *yourself.*

EXTRAVAGANT: Throwing out a tea bag after using it only once.

FLIRT: A girl who believes it's every man for herself.

FRUSTRATION AND PANIC: Frustration is the first time you discover you can't do it the second time, and panic is the second time you discover you can't do it the first time.

HIGHWAY ROBBERY: The price of new cars.

HINDSIGHT: What a woman should have before wearing slacks.

HOLLYWOOD HOUSE: A swimming pool surrounded by mortgages.

259

HONESTY: Fear of being caught.

A LIBERAL: A man who has both feet firmly planted in the air.

MARRIAGE: The hangover that lasts a lifetime.
Not a word—a sentence.

MINI-SKIRT: Tempt-dress.

MINK: A tranquilizer for women.

MONEY: The poor man's credit card.

MOTHER-IN-LAW: Comes for a six-month visit—twice a year.

NOODNICK: A naked Santa Claus.

ORATOR: The fellow who is always ready to lay down your life for his country.

ORGY: Group therapy.

PEDESTRIAN: Man with one car and family of grown children.

PERFECT MAN: Your wife's first husband.

PETTING: The study of the anatomy in braille.

PHILANTHROPIST: One who returns publicly what he stole privately.

PRACTICAL NURSE: One who marries a rich patient.

PROTEIN: A call-girl too young to vote.

RACE HORSE: Can take several thousand people for a ride at the same time.

RADICAL: Anyone whose opinions differ from yours.

ROTISSERIE: A ferris wheel for chickens.

RUSSIA: Where a guy can talk his head off.

SINNER: One who gets found out.

SOCIAL SECURITY: Where the government guarantees you a steak in your old age—when all your teeth are gone.

SOCIALIZED MEDICINE: When women get together and talk about their operations.

STOCK MARKET: Is like a Sultan—touching new bottoms too often lately.

TANGERINE: A loose-leaf orange.

TOPLESS WAITRESS: Wild waist show.

UNTOLD WEALTH: That little bit the income tax people never hear of.

VICIOUS CIRCLE: A wedding ring.

WOLF: A boudoir commando.

Democrats
(*see Republicans, Politics, etc.*)

I made so much money betting on the Democrats—I became a Republican.

Both candidates are ready and willing—now if we could only find one that's able.

The Democratic state senator announced that he is perfectly familiar with all the questions of the day—the trouble is he doesn't know the answers.

They elected him to Congress—anything to get him out of town.

The Democrats were pretty smart. Every place the Republicans went they left big tips and said "Vote Republican." But the Dems were smarter. They left no tip and said, "Vote Republican."

REPUBLICAN: "Remember, the worm will turn."
DEMOCRAT: "So what, it's the same on both ends."

Dentists

A Tulsa, Oklahoma, oilman rushed to his dentist for an examination. The dentist dove into the Oilionaire's mouth and said, "Perfect, man, perfect! You don't need a thing." "Well, drill anyway, doc," the patient drawled, "I feel lucky this morning."

The dentist examined the nervous lady and finally said, "It looks like I'll have to pull your tooth." The woman squealed, "I'd rather have a baby!" The doctor countered, "Make up your mind, lady, before I adjust the chair."

"But how could you bite yourself on the behind?"
"I sat on my false teeth!"

The actor was very nervous as he sat down in the chair. "I want gas," he insisted, "I can't take pain. What kind of gas do you have?"
"For you I suggest mustard gas," the dentist said; "it goes good with ham."

The playbore never forgave the chorus girl. He sent her to the dentist to have her teeth capped and paid for it, too. Then she decided to find herself a younger and richer boy. Everytime he met her after that, she grinned at him as she passed. "She's laughing at me," he hollered, "with *my* teeth."

You may be a painless dentist—but this is gonna hurt—I don't have the money.

"Darling," one lady meowed to another, "such beautiful teeth—are they really yours?"
"Sweetie," the other scratched back, "of course—do you want to see the summons from my dentist?"

"I'm dining with the upper set tonight."
"Better take your lowers, too, the steaks may be tough."

The dentist approached the patient, who let out a scream. "What are you hollering for?" the dentist asked. "You're not even in the chair yet."
"I know, doc," he answered, "but you're stepping on my corn."

1ST MAN: "She has teeth just like pearls."
2ND MAN: "Yeah . . . she and Pearl got them at the same dentist's."

PATIENT: "Hey, that wasn't the tooth I wanted pulled."
DENTIST: "Take it easy. I'm coming to it."

PATIENT: "Have you been a dentist very long?"
DENTIST: "No, I was a riveter till I got too nervous to work high up."

"That's all right," the dentist said, "you don't have to pay me in advance."
"What advance?" the patient answered. "I'm just counting my cash before you give me gas!"

I finally broke my husband out of the habit of biting his nails—I hid his teeth.

He's a careful dentist—he pulled my teeth with great pain.

Her teeth are her own—I was with her when she bought them.

261

There is a rich Texan who has a different dentist for every tooth.

"Why are you buying all those old magazines?"
"I'm studying to be a dentist."

PATIENT: "This may hurt a little—I don't have the money."

My dentist charges five dollars a cavity—I gave him five dollars and he gave me a cavity.

Her teeth are so far apart—when she smiles she looks like a picket fence.

Now I know why she smiles all the time—her teeth are the only things that aren't wrinkled.

"I've got to reduce," she said to the dentist. "Will you yank out my sweet tooth?"

Sign in dentist's office: "Get your 1968 plates here."

Diet
(see Doctors, etc.)

A diet-conscious lady he knows once weighed 180 pounds, but now weighs only 85 pounds . . . casket and all. . . .

The prayer of a small girl: "Please, Lord, can't you put the vitamins in pie and cake instead of cod liver oil and spinach?"

No-Cal Hair Tonic—for fatheads.

Eat all you want—chew—but don't swallow.

This is a story that happened about 700 years ago in Asia. Nasreddin Hoca had a donkey with a voracious appetite. He wondered if by gradually reducing the animal's food every day it would not be possible to condition the animal to get along without any food at all. This interesting experiment was continued for several weeks, but a few days after all food had been stopped, the donkey tor led over and died, to the great chagrin of Nasreddin Hoca, who sadly murmured: "What a pity that he should have died just when he was getting accustomed to hunger."

"No rich foods, no meat, no drinks," the doctor prescribed to his patient; "that should save you enough money to pay my bill."

Eat all you want of everything you don't like.

Sign in reducing salon: "Rear today—gone tomorrow."

If you are really set on losing weight —put the scale in front of the refrigerator.

"Take a look, doc," she beamed. "I dropped twenty pounds."
The doc looked and sighed, "You didn't drop them far enough."

The salesman and his wife arrived in California on a combined business-pleasure trip. He ordered the biggest and most expensive dinner he could afford. His wife made some fast calculations. "Frank," she warned, "that adds up to about 1,200 calories."
"So what?" Frank answered. "I'll put them on my expense account."

The doctor told her she could eat anything she liked—and as much of it as she wanted for every meal. She chose strawberries and sour cream. When she came back to the doctor she was thirty pounds heavier. "I don't understand it," the doctor said. "Did you do what I told you—did you eat strawberries and sour cream every meal and nothing else?"

"Definitely," she said. "After every meal—I ate strawberries and sour cream."

Americans have more food to eat than people of any other nation on earth, and more diets to keep us from eating it.

I just quit my onion diet. I lost ten pounds and twelve friends.

The best exercise to lose weight is to shake your head back and forth "NO."

Diets are strictly for those who are thick and tired of it.

Dieting will not help him lose his fat head.

The best way to lose weight—isn't nearly so much fun as the worst way.

Newest invention: a candy bar with lettuce inside—for women on a diet.

His doctor put him on a seven-day diet—but he ate the whole thing in one meal.

Dean Martin on the drinking man's diet: "I don't know about the rest of your body, but it sure makes your head lighter."

The second day of a diet is always easier than the first. By the second day you're off it.

He was put on a diet of chicken fat —it cuts the grapefruit.

The best way to stay on a diet is to keep your mouth and the refrigerator closed.

Well, it took a lot of will power—but I finally gave up trying to diet.

Doctor to overweight patient: "Here, follow this diet—and I want to see three-fourths of you back in my office for a checkup in two months."

We were standing on a local corner near one of those penny scales when a husband and wife approached. He jumped on the scale and dropped in a penny. "Listen to this fortune," he said enthusiastically to his wife as she peered over his shoulder. "It says I'm bright, resourceful and energetic and that I will go on to great success." "Yeah"—she returned. "It's got your weight wrong, too."

Fat makes you more law abiding. For example, very few overweight men make successful bank robbers. They have too much trouble waddling away from the scene of the crime.

Totie Fields says she's not overweight, she's just short for her weight. She should be seven feet eight inches tall.

There are minus 20 calories in a stalk of celery—it actually has 5 calories but you burn up 25 just chewing it.

Just when you get to the point when menu prices don't matter—calories do.

When I first met my wife she was always on a diet—she had an hourglass figure; but now she's let the sand settle in the wrong end.

Today half the population is trying to lose weight. This applies to both men and women. One of the best ways to lose weight is to eat yogurt. It's a magic food made from unwanted milk.

I knew of a couple who went on a yogurt diet. They ate nothing but yogurt for 6 months. When they started he weighed 264 pounds and she weighed about 130. But after eating yogurt for only 4 months, the husband lost 140 pounds and his wife disappeared completely.

In the interest of physical culture, I subscribed to one of those body building magazines. My mailman brought me 10-pound weights, then 20-pound weights, then 50-pound weights. And it was amazing; in less than three weeks, you should have seen the muscles on my mailman.

I have a friend who doesn't diet and never gains an ounce . . . he eats six meals a day. An average meal would consist of 2 steaks, 4 pounds of potatoes, 3 hamburgers, an apple pie, a malted, an ice cream soda and a hot fudge sundae . . . and he still weighs the same 475 lbs.

When a woman goes on a drastic diet, she has either one or both of these objectives in mind: to retain her girlish figure—or her boyish husband.

Sandwich spread: what you get from eating between meals.

If you are thin, don't eat fast. If you are fat, don't eat. Fast.

There are certain compensations for overweight women. Men do not suspect them and other women do not fear them as competition.

Travels of a French fried potato: in your mouth a second, in your stomach four hours, on your hips the rest of your life.

Phyllis Diller

"Everybody says I'm a beautiful person *inside*. Leave it to me to be born inside out."

"Phyllis has that rare beauty that drives men sane"—says an admirer.

"I call my neighbor Mrs. Clean. I finally found out why her laundry looks so much whiter than mine—she washes it."

"I'll never forget my first fur. It was a modest little stole. Modest?—people thought I was wearing anchovies."

"Don't call a baby-sitter who knows your children—she won't come."

"Don't taste the food while you're cooking it—you may lose the nerve to serve it."

"It takes a heap of livin' to make a house a home."

Bob Hope says: "Phyllis Diller is the lady with a thousand gags. One thousand and two—I forgot her face and figure."

"I can't work with my hair out of place—do you have a screwdriver?"

"The other night a Peeping Tom begged me to pull down my window shade."

"My husband has always felt that marriage and a career don't mix—that is why he's never worked."

"When I go to the beach in a bikini even the tide won't come in."

"My husband says he's learning karate to defend my honor. I told him to mind his own business."

"My husband once tried to run out on me—but the police arrested him for leaving the scene of an accident."

"I lost a beauty contest—and it was *fixed!*"

"We're at a cheap hotel, but it has a continuous floor show—mice!"

Talking about her driving: "Who would give me a license?! I got two tickets on my written test."

Diplomats

A diplomat is a man who can tell you to go to Hell so tactfully that you look forward to the trip.

A diplomat is a man who when asked to name his favorite color answers—"plaid."

Diplomacy is the ability to take something and act as though you were giving it away.

A diplomat is a person who can talk interestingly for an hour—and say nothing.

A diplomat is a man who can convince his wife she looks vulgar in diamonds.

A diplomat is a man who can convince his wife she looks fat in a fur coat.

If you want to deceive a diplomat, speak the truth—he has had no experience with it.

Divorce
(*see Marriage, Court Rooms, Judges, Alimony, etc.*)

Not fit to be tied.

The only grounds you need for divorce is—marriage.

They were mis-pronounced man and wife.

For the man who has everything—a divorce.

Love will find a way—*out.*

I got custody of the kids—she got custody of the money.

Special Cocktail: Divorce on the rocks.

The only thing they had in common —was her.

They were married three years—and the only time they were seen together was in court.

She didn't marry him for his money —but she sure is divorcing him for it.

Statistics prove that one out of every ten couples get divorced—the rest fight it out to the bitter end.

She divorced him because he had a will of his own—and it wasn't made out to her.

A divorce was inevitable; she was always complaining about the housework—she didn't like the way he did it.

HUSBAND: "I want a divorce—my wife called me a lousy lover."
JUDGE: "You want a divorce because your wife called you a lousy lover?"
HUSBAND: "No, I want a divorce because she knows the difference."

The worst thing about a divorce is that somewhere—perhaps miles apart —two mothers are nodding their heads and saying, "See—I told you so!"

The Hollywood star was so sentimental—she wanted to get divorced in the same dress in which her mother got divorced.

She couldn't afford a divorce—so she shot him.

Reno: The great divide.

Doctors
(*see Diet, Psychiatrists, Analysis, Hospitals, Dentists, Nurses*)

I feel awful tonight. I went to the doctor's office this afternoon to talk to him. As soon as I walked into the office, the nurse said, "Take off your clothes." I went into another room and there was another guy there with his clothes off. I said, "This is ridiculous, I only came in here to talk to the doctor and they made me take my clothes off." He said, "What are you kickin' about ... I'm the doctor!"

PATIENT: "All the other doctors differ from your diagnosis in my case."
DOCTOR: "I know—but just wait—the post-mortem will prove I'm right."

DOCTOR: "Your husband will never be able to work again."
WIFE: "I'll go up and tell him right away—it'll cheer him up."

I was feeling a little run-down so I went to visit a doctor someone had recommended to me. I think his name was Kronkeit. He looked me over and said, "Mr. Jones, I don't know how to tell you this but you only have four hours to live. Is there anyone you'd like to see?" I said, "Yeah, another doctor!"

I know a doctor so egotistical that when he takes a woman's pulse—he subtracts ten beats for his personality.

"I don't get it," said one pretty girl as she took off her clothes. "I tell the doctor my sinus is bothering me and he asks me to strip." A naked redhead with a satchel on her lap replied, "My case is even more puzzling. I'm here to tune the piano."

My doctor sure put me back on my feet—when I got his bill I had to sell my car.

"Calling Dr. Fink—Calling Dr. Fink —Your patient refused to take the medicine you prescribed—He got well and went home."

A friend showed up at my party minus an appendix.
"I didn't know you had appendicitis," I said.
"I didn't, but I had to run into my doctor's office to use his phone—and how could I leave without buying something?"

"How are you feeling?" Dr. Gilbert asked his patient as the beautiful blonde nurse stood by.
"I want to go home to my wife!"
"Oh," the doc said, "still delirious, huh?"

The patient called the doctor at 2 A.M. He was distraught: "I can't sleep, doc. It's that bill I owe you—I can't pay it—it bothers me so much I can't sleep."
DOCTOR: "Why did you have to tell me that? Now *I* can't sleep!"

She met the doctor in the lobby. "Doctor," she groaned, "I feel terrible; my head hurts, my shoulder is killing me, it's hard for me to walk on my paining feet, and even my adam's apple is rotten."
"Well," the doctor suggested, "why don't you come around to see me."
"Maybe," she said pensively. "Maybe next week if I'm feeling better."

266

A doctor is a success when he makes enough money to be able to tell a patient there's nothing wrong with him.

DOCTOR: "You'll have to cut out women or liquor."
PATIENT: "Well, then, I'll give up liquor —I can always drink when I'm old."

The nearsighted doctor treated the patient for varicose veins for a year— before he found out that the patient's fountain pen leaked!

"If my doctor could see me now with this champagne and caviar, he'd go crazy!"
"Why—are you supposed to be on some kind of diet?"
"No—I owe him $500!"

DOCTOR: "If I find the operation necessary—will you have the money?"
PATIENT: "If I find I don't have the money—will you find the operation necessary?"

PATIENT: "My right foot hurts."
DOCTOR: "It's just old age."
PATIENT: "But my left foot is just as old—how come *it* doesn't hurt?"

The girl told the doctor she was too embarrassed to get undressed—she was so shy.
"Okay." The doc understood. "I'll put out the lights—you can undress in the dark."
When she was naked, she asked, "Where will I put my clothes?" as she groped in the dark.
"Right here next to mine," the doctor suggested.

Dogs
(*see Animal Stories*)

I've got a sheep dog. He doesn't have fleas—he's got moths.

I sold my dog for $100,000—I got two $50,000 cats for him.

"My dog runs after cars."
"So what, a lot of dogs chase cars."
"Yeah, but my dog catches 'em."
"So what, he can't drive."

They say barking dogs never bite. I know it—and you know it—but does the dog know it?

"My dog may not be pedigreed and all that, but he's a hell of a watch dog. No stranger ever gets anywhere near our house without our Fido letting us know."
"What does he do? You mean he growls and bites?"
"No—he crawls under our bed."

They tell me that dog is worth $50,-000. I still can't believe he could save up that much.

GREAT DANE: The kind of puppy that has the house broken before he is.

Do-It-Yourself

If you really want to make some money, come up with a book on "How NOT to do it yourself."

Draft
(*see Army, War, Air Force, etc.*)

Two prison mates were B.S.ing in their cell. One said: "How come I only burned up my draft card and was sentenced to life—while you killed somebody and they gave you only four years?"
"That's because the guy I killed was a draft card burner."

He tried everything to get out of the draft. Even developed a limp, till he believed it himself. He practiced every day. When he got to the draft board he exhibited his limp.

"Don't worry," said the head of the board as they inducted him, "where we're sending you it's hilly."

He hid in the cellar to avoid the draft. When his eyes got used to the darkness, he saw his grandfather hiding in a corner. "What are you doing here?" the lad asked.

"They need generals, don't they?" the old man answered.

I got a letter from the draft board notifying me of its change of address. I wrote back, "Fellows, you don't have to tell me every time you make a move. I know if I want you, you'll know where to find me."

If they take him—it's total war— they would draft the draft board first.

One guy told the draft board he couldn't go because of a pain in the back. They said, "The pain will go— and you with it."

I don't know if I'm going but the draft board did send me a letter saying, "Don't start to read any continued stories."

I think the President is making a mistake in not drafting married men— after all, these are the only recruits who will really know how to take orders.

A young man of 18 was notified by the draft board that they wanted him in the army. When he told his mother she made the scene of all time.

"My bambino," she cried, "my little-a-boy. They take-a my bella bambino!"

"Why are you talking like that, mom?" the son asked. "You're not even Italian."

A nineteen-year-old reporting for his physical was classified 1A by the examining doctor who happened to be his family doctor.

"Your hay fever seems better," the doc said.

"That's pretty strange," the youngster said angrily. "When I was paying you ten dollars a visit—you always found it worse."

The karate expert was drafted and the first time he saluted—he knocked his brains out.

There was the fainthearted college student who was afraid to burn his draft card—so he boiled it.

DRAFT BOARD: The world's largest travel agency.

Young man to draft board: "But you've got to take me—I've told my boss what I think of him—I've proposed to three girls—and I sold my car."

"I just received a notice from my draft board—they burned my draft card."—Bob Hope

Dreams

WIFE: "I dreamed you bought me a fur coat."

HUSBAND: "Well, go back to sleep and wear it in good health."

Never mind what my dreams mean, doc, just get me their phone numbers.

He fell in love with the girl of his dreams—and she turned out to be a nightmare.

It doesn't hurt me if my wife dreams about being married to a millionaire— as long as she doesn't do it while she is out shopping.

268

I dream about beautiful girls—but you should see the kind I get.

"I dreamed last night that I was with Brigitte Bardot—she was kissing me—hugging me—"
"Then what happened?"
"Then it was time to get up—but I'm going to sleep early tonight."

I dreamed all night I was eating shredded wheat—when I awoke, half the mattress was gone.

The doctor gave the insomniac a handful of pills. "This red pill," he explained, "will make you dream of Brigitte Bardot. The pink one will make you dream of Sophia Loren, and the yellow one will make you dream of Elizabeth Taylor."
"Good," said the patient, "I'll take two of each—and don't bother to wake me for two weeks."

Drinking
(*see Bars, Restaurants, etc.*)

Jackie Gleason says: "Drinking removes warts and pimples—not from me—but from those I have to look at."

Everybody says Dean Martin always has a glass in his hand. That's not true. I never saw him with a glass in his hand—a bottle yes.

Somebody gave Deano a hot foot—he burned for four days.

It's not true that Martin spells his home town "*STEW*BENVILLE."

Phil Harris breathed on my suit—it was the best cleaning job I ever had.

Joe E. Lewis isn't a heavy drinker—he only weighs 140 pounds.

A heavy drinker was regaling his friends with his early life and the hard times he had. "Things were so bad," he recalled, "that sometimes I had to live for days on nothing but food and water."

A husband returned home late one night in a rather inebriated state and handed the wife his pay envelope. She opened it, looked inside and shouted, "This is only half your salary. Where's the rest of it?" "I bought something for the house," he explained. "Oh, how nice," smiled the spouse. "What'd you buy?" To which her husband replied, "A round of drinks."

To avoid a hangover—keep drinking.

Lovable clown Joe E. Lewis has been warned many times about his drinking. "Don't worry about a thing," is Joe's answer. "I'm responsible for a new surgical technique. After my last operation, instead of stitches they used corks."

W. C. Fields, well known for his light eating and heavy drinking habits, once said, "I never like to eat on an empty stomach." A friend once introduced him to brandied figs. Said Fields, "I never ate so much to drink in my life."

One of Gleason's fans was astonished to find the Great One imbibing pretty good at a bar. "I thought you were a man of regular habits," the man scolded. "I am," Jackie retorted. "Drinking is one of my regular habits."

"They say drinking shortens a man's life."
"Yes—but he sees twice as much in the same length of time."

He only drinks to calm his nerves,
And steadiness improve;

269

Today he got so steady
He couldn't even move.

Oil and alcohol *do* mix—but it tastes lousy.

A terrible argument was taking place between a man and wife when the stranger entered the bar. He edged his way in between the fighting couple and said to the bartender, "I want something long, cold and full of gin."
"Here, buddy," offered the man who was losing the argument, "take my wife."

"I went to a dozen different bars this afternoon, but I couldn't get what I wanted."
"That's funny. What did you want?"
"Credit."

The elderly gentleman went to see the doctor, who noticed his hands shaking violently.
"You must drink a lot," the doctor said.
"No," said the old man, "I spill most of it!"

She's eighty-five years old and doesn't need glasses—drinks right out of the bottle.

He gets drunk on Scotch tape.

The Red Cross rejected his blood donation—his plasma had an olive in it.

He has no respect for old age—unless it's bottled.

The only way he opens a conversation is with a corkscrew.

He never has a hangover—he stays drunk.

So he's a hypochondriac—but Irish coffee with Sanka?

I got a telegram from Joe E. Lewis, but I couldn't read it—the light was bad and I'm afraid to light a match around it.

It's a lie about how much Dean drinks. I've known him a long time and I never saw him take a drink until dinner time. In fact, I had dinner at his house and you never saw such a banquet—but who can eat that much at eight o'clock in the morning?

Show me a man who can eat, drink and be merry—and I'll show you a fat, grinning drunk.

DRUNK: "Why didn't you wake me at 7:30?"
OPERATOR: "Because you didn't get to bed until 8."

Joey Bishop says he gave Dean Martin a lighter—and he drank it in one gulp.

He drinks like a fish—too bad he doesn't drink what a fish drinks.

Dean Martin cut his finger—it's the first time I ever saw blood with a head on it.

Problem drinkers—are those who never buy.

Dean Martin wants to buy Alcatraz. He always wanted a house on the rocks with water on the side.

Don't take another drink—your face is already blurred.

Drive-In Theatres

My aunt went to a drive-in movie and became the first woman ever to be run over on the way to the bathroom.

No matter how bad the movie at a drive-in theatre, most patrons love every minute of it.

He's so rich he goes to drive-in theatres in a taxi.

The husband and wife went to see the latest Brigitte Bardot movie at the drive-in. They were late arriving, and as they drove up to the attendant the husband said, "Will we get to see a complete performance?" "No, sir," he said, "you won't. But I reckon you'll come closer to it than in any other movie I can think of."

He showed her a lot of love and affection. He took her to a drive-in movie and let her peek into the other cars.

Pretty soon all the drive-in theatres will be open—and people will quit watching movies again.

The owner of a drive-in theatre said to his partner, "If business gets any worse, we'll have to start showing pictures."

At a drive-in theatre even after the murder mystery is over, nobody knows who did it.

I saw a championship fight at a drive-in theatre but it was sort of confusing. Most of the time I was watching the wrong clinches.

A funny thing happened at this drive-in theatre—a fellow drove in all alone.

This picture at the drive-in was so sad—there wasn't a dry windshield in the place.

There's a new drive-in theatre screen: The manager puts one around each car.

When the teener asked his old man for the car to take his girl to a drive-in theatre, pop said, "But it's so foggy!" The kid explained, "That's nothing —we've already seen the picture."

Driving
(see Cars, Traffic, Accidents, etc.)

Best way to stop noise in a car is to let her drive.

It was one of those new low foreign cars—he stuck out his hand to make a left turn and ruptured the cop on the corner.

Latest model cars have modern devices to safeguard the lives of pedestrians. If a car runs over you, the exhaust sprays you with penicillin and a get well card drops on your chest.

"My wife is *the* woman driver. I saw her driving down the street—only 30 miles an hour—but it was on the sidewalk—I ran into my building—shut the door—ran into the elevator—shut the door—ran into my closet—shut the door—it didn't help—she hit me!"

George Gobel was asked to come up with a slogan over the July 4th weekend to encourage safe driving. George suggested: "Ladies and Gentlemen, this is a holiday weekend. The National Safety Council estimates that 524 people will be killed. So far only 185 have been killed. Some of you folks aren't trying."

271

Sign in used car lot: "If your headlights are out of order—don't stop to have them fixed at night—just put your radio on real loud. This will help drown out the noise of the crash."

She's a great driver—gets 20 miles to a fender.

Is the white line in the center of the road really for bicycles?

My wife never stops for a red light when she's driving. She says, "You see one or two, you've seen them all."

Nothing confuses a man more than driving behind a woman who does everything right.

The woman driver made a right turn from the left lane, and smashed into another car. "Why the hell didn't you signal?" the angry motorist screamed.
"Sir," she answered haughtily, "why do I have to signal—I always turn here."

The husband complained that his wife ran over his golf sticks.
"I told you," she said, "not to leave them on the porch."

When it comes to parking—she does a bang-up job.

Riding on the freeway is like Russian roulette—you never know which driver is loaded.

Drug Stores
(*see Doctors, Pills, etc.*)

CUSTOMER: "You made a mistake in that prescription I gave my mother-in-law. Instead of quinine you used strychnine!"
DRUGGIST: "You don't say? Then you owe me twenty cents more."

CUSTOMER: "I can't sleep at night—the least little sound disturbs me. I'm a victim of insomnia. Even a cat on our back fence distresses me beyond words."
DRUGGIST: "This powder will be effective."
CUSTOMER: "When do I take it?"
DRUGGIST: "You don't. Give it to the cat in milk."

"A mustard plaster."
"We're out of mustard, how about mayonnaise?"

"Sir, you gave my wife arsenic instead of sleeping powder!"
"That's all right—you only owe me another ten cents."

We got a new wonder drug—it's so powerful—you have to be in perfect health to take it.

DRUGGIST: "Well, Charlie, did that mudpack improve your wife's appearance?"
CHARLIE: "It did for a few days—but then it wore off."

"He's a great druggist, isn't he?"
"Yes, but I think he makes the chicken salad a little too salty."

These new miracle drugs sound so good—I'm sorry I'm healthy.

Dull
(*see Bores*)

His life is so dull—he looks forward to dental appointments.

Stay with me—I want to be alone.

His tombstone should read: "Died at 20—buried at 60."

This town was so dull—the Howard Johnson's stand had only one flavor.

Get brainwashed—in your case it might help.

My home town is so dead—they don't even ring the curfew at 8 P.M. any more. It kept waking everybody up.

Dumb

She's so dumb—she has to take her sweater off to count to two.

He wanted to write Happy Birthday on a cake—for three hours he tried to get the cake into his typewriter.

The only thing that can stay in his head more than an hour—is a cold.

It takes her an hour to cook—minute rice.

The chorine was a little confused as she faced the lawyers on the witness stand. "Do you mind," she cooed to the judge, batting her baby blues, "if I tell my story in my lawyer's own words?"

"I was so surprised when I heard it," he screamed, "I couldn't believe my eyes."

He doesn't have an inferiority complex—he's just inferior.

If he said what he thought—he'd be speechless.

He has a brain—but it hasn't reached his head.

Offer him a penny for his thoughts —and you're overpaying him.

He's so dumb he had the seven-year itch for eight years.

She had a 38 bust and an I.Q. to match.

HE: "I suppose you think Barnum and Bailey are married to each other."
SHE: "What difference does it make— as long as they love each other."

He was so dumb it finally sent him to the hospital—he threw a cigarette butt in a manhole and then stepped on it.

He was so dumb that it killed him. He bet his friend that he could lean further out of a window . . . he won his bet!

He saw a moosehead hanging on a wall and said to the host, "May I go in the next room and see the rest of it?"

The model was telling her friend about a strange man who got on at the same station with her and "hugged me and kissed me until he had to get off."
"Didn't you say anything to him?" asked her friend.
"I should say not," said the model. "I never talk to strangers."

"Have you seen a crazy man?" inquired the man out of breath.
"What does he look like?" asked the policeman.
"He's very short," said the man. "Only six feet four, and he's very thin. He weighs about four hundred pounds."
The cop peered at him peculiarly. "If he's short how could he be six feet four and if he's very thin, how could he be four hundred pounds?"
"I told you he was crazy," answered the man.

He was the flower of manhood—a blooming idiot.

He got an idea—beginner's luck.

The politician is so dumb—when you ask him his name—he calls a conference.

LOIS: "Well, I'm falling in love and I think I should go to a palmist or a mind reader. Which would you suggest?"
DORIS: "You'd better go to a palmist—you know you've got a palm."

WIFE: "I lost my bank book—but don't worry. I took the precaution of signing all the checks as soon as I got them—now they're no use to anybody."

She thinks a mushroom is a place to love.

She couldn't tell which way our elevator was going if she had two guesses.

Why is it every time I wash ice cubes in hot water—I can't find them?

If anyone said hello to her—she'd be stuck for an answer.

He spent two weeks in a revolving door—looking for a doorknob.

They say it pays to be ignorant—so how come I'm broke?

I may look dumb—but that doesn't mean I'm not.

"This match won't light."
"What's the matter with it?"
"I don't know—it lit before."

He gave his wife a washing machine for her birthday but he had to get rid of it—every time she got into it—she came out black and blue.

He doesn't know the meaning of the word defeat—besides thousands of other words he doesn't know the meaning of.

He didn't know the meaning of the word fear—until he looked it up.

He changed his mind—but it didn't work any better than the old one.

She wouldn't accept tickets for a door prize—she says she doesn't need a door.

He thinks a naturalist is a crap shooter who only throws sevens and elevens.

Ears
(*see Faces, Heads, etc.*)

The only time she washes her ears is when she eats watermelon.

All day long I heard a ringing in my ears—then I picked up the phone and it stopped.

"That hat fits you nicely."
"Yes, but what happens when my ears get tired?"

He's a big ear doctor—he only looks into big ears.

Her mouth was so big, every time she yawned—her ears disappeared.

Education
(*see Juvenile Delinquents, Kids, Children, Schools, Colleges, Universities, etc.*)

They now have an "educational toy." It's a little too complicated for a kid but it's designed to help the child adjust to the world of today. No matter how he puts it together—it's wrong.

I remember when aid to education used to be the father.

My son, who is nine years old, goes to a very progressive school—he dates his teachers.

Education is wonderful—it helps you worry about things all over the world.

Education is what a man gets when he sits in his living room with a group of teenagers.

Woody Allen says: "I had a terrible education. I attended a school for emotionally disturbed teachers."

Education is very important. A good education enables you to work for someone who has no education at all.

"I spent $15,000 dollars on my daughter's education," the businessman was complaining to his partner, "and she marries a bum who only makes 3,000 a year."
"What are you complaining about?" the partner asked. "You're still getting 20 per cent on your money."

I was a teacher in one of those progressive kindergarten schools. I didn't realize how progressive it really was until two of the kids got married last month.

One mother to another: "I never realized the value of education until the children went back to school."

A teacher is a person who used to think he liked children.

Efficiency Experts
(*see Office, Executives, etc.*)

If all the efficiency experts would be laid end to end—I'd be in favor of it.

The efficiency expert scrutinized the salesman's expense account. "How the hell could you spend twelve dollars a day for food in Augusta, Georgia?"
"Simple," the salesman answered, "you just miss breakfast."

He went crazy giving pep talks to rabbits.

EFFICIENCY EXPERT: A guy smart enough to tell you how to run your business—and too smart to start his own.

Ego
(*see Actors, Hollywood, etc.*)

He's so conceited—he has his X rays retouched.

He's carrying on a great love affair—unassisted.

Zsa Zsa Gabor talking about her third husband, George Sanders: "When I was married to him we were both in love with him; I fell out of love with him—but he didn't."

He likes you to come right out and say what you think—if you agree with him.

An egotist is a guy who tells you all the things about himself that you wanted to tell about *yourself*.

Mohammed Ali was explaining to me that he used to brag about being the greatest because it was good box-office and he was climbing and had to get attention. "Now," says the heavyweight champ, "I am not so show-offy. Don't misunderstand, I'm still the greatest, but I'm more modest about it."

I insist I am not conceited—although, you realize—I have every right to be.

I'm afraid I'm unfaithful—I don't love myself as much as I should.

His head is getting too big for his toupee.

Every time he looks in the mirror he takes a bow.

Every time he opens the refrigerator and the light goes on—he takes a bow.

He's suffering from "I" strain.

He's a self-made man who adores his maker.

He's a guy who, when he reads a story and doesn't understand it, figures it must be a misprint.

When he hears a clap of thunder—he takes a bow.

I know I'm not the most handsome man in the world—but what's my opinion against millions of others?

"One of my chief regrets during my years in the theatre is that I couldn't sit in the audience and watch me."—John Barrymore

George Gershwin praised his mother by explaining, "She is so modest about me."

One columnist murdered a comic in his column without using his name. The comic threatened to sue:
"But," his wife said, "he didn't mention your name."
"That's it," he hollered, "nobody'll know it's me!"

He'll never change his religion—he thinks he's God.

Her body has gone to her head.

He has never said a kind word about anybody—that's because he only talks about himself.

Conceit is God's gift to little men.

Elections
(*see Politics, Republicans, Democrats, etc.*)

The Britisher couldn't understand why we keep our bars closed on election day. "At home we keep the bars open," he said. "We figure nobody is going to vote for those candidates sober."

The Republicans left big tips and said, "Vote Republican." The Democrats were smarter—they left no tips and said, "Vote Republican."

The sign in the voting booth in Moscow reads, "Vote Communist—the life you save may be your own."

To tell the truth, I do not believe in political jokes—too many of them have been getting elected.

I never vote for the best candidate—I vote for the one who would do the least harm.

Employment
(*see Office, Work, Executives, Bosses, etc.*)

"What's the idea of that cross-eyed man for a store detective?"
"Well, look at him! Can you tell who he is watching?"

If at first you don't succeed, you're probably not related to the boss.

The four partners had a meeting about the stenographer who filled a sweater better than she did her job. "Which one of you took her out?" one of the partners asked. Three of them raised their hands, including himself. The man who didn't raise his hand was told, "Well—if you're telling the truth, *you* fire her."

The trusted employee had stolen half a million dollars over a period of years. And he was a relative yet. When the big boss found out he fired him immediately. "I'm not going to put you in jail," he said. "I don't want a scandal—it would break your mother's heart—and it wouldn't help our firm either."

The employee replied, "I admit I robbed you of a lot of loot—but I now have a big home, two cars, and every luxury I could want. I don't need a thing—why hire somebody else and have him start at the beginning?"

His idea was to get an employee who was not more than twenty years of age but with thirty years' experience.

He fired his secretary because of lack of experience. All she knew was typing, shorthand, and filing.

She failed the typing test but passed the physical.

She likes her job—lots of opportunities for advances.

She has a great future. She's really going places—with the boss.

The lady of the house reprimanded the maid: "Look at the dust on this desk," she said. "It must be at least two months old."

"Then don't blame me, madam, I've only been here two weeks."

He gave the new maid the special list of dishes that his mother-in-law liked. "The first time you serve one of them," he said, "you're fired."

I just got a big television part—I'm gonna be scorekeeper on "Peyton Place."

"You never worked in a precision factory and you want two hundred a week?"
"Sure—the work is harder if you don't know how to do it."

My brother got a job as a lifeguard in a car wash.

Engaged
(*see Romance, Love, Dates, etc.*)

If I had all the qualities you want in a man—I wouldn't be proposing to you.

When the two teenagers were turned down by the Marriage License Bureau, they asked, "Could you maybe give us a beginner's license?"

"The ring is nice," she said hesitatingly, "but it is small, darling."
"So what?" he tried to overcome it. "After all, we are in love and you know the old saying—'Love is Blind.' "
"Yes—but not *stone* blind "

"Be honest with me—are you marrying my daughter for my money?"
"To level with you—we're both taking a chance. How sure am I that you won't go broke in a couple of years?"

The period of engagement is like an exciting introduction to a dull book.

Ethnic Humor
(*see chapter on Censorship, International Humor, Dick Gregory, Jewish Humor, Integration, Myron Cohen, etc.*)

Ethnic humor is a vulgar caricature of a people that is put down here strictly as a comic history of a bygone era in comedy. Today it is very rarely used—where once it was *the* form of comedy. Even today, in the right hams and the right time and place— you could get killed.

St. Patrick's is the day on which the Irish march up 5th Avenue and stagger down 6th Avenue.

"What's an Irish seven-course dinner?"
"A boiled potato and a six-pack of beer!"

"How do you tell a bride at an Irish wedding?"
"She's the one in the maternity dress."

An Irishwoman who had reached the age of 102 was giving an interview about her longevity, when one of the reporters asked her if she had ever been bedridden. "Oh yis," she answered, "many times, me bye—and once on a sleigh."

"Why is Santa Claus Polish?"
"Who else would wear a red suit?"

"Who has an IQ of 200?"
"Poland."

"What is a dope ring?"
"Six Polacks sitting in a circle."

"What do you call removing a splinter from a Polack's behind?"
"Brain surgery."

The Scotsman was awakened to find that his wife had died during the night. Frantically he called down to the maid, "Marta—boil only one egg for break fast this morning."

"My Scotch boy friend sent me this picture."
"How does it look?"
"I don't know, I haven't had it developed yet."

In Israel they have a slogan in the navy that goes: "Don't give up the ship—sell it."

The unkempt Arab rug peddler was making his way down a Parisian boulevard trying to sell his wares.
"Will you buy a carpet, monsieur?" he pleaded to a passing tourist.
"No, no!" snapped the tourist, drawing back. "They stink!"
The Arab drew himself up in proud indignation. "How dare you say that!" he cried. "I'll have you know, monsieur, that my carpets do not stink! It's me!"

Tony opened his lunch box every day and found a peanut butter sandwich. Each day he threw it away hollering, "I no lika peanut butter sandwiches." After watching this for five days in a row, his co-worker asked, "If you no lika peanut butter sandwich, why you no tell your wife no make you peanut butter sandwich?"
"What wife?" Tony screamed. "I make my own sandwiches."

"Was I brought here to die?" he asked when he opened his eyes in the hospital.

"No," answered the Australian, "you were brought here yester-die."

The Irishman was really loaded. "Don't you know drinking shortens a man's life?" his doctor told him.

"Yes," he hic'd, "but he sees twice as much in the same length of time."

The Scotsman celebrated New Year's Eve with his wife. They got themselves a pip of a drunk by going around in a revolving door all night.

"I wish you'd get something for that cough o' yours," the Englishman barked. "That's the second time you've blown out the bloomin' candle."

Tonto and the Lone Ranger were surrounded by Indians when the Lone Ranger turned to Tonto and said, "We're in trouble, Tonto."

To which Tonto replied, "You mean *you're* in trouble, white man."

Dick Gregory says there is nothing to the rumor that Georgia is passing a law banning mixed drinks.

"I'll say this about living in an all-white suburb," says Dick. "Crabgrass is *not* our biggest problem."

"What would you call a 6-foot-4 Negro with a knife in his hand?"
"Sir!"

"Why do Italians talk with their hands?"
"Because they can't stand each other's breath."

Two women met at Grossinger's: "What happened with your sons?" one asked.

"Morris is in the dress business," she said. "He makes a fortune—sends me the whole winter to Florida, gives me $200 a week just for spending money—a millionaire that boy."

"And Irving?"

"He became a Rabbi—by me that's not a business for a Jew."

When John married Theresa, they moved into a brand new old flat in Harlem. The first pieces of furniture the husband brought home were a sewing machine and a full-length mirror.

"What's all that junk?" the wife asked.

"That's no junk—you take your choice. You take the sewing machine, and go to work, or you take the mirror and sit down and watch yourself starve."

TEACHER: "Now, children, I want you to write your name in your primers."
ABE: "Are you kidding? That will kill the resale value."

"What's the definition of a nymphomaniac?"

"A Jewish girl who will go to bed with a guy after she's had her hair done."

"How can you tell the difference between a Jew and an Italian?"

"The Jew is the one in the Italian suit."

"How can you tell an Italian movie star from an American movie star?"

"She's the one with the mustache."

"Who put the twenty-two bullet holes in Mussolini?"

"Five thousand Italian sharpshooters."

"How do you tell the bride at an Italian wedding?"

"She's wearing something old, some-

279

thing new, something borrowed, something blue, something pink, something purple, something orange, something yellow. . . . "

The waiter dropped a tray of drinks on Mac Phearson—it was the first time the drinks were on him.

You can always tell when you're passing a Scotsman's house—no garbage cans.

I don't believe the one about the young Scot who murdered his parents so he could go to the orphans' picnic.

"What is matched Puerto Rican luggage?"
"Two shopping bags from the same store."

"What happens to garbage in Italian restaurants?"
"They serve it in Spanish restaurants!"

"How was the limbo invented?"
"A Puerto Rican sneaking into a pay-toilet."

One thing you never heard of is a Puerto Rican suicide. You can't kill yourself jumping out of a basement window.

"What is the recipe for baking a Hungarian cake?"
"First you steal two eggs. . . . "

The Englishman laughs at a joke three times. Once when he hears it, once when it is explained to him, and once when he understands it.

LORD FARTHING: "I hear they buried your wife."
LORD SCHMATE: "Had to—dead, you know."

The British missionary was trying to convince the Hindu to join Christianity: "Wouldn't you like to go to Heaven when you die?"
"Not me," said the Hindu. "If Heaven were any good—you British would have grabbed it years ago."

Etiquette
(*see Modest*)

Etiquette is learning to yawn with your mouth shut.

Etiquette is knowing which finger to use when you whistle for the waiter.

Etiquette is the noise you don't make when you eat soup.

The well-bred man steps on the cigarette so it won't burn the rug.

A bird in the hand is bad table manners.

Every time she throws a cup at her husband—she takes out the spoon.

He had the manners of a gentleman —I knew they didn't belong to him.

There is no man so bad that a woman cannot make him worse.

"Is my face clean enough to eat with?"
"Yes, but you'd better use your hands."

Social tact is making your company feel at home, even though they wish they were.

"He's just bashful. Why don't you give him a little encouragement?"
"Encouragement? He needs a cheering section!'

He eats with his fingers and talks with his fork.

He died an unhappy death. He was afraid his last breath would be a hiccough, and he wouldn't be able to say, "Excuse me."

"Do you know what to do with crumbs at the table?"
"Sure, let them stay there."

"What is the first thing you do when you get up from the table?"
"I put on my shoes."

"You know, I think there's something wrong with my boss's eyes."
"How's that?"
"When I went into his office this morning he asked me three times where my hat was—and it was on my head all the time."

"Stop! Act like a gentleman."
"Sorry, but I don't do imitations."

"This man is following me around and he's been doing that for fifteen minutes. Tell him to stop."
"Don't be silly. That's the butler and he's trying to serve you cocktails."

"When I sneeze I put my hand in front of my mouth."
"Really, Phil? Why do you do that?"
"To catch my teeth!"

My boy friend is so polite he always knocks on the oyster shells before he opens them.

Another thing, the next time you butter your bread: when you finish buttering it, don't fold it and then eat it.

He embarrassed us—he drank his soup and six couples got up and danced.

"When you yawn, you put your hand to your mouth."
"What? And get bitten?"

She's very proper. She won't even look at things with a naked eye.

Executives
(*see Bosses, Business, Office, etc.*)

He is so dedicated to his work that he keeps his secretary near his bed in case he gets an idea during the night.

A good executive is a man who believes in sharing the credit with the man who did the work.

An executive came home one night and slumped unhappily into his favorite chair. Noticing his state, his wife asked what was wrong. "Well," he moaned, "you know those aptitude tests I'm giving over at the office? I took one today and it sure is a good thing I own the company."

A good executive never puts off for tomorrow—what he can get you to do today.

He's a perfect executive; when he's dictating to his secretary—he always ends a sentence with a proposition.

The big executive wolf was chasing his secretary for weeks. "Tonight's the night," he warned her, "we go to my apartment."
"I'm very didactic and pithy in my refusal of your derogatory, vituperative, and vitriolic proposition."
"I don't get it," the big shot said.
"That's what I've been trying to tell you!" she answered.

He doesn't believe in wasting time with secretaries. He uses the old saying, "If at first you don't succeed—fire her."

I hired a gorgeous secretary but I had to let her go—she came in the office one day and I told her to sit down and the silly girl looked for a chair.

Executive ability is convincing your wife you hired your pretty secretary for her ability.

Exercise

"I get plenty of exercise," says Jackie Gleason. "Immediately after waking I always say sternly to myself, 'Ready, now. Up. Down. Up. Down.' And after three strenuous minutes I tell myself, 'Okay, boy. Now we'll try the other eyelid.' "

Eyes
(*see Faces, Head, etc.*)

The height of embarrassment: Looking through a keyhole—and seeing another eye.

My eyes were never any good—and I got a wife to prove it.

He had bad eyesight until he was sixteen—and then he got a haircut.

I lost my glasses and I can't look for them until I find them.

I knew I needed glasses when I walked into the closet and said, "Down."

I knew I needed glasses when I passed my wife and said, "Good evening, sir."

It was so windy in Chicago—I spit in my own eye.

She had something that would knock your eye out—a husband.

"Do you close your eyes when you kiss?"
"No, I have to be on the lookout for my husband."

I like to live in a small town. I don't have to keep an eye out for my wife—the neighbors do it for me.

Let's wash the windows, mother—the neighbors are straining their eyes.

A wolf is a guy who takes out a sweater girl and tries to pull the wool over her eyes.

I'm not saying she's cockeyed—but she can look at a tennis match without moving her head.

Faces
(*see Ugly, Eyes, Noses, etc.*)

"I have the face of an 18-year-old."
"Well, give it back—you're getting it all wrinkled!"

Is that your face or are you celebrating Halloween?

The last time I saw a face like that was on an iodine bottle.

She had a face like a flower—cauliflower.

She had a winning smile—too bad she had a losing face.

The only time her face gets washed —is when she cries.

A man falls in love with a beautiful face and then makes the mistake of marrying the whole girl.

He has such a long face—the barber charges him twice for shaving.

She had an Early American face—she looked like George Washington.

Some girls have dishpan hands—she's got dishpan face.

She looks like a million—but nobody can be that old.

Family
(*see Parents, Marriage, Children, Kids, Juvenile Delinquents, etc.*)

Every family should have three children; if one turns out to be a genius—the other two can support him.

When I was six my family moved—but I found them again.

Her family was so exclusive; they didn't come over on the Mayflower—they had their own boat.

He didn't come from a good family—he was sent.

Our family had more trouble than a soap opera.

A family man is one who has replaced the money in his wallet with snapshots of the wife and kids.

She comes from such an old family—it's been condemned.

Molly Picon tells about her childhood: "My grandmother raised eleven children in four rooms in Philadelphia."
"How did she manage?" she was asked.
"Easy—she took in boarders."

I came from a family of ten kids. I used to come home late—so ı could sleep on top.

Farming

A farmer had such a pretty wife that he couldn't keep his hands off her—so he fired the hands and bought a tractor.

A farm is a hunk of land; if you get up early and work late you can make a fortune—if you strike oil.

Now I know why the cow jumped over the moon—the farmer had cold hands.

He's a gentleman farmer—owns two station wagons and a flower pot.

She was only a farmer's daughter—but she tried every salesman's samples.

"I heard you shot twelve ducks—were they wild?"
"No, but the farmer was."

Men's Fashion

I like the suit you're wearing—who shines it for you?

His suit looks like a million—all wrinkled and green.

I like your suit so much—like it was cut from an old sofa.

He rides the subway just to get his suit pressed.

My new blue serge suit picks up everything but women.

He looks like a torn page out of *Esquire*.

You like my suit? Very reasonable. Only two payments and a change of address.

283

"That hat fits you nicely."
"Yeah, but my ears are tired."

My raincoat has a waterproof label; the label is waterproof—but not the coat.

"The suit fits you like a glove."
"I wish it could fit like a suit."

It's terrible to see men looking like girls with the long hair and all. You can't tell the difference. I was sitting in a restaurant when a girl came in. I turned to the person at the next table and said, "Isn't it terrible how boys look like girls these days?"
"That's my son," she said, pointing to the girl.
"Oh, I'm sorry, I didn't know you were the mother."
"I'm not," my neighbor said indignantly, "I'm the father."

"How do you get into those tight pants?"
"Very carefully."

Blue serge suits are very handy—for removing dandruff from your hair.

Women's Fashion
(*see Twiggy, Mini-Skirts, Topless, Waitresses, Figures, etc.*)

She's been married so many times—the wedding dress is her native costume.

A wise man never laughs at his wife's old clothes.

Gals who buy sweaters: "The right size is the tight size."

"Who made her dress?"
"The police."

I gave her a three-piece sweater set for Christmas—two needles and a ball of wool.

Some women show a lot of style and some styles show a lot of women.

They say long dresses pick up germs —you should see what those short dresses pick up.

She always wears a play suit—but she means business.

If her dress were any shorter—it would be a collar.

Girls' fashions may change—but their designs are the same.

FASHION NOTE: Women will be wearing the same thing in brassieres this year.

Women's dresses keep going higher and higher—you wonder what they'll be up to next.

There are two types of sweater girls: the type that knits them—and the type that fits them.

"This dress is a little too long for me —do you have anything shorter?"
"Try the belt department!"

A new fur will do a lot for a girl—and a girl will do a lot for a new fur coat.

There are millions of reasons why women dress the way they do—and all of them are men.

When the wife wears the pants—some other woman wears the fur coat.

The only thing getting longer in women's clothes—are the shoulder straps.

284

She talked him into buying her a new dress—then he tried to talk her out of it.

All a sweater does for her is make her itch.

Pajamas are great on a honeymoon —in case of fire.

Her dress kept everybody warm but her.

A woman's dress should be like a barbed-wire fence—serve its purpose without obstructing the view.

"This piece of lace on my dress is sixty years old!"
"Beautiful—did you make it yourself?"

Some of the bathing suits look like they haven't been delivered yet.

She looks like she was poured into that dress—but forgot to say "when."

Either her dress is too short—or she's in too far.

If that dress she's wearing was cut any lower—she'd be barefoot.

Gina Lollobrigida doesn't like miniskirts. "It is better for men to discover," she says, "than for women to reveal."

"I want a pair of shoes with low heels."
"To go with what?"
"A short fat bald millionaire."

If women dressed to please their husbands—they'd wear last year's clothes.

With those new mini-skirts, and low-cut dresses—I don't know if she's trying to catch a man or a cold.

Her neckline is where her waistline was.

Nobody asks her to remove her hat at the movies—it's funnier than any picture.

The latest in women's fashions are dresses made of newspaper. Can you imagine a man arrested as a masher just because he wanted to read the fine print?

Fred Allen commented on a woman's hat: "There's a creation that will never go out of style—it will just look ridiculous year after year."

Those stretch ski pants the girls are wearing this season come in three sizes: small, medium, and don't bend over.

Your dress should be tight enough to show you're a woman and loose enough to show you're a lady.

To women who wear slacks: "Does your end justify your jeans?"

Those new paper dresses will be used to wrap some very nice packages.

Fat

I know a girl so fat—I gave her a belt for Christmas and she used it for a wristwatch.

He went on a three-week diet and lost twenty-one days.

Jackie Gleason to Twiggy: "I ate more than you for breakfast."

He has so many double chins—he needs a bookmark to find his collar.

They say fat people are good-natured. They have to be. They're too heavy to run and too fat to fight.

She more than kept her girlish figure —she doubled it.

She got the dress for a ridiculous figure—*hers*.

When the fat woman got on the bus, she called out, "Isn't anybody going to offer me a seat?"
One little fellow got up and said, "I'm willing to make a contribution—anybody else?"

I won't dare say she's built like a truck—but I did notice that nobody ever passes her on the right.

She brags that she's got the figure of a girl. That's true—a fat girl.

She brags she's got a schoolgirl figure —but how the hell do you find it under all that fat?

Did you hear about the fat man who bought a sports car and had to have it let out?

I'm not saying she is fat—but I've known her for five years and I still haven't seen all of her.

She was so fat she could answer the front door without leaving the kitchen.

She's so fat she has to put on a girdle to get into her kimono.

She is so fat—she is two inches taller when she lies down.

She is so fat she has to go through a revolving door in two trips.

She's so fat, when she walks down Park Avenue it becomes a one-way street.

She's so fat she wears two girdles— an upper and a lower.

"I got her a present last week and she can't fit into it."
"Well, get her a larger dress."
"What dress? It's a Volkswagen!"

Is he fat? He had the mumps for three weeks before he found out about it.

I had a funny experience with this fatso the other night. I was sitting in the dark and I thought I was necking with her—but all the time I only had hold of her arm.

He was born when meat was cheap.

Totie Fields

"I'm not really fat—I'm just short for my weight! I should actually be about 8 foot 6 inches."

Phyllis Diller and I are going to do "The Odd Couple."

Totie Fields admits she's putting on weight. "All I can tell you," Totie says, "is that the other day I got on a weighing machine that stamps your weight on a card. When the card came out, I read it, and it said, 'Come back in ten minutes—alone.' "

Totie says she has an 18-inch waist —"through the center."

Two-hundred-pound Totie Fields says, "I went on a crash diet: I walked into a truck and you ought to see it—a mess."

W. C. Fields
(*see Drinking, Hollywood, Comedians*)

"After two days in the hospital—I finally took a turn for the nurse."

W. C. Fields, well known for his light eating and heavy drinking, used to say, "I never like to eat on an empty stomach."

A friend once introduced him to brandied figs. Said Fields, "I never ate so much to drink in my life."

"Every time I see you—you have a bottle in your hand," the lady said to Fields.
"You don't expect me to keep it in my mouth all the time, do you?"

"It was a woman who drove me to drink—and you know, I never even thanked her."

W. C. Fields was most proud of his drinking ability. He once challenged Mark Hellinger to a brandy-drinking contest. "I got Mark so plastered," he bragged the next day, "it took three bellboys to put me to bed."

"Talk about nitwits, when I said hello to this idiot—he couldn't even think of an answer."

His secretary kept annoying him while he was drinking—which was all the time. "The head of the studio wants to talk to you," the secretary said. "He's called you five times."
"Give him an evasive answer," Fields said. "Tell him to drop dead."

Mae West and W. C. Fields were starred in several pictures but there was always the fight about billing. "If you weren't such a ham, you'd have to admit that never in history is a man billed before a lady," argued Miss West.
"Oh yeah? How about Mister and Missus?"

A Hollywood columnist printed the false news that W. C. was dead. The comedian called the editor in a rage. "I hope you noticed," he screamed, "that your foul newspaper announced this morning that I was dead."
"I did—may I ask where you're calling from?"

Some young man came to the door of W. C. Fields' home in California and claimed he was his son.
Fields decided to talk to him. "Have a drink," he offered the youngster.
"Thanks," said the boy, "I'll have a Coke."
"Coke?" hollered Fields to his valet. "Throw this bum out—he's no son of mine."

Fights
(see Marriage)

I had a terrible fight with my wife I said, "You know, you're going to drive me to my grave." In two minutes she had the car in front of the house.

"Where did you get that black eye?"
"I got beat up for kissing a bride."
"But I thought that was permissible."
"But this was two years after the ceremony."

He had a big battle with his wife and was so unhappy.
"What happened?" I asked.
"I had a rough one with my old lady; she promised she wouldn't talk to me for thirty days."
"Well then," I said, "you should be happy."
"What happy?—This is the last day."

They had been fighting for twenty-five years. On their silver anniversary she said, "Well, old man, how are we gonna celebrate?"
"How about two minutes of silence?"

The only person who listens to both sides of an argument—is the woman in the next apartment.

"I can't work—my wife broke a leg."
"What's that got to do with you?"
"It's my leg she broke!"

Morris had a terrible fight with his wife and moved out to a hotel. All day he brooded, but by dinner time he was hungry and sorry—so he called her.
"Hello, Sarah, what are you making for dinner?"
"What am I making, you bum? Poison I'm making!"
"So make only one portion. I'm not coming home!"

He had a terrible fight with his wife and was complaining to a pal what a drag she was.
"But," his friend tried to be nice, "she must have some redeeming features?"
"Yeah," he admitted, "she does my washing and ironing."
"What's bad about that?"
"Yeah—but what a price to pay for laundry!"

The movie queen got a call from the columnist: "I want to check on a rumor before I print it—the story is that you and your fifth husband haven't been getting along too well."
"Absolutely ridiculous!' the star exploded. "We did have a few words and I shot him. But that's as far as it went."

Everybody loved the Broadway couple, a perfect match. You could never tell who would come out the winner nightly.

For a number of years we were deliriously happy—and then we met each other.

Never hit a man when he's down—he may get up.

"Why did you hit your wife with the chair?"
"Because I couldn't lift the piano!"

They're taking him to the hospital for beating his wife.

Figures
(*see Twiggy, Mini-Skirts, Fashions, etc.*)

She's got an hour-glass figure—and I can't wait till my hands reach ten-thirty.

If I told you that you had a beautiful body—would you hold it against me?

She's built like the brick wall of China—and nobody has climbed it, either.

She's 40-23-36—but unfortunately not in that order.

The way she's built—it takes her hours to get her feet wet under a shower.

She's got an hour-glass figure but all the sand has sifted to the bottom.

The only thing a low-cut dress does for her is show off her jewelry.

We should send our aid program to her—she has more underdeveloped areas than any country in Asia.

She eats so much—she's got a figure eight.

She needs falsies to look flat-chested.

If she had any hindsight—she'd never wear any slacks.

288

She reminds you of a deck of cards: pretty mixed up—but is she stacked.

She's well-reared—and looks good in the front too.

The only thing a sweater does for her is keep her warm.

She's a perfect model—for a mountain.

She's a perfect model—for a scarecrow.

She's a perfect model—for a fountain pen.

She's built like a guitar—upside-down.

"Swimming is good for the figure."
"Yeah? Did you ever see a duck?"

She's built like a used nail file—she looks like Raquel Welch after taxes.

She's so bowlegged—she could walk down a bowling alley while the game is going on.

That Twiggy has a 36 figure: 12, 12, and 12.

She's the only girl I know with two backs.

Boy Scouts have a new way of starting fires—they rub two Twiggies together.

When Twiggy stands sideways—she is marked absent.

She doesn't·even cast a shadow.

The best camouflage for a woman's bowlegs is a low neckline.

When a man looks a woman straight in the eyes, she'd better do something about her figure.

Very often the girl with a lot of horse sense has the figure to go with it.

Flowers

What do you send to a sick florist?

She was only a florist's daughter—but she was potted all the time.

When a man brings his wife flowers for no reason—there must be a reason.

Flying
(*see Airplanes, Air Force*)

There's still a bit of risk in aviation—the taxi ride from the city to the airport.

He won't fly on account of his religion—he's a devout coward.

I get air-sick when I lick an air-mail stamp.

Every year it takes less time to fly across the ocean and longer to drive to work.

Fog
(*see Smog, Air Pollution, etc.*)

The fog is so thick in England, the farmers have to milk the cows by radar.

It's so foggy in San Francisco that on a clear day you can see the fog.

1ST MAN: "She's the most beautiful woman in the world and yet I've never been able to really see her."
2ND MAN: "Why not?"

289

1ST MAN: "Every time I look at her my glasses fog up!"

It's so foggy in England, I was ten years old before I met my mother. And ten years later I found out she was my father wearing a kilt.

Mayor Lindsay did something about the fog in New York City. He put up all the street signs in braille.

It was so foggy in L. A. the tourists felt the sights and went home.

Food
(*see Cooking, Restaurants, etc.*)

He missed his wife's cooking—every chance he got.

She is such a bad cook, when she takes food on a picnic—I feel sorry for the ants.

She ordered a large pizza pie with anchovies, peppers and mushrooms and all the rest. When it was ready, the counterman asked, "Shall I cut it in twelve pieces or eight?"
"Eight pieces," said the gal firmly. "How on earth could I ever eat twelve pieces of pizza?"

Canapes are a sandwich cut in twenty-four pieces.

My wife is such a great cook she has to call in the repairman to fix a TV dinner. She constantly serves leftovers. It's like eating re-runs.

Comic Alan Drake says a lot of comedians talk about their wives' cooking. "My wife's cooking isn't so funny. Anything that brings you that close to death is a very serious matter."

If I eat candy I get sick—if I eat garlic I get lonely.

Never has so much Chicken à la King owed its existence to so few chickens.

A friend of mine told me his wife is a terrific cook—just the other night he came home and found a truck driver eating there.

Fortune Cookie Slogans

The message in the fortune cookie read, "You will meet a cute redhead. You will give her money. She is our cashier."

"You have a great future—but not in your business."

"Don't eat the egg roll."

"Regardless how dumb woman can be—she always has bride ideas."

Chun King say: "If at first you do not succeed—marry boss's daughter."

"Smart woman. She never let fool kiss her—or kiss fool her."

"Brain of average woman is divided in two parts—dollars and cents."

"Every man he like to see broad smile—especially if broad she smile at him!"

"Give housewife an inch—and she sure to make whole family go on diet."

"Wife she is living proof that man can take joke."

"Husband he is living proof that woman can take joke."

"Tactless man he is man who voices what everybody else is thinking."

"Many husband he feel that what his wife not know won't hurt him."

"Girdle is accessory after the fat."

"Statistics show that the general run of pedestrians—is too slow."

Phil Foster

"I feel that certain jokes have been around long enough and used long enough, so I figure we form a joke Hall of Fame. All the old jokes will be retired, given a number, and laid to rest in the Hall of Fame, never to be used again.
Here are my contributions of jokes that are up for the "Hall of Fame.""

"Do you know how to drive a baby buggy?"
"No."
"Tickle its feet."

Guy walks in drugstore, says to clerk, "Make me a malted."
Clerk says, "Poof, you're a malted."

RESTAURANT OWNER: "Do you like the food?"
PATRON: "I could get more nourishment biting my lip!"

"Inflation is really here. I gave my kid a nickel and he thought it was a medal."

"Now that the war is over you can get parts for your head."

"Were you born in Brooklyn?"
"Yes."
"What part?"
"All of me."

"Did you get a haircut?"
"No, I got all of them cut."

"My uncle slept in the chandelier. He was a light sleeper."

France
(*see International Humor chapter*)

Big sign in front of the George V hotel in Paris: "Yankee go home—but not until you've done all your shopping."

The shopping center is called, "Rue de La Pay-through-the-nose."

The only way to get a kid to take medicine in France is to put it in his wine.

My friend laughed when I spoke to the waiter in French, but the laugh was on him. I told the waiter to give him the check.

TOURIST: "I took my wife to the Folies Bergere. That's like taking a meatball to a twelve-course dinner."

In France, the postman isn't the only working person who has to walk the streets to pick up the male.

Things must be getting tough in France. I just got a postcard from Paris —and there was writing on it.

In France, the men like to stay out until the "Oui" hours of the morning.

Friends

His best friend was cheating with his wife and when the wife died, the best friend really took it to heart. It was the husband who consoled the friend: "Don't worry, I'll get married again!"

He always does his best—friends.

291

You can depend on him. He's always around—when he needs you.

A friend in need—is a pest.

If you ever need a friend—buy a dog.

He's a close friend—he parts with nothing.

He hasn't an enemy in the world—and none of his friends like him.

Two friends were having a friendly argument. "Aah, you don't know how to make love."
"I don't, huh?—Ask your wife!"

"Guess I'll be going now—don't trouble yourself to take me to the door."
"It's no trouble—it's a pleasure!"

If you help a friend when he's in trouble he'll never forget you—especially when he is in trouble again.

He has friends he hasn't even used yet.

When a fellow needs a friend—he sometimes makes the mistake of getting a wife.

Joe Frisco

Joe Frisco was one of the most fabulous characters of the 20th Century. His was a rare type of humor—quoted wherever showpeople gather.

Stuttering Joe Frisco was working at Charley Foy's famed nitery in California. Charley was complaining to his cast one night that he was suffering from thieves. "I've just lost a whole chicken," scowled Foy accusingly.
"D-d-don't look at m-me. I d-d-

didn't take it," retorted Frisco. "If you don't believe it, w-w-w-weigh me!"

The tout was complaining to Joe that he hadn't won a single race either with or for a wealthy sucker. "He gives me a thousand dollars a race to bet for him," he cried, "and I've given him twenty-three straight losers."
"G-g-g-get away from that b-bum," snarled Frisco, "h-he's unlucky for you."

Joe was working at Grace Hayes' lodge in Hollywood and as usual was across the street in the diner—making bets on the ponies. It was a celebrity night and Grace introduced Lawrence Tibbett. The world-famous baritone started to sing his famous "Glory Road," and his magnificent voice was booming around the room as Joe entered. "Th-th-there's a guy with a v-v-v-voice!" he said as he approached Miss Hayes. "W-w-why don't you s-s-sign him up—p-p-put him in the show."
"You dope," Grace explained, "that man's name is Lawrence Tibbett."
"Th-th-the hell with it!" screamed Joe. "Ch-change his n-name, put him in the sh-sh-show."

Once a Western Union boy who stuttered worse than Joe came to his room to take a telegram. "Go-go-go back to the office," Joe warned him, "and tell them to s-s-s-send me a straight man."

During the First World War a monster benefit was staged at the Metropolitan Opera House. There was almost no entertainer of any prominence who was not there. All three Barrymores were on the bill, and Al Jolson—everybody.
Big as they were, however, there was one who seemed to top all in importance—Enrico Caruso. The other stars

had a respect for him that amounted to awe. As Caruso stood in the wings waiting his turn, nobody actually had the courage to address the great man himself—that is, nobody but Frisco. "Hey, C-c-caruso," he said, "don't do D-D-D-Darktown Strutters Ball—that's my n-n-number and I follow you."

Joe was in his room at the Edison Hotel in New York when the phone rang. It was his manager with an offer of three thousand dollars a week to open at the Palace Theatre. "Are you k-k-kidding?" Joe barked. "You k-k-know my price is four thousand."

"I'll see what I can do," the manager said, "but come on over to my office and we'll talk it over."

"Wh-wh-what—and get locked out of my room?"

Joe was at his unhappiest and a friend suggested he go to an analyst.

"Are you k-k-kidding?" he growled. "I re-re-refuse to p-p-pay anyone thirty dollars an hour j-j-just to squeal on my p-p-parents."

Funerals
(*also see Tombstones, Death, Cemeteries*)

A group of people were seated in a local barbershop attempting to eulogize a citizen who had just died. For years the fellow had been the most hated man in town and no one could think of anything good to say about him. Eventually, after more than an hour of silence, the barber spoke up. "You know," he said, "I must admit he wasn't a hard man to shave."

A New York newspaper, in an article on air-raid procedures, stated: "Funeral coaches also must park, but the occupants may remain in them."

A New Hampshire farmer had been urged to attend the funeral of his neighbor's third wife. "But I'm not going," he announced to his own spouse. "Goodness sakes, why not?" she asked. "Well, Mary, I'm beginning to feel kind of awkward about goin' so often without anything of the sort to ask him back to."

FINNEGAN: "At my funeral I want you to pour a bottle of Irish whiskey over me grave."
SHAYNE: "Sure—but would you mind if I passed it through me kidneys first?"

He went to Florida for his health but after two weeks he died, and his body was shipped back home for the funeral. Two of his friends came to see him as he lay in his casket.
"Doesn't he look wonderful?" one said.
"Yeah," said the other, "those two weeks in Florida sure did him a world of good."

Furs
(*see Fashions, Clothes, Shopping, etc.*)

It seems there's a New York furrier who has been trying to get a longer lasting, cheaper fur by mating a mink with a chimpanzee, but it doesn't work —the sleeves are too long.

Right before I went on the air one night, I was handed this note: "Will the man who found a fur coat here in the studio last week please return the blonde that was in it."

This customer came into my show room and said he wanted something in a mink—my model.

Cross mink with kangaroo to get fur coats with pockets in them.

1ST GIRL: "That's a gorgeous fur coat you're wearing. What did you do for it?"

2ND GIRL: "Just shortened the sleeves."

She says that coat is dyed mink. From the looks of it, it must have died a horrible death.

1ST GIRL: "How did she get a mink coat?"

2ND GIRL: "The same way the minks get them."

The only way you can get a mink nowadays is to be like a fox and play cat and mouse with a wolf.

Zsa Zsa Gabor
(see Double Acts chapter)

I'm tired of Dear Abby, Doris Blake, and the rest of the sob sisters always trying to solve the problems of the poor and the lonely. Nobody ever worries about the rich. I think we ought to give a little thought to the overdog for a change. What we need is an advice to the wealthy column. I recommend Zsa Zsa Gabor, about whom Oscar Levant once said, "She does social work among the rich."

It was Matthew, or Mark, or John, or it might have been Sargent Shriver who said: "The poor ye always have with us," but it was Zsa Zsa Gabor who said: "God help the rich—for the poor can beg." Or was that Voltaire? Then again it could have been Rocky Graziano. At any rate, I do know that Zsa Zsa is the best equipped to give advice to the richlorn.

If you need convincing that Zsa Zsa is the Prophet of the Prosperous, here are some actual letters that she has received—as well as her answers:

"Dear Miss Gabor:

Perhaps I shouldn't be writing to you with this kind of a problem. It may be I should see a doctor—but I hope you can help me.

I have a boyfriend who, whenever I see him, makes my face turn red, my blood pressure go up, and I feel a strange sensation all over. What should I do?"

ZSA ZSA'S ANSWER: "Sounds to me like you did it already."

"Dear Miss Gabor:

I have been engaged to a man for the past four years. During that time he has given me a beautiful mink coat, much jewelry, some gorgeous black lingerie, a horse, a stove, and a little foreign car. We are no longer engaged. What do you think would be the proper thing to do?"

ZSA ZSA'S ANSWER: "Send back the stove."

"Dear Miss Gabor:

I have been keeping company with a very charming, handsome man who owns over 100 oil wells in Oklahoma and a gold mine in Colorado. He is very generous, but lately he seems to have lost interest in me. What should I do?"

ZSA ZSA'S ANSWER: "You seem to have a very serious problem: You said he has 100 oil wells and a gold mine? I must handle this man personally—send me his name and address."

PROFESSOR ZSA ZSA LECTURES TO ALL WOMEN: "Husbands are like fires—they go out when unattended."

"A smart female is one who quits playing ball when she makes a good catch."

"The only way to cure a man in love is marriage—and if that doesn't cure him—nothing will."

"I have come to the conclusion that all men between the ages of 15 and 95 have the same attitude about sex— *they like it!*"

Zsa Zsa talks to you right from her chest—and that's *very* nice talk— always straight and to the point. "That ring is very vulgar," an acquaintance said to her about her new engagement ring that was about forty carats.
"If I didn't have it," Zsa Zsa scratched back, "I vould also think it's vulgar."

Zsa was talking about her third husband, George Sanders: "When I was married to him, we were both in love with him—I fell out of love with him— but he didn't."

QUESTION: "My boy friend curses, drinks, and smokes—what should I do?"
ZSA ZSA: "Don't reform him. I know a woman who got her feller to give up smoking, cursing, drinking, chewing, and gambling, and when she got finished with him—he decided she wasn't good enough for him."

I saw a baby picture of Zsa Zsa lying on a bearskin rug—wearing a wedding gown.

Gambling
(*see Las Vegas, Horse Racing, etc.*)

Las Vegas is a wonderful town. You can't beat the climate, the food, or the crap tables. I even lost money on the stamp machine.

I wouldn't say the roulette wheel was crooked, but how come the table says "Tilt"?

One gambling hotel in Las Vegas will send a table and dealer to your room. "That's what we call room service here," the manager bragged.

It's still tougher to make a six with two threes than a Gabor with two Zsas.

Nevada is famous for its gambling. This is one place where money isn't everything—if you stay there long enough, it's nothing.

Man in Reno, Nevada, was spending his vacation at the crap tables getting an indoor tan. He wired his partner, "Having a wonderful time—wish I could afford it."

"How come he's so lucky at cards and such a bust at the race track?"
"He can't shuffle horses."

Lady Godiva put everything she had on a horse.

Nobody could ever get as loaded as the dice in that joint.

One horseplayer to another horseplayer: You said he was a great horse and he sure is. It took eleven other horses to beat him.

As your plane approaches Las Vegas the stewardess says: "We are now approaching Las Vegas. Please fasten your money belts."

The trouble with hitting the jackpot on a slot machine is that it takes so long to put the money back in the machine.

Max Asnas was driving to the Jamaica race track in a hurry when a cop stopped him and barked, "Where do you think you're going?"
"I'm sick," Max replied.
The cop peered into the car and saw the racing forms.
"Sick, eh? It looks like you're going to the race track."

295

Max moaned, "Oy! Is that a sickness."

In Las Vegas, everything is touched with the gambling fever. The undertaker was complaining that business was bad. "With the exception of a few night club comics, nobody is dying here lately," he cried.

I felt sorry for him until I walked in the back of the funeral parlor and saw six stiffs lying there. "Why, ya bum!" I screamed. "I thought you said business was lousy—what about those six stiffs you got back there?"

"SSSHHH," the undertaker silenced me, "five of them are shills."

He observed Be Kind To Animals Week: all the money he earned—he gave to the horses.

"No cheating now," the gambler said; "I want you to play these cards straight—'cause I know what I dealt."

Garment Center
(see Executives, Models, Business, Fashions, Bosses, etc.)

At one cocktail party on 7th Avenue, one clothing man spied a tray of canapes. "Dig the dinner swatches," he noted.

Things are so bad in the Garment Center—the manufacturers are laying off their sons-in-law.

The young son of a dress manufacturer was asked by his teacher to tell how many seasons there were. "Two," the boy said quickly, "busy and slack."

"I hear you had a fire?"
"Sh—it's Thursday!"

"How's business?"
'Business is like sex: wnen it's good

it's wonderful and when it's bad—it's still pretty good."

"I have a hundred suits," the cloak and suiter was bragging, "and they're all pending."

The nicest thing about money is that it never clashes with anything you're wearing.

The dress manufacturer sent this letter to one of his customers: "Dear Sir, after checking our records, we note that we have done more for you than your mother did—we've carried you for fifteen months."

I'm overpaying him—but he's worth it.

A garment manufacturer invited his new model to join him at his cottage for the weekend.
"Wonderful," she said, "and I'll bring my boyfriend."
"Your boyfriend?—what for?"
"In case your wife wants to have some fun too."

He interviewed the model for a job in his showroom. When he took all her measurements and qualifications he then asked, "Where can I get hold of you?"
"I don't know," she giggled, "I'm awfully ticklish."

When the designer was fired, he challenged his boss, "And who are you going to find to fill my vancancy?"
"You're not leaving a vacancy."

BOSS: "This is the last straw. You're through—fired!"
CUTTER: "Fired?—I thought slaves were sold."

The Garment Center boss had to finally fire his secretary because she lacked experience—all she knew was typing, shorthand, filing and book-keeping.

MAX: "I'm in big trouble. I'm about to go bankrupt—unless I can raise some cash—and I haven't the slightest idea where I'm going to get it from."

SAM: "I'm glad to hear it—I was afraid for a minute you might have an idea you could borrow it from me."

Ghosts

There's only one way to get rid of a ghost—ask him for a contribution.

"I want to be buried naked," the scoundrel told his wife. "Where I'm going I don't need any clothes—it's pretty hot down there."

After he died, his ghost floated down the chimney and sat on his wife's bed. "I'll need my clothes and heavy underwear after all," the ghost said. "There are so many rich characters down there—they had to put in air-conditioning."

Gifts
(*see Xmas, Birthdays, Anniversaries, etc.*)

Do you know what I got for Father's Day? The bills from Mother's Day.

I'd like to buy some flowers for the girl I love—but my wife won't let me.

I'd like to get something for my wife —but nobody will make me an offer.

I gave her a going-away present— but she still won't go away.

Every time I buy her a present, she gets so excited, she can hardly wait to exchange it.

She's a good girl. She won't take gifts from men—she insists on cash.

I gave my wife a ten-dollar gift certificate for Christmas. She used it as a down payment for a three-thousand-dollar diamond ring.

What do you give a man that's got everything? An accountant to tell him how to keep it.

What do you give a guy who's had everybody?

He not only wants everything for nothing—but he wants it gift-wrapped.

Gigolos
(*see Playboy*)

The girls are always falling at his feet—the kind he gets are too weak to stand up by themselves.

GIGOLO: A hired hand.

Girls
(*see Women, Wives, etc.*)

Girl who says she'll go through anything for a man—usually has his bank book in mind.

The salesgirl at the perfume counter leaned over toward her young customer and warned: "Let me give you a word of advice—don't use this if your bluffing."

"How did you meet her?"
"I opened my wallet and there she was."

"The water is fine this morning," she said to her traveling companion in Miami Beach—"full of men."

297

"What has she got that I haven't?"
"Nothing—only she groups it better."

The young doll announced that she was marrying the antiquated millionaire. "I'm not giving up my youth," she explained, "just pawning it."

SHE: "After we are married I will share all your troubles and sorrows."
HE: "But I have no troubles and sorrows."
SHE: "Well, you will have after we are married."

She's the kind of girl who rides home from a walk.

She's a home-loving girl—anybody's home.

Every time I meet a girl who cooks like my mother—she looks like my father.

When she got her first mink coat, she spent hours describing it to her girlfriend and days explaining it to her mother.

"You can have a good time with her even if you play your cards wrong."

"Are you married?"
"No."
"Why?"
"I'm waiting for somebody besides my mother to ask me."

Then there was the stuttering girl who started to tell the man about her past and finished to find him in it.

I saved my girl from being attacked last night—I controlled myself.

The modern girl has what it takes—to take what you've got.

She's a nice girl: Won't take gifts from men—insists on cash.

She's the kind of girl you take to the movies when you want to see the picture.

Glamour
(see Fashions, Playgirls, Playboys, Society, etc.)

The ony polish she has is on her fingernails.

She threw me the rose in her hair—I caught it and threw back her hair.

The dress looked good—considering the shape it was on.

Her disposition was so sour—even her face cream curdled.

Her dress fits her like a glove—a catcher's mitt.

Her neckline keeps going down and her hemline keeps going up—I'd like to be there when they meet.

George Gobel

"Our program tonight is being sent to our fighting men in Murphy's bar."

"For my birthday my wife sent me forty cuff links. Trouble is I have no shirts with French cuffs. So I had to have my wrists pierced."

"I was on a tough horse, boy. I got up on him and all of a sudden he kicked so hard that he caught his own hoof in one of the stirrups. I said, 'Horse, if you're getting on I'm getting off.'"

"A lot of people ask me why I keep my left hand in one spot on this guitar, when other guitar players move it all around. Well, you see they're looking for a chord. I found it."

"I had to take my kid to a psychiatrist, who said he was a neurotic. I mean paranoic. I mean . . . well, he steals!"

"Had a terrible thing happen in the garden. I found a bachelor button in my black-eyed Susan's bed."

"I had this idea to make the Great Wall of China into a handball court."

"I make all the big decisions in my family and my wife makes the small ones. She decides where we go out, whether to buy a car, etc.; and I make the big ones—like whether to admit Red China."

Golf
(*see Sports, Liars*)

CADDIE: "Sir, you've been losing so many new balls—why don't you use an old ball?"
GOLFIE: "I never had an old ball."

There were golf sticks on top of the funeral car as it passed the candy store. "He really must have loved golf," one sportsman remarked.

"Still loves golf," said his friend. "That's his wife—after the funeral he goes right to the golf course."

This fellow loved to play golf. Every day when he closed the butcher store, he ran to the golf course. One day, he and a friend were on the green when a funeral procession passed by. The butcher took off his cap and stood at attention until the funeral procession passed out of sight. His friend was amazed and asked, "Are you always so touched and so sentimental at the sight of a funeral?"

"No," answered the butcher, as he swung at the ball. "But that was my wife and we would have been married twenty-seven years tomorrow."

"Say, caddie, why do you keep looking at your watch?"
"It isn't a watch, sir, it's a compass."

"A terrible course, caddie, a terrible course."
"Sorry, sir, but this isn't the course. We left that an hour ago."

"Charlie plays a fair game of golf, doesn't he?"
"Yes—if you watch him."

Two movie producers decided to play golf for the first time. On the way to a country club they purchased all the necessary equipment—shoes, sport togs, clubs and so forth, then checked in at the club. "I'm sorry," the starter told them, "but you can't play today."
"But why not?" they protested. "Look, we're all ready. New clubs, everything."
"Sorry," repeated the starter, "but you can't play today. There aren't any caddies."
The producers looked at each other. "So who cares?" said one. "For one day we'll take a Buick."

I found something that can take five points off your game—an eraser.

The manufacturer was taking his first lesson in golf. "The first thing you do is hit the ball in the direction of that first hole," the pro explained. The cloak and suiter took one swing and by luck the ball fell within one foot of the hole. "Great," said the golf pro.
"What do I do now?" the manufacturer asked.

299

"Now, you have to put the ball in the little hole—one foot away."

The man looked disgusted. "Now he tells me," he said.

In Israel you start the golf game from the 18th hole and go backwards.

Nothing counts in golf—like your opponent.

I'm a two-handicap golfer—I have a boss who won't let me off early and a wife who keeps me home on weekends.

By the time a man can afford to lose a golf ball—he can't hit that far.

One fellow at this club just trims everybody on the course. A big, strapping fellow, he can hit the golf ball a ton and has everybody down not only because he's so good, but because he brags about it. Finally, one duffer gets an idea. He reads somewhere that an animal trainer has taught a gorilla how to play the game. He calls up the trainer and makes a deal to bring the gorilla to the club.

"Is this gorilla really that good?" he asks.

"Good!" exclaims the trainer. "He can hit a golf ball 450 yards!"

The next day the gorilla shows up and the match is set up with the club champ. The gorilla picks up a driver and tees off. True to the claims, the ball sails 450 yards through the air and drops four inches from the cup. The club champ is wide-eyed. The other players are ecstatic. The caddie hands the gorilla a putter. He swings and hits the ball 450 yards.

If you break one hundred, watch your golf. If you break eighty, watch your business.

Two old gals joined each other on the golf links every month. On this particular day, one of the gals strode to the first tee, pulled back her club, closed her eyes and swung with all her might. The ball hooked off to the side, ricocheted off several trees and took a fantastic bounce onto the green and into the cup for a hole-in-one. Her friend turned and frowned. "Sylvia, you sneak," she said angrily, "you've been practicing."

Goofs .

When you're on the road for Uncle Sam—you meet royalty as well as people, and you've got to be prepared for both.

Where would we know from royalty? Did we have a changing of the guard in front of my father's temple in Brownsville, Brooklyn? Did we curtsy and bow over an egg cream at the candy store on Pitkin Avenue? You had protocol in your three-room apartment in the Bronx?

Protocol? We didn't even have steam heat! If you want to know something, my grandma would have thought I was coming up in the world if I just met an assistant manager from somewhere.

Our troupe had been briefed that in Moslem, Buddhist, and Hindu countries, we shouldn't whack anyone on the back—especially, particularly, and definitely not royalty. As it turned out we remembered the warnings just a couple of physical contacts too late.

Now, take for instance the Crown Prince of Afghanistan. He loved us. He came back four times to see the show. His Highness was anxious to meet everyone in the cast.

On the fourth trip around I introduced his Royal Highness to Al Williams of the Step Brothers, who were the dancing stars of my show. Our exuberant dancer gushed, "I sure am delighted to meet you, sir, and I hope I can play your country some day." I jumped in quickly, "But this *is* his country." Al threw his arms around the Royal One and apologized, "Gee, I'm sorry, Prince-y, you don't look like a local."

Then there was the night in Katmandu, Nepal. "Flash" McDonald of the Steps was holding court at one of our after-show suppers at the Palace. He was telling a joke and didn't get any response from a handsome gentleman at this table. Undaunted, our boy smashed him across the shoulders with a "Dontcha get it, mac?"

"Mac" turned out to be his Imperial Majesty—the King of Nepal.

We were invited to honor then President Eisenhower at a dinner in Hawaii given by Governor Quinn.

The tables were heaped high with assorted tasties arranged in the form of Marine Corps and White House emblems in honor of the President. It all looked good enough to eat. Since I just happened to be starving, I immediately commenced vacuuming up foodstuffs before I noticed that nobody else was even nibbling. "Maybe they ain't hungry," I said to Cindy, already elbow deep in the White House that was made of chicken.

"Guess not," agreed Cindy, who'd already gnawed halfway through the Marine Corps hat made of shrimp.

I ignored the stares. I just figured the other guests had recognized me and couldn't tear their eyes away from me. I was just in the process of busting up my fourth flag when I noticed Merriman Smith, the UPI man, gesticulating to me wildly.

"Not now." I shook my head. "Can't you see I'm eating?"

"I know," he growled. "That's what I want to see you about. Don't you know it's not protocol to touch any food until the President has at least seen it?"

I wiped the cocktail sauce from my ruby lips and went to work. I must say it was very embarrassing trying to form Marine Corps hats, anchors, and flags out of olive pits, shrimp shells, chicken bones, and other missing parts.

Later, while I talked to the President, Cindy was in a corner chatting happily away with a very nice lady named Barbara. She never did catch the last name because Barbara had said she read Cindy's columns and loved her on TV and naturally my lovely but hammy wife had blocked out everything else but that. It was strictly on a first name basis all the way. It was Cindy and Barbara—Barbara and Cindy.

Merriman and I inched over just as Barbara asked, "Where did you get your gorgeous gown, Cindy?" Said Cindy, strutting like a peacock, "It's an original—it's a Scaasi."

"Oh, I know all about Scaasi," said Barbara. "My mother-in-law has several."

"Oh yes?" gushed Cindy. "Well, Scaasi charges a fortune—your mother-in-law must be loaded, honey. What does she do?"

"Barbara," the very dear friend, was Barbara Eisenhower, Mamie's daughter-in-law.

Like them theatrical folks say, "We closed in New Delhi, India"—and we almost closed India altogether.

Since Uncle Sam was picking up the tab for this cultural exchange trip, naturally the commercial was, "Let's be friends."

At the end of our four-hour show we pushed about 500 balloons into the audience—red, white and blue, of course, with the legend on each balloon, "JOEY ADAMS SHOW—U.S. A." Everybody jumped for these precious balloons, from the Kings and Queens, Presidents, and Ambassadors to the peasants or the nationals. It was organized confusion. When the excitement died down, I walked front and center, as the band and troops behind me subtly played "God Bless America," and made with my friendship commercial.

We repeated this in every country from Afghanistan to Nepal to Cambodia to Laos and points East. Now there were 20,000 Indians in this New Delhi audience. In addition to Madam Gandhi, Mr. Nehru, and every Ambassador from all over the world, as well as Kings, Queens, and Prime Ministers from all over Southeast Asia and Europe.

As usual, at the end of this show we sent the hundreds of balloons into the audience. Everybody jumped for them. And when all quieted down, I walked front and center, put my straw hat over my heart and said the words I had uttered at hundreds of shows, for our President. "I hope that the friendship, fun and love that is here today will always be there between all of India and all of America."

Just then, an Indian in the third row pulled back his right fist and punched an American smack in the mouth. "You dirty bum," he shouted as he threw his haymaker, "you stole my balloon."

They dragged the exponents of "brotherhood between nations" backstage to patch them up. I finished my stirring speech of love and friendship to my busted-up, banged-up, bruised and bleeding audience of two—one Indian and one American.

Anybody can goof—and they do. I was there when one of our State Department geniuses introduced "The Duck and Dooches."

One night-time TV star was talking about Adam Clayton Powell. As he closed—almost for good—he said, "Keep the baby, faith."

Once when Cindy and I were in London, England, my dear wife announced that she'd like to see their famous underground. Her "like" is tantamount to a command. So we donned our evening clothes and went into the hole at Piccadilly Circus, the nearest subway entrance. I bought two tickets and after passing the turnstile immediately threw them away.

"Why are you throwing them away, old sock?" Cindy asked. "Why do you think they give you tickets? It's probably like the Jersey turnpike. If you travel a certain amount of stations you must pay more money or something."

"What do you know?" I answered, thereby settling the whole discussion. "Furthermore, we're only going one station."

"Yeah, but how do they know that?"

"Let's not argue," I said firmly. "What's the big deal about a couple of lousy subway tickets?"

One stop and we fought our way out of the train and jauntily walked out of the exit.

"Your tickets, sir," said the guard politely.

Cindy laughed hysterically. "What tickets?" I asked, annoyed. "I threw them away."

Cindy's laughter now seemed maniacal.

Immediately the guard's smile turned into a smirk. He looked at me as if I were a Nazi spy and my wife an escaped lunatic.

The old man breathed heavily as if he'd been there since the time of Queen Victoria and his uniform hadn't been cleaned since.

"Where'd you come from?" the man with the walnut face asked.

"From the United States," I said defiantly.

"On this line?"

I will never forget the time I was left with Kosher egg on my face in Israel. I was honored by the State of Israel at the King David Hotel in Jerusalem. I not only had starched shirt but starched lapels as well. Cindy had sequins in her nose. But David Ben-Gurion who did the honoring wore an open sport shirt—with figures yet.

I told the Prime Minister how honored I was and how thrilled I was that he would be so informal. He said if he could help it he would never wear a tie.

For the rest of our trip in Israel I said to my wife, "Forget it—no more ties for me." Two weeks later we were at the Magiddo Hotel in Haifa. They were advertising a Saturday night dance. We thought it would be fun for us to go to this typical Saturday night dance like any sabras—no guides, photographers or interpreters—just act like two Israelites.

We paid for the tickets like everybody else—and I presented them at the door. "I'm sorry," the ticket taker said. "You can't come in without a tie."

"Are you kidding?" I screamed, "David Ben-Gurion, the Prime Minister—the head man of Israel—never wears a tie."

The ticket taker answered, "David Ben-Gurion never comes to our Saturday night dances."

I still have nightmares when I think back on that first night in Cambodia. The Queen was honoring the Joey Adams troupe and was decorating Cindy and me with the Peace medals. I was the first to be pinned by the Queen.

I was glowing like Her Majesty had just conferred knighthood upon me. I jammed my hand in my blouse "à la Napoleon" and thought, "Sir Joey Adams." To Al Williams standing next to me I gloated, "So far I've been honored by two Kings and three Queens."

"One more King," Al said, "and you can go gin."

Suddenly I heard a blood-curdling scream like something out of a Bela Lugosi movie. I was frozen to the spot. When I came to, I saw that it was Cindy and she was bleeding from her chest. The Queen had accidentally stabbed her with the medal when she pinned it on her. Cindy retreated back to the hotel to pet her medal and lick her wounds.

Gossip

Two women were talking. One said to the other, "I told you about Mildred —she got mixed up with what's-her-name and she and what-do-you-call him wound up at you-know what and you should see what happened to you-know-who—I told you the story before, didn't I?"

"Yes—but this is the first time I heard all the details."

She never repeats gossip—she starts it.

She listens to both sides of an argument—but only if it's on a party line.

She'll never tell a lie—if the truth will cause more damage.

"I hope I can live up to all the things you said about me."

"Well, I had to live down the things you said about me!"

"You can't believe everything you hear."

"No, but you can repeat it."

She says she's a virgin—but she's not a fanatic about it.

She picks her friends—to pieces.

303

Billy Graham

One of Billy Graham's most effective means of communicating his ideas is through parables such as the following:

"I heard the story of a man who walked along a road, tired, weary, and discouraged. He could hardly put one foot ahead of the other. A neighbor overtook him in a wagon and invited him to ride with him. As they rode along together his neighbor noticed that the tired, weary man still carried a heavy sack of grain on his back.

" 'Put that down,' he said. 'You don't need to carry that.'

"The tired man said, 'Oh, it's enough for you to carry me, let alone this sack of grain.'

"There are thousands of you who have turned to God, but you are still carrying your burdens. But God begs you: 'Cast all your care on Me, for I care for you.' "

"I heard about a man some time ago who had a watermelon patch, and some young rascals in the community were stealing him blind.

"So he said, 'All right, I'll get 'em.' So he put up a sign in his watermelon patch that said, 'One of these melons is poison.' He went to bed and got up the next morning, and sure enough they hadn't stolen a watermelon. Everything was the same, except the sign had been changed. It now read, 'Two of these watermelons is poison.' "

"Well, I heard about a man who had read a book review on Bridie Murphy and the transmigration of souls. He was helping his wife with the dishes and he asked his wife, 'Does that mean if I die I will come back to this world in another form?'

" 'Yes, that's what it means,' his wife said.

" 'Do you believe if I were to die, for example, I would come back as a worm?'

" 'Sweetheart,' she replied, 'you are never the same twice.' "

"The smallest package I ever saw was a man wrapped up wholly in himself."

"A woman once told me all her little boy needed was a pat on the back. I told her if it was low enough and hard enough, it would do him some good."

"About the only time some people get on their knees is when they tune their television sets."

"I heard about a fellow some time ago who was talking to a friend of his, and he said, 'Boy, my wife is an angel.'

"The friend said, 'You're lucky, my wife is still living.' "

Dick Gregory

"You always see pictures of those Ku Klux Klanners wearing pointed hoods. Those hoods are flat! It's the heads that are pointed."

"People keep telling me some of their best friends are colored. Let's face it. There just aren't that many of us to go 'round! Personally, I like Negroes. I like them so much I even had them for parents."

"If it weren't for bad luck, I wouldn't have no luck at all!"

"There's only one difference between the North and South. In the South they don't care how close I get, so long as I don't get too big. In the North, they don't care how big I get, as long as I don't get too close."

"People keep talking about the white race and the black race—and it really doesn't make sense. I played Miami, met a fellow two shades darker than me—and his name was Ginsberg! Took my place in two sit-in demonstrations —nobody knew the difference. Then he tried for a third lunch counter and blew the whole bit . . . asked for blintzes."

Dick spares no one with his scalpel: "The NAACP is a wonderful organization. Belong to it myself. But do you realize if tomorrow morning we had complete integration, all them cats would be outta work?"

"You know why Madison Avenue advertising has never done well in Harlem? We're the only ones who know what it means to *be* Brand X!"

When Dick answers hecklers they go away bleeding:
"Why do you heckle me? You want excitement? Go down to the NAACP and ask for the white washroom."

"Man, trying to get you to shut up is like trying to explain integration to a lynch mob."

"Don't just sit there and heckle me. Pay your check. Burn your cross and leave."

"If it weren't for Abe Lincoln—I'd still be in the open market."

Gypsies

Rich Gypsies opened a chain of empty stores.

I know a Gypsy who inherited a million dollars—so he moved into a store on Park Avenue.

She was a sort of modernistic fortune teller—she read tea bags.

It's easy to tell a Gypsy fortune teller. Every time you go into one of their stores—you walk out without your fortune.

She was a great fortune teller; she not only read my mind—but slapped my face as well.

SIGN IN GYPSY TEA ROOM: "We predict anything but the weather."

Buddy Hackett
(see "Comedians" chapter)

When Donald O'Connor took Buddy to his first Japanese restaurant for sukiyaki, he followed the custom of removing his shoes when he entered, and sat on the floor with everyone else. After his first mouthful, he wanted out, and commented: "Now I'm hip to the bit about taking your shoes off. This food is so lousy, they're afraid you'll kick 'em!"

"My idea of really having arrived is to be able to hire a Japanese houseboy. But what am I going to do with him in one room? When I say, 'That's all,' where can he go? He lives in. Unless he hangs out of the window by his fingertips. I live in a basement—he has to hang up!"

When the boy comic signed his first picture deal with Universal, he commented, "This is a strange contract. The foist clause forbids me to read the rest of the paper!"

"I remember I was driving and I hit a motorcycle cop. He walked over to me with a big grin on his face ear to ear—he had the handlebars stuck in his mouth."

"All my wife wants from my life is to take out the garbage. When I'm away on a trip she mails me the garbage."

"I married a very young wife. She was seventeen. I tell you the truth, I didn't know whether to take her on a honeymoon or send her to camp."

"Beautiful girl walked into a Chinese restaurant and sat down. The waiter was quite taken by her and after taking her order walked back into the kitchen and said to the chef, 'Boy, there's a girl out there built like the brick Wall of China.'"

Hair
(*see Bald, Barbers, Head, Faces, etc.*)

I had bad eyesight until I was ten—and then I got a haircut.

Old redheads always die—they never fade away.

Do you want a haircut—or just a change of oil?

Baldness is neat.

Her hair is so tight—she can't shut her mouth.

She looks like a doll—her hair is pasted on.

He wore a hearing aid for three years—until he took a haircut and he was cured.

Redheads who don't frequent the beauty parlor too often—soon show their true colors.

Marty Ingels said to Phyllis Diller: "I hear your hair's just been set—what time does it go off?"

Hands

She said she would slug the next guy who takes things in his hands.

A farmer had such a pretty wife that he couldn't keep his hands off her —so he fired his hands and bought a tractor.

"May I sit on your right hand at dinner?"
"I may need it to eat with—but you may hold it for a while."

Ten years ago I asked for her hand —and it's been in my pockets ever since.

Happiness

Happiness is when you invite your in-laws to dinner and they can't make it.

Happiness is when your son marries a boy of his own faith.

Happiness is when your girl sees you out with your wife and forgives you.

Happiness is when your wife gets in the wrong line at the bank and makes a deposit.

Happiness is when you have ten cents in front of a pay toilet.

Happiness is when you're accused of rape at the age of seventy.

"Happiness is when they stop telling those lousy Polish jokes," says Prince Stanislas Radziwill.

Happiness is your husband—who doesn't suspect a thing.

Happiness is a wife and a lighter that both work.

Happiness is a warm puppy—doing it on somebody else's lap.

Happiness is getting the baby to bed —when she's nineteen years old.

Happiness is a belch after a Hungarian dinner.

Happiness is when you love your neighbor and her husband is on the road.

Happiness is when an old man marries a frigid woman.

Happiness is your mother-in-law having her face lifted so tight—she can't open her mouth.

Head
(*see Faces, Bald, Hair, Eyes, etc.*)

She has a good head on her shoulders—but it would have looked better on her neck.

I had so much gold in my teeth— I had to sleep with my head in a safe.

No wonder he's got a cold—he's got a hole in his head.

She's got a good head on his shoulder.

He's so bald—his head keeps slipping off the pillow all night.

He got a splinter in his finger—he scratched his head.

He's so bald his neck looks like it's blowing bubble gum.

Health

I need help with my toothbrush.

I drank to everybody's health so often—I ruined my own.

It's so healthy here—they had to shoot a guy to start a cemetery.

His wife's health has him worried— it's always good.

Some girls who are the picture of health—are just painted that way.

She is so pale—the only way she can get some color in her face is to stick her tongue out.

She's got a lovely color—green.

A little honey is good for your health —unless your wife finds out.

"Do you believe kissing is unhealthy?"
"It would be now—here comes my husband!"

Hecklers
(*also see Insults, Squelches, and chapter, "The Hecklers"*)

Next time you give your clothes away—stay in them.

In your case—brain surgery would be only a minor operation.

Morey Amsterdammed to a pest, "You should have been born in the Dark Ages—you certainly look awful in the light."

Henny Youngman to a bore: "When you were born, something terrible happened—you lived."

Some day you'll go too far—and I hope you stay there.

If you have something to say—shut up.

"I wish," he said to his nagging wife, "Adam had died with all his ribs in his body."

"Sir, you are annoying the man I love."

Stick around while I get loaded—it will make you very witty.

He comes from the gutter and he's homesick.

If I need a stooge—I'll get one with a college education.

There are only three things that hiss: a goose, a snake, and a fool—come forth and be identified.

Sir, some day you're going to find yourself—and will you be disappointed.

Have you ever been to the zoo?— I mean as a visitor.

I need you like Venice needs a street sprinkler.

You're perfect for hot weather— you leave me cold.

Henpecked
(*see Modest, Marriage, Husbands, Wives, etc.*)

He was a bold henpecked husband. He almost opened his pay envelope to see if he got the raise his wife asked for.

He brags that his wife deserves all the credit for stopping him from gambling away his salary—she spends it before he gets it.

"If you have something to say," she barked, "shut up."

He divorced his wife a year ago and is still afraid to tell her.

He runs things around the house— like the vacuum cleaner and the lawn mower.

You can always tell a henpecked husband in a fight—he's the one holding his wife's coat.

The only time he opens his mouth around the house is to yawn.

He's a man of conviction—after he knows what his wife thinks.

She leads a double life—his and hers.

When she wants his opinion—she gives it to him.

His parrot talks more than he does.

Hick Towns
(*see Small Towns*)

Where everybody knows whose check is good and whose wife isn't.

I don't have to keep an eye on my wife—the neighbors do it for me.

You have to widen the street to put the white line down the middle.

If you see a girl dancing with a man old enough to be her father—he is.

When the train stops at the station —the engine is out in the country.

The town is so small—they have the "Come Again" sign painted on the back of the "Welcome" sign.

It's a place where there's nothing doing every minute.

You use your electric razor and the street lights dim.

The real news comes over the fence —not over the radio.

The town is so small—the barber shop quartet consists of three people.

It's where people go to church to see who didn't.

Where they buy a newspaper to verify what they heard earlier on the telephone.

The only thing open all night is the mail box.

So far from civilization—the TV sets are run by gas.

They hired a traffic cop and then went out to find him some traffic.

Town so small—to have a village idiot—we all had to take turns.

They had a single traffic light—that changes once a week.

It was such a small town—the Howard Johnson's stand had only one flavor.

Hillbillies
(*see Farming, Small Towns, Hick Towns*)

The city boy was being led through the swamps of Georgia. "Is it true," he asked, "that an alligator won't attack you if you carry a flashlight?"

"Wal, now, that all depends," drawled his hillbilly friend, "on jest how fast you carries it!"

A Louisiana farmer had fifteen children, all boys. And when they came of age, they all voted the straight Democratic ticket, just as their pappy, grandpappy, and great-grandpappy had always voted. But someone at the polling booth discovered that one of the boys had done the unforgivable. He had voted Republican!

"Hey, Ephraim," demanded the country campaign manager, "whut th' hell's the idee o' lettin' yo' boy Lucifer vote fer them dang Ree-publicans?"

"Aw, t'ain't mah fault," grumbled Eph. "I tried to brang 'em all up right in the fear of the Lawd, an' to vote straight Democratic, but you seen whut happened. That Lucifer, the dirty cowpoke, he larned how t' read!!"

"Ain't you heered?" asked Clem. "We're havin' a big raffle fer Widder Hawkins. How 'bout you buyin' a ticket?"

"I'd shore like to," whined Lum, "but I dasn't. My wife wouldn't let me keep her effen I won her!"

One Tuesday morning Clara Mae went to the depot and saw Uncle Crawfish standing there with a suitcase in one hand and a Bible in the other. "Whar you goin'?" Clara Mae asked.

"Figured on goin' to El Dorado," admitted Uncle Crawfish with a blushing grin. "Heered tell that there town is plumb full of dancin' gals a-hootin' and a-hollerin' and a-histin' their skirts and drinkin' corn-likker. What's more, they got fiddlers, community sings, and all kinds of carryin's-on . . . So, I'm a-goin' there jest to see for myself!"

"But why are you takin' thet big Bible?" asked Clara Mae.

"We-ell," drawled Uncle Crawfish, "if it's as good as I been a-hearin', I aims to stay till Sunday!"

A Tampa hostess was entertaining her aristocratic friends from the

North. "I believe that Southern spoon bread was the most delicious morsel I've ever tasted," enthused one Northern lady. "My dear, I must have the recipe."

"I'll call in ouah new cook," assured the Southern lady. "She's a backwoods country woman, but I do declare, she sho' can cook. Pearline, come in here, please."

Pearline entered, wiping her hands and putting on her shoes. When asked for the spoon bread recipe, she answered: "Wal, I don't prezackly know whut I use. I jist kinda make spoon bread by instink. I puts a dab o' hawg lard, a nubbin o' cawn-meal, a cat sneeze o' salt, some water, an' a . . ."

"How much water?" she was asked.

"Wal, I allus puts in the same amount," Pearline stated. "I squirts in exackly one mouthful of water!"

He was taking his wife home from the hospital after she had given birth to his twelfth child, when the doctor met him in the corridor. "Well, goodbye folks," the doc said. "I guess I'll be seeing you again next year."

"Won't be a-seein us no mo," the hillbilly answered.

"Oh, come now," the doc said, "I've been seeing you every year for the past twelve years since you're married."

The wife said, "I know, but me 'n' me ole man jist found out what's a-causin' 'em."

A mountaineer and his young wife came into town on their weekly shopping spree. The husband was carrying a week-old baby in his arms.

"Yore's?" asked his friend Clem.

"Ah reckin," he answered. "Leastways, it wuz caught in my trap."

"Why don't you marry me, Annie Mae?" the country boy pleaded. "There isn't anyone else, is there?"

She looked at his ugly kisser and his dirty overalls.

"Oh Clem," she sighed, "there must be!"

DOCTOR: "Your wife is going to have a baby."

HILLBILLY: "I ain't a bit surprised," he said spitting out a mouthful of tobacco juice. "She's had every opportunity."

A rich hillbilly died and left his money in trust for his wife. Only trouble is—she can't touch it till she's twelve years old.

Down in Kentucky the girls get married so young that after the ceremony they don't kiss the bride—they burp her.

Hippies
(*see Beatnik and Bop Humor*)

This hippie came to the party incognito—he took a bath.

A hippie's home is one in which, no matter what time of day it is, you can always take a shower.

His place is such a mess—the phone rang and he couldn't find it.

"What's a hippie?"
"Those characters with dirty pants, filthy sandals. long shaggy hair and dirty sweatshirts."
"Oh them. We call them slobs."

The hippie maid comes in every day and dirties up a little.

The headwaiter stopped the two hippies at the door. "You can't come in here without a tie," he insisted. They returned fifteen minutes later. Only one was wearing a tie.

"What about him?" the headwaiter demanded of the one without a tie.

"Him?" replied the hippie. "That's my wife."

I went to a hippie wedding in Greenwich Village—and they gave the bride a shower—just before the wedding.

The hippie was sitting in a barbershop. After an hour the barber said he was ready to cut his hair. "But I don't want a haircut," replied the kid whose long hair covered his face and reached his shoulders.

"Then what are you doing here?" the barber asked.

"Hiding from my father," said the hippie. "He'd never think of looking for me in a barbershop."

A Japanese hippie went crazy—he went looking for RSD.

The hippie weighed 185 pounds— till he took a bath—now he weighs 120.

The hippie rented a room and turned it into a hotel.

The boy and girl hippie got married in a bathtub—it was a 2-ring ceremony.

Holidays
(*see Birthdays, Anniversaries, etc.*)

My most embarrassing moment was on Halloween when I told the girl with the body to remove her mask and it turned out to be the hostess and she wasn't wearing a mask.

What's so wonderful about Columbus discovering America? It's so big —how could he miss it?

What I want to know is—if George Washington was such an honest man— how come they close the banks on his birthday?

Yom Kippur is the one day of the year when the Jewish people fast. Levy was surprised to see Cohen eating in a restaurant—and oysters yet! "Oysters? On Yom Kippur?" queried Levy with raised eyebrows.

"What's wrong?" answered Cohen. "Yom Kippuh has an 'R' in it."

COP: "Where do you think you're going?"

DRUNK: "Hic, I'm comin' home from a Noo Yearsh Eve party."

COP: "Are you kidding? New Year's was three weeks ago."

DRUNK: "I know. That'sh why I figgered I better be gettin' home."

I celebrated Lincoln's birthday by going through his tunnel, and it wasn't easy—I don't have a car.

A: "How was your turkey?"

B: "Terrible."

A: "Why?"

B: "The stuffing we put into him seemed to be the only food he ever had."

The out-of-work comic was complaining, "To make a couple extra bucks I took the job at the department store. On Thanksgiving I dressed like a pilgrim, on Christmas I dressed like Santa Claus, but I'm finished with holidays. Easter's comin' and I ain't gonna lay an egg for nobody!"

The old gentleman was cautioning the little girl. "Never hesitate about giving presents on Christmas. Don't you know that for every Christmas present you give away, two will come back?"

311

"I'll say," said the kid. "Last Christmas my father gave my sister away in marriage and this Christmas she and her husband came back."

Every Lincoln's birthday, the actor who played Lincoln in many stage plays dressed up like his idol. As he passed the Palace Theatre in the garb of the Great Emancipator, one sidewalk heckler piped up, "He ain't gonna be happy until he's assassinated."

"We only celebrate three major holidays here, suh," bragged the Texan. "The battle of the Alamo, Sam Houston's birthday, and January 20th."
"What's January 20th?" asked the visitor.
"That's the day the new Cadillacs come out, son."

St. Patrick's Day is the wearing of the green and April 15 is when they take your green.

There's an old legend that the statue of Christopher Columbus on New York's Columbus Circle comes to life every year on his birthday. One day, the story goes, a reporter asked Chris, "If you could really come alive after all these years of being a statue, what is the first thing you'd want to do?"
"Kill about twelve million pigeons," answered Columbus.

The soldier boy was so unhappy. "But this is Christmas," I tried to cheer him up, "Santa Claus and all that."
"What Santa Claus?" he cried. "Twenty years ago I asked Santa for a soldier suit—now I get it."

New Year's Eve—our guests pass out the same time as the old year.

He had a wild time. He spent New Year's Eve with the biggest spender in town—his wife.

Mort Sahl says the new national holiday is Beat Wednesday, when all the people in the coffee houses go to work for one day.

At exactly twelve midnight on New Year's Eve, a celebrant stood on top of the Times building and dumped a big vat of Italian food on all the revelers.
His friend looked up at him and screamed, "I told you confetti, you fool, not spaghetti."

Last March 17th, a delegation of St. Patrick's Day marchers marched up to the Capitol in Washington to talk to the President. Said one son of Erin who was the spokesman, "How can we have the wearing of the green when your income tax boys take it away two days before?"

Some smart boys in Washington said we ought to declare income tax day on April 15th an official holiday.
What good is it—we'll have no money to celebrate with.

The New York night club was particularly crowded one Armistice Day. The club was filled with boys and girls in uniform. One young man approached the host-comedian and asked for a good table because "I'm just out of uniform."
He was very solicitous. "What branch of the service were you in, young man?"
"I'm a bellhop," he replied.

FIRST MAN: "The Chinese settle all their debts on New Year's day."
SECOND MAN: "Yeah, but they don't have a Christmas the week before."

The bright young thing approached the clothier's counter and asked the clerk, "What would you suggest is suitable for a distinguished gentleman on Valentine's Day?"

"Well, ma'am," replied the clerk, "how about something nice in ties?"

"No, I don't think so," said the girl. "You see, he has a beard."

"Oh, I see," continued the clerk. "Then how about a fancy vest?"

"N-no," hesitated the girl. "You see, it's a rather long beard."

The clerk sighed wearily. "Well, how about carpet slippers?"

Hollywood
(*see Movie Actors, Ego*)

In Hollywood—marriage is sufficient grounds for divorce.

The official Hollywood drink—marriage on the rocks.

So these Hollywood kiddies were playing house. Said one: "We're going to have a big family—I want three fathers and three mothers."

A Hollywood marriage is a good way to spend a weekend.

When I first went to Hollywood I was such a square, I went to motels and I slept in them.

Hollywood is where the pople accept you for what you're not.

It isn't that I don't like the people in Hollywood; it's just that I don't like the Hollywood in people.

Hollywood people are really lucky. Can you imagine if they had to pay taxes on the money they claim they make?

Did you hear about the very sentimental Hollywood star who wanted to get divorced in the same dress in which her mother got divorced?

He was the proudest kid in the school —he had the most parents at the P.T.A. meeting.

Her career began when she became too big for her sweaters—and ended when she became too big for her britches.

And you said their marriage wouldn't last—they left the church together, didn't they?

The Hollywood starlet was married so many times—she has a wash and wear bridal gown.

In Hollywood the bouquet lasts longer than the groom.

In Hollywood it's impossible to have a secret marriage—the divorce has to come out.

The small-time producer was so excited with the success of the Ten Commandments that he wanted to do a sequel, so he called Henny Youngman —the King of the One-Liners.

The actress was introducing her eighth husband to her daughter by her first husband: "Darling, I want you to meet your new daddy—say something to him."

"All right," the kid obeyed. "Daddy, will you please sign your name in my visitor's book?"

Hollywood is where couples stop going steady—after the wedding.

The sexy movie star was complaining to her cameraman, "How come you never photograph my best side lately?"

"How can I?—you're always sitting on it."

Hollywood friendships don't last— they usually end up in marriage.

He'd divorce his wife—but he doesn't need the publicity right now.

A typical Hollywood marriage is one where the bride is inclined to keep the bouquet and toss the groom away.

Homes
(*see Suburbs, Apartment Houses, Alan King*)

Home cooking is where a man thinks his wife is.

He lives in a beautiful home—overlooking the rent.

Running water in every room is fine —if it doesn't come through the roof.

My cellar is so damp, when I laid a mousetrap—I caught a herring.

Their house is so dirty—last week their dog buried a bone in the rug.

I saw a model home yesterday—but she wouldn't let me in.

I'm not saying our builder was cockeyed—but who ever heard of walking downstairs to the attic?

Our house is so old we had to paint it before the building inspector would condemn it.

Our house is so old—we never know when people upstairs are going to drop in on us.

Honesty
(*see Lies*)

He's as straight as a scenic railway in an amusement park.

I wouldn't say he's a liar, but when it comes time to feed his hogs—he has to get somebody else to call them for him.

"I swore to tell the truth, but every time I do—some lawyer objects."

He's as honest as falsies.

A lie never passes his lips—he talks through his nose.

Honesty and sagacity: Honesty means you must always keep your word under any circumstances. Sagacity means you never give it.

Honesty is fear of being caught.

With men a lie is a last resort—with women, it's first aid.

After the witness was sworn in the judge reminded him, "Remember, you swore to tell the truth."
"Yes, sir, I remember."
"And do you know what to expect if you don't tell the truth?"
"Yes, judge, I expect to win the case."

I've met this man in places where any honest person would be ashamed to be seen.

If Washington was so honest, how come the banks close on his birthday?

Never trust a girl who says she loves you more than anybody else in the world—it means she's been experimenting far and wide.

He's so crooked he has to screw his socks on.

Honesty is the best policy—except when you're trying to collect on your insurance policy.

An honest man is one who's never been caught.

Honeymoon
(*see Brides, Marriage*)

The honeymoon is over when a quickie before dinner means a cocktail.

A honeymoon is just a vacation a man takes before going to work for a new boss.

I knew the honeymoon was over— she refused to help me with the dishes.

They had to call off their honeymoon—couldn't find a baby sitter for the two weeks.

"Does your husband snore?"
"I don't know—we've only been married for three days."

INTERMISSION: When newlyweds are going out for breakfast.

Bob Hope
(*see Comedians*)

"In Russia you don't watch television—television watches *you*."

"I've gotten so many honorary degrees at so many universities—I've been a doctor so many times that I'm starting to resent Medicare."

"My friend plays a wild game of golf. He got up to the first hole—hit one into the woods. On the ninth he hit one in the lake. On the next hole he hit a new ball into the woods again. I said: 'Why don't you use an old ball?' He said, 'I never had an old ball!' "

"This plane was so old—Richard Arlen was flying it. I don't mind an open cockpit, but when you have to go out on the wing to the restroom—that's too much."

"When Cassius Clay was born—he was a six pound mouth."

"The last guy Phyllis Diller stirred up was Batman. He took one look and flew away."

ABOUT IKE: "The General plays golf like a military man. Every time he gets on the green he strokes the ball towards the hole and hollers—'Fall in!' "

ABOUT TRUMAN: "He runs the country with an iron hand and plays the piano the same way."

ABOUT LBJ: "The White House is in great shape—except for the holes under the President's desk. You know how some executives doodle? LBJ drills for oil."

ABOUT JFK: His father gave him a choice: "You can either run for President—or go to camp."

"The Pentagon in Washington has a new emblem—crossed shovels on a field of red tape."

Horse Racing
(*see Race Track, Sports, Golf, Gambling, Bookmakers, etc.*)

KID: "Daddy, which runs faster, horses or trains?"
FATHER: "Trains, of course."
KID: "Then why don't you bet on trains?"

I don't mind if my horse loses—but when he comes to the grandstand and asks, "Which way did they go?"

He finally figured out a way to beat the first four races—he doesn't show up until the fifth.

"Did you bring the money?" one horse fan asked the other.
"No," his buddy replied, "my wife blew it on the rent."

No horse can go as fast as the money you bet on him.

First time I saw a horse run sixth in a five horse race.

Hospitals
(*see Doctors, Hypochrondriacs, Psychiatrists, etc.*)

DOCTOR: "You're running a high fever —104."
STOCK BROKER: "When it reaches 105 —sell."

DOCTOR: "You're running a high fever —104."
SPORTSMAN: "Is it a world record?"

DOCTOR: "You're running a high fever —104."
HYPOCHONDRIAC: "Goody—how many medicines may I have?"

PATIENT: "Are you sure I'll make it, doc? I've heard of a case where they treated one guy for arthritis and he died of yellow fever."
DOCTOR: "Ridiculous—if I treat a patient for arthritis—he dies of arthritis."

PATIENT: "Doctor, I'm going nuts. All day long I keep talking to myself."
DOCTOR: "You're not crazy if you talk to yourself—only if you listen."

I wouldn't say he was unpopular— but he was in the hospital for three months and only received one get-well card and that was from the Blue Cross.

Sophia Loren was taken to the hospital with a very bad chest cold— the doctor who treated her is recovering nicely.

Sophia Loren was taken to the hospital with a very bad chest cold—those germs sure know how to live.

NURSE: "Your pulse is steady as a clock."
PATIENT: "You got your hand on my wristwatch."

What a swanky hospital—you have to be well before they let you in.

I know a fellow who just got out of the hospital. He tells me he got more than 500 get-well cards from Blue Cross alone.

He's got young blood—but he keeps it in an old container.

The medical world has its problems. It's hard to give a man shock treatment once he's seen his wife in curlers.

Hot
(*see Weather, Cold*)

It's been so hot lately, burglars are only breaking into air-conditioned apartments.

It's so hot—everybody is reading fan mail.

It's so hot—Indians are wearing sheets instead of blankets.

It was so hot I took 4-way cold tablets and none of them knew which way to go.

On a blistering hot day when Morey Amsterdam and his wife had guests for dinner, Kay asked little Kathy, then eight, to say the blessing. Embarrassed, she said, "But Mommy, I don't know any."

"Oh—just say what you've heard me say," Kay Amsterdam said.

Obediently she bowed her head and said, "Oh, Lord, why did I invite these people here on this hot day?"

She's perfect for hot weather—she leaves me cold.

Hotels
(see Apartment Houses, etc.)

The man complained to the manager of a small-town hotel about his accommodations. "This is the best we have," said the manager defensively. "This is the royal suite."

The man cracked, "The last royalty that slept here must have been King Kong."

This hotel was so swanky—even the guests had to use the service entrance.

It was so exclusive—even the room service number was unlisted.

One hotel I know was so bad off— the chambermaids were stealing towels from the guests.

MANAGER: "Is there any time you want to be called in the morning?"
GUEST: "No, thank you, I always wake up every morning at seven."
MANAGER: "Then would you mind waking the clerk?"

Herb Shriner says, "There was only one hotel in my home town. It wasn't much but at least it had a bridal suite. That was the room with the lock on the door."

"This is the house detective. You got a lady in there?"
"Just a minute—I'll ask her."

My room was so small—I had to use a folding toothbrush.

My room was so small—when a girl came in she had to lie down.

My room was so small—if you dropped a toupee, you'd have wall-to-wall carpeting.

BELL BOY: "Carry your bag, sir?"
MAN: "No, let her walk."

One must have references—two must have luggage.

A family hotel—everyone's your wife.

They advertised: "Every room on the ocean." When high tide came up— mine was in it.

My room was so small, I dropped my handkerchief and it became a wall-to-wall rug.

Why are hotel room walls so thin when you sleep and so thick when you listen?

HOTELS: Where you give up good dollars for bad quarters.

"$285 for one night?" the man asked as he was checking out.
"You were here one night," the clerk answered, "but your wife has been here for six months."

The room was so small when he closed the door the knob got in bed with him.

The room had a great view—on a clear day you could see the dresser.

317

The room had a great view—if you looked *up*.

Hunting
(*see Safari*)

"Once when I was out hunting with my rifle I ran across a big black bear. He grabbed the rifle out of my hands and pointed it at me."
"What happened?"
"What could happen—I married his daughter."

A few weeks ago I went out on a hunting trip with a friend of mine in the clothing business. We were walking through the woods when all of a sudden a huge bear came out from behind a tree and leaped at me. I screamed, "Help me, is that a bear?" My friend said, "How should I know? Do I deal in furs?"

"If an elephant charges you, let him have both barrels at once."
"And the gun, too, as far as I'm concerned."

"I shot this tiger in India. It was a case of me or the tiger."
"Well, the tiger certainly makes the better rug."

The hunter had been lost for three days. He was hungry, weary, and ready to fall down when he saw his friend, a fellow hunter. "John," he yelled with all the energy left in him, "John—it's me! Thank God—I've been lost for three days."
"Take it easy," John answered, "I've been lost for two weeks."

The hunter returned from one of his trips and admitted reluctantly that he shot his dog.
"Was he mad?" his friend asked.
"He certainly wasn't happy."

This hunter bought a little sports car —just so the deer on the fender would look bigger.

A baby lion was chasing a hunter around a tree in Africa. Mama lion said to the baby lion, "Junior, don't play with your food."

The hunter was completely lost and screamed at his guide, "You told me you were the best guide in New Hampshire."
"I am—but I think we're in Canada right now."

Husbands
(*see Women, Marriage, etc.*)

In all the years I've been married, I've never stopped being romantic—if my wife finds out, I'm dead.

A husband is a lover who pushed his luck too far.

He wears the pants in the house— under his apron.

He married her for her money—and he's earning every dollar of it.

If they had had electric blankets and sliced bread when I was a kid, I never would have gotten married.

He's been given six months to live; that's how long his wife will be away on her trip to Europe—and with her mother, yet.

He'd never be what he is today without her—busted.

The man who brags that he runs things around the house is probably referring to the lawn mower, vacuum cleaner, and the washing machine.

One husband complained: "I don't get along with my wife—she understands me."

A husband would like to believe he could do all the things his wife suspects he does.

When George died, his friends inquired if he left his wife much. "Almost every night," wailed his wife.

Like the wolf who died while he was cheating on his wife. When they broke the news to his spouse, she remarked, "At least I have one consolation. I know where he is tonight."

Bigmouth that he was, he was bawling his wife out on the street, and when she finally answered him, she barked, "We're paying two hundred dollars a month rent. Why can't we fight inside?"

The habitual thief was so thoughtful of his wife. When he was arrested and was riding in the patrol wagon, he pleaded, "Could we stop off and tell the wife where I am so she won't worry?"

The girl quit her job as governess because, she complained, "The children were too backward and the father was too forward."

A husband may not be the best informed of men—but he is the most.

A husband is a man who gave up privileges he never knew he had.

A husband is a man whose wife knows his jokes backwards and tells them that way—just before he tells them.

He knows when to take out the garbage—when his wife tells him.

His wife has changed a lot since they were married—his habits, his friends —his love.

A perfect husband—is the man next door.

He lets his wife think she has her own way—and then lets her have it.

He was so generous. "It's your birthday," he said to his wife grandly; "run around to some smart shops and pick out a few nice things for yourself— but don't get caught."

"Boy," the husband said to his wife on the cruise ship, "this could be such a romantic night if we weren't stuck with each other."

Seems like yesterday I got married. I wish it was tomorrow. I'd call the whole thing off.

My wife used to say to me, "OK, so I like to spend money. Name one other extravagance."

The frustrated horse player kept hollering at his wife: "You keep blowing my salary on luxuries like rent and food."

WIFE: "Why don't you make love like Cary Grant does and all them guys on the screen?"
HUSBAND: "Are you kidding? Do you know how much those guys are paid to do that?"

"I just got a dog for my wife," one husband told the other.
"I'd like to make a swap like that myself."

319

Hypochondriacs
(*see Hospitals, Doctors, Psychiatrists, etc.*)

It's easy to spot a hypochondriac. He's the guy who can read his doctor's handwriting.

The only sickness you get from a hypochondriac is a pain in the neck—or lower.

There are only two people in the world that can read a doctor's writing —a pharmacist and a hypochondriac.

A frustrated hypochondriac is a guy who just found he's allergic to medicine.

He feels lousy until he finds a doctor who tells him he's sick—then he feels good.

Then there's the romantic hypo— he can read a fever chart better than a Wall Street broker. He has girls in his little black book, classified according to the degrees they make his temperature rise.

"That doctor," said the hypochondriac, "he says there's nothing wrong with me—he just doesn't like me personally. He says I have a persecution complex. That's a lie—he says that only because he hates me."

When he smells flowers—he figures there must be a funeral nearby.

He won't kiss a girl unless her lipstick has penicillin in it.

She takes drugs they don't have a disease for yet.

He's so full of medicine—every time he sneezes—he cures somebody.

The Indian hypochondriac sends up filtered smoke signals.

The far-out hypochondriac only smokes filter-tipped marijuana.

When he serves highballs—he uses thermometers as mixers.

Income Tax
(*see Taxes*)

Income tax forms are down to only two lines now: "What did you make in 1968?—Send it."

The man wrote a letter to the income tax bureau. "I haven't been able to sleep since I cheated on last year's income tax. Enclosed please find one thousand dollars. If I find I still can't sleep, I'll send you the rest of the money."

An angry man ran into the post office and shouted to the postmaster, "For some time I've been pestered with threatening letters. I want something done about it!"

"I'm sure we can help," soothed the postmaster. "That's a federal offense. Have you any idea who's sending you these letters?"

"I certainly do," barked the fellow. "It's those pesky income tax people."

FRIEND: "Which of your works of fiction do you consider best?'

AUTHOR: "My last income tax return."

Tax collectors and psychiatrists are giving out the same advice: "It's no good for a man to keep too much to himself."

HARRY: "Poor Sam, he was ruined by untold wealth."

SOL: "Yeah, he should have told about it in his income tax report."

New income tax forms are being printed on Kleenex. That's to make it comfortable for you when you pay through the nose.

If you pay your income tax you go to the poorhouse and if you don't pay, you go to the jailhouse.

An income tax form is very much like a Chinese laundry list—you've got to lose your shirt with either one.

"How come you're putting down your baby as a dependent? It hasn't been born yet."
"I know, but it was part of last year's work."

Income tax is the fairest tax of all —it gives everybody an equal chance at poverty.

It takes more brains to make out your income tax than to make the income.

He refused to pay his income tax in four installments like everybody else. He insisted on paying it all in one lump sum. "My heart," he explained, "can't take it four times a year—one hurt and I'm through with it."

The Internal Revenue is the world's most successful mail order business.

There are only two things you can be sure of: death and taxes—too bad they can't come in that order.

If you have untold wealth—you can expect a visit from the income tax boys.

You sure got to hand it to those Internal Revenue boys—they'll get it anyway.

Save your pennies—the dollars go to the income tax boys.

You don't know when you're well off—but the income tax boys sure do.

The income tax has made more liars out of the American people than golf has.

He had so much money—he told his accountant *not* to cheat on his tax.

My wife and the income tax people have a lot in common—all they ever think about is money.

I put eight of my relatives down under contributions—if they are not an organized charity, I don't know what is.

Income tax time—when millions of Americans test their powers of deductions.

WOMAN TO CLERK: "I do hope you'll give my money to some nice country."

Indians

The Indian out West was leaning against the post. Not that he was tired, but he was just resting because he didn't want to get tired. The tourist approached him and disturbed him: "Why don't you get a job and invest your salary, make a lot of money and then you won't have to work any more?"
The Indian grunted, "Why go through all that? I'm not working now."

I wasn't there but they say it's a true story. When Columbus landed, a couple of Indians watched as they unloaded their cargo. Columbus himself approached the two redskins. "Bueños dias," he greeted them.
One Indian turned to the other and said, "There goes the whole damn neighborhood."

With all the juvenile delinquency, crime, muggings, killings, strikes, bombings, and uprisings going on—I think maybe the Indians should have had some stricter immigration laws.

321

Will Rogers said, "America never lost a war or won a conference." You might add "except in the case of the Indians." They are the only ones we ever beat that didn't come out ahead.

"I felt like Custer, I never saw so many Indians," the tourist was telling the gang at the office when he came back from New Mexico. "There were Indians to the right of me, Indians to the left of me, and Indians in front of me."
"So what did you do?" his secretary asked.
"What could I do? I bought a blanket!"

A tourist driving through Arizona stopped by an Indian selling blankets. "How much?" he asked.
"Fifty dollars," said the Indian.
"I'll give you ten," said the tourist.
"Oh no, brother—no more deals like Manhattan."

An Indian chief, head of a Nevada tribe, drove into Las Vegas for a bit of gambling and was wiped out quickly. He climbed to the top of Mt. Charleston and sent smoke signals to his tribe asking for money.
The tribe signaled back, "For what reason do you need money?"
Before the chief could reply, a group of scientists from the Atomic Energy Commission detonated an atomic charge in the desert. A tremendous mushroom of smoke rose from the earth, darkening the sky.
Promptly the tribe signaled, "All right, all right, sending the money—just don't holler."

Two Navajo Indians were in New York. The Indians kept staring at the closely grouped Con Edison smoke-stacks belching smoke. The first Indian asked his friend: "What is smoke signal saying?"

"Hard to understand," the other Indian grunted. "Everybody talking at same time."

Inflation
(see Money, Banks, Business)

Americans are getting stronger. Twenty years ago it took two people to carry ten dollars' worth of groceries. Today, my child can do it.

If there isn't inflation, how come the supermarket has offered to buy back at twice the price groceries I bought there last week?

Inflation is when you earn four dollars per hour, and in the supermarket your wife spends at the rate of six dollars per minute.

I don't know if we'll ever cure poverty, but the way taxes and prices are going, we're sure to cure wealth.

Balance economy note: Crime may be up, but don't forget . . . arrests and convictions are down.

Anyone who sits around the house worrying about inflation is crazy. He should be out there, frantically buying things before prices go up again.

I know there's inflation—you know that penny candy? It's now a nickel.

Even 2¢ plain is selling for 10¢.

Just when you think you can make both ends meet—somebody moves the ends.

"Darling," the wife complained to the husband, "you're making it slower than I can spend it again."

They say dollar bills carry germs. That's ridiculous. Even a germ couldn't live on a dollar these days.

If you don't know what's up—you haven't been shopping lately.

Prices are so high—if you spend five dollars they ring up "No sale!"

"The nation is prosperous as a whole —but how much prosperity is there in a hole?"—Will Rogers

There are things that money can't buy—like for instance the same things it bought last week.

The husband was complaining about the act of having a baby. "Look at this hospital bill," he shrieked. "When I was born it cost nothing; now, over $600—for one baby." "True," the wife answered, "but think how long they last."

Everything has gone up. Yesterday's penny-pincher now uses a dime.

They call it take-home pay because there is no other place you can afford to go with it.

The way the world is now: a book on *How To Be Happy Without Money* costs ten dollars.

INFLATION: When nobody has enough money because everybody has too much.

Inflation is after you get enough money to buy something—it isn't enough.

The best proof that appearances are deceiving is that the dollar bill looks exactly the same as it did fifteen years ago.

Insults
(*see Hecklers, Squelches, etc.*)

All she has to do to dominate the conversation is to leave the room.

Sex siren? She couldn't lure you out of a burning building.

He has so little personality—he worked a color TV show and came out in black and white.

An insult is like a married man coming home with lipstick on his collar —it's hard to laugh off.

The summer resort was so seedy-looking, it didn't even look good in the advertising folder photos.

The self-styled Romeo with the self-made toupee tried to make the hard-to-make girl. She wasn't having any of his lip or his rug, and finally squelched: "This is the first time I've ever seen broadloom ear-to-ear." She continued, "You're the only guy I've ever met with a nine-by-twelve head." And then finished him off with: "When you have a party, I'll bet you roll up your head!"

The picture was so bad that one critic murdered, "A stinkbomb was exploded in the theatre but wasn't noticed until the show was over."

Gene Baylos heckled the food at a restaurant: "I think they're putting makeup on the roast beef."

The noisy diner was banging on the table with his cutlery. "The service here is lousy," he bellowed. "Look at my glass, it's empty. What've I got to do to get some water?" The quiet waiter leaned over and whispered, "Why don't you set fire to yourself?"

I'm very proud to be considered a friend of his—and it isn't easy to be a man's only friend.

He's a fine newspaperman—he's "A" in my book. In fact, I think most of them are A.A.

323

The most pleasant thing to say about him is that he has B.O.

His performance was out of this world—and I hope he joins it.

I think the world of him—and you know what I think of the world.

They have nothing in common—except they both are.

He's not himself today—and it's a great improvement.

She's in love with him—and so is he.

He's very important—men like him don't grow on trees—they usually swing from them.

TO A BAD AUDIENCE: "You've been a great bunch of seats."

Insurance

My father-in-law is in the insurance business. He sold me a twenty-year retirement policy—at the end of twenty years—he retires.

A fellow who lives in the city most of the year but summers in Maine was surprised one winter day when he received a call from the caretaker of his summer place. "There's a bad forest fire up here," he was informed, "and it looks like your house might get burned down."

"My goodness!" the homeowner exclaimed. "Is there anything I can do?"

"Well," the caller replied, "I thought maybe you might want to put more insurance on the house."

A man went into the insurance office to report that his car had been stolen and he would like to get his money. The insurance executive was polite but firm: "Sorry, we do not give you money; we replace the car with a new one."

The man answered indignantly, "If that's the way you do business. you can cancel the policy on my wife."

My grandfather took out a million dollars' worth of life insurance. It didn't help him—he died anyway.

He sold me group insurance—but the whole group has to get sick before I collect.

When I was sick my husband sat up all night and read to me—my insurance policy.

The dear little old lady lost her jewelry and put in a claim for $3,000. After a cursory examination, and since it was her first loss, they paid her in full.

Three weeks later, after she cashed the check, she found her jewels. She immediately sent a letter to the insurance company: "I found my jewelry. Thanks for everything, anyhow, but I didn't think it was right for me to keep the jewelry *and* the money, so I sent the money to the Salvation Army."

"I'll buy that bracelet for $5,000," the man told the lady.

"Are you joking?" she countered. "The insurance company is offering more than that as a reward."

The lady sent a letter to the insurance company. "I'm happy to announce that my husband who was reported missing—is now definitely deceased."

Life insurance is something that keeps a man poor all his life so he can die rich.

"But lady, you can't collect the life insurance on your husband—he isn't dead yet."

"I know that—but there's no life left in him."

She called her insurance man: "Charlie—I'm very angry with you. You insured me against accidents and so far I've had three in ten days."

Did you hear about the bandit who walked into an insurance office—and escaped without buying any.

If you don't stop nagging me—I'll let my insurance lapse.

My husband doesn't carry life insurance. He carries fire insurance—he knows where he's going.

Fun is like life insurance—the older you get, the more it costs.

This insurance company gives you double indemnity. If you die in an accident—they bury you twice.

Mr. Davis took out an insurance policy for $25,000 and three months later he passed on. When the insurance agent brought his widow the money, he suggested she take out insurance for her three children.

"It's a good idea," she agreed, "after all, my husband—he listened to you and he had luck."

"But mother, why can't I go in swimming?"

"Because it's too deep."

"But daddy is swimming."

"He's insured."

I have so much insurance—if anything happened to me, Lloyds would have to leave London.

Integration
(*see Restricted, Religion, Ethnic Humor, Dick Gregory, Flip Erikson, etc.*)

A guy walked into a Chinese restaurant and saw a Negro waiter. Surprised, he asked what was the specialty of the house. The Negro waiter said, "Pizza."

The guy said, "Pizza in a Chinese restaurant?"

Waiter said, "Well, this is a Jewish neighborhood."

Harry Hershfield was in a small Southern town speaking at a U.J.A. dinner. "I can't understand people hating each other," one woman said to him. "Look at me—I'm living in the South thirty years—I'm not anti-semitic to the colored people."

He got up a petition to send the Indians back to where they came from.

Intermission

When newlyweds come out for breakfast.

At a college dance when everyone comes inside to rest.

She doesn't dance too well—but can she intermission.

International
(*see also "International Humor" chapter, Russia, France, Israel, Travel, etc.*)

You know what kills me? Everybody says if you go to Paris you get cheated. But the only time I got gypped all the time I was in Paris was when I bought some French postcards from a fella: I paid the guy and I never got the pictures . . . they burned up changing hands.

325

You know what disappointed me in Europe? The Swiss bell-ringers. They're women who ring bells and yodel. We have the same thing over here—we call 'em Avon Ladies.

The story was told of an American, Frenchman, Chinese, and Scotsman drinking beer. A fly fell into each of the four glasses. The American tossed his drink away. The Frenchman drew out the fly and drank the beer. The Chinese tossed away the beer but ate the fly. The Scotsman drank his beer, but sold the fly to the Chinese.

Adolf Hitler was discovered hiding in Buenos Aires, so the anecdote goes, by two aged Nazis who told him he must take over Germany.
"But I'm a fugitive," he protested.
"We can fix everything," they said. "You have to do it for the Fatherland."
Hitler thought it over. "All right, for the Fatherland I'll do it," he said, "but this time the nice guy stuff is out."

Although most of Castro's foreign trade has collapsed, he's doing a booming business in one area—exporting Cubans.

England finally has something it can beat Germany at without our help—soccer.

No, the Chinese should not be allowed to join the U.N.—You know the Chinese, once they vote, an hour later they want to vote again.

I know a restaurant that serves only Chinese and German food—an hour later you're hungry for power.

Russia is the only country in the whole world that kept its word about practicing disarmament: It disarmed Poland, Hungary, East Berlin.

I took some French lessons and my French is so good—I find myself rude to Americans.

To identify some items in Europe: If it's cold, it's soup—if it's warm, it's beer.

People who say the American dollar doesn't go far are nuts—it goes to Afghanistan, India, Vietnam, Pakistan.

Inventions

A scientist crossed a potato with a sponge. It tastes terrible but it holds a lot of gravy.

Old maids can now buy cellophane mattresses, so they don't have to jump out of bed to see who's underneath.

He invented a new drug that cures penicillin.

A double-decker bathtub for people who like to sing duets.

I just invented something that cooks, cleans, washes the dishes, and scrubs the floor—it's called a wife.

I invented a spot remover that removes spots left by spot removers.

I invented an alarm clock that doesn't ring—for people who want to sleep late.

I'm working on a big invention right now—color radio.

He invented an automobile powered by electricity instead of gasoline. "I went from California to New York and all it cost was $3.40—but it was $32,-000 for the extension cord."

I love that invention of the electric toothbrush—now I only have to see my electrician twice a year.

Father invented a house with the basement on top of the roof—so in case we lose something, we don't have to turn the house upside down looking for it.

This dern new-fangled house you done sent me ain't no good. In fact, it's plumb lousy. I think mebbe I put it up wrong. Leastways, everytime I step out the front door, I fall off the roof!

Plant pickles upside-down and instead of warts they will have dimples.

To make pickles look like bananas, buy a can of yellow paint.

The new invention on the market is a combination toothbrush and pliers. If you don't want to brush your teeth —pull them out.

Cellophane window shades so your neighbors don't have to worry about what's going on.

A built-in alarm clock that doesn't ring—for people too lazy to get up to look for a job.

Plastic termites for people with modern homes.

Furniture in Early American style: At six in the morning, an Indian, sitting on your dresser, wakes you up.

For people who are dispossessed often, have your interior decorator make you drapes that match the sidewalk.

Stuff your mattress with billiard balls—it's easier to roll out of bed. When you get up the next day, you don't have bags under your eyes—just side-pockets.

"He has an airplane that can stay in the air for sixty-five days without petrol or oil."
"That's not possible—he'd have to come down on account of the law of gravity."
"He went up before the law was passed."

He crossed a tiger with a parakeet. He doesn't know what it is—but when it talks you listen.

A rocking chair—with a seat belt.

She has a new gadget that does all the housework—it's called a husband.

He invented a soap that leaves your hands whiter than new—but your wash comes out rough and red.

I just invented a new refrigerator with peepholes for people who want to make sure the light goes out.

He invented an electric sundial.

Irish
(*see International Humor chapter*)

"Now we got quite a big family," Pat was telling his pals at work. "One brother is a Bishop and oim the best bricklayer in all of Ireland."
"Yop," said one listener, "I guess we all can't be the biggest."
"No sor," Pat agreed, "me poor brother—he couldn't do this to save his loif."

FATHER DONOVAN: "I will pray that you will forgive O'Brien for hitting you with that bottle."
CLANCY: "Sure and yer Holiness might be wastin' yer time—why not wait till oi get well—an' then pray for O'Brien."

327

"Tell me, Pat, is it true that you will be buried in an English cimmiterie?"

"Glory be to God—oid rather die first."

"Faith and oi niver saw such a blackened oiye. Dun't tell me yer let that little shrimp of a man Clancy O'Donovan do that to ye?"

"Please, I will not have ye shpeke disrespectfully of the dead."

JUDGE: "Patrick Donovan, you've been brought here for drinkin'."

PATRICK: "Well, yer highness, wot er we waitin' fer—le's git started."

"Begorrah, oid give me life savings if I knew where I was goin' to die."

"Sure now, faith, an' whut good would it do yez if yez knew?"

"Plenty—oid shtay away from that place."

Israel
(*see International Humor chapter*)

Jerry Shane says that Israel's new TV station has a symbol of their own. Instead of the NBC peacock—they have a boiled chicken sitting in a pot of soup. And they've changed the name of some of the shows. "The Price is Right" is called "Is that the best you can do?" and "Peyton Place" is called "A Shame for the Neighbors."

Sense of humor sign at the port in Haifa: "Don't give up the ship—sell it."

"The war can't last more than two months."

"How do you know?"

"My husband just joined the army and he's never held a job for more than two months in his life."

A tourist asked the taxi driver in Jerusalem to take him to the Wailing Wall—so he took him directly to the income tax building.

The junk dealer rang the bell and the husband answered. "Do you have anything I can pick up?" the junk dealer asked.

"Come back later," the husband growled, "my wife's not here."

ADVERTISEMENT IN LOCAL PAPER IN HAIFA: "You may have a friend at Chase Manhattan—but at our bank you have family."

The first Jewish soldier ever to be court-martialed. He missed the war—he overslept.

ISRAEL ENLISTMENT POSTER: "Join the Army and see the pyramids."

Did you hear about the new Arab war maps? You look at them and they fold.

An Israeli soldier apologized for capturing only 6 tanks and 200 prisoners: "After all, my husband wasn't with me."

A picture of the Arabs practicing war maneuvers—throwing their hands in the air.

Two foot soldiers in Jerusalem are talking over a saucer of tea.

"What's our goal today?"

"We capture the Suez Canal."

"Good—but what will we do in the afternoon?"

The Arabs fought until the first man.

QUIZ: "How do you know an Egyptian flag when you see it?"

ANSWER: "It's all white."

The Arabs complained to the U.N. that the war was unfair: "Israel has two million Jews and we ain't got any."

Morey Amsterdam is writing the world's thinnest book: *Arab Military Victories.*

Larry Gore's hilarious *Blintzkrieg '67* has these observations:

"The Jews don't want the Suez—there's no boardwalk."

"The Israelis had to win the war that quickly because they can't carry guns on the Sabbath."

"Of the 659 casualties announced by the Israelis only 159 are real casualties —the rest are pledges."

Italy
(*see International Humor chapter and Ethnic Humor*)

The wonder of Italy: How one country could turn out such small cars and such big women.

Two great things have come out of Italy in the last ten years and Sophia Loren is both of them.

Two great things have come out of Italy in the last decade and Gina what's-her-name has both of them.

Sophia is four feet, six inches tall— lying flat on her back.

Jealousy

I knew a bride who was so jealous —she had male bridesmaids.

George Jessel
(*see Dais, Speakers, Roast of the Town chapter, etc.*)

Jessel has very often doubled at two eulogies in one day. He is proud that he is known as the greatest orator at these funerals. Once, at a particularly tender moment during his eulogy, he accidentally glanced down on the deceased in the coffin. "My God," Jessel gasped, "I *know* this man."

Jack Benny tells about the time George delivered the eulogy for James Mason's cat. "When Jessel finished eulogizing the cat there wasn't a dry eye—I never knew that cats did so much for Israel and the Democrats."

Jessel says, "I have been requested to perform at every type charity— Catholic, Jewish, and Protestant. The Moslems I'm not so close to at the moment. However, if they asked me to perform for Nasser, I would gladly do it—like perform at his eulogy when he passes on."

George's favorite story is about the widow who was selling her husband's practically new Cadillac for fifty dollars. "Why?" somebody asked her.
"In my husband's will," she explained, "he asked that this new Cadillac be sold and the proceeds be given to his beautiful young secretary. I am following his wishes—to the letter."

"No one would say a word for Charlie Green, who passed away. The preacher pleaded. Finally one man said, 'Awright, open the lid—I'll talk.' He looked at the body: 'Brother Green is dead and that's a good thing. He was seventy years old. He should have died sixty-five years ago. He was the meanest man in town—he stole milk from children, put widows out of their homes. But next to his brothers Frank and John who are still alive, he was an *angel.*'"

329

Jessel was signed to do a tour with Eddie Cantor. When they arrived in Bridgeport, George noticed the billing: "Eddie Cantor with George Jessel." "What the hell kind of conjunction is that? 'Eddie Cantor *with* George Jessel,' " he screamed at Manager Irving Mansfield. Irving promised to change the conjunction. The next day the marquee read, "Eddie Cantor *but* George Jessel."

Jessel was always broke and Cantor had millions. Jessel enjoyed spending his money but he was bugged that Cantor was such a good businessman. One day he walked out of his dressing-room door and saw a big sign with the legend "Jesus Saves." Under it he wrote in ink: "But not like Cantor."

George Jessel was talking about, "That idiot—I told him how to run his studio."

"So, what happened?"

"Nothing, we parted good friends. He boarded his yacht—and I took the subway home."

Jewish Jokes

(*see Ethnic Humor, Israel, chapter on International Humor, Integration*)

Someday there may be a Jewish President of the United States. I can just see the pitcure: 1984—a man calls the woman in the Bronx and says, "Congratulations, your son just became President of the United States!"

"So what?" she answered. "Better he should be a doctor."

The President thought he was calling Arthur Goldberg's house in Chicago. "This is the President," he said to the little Jewish lady. "From what synagogue?" she asked.

This synagogue is so orthodox that during Rosh Hashana and Yom Kippur they have a big sign out front that says, "Closed for the Holidays."

There is only tradition in Jewish life. My father has been going to the same theatre for fifty years. Lately it's become a Spanish theatre—but he still goes. When he's coming out the other day I asked, "Pop, what are you doing here? You don't understand Spanish."

He answered, "Did I understand English?"

"Mom," the boy said, "I'm getting married—and the girl is not Jewish."

"So what?" she said. "I'm modern. Just don't tell your Uncle Irving—you know how narrow-minded he is. But about me you don't have to worry—because I'll kill myself anyway."

"The rabbi told us a fantastic story in synagogue today," the boy told his father. "The Jews were chased out of Egypt and they came to the Red Sea. When they saw the Egyptians following them they built a bridge over the Red Sea and went over in safety. But when the Egyptians kept coming, the Jews put dynamite under the bridge and when all the Egyptians came on top of the bridge, the Jews blew up the bridge and all the Egyptians fell in the Red Sea and were drowned."

Father said to the kid, "The rabbi told you this story?"

"No, but if I told you what the rabbi told us—you'd never believe it."

Morey Amsterdam tells about a Jewish Western being shot in a delicatessen in Dodge City:

"It's called 'Frontier Heartburn'— and it's a gas. In one scene the hero is seen drinking tomato juice and borscht. It's called a Bloody Sarah."

Shlamiel and Shlamazel: the big difference is: A Shlamiel drops the soup in the lap of the Schlamazel.

CUSTOMER: "Will this mink be ruined in the rain?"

FURRIER: "Did you ever see a mink with an umbrella?"

The teacher called the roll at the first grade classroom. "Johnny Murphy."

"Here, teacher."

"Pamela Andrews."

"Here, teacher."

"Abraham Rabinowitz."

"I'll give 100 dollars."

A guest at a summer resort on the Borscht Belt was taking free dancing lessons every day. At the end of one of the sessions he sat down exhausted next to a friend who was engrossed in the *New York Times*.

"What do you think of this Sukarno?" the studious one asked, banging the paper.

"Please," said the dancer, "I'm having enough trouble with the rhumba."

Two Jewish ladies met at a luncheon. "So, how's everything?" the first asked.

"Eh!—and how's by you?"

"Nu!—and your husband?"

"Mmmmm—and your children?"

"Ahhhh!—"

"Well, good-bye—it's good when two friends meet like this and talk out the heart."

Two elderly Jewish gentlemen sat in silence for an hour rocking back and forth on the porch of the Miami Beach hotel. After an hour or more of silence, one sighed out loud and said, "Oy." His friend answered, "You're telling me."

"Close the window—it's cold outside."

"So, I'll close the window it'll be warm outside?"

The woman called her husband to her side as she lay dying. "Max," she confessed, "before I die—I must tell you, I've been untrue to you."

"So—why do you think I gave you poison?"

The mother caught her daughter making love in the living room. "Out!" she screamed. "You'll leave this house right now—and don't come back till you're a virgin."

SECRETARY: "Mr. Graham, your mother, Mrs. Goldberg, is calling you."

GRAHAM: "Mom—where were you last night? We expected you at my new apartment. What happened to you?"

MOTHER: "I came there about 6 o'clock and I sat in the lobby until 10 and then I went home."

GRAHAM: "But mom, why didn't you come upstairs to my apartment?"

MOTHER: "I couldn't remember your name."

LADY IN ELEVATOR: "Just a second—hold it—please—don't close the door—we're going down without mine husband."

OPERATOR: "Don't get excited lady—this ain't the *Titanic!*"

MAN: "Mamma, I haven't much time, but before I go, I want to tell you that after I'm gone, you should give the house in the country to our daughter Ethel."

WIFE: "Ethel? What does she need that big house, they have no children—better you should give the house to Doris."

MAN: "OK, mamma—now you'll see that the store should go to our son Jack."

WIFE: "But papa, you know Jack, he's no good in the store. He'll run it

331

down—better you should give the store to Joey."

MAN: "OK, mamma—but the new car I would like for our son Freddy."

WIFE: "Freddy!—you know Freddy— with his reckless driving—he'll ruin it—better you should give the new car to Jack."

MAN: "Mamma—who's dying—me or you?"

LBJ

President Johnson was asked by a reporter what his golf handicap was. He answered: "I don't have any—I'm all handicap."

"I see in the papers that Barry and Rocky have decided to cut down their appearances in California. This reminds me of the fellow down in Texas who told his friend he was thinking of running for sheriff against Uncle Jim Wilson. 'What do you think?' he asked.

" 'Well,' said his friend, 'it depends on which one of you sees the most people. If you see the most, Uncle Jim will win. If he sees the most, you will win.' "

As Calvin Coolidge said, "You don't have to explain what you don't say."

"This is a moment that I deeply wish my parents could have lived to share. My father would have enjoyed what you so generously said of me, and my mother would have believed it."

Once when he was called "The luckiest man alive," he answered, "Yes, and I find the harder I work, the luckier I get."

"This is one of the best introductions I ever received—if not *the* best—except once down in the hills of Tennes-

see and the Governor was supposed to introduce me. He didn't show up—and I had to introduce myself."

LBJ loves to tell preacher stories. Of course, there are no preachers like the ones in Texas. He tells the one about the preacher who dropped his sermon before the service one Sunday and watched horrified as a dog chewed it up. "I'll have to preach God's word today," he told the congregation, "but next week I hope to do better."

My favorite story about LBJ is the time he had a group of pals over to a barbecue on his ranch. Like all Texans, he was bragging. "I got 3,000 head of cattle on this ranch." His neighbor interrupted, "Mr. President, I don't want to bring you down—but this is Texas: every rancher in Texas has at least 3,000 head of cattle." And the President said, "In his refrigerator?"

Another time the President was "on" as usual, and as usual was telling his tall stories as Texans do. "I had a neighbor here in Johnson City that had 100,000 head of cattle on his ranch— no bodies—all heads."

Lynda Bird caused the comics to come out with their full artillery. "I had a hunch Lynda Bird was here tonight," Bob Hope said at a Hollywood show. "I was frisked twice on the way in."

Johnny Carson said: "Two secret service men interrogated me today. Nothing important. Just wanted to know if I didn't want to renew my subscription to McCall's."

They describe LBJ by saying he is tall, dark and has some fourteen million dollars. That and the fact that he is a Texan have brought out all kinds of stories. Who cares if they're true.

The President would be the first to say they are amusing.

"He's the luckiest Texan of them all —his 1,000 head of cattle suddenly started gushing oil."

The story goes that LBJ was bragging that his state never had bad times. "But surely you felt the great depression of the 1930s?" a detractor asked. "No, we didn't," the President replied. "However, we did enjoy one of the poorest booms we had ever known."

When LBJ started his anti-poverty program (in Texas it applies to anybody who makes under a million a year), every true Son of the Lone Star State said: "He's trying to make this the the United States of Texas."

In Texas they tell the story of how Everett Dirksen, Senate minority leader, at one time was supposed to imitate Johnson in everything he did. LBJ bought a cane—so did Dirksen. LBJ bought a Cadillac—Dirksen followed suit. LBJ got mad—he installed a phone in his Cad. Dirksen found out, had his own phone installed in his car —and decided to rub it in by calling LBJ one morning as both men were in their cars.

"Hello, Lyndon," Dirksen said. "Guess what—I'm calling you from my car!"

"What's that, Ev?" asked LBJ. "I can't hear you. Will you hold a minute? My other phone is ringing."

When LBJ decided he wasn't running again he became a hero overnight. "Sure," LBJ admitted, "everybody loves his mother-in-law when she says she's leaving."

Jokes
(see Comedians, chapters in Part I on Wits, Comedians, Storytellers, etc.)

I hope you live to be as old as your jokes.

He'd be the most popular man in TV if he were as well-known as his jokes.

A wife laughs at her husband's jokes —not because they are clever—but because she is.

I'm not going to stand here and tell you a lot of old jokes—but I'll introduce the next speaker who will.

Not all bum jokes are about hoboes.

I think there's company downstairs —I just heard mamma laugh at one of papa's jokes.

Judges
(see Court, Lawyers, etc.)

The judge was trying a case concerning some dice players. "Will all the crapshooters step to the bar?" he said. Six men stepped forward, when only five were involved. "What are you doing here?" the judge asked the sixth man. "What's the matter?" said the man. "Ain't my money good?"

A man had been found dead and the jury was puzzled as to what caused his death. The judge finally explained: "It was an act of God under very suspicious circumstances."

"Why don't you settle this case out of court?" the judge asked the two men before him. "That's just what we were doing," replied one fellow, "when the police came and interfered."

The noted jurist was asked how he comes to a decision. "Oh," he said, "I listen to the plaintiff and then I make my decision." "Don't you ever listen to the defendant?" he was asked. "I used to," he said, "but that mixes me up."

An old Southerner who could trace his ancestry back to the time when Lee fought Grant was hauled into court for vagrancy. Brought before the judge, he was asked his name. "It's Colonel Zeth Eaton," he replied. "And what does the 'Colonel' stand for?" the man on the bench asked. "That 'Colonel' is kinda like the 'Honorable' in front of your name," the old man answered, "it doesn't mean a damn thing!"

JUDGE: "You'll have to carry your plea for clemency alone—the Governor has been indicted himself."

A Michigan circuit judge tells about a divorce suit he handled recently. "I think you might as well give your husband a divorce," he advised the wife. "What!" shouted the lady. "I have lived with this bum for twenty years, and now I should make him happy?"

As soon as the judge sentenced the hardened criminal to twenty years in prison, he rushed out of the courthouse. "Where are you going?" his clerk asked. "Are you afraid of his gang?"
"No, I'm going over to rent his apartment."

The judge was soft and gentle. "Have you ever been sent to prison?"
"No," the penitent prisoner cried, tears running down his cheeks. "No, your honor."
"There, there, don't cry," said the judge compassionately. "You're going there now."

"You are lying so clumsily," the judge said to the witness, "that I would advise you to get a lawyer."

JUDGE: "Well, gentlemen, has the jury reached a verdict?"
FOREMAN: "Your honor, we have discussed this case hither and yon, backwards and forwards, upside-down and rightside-up, and after careful deliberation we have come to the conclusion—*we shouldn't mix in!*"

Juvenile Delinquents
(*also look under Children, Kids, Teenagers, Colleges, Universities, etc.*)

The two tough kids were watching the newcomer to the neighborhood walking down the street. One said to the other: "You grab one leg, I'll grab the other—and we'll make a wish."

One tough kid in the Williamsburg section of Brooklyn has his own racket. He takes sparrows, dips them in peroxide and sells them as canaries!

In school, in that same section, if a kid raises his hand, they think it's a holdup.

You think the kids of today are rough? One day when I was a kid, I walked into the house, my nose was bleeding, my arm was in a sling, and two teeth were knocked out. My mother said, "What happened?" I said, "Some kid pushed me off the roof." She said, "Good—for a minute I thought you were fighting again!"

When my father came home he got mad, so I ran under the bed. He said: "Come out from under the bed." I said: "You're gonna hit me." He said: "I'm not gonna hit you." I said: "Promise?" He said "I promise!" The minute I came out from under the bed —wham—I got it right in the nose! I said: "But Dad—you promised." He said: "That'll teach you not to trust anybody, especially your father!"

The delinquents of today are the same as the delinquents of fifty years ago, only they have better weapons.

He carries a blackjack in his pencil box.

It was a very old-fashioned school— you had to raise your hand before you hit the teacher.

The kid was playing hooky from school. The father told the kid to go out and get a job. The problem child decided to be a bookmaker in his neighborhood. Instead of money, he dealt in pebbles.

One day another kid who was gambling with him came around with a big rock. "I better not take his bet," said the young bookmaker, "he must know something!"

The place to stop juvenile delinquency is in the high chair—not the electric chair.

A town was having a juvenile delinquency problem. The kids kept having gang wars in the alleys. So the city fathers built three beautiful playgrounds. Now they have the gang wars in the playgrounds.

I remember when kids used to cut classes instead of teachers.

The teacher was telling about this one kid in her class who drinks, smokes marijuana, curses and kicks her everytime he comes in and goes out of the class. What bothers her the most— is that this kid is the only one who has a 100 per cent attendance record in her class.

The kid set fire to his teacher's desk, stabbed the principal, robbed three of the kids in her class and was caught in the little boys' room smoking hashish. His teacher handled the situation. Of course, you're not allowed to touch the little doll—but she wrote a very strong note to his psychiatrist—with a copy to his parents.

They were a gang of rich delinquents. These kids are so well educated that when they write dirty words on the men's room walls—they're in Latin.

Never give the boy all the allowance you can afford—keep some to bail him out.

He could go to any reform school in the country on a scholarship.

His parents almost lost him as a kid —but he found his way home.

Karate

He learned to deliver karate blows with his bare feet. But he got into a fight recently, and while he was taking off his shoes and stockings, the other guy broke him in half.

I'm a karate student—the lessons are only $200 a year, but I break $2,000 worth of boards.

The Wit of John F. Kennedy

At a fund raising dinner: "I am deeply touched—but not as deeply touched as you have been by coming to this dinner."

"I appreciate your welcome. As the cow said to the Maine farmer, 'Thank you for a warm hand on a cold morning.'"

On one of his trips to California the President was asked by a little boy: "How did you become a war hero?"
"It was absolutely involuntary. They sunk my boat."

335

When he appointed his brother he answered his critics: "I see nothing wrong with giving Bobby some legal experience as Attorney General before he goes out to practice law."

At a dinner in Washington he said: "I have just received the following letter from my generous daddy. It says, 'Dear Jack: Don't buy a single vote more than is necessary. I'll be damned if I'm going to pay for a landslide.' "

After RFK was in office a few weeks, the President joked: "Speaking of jobs for relatives—Master Robert Kennedy, who is four, was in to see me today, but I told him we already had an Attorney General."

JFK was a great storyteller and loved to tell the one about "the Russian who ran through the Kremlin hollering, 'Khrushchev is a fool. Khrushchev is a fool.' He was sentenced to twenty-three years in prison—three for insulting the party secretary, and twenty for revealing a state secret."

He kidded his religion, "I asked the Chief Justice of the Supreme Court whether he thought our new educational bill was constitutional and he said, 'It's clearly constitutional—it hasn't got a prayer.' "

Instead of kicking, he delighted in ribbing those who opposed him. One time in Columbus, Ohio, he received a tremendous ovation at a dinner. When the cheers finally subsided he said, "There isn't a town in America where I get a bigger hand and a smaller vote than Columbus, Ohio."

Kids
(*see Children, Juvenile Delinquents*)

A little boy tried to buy a ticket to the movies and the cashier asked why he wasn't in school. "I don't have to go," he announced. "I have the measles."

Strike your child every day. If you don't know why—he does.

Little Patty Lamm, the seven-year-old daughter of a Cleveland publicist, was painting something when her father walked in and asked what it was. She said, "I'm painting a picture of God."
"Darling," said Pop, "it's very sweet of you, but nobody ever saw God and nobody knows what He looks like."
"Well," said the little doll, "*now* they'll know."

FATHER: "Always you ask me questions. What would have happened if I asked so many questions when *I* was a kid?"
SON: "Maybe you'd be able to answer some of mine."

FOND MOTHER: "Quiet, dear, the Sandman is coming."
MODERN CHILD: "Okay, mom, a dollar and I won't tell pop."

"My, grandpa, what a lot of whiskers! Can you spit through them all?"
"Yes, sonny, I can."
"Well, you'd better do it now, cause they're on fire from your pipe."

Two Movieland children, both offsprings of much married, much divorced parents, got into a fight about the abilities of their respective mothers. The argument really got hot and one kid said, "Well, anyway my father can lick your father."
"Are you kidding?" said the other kid. "Your father *is* my father."

"Why don't ya treat your Pa with more respect?"
"I'm disappointed in him. Ma tells me the stork brung me."

ALICE: "Auntie, were you ever in a predicament?"
MAIDEN AUNT: "No, dearie, but Heaven knows, I've tried."

MOTHER: "Where do bad little girls go?"
GIRL: "Most everywhere."

He lives in such a ritzy neighborhood that the local juvenile delinquents scribble naughty words on the sidewalk—in French.

A three-year-old was struggling with the back button on his new long-underwear. Finally he gave up, trotted up to his mother and said: "Mommy, open my bathroom door, please."

A little boy asked his mother if he could watch the solar eclipse. "Okay," she replied, "but don't go too close."

Two kids were on the corner and a little girl walked by.
One said, "Her neck's dirty."
Other one said, "Her does?"

Did you ever hear the cutie about the lady who sent her four-year-old son to a progressive summer camp? On visiting day she found him all agog about having gone swimming in the camp pool. "But how did you do that?" she asked. "I forgot to pack your bathing trunks." "We went in naked!" the tot explained. "Did the little girls go in naked too?" asked the mother excitedly. "Goodness no, mother!" the tyke replied. "They wore bathing caps."

"All the neighbors complain about our Freddy," said his mother, "and unfortunately they've got good cause because he's a little rascal!" "Then I'd better buy him a bicycle," said his father. "Why, do you think that will improve his bad behavior?" asked mother. "Well, no," said father, "but it will distribute it over a wider area."

A father asked his twelve-year-old son to make a list of the nine greatest men in America. The lad began writing. A few minutes later, the inquisitive parent asked, "Well, how're you getting along?" "I've got nine of them already," the kid smiled, "but I can't make up my mind who to put down for third base."

A little boy looked at his mother's fur coat and remarked, "How that poor beast must have suffered so that you might have that coat." His mother answered, "Shut up, you shouldn't talk about your father that way."

A little boy asked his father, "Daddy, who gave me my bicycle for Christmas?"
"Santa Claus, of course."
"Well, Santa was here this morning and said another installment is due."

"Why, I'm ashamed of you, my son," the father screamed at his lazy offspring. "When George Washington was your age, he had become a surveyor and was hard at work."
"And when he was your age," shot back the lad, "he was President of the United States."

A young kid was being enrolled for a progressive school and received an application blank. At the top was the question, "Is your child a leader?" His mother wrote, "No, but he's a good follower." A week later the mother got a letter from the school. "Your child has been accepted for the class of '69 which is comprised of fifty-eight leaders and your son."

The day the kid was confirmed the father decided to have a heart-to-heart talk to him. You know today you are a man, etc. Then he told him about the birds and the bees. Later, the young Bar-Mitzvah boy told his friend, "You know the thing people do when they want babies? Well, birds and bees do the same thing."

Visitors in the house, and the kid yells down: "Maaaa—there's only clean towels in the bathroom—shall I start one?"

MOTHER: "Willie, the canary is gone."
WILLIE: "Gee, that's funny. It was there this morning when I vacuumed the cage."

"Sonny, did you get my suit from the tailor?"
"He refused to give it to me without the money, pop."
"Didn't you tell him I thought you were too young to carry money?"
"Yeah, but he said he'll keep the suit till I get bigger."

The youngster was always stealing candy. The cop decided to teach him a lesson and put him in jail for a few hours—he put him in a cell with a hardened criminal to scare him so he would never do it again.
"What are you in here for?" the hood asked.
"For stealing candy!" the kid said.
"And they give you a rap like that for stealing candy?" the mug asked. "Why don't you rob a bank?"
"I don't get out of school till 3 o'clock," the kid explained.

A boy of eight attending class at dancing school was taught by the instructor how to bow at the waist and ask a girl to dance. Twenty minutes later the same little boy approached the same instructor. "Sir," he said, "I have a question. Now, how do I get rid of her?"

A New York youngster is one who identifies the world's zones as the Arc-

tic, Antarctic, Temperate, Torrid and Towaway.

Jessel says kids are taking LSD so they can fly to Israel.

Virginia Graham told of her three-year-old grandson who looked out the window and saw lightning for the first time. "Look, ma, God just took my picture."

Some parents want their kids to play the piano instead of the violin because it's harder to lose a piano.

Alan King
(*see Suburbs, "Comedians" chapter*)

"I'm paying so much insurance to take care of the future that I'm starving to death in the present."

"Those moving men—they always show up jolly, gay and full of spirits—about a fifth apiece."

"My wife loves bargains. What a great shopper. One time she went out window shopping—came home with seven windows."

"Anybody who owns his own home—deserves it." Which happens to be the title of his book.

"At all suburban supermarkets they always have a big sign out front which reads, 'Ample parking.' I've figured out that Irving Ample is the owner; he's the only one who can get in the damned lot."

"If there's anything my kids need, it's a new toy. They're already stocked up like an arsenal. My oldest boy, Bobby, has 37 pistols, 48 rifles, and 3 Thompson machine guns. In case of an invasion, he could hold out for a month. They even invited him to the disarmament conference. If any more toys come in the house, we'll have a bigger armed force than NATO."

"A little old lady was on a park bench in the Bronx. A neighbor admired her two little grandchildren and asked how old they were. The little old lady said: 'The lawyer is four and the doctor is six.' "

"Romeo and Juiet got married. They spent one night together and the next day he committed suicide. Then she committed suicide. I'm trying to figure what went on in that bedroom."

Imagine if they had to live in the suburbs like normal people—*normal?*

"Aren't you going to shave, Romeo?"
"It's Saturday—why should I shave?"
"Because my mother is coming over —that's why."
"Your mother doesn't shave on Saturday, either."
"And on your way out, take out the garbage."
"Who's going out?"
"You are. My mother wants you to pick her up."

Kissing
(*see Love, Romance, Dates, etc.*)

I take my wife everyplace—it's better than kissing her good-bye.

HE: "Do you believe kissing is unhealthy?"
SHE: "It will be now—here comes my husband."

"Darling, may I kiss your hand?"
"Sure, but don't burn your nose on my cigarette."

She had such buck teeth that every time she kissed him she combed his mustache.

"How did you learn to kiss like that?"
"I used to blow up footballs!"

"She swears she's never been kissed."
"That's why she swears."

She asked me if I knew anything about kissing. Which is rather odd because I was kissing her at the time.

Put some lipstick on—I got to have a target.

Never let a fool kiss you or a kiss fool you.

He who kisses and runs away will live to kiss another.

His kisses were so hot it burned up her husband.

"What would you say if I told you I don't believe in kissing?"
"Good-bye."

Before marriage a girl has to kiss her man to hold him—after marriage she has to hold him to kiss him.

A man who can drive safely while kissing a pretty girl—isn't giving the kiss the attention it deserves.

It takes a lot of experience for a girl to kiss like a beginner.

"Is your daddy home?"
"No, sir, he hasn't been home since mother caught Santa Claus kissing the maid."

He hasn't kissed his wife in years— but he shot the man who did.

"Have you kissed the bride?"
"No, not lately."

"Kisses are the language of love."
"Well, speak up!"

I don't mind girls who kiss and tell
—it's good advertising.

"I got this black eye and broken nose for kissing the bride after the ceremony."
"But isn't that the usual custom?"
"Yeah, but this was *three years* after the ceremony."

A kiss is no use to one—yet absolute bliss for two. The little boys get it free, the young man has to ask for it, the old man has to buy it.
The baby's right, the lover's privilege, and the hypocrite's mask.
To a young girl: faith; to a married woman: hope; to an old maid: charity.

Kissing a girl is like opening a bottle of olives; once you get one—the rest come easy.

A kiss is a pleasant reminder that two heads are better than one.

Kosher
(*see Israel, Jewish Jokes, Borscht Belt Laughs, Ethnic Humor, etc.*)

The two Irishmen passed a restaurant that advertised kosher food. One said, "What's that sign mean?" The other replied, "To you it means nothing, to me it means nothing, but to the Jewish people, that's Duncan Hines."

Kosher food means you can't mix dairy with meat at the same time. You have to wait six hours after eating meat to have dairy. So, you can't have cream with your coffee after a meat dinner. When I worked in the Catskills and

the place was strictly kosher, I figured out an ingenious idea. I bought a new fountain pen, filled it with sweet cream, smuggled it into the dining room—and charged twenty-five cents a squirt to all who wanted cream in their coffee.

Landlords
(*see Apartment Houses*)

"Was your landlord put out when you asked him to trust you for another month?"
"No indeed, *I* was."

"The landlady was over to the house and she gave father three days to pay the rent."
"What did he do?"
"He took Fourth of July, Easter, and Christmas."

The American tourists were being guided through an ancient castle in Italy.
"This place is over 500 years old," the guide was showing off his lessons; "not a stone in it has been touched, nothing fixed—nothing replaced—in all these years."
"Well," said one of the tourists from New York, "they must have the same landlord I got."

The Greenwich Village apartment had three washrooms: His, Hers, and Come As You Are.

Give a landlord an inch—and he rents it.

Languages
(*see "International Humor" chapter, also Scotland, Italy, France, Israel, etc.*)

English is called the mother tongue because father seldom gets to use it.

Kisses are the language of love—and you talk to anybody.

Nobody cares how bad your English is—if your scotch is good.

"Did you have any trouble with your French when you were abroad?"
"No, but the French did."

Girls shouldn't be allowed to study foreign languages—one tongue is enough for any woman.

SIGN AT TAX OFFICE: "Watch your language."

Opera in English is a fine idea—it helps you understand what's boring you.

He speaks Spanish like a native—a native Hungarian.

Las Vegas
(*see Gambling*)

Better known as Lost Wages, Nevada.

I go there every year to visit my money—and leave a little interest.

Nevada is nice if you're a slot machine. The one-armed bandits grab your money faster than the income tax boys.

If you're too sick to come downstairs, they send a dealer to your room—that's what they call room service in Vegas.

Women dealers in some spots: you know they ain't giving up anything—only taking.

Hope they have more luck with my money than I did.

Wouldn't say roulette was crooked—but how come the table said "TILT"?

Las Vegas set me back ten days socially and four years financially.

Only place you can get tan and faded at the same time.

Nobody forces you to gamble. Nobody forces you to have sex either—but it's more enjoyable.

They don't force you to gamble—but they registered me at a blackjack table and gave me a room with an adjoining roulette.

Money isn't everything—and if you stay here long enough—it's nothing.

As I got off the plane in Vegas, I dropped my bag—two seconds later I was faded.

Sure it's crowded in Las Vegas—nobody's got the money for plane fare out.

During a recent convention of atom scientists in Las Vegas, one of the professors spent all his free time at the gambling tables. A couple of his colleagues were discussing their friend's weakness.
"Costa gambles as if there were no tomorrow," said one.
"Maybe," commented the other, "he knows something!"

SIGN ON ENTERING LAS VEGAS: "Keep Las Vegas Green: Bring Money."

DEFINITION OF LAS VEGAS: Where the odds are you won't get even.

All the hotels are gorgeous—you can't tell the difference—it's like comparing one vacuum cleaner to another.

341

Laughter

"An onion can make people cry—but there has never been a vegetable invented to make them laugh."—Will Rogers

"God's greatest gift to man is the joy of laughter. We laugh before we speak—we laugh before we walk."—Ken Murray

"Laughter is the sensation of feeling good all over—and showing it principally in one spot."—Josh Billings

"Laughter is sudden glory."—Thomas Hobbes

MAN: "Why do you suppose women don't have a sense of humor?"
WOMAN: "God did it on purpose—so that we may love you men instead of laughing at you."

"The human race has only one effective weapon and that is laughter."—Mark Twain

Fred Allen said: "It is bad to suppress laughter: It goes back down and spreads your hips."

Laundry

The only trouble with some of these laundries is that they don't leave enough shirt on the cuffs.

"Here, look what you did."
"I can't see anything wrong with that lace."
"Lace? That was a sheet!"

"Our new Minister is so wonderful. He brings things home to you that you never saw before."
"I have a laundryman who does the same thing."

"Your laundry is back."
"Oh, thanks."
"Yeah, they refused it."

The Chinese laundry does a good job with my shirts, but an hour after I take them out—they're dirty again.

Sign in laundry: "We do not tear your laundry with machinery—we do it carefully by hand."

My laundry lost the buttonholes from my shirts.

This laundry is so swanky—you have to wash it before they will accept it.

SIGN IN LAUNDRY: "Drop in and drop off your clothes."

SIGN IN LAUNDRY: "Don't kill your wife —let us do the dirty work."

My car just came back from the car wash—and all the buttons on the dashboard are missing.

Marriage is the most expensive way to get your laundry free.

"Who does your laundry?"
"Nobody—I tear the buttons off myself."

My laundry never lost a single button—sleeves, yes—but no buttons.

I made a deal with my laundry: I'll send them back all their pins—if they'll send me back all my buttons.

Lavender Boys

The newspaper stories claim that one out of every six British men is a homosexual—and they still claim there will always be an England.

This boy has something up his sleeve —it's a hanky.

The Martian landed in Greenwich Village and lisped to the lavender boy he met, "Take me."

He was a Boy Scout until he was sixteen—then he became a Girl Scout.

When he mentions "Daisey" in his sleep—he's definitely talking about flowers.

The two lavender boys were living together in an apartment overlooking the rent and were happy until one day one of them was found lying dead in an alley. The police questioned the living doll.

"All I know, dears," he confessed, "is that he said he was going to fly to Africa; so he opened the window and jumped."

"Why didn't you stop him?" growled the detective.

"I thought he could make it."

He would rather swish than fight.

It was the lavender lad's thirteenth birthday. A friend, unaware of this, called and suggested they get together.

"I can't see you today," said the Bar-Mitzah boy, "today I am a man— but I'll see you tomorrow, sweet."

When I get a brand new hair-do,
And a new pair of shoes and a bag.
I float on the air like clouds do,
I enjoy being a fag.

He is so distinguished looking—he turned prematurely gay.

They had a call for chorus boys and 150 odd fellows showed up.

Christine must be a woman—what man would talk so long about an operation?

A Greenwich Village sign shouts: ' Guess your sex—25¢."

Lawyers
(see Court, Judges, etc.)

A lawyer was questioning a witness in a murder case. "Did you say that she shot him at close range?"

"Yes."

"Were there any powder marks on him?"

"Sure," came the reply. "That's why she shot him."

The story is told of the lawyer's wife who was complaining about the way their home was furnished. "We need chairs, a dining room set and a new lamp."

"Listen," her spouse told her, "one of my clients is suing her husband for divorce. He has a lot of money and as soon as I finish breaking up their home, we'll fix ours."

A lawyer is a fellow who is willing to go out and spend your last cent to prove he's right.

TOMBSTONE: "Here lies a lawyer and an honest man." And who'd ever think there'd be room for two men in that one little grave?

The Hollywood couple didn't want to get a divorce until their son passed his bar exams—they wanted to be his first case.

Big lawyer—just because he tried to break her will.

"Are you badly injured?"
"Can't tell till I see my lawyer!"

The Hollywood lawyer was without a client for so long that he divorced his wife just so he would have a case.

343

Am I legally married if the shotgun wasn't loaded?

"I wish you had an alibi."
"So do I—then I wouldn't need you."

A lawyer tore excitedly into court and asked that a new trial be granted a client found guilty the day previous. "I've uncovered new evidence," declared the lawyer.
"Of what nature?" asked the judge.
"My client," the lawyer told him, "has an extra six hundred dollars. I ony found out about it this morning."

The lawyer had just won a speedy acquittal for a wealthy businessman charged with bigamy. "You're a free man," said the lawyer. "Go on home to your wife."
"Which one?" enthused the acquitted.

"I never saw such an ugly group of criminal types," the new secretary said to the judge in the police court. "Is it the same every day?"
"I guess so," the judge answered, "those are the lawyers."

The ex-lawyer was making a big speech to a group of assembled young attorneys. "As soon as I realized this was a crooked business—I got out of it."
"How much?" asked one young attorney in the rear.

Satan and St. Peter had a big beef, and St. Peter threatened to sue.
"Are you kidding—where are you gonna get lawyers up there? They're all down here."

"They can't put you in jail for that."
"Is that so? Where the hell do you think I'm calling from—the candy store?"

"When I was a kid," the lawyer was reminiscing, "I wanted to be a pirate."
"Congratulations," said the client.

The lawyer attacked him unmercifully. "Aren't you ashamed—a common smuggler."
"At least," the witness answered, "I'm better than my father."
"What did he do?" the lawyer asked sarcastically.
"He was a shyster lawyer," he snapped.

What a lawyer! He got the jury so confused—they sent the judge up.

This cheap attorney became a divorce lawyer—so he could get his women free.

LAWYER: A person who helps you get what's coming to him.

Somebody figured it out—we have thirty-five million laws trying to enforce the Ten Commandments.

"I swore to tell the truth," the witness said to the judge, "but every time I do some lawyer objects."

One of the law partners went on a vacation and left his associate to complete the case. When he won for his client, he wired his partner, "Justice has triumphed." The vacationing lawyer wired back, "Appeal the case at once."

The lawyer's client was convicted on a robbery rap and sentenced to ten years in jail. The attorney visited the client soon afterwards and told him, "Now, listen, don't worry about a thing! I'm going to get you a new trial. I've got new evidence. We got a change of venue. We'll get you a completely new deal and get you free. Don't worry about anything. In the meantime, if you get a chance, try to escape."

Laziness

Nathan's wife tells of his discomfiture the time the sheriff's funeral passed their gate. "It was a grand sight," she said.

"Nathan was restin' in the hammick when it went by. I come out and told him who all was in the carriages and autymobiles, and his kinfolk wavin' to him. Nathan was kinda peeved. 'Just my luck,' he said, 't' be facin' th' other way.'"

He's so lazy—he stands with a cocktail shaker in his hand waiting for an earthquake.

"He's so lazy—he's been sitting there all day doing nothing."
"How do you know?"
"I've been sitting here watching him."

"I love to lie in bed in the morning and ring for my valet."
"I didn't know you had a valet."
"I don't—but I have a bell."

"He's carrying two loads of bricks and you're only carrying one."
"Sure—he's too lazy to go back twice."

He says he has a bad case of insomnia—he keeps waking up every few days.

Whenever he feels like exercising—he lies down till the feeling goes away.

Even if he was robbed—he wouldn't go for the cop unless it was downhill.

He never puts off for tomorrow—if he can put it off forever.

He's too lazy to walk in his sleep—he insists on being carried.

He refuses to drink coffee in the morning—it keeps him awake all day.

The first thing he does when he gets up in the morning is take a sleeping pill.

He doesn't know how long he's been out of work—he can't find his birth certificate.

He found a great way to start the day—he gets back in bed.

He puts in a good day's work—in a week.

He was so lazy—he wouldn't even help his mother-in-law out of his house.

If his ship ever did come in, I doubt if he'd bother unloading it.

There ought to be a better way to start the day than by getting up in the morning.

Legs
(*see Figures*)

I've seen better legs on my kitchen table.

I've seen better looking bones in soup.

She was so bowlegged—we hung her over the door for good luck.

She's got a very unusual figure—her seams are straight—but her legs are crooked.

"You're stockings are wrinkled."
"I'm not wearing any."

My girl is so bowlegged, when she sits around the house—she sits around the house.

She is so bowlegged—she can get out of a car on both sides at the same time.

Jack E. Leonard
(*look under Comedians, Insults, and Don Rickles*)

I won't tell you how much I weigh—but don't ever get in an elevator with me unless you're going down.

You have a nice voice—one of these days it will reach your throat.

You have a nice personality—but not for a human being.

He hasn't an enemy in the world—but all his friends hate him.

Joe E. Lewis is the only man with an honorary drinking license.

ABOUT SINATRA: "You're an Italian exclamation point!"

ABOUT RICHARD BURTON: "He's here courtesy of Simmons Mattress Co."

CARMINE DE SAPIO: "The Italian Boss Tweed."

GENE AUTRY: "He's so rich he owns a Cadillac horse."

PERRY COMO: "I always enjoyed your voice—even when you worked under the name of Bing Crosby."

TO STEVE ALLEN: "I could stand up here and be very funny—but I don't want to change the format of your show."

TO GLEASON: "Go lie down on your cots."

I'm so fat—when I walk down the street—I *am* the street.

Sam Levenson

Everybody knows that Sam Levenson was a schoolteacher and, as such, has had some very odd experiences, so I think we'll let Sam tell this one:

"When I was teaching school in Brooklyn, one of my assignments was 'Hall Patrol.' During one of my routine checks of the staircases, I found this big fifteen-year-old fondly squeezing the life out of an attractive young lady. I pulled him away angrily. 'What on earth do you think you're doing?' Without even so much as a blush he came back with, 'It's OK, Mr. Levenson, she lives on my block.' "

"Say, by the way, Max," said his old friend Sam, "I hear there is congratulations coming to you—a new son-in-law?"
"It's more trouble than congratulations—he can't drink and he can't play cards."
"So if he can't drink and he can't play cards—this you call trouble?"
"Yes! He can't drink—and *he drinks*; he can't play cards—and *he plays!*"

A verbal agreement isn't worth the paper it's written on.

LADY TO BEGGAR: "Aren't you ashamed to stand here begging on the street?"
BEGGAR: "What do you want, lady; I should open an office?"

Panicky lady as train is pulling out: "Mr. Conductor—if I run will I catch the train?"
"Lady, if you run—you'll pass it."

The clerk at the post office refused his package: "It's too heavy; you will have to put more stamps on it!"
"And if I put more stamps on it—that will make it lighter?"

"I have succeeded in business because of two principles—honesty and wisdom. Honesty means simply that if you promise to deliver a shipment of goods on the 15th of April, come hell or high water you deliver the shipment."
"And wisdom?"
"Wisdom means—'Dope! Who asked you to promise?' "

Our menu at mealtime offered two choices—take it or leave it.

"Sixty dollars for a hat?" he hollered to his wife. "Don't you know it's a sin to spend sixty dollars for a hat?"
"What do you care? The sin is on my head!"

He turned down the man who asked him to give to the local charity: "I have my own to give to!"
"If you will pardon me," the solicitor replied, "from what I have heard, you don't give to your own, either."
"Aha! That's just it—if I don't give to my own—I should give to total strangers?"

"And mothers are great. When I was teaching a mother once wrote me a note about her son. It said, 'If Gregory is a bad boy, don't slap him, slap the boy next to him. Gregory will get the idea.' "

Joe E. Lewis
(see Drinking)

TO A NOISY PATRON: "A man with your mentality should have a much lower voice."

TO A LOUDLY DRESSED PEST: "You leave a bad taste in my eyes."

ABOUT A HAM ACTOR: "He's so unpopular that if he stood on the Israeli-Jordan border he'd be shot at from both sides."

TO A DRUNK AT THE BAR: "Sir, when you drink you forget your manners. Last night when you left you stepped on my fingers."

JOE E.'S DESCRIPTION OF GEORGIE JESSEL: "He's a man who just reached middle age for the third time."

ABOUT BOOZE: "I once quit drinking—it was the most boring ten minutes of my life."

"I don't feel well lately—my doctor found too much blood in my alcohol stream."

TO A VOCAL PEST: "It's nice hearing from you—next time send me a post card."

AFTER A FIVE HOUR OPERATION: It was wonderful—first good night's sleep I've had in three years."

BAR: "They've redecorated the bar—they put new drunks around it."

WEALTH: "I've been rich and I've been poor. Believe me—rich is better."

"They asked me about doing a Western series for TV. They're going to call it 'Frontier Drunk.' "

"I never drink on New Year's Eve. That's Amateur Night."

"They did the story of my life in the movies but they couldn't do the true story. Paramount Pictures didn't have a liquor license."

"In the movie of my life story there's one scene in which I refuse a drink. They had to get a stuntman to play me."

"I told my doctor I drank to quiet my nerves. He said, 'Nobody's nerves are that noisy.' "

"I've donated my liver to science after I die. They were thrilled. They were so happy to get one already pickled."

"Someone asked me what my drinking capacity was. Well, I don't know for sure, but I'm about 2,000 swallows ahead of Capistrano."

"I woke up at the crack of ice and I've been cold drunk all day. My pianist, Austin Mack, is the one who really drinks. He was so drunk, as I was leaving the club last night on the way out he stepped on my fingers. I hate a guy who falls on top of me when he's drunk."

"I used to be a test pilot for Seagram's."

"When my doctor took my blood test he offered me sixty dollars a case."

"Las Vegas is the only town in the country where you can have a good time without enjoying yourself."

"Anyone who takes me for a darn fool—makes no mistake."

Joe E. Lewis tells about the guy, a casual race track acquaintance, who said: "Could you lend me ten bucks?" Lewis took a chance, and at the end of the day received his ten-spot back. The next day, the same bloke made another request—this time for twenty, and after the seventh race, refunded the loan. On the third day when he asked him for thirty, Joe waved him away. "Nuthin' doin!" said Joe. "You fooled me twice!"

"A man who has $11,000,000 is just as happy as a man who has $12,000,-000."

"I was feeling lousy in the hospital, then I took a sudden turn for the nurse."

To a ringsider who had fallen asleep at the table: "I didn't mind your going to sleep while I was doing my act but you hurt me when you didn't say good night."

To Jackie Gleason: "Jackie, you belong in Hollywood, and the walk will do you good." When Jackie heckled back: "Jackie, you are not obligated to answer back and so far neither are you equipped."

And Joe E. christened Ed Sullivan "The Man With the Golden Gums."

To an attorney: "I studied at the bar too, but I flunked martinis."

Liar

"Have you seen one of those instruments to detect falsehoods?" "Seen one? I married one."

"Can you tell by your husband's face if he's lying?" asked one wife of another. And the other snorted, "Yes, if his lips are moving, he is."

"That man is going around telling lies about you."
"I don't mind—but I'll break his head if he begins telling the truth."

He tells more lies than a girdle.

He not only kisses and tells but most of the time he tells when he doesn't kiss.

He lies on the beach in Hawaii—about what a big man he is in his home town.

I don't even believe him when he swears he's lying.

The irate husband was complaining that his wife was a liar.
"What makes you say that?"
"She came home early this morning and told me she spent the night with Margie."
"How do you know she was lying?"
"Because *I* spent the night with Margie."

No man has a good enough memory to make a successful liar.

If George Washington never told a lie, how come he got elected?

Licenses

I'm not saying she is fat—but two more pounds and they will make her wear license plates.

She's been married so many times she carries a license made out, "To Whom It May Concern."

Our parking attendant is very happy. After ten years on the job he's getting his driving license at last.

When you are run down, the best thing you can take is the license number.

Life

Life begins at forty—but you'll miss a lot of fun if you wait that long.

We should all live within our means —even if we have to borrow the money to do so.

Whiskey may shorten your life—but you'll see twice as much in half the time.

You could write the story of his life on a piece of confetti.

Many women marry a man for life —and then discover he doesn't have any.

Life insurance is something that keeps a man poor all his life—so he can die rich.

"I gave you the best years of my life."
"Those were the best?"

Do my life story—I might have lived.

DOCTOR: "Have you been leading a normal life?"
PATIENT: "Yes."
DOCTOR: "Well, you'll have to cut it out for a while."

There's one good thing about life— it's only temporary.

Limericks
(*see chapter on Limericks*)

A naked young lady called Belle,
Walked the streets while ringing the bell,
When asked why she rang it,
She answered, "God dang it!
Can't you see I have something to sell?"

I knew a young lady named Smith
Whose virtue was largely a myth.
She said, "Try as I can,
I can't find a man,
Whom it's fun to be virtuous with."

A lavender man named O'Day
As a TV contestant made hay,
On a passionate spree,
He kissed the emcee,
So they chose him Queen for a Day.

349

There was a young girl from St. Paul,
Wore a newspaper dress to a ball.
But the dress caught on fire,
And burned her entire,
Front page, sporting section, and all.

There was a young swish they called
  Bloom,
Who took a lez to his room,
They argued all night,
As to who had the right,
To do what and where and to whom!

There was a young lady called Honey,
Who made like a cute little Bunny,
And male callers galore,
Lined up at her door,
To take turns at paying her money.

There was a young girl from Port
  Chester,
Whose boy friend kissed and caressed
  her,
But she said that his throes,
Would ruin her clothes,
And so he completely undressed her.

A horse-loving lady named Maud
At love was a terrible fraud,
With the boys in the stable,
She was willing and able,
But in bed with her spouse she was
  bored.

Underdeveloped young Joe,
Told his girl—nymphomaniac Flo,
"I do like the sport,
But let's cut this thing short,
Cause this is as far as I go."

There was a young lady named Gloria,
Whose boy friend said, "May I ex-
  plore you?"
She replied to the chap,
"I will draw you a map
Of where others have been to before
  ya."

There was a young lady from space,
Whose corset grew too tight to lace,

Her mother said, "Nelly,
There's more in your belly,
Then ever went in through your face!"

Abraham Lincoln

Lincoln's wife Mary Todd came
from a "high-toned" family. "Do the
Todds spell their name with one D or
two Ds?" someone asked.
"One D is enough for God," Mr.
Lincoln said, "but the Todds need
two."

Commenting on another lawyer he
said: "He can compress the most words
into the smallest ideas better than any
man I ever met."

Asked how he felt after a political
loss in 1862, Mr. Lincoln answered:
"Somewhat like the boy in Kentucky
who stubbed his toe while running to
see his sweetheart. The boy said he was
too big to cry, and far too badly hurt
to laugh."

"A woman is the only thing I am
afraid of that I know will not hurt me."

"My father taught me to work—he
did not teach me to love it."

"Public discussion is helping to
down slavery. What kills a skunk is
the publicity it gives itself."

The cleric, talking for the delegation, kept quoting at length from the
Bible to prove his points. When Lincoln couldn't take it much longer he
spoke up:
"Well, gentlemen, it is not often that
one is favored with a delegation direct
from the Almighty!"

In one of the Lincoln–Douglas debates, Mr. Douglas taunted Lincoln
with the fact that the first time he met

Lincoln he was in a store were Lincoln was selling whiskey.

Honest Abe replied by saying: "What Mr. Douglas said is true. I did keep a grocery, and I did sell cotton, cigars, and, sometimes, whiskey. But I remember in those days, that Mr. Douglas was one of my best customers. Many a time I have stood on one side of the counter and sold whiskey to Mr. Douglas on the other side, but the difference between us now is this: I have left my side of the counter—but Mr. Douglas still sticks to his as tenaciously as ever."

When a temperance group complained to President Lincoln about General Grant's whiskey drinking, Abe replied, "Find out the brand General Grant uses—I'd like to send some to my other generals!"

"I don't know who my grandfather was—I'm more concerned what his grandson will be like."

Somebody pointed to Lincoln and said, "He's a common-looking man." Honest Abe overheard him. "The Lord prefers common-looking people," he addressed the man; "that's why He made so many of them."

Lingerie
(*see Fashions, Clothes, etc.*)

With all those feminine falsies—a guy never knows what he's up against.

A girdle doesn't change a woman's weight. It only moves it to a more interesting location.

SIGN IN GIRDLE SHOP: "The world is in bad shape—must you be too?"

A girdle is a device to keep an unfortunate situation from spreading.

A shoulder strap is a piece of ribbon that keeps an attraction from becoming a sensation.

A girdle is the difference between facts and figures.

They now have an "Irish girdle"— it is so tight, you'll turn green.

A girl who tries to talk her boy friend into buying her a silk nightgown —usually ends up with her boy friend trying to talk her out of it.

Art Linkletter
(*see Jokes for Children, Children, Kids, Parents, etc.*)

"I asked one kid if he knew the meaning of the saying, 'The early bird gets the worm.' "

"He replied, 'They're welcome to it—I ate one once and it tasted like cold spaghetti.' "

"I asked a youngster, 'Where did your parents meet?'

" 'They were roommates at college,' was the killer."

"My favorite definition of a child: An object halfway between an adult and a television set."

"Religious stories have a special meaning for kids. One seven-year-old recited the story of David and Goliath —how David hit the big giant in the forehead with his slingshot and the giant Goliath fell dead.

" 'What does that teach us?' I asked the boy.

"He said, 'Duck.' "

Mr. Linkletter, who has been doing an afternoon show for years, swears he received this letter: "Mr. Linkletter, I always watch you when I'm sick."

Art Linkletter's *Kids Say the Darndest things:*

ART: "How do you get money?"
KID: "I get a nickel every day I don't have a damp bed."
ART: "How are you doing?"
KID: "I made a dime last week."

ART: "What do you think a rich man is?"
KID: "A bachelor."

ART: "What do you want to be when you grow up?"
KID: "Nothing—I don't want to grow up."
ART: "How come?"
KID: "Because of all the bills you have to pay at the end of the month."

Losers

He's a born loser. When he tries to whip cream—the cream wins.

A loser is a guy who sticks his hand out to make a left turn—and hits a cop right in the mouth.

A loser is a gigolo with chapped lips.

A loser is a politician with laryngitis.

"You're a loser," she said. "I can't marry you—I want a star!"
"Are you kidding? If I had all the things you expect in a man—who would want you?"

He's in a hole more often than a gravedigger.

He should learn a trade to find out what kind of work he is out of.

He's a jack-of-all-trades—and out of work in all of them.

He's as broke as a pickpocket in a nudist camp.

He started at the bottom—and stayed there.

He gives failure a bad name.

He never makes the same mistake twice—he always finds new mistakes to make.

A loser is a Hindu snake charmer with a deaf cobra.

He has that certain nothing.

He's selling furniture for a living—his own.

All a pickpocket could get from him is practice.

LOSER: is a girl who puts her bra on backwards and it fits.

Love
(*see Romance, Dates, etc.*)

If all the world loves a lover—how come they have cops in Central Park?

The salesgirl approached the customer in the department store. "What is your pleasure, sir?"
"My pleasure is making love, but I came in here to buy a hat."

Business is like making love—when it's good it's very good and when it's bad, it ain't bad.

He showed her a lot of love and affection. He took her to a drive-in movie and let her peek into the other cars.

A woman set out to reform her fiance. She got him to give up smoking, then swearing, drinking, chewing tobacco, and gambling, and when she finally finished with him, he decided she wasn't good enough for him—so he jilted her.

ZSA ZSA GABOR: "Ven I vas married to George Sanders, ve vere both in love with him. I fell out of love with him —but he didn't."

"Love is a mutual misunderstanding."—Oscar Wilde

Love starts with a fever—winds up with a yawn.

Love is the thing that makes the heart light and the parlor dark.

Some of his greatest love affairs have involved only one person—himself.

"One should always be in love—that is the reason one should never marry." —Oscar Wilde

Always remember, the heart is a muscle; you're never really in love— you're muscle-bound.

Love is valued highest during the days of courting and the days in court.

"Would you call for help if I tried to kiss you?"
"Do you need help?"

He was in love with a twin. "Did you ever kiss the other by mistake?" his friend asked.
"Are you kidding?" he answered. "Her brother has a mustache."

Many a young couple who have nothing in common—fool around until they do.

SHE: "You don't love me anymore— I'm going back to my mother."
HE: "Don't bother—I'll go back to my wife."

She laughed when I sat down to play—how did I know she was ticklish?

When he finally proposed—she was so excited—she fell out of bed.

"Is she his first love?"
"Oh no, only his first wife."

How about coming to my apartment and putting your shock-proof watch to the test?

In coffee, it's taste; in whiskey, it's age; in a car—it's uncomfortable.

"Why don't you buy me a mink coat? I'm always cold."
"That's why!"

"Darling, will you love me when I'm old and gray?"
"Well, don't I?"

"So you fell in love with him at second sight?"
"Yes, when I first met him I didn't know he was rich."

"Love is blind."
"But my neighbors aren't—pull down the shades!"

She: "I nearly fainted when the fellow I went out with asked me for a kiss."
He: "Baby—you're gonna die when you hear what I have to say!"

She'll get along—she always does the wrong thing at the right time.

I told him I worshipped my figure— and he tried to embrace my religion.

What a wonderful night. The moon was out—and so were her parents.

Love cures people—both the ones who give it and the ones who receive.

353

"Do you neck?"
"That's my business."
"Oh, a professional!"

"Do you believe in free love?"
"Have I ever given you a bill?"

Shortest bedtime story: "Move over!"

She makes love cafeteria style—you help yourself.

Love is a trap—you fall into it.

Love is like hash—you have to have confidence in it to enjoy it.

Did you hear about the sleepy bride who couldn't stay awake for a second?

Al Capp, when asked about his opinion of the free love societies, said, "The price is right."

LSD

"Now they have LSD with platform-mate—you take the same trip, but you go three miles farther."

"Some guy at a party asked me if I wanted to 'take a trip' so I went home and got my baggage."—Milt Moss

This Japanese hippie went crazy looking for RSD.

Luck

He had tough luck. He had a check for ten dollars and the only person who could cash it was a fellow to whom he owed nine dollars.

NED: "Why do you call Ted the luckiest man you ever knew?"

RED: "He's got a wife and a cigarette lighter—and they both work."

An engineer friend of mine, when taking his shower, slipped on the soap. Then he tore his shirt while he was putting it on. On the way out of the house he fell down the stairs. He finally got out on his run, and as he was traveling sixty miles per hour he looked ahead, and there he saw another train coming toward him at the same speed on the same track. He turned to the fireman and said, "Joe, have you ever had one of those days when everything went dead wrong?"

"Friday is very unlucky."
"What makes you think that?"
"Well, Washington, Napoleon, and Lincoln were all born on Friday and look at them now—all dead."

"Is it unlucky to postpone a wedding?"
"Not if you keep postponing it."

"My wife took everything and left me."
"You're lucky—mine didn't leave."

"My wife has the last word."
"You're lucky—mine never gets to it."

Lenny Kent talks about his bad luck: "Last week my uncle died and left me a barber shop—in Cuba. And last year when I went to Italy, I got a ticket in Venice for swimming against the tide."

"My wife is an angel."
"You're lucky—mine is still living."

I've had bad luck with both my wives —the first divorced me and the second won't.

I heard you are getting a divorce— who is the lucky man?

I've been married for seven years—I knew I shouldn't have broken that mirror.

Walking under a ladder can be lucky—if there is a girl on it.

Maids
(*see Employees, Work, etc.*)

"Is it true my old maid is working for you?"

"Yes, but don't look so worried—I don't believe a word she says."

He gave the new maid the special list of dishes his mother-in-law liked. "The first time you serve one of them," he warned, "you're fired."

The lady asked for a reference for the maid. "Was she a steady worker?" the woman wanted to know.

"Steady?—She was motionless."

The maid had been happily employed with the same family for ten years. One day she announced she was quitting because she was pregnant.

The mistress said, "Rather than lose you, we'll adopt the child."

A year later the maid again found herself "that way" and told her mistress, who again adopted the baby rather than lose her.

This happened a third time. Help was hard to get, so the mistress again volunteered to adopt the child.

And the maid said, "Oh, no, not me—I won't work for a family that has three children."

My maid works a three-day week. But it takes her five days to do it.

I'm really in trouble—the maid caught me kissing my wife.

MADAME: "Marta, look at the dust on that shelf—it must be at least six weeks old."

MAID: "Well, don't blame me—I've only been working here for three weeks."

The woman of the house was showing the new maid around. "Now these marble floors must be washed every day."

"Madam," said the former maid, "I get on my knees—only to pray."

"Our maid is dishonest," she told her husband. "Two of the towels we swiped from the Hilton are missing."

I've had the same maid for years—she doesn't believe in changing after she went to the trouble of teaching us her ways.

I was explaining to my new maid that sometimes I bring home extra guests and that she will have to be prepared for such an emergency.

"I'll be ready," she answered. "I'll keep my bags packed."

I had to get rid of my maid—she kept handling china—like Russia does.

"How long has your maid been with you?"

"She never has—she's been against us from the start."

I'm not knocking my maid—especially since I know she'll be reading my books—but she is a little lax in taking messages. I even offered to send her to school to learn how to be a better housekeeper.

"Sir," she said, "why should I go to school? I already know how to do more things than I want to do."

Dorothy Parker's maid quit when she came in one day and found an alligator in the bathtub. She left this note for Miss Parker: "I have resigned. I refuse to work in a house where there is an alligator in the bathtub. I would have told you this before—but I did not think the matter would ever come up."

Manners
(*see Society, Snobs, etc.*)

A bird in the hand is bad table manners.

"Is my face clean enough to eat with?"
"Yes, but you better use your hands."

She's very proper. She won't even look at things with a naked eye.

So polite that when she threw a cup of hot coffee at him, she took the spoon out first.

He embarrassed us—he drank his soup and six couples got up and danced.

She blushes if somebody says intersection.

The man walked into the bathroom by mistake where a lady was taking a bath. He calmly tipped his hat and said, "Pardon me, sir"—and left quickly.

He had the manners of a gentleman. I knew they didn't belong to him.

Short skirts tend to make men more polite—did you ever see a man get on a bus ahead of one?

When a man opens the door of his car for his wife you can be sure that either the car is new—or his wife is.

The woman said she wanted a divorce because her husband had bad manners. "He always holds his little pinky out when he holds a cup of tea," she complained.

"My dear lady," the judge explained, "in society it's proper to hold your little pinky out when you're drinking tea."

"With the teabag hanging from it?"

Marriage

(*see Henpecked, Divorce, Husbands, Wives, etc.*)

MARRIAGE: The only cure for love.

Marriage is something like the measles—we all have to go through it.

MARRIAGE: Strange bedfellows—more often.
Strained bedfellows—most often.
Estranged bedfellows.

Marriage vows should be changed to fit the crime:
Actor: "Do you promise to love, honor, and applaud?"
Businessman: "Until debt do us part."

"I've never thought about divorce—murder yes."

Some Greek said it so don't blame me: "I never married—and I wish my father never had."

"I see no reason why you can't marry my daughter if you can support a family," the girl's father told the boy.
"I'm prepared to do that," said the anxious lad.
"Good," replied her old man, holding out his hand. "Counting my daughter—there are seven of us."

"How is your daughter's marriage working out?"

"Fine. Of course, she can't stand her husband—but then there's always something, isn't there?"

It is better to marry for money than for no reason at all.

They found a plan that works—one night a week he goes out with the boys —the other six, she does.

"I want you to stop picking on Kay —the man who marries her will get a prize."
"Well, if I were a man I'd make her show me the prize first."

"No wonder I'm sick of marriage! Tommy hasn't kissed me once since the honeymoon."
"Why not divorce him?"
"But Tommy isn't my husband."

"Is it true married men live longer than single men?"
"No, it only seems longer."

He had been married twenty-five years and was giving advice for a happy marriage: "First maintain the right to spend at least one night a week with the boys—and then don't waste it with the boys."

I got married because I wanted a large family. And I got one—my wife's.

He said he'd go through hell for her so she married him and he had to go through with it.

Marriage is an institution that teaches a man regularity, frugality, temperance, patience, and many other virtues he wouldn't need if he had stayed single in the first place.

She married him until "Debt do us part."

Women are fools to marry—but what else can a man marry?

He was unlucky in both his marriages—his first wife left him—and this one won't.

She's been married so many times— the wedding dress is her native costume.

Married life is great—it's my wife I can't stand.

My wife and I have been happily married for ten years. We go out twice a week: restaurant, nightclub—soft music, good food, candlelight. She goes out Tuesdays—I go out Fridays.

Statistics prove that single men die more quickly than married men. Therefore, if you are looking for a long, slow death—get married.

Woman to judge: "That's my side of the story—now let me tell you his."

It takes two to make a marriage— a bride and her mother.

He was married five years and never told anybody—he likes to keep his troubles to himself.

The man who thinks most seriously about marriage is the one who is already married.

"The secret of a happy marriage," she told her husband, "is in doing things together. Like opening a joint bank account."

Happy marriage is unselfishness, share and share alike. For example, every night my wife and I order two brandies and two coffees after dinner. She takes the two brandies and gives me the two coffees.

357

The couple agreed for their tenth anniversary to take a motor trip. In their ten years of married life this was the first thing they ever agreed on. They decided to do it for a novelty—they had never fought in an automobile!

On their way to Canada they quarreled, and on the way back they screamed at each other. En route home, they passed a farmhouse and saw a donkey braying. "Isn't that one of your family?" he said spitefully.

"Only by marriage, dear," she answered sweetly.

She was disgusted with the bum. Married life with him was just a bed of razors. "If only I were the wife of a millionaire," she complained.

"You mean, if only you were the widow of a millionaire," corrected her mother.

The wedding was just over. The reception was in full bloom. For want of something to say, the young man said to the fine-looking woman at the bar, "Are you a friend of the groom's?"

"I should say not," she hiccuped. "I'm the bride's mother."

"You said this restaurant was under new management. How come Mr. Katz is still here?"

"Yes—but he got married yesterday."

JIM: "Did you marry that girl you were going with or do you still do your own cooking, serving, and cleaning?"

FRANK: "Yes to both questions."

The doctor said to me, "You're ill, you need a quiet life; I shall prescribe a sleeping pill. But give it to your wife."

If it weren't for my wife, we'd be one of the nicest couples in town.

The difference between a husband and a lover is—night and day.

Entirely too many women get all excited about nothing—and then marry him.

He's married and has twelve children. He must like kids—or something.

My husband stays home so much—we practically live there.

Everything he had was in his wife's name—even his tombstone had her name engraved on it.

Married men may not be the best informed men—but they are the most.

They were married for twenty-five years and had their biggest argument on the day of their silver anniversary. She never hit harder or lower: "If it weren't for my money, that TV set wouldn't be here. If it weren't for my money, the very chair you're sitting on wouldn't be here!"

"Are you kidding?" he interrupted. "If it weren't for your money—*I* wouldn't be here!"

The unhappy man was complaining to a pal: "I had a big beef with my wife—she promised she wouldn't talk to me for thirty days."

"Then you should be happy."

"What, happy? This is the last day."

Marriage is like a warm bath—once you get used to it, it's not so hot.

"I'll tell you one thing—I'm master in my house."

"Shake—my wife is away, too."

Martians

(*see Outer Space, Astronauts; also "Monologue" chapter, Off-Beat Humor*)

A Martian landed in Las Vegas in front of a slot machine. Just then the machine revolved noisily and hit the jackpot. Coins came pouring out. Turning to the machine, the Martian said, "You shouldn't be out with a cold like that."

Me, I know one thing. A woman will never be the first human being to set foot on the moon on accounta she won't know what to wear for the event. We are so close to it now, one guy is already manufacturing pills to relieve "space-sickness."

Bob Hope has his bags packed; he has ordered his space suit and will travel. When Robert returns to earth his first joke must be about the difference in our women:
"The women on Mars have their bosoms in the back—it doesn't make 'em more attractive, but it's better for dancing."

One Martian ambled into a drug store and cornered the gaily lit-up juke box. Giving it the once-over he crooned, "What's a doll like you doing in a joint like this?"

Two gents from outer space zoomed into New York for a night on the town. Sidling up to a fire hydrant one queried, "Where is your leader?" His buddy heckled, "What are you asking him for—can't you see he's just a kid?"

A woman carrying a portable TV set was approached by a visitor from the moon: "Do you always carry your child by the neck like that?"

The Martian strode up to a grand piano in the Wurlitzer window and snarled, "Wipe that grin off your face."

The Martian landed at a hotel in Vegas, walked over to one of the dealers and said, "Take me—to the cleaners."

Groucho Marx

Groucho Marx lets his quips fall where they hurt. He dropped by to see Abel Green, the editor of *Variety*, who was out. So Groucho left his marksmanship: "Was in to see you—glad I missed you." He even used himself as a target. When asked to join the Friars' Club, he answered, "I wouldn't belong to any organization that would have me for a member."

"She's her own worst enemy," Harpo remarked.
"Not while I'm alive, she isn't," Groucho said.

Groucho and a friend grabbed for the lunch check. Groucho lost and won the check. "Either you're losing your grip," he said to the friend, "or I don't know my strength."

"What's your pleasure?" the waiter asked him.
"Girls!" Groucho answered. "What's yours?"

My girl is a human gimmie-pig.

He's a falsie manufacturer—he lives off the flat of the land.

I met a lady inventor the other day —and I'm glad he invented ladies.

I'm an ordinary sort of fellow—42 around the chest, 42 around the waist, 96 around the golf course, and a nuisance around the house.

359

Groucho was admiring the stacked young tennis star and asked about how she gets in shape for her future tournaments. "I have to improve my form and speed," she answered.

"If your form improves," Groucho said leering, "you are going to need all the speed you can muster."

I find TV very educational; every time somebody turns on a set—I go in the next room and read a book.

When an actress arrived at a Hollywood party in a very sexy tight gown cut down to her shoe-buckle, Groucho looked her over and said, "One false move—and I'll appreciate it."

Introducing a picture at a premiere Groucho announced, "Every once in a while Hollywood makes a great picture, a distinguished film, a movie which is a work of art. Unfortunately, this isn't the picture we are about to see."

A GI told Groucho Marx that he was looking for a girl who didn't drink, smoke, swear, or have any bad habits. "What for?" asked Groucho.

America is the only country in the world where you can go on the air and kid politicians—and where politicians go on the air and kid people.

Mean

My mother-in-law is so unhappy because she doesn't have a fortune with which to disinherit me.

He's got such a long face—his barber charges him twice for shaving him.

You're so mean you only give one finger when you shake hands.

When I cut my finger she cried over it—just so she could get salt in the wound.

He throws Mexican jumping beans to the pigeons in the park.

A Russian was being led off to execution by a squad of Bolshevik soldiers on a rainy morning. "What brutes you Bolsheviks are, to march me through the rain like this."
"How about us? We have to march back."

Speaking of public enemies, I know a guy who gets up at 4 A.M., leans out the window and whistles to wake up the birds.

My uncle watched him go down twice and when the man came up for the third time, my uncle said, "When you go down the next time, see if my bait is still on the hook."

He's so mean he'd send a get well card to a hypochondriac.

He's so mean that if he killed himself he'd get the right man.

"Honestly, if I could trade places with Rock Hudson or Tab Hunter right this minute, I wouldn't do it."
"I know you wouldn't. You never do anything to please me."

He is so mean he tears the month of December off his calendars to fool his children.

He was so mean he put a tack on the seat of the electric chair.

He has a disposition like an untipped waiter.

He had three phones installed—so he can hang up on more people.

First thing she does when she gets up is brush her teeth and sharpen her tongue.

When he wants your opinion—he'll give it to you.

It's not his money that counts—people hate him for himself alone.

He's the meanest kid in town—he locks the bathroom door the nights grandpa has his beer parties.

He folds his newspaper in the subway so the man sitting next to him can only see half the headline.

You couldn't warm up to him if you were cremated together.

The only people who would enjoy working for him would be grave diggers.

He's not a bad guy—until you get to know him.

Lou Holtz talked about the former head of a picture company: "He started as a poor louse; later he became a multimillionaire—but success didn't change him."

My mind is made up—so don't confuse me with the facts.

He hasn't been himself lately—if only he would stay that way.

He'll face the music—if he can call the tune.

Memory
(*see Absent-Mindedness*)

My memory is excellent. There are only three things I can't remember: I can't remember faces, I can't remem-ber names—and I forget what the third is.

She's so old she doesn't learn history —she remembers it.

She's got a memory like an elephant —and a shape to match.

An elephant never forgets—but what has he got to remember?

I'll never forget the day I first met my wife—although God knows I've tried.

A good memory is what keeps a good chaperone awake.

Men
(*see Husbands*)

A man is incomplete until he's married—and then he is really finished.

By the time most men learn how to behave themselves—they are too old to do anything else.

Married men make the best salesmen —they are used to taking orders.

By the time a man can read a woman like a book—he's too old to start a library.

All men are born free and equal—but some of them get married.

When a man falls in love with himself—it is the beginning of a lifelong romance.

A man doesn't know what real happiness is until he's in love—and then it's too late.

Not all men are fools—some are bachelors.

Many women marry a man for life —and then find out he doesn't have any.

He's a man of rare gifts—hasn't given one in years.

A man who refused to fight used to be called a coward—today they call him a bachelor.

Men are fools to marry—but what else can we marry?

When men drink they do it for two reasons. Either they have no wife to go home to, or they have.

"Have you noticed that most heroes are married men?"
"Every married man is a hero."

He is a man of letters—he works for the post office.

Miami Beach

I worked at a hotel that has a wall-to-wall ocean. It's so swanky even the owners have to use the servants' entrance.

The Caledonia is this year's Hotel. But I stayed at next year's hotel—it's called "Under Construction."

It's so modern—the elevators stand still and the floors move up and down.

They have plenty of hotels planned but they're running out of names. One guy is building two hotels—he'll call them "HIS" and "HERS."

One hotel in Miami Beach was robbed—they stole forty canes.

All day long you lie in the sand— about how much money you've got.

It's so warm in Miami Beach, every-body sleeps under one blanket—what a wonderful way to make friends.

So much money in Miami Beach— girls are coming home with green sun-burns.

Sign in Miami: "Keep Florida Green—bring money."

Jackie Mason's Miami Beach

"You see," Jackie Mason said triumphantly, "like I said, this is all propaganda. This black headline in the *Miami News*: 'ICE, SNOW, AND WILD WIND—VICIOUS STORM HITS CHICAGO.' You think after seeing this anybody's going to check out and go home to freeze? They'll hock everything not already hocked to stay a few days longer. How'd they get here in the first place? That Irishman on TV hooked 'em by yelling 'Come on down!' giving you the idea, by the background, that the sun was shining and the water was warm enough to swim in. It was. Where was the com-mercial filmed? In Puerto Rico."

"I think Miami Beach is the most spectacular resort in the world, better even than the Riviera, Majorca, the Chinese Volga, and the Concord. It's got the best hotels, the finest foods, the most activities. But if you come down here for a tan, forget it. The only time the sun really shines all day is the day you pack to go home. If you want the sun every day, start packing every night before like it's going to be your last day."

"I like to watch those palefaces run to the beach or cabana club every morning when I'm going to my room to sleep. They douse themselves with olive oil, cod-liver oil, 3-in-1 oil, and

362

then change their oil every thousand miles. Then the clouds part, the sun peeks out and they shout, 'It's out! It's out!' Eight seconds later it's dark again and they all slump back to their $50-per day rooms, turn on the radio or TV and hear it's 90-in-the-shade in New York and to come on up."

"Me, I've got a special rate. I only pay thirty-five dollars a day, double-occupancy. Single, I rent out the other half of my bed for twenty-five dollars a night, twenty if it happens to be a girl. But who needs this expense? Back home I sleep for eight cents and sleep a lot better. Here I keep one eye open to see what I'm paying thirty-five dollars for. I also pay an accountant to stay with me to find out what every nap costs me."

"I will say this for myself, I'm conservative. I've got a room with a view —of another room. For a room with an ocean view you pay twice the price. Like, it's worth a fortune to look at the ocean. Who spends the day staring at the ocean? Not even the lifeguards. No, it's like I say. You spend all your money trying to sleep and as soon as you get up you're wiped out. You just about have enough left to order room service for a budget-priced breakfast, twenty-three dollars, plus tax, minimum, five dollars for a contribution to B'nai B'rith and a tip. For what breakfast costs here I can eat in Brooklyn for a week and have enough left over for a down-payment on another trip to Florida."

"The whole concept of a suntan is a status symbol. Somehow, in this country, if you're brown you have a rough time of it; but if you turn brown, you're a sensation. It's a sensational color if you get it in Miami Beach, but if you got it in Alabama, it's no good. Notice when a tourist gets back from Miami

he can't wait to show off his tan? He even calls and talks to people he's never met, to say, 'Hello. See my tan? You should have seen it yesterday, it faded on the plane.' No matter how dark he is he apologizes for not being as dark as he was. He lies in the sun all day and at night if you nod to him he warns 'Don't touch me. Every part of my body hurts.' This pain, I figure, costs him maybe eight hundred dollars a week, without pencillin."

"I don't say the food here isn't worth talking about. Talking about, yes, but eating, that's different. It's staged like maybe Mike Nichols or June Taylor or David Merrick might do it. Every meal is cast with two waiters, a captain, and if you're above the eighth floor, a maitre d' on a Honda. Even if you order a cold glass of water they light up a sterno and send smoke signals to the kitchen that they've located another sucker. This flambeau stuff makes everything look expensive. Even hominy grits and hush puppies, flambeau, runs into four figures."

Mind

I had my mind made up to stay home with her—but she had her face made up to go out.

"They say too much lovemaking affects the mind."
"You're crazy."

First I couldn't get her off my mind —now I can't get her off my hands.

He's got a photographic mind—too bad it never developed.

He went to a mind reader—and was only charged half-price.

"I've changed my mind!"
"Thank goodness—does it work better now?"

Mini-Skirts
(*see Fashion, Figure, Topless, etc.*)

Some women dislike mini-skirts, "Because they came into fashion too late—by twenty years and forty pounds."

The only thing a mini-skirt does for her is give her cold knees.

She doesn't have the legs for mini-skirts—only the nerve.

If her dress were any shorter—it would be a collar.

Either her dress is too short—or she's in too far.

She was so short—her mini-skirt dragged the floor.

I've seen her in a mini-skirt and believe me—I've seen better bones in soup.

The mini-skirt did one thing for her in winter—it gave her chapped thighs.

Those skirts keep getting higher all the time—I wonder what they'll be up to next?

The skirts are getting shorter and the neckline lower—I'd like to be here when they meet.

With today's fashions you can't tell if a girl is wearing a high mini-skirt or a low lobster bib.

Gina Lollobrigida doesn't like the the mini-skirts. She says, "It is better for men to discover than for women to reveal."

In the old days, if you wanted to know if a girl had knock-knees, you had to listen.

Sign in a shop selling mini-skirts: "Buy Short!"

As I see it, there are three kinds of mini-skirts: mini, micro and don't bend over.

Mini-skirt: calculated risqué.

Mistress
(*see Playgirls*)

A mistress is like a wife—only you don't have to do the dishes.

They were married thirty-two years and he took her to a restaurant to celebrate. "See that girl over there, the blonde? You might as well know, that's my mistress," he confessed.
"After thirty-two years, you bum, you got a mistress?" she squealed.
"Not only that, but see the brunette with the bangs?—that's Pincus' mistress."
"Pincus," she hollered, "that little shrimp—he got a mistress?"
"And that redhead, see her?—that's Kline's mistress."
"That little fat pig; he got a mistress? You know something, Max—I like ours the best."

Difference between wife and mistress is night and day.

Mistress—a cutie on the Q.T.

I had a gorgeous apartment in the Village—but my louse expired.

Modesty
(*see Henpecked*)

He is so modest he carries extra fuses around with him just in case his girl's lights go out.

She's so modest she blindfolds herself while taking a bath.

She's so modest she pulls down the shade to change her mind.

He told her he wasn't himself tonight, so she beat him up because she doesn't allow strangers in the house.

OLD MAID: "This isn't your room."
DRUNK: "That's all right, I'm not myself tonight."

He was always very shy. Even his tombstone reads, "Pardon me for not rising."

He's so shy he wouldn't open an oyster without first knocking on the shell.

It's easy to pick out the married man—he's the one that's listening.

The church is so small and she is so modest—that when the minister says "Dearly Beloved"—she blushes.

I hate to say it, but I'm unfaithful. I don't love myself as much as I should.

I wouldn't be seen with a girl who would go out with a guy like me.

The pianist was so shy—he used to play the piano from the inside.

I'm tops in humility.

Money
(*see Rich, Poor, Banks, Business*)

Be sure and save your money—you never know when it may be valuable again someday.

Even if money could buy happiness, think what a luxury tax there would be on it.

United States money not only talks —it has learned to speak every foreign language.

You can't see his hidden charms— his money is in Swiss banks.

A man after buying a ticket to a show walked off without picking up his change. The customer next in line asked the cashier what she did in a case like that. "I rap on the window with a sponge," she replied.

"Money doesn't bring happiness."
"Can you prove it?"
"Sure. You take a guy with forty million dollars. He ain't happier than a man with thirty-nine million."

A certain producer brags about the fact that he came to this country without a dime in his pocket—and now he owes more than $50,000.

Money may talk, but it seems to be very hard of hearing when you call it.

Having a little financial trouble— I'm two cents overdue on my library card.

The salary we used to dream of is the one we can't live on today.

You don't marry for money—you divorce for it.

Money can't buy love—but it can put you in an excellent bargaining position.

MODEL: "The great thing about money —it never clashes with anything you're wearing."

"She married a man who is ninety and has a million dollars."
"What's the idea of marrying a man ninety years old?"

"If someone handed you a check for a million dollars would you stop and examine the date?"

1ST MAN: "Since he lost his money half his friends don't know him anymore."
2ND MAN: "And the other half?"
1ST MAN: "They don't know yet that he's lost it."

Money can't buy happiness, but it will get you a better class of enemies.

Money is the root of all evil, but so far no one has found a better route.

"When I came to New York I had only a dollar."
"How did you invest the money?"
"I used it to send a wire home for more money."

It all happened while she was under the influence of money.

"How did you make all your money?
"I formed a partnership with a rich man."
"How did you do it?"
"He had the money and I had the experience."
"And was it a successful business for you?"
"Immensely so. When we dissolved a year later, I had the money and he had the experience."

There is only one way to balance the budget—tilt the country.

He's money-mad. He hasn't got a cent—that's why he's mad.

We should all live within our means —even if we have to borrow the money to do so.

It's true that opposites attract. A poor girl is always looking for a rich man.

When she goes shopping—she comes home with everything but money.

Don't marry for money—you can borrow it cheaper.

My wife found a new way to save her money—she uses mine.

Nowadays if someone pays in cash you get suspicious—you figure his credit is no good.

A child who knows the value of a dollar these days—must be mighty disappointed.

A dollar goes very fast nowadays— but not very far.

People are funny; they spend money they don't have to buy things they don't need—to impress people they don't like.

It's never the woman who pays—she just charges and charges.

After paying for the wedding— about all a father has left to give away is the bride.

MONEY: The stuff that makes a dirty old man—a man-about-town.

"My husband and I like the same thing—only he likes to save it, and I like to spend it."

Wife: "We always have too much month left at the end of our money."

It may be the woman who pays—but she's using some man's money to do it.

What may have spoiled today's younger generation is the sign most of them were born under. The dollar sign.

The reason for tight money is that too many pay checks are cashed in taverns.

Corbett Monica

ABOUT TV: "I was on the Joey Bishop show for three years. If you didn't see it, don't grieve. When we went off the air we had a very unusual rating—we owed CBS nine points."

HOLLYWOOD: "Living in New York most of my life—when I went to California it reminded me of two Newarks."

ETHNIC HUMOR: "Crossed a Jew with a Pollack—he's a janitor but he owns the building."

DIET: "He put saccharine in everything: ice cream, coffee, tea—now he's got artificial diabetes."

One woman got up in her weight-watching class and announced, "I just got rid of 175 pounds of excess flab—I divorced my husband."

USED CARS: "The salesmen was bugged by the prospective non-buyer who asked, 'And what's the 320 H.P. mean?'

'That's horse power.'

'That means it's got a lot of horse power?'

'Let's put it this way; if you get a flat —you've got to shoot it.' "

HOTEL: "My room was so small—you could only smoke regular cigarettes."

CARS: "I have a new Japanese car; it runs terrible—but what a radio!"

CHILDREN: "The teacher asked me to fill out an application for my son at the private school. One of the questions was, Is your son a leader or a follower?

I answered, 'A leader—but if not, he'll be a loyal and faithful follower.'

A week later I received a letter from the teacher, 'We have a class of fifty, forty-nine leaders and your son.' "

MARRIED LIFE: "Married men live longer than single men—so if you single fellows want a slow death...."

WAITED TO APPEAR AT A BENEFIT: "I waited so long to go on I shaved twice."

AFTER STACKED GIRL FINISHES HER SONG: "Did you see the voice on that girl?"

Discussing his recent unsuccessful opening on Broadway: "Put it this way —when the show opened, I was double-parked outside. When it closed, I hadn't gotten a ticket yet."

Mothers
(see Family, Parents, Marriage, Mothers-in-Law, Children, Kids, etc.)

This is Mother's Day and I hope everybody remembered to send some mother a present. . . . Everybody in show business remembers Mother's Day. . . . Dean Martin sent his wife some flowers . . . not exactly flowers . . . it was four roses . . . and Doctor Kildare sent his mother a beautiful heart . . . of course it was still beating!

A salmon lays three thousand eggs a year and nobody remembers it on Mother's Day.

The mother said to her daughter, "Marriage is give and take—if he doesn't give you what you want—take it!"

"If you don't do your lessons, I'll break every bone in your body," the mother said to her ten-year-old son.
"Who do you think you're talking to—Daddy?"

The cop arrested the young teener for wearing the scantiest bikini—to tell the truth, it looked like three colored Band-Aids. "What would your mother say if she saw you in the outfit?" the sergeant asked.
"She'd be furious," she answered, "it's her suit."

One of the most wonderful gifts to send a mother-in-law on Mother's Day is her daughter.

On Mother's Day her husband presented her with a beautiful skunk coat. "I can't see how such a beautiful coat comes from such a foul-smelling beast," said the mother.
"I don't ask for thanks, dear," said her husband, "but I do demand respect."

Mothers-in-Law
(*see Family, Parents, Husbands, Lovers, etc.*)

"Every comic knocks his mother-in-law, good or bad. Not me; I'm married fifteen years and my mother-in-law has been living with me fifteen years, and she can live with me forever—what can I do—it's her apartment."

The shortest distance between two points—is the route a groom takes when driving his mother-in-law home.

The daughter called her mother and cried that she wanted to come home to her house.
"How will that punish him?" she asked. *"I'll* come to *your* house."

"My mother-in-law won't stay in this house another moment unless we get rid of the mice. Say, where are you going?"
"To get rid of the cat."

My mother-in-law is a very good cook. I usually get two of her favorites: "cold shoulder" and "hot tongue."

NEW BRIDE: "George is perfectly wonderful to me, mother. He gives me everything I ask for."
MOTHER: "That merely shows you're not asking enough."

WIFE: "I suppose you wish I'd go home to mother."
HUSBAND: "I wouldn't wish that on anyone."

Adam had no mother-in-law. That is how we know he lived in Paradise.

"Hello, Higbee. Off on a pleasure trip?"
"Yes, I'm taking my mother-in-law home again."

"What's wrong? You look sad."
"I just wrote a good mother-in-law joke."
"Didn't the editor like it?"
"I don't know. My mother-in-law saw it first."

"Do you mean to tell me you've been married for five years and your mother-in-law has only been to visit you once?"
"Yeah. She came the day after we were married and never left."

My mother-in-law was kidnapped last week. The kidnappers said if we didn't send twenty-four thousand dollars quick we would have to take my mother-in-law back.

He divorced his wife and married her sister because he didn't want to break in a new mother-in-law.

He sent his mother-in-law a present on Mother's Day—her daughter.

A friend of mine got married just two weeks ago. His mother-in-law moved in right away, and already that marriage is broken up. The fella likes his mother-in-law all right. But he just can't stand his wife.

The best way to send your wife home to her mother—is to send her mother with her.

If I had it to do over again, I would marry a Japanese girl. They are very pretty, obedient, graceful, loving—and your mother-in-law is in Tokyo.

A mother-in-law is never outspoken.

Mouth
(see Head, Faces, etc.)

There's a Russian singer who sings through his nose—he's afraid to open his mouth.

He has such a big mouth—he can eat a banana sideways.

My wife has her hair pulled back so tight—she can't shut her mouth.

Her mouth is so small—she uses a shoe-horn to take an aspirin.

Now, Junior, say "ah"—so the doctor can take his finger out of your mouth.

Her mouth was so big, when she smiled she got lipstick on her ears.

Her mouth is big enough to sing duets.

Movies
(see Hollywood, Actors, etc.)

I made a picture—it took seven days to make—with retakes. I posed longer for my graduation picture.

It's the most expensive picture they ever made in Hollywood—it cost 2 million just for the intermission.

Sophia Loren got a chest cold—man, those germs sure know how to live.

They shot the picture in a hurry—previewed it and then shot the director.

I made a couple of pictures while I was out there, but I had to stop. My Brownie broke.

I dropped in to see your latest picture—I wanted to be alone.

She had a quiet wedding with only the press agents of the immediate family present.

HOLLYWOOD: Where movie stars wear dark glasses to night spots so they won't be inconspicuous.

"Have you any friends in Hollywood?"
"I won't know until after my picture is previewed."

The best way to enjoy a motion picture is to send your girl's parents to the movies.

FRIEND: "I'm so sorry I couldn't come to your wedding."
MOVIE ACTRESS: "Never mind . . . you'll come to my next one."

WIFE: "Why don't you ever make love to me like Gregory Peck did to that girl in the movie?"
HUSBAND: "Do you know how much they have to pay him for doing that?"

I saw your latest picture, but the seats were so uncomfortable, I couldn't sleep.

A visiting Hollywood quickie producer didn't have enough money to tip at the Copa—so he gave the waiter the lead in his next picture.

"You say you want me to play a mob scene in my next picture?"
"Yes. You're to meet all your former lovers."

1ST MOVIE ACTRESS: "That's a very unusual necklace you're wearing."
2ND MOVIE ACTRESS: "Yes, I made it entirely out of my old wedding rings."

I wanted to be tested to play the old Clark Gable parts; the only trouble is—my old parts don't work like Clark Gable's did.

No wonder Sophia Loren is getting all those terrific parts—look at all those terrific parts she had to start with.

The picture was so bad—people were waiting in line—to get out.

Even the French are starting to make unusual pictures—I saw one where the boy and girl were married.

"Every time I go to the movies some fat old lady sits next to me munching popcorn."

"Why don't you change seats?"
"I can't—it's my wife!"

Wouldn't it be nice if you could go to the movies and see a picture as good as the one that's coming next week?

She asked me to hold her seat in the movies—then she got angry when I did.

Music
(*see Opera, Ballet, Theatre, Show Business, etc.*)

Benny Goodman played his clarinet at the Andrew Goodmans' party. During the supper a lady was chatting with Goodman when someone shattered a champagne glass on the parquet floor. "What was that?" the lady asked.
Goodman replied: "C-sharp."

Some girls are music lovers—others can love without it.

DEFINITION OF A TRUE MUSICIAN: When he hears a lady singing in the bathtub—he puts his *ear* to the keyhole.

"Are you fond of music?"
"Yes, but keep right on playing."

Musicians who play by ear should remember we play the same way.

WIFE: "The papers say that the concert we went to last night was a great success."
HUSBAND: "Really? I had no idea we enjoyed it so much."

"What is your occupation?"
"I used to be an organist."
"And what made you give it up?"
"My monkey died."

"As soon as you started playing the piano at the party, twenty people stopped talking."

"Is that so?"

"They fell asleep."

1ST MAN: "Look at Mozart. At the age of four he was already composing symphonies."

2ND MAN: "Well, what else could he do? He was too young to go out with girls."

1ST MAN: "That's not a Caruso record. The man is singing in German."

2ND MAN: "Yes, the record was translated."

A famous maestro had a tough time deciding whether to marry a very beautiful but stupid girl or a rather painful-looking creature who was blessed with a magnificent voice. Art triumphed. He married the soprano. The morning after their nuptials, he woke, took one look at his bride, nudged her and shrieked, "For God's sake—sing."

FRIEND: "Your voice surprises me."

VOCALIST: "I studied and spent one million dollars to learn to sing."

FRIEND: "I would love to have you meet my brother."

VOCALIST: "Is he a singer too?"

FRIEND: "No, he's a lawyer. He'll get your money back."

STRANGER: "Does your orchestra ever play by request?"

ORCHESTRA LEADER: "A lot of times."

STRANGER: "Ask them to play pinochle."

He is known as the Van Gogh of the sax players—because he doesn't have an ear.

"Do you know Shostakovitch's Fifth?"

"I don't know—was it a boy or a girl?"

"Do you know Shostakovitch's Fifth?"

"It's a great bottle of booze."

A trumpet player was rehearsing late one night when there was a knock on his door. He opened it and found an enraged neighbor who asked, "Do you know there's a little old lady sick upstairs?"

"No," replied the musician, "but if you hum a few bars, I'll fake it."

A bandleader asked a pianist to give piano lessons to his son. "Do you know the scale?" the pianist asked at their first session.

"Yes sir," the nine-year-old answered, "one hundred bucks a week for sidemen and double for leader."

He's a spiritualistic musician—whenever he plays he hears rappings on the walls.

I've heard prettier music come out of leaky balloons.

She was only a musician's daughter —but she wouldn't respond to any overture.

My brother is still in the house playing a duet—I finished my part first.

He has a very unusual voice—it's like asthma set to music.

If you want to remember his voice—tear a rag.

One of the finest orchestras in the country—in the city they are not so good.

For a five-piece band—they really sound like four.

One of the great bands of the day—at night they are not so good.

Every time I play the accordion I cry like a baby—the accordion keeps pinching my belly.

Just once, I'd like to see Dagmar play the accordion.

"What do you have to know to play the cymbals?" a fan asked conductor Sir Malcolm Sargeant.
"Nothing," he answered, "except when."

Names

I call him "Label" because he sticks so close to the bottle.

I call her "Muscles" because she's on everybody's arm.

I call her "Hershey Bar" because she's half nuts.

I call her "Easter Egg" because she's hand-painted on the outside and hard-boiled on the inside.

I call her "Luke" because she's not so hot.

I call my wife "Congress" because she's always introducing new bills in the house.

I call him "Dynamo" because everything he has is charged.

I call her "Baseball" because they threw her out at home.

She calls me "Girdle" because I'm always creeping up on her.

I call her "Domino" because everybody plays with her.

I call her "Dollar" because she is wrinkled and green.

I call him "Ceiling" because he's always plastered.

I call her "Baseball" because she won't play without a diamond.

I call her "Booby-Trap" because when you touch her she goes off.

I call her "Poison Ivy" because she's something awful to have on your hands.

I call her "Appendix" because everybody takes her out.

I call her "Doorknob" because she's had plenty of hands on her.

I call him "Paul Revere" because he's always horsing around.

Neighbors
(see Suburbs, Apartment Houses, Small Towns, Hick Towns, Friends, etc.)

WIFE: "Our neighbors don't have a TV set, or a grand piano, or a Cadillac."
HUSBAND: "Yeah, but they must have a bank account."

If we keep up with the neighbors, we'll fall behind—with the creditors.

Our neighbors have never heard an angry word come out of our apartment —we've had the walls soundproofed.

Our neighbor had her husband put out of the house—because he clashed with the drapes.

He loves his neighbors—wives.

It's pretty hard to keep up with the Joneses—especially when they are newlyweds.

Enough is what would satisfy us—if our neighbors didn't have more.

Anything you tell a woman usually goes in one ear and out to the neighbors.

If you help your neighbor when he's in trouble he'll never forget you—especially the next time he's in trouble.

The housewife told the salesman she wasn't interested in a vacuum cleaner, "But see my neighbor next door—I borrow theirs and it's in terrible condition."

The best way to love thy neighbor is when her husband is out of town.

Not only is she the most respected lady in the neighborhood—but the loneliest.

One figure that's always on the up-and-up is a woman's estimate of her neighbor's age.

Let's wash the windows, mother—the neighbors are straining their eyes.

"Love is blind."
"But our neighbors aren't—pull down the shade."

When she sings I always stand out in the yard—I don't want the neighbors to think I'm beating her.

Opportunity knocks once and the neighbors the rest of the time.

"Love thy neighbor as thyself—but don't take down the fence."—Sandburg

Newspapers

Letter to Subscription Department, the *New York Times*:

"My son has been reading the *Times* since his confinement to a mental institution. Now that he is cured, I wish to cancel his subscription."

A small town is a place where they buy a newspaper just to verify what they heard over the phone.

I was a beautiful child; my parents used to have me kidnapped—just to see my picture in the paper.

"My father is wealthy—he owns a newspaper."
"So what—a newspaper is only ten cents."

Excuse me, sir, are you reading that newspaper you're sitting on?

Did you hear about the reporter for a Tel Aviv newspaper who got a big scoop and raced into the pressroom yelling, "Hold the back page!"

I have printer's ink in my veins—which is a pain, since all our cheap relatives don't bother to buy ink any more. They just fill their pens in me.

My favorite gentleman of the press is a Bronx tailor.

Vital Statistics Note in a Small-Town Newspaper: "Due to the shortage of paper a number of births will be postponed until next week."

REPORTER: "Do you think I should put more fire into my articles?"
EDITOR: "No, vice versa."

The reporter came back from covering the campaign trail.
EDITOR: "Well, what did the candidate have to say today?"
REPORTER: "Not a thing."
EDITOR: "Good, then we can keep it down to a column."

373

I used to be an old newspaperman—but I found that there was no money in old newspapers.

Night Clubs

It was so crowded I was dancing cheek to cheek with the girl behind me.

Some men make the best chorus girls.

When a chorus girl starts sewing tiny garments—chances are she's mending her costume.

They keep the lights very low—so you can't see the prices on the menu.

Bored wife to husband in noisy night club: "Why can't you be like other husbands and never take me anyplace?"

I worked in a night club where the service was so bad that one time the waiters went out on strike, and it was two weeks before anyone knew the difference.

Two women were sitting in a night club on a chilly day. When one finished her drink, she set her glass down, and said to her companion, "You having another?"
"No, dolling," she answered. "It's just the way my coat is buttoned."

Noses

In Alaska they kiss by rubbing noses—Jimmy Durante could be king up there.

A bird in the hand is worthless—when you want to blow your nose.

She had such a turned-up nose—every time she sneezed, she blew her hat off.

You've heard of nose drops? Well, hers did.

She's had her face lifted so many times—she talks through her nose.

I'm not saying he has a big nose—but he's the only man who can smoke a cigar under a shower.

"Is that perfume I smell?"
"It is—and you do."

Is that your nose or are you eating a banana?

Nudists

You can always spot a Peeping Tom at a nudist colony. He's the guy sneaking looks at the girls passing by outside.

The two engaged nudists decided to break it up—they'd been seeing too much of each other.

FRIEND: "How are things at your nudist colony?"
OPPORTUNIST: "Well, pretty good. I opened up a little store out there. I'm selling underthings to the nudists."
FRIEND: "What kind of underthings could you sell to nudists?"
OPPORTUNIST: "Cushions!"

He's as careful as a nudist crossing a barbed-wire fence.

He was asked to grow a beard so he could go to the village for supplies.

Where does a nudist put his keys after he locks his car?

374

Where do you pin a medal on a heroic nudist?

At a nudist wedding—you can always tell who the best man is.

The maid answered the door—I could tell it wasn't the butler.

The nudist picture got four stares.

The nudist bride didn't go in the sun for three months—she wanted to get married in white.

The Martian landed in a nudist colony and hollered, "Take me to your tailor."

One thing about being a nudist—you don't have to hold your hand out to see if it's raining.

What a nudist camp. They wouldn't let people in with tattoos. Claimed the pictures spoiled the view.

Another advantage of being a nudist—you don't have to sit around in a wet bathing suit.

You're as popular as poison ivy in a nudist camp.

A friend was a guest at a nudist colony. He was watching a volley ball game between two all-girl teams who were fully dressed in the nude. A group of gaping males stood watching the game. My friend walked over to the male cheering section, tapped one of them on the shoulder and asked, "Excuse me—can you tell me the score?"

He has the biggest handicap in the nudist colony—he's nearsighted.

He's been watching her at the nudist camp—he wishes he could see her in a sweater.

She is the girl with the biggest problem in the camp—she's a bleached blonde.

This woman was taking a bath, heard the doorbell ring, went nudely to the door and asked who was there. "Blind man," a voice replied. Martha opened the door to a stalwart fellow who said, "Where do I put these blinds?"

Nurses
(also see Doctors, Hopsitals, Psychiatrists, etc.)

The head nurse was showing the pretty young graduate from nursing school the hospital. As they were walking, the head nurse stopped in front of a door of the men's convalescent section. "This is a really dangerous ward," she remarked. "These patients are almost well."

The conceited young man had been in hospital for some time and had been extremely well looked after by the pretty young nurse. "Nurse," said the patient one morning, "I'm in love with you. I don't want to get well."
"Don't worry," replied the nurse cheerfully, "you won't. The doctor's in love with me too, and he saw you kissing me this morning."

DOCTOR: "Nurse, where's the man who belongs in this bed?"
NURSE: "He couldn't get warm—so I put him in with that lady who's running 104."

The nurse was nicknamed "Appendix" because all the doctors wanted to take her out.

DOCTOR: "I notice that 205 isn't chasing you any more. How did you do it?"

NURSE: "Easy—I took the tires off his wheelchair."

The doctor walked into the hospital room and found his patient in bed with his nurse. "What are you doing?" screamed the medical man. "You're a very sick man!"
"That sick I'm not."

"Where you been? I haven't seen you for a long time."
"Around. You know I had an accident three years ago and I'm still suffering."
"How come?"
"I married the nurse."

"You shouldn't be up," the nurse said; "you'll break your stitches."
"Then why do you use such cheap thread?"

The doctor was furious when his beautiful nurse broke their engagement. "He insisted I give him back all his presents," she revealed to her girl friend.
"You're joking!" she said in horror.
"Not only that," said the nurse, "but he sent me a bill for fifty-one visits."

"I'm sorry I can't go out with you tonight," the nurse said, "but I'm afraid to leave the baby with her mother."

Off-Beat Humor
(*see also Martians, Crazy Mixed-Up Humor, etc.*)

The mechanic was caught in the big wheel, whirled around for what seemed an eternity, and then thrown about fifty feet away. His co-worker rushed to him and put his head on his lap. "Speak to me," he pleaded. "Johnny, are you okay? Speak to me."
"Why should I speak to you?" he said as he opened his eyes. "I just passed you a couple of hundred times and you didn't speak to *me*."

I know a fella who invented a twelve-foot pole for guys who can't touch a girl with a ten-foot pole.

She was suffering from an enlarged navel—she carried the flag in the parade.

"Why didn't you call me?"
"You have no phone!"
"No, but you have."

He has a fine-tooth comb—the only man I know who combs his teeth.

I fooled the house detective. When he knocked—I had less than ten points.

He jumped into a cab and screamed, "Follow that cab in front of us."
"I have to," said the cabby. "He's towing us."

The hearing aid was too expensive—so he bought a plain piece of wire and stuck it around his ear. "Do you hear better with that wire?" a friend asked. "No—but my friends talk louder."

They now have a new Chinese deodorant—the trouble is that one hour after you use it, you're offensive again.

This fellow complained to the clerk in the broken-down motel, "There's no ceiling in my room."
"That's all right," the clerk answered, "the fellow upstairs doesn't walk around much."

The town I come from is so small, when I plug in my electric razor—the trolley stops.

I got a friend who has a peculiar way of estimating time: "I knew thirty seconds had passed because I was half-way through my minute steak."

MAN TO GRASSHOPPER: "Are you aware that they have named a drink after you?"
GRASSHOPPER: "You mean they have a drink called Charlie?"

I have discovered a cure for which there is no disease.

My parents were too poor to have children—so the people next door had me.

"You and your damn suicide attempts—look at this gas bill!"

OCULIST: "I want you to read that eye chart, please."
LADY: "Would you be so kind as to read it for me? My sight is not very good."

"My father planted a tree in our living room."
"That's ridiculous."
"I know—but it keeps our dog off the streets at night."

"My brother ran a hundred yards in six seconds."
"You're crazy—the world's record is more than nine seconds."
"My brother knows a short cut."

I knew my wife was getting thin when we walked into a restaurant arm-in-arm, and the headwaiter said, "You'll have to check your umbrella."

An angry mother took her nine-year-old son to the doctor's office and asked: "Is a boy of nine able to perform an appendix operation?"
"Of course not," the doctor said impatiently.
The mother turned to the boy in anger and screamed at him, "So who was right? Put it back!"

The doctor rushed out of his study and instructed his wife, "Get me my bag at once!"
"What's the matter?" she asked.
"Some fellow just phoned and said he couldn't live without me."
The wife thought a few seconds. "Just a moment," she said gently, "I think that call was for me."

After a man had had a few dry martinis, he praised the bartender:
MAN: "Such genius deserves a reward." (With this remark he takes a live lobster out of his pocket.) "Here, take this with my compliments."
BARTENDER: "Why, thanks. Can I take it home for dinner?"
MAN: "No, no. He's already had dinner. Take him to a movie!"

HE: "Can't we keep our marriage a secret?"
SHE: "But suppose we have a baby?"
HE: "Oh, we'll tell the baby, of course."

Office
(see Business, Executives, Efficiency Experts, Work, Automation, Computers, Employment, etc.)

The man was trying to locate his friend John Sexauer. He called every office in town and finally reached one busy operator. "Do you have a SEX-AUER there?" he asked. "Sexauer?" she barked. "We don't even have a coffee break!"

A young miss just out of business school was filling out an application form (her own form was already filled out) in one of New York's larger advertising agencies. She went through it fine, but when she came to the heading called "Sex" she hesitated. Finally, she decided to answer. "Once in a while," she wrote.

I'm afraid I'll have to fire my typist— she's always interrupting my dictation and asking me to spell the simplest words—and it just gets embarrassing to have to keep saying, "I don't know."

"Okay," the executive said to the sexy brunette secretary, "you're hired —now would you like to try for a raise?"

"You'll like it here," the steno said to the new girl, "lots of chances for advances."

As soon as that struggling stenographer quits struggling—she'll discover that she doesn't have to be a stenographer.

Give a man enough rope and he'll claim he's tied up at the office.

She's the best little secretary he ever got his hands on.

Secretary: "I did try getting in on time—but it makes it such a long day."

She's the main squeeze in the office.

A secretary was leaving for her summer vacation. She warned her substitute, "While I'm gone you'll continue on everything I was working on—but that does not include Mr. Davis!"

"Fantastic," the office manager said to the stenographer; "you've been with us only two weeks and you're already three months behind in your work."

Boss introducing new sexy file clerk: "She sorts out the men from the boys."

"How long did you work for your last boss?"
"Until I got him."

"How come you're only having a sandwich—are you on a diet?"
"No—on commission."

"I have a very efficient secretary— she hasn't missed a coffee break in ten years."

His stenographers have to have a lot of experience with shorthand—and long arms.

"My union is fighting for a four-day week."
"Okay—but who's gonna pay for the two coffee breaks and the lunch hour I'll be missing?"

The absent-minded office manager pulled the typewriter down on his lap —and started to unfasten the ribbon.

She can operate all the office machinery great—the cigarette machine, the coffee machine. . . .

Old Age
(see Age, Old Maid, etc.)

He really goes in for athletics— rides horseback every day—except for the last two weeks in August. That's when the guy who puts him on and takes him off goes on vacation.

The ninety-five-year-old man married the ninety-three-year-old woman —and they spent the first three days of their honeymoon just trying to get out of the car.

Sinatra, Cugat, Justice Douglas, Cary Grant, and Henry Fonda married pretty girls dozens of years younger. I can't wait till *I* get old.

He's eighty-three and he still chases girls. He can't remember why—but he still chases girls.

He's at the age now—when he goes out with a girl—he can't take yes for an answer.

An eighty-five-year-old man was complaining to his friend. "My stenographer is suing me for breach of promise." His friend answered, "At eighty-five, what could you promise her?"

He's so old he gets winded playing chess.

He still chases girls but only if it's downhill.

He is at the age when a pretty girl arouses his memories instead of his hopes.

A recent story concerns the old lady who tottered into a lawyer's office and asked for help in arranging a divorce. "A divorce?" asked the unbelieving lawyer. "Tell me, Grandma, how old are you?"
"I'm eighty-four," answered the old lady.
"Eighty-four! And how old is your husband?"
"My husband is eighty-seven."
"My, my," said the lawyer, "and how long have you been married?"
"Next September will be sixty-two years."
"Married sixty-two years! Why should you want a divorce now?"
"Because," Grandma answered calmly, "enough is enough."

Harry Hershfield says he went to see his doctor on his eighty-second birthday and explained he wanted to get married. "Will I be able to expect an heir?" he asked. The doctor, after examining him, explained: "You're heir-minded—but not heir-conditioned."

Georgie Jessel was going with an older girl, that is, older than his godchild who was three. He was crazy about her but he didn't know what to do with her after they married: take her on a honeymoon to Europe—or send her to camp.

An eighty-two-year-old man married a teenager. For a wedding present he gave her a "do-it-yourself kit."

She looked like a million—every day of it.

Old Maid
(*see Age, Old Age*)

The old maid was asked which she liked most in a man—brains, money, or appearance, and she answered, "Appearance—and the sooner the better."

The old maid found a thief under her bed. She held a gun on him and called the police. "Please send a cop over—in the morning."

OLD MAID: (calling fire department) "A man is trying to get into my room."
FIRE DEPARTMENT: "You don't want the fire department—what you want is the police department."
OLD MAID: "I don't want the police—I want the fire department—a man is trying to get into my room—and we're on the second floor and he needs a ladder."

Did you hear about the mean ventriloquist who went around throwing his voice under the beds of old maids?

379

An old maid rang the fire alarm and twenty firemen responded. When they arrived, she said: "There's no fire, so nineteen of you can go back."

She knows all the answers—but nobody has ever asked her the questions.

The old maid attended a wrestling match and one of the wrestlers was thrown in her lap. She held onto him for dear life yelling, "Finders keepers!"

Two old maids ran a drug store. A man walked in and said, "I'd like to see a male clerk."
One old maid answered, "I'm a registered pharmacist. You can tell me all your troubles."
The customer explained, "I'd like some sort of pill to calm me down. I have a terrible habit. Everytime I see a girl, I wanna make love to her. What can you give me?"
The old maid replied, "Just a minute, I'll discuss it with my sister."
About five minutes later she returned. "Well?" said the man.
"My sister and I," said the old maid, "decided to give you the drug store and seven hundred dollars."

Two old maids were sitting in the insane asylum. One said, "Y'know, I feel like having a man hug me and kiss me and make love to me!"
To which the other replied, "Oh, now you're talking sense. You'll be outta here soon!"

When there is an old maid in the house—a watchdog is unnecessary.

Opera
(*see Music, Ballet, Shakespeare, Theatres, etc.*)

I go to the opera whether I need the sleep or not.

Opera is Italian vaudeville.

Opera is where you get stabbed and instead of bleeding—you sing.

"Do you know Madame Butterfly?"
"I knew her when she was a cocoon."

"How do you remember all the words in the opera?"
"I just tie a little string around my finger."

"Can you hear the singing?"
"No, these are good seats."

If you close your eyes—can't you just imagine you're at home with the radio on?

The trouble with opera is that there is too much singing.

They are going to do more operas in English—then you'll understand what's boring you.

As far as the performance was concerned, it was some of the best bracelets we ever heard. We spent the first act looking at ermine and for the rest we just let our eyes slum a bit. It was truly a night at the opera, but personally we enjoyed it much better with the Marx Brothers.

A girl worker in a Moscow factory asked her lady boss, "Madame Troika, can I quit early tonight? I'm going to the opera."
"Never call me Madame. We are all alike here—I don't want to hear that Madame again—understand? Now what opera are you going to see?"
"Comrade Butterfly."

Opportunity

This was a persistent customer: "You mean to tell me that if President Johnson wanted to see this show tonight, you couldn't manage to scrape up a ticket for him?"

"Yes," came the admission, "if President Johnson needed a ticket, we'd have one for him."

"Well," shot back the insistent one, "I got news for you—President Johnson isn't coming and I'd like to have his seat."

"You know why I'm a failure? The one time and the only time opportunity ever knocked on my door, I didn't answer. I thought it was the house detective!"

Opportunity knocks, but last night a knock spoiled my opportunity.

An elderly lady was introduced to Dr. Klein at a party. At her first opportunity she cornered the gentleman and said, "Doctor, I'm so glad to meet you. Let me ask you a question. Lately I get a terrible pain here in my side when I raise my arm like this. What should I do about it?"

The gentleman answered, "I'm very sorry, madam, but you see I'm not that kind of a doctor. I happen to be a doctor of economics."

"Oh," said the old lady. "So tell me, doctor, should I sell my General Motors?"

"Most people don't recognize opportunity when it knocks—because it comes in the form of hard work."—H. L. Mencken

This is about the family that went picnicking on a Sunday afternoon. They found a lovely green spot in the country, spread out the tablecloth and covered it with sandwiches, hard-boiled eggs, etc. Impressed by the beauty of the place, they were puzzled by the flags with numbers they saw at various points in the distance. Midway through their picnic, a gentleman strode angrily toward them.

"Just what do you think you are doing?" he exploded. "Don't you realize you are sitting on the fifteenth green of the most exclusive golf club in the country?"

Papa swallowed his hard-boiled egg and sarcastically answered, "So, this is the way to get new members?"

Optimists
(see Pessimists)

An optimist is a man who goes to the window in the morning and says, "Good morning, God." A pessimist goes to the window and says, "My God, it's morning!"

An optimist is a guy who falls off the Empire State Building and on the way down he keeps saying: "Well, I'm not hurt yet!"

An optimist is somebody who hasn't been reading the paper or listening to the news lately.

An optimist sits in the balcony and winks at the chorus girls.

Two good friends, one an optimist, the other a pessimist, were in an automobile accident, and were lying in the street waiting for the ambulance. "I feel like all my bones are broken," groaned the pessimist. "So," said the optimist, "think how lucky you are you are not a herring."

He starts working on crossword puzzles with a fountain pen.

381

He got married when he was seventy-five and then looked for a house near a school.

OPTIMIST: He keeps going down to City Hall to see if his marriage license has expired.

An optimist is a guy who expects his wife to help him with the dishes.

He married his secretary and thinks he can continue to dictate to her.

An optimist is a man who doesn't give a darn what happens as long as it doesn't happen to him.

An optimist is a man who will leave his door unlocked and hopes his wife walks out on him.

A man who thinks marriage will end his trouble.

A man who thinks a woman will hang up the phone just because she said good-bye.

He goes into a restaurant without a cent and intends to pay for the meal with the pearl he expects to find in the oyster.

Organizations

Mr. Cohen belonged to an organization with many social benefits. Each person in the club was asked to buy a plot at a reduced rate—sort of a group plan so they could have a place to live when they died. When the organization found that it wasn't paying off too well, they asked the president to talk to the delinquent members, and Cohen was first to be called. "You bought a plot twenty-five years ago," the president began, "and you haven't paid for it yet." The member looked askance. "I didn't use it," he answered. "Who stopped you?" was the topper.

Somebody asked W.C. Fields, "Do you believe in clubs for women?"
"Yes—if every other form of persuasion fails."

He was thrown out of the club—they dismembered him.

Groucho Marx was invited to join an actors' club. "I wouldn't belong to any organization," he answered, "that would have me for a member."

He belonged to so many organizations and paid dues in all of them. When he died he insisted they put on his tombstone, "Clubbed To Death."

"I thought you were going to the lodge meeting tonight?"
"It's been postponed—the wife of the Grand Exalted Invincible Supreme Potentate wouldn't let him out tonight."

Secretary of women's club: "The report on 'Solving World Problems' will be delayed because three members couldn't get baby-sitters."

Outer Space
(*see Astronauts, Martians, Off-Beat Humor, Crazy Mixed-Up Humor, Dumb*)

If the President is looking for extra revenue—let him tax all those Martians running around looking for their leader.

The Martian came home late for dinner at his home on Mars. "Couldn't help it, dear," he explained to his wife. "I was caught in a traffic jam near Cape Kennedy."

382

They are already manufacturing pills to relieve "space-sickness."

The women on Mars have their bust in the back. It doesn't make them more attractive—but it's better for dancing. Especially when you put your arm around her.

An astronaut landed on the moon and saw a gorgeous twenty-foot girl. He approached her and said, "A ladder now—your leader later."

So this Martian came to earth, stepped into a taxi and said, "Take me to your leader." "Sorry," said the cabby, "I'm pulling into my garage."

A Martian stopped a man on the street and told him, "Take me to your leader."
"Oh, I can't," he answered. "She's in Florida with my mother-in-law."

Travel is now really out of this world.

A space ship landed on 5th Avenue and out popped a neurotic Martian who stopped a fellow and said, "Take me to your leader's psychiatrist."

Advice to space travelers: "Don't look down."

A Venutian space ship landed in a sand trap on a golf course in California. "What do I do now?" the pilot radioed the boss on Venus. The answer came back, "Use a seven iron, stupid."

It's dangerous work—only married men should be sent to the moon—single men have something to live for.

The Martian was kissing and hugging the traffic signal when it quickly changed from "Go" to "Stop." The Martian snickered, "What do you expect? American women are all teasers!"

The man from Mars came upon a roller towel dispenser in the men's room. He looked around, embarrassed, and whispered to the dispenser, "Madam, you slip is showing."

A man from Venus saw a wire mesh trash basket on a street corner. "What are you trying to prove?" he said to the basket. "With those flimsy clothes—you'll freeze to death!"

An odd-looking Martian from Mars played all night at the crap table in Vegas. Nobody noticed him until he made fifteen consecutive passes.

"Are you from Mars?" he asked the green man.
"Yeah," he answered.
"Are you all green like that?"
"Yeah."
"You all got antennas sticking out of your ears like that?"
"Yeah."
"You all got like round black caps in the middle of your head like that?"
"Only the orthodox."

The pair of newly arrived Martians stood on a corner looking at the traffic light.
"I saw her first," one insisted.
"So what?" his friend reasoned. "She winked at me."

Did I tell you about the Venusian who entered a Las Vegas gambling room and said, "Lead me to your taker."

The man from outer space landed in a nudist colony, and said to the nearest man, "Take me to your tailor."

When the space ship landed on a Texas oil field, the Texan offered any price for it. He bought it for $750,000 from the owner. After the transaction the space ship owner laughed to his

383

friend, "Wait till he finds out it's last year's model."

Wouldn't it be the scandal of all time if the first couple we see on the moon are Judge Crater and Amelia Earhart?

Mr. and Mrs. Mars were passing a hardware store. Like all wives anywhere, she stopped to look in the window and admired the paints. "No dice," said the husband; "your old coat will just have to last another season."

The Venutian was bragging about "My son the Univac—he's not only handsome—but he's got brains as well."

A Martian walked over to the lamppost and said, "Before you take me to your leader—how about okaying my credit card?"

You know why the Russians are leading the race for outer space? They're all trying to get the hell out of there.

It looks like the Russians may have the first man on the moon. They wouldn't be able to get him back— but that's one of the inducements.

Parents
(*see Kids, Children, Marriage, Juvenile Delinquents, Wives, Husbands*)

PA: "The man who marries my daughter will need a lot of money."
HIM: "I'm just the man then."

FATHER: "You're getting too old to play with the boys."
DAUGHTER: (innocently) "I don't have to any more, father."

FATHER: (to daughter's boy friend) "Remember, young man, the lights are put out in this house at eleven o'clock."
BOY FRIEND: "That's fine by me, sir."

FATHER: "My son, I am a self-made man."
SON: "Pop, there's one thing I like about you. You always take the blame for everything."

"I'll teach you to make love to my daughter."
"I wish you would. I'm not making much headway."

Some young boys were bragging about their fathers. One said, "My father's a great magician. He can walk down the street and turn into a saloon."

A young boy boasted about his father to his friends. "My father was the first man to fly 10,000 feet with a stick in his hands." "Oh, was he a flyer?" "No," the boy said, "the poolroom blew up."

Mother let the maid go—'cause daddy wouldn't.

The worried mother told the doctor, "My son insists on emptying ashtrays." "Well, that's not unusual," the doctor said. "Yeah," the mother said, "but in his mouth?"

TEACHER: "How do you like your new home, Johnny?"
JOHNNY: "Great. It's so big all of us have our own rooms, except for mom . . . she's still in with dad."

My mother had some women's ailment and so she went to see her nephew, who was a gynecologist. After the examination was over she looked him straight in the eye and said, "Tell me, does your mother know how you make a living?"

Due to the tax advantages of a partnership, Crosby has his family set up as a partnership. When the Internal Revenue office questioned Kathy Grant if she was actively engaged in the partnership she said, "Of course . . . I'm producing new partners."

"Your face is clean," the mother said, "but how did you get your hands so dirty?"
"Washing my face," replied the young boy.

She's raising her kids by the book—*Peyton Place.*

"Daddy, why did you marry mommy?"
"Ah, so you're wondering too!"

"Son," mother said to her son on his sixteenth birthday, "you can always come to mother about everything. If you ever start smoking or drinking, come to mamma and tell her. I don't want to hear it from the neighbors."
"Don't worry, mom," the kid said, "I gave up smoking and drinking a year ago."

The toughest thing about homework is getting mom and pop to agree on the same answer.

The mother was enjoying her cry at her daughter's wedding. "Don't think of it as losing a daughter," her husband consoled her, "think of it as gaining a bathroom."

They're engaged—but they are not getting married because they're not good enough for each other—I know because I've been talking to both families.

"Hey, pop," the kid quizzed the old man, "how come a Coke will spoil my dinner but a martini gives you an appetite?"

By the time the couple can really afford to have children—they are having grandchildren.

Parking
(*see Traffic*)

The meek shall inherit the earth, but it's the bold who will end up with the parking spaces.

It's very difficult to get a parking ticket in N. Y.—first you have to find a place to park.

The Long Island Expressway is the longest parking lot in America.

There are more cars in New York than all of Europe. There are more cars in Long Island than all of England. We will have to park overseas.

I spent two weeks in Los Angeles, one week in San Francisco, three weeks in New York—I couldn't find a place to park.

COP TO MOTORIST: "I'd give you a ticket if I could find a place to park my motorcycle."

While you're laughing—they are towing away your car.

Party

This fellow crashed the party. He was there about ten minutes when a dignified gentleman walked over to him and said, "Who are you?"
The crasher beamed. "I'm with the groom."
"I've got news for you, kid," said the gentleman, "this is a wake!"

Xavier Cugat tells the story about the girl, wearied by a long drive, who stopped into a motel looking for a room. The clerk told her that the last room had just been occupied but that there was a couch there, and if the man didn't mind her lying down on the couch, it was all right with him. In desperation, she knocked on the door and said to the man, "Look, you don't know me, I don't know you, we don't know them, they don't know us. Can I please bunk on your couch for a while? I won't bother you."

"Sure," he said, and went back to sleep.

A little while later, she woke him up and said, "Look, you don't know me, I don't know you, we don't know them, they don't know us, do you mind if I just sleep on top of the bed? I won't bother you."

"Okay," he said, and fell asleep again.

A short while later, she said, "Look, I don't know you, you don't know me, we don't know them, they don't know us, whaddya say we have a party?"

"Look," the man said, "if I don't know you, you don't know me, we don't know them, they don't know us—who the hell we gonna invite to the party?!"

The hostess was so anxious for everybody to have a good time. "You're head of Alcoholics Anonymous, aren't you?" she gushed.

"No," he said, "I'm head of the vice squad."

"Oh," she giggled, "I knew there was something I wasn't supposed to offer you."

At his parties, once the ice is broken —the furniture and the dishes go next.

Nothing is more embarrassing than to be seen at a party you wouldn't be caught dead at.

You can always tell a host at a party —he's the one watching the clock.

A fool and his money—are some party.

They were invited to a masquerade party. "What'll I wear?" the husband asked.

"Go sober," she said, "that'll fool everybody."

"I notice your husband serves the stuff but he doesn't drink a drop himself."

"I don't permit it. As soon as he gets loaded—he starts bringing out the good stuff."

There are two kinds of party-goers— one wants to leave early and one wants to stay late. The only trouble is—they are usually married to each other.

A man can always tell what kind of time he has been having at a party by the look on his wife's face.

He was such a bore and pest that people used to have parties—just not to have him.

Every time he comes to town they want to give him a party—a farewell party.

Going to a party with your wife— is like going fishing with the game warden.

"They laughed as I stood up to sing. How did I know I was under the table?"

At the party they gave out door-prizes—one fellow won four doors.

COCKTAIL PARTIES: Where they cut sandwiches and friends into little pieces.

We hate to eat and run—but my husband is still hungry.

I'm tired. I think I'll flirt with some stacked broad—so my wife will insist we go home immediately.

"To get fifty people to a cocktail party," said Elsa Maxwell, "in New York you have to invite one hundred. In Hollywood, you invite twenty."

Percentage
(*also see Business*)

"I buy a piece of merchandise for one dollar and I sell it for four dollars —you think three per cent is bad?"

The agent was angry at the actor—because he got 90 per cent of *his* money.

"I'm here on a percentage deal—I get ten per cent of everything over 50 thousand dollars a day."

"I get ten per cent of the gross—Irving Gross—he's a waiter here."

PROF: "Did you know that the human body is made up out of 92 per cent water?"
STUDENT: (Looking at stacked girl at the next desk) "Yeah, but look what she did with her eight per cent."

SLOGAN OF INVESTMENT COMPANY: "You can eat better on ten per cent —but you sleep better on five."

A rating service called ten thousand men to query, "Who are you listening to right now?" And 83 per cent of them answered, "My wife."

"Ninety-eight per cent of the men love marriage."
"Yeah—but I keep running into the other two per cent."

Eighty-seven per cent of all accidents happen in the home—that accounts for the 6,000 babies born every hour.

"I make a fortune, but I can't seem to make all ends meet—I'm always in trouble."
"Why don't you budget your money?"
"I do—30 per cent for rent, 20 per cent for food, 20 per cent for clothing, 20 per cent for amusement, and 40 per cent for girls."
"But Charley, that makes 130 per cent."
"I told you I'm always in trouble."

Personality

She's got a personality like a dunked tea bag.

He has the personality of an alligator handbag.

He is vulgar, loud, arrogant, and has bad breath. And those are his good points.

He has the personality of a social disease.

He has the personality of the inside of a fountain pen.

He has the personality of a loose sneaker.

He couldn't make the winners laugh in Las Vegas.

He has the personality of an enema bag.

He's got a personality like a shoe box.

Pessimists
(*see Optimists, Definitions, Daffynitions*)

Must tell you about the man who was looking so glum and despondent that a friend asked, "Morris, what's eating you? You look like last month's balance sheet."

" 'What's eating me,' he asks! Remember two weeks ago, my Tante Razel died and left me $50,000?"

"Yeah, I remember, so what's so awful?"

" 'What's so awful,' he asks! Remember last week my Uncle Chaim died and left me $75,000?"

"I remember that too, but what's bad about that?"

"What's bad about it? . . . This week, nothing!"

A pessimist read his horoscope which said, "Make new friends and see what happens." He made three new friends and nothing happened. Now he complains he's stuck with three new friends.

He's such a pessimist he even complains about the noise when opportunity knocks.

He never worries about tomorrow— he knows everything is going to turn out wrong.

If you tell him life begins at forty, he answers, "So does arthritis."

Prince Philip

I have very little personal experience of self-government. I am one of the most governed people you could hope to meet.

The only active sport which I follow is polo—and most of the work's done by the pony.

Prince Philip explained his short visits to countries this way: "When you start blocking up traffic—well, the first day people enjoy it, but by the third day they get bloody tired of it. The art of being a good guest is to know when to leave."

We are certainly not a nation of nitwits. In fact, wits are our greatest single asset.

Visiting a textile group, Prince Philip greeted the chairman of the knitting division: "So you're the head knit!"

The Queen couldn't be here tonight. She had to stay home this time because I'm afraid she is not quite as free as I am to do as she pleases.

In a speech to a graduating class: "It is traditional on these occasions for me to give you a bit of advice which you will equally traditionally ignore."

In a normal way, I am not noticeably reticent about talking of things about which I know nothing.

The head of the bowling club in Brazil summoned all the English he could in presenting Prince Philip with an emblem: "Balls, you know."

Prince Philip smiled pleasantly and answered: "And balls to you, sir."

Phonies
(*see Cads, Playboys*)

Give him a free hand and he'll stick it right in your pocket.

He never goes back on his word— without consulting his lawyer.

He never forgets a favor—if he did it.

388

If you lend him money, you never see it again—and it's worth it.

He's as phony as a dentist's smile.

He's as phony as the story of a prostitute.

I never forget a face—but in this case I'll make an exception.

A phony is the fellow who gets away with things you'd like to do but don't dare.

He's as phony as a candidate running for office.

He's as phony as your mother-in-law's smile.

Instead of giving a girl a present—he gives her a past.

Instead of counting his blessings—he counts yours.

Photography

One thing about children—they never go around showing snapshots of their grandparents.

She's so fat, when the photographer takes her picture—he charges her group rates.

If you look like your passport photo—you're not well enough to travel.

She's got a photographic mind—too bad it never developed.

There are so many tourists that they are getting in each other's snapshots.

He is the only fellow who looks as bad as his passport photo.

OFFICER: "He's a camera fiend of the worst kind."
JUDGE: "But you don't arrest a man because he has a mania for taking pictures."
OFFICER: "It isn't that, your honor—he takes the cameras."

A family man is a man who has replaced the money in his wallet with snapshots of the wife and kids.

"This picture doesn't do me justice."
"You don't want justice—you want mercy!"

Her picture has to be taken with a very fast camera—if you want to catch her with her mouth closed.

"Here is a picture of my bride!"
"She must be very wealthy!"

I still don't see why she broke off the engagement. She showed him a picture of her father holding her on his knee when she was a child. All he asked was, "Who is the ventriloquist?"

"Do you make life-size enlargements from snapshots?"
"That's our specialty."
"Good—let's see what you can do with this picture of the Grand Canyon."

Pickets
(*see Unions*)

The woman called the owner of the store: "Will you please call my husband, Mr. Frank Kline, to the phone?"
"We have no Frank Kline working here," the manager explained.
"I know," she said, "he's outside picketing the store."

A picket was walking up and down a busy street carrying a blank sign. A friend asked, "What's the idea?"

The picket replied, "I'm looking for a sponsor."

When they arrested the troublemaker while he was parading with a blank sign, he blurted out, "I've been looking for a cause—this looks like it's it."

A New York sign painter who made a specialty of lettering signs for union strikers was picketed by men who wore signs saying, "These signs were not painted by the firm we are picketing."

This teacher scolded the pupil: "If you don't learn to write—nobody'll be able to read your picket sign!"

Pills
(*see also Doctors, Nurses, Drug Stores*)

Henny Youngman claims his wife is hooked on LSD—lox, salami and danish.

Have you heard about the lady who confused her contraceptive pills with her saccharin tablets? She just had the sweetest baby.

My doctor has given me so many white pills, blue pills and pink pills—I now take red and green ones to direct traffic.

He took so many saccharin pills—he now has artificial diabetes.

A pill is a gadget to be used in any conceivable circumstances.

Plastic Surgery
(*see Doctors, Nurses, etc.*)

"Five thousand for having my face lifted? Doctor, that's robbery! Isn't there anything cheaper I can try?" "Try a veil!"

Since I had my nose lifted—my mouth don't work so good.

My uncle had his face lifted—with a piece of rope around his neck.

Playboys
(*see Playgirls*)

A handsome young playboy showed up at his favorite bistro swathed in bandages. "What happened to you?" asked a friend. "I held up a train," said the playboy. "You?" exclaimed his friend. "Held up a train?" "Yeah," came the laconic answer. "It was a bride's train, and it seems I held it up too high!"

An amorous playboy had cornered his girl in the back seat of the sedan and was eagerly trying his hand at her. She kept resisting and pushing him away. But still he persisted. Finally, she became annoyed and gave him a violent shove. "Lester," she said, smoothing her skirt, which had fallen to the floor during the struggle, "I don't know what's come over you. You've always been so restrained and so gentlemanly." "Yes, I know," said Lester apologetically, "but I just can't help it. I'm trying to give up smoking."

When she told her father she was pregnant and the man was the rich Charlie Brown—the old man rushed out gun in hand.

The playboy calmed him down: "Don't get upset—if it's a boy, I'll settle $50,000 on them—if it's a girl, $100,000."

The old man thought a bit. "And if it's a miscarriage," he asked, "does she get another chance?"

Even as an infant—he grabbed for the nurse instead of the bottle.

He collects old masters and young mistresses.

Man who can read girls like book—usually like to read in bed.

The average man likes to give a girl a present—while the playboy would rather give her a past.

They say Socrates had one wife and one hundred mistresses. I guess he was the original Playboy philosopher.

He can look at a girl's future and tell what kind of a past she's going to have.

He's real broad-minded. In fact, he thinks of nothing else.

Playgirls

Many a girl has made it to the top—because her clothes didn't.

She is looking for an older man with a strong will—made out to her.

When she found out the millionaire was a hunter, she announced to him that she was game.

She is known by the company that keeps her.

She doesn't mind if he's a cad—as long as his convertible is too.

SECRETARY: "Where did you get that beautiful mink coat? I've been struggling for years to get one!"
PLAYGIRL: "Darling, you mustn't struggle."

Say, that's a beautiful chinchilla—how much did you *play* for it?

The only time she says "Stop" is when she's sending a telegram.

She's the good time that was had by all.

She believes it's every man for herself.

She's had more hands on her than a doorknob.

A fond mother, whose daughter had not come home at the usual time, grew worried at her absence, so she telegraphed five of her daughter's best friends, asking where Mary was. Shortly after her daughter's return, the answers to her telegrams arrived. Each one read, "Don't worry, Mary is staying with me tonight."

Everybody has her number—if not, they can get it on the wall of every phone booth and men's room in town.

When she reached seventeen her voice started changing—from NO to YES.

She's so kind to animals, she'd do anything for a chinchilla or even a mink, or as a last resort—a fox.

When she gets up in the morning she feels like a new man.

"Why do you have so many boy friends?"
"I give up!"

MAN: "What do you give to a man who has everything?"
PLAYGIRL: "My phone number."

For Christmas she wanted an Italian sports car—with the Italian sport still in it.

391

She likes men who lay their cards on the table: Diner's Club, American Express, Carte Blanche.

FRIEND: "I'm gonna marry a real go-getter."
PLAYGIRL: "Not me—I want a man who's already got it."

I gave him up—I can't afford anybody who can't afford me.

Her baby came from a long line that she listened to.

She owes everything to the director who made her.

She doesn't care for a man's company—unless he owns it.

PLAYGIRL AT PERFUME COUNTER: "Do you have something that will bring out the chinchilla in a man without disturbing the wolf?"

The playgirl was asked: "What do you give a man who has everything?" She replied: "Encouragement, dear, encouragement."

Poems
(*see Limericks*)

I bought my girl a pair of garters,
In the five and ten,
She gave them to her mother,
It's the last I'll see of them!

When nature spelled him out,
She made a sad mistake,
And spelled him with a double "D,"
A most horrific fate,
She meant him for a ladies' man,
But a laddies' man was he!
A sad mistake, a horrific fate,
To be spelled as he with a double "D."

I met a little shop girl,
Her name was Tillie Gall,
And every time I kissed her,
She asked: "Will that be all?"

If I should run for office,
I wouldn't be a dope,
I'd only kiss the babies who,
Are old enough enough to vote.

Burning his candle at both ends,
Makes him look like a fright,
Watching the office clock all day,
And television all night!

To drink and drive and still survive,
My friend, the safer scheme,
Is pour the whiskey in your tank and
drink the gasoline.

It's easy to grin when your ship
comes in,
And you've got the stock market beat.
But the lad worthwhile is the man
who can smile,
When his shorts are too tight in the
seat.

A pink brassiere was the gift he gave,
To the gal he loved and trusted.
But she sold the thing for
cold hard cash,
For she was a gal flat-chested.

Mamma saw a light by chance,
That made her pale and wan;
The maid was pressing papa's pants
And papa had them on.

Jack be nimble, Jack be quick,
Jack jumped over the candlestick.
Alas, he didn't clear the flame,
And now he's known as Auntie Mame.

Kiss me, darling,
Hold me tight,
I want to get some practice,
For my date tomorrow night.

392

I met a girl the other night,
It was strictly fun, no sorrow.
How could I forget that sight,
The case comes up tomorrow!

An oversexed lady named Bright,
Insisted on six times a night,
A fellow called Fedder,
Had the nerve to wed her—
His chance of survival is slight.

Sweet Vivian's a golfer,
Which causes quite a stir,
'Cause all the men are anxious,
To play a round with her.

Police
(*see Crimes, Court Rooms, Lawyers, etc.*)

"You're wanted for a safecracking job."
"Fine! I'll take the position."

POLICE SERGEANT: "You here again?"
HE: "Yeah. Any mail?"

GIRL: "Stop that man: he wanted to kiss me."
COP: "That's all right, miss. There'll be another along in a minute."

I showed the cop the badge I got for doing the police benefit. Until then I never knew what to do with the badge —and it had eight points in it, too.

"How could you let him get away?" the sergeant screamed at the rookie cop. "Did you watch all the exits like I told you?"
"Yes, sir—but he must have left by one of the entrances."

A former salesman became a police officer. After his first day on the job he told his wife, "This is a much better job. The pay may not be as big—but the customer is always wrong."

"You idiot," the cop said to the driver, "how could you hit a man in broad daylight going twenty miles an hour?"
"I'm sorry—my windshield is covered with safety stickers."

"Well, if I was speeding," the woman driver said to the motorcycle cop who finally caught her, "so were you."

An actress I know walked into the homicide division of the police department. "*Please* tell me," she asked, "who do I see to apologize for shooting my husband?"

A policeman in each subway station has been of big help. Up until today— not one train has been stolen.

COP TO MOTORIST: "I'd give you a ticket—if I could find a place to park my motorcycle."

The bridge party was going along fine—until the cops looked under the bridge.

"Let's hurry into the patrol wagon, mother, or we'll never get a seat."

Dad is always bothered by flat feet —they keep giving him speeding tickets.

My uncle is now with the police— they finally caught up with him.

Nothing will improve your driving— like having a police car following you.

The baby was born in a taxi and the policeman was pressed into duty. The husband begged the cop to help. A smack on the backside and the child let go with a yell that could be heard around the block. Now the father really got hysterical and started hollering, "Police brutality!"

393

A Southern town has this poster with the legend: "Help support your local police—bribe them."

Politics
(*see Republicans, Democrats, etc.*)

If any more actors get into office in California, that will be the only state in the union with their own marquee.

The Democrats were smarter this election. Every place the Republicans went they left big tips and said, "Vote Republican." The Dems were smarter —they left no tips and they said, "Vote Republican."

Hermione Gingold says it wouldn't do any harm to have more actors in politics—politicians are such bad actors.

Every American has a chance to become President—that's one of the risks he has to take.

He never voted—he wouldn't know how to vote—he doesn't even pull the curtain when he takes a shower.

I'm glad George Murphy and Ronald Reagan won—now I don't have to watch them in pictures.

Georgie Jessel buried Presidential hopeful Thomas E. Dewey with one sentence—at a Madison Square Garden rally: "Yes, Dewey is a fine man, and so is my Uncle Morris. My Uncle Morris shouldn't be President and neither should Dewey. Good night."

So what if Rockefeller loses New York State? He can always buy New Jersey.

I like the straightforward way you dodged all those issues.

FANNY: "Why don't they ever have a woman President?"
ESTHER: "A President has to be over forty years of age and a great leader of men—and you know as well as I do that no man would follow a woman after she's forty years old."

He was an unsuccessful politician, poor but dishonest. He went to his ward leader. "I have thirty votes in my family and I control two hundred more. Why can't I be an Assemblyman?"

After a little persuasion, the leader ran him for office, and he was elected. Two years later he was back again with a request to become a Congressman. The leader granted this request, too, and he was elected. Four years later he asked to be run for Governor. Again the leader consented and again he won.

Soon he was back again and said to the boss, "You must do me another favor."

"What now?" screamed the head politician. "I made you an Assemblyman, I made you a Congressman and I made you a Governor. What do you want me to do now? Make you President?"

"No," whimpered the Governor, "make me a citizen."

"What do you think is to blame for all our problems with the countries in Europe?" asked the interviewer of the Senator. "The trouble with American foreign relations," replied the Senator, "is that they're all broke."

They don't have to tell lies about each other—the truth is bad enough.

If actors keep going into politics we may get the next election results from a Price-Waterhouse envelope.

FIRST CITIZEN: "It must be terrible for two great political leaders to split."

SECOND CITIZEN: "Not if they split 50-50."

He stands for what he thinks people will fall for.

The debate was hot and heavy when he hit below the belt: "What about the powerful interests that control you?" "You keep my wife out of this."

The judge died and a lawyer rushed over to the club leader offering himself as a candidate to take the dead judge's place. "I have no objection," the leader said, "but you'll have to arrange it with the undertaker."

That new South American President is a fine man, wasn't he?

I know one Congressman so unpopular that one year he ran unopposed—and still lost.

Mayor Lindsay would rather be in show business. I hear he asked Mike Nichols to direct his next election campaign.

I voted five times, but they can't do anything to me—I'm not a citizen.

They elected him to Congress—anything to get him out of town.

"We hang the petty thieves and appoint the great ones to public office." —Aesop

George Washington is the only man who didn't blame the previous administration for his troubles.

Mayor Lindsay has been doing more shows than any of the comics in town. When his secretary reminded him to be at City Hall at 10:30 A.M. he asked, "Why? What's playing there?"

One of those staunch, rabid Democrats was making his point: "I don't think you'd vote Republican if the Good Lord himself were running on the Republican ticket."
"I should say not—he'd have no business to change now."

When Winston Churchill was asked about what great qualifications were most essential for a politician he said, "It's the ability to foretell what will happen tomorrow, next month, and next year—and to explain afterward why it didn't happen."

One Congressman to another: "I'd hate to have to go out and make a living under these laws we just passed."

George Romney, as a young campaigner, showed that he knew how to win votes. Stumping the Detroit suburbs, he stepped into a police station and found a patrolman booking a prisoner. Romney's comment to the officer: "I see you got one. Good for you." Then to the prisoner: "I hope everything works out all right."

1ST WOMAN: "What do you think about Red China?"
2ND WOMAN: "Only on a white tablecloth."

One Senator coming out of the Capitol to another: "You spend a billion here, a billion there, and the first thing you know it adds up."

Politics, or
How I Roast the Politicians
by Joey Adams

"Rockefeller said he wouldn't be drafted," I said about the Governor who was sitting next to me. "He meant the army."
The occasion was the Governor's

dinner for scholastic achievement at the Hilton Hotel. It was the day Nelson Rockefeller chose to run. "I know why he decided to go for the Presidency," I continued. "His brother Winthrop wants to be Attorney General." The Governor loves to be ribbed and will often invite me to roast him publicly, and of course, I am happy to please him: "I can't understand why he wants the job—it means he'll have to move into a smaller house. He's so rich, he'll have to put the White House in his wife's name.

"One thing about Rocky, he treats his kids like any normal children. When his new boy was born he gave him an ordinary set of blocks—51st Street, 52nd Street, 53rd Street. . . . Rockefeller has a ranch in Venezuela—in fact, his ranch *is* Venezuela. Rocky is so rich, he sends care packages to Kennedy."

In this era of masochistic comedy, our most famous personalities have accepted testimonials just to be carved to pieces by murderers who don't get the chair, unless it's the center one on some dais, to trigger the slaughter of a poor suspecting guest. This honored guest is sworn to take it. It's laugh and the world laughs with you—cry and you're a poor sport.

Mayor John Lindsay of New York is the easiest target of all because he likes to be a comedian himself. While Reagan, Murphy, and Shirley Temple were switching to politics, Lindsay was looking to get into show business. After the mayor's speech for the AGVA Youth Fund at the Americana Hotel I said, "You were very funny, John—not tonight—at City Hall. You are one of the funniest mayors in America."

"Lindsay," I said with my arm around the Mayor, "is still a non-candidate for President or Vice-President but the truth is he would rather play the Latin Quarter than City Hall. In fact,

he just hired Mike Nichols to direct his next election campaign."

"But that doesn't mean he doesn't take care of his city. He just worked out a great scheme to alleviate traffic in New York—he's making the entire city one way north—then it becomes Connecticut's problem."

A sense of humor is what makes you laugh at something that would make you mad if it happened to you. But given the choice, politicians would rather be rapped than ignored. You can always pick out politicians by the glazed look that comes into their eyes when the conversation wanders away from themselves. And anyway, there is nothing they can do about it—"He who laughs last—is a loser."

"You have my vote, Senator Goldwater," I said to the Presidential candidate, "but I also voted for Tom Dewey, Alf Landon and Wendell Willkie."

Barry Goldwater laughed the loudest when I said, "You remember his slogan—'In your heart you know he's right.' The trouble is he's so far right he's on a bias."

Senator Goldwater said in his speech, "I'd rather be right than President."

"Don't worry," I concluded, "you'll never be either."

The biggest asset a candidate needs is to be able to take it. And the bigger you are the bigger the target.

"Robert F. Kennedy does not want to be President," I said to the thousand men who had come to honor the late Senator. "He wants to be King." Of course, Bobby's laugh was the loudest and the longest. He often called me to rib him publicly. It made him one of the boys.

Kennedy's pals told me that I could go the limit. R.F.K. insisted that he be treated like any other fall guy. I unloaded my biggest guns:

"Bobby wants to be President—and he does have lots of experience. His first job out of school was counselor at camp—his second job was Attorney General.

"When he ran for Senator his father cautioned him, 'Don't worry, son. If you lose New York—I'll buy you New Jersey!'

"Bobby is five foot 7 inches tall—when he takes a haircut—he's five foot two. And he just doesn't take a haircut. First he gets an estimate—then he takes gas.

"Senator Kennedy is really smart. He likes to have residences all over the country. Just in case he decides to run from anyplace. He has a house in New York. A house in Maryland. A house in Massachusetts. And right now he has his eye on 1600 Pennsylvania Avenue. But the word I get is that the present tenants still aren't ready to move.

"They called him a carpetbagger when he ran for Senator from New York. They said he didn't know New York at all. All lies. So what if he thought that Rockefeller Center was the Governor's navel?

"Bobby now has a vigorous image for the Youth of America—and he's produced a good many of them. When he comes home he doesn't ask 'What's new?' He asks, 'Who's new'?"

Republican leader Len Hall has come under my scalpel many times. Len ran the campaign for President Eisenhower. But he since has bombed out with Goldwater, Nixon and Romney. Naturally, I used this to advantage.

"May I suggest," I faced Hall at one Fall Guy Luncheon, "that you run Nasser's campaign. If you could do for his career what you did for Romney, Nixon and Goldwater—"

"Hall," was my final stab, "has taken our biggest names and made unknowns out of them."

The Fall Guy Luncheons at the Garden City Hotel in Long Island have roasted everybody from Robert Moses to Guy Lombardo. Hundreds of businessmen, politicians and executives show up to make sure my roast is well done.

"It's been said that Robert Moses is the greatest public servant in the history of our town," I said about the controversial head of the World's Fair, "and now I'd like to introduce the man who said it—Bob Moses."

I had my hand on his shoulder when I remarked, "The only way to get in touch with him—you have to write him on a *tablet*—he thinks he's the *real* Moses."

"Richard Nixon," I suggested to a mixed group of Republicans and Democrats, "couldn't win if he ran unopposed. He couldn't carry the south if he came out for slavery."

"Naturally," I always say, "I only give the big needle to my friends." Which is the excuse to open all the wounds before I sew them up again.

"Nixon," I said lovingly, "is a nice man. My Uncle Morris is also a nice man. My Uncle Morris shouldn't be President—and neither should Nixon.

"I must admit that I'm the one who suggested that he run. In fact, I remember the exact words I used—I said, 'Richard, you got about as much chance to be President as I have.

"The former Vice-President," I suggested, "has been ready and willing to run for the Presidency for years. Now if he were only able."

I once said about Thomas Dewey, the stuffy almost-President of the United States, "Dewey is a great man —people often compare him to St. Paul—one of the dullest towns in America.

"You never hear about Governor Dewey's family—they are doing their best to keep it quiet."

Senator Gene McCarthy is a new target for the sharpshooters. "He is perfectly familiar with all the questions of the day," I said. "The trouble is he doesn't know the answers.

"I like the straightforward way he dodges all the issues—he's full of indecision."

Of course, I always smile lovingly at a candidate when I explode. Then I must finish with a compliment: "I predict that Senator Gene McCarthy will be the next President of the United States—but I also predicted that Zsa Zsa Gabor would join the Peace Corps."

Another happy target is Mayor Sam Yorty of Los Angeles. "Sam," I said, "has finally solved the smog problem in Los Angeles—he's putting up the street signs in braille—now the tourists can feel the sights and go home."

"He speaks straight from the shoulder," I said about Governor Reagan. "Too bad his words don't start higher up."

The former song and dance man is another easy foil. "When you talk about Governor Reagan running for President," I said at a dinner the other day, "you should mention experience, knowledge and ability—because those are three things he hasn't got.

"I'm sorry that his contemporaries couldn't be here tonight. People he went to school with, like Francis X. Bushman, Alice Faye and the ever popular Mae Busch.

"I hope he wins," I said affectionately, "and stays in politics—now I won't have to watch him in pictures any more.

"Reagan," I proclaimed, "made so much money betting on Democrats—he became a Republican."

There are no sacred cows in politics. I once introduced Congressman Adam Clayton Powell as "The handsomest, most talented and most dynamic member of Congress—that's all admitted. And he's the one who admits it."

"Cargo," I said, facing the smiling Governor of New Mexico, "is one politician who doesn't mind when you tell lies about him—it's the truth he doesn't want to hear."

"Much has been said and written about Mayor Daley," I said in introducing the Chicago boss, "and he is here tonight to deny it."

If you get a reputation as the Big Needle, the politicians think you don't like them—if you don't throw a few barbs when you introduce them or talk about them. Sometimes their campaign managers suggest a punch line. Even the candidates themselves have put scalpels in my mouth.

Vice-President-hopes-to-be-President Hubert Humphrey is a marathon talker. One of his aides suggested a line which I switched when I followed one of his one-man debates: "I finally found out why talk is cheap—there's more supply than demand."

When LBJ decided he's had it and HHH decided he hasn't I said, "Every American has a chance to be President—that's one of the risks he has to take.

"Hubert Humphrey," I said, "has been around the President for years and is very familiar with all the questions of the day—the trouble is he doesn't know the answers.

"I think HHH is the greatest. And that's not only my opinion—it's his too."

If I didn't like him I could never say, "People say our Vice-President is in the shadow of our President—but that's not true. They even have a Hubert Humphrey doll on the market now. You wind it up and for four years it does nothing.

"Our Vice-President is an authority on what's going on around the world. 'The trouble with our foreign relations,' says our future President, 'is that they're always broke.'"

Nobody respects or loves our President more than I. But if I didn't throw a line at him he would think I was ill. When the polls recently showed that LBJ's popularity was increasing every day, I said, "That's no surprise—even your mother-in-law is popular when she says she's leaving."

A politician is one who goes to great lengths to say nothing; then complains when no one quotes him.

Poor
(*see Money, Rich, etc.*)

One thing about being poor—it's inexpensive.

There is one advantage to being poor —the doctor will cure you faster.

To paraphrase Honest Abe, "The Internal Revenue Bureau must love the poor people—it's created so many of them."

He's such a poor psychiatrist—whenever he gets a patient, he has to run out and rent a couch.

They're never going to cure poverty —but the way taxes are going up—they're sure going to cure wealth.

He took a taxi to court where he had filed for bankruptcy—then he invited the cab driver in as a creditor.

Between the new taxes, inflation, and the stock market, we are creating a new class of nouveau poor.

He was the pet of the family—they were too poor to have a dog.

I was so poor as a child, I was made in Japan.

The Texan was so poor that the telephone in his Rolls Royce was on a party line.

The poor little boy was born on the Lower East Side of poverty-stricken parents. He grew up and married a neighborhood girl and had three children. He struggled for years but suddenly his luck changed and he became a billionaire. He bought homes in Paris, Beverly Hills, Hong Kong and the Riviera—but he never forgot.

Every year he returns to the Lower East Side—just to visit his wife and children.

All this talk of war on poverty inspired one Chinese restaurant in Chinatown to come out with *misfortune* cookies.

Popularity

She's so unpopular—she comes home with the same lipstick she started out with.

She is so unpopular—her phone doesn't even ring when she's in the shower.

She is so popular—she has her number in the yellow pages.

He'd be more popular if he were as well-known as his jokes.

She gets more phone calls than a bookie and more visitors than a fair.

Best thing about those new popular songs—they're not popular long.

The popular girl is the one who waxes her zipper to make it work smoothly, silently, and conveniently.

Presidential Wit
(*Also look under FDR, LBJ, Kennedy, Truman, etc.*)

CALVIN COOLIDGE: Once when Mrs. Coolidge wasn't able to go to church with the President on Sunday, she asked him at lunch what the sermon was about.

"Sin," he said in his usual talkative manner.

"Well, what did he say about sin?"

"He was against it."

HERBERT HOOVER: Mr. Hoover was asked once, "What do retired Presidents do?"

"Madam, we spend our time taking pills and dedicating libraries."

ULYSSES S. GRANT: "I only know two tunes; one of them is "Yankee Doodle," and the other isn't."

THOMAS JEFFERSON: "Never buy what you do not want because it is cheap; it will be dear to you."

THEODORE ROOSEVELT: "I think there is only one quality worse than hardness of heart and that is softness of head."

WILLIAM HOWARD TAFT: President Taft was campaigning in hostile territory. Somebody threw a cabbage at him. It rolled in front of the President's feet. "I see," he said, "that one of my adversaries has lost his head."

WOODROW WILSON: "A conservative man is a man who just sits and thinks, mostly sits."

DWIGHT DAVID EISENHOWER: "Gosh, someone around here is always feeding me those 'folksy' phrases. Hell, I'm folksy enough as it is, without their trying to make matters worse."

Prostitutes
(*see Mistress*)

Doctor to woman of ill-repute: "Sorry, you'll have to be on your feet for two or three days—but don't worry, I'll have you back in bed in no time at all."

Three women of Shady Lane were brought before the bar of justice for soliciting. At the same time a little peddler was brought before the court for peddling without a license. "What do you do for a living?" the judge asked the first girl.

"I'm a milliner."

"For not telling the truth—thirty days."

The next girl said she was a dressmaker. The judge give her thirty days for lying. The third girl admitted she was a prostitute. "That's all we care about in this court: truth. Suspended sentence," he barked. Next came the little peddler. "What do you do for a living?" the judge asked.

"To tell the truth," he answered, "I'm a prostitute."

The man went to the "House" and asked for Elsie. Before he left he gave her 200 dollars. She was so pleased and welcomed him the next day. Again he gave her 200 dollars. He did the same thing the third day.

"I never met a customer like you," she admitted. "Three days in a row you give me 200 dollars. How can I ever thank the person who sent you to me? Who recommended me?"

"Your sister in Hungary gave me 600 dollars to bring to you."

"I'm not going to no more psychiatrists," said the call girl. "I just don't see any future in going to a guy who tells me to lie down on a couch and then sends me a bill."

The shady lady in town, after piling up "fins" and sins, decided to salve her conscience by giving away a sizable sum to the local Community Chest, which had a drive for funds. She called up the committee chairman and said, "Honey, I'd like to make a donation of five thousand bucks to the Community Chest."

The chairman, aghast at her audacity, said frostily, "Madam, and I don't use the term loosely, I wouldn't dream of taking your money. We don't need that kind of money," and slammed the phone down.

A week later she called again and upped the ante to ten thousand. Again he refused and hung up.

A few days passed and this time she called with an offer of twenty-five thousand dollars. At this, the chairman called the committee together and asked them what he should do. One of the men spoke up and said, "Take it, jerk, it's our money anyway!"

A voluptuous redhead walked up to the window in the bank and plunked down fifty twenty-dollar gold pieces. A big grin appeared on the teller's face and he said, "Naughty girl, you've been hoarding, haven't you?"

"Listen, wise guy," snapped the redhead, "it's none of your business how I earned this money; all you got to do is deposit it!"

I'm not sure what she does for a living—but I do know she was asked to leave her hotel because she entertained more enlisted men than the USO.

I lived in one house of ill-repute for two weeks—now that's what I call room service.

Abe was fifty-eight years old and his doctor just told him that he either retired or expired. Confronting his fifty-five-year-old wife, Molly, with this tale, and the fact that they had nothing in the bank, depressed Abe.

MOLLY: "Don't worry, Abe. I'll support us."

ABE: "But Molly, you're fifty-five and you never did a day's work in your life. What are you going to do?"

MOLLY: "I'll walk the streets. That every woman knows how to do."

With that remark Molly left the house and returned at 5 A.M., and handed Abe a roll of bills and some change. Gleeful and surprised, Abe counted the money of her night's work.

ABE: "Eighteen, nineteen, twenty dollars and four dimes. You did all right, Molly. But tell me, who gave you the dimes?"

MOLLY: "They all did."

She went berserk—she worked in the brothel for three years—and then found out the other girls were being paid.

This one woman of ill-repute refuses to admit married men to her house. Her motto is, "I cater to the needy—not the greedy."

Proverbs
(*see Quotations, Sayings, etc.*)

Do unto others—before they do unto you.

People who live in glass houses—should use their neighbor's bathroom.

Be kind to the lady you're married to—the wife you save may be your own.

A fool and his money—are some party.

Opportunity knocks but once—if the house detective doesn't beat him to it.

A woman's word is never done.

To err is human—but it feels divine.

All the world loves a lover—except her husband.

This is still a free country—where a man can do as his wife pleases.

It is better to have loved and lost—much better.

The ten best years in a woman's life come between 28 and 30.

A man is only as old as he looks—and if he only looks, he's old.

Pretty soon all the drive-in theatres will be open and people will quit watching movies again.

Most of us spend a lifetime going to bed when we're not sleepy and getting up when we are.

There's no fool like an old fool—he's had more experience.

Two heads are better than one—except during a hangover.

Money talks—but all I ever hear it say is good-bye.

Talk is cheap—except when you want to hire a lawyer.

Marry in haste—and repent at her lawyer's.

It takes two to make a quarrel—and the same number to get married.

Psychiatrists
(*see Doctors, Nurses, Hospitals, Analysis, etc.*)

The psychiatrist asked the troubled man how long he had been thinking he was a dog. "Since I was a puppy," the man replied.

The man relaxing on the couch said, "You know the girl whose hair I used to stick in the inkwell?"
"Oh yes," the psychiatrist said. "Ever see her?"
"Only when I want to fill my fountain pen," the man said.

A psychiatrist is a guy who uses other heads to make money.

One chap had a distinct fear of telephones. When they rang, he just wouldn't answer. But the psychiatrist took care of that. After considerable analysis the man was cured. Now he answers the phone whether it rings or not.

A beautiful girl walked into the psychiatrist's office and he leaped at her, kissing her. When he pulled away he said, "Well, that takes care of my problems, now what's on your mind?"

"My husband beats drums all day."
"So what, nothing wrong in playing drums, thousands do it—even professionally."
"From the inside?"

How rich can they get? This couple have a sleep-in psychiatrist and she likes it.

"What's your trouble?"
"I prefer bow ties to long ties."
"So what? Thousands of people prefer bow ties. In fact—so do I."
"You do? How do you like yours—fried or boiled?"

I feel badly about the cowboy star who had to kiss his horse at the end of every picture. Now he's beginning to look forward to it—and it's a male horse, too.

Two psychiatrists met in the lobby. One said hello. The other kept walking, then stopped. "I wonder what he meant by that?" he asked himself.

"I have twelve children and just found out my husband doesn't love me."
"Imagine if he *did!*"

"I don't drink or smoke or go with girls—and I'm going to celebrate my eighteenth birthday tomorrow."
"How?"

"I've been troubled for years by a superiority complex."
"So, why don't you take treatments?"
"I can't—it belongs to my mother-in-law."

There's a psychiatrist who has hit on a new kind of shock treatment—he sends the bill first.

Know the difference between a neurotic, a psychotic, and a psychiatrist? The neurotic builds castles in the air, the psychotic lives in them, and the psychiatrist collects the rent.

A guy went to a psychiatrist and said, "Doc, don't waste my time. I got two questions. Just answer them. First, could I possibly be in love with an elephant?"
"Of course not," said the doc. "Now what's the other question?"
"Where can I get rid of a rather large engagement ring?"

Harry Hershfield tells it: Sam Schwartz went to an analyst who said, "What can I do for you?" Sam Schwartz replied, "What can *you* do for *me?* I'm Napoleon! I have my army ready, we're going to attack France again! You can do nothing for *me*. It's my wife, Josephine. She keeps telling people her name is Mrs. Schwartz."

These were his terse instructions: "And when you check out of this hospital, come and see me in my private office."
A week later, bedraggled and worn and his face a chlorophyll green, Eddie went to see the doctor. "Good grief," he exclaimed, "what happened?"
"You and your lousy instructions!" Eddie moaned. "I cut out the starches and sweets, but the one cigar a day damn near killed me. You see, doc, I never smoked before in all my life."

This fellow awoke one morning and discovered lilies growing right out of the top of his head. He ran right down to his psychiatrist's office. The head-shrinker stared at the flowers. He said, "Why, this is fantastic. Now where on earth do you suppose those flowers came from?" The guy yelled, "Look at the card! See who sent them!"

Which reminds me of the Sam Levenson story about the woman who confessed to the psychiatrist that her husband blew smoke rings during the day. The psychiatrist said, "Lots of men do that."
"But," said the woman, "my husband doesn't smoke."

"Lie down here on the couch," her psychiatrist said.
"I'd rather not—that's how all my trouble started."

A man dressed in mid-eighteenth-century garb approached a psychiatrist and told him, "I'm Abraham Lincoln." Then he whispered, "Doc, I've got a serious problem. I think my wife's trying to get rid of me. She keeps insisting that I take her to the theatre."

A man visited a psychiatrist because he thought he was President Nasser. The head-shrinker assured him that it wasn't too serious a delusion. "A lot you know," moaned the man. "I happen to be Jewish."

A psychiatrist was explaining to her patient. "Now, you mustn't continually say you're Adam. It's just nonsense and an absurdity of your mind. You couldn't have been the first man." "Skip the long talk, doc, that's what caused all the trouble between me and my wife."

A fellow ran into a psychiatrist's office and told the head-shrinker, "My girl friend thinks she's a rabbit."
"Bring her in," suggested the dome doctor, "I think I can help."
"You certainly can," said the man. "If she comes to see you, don't cure her."

He calls himself "The Friendly Psychiatrist." He lies down on the couch with you—they call this socialized medicine.

There is nothing wrong with a psychiatrist that a few wealthy neurotics can't remedy.

"You've done me a lot of good," she said to the psychiatrist as she shot him, "but I'm afraid now you know too much."

PATIENT: "I've been misbehaving and my conscience is bothering me."
DOCTOR: "I see—and you want something to strengthen your will power?"
PATIENT: "No—something to weaken my conscience."

Two psychiatrists met on the street and one said to the other: "You're fine —how am I?"

I go to a very poor psychiatrist. He can't afford a couch—uses a cot.

My psychiatrist is very busy—he has an upper and lower berth.

Two Hollywood characters ran into each other at the door of their psychiatrist's office. "Hello, dere," said one. "Are you coming or going?"
"If I knew that," said the other, "I wouldn't be here."

Punch Lines
(also look under Sayings, Proverbs, Quotations, etc.)

Things are so bad in the garment center—the manufacturers are laying off their sons-in-law.

Things are so bad, one store on 6th Avenue had a sign reading "PRE-FIRE Sale."

A drunk dropped a penny in the sewer and looked up at the clock atop City Hall to see how much he weighed.

The greatest points of interest in Las Vegas continue to be 7 and 11.

There's a new perfume in Europe that's guaranteed to drive the Europeans crazy—it smells like American money.

When a woman gains too much weight, it's a crime—so—she buys a girdle to make the punishment fit the crime.

Much of the name-dropping done in Hollywood is done in the divorce courts.

We're going to have all honest politicians from now on—there is nothing left to steal.

It happened while she was under the influence of mink.

Took her four years to get a sheepskin and one night to get a mink.

She gave him a choice of a new bracelet or a nervous breakdown.

I thought I saw the handwriting on the wall—till I realized I was in a men's smoking room.

Quizzes

I saw one contestant on TV win a radio, TV set, washing machine, automobile and refrigerator—and he was one of the losers.

Groucho once asked a model who appeared on his quiz show about her most exciting experience. The girl couldn't come up with one. "A model with no exciting memories?" Groucho said unbelievingly. "What are you modeling—clay?"

These days the quiz shows give away laughs instead of big money. I remember one quiz show where the sponsor had to give up his business after only three weeks on the air—by mistake they gave away his factory.

Now you win things nobody can use. One couple on their honeymoon, married only three days, won an electric blanket. But they couldn't use it—he was A.C. and she was D.C.

I remember once on a quiz show a fellow won a trip to New Zealand. That was six years ago. Last I heard he was still in New Zealand—trying to win a trip back.

On one TV quiz show, a woman won a vacation and dropped dead from the shock. But the sponsors kept their word and they sent her body to Bermuda for two weeks.

Playgirls never go into quiz contests—they can get what they want by merely answering only *one* question.

My friend Jan Murray had the greatest idea for the biggest give-away program of them all. It's called "State Your State." You hold up a handful of dirt. If the contestant guesses what state the dirt is from—you give him the whole state. You play that for fifty weeks, and then you move on to Europe. Imagine winning Russia—who would want it?

They now have a new twist in quiz shows. They call you up on the telephone and if you are home—they borrow twenty dollars from you.

Quotations
(also look under Sayings, Proverbs, Punch Lines)

GENERAL CUSTER: "I never saw so many Gahdam Indians."

MOTTO FOR SUBWAYS AND BUSES: "The public be jammed."

TOMMY MANVILLE: "The trouble with men is they know all about women but nothing about wives."

MOREY AMSTERDAM: "My wife is an interior decorator—she wants to get rid of me because I clash with the drapes."

GEORGIE KAYE: "A psychiatrist is a man you see when you're going crazy—and he helps you."

JIM BACKUS: "Many a man owes his success to his first wife—and his second wife to his success."

VIRGINIA GRAHAM: "Men and women are equal—but don't let him know it."

405

CHARLES BOYER: "I'm French, so I never discuss politics, cooking, or women. I simply enjoy all three."

OSCAR WILDE: "Morality is simply an attitude we adopt toward people whom we personally dislike."

TALLEYRAND: "I'm not interested in facts—I want the truth."

JOHN BARRYMORE: "Brides aren't happy—just triumphant."

PHILIP WYLIE: "In the old days men rode chargers—now they marry them."

ARTHUR GODFREY: "Common sense gets a lot of credit that belongs to cold feet."

SHOLEM ALEICHEM: "If somebody tells you you have two ears like a donkey, pay no attention. But if two people tell you—buy yourself a saddle."

DALE CARNEGIE: "Success is getting what you want—happiness is wanting what you get."

WINSTON CHURCHILL: "Eating words has never given me indigestion."

AMOS AND ANDY: "Relatives is like radishes. Just when you think you has heard the last of them—there they are again."

OSCAR WILDE: "If one could only teach the English how to talk and the Irish how to listen, society in London would be more civilized."

MAURICE CHEVALIER: On how it feels to be eighty: "Not so bad, considering the alternative."

HAITIAN PROVERB: "Do not insult the mother alligator until after you have crossed the river."

MARK TWAIN: "Few of us can stand prosperity—another man's, I mean."

BENJAMIN FRANKLIN: "In three days guests, like fish, begin to stink."

FRED ALLEN: "There's a little good in everybody. In fact, even a Mickey Finn has a couple of good drops of whiskey in it."

AVA GARDNER: "Petting is the study of the anatomy in braille."

TALLYRAND: "She is intolerable—but that is her only fault."

GEORGE BERNARD SHAW: "Do not do unto others as you would that they should do unto you. Their taste may not be the same."

JOHN BARRYMORE: "You never realize how short a month is until you pay alimony."

JOHN RUSKIN: "Remember that the most beautiful things in the world are useless—like peacocks and lilies for instance."

MONTAIGNE: "A good marriage would be between a blind wife and a deaf husband."

WILSON MIZNER: "The days just prior to marriage are like a snappy introduction to a tedious book."

FRANKLIN: "God heals and the doctor takes the fees."

GENE FOWLER: "A fool and his money can go places."

MARK TWAIN: "Be good and you will be lonely."

BALZAC: "A husband and wife who have separate bedrooms have either drifted apart or found happiness."

406

AARON BURR: "The rule of my life is to make business a pleasure—and pleasure my business."

OSCAR WILDE: "Plain women are always jealous of their husbands. Beautiful women never are. They are always too busy with being jealous of other people's husbands."

OSCAR WILDE: "Men marry because they are tired—women because they are curious—both are disappointed."

GEORGE BERNARD SHAW: "It is dangerous to be sincere—unless you are also stupid."

OSCAR WILDE: "I can resist everything except temptation."

THE TALMUD: "Tongue in the mouth of woman is one of God's less agreeable blunders."

MELINA MERCOURI: "In Greece we're too poor to go to psychiatrists—we have friends instead."

Race Track
(*see Gambling, Bookmakers, Horse Races, etc.*)

I'm going to the race track today. I hope I break even—I really need the money.

Railroads

The railroad was known for its slowness, but they decided to speed up its service—so they put the stations closer together.

CONDUCTOR: "Madam, are all these children yours or is it a picnic?'"
WOMAN: "They are all mine and believe me, it's no picnic."

"For gos! sakes, conductor, let me off at the next stop. I thought this was a diner."

"Hello! Grand Central? Do you have a sleeping car? Well, wake it up!"

Some people buy auto parts and some live near railroad crossings.

Rape
(*also see Sex, Prostitutes, Love, Romance*)

A man is tried for rape—found guilty of assault with a lively weapon.

"Are those real diamonds?"
"If not—I've been raped."

Ethel was having a baby and confided to her girl friend. "How did it happen?" she asked.
"Well," she explained, "I was watching a Republican parade on 5th Avenue when two guys pulled me into a hallway."
"Why didn't you scream?" asked her confidante.
"What? And have the Republicans think I was cheering for them?"

Real Estate
(*see Suburbs, Homes, Apartment Houses, etc.*)

A sign in front of a real estate office: "WE HAVE LOTS TO BE THANKFUL FOR!"

This afternoon I went over to the real estate office to see a model home but she had already left.

When a real estate agent asked a woman if she wanted to buy a home, she said, "What do I need a home for? I was born in a hospital, educated in a college, courted in an automobile and married in a church. I live out of paper bags and delicatessen stores. I spend my mornings at the golf course, my afternoons at the bridge table and my evenings at the movies. And when I die, I'm gonna be buried at the undertaker's. I don't need a home—all I need is a garage!"

He lived in a very fashionable part of town but he decided he wanted a change. So he called a real estate agent and told him to put his home up for sale.

The very next Sunday, he read the For Sale ad in the *New York Times* and called the agent immediately. "I'm not going to sell my house," he informed him; "your ad convinced me it's just the kind of house I want."

REAL ESTATE AGENT: "First you folks tell me what you can afford, then we'll have a good laugh and go on from there."

The real estate salesman was showing the dilapidated house to a prospective buyer. It looked like one blow would make it collapse like an accordion. "You can do a lot with this place," he enthused.
"Yeah," said the non-buyer, "if you're handy with money."

"You built that house upside-down."
"No wonder I keep falling off the porch!"

"This wall is awfully thin. I can look right through it."
"That's no wall, that's a window."

"How do you like my house as a whole?"
"As a hole it is all right, but as a house no good."

We got an unusual sunken living room. It's still sinking.

It's really a waterproof house. After a rain not a drop leaks out of the cellar.

Records
(*see Books*)

My record is a big smash—I just found out Roulette threw them out of the window.

I'm on the Roulette label. If we do well—they may take me off the label and put me on a record.

I make records because disc jockeys can't spin my books.

My record has been on the radio—it's also been on the chair, on the table, and on the bed.

They now want me to make some recordings with Mickey Spillane—long slaying records.

My records are available in gas stations, meat markets, and pet shops—so far no music stores.

Royalties from my records go to a very good cause—my wife.

Relatives
(*see Mothers-in-Law, Husbands, Wives, Kids, Children, etc.*)

Most relatives live beyond your means.

Blood is thicker than water—and relatives are always punching each other in the nose to prove it.

"Fish and relatives begin to smell bad after three days."—George Bernard Shaw.

My mother always went shopping with a baby carriage and it was two years before I found out a head of lettuce wasn't my brother.

1ST ENGLISHMAN: "My cousin has been staying at my house for six months. I just can't seem to get rid of him."
2ND ENGLISHMAN: "Maybe you should drop him a hint or two?"
1ST ENGLISHMAN: "Oh, I do. . . . Every time I see him I run up to him and say, 'Well, so long.' He just stands there smiling and says, 'Well, hurry back, old man.'"

1ST MAN: "Have you any poor relations?"
2ND MAN: "Not one that I know."
1ST MAN: "Have you any rich relations?"
2ND MAN: "Not one that knows me."

Of all my relations—I like sex the best.

There were ten kids in my family—I never slept alone until I got married.

A harassed husband runs frantically into a drug store.
HUSBAND: "Quick, give me some arsenic for my mother-in-law!"
DRUGGIST: "Have you got a doctor's prescription?"
HUSBAND: "No, I haven't . . . but here's a photograph of her."

The patient lay on the psychiatrist's couch and explained to his doctor that he was haunted by visions of his departed relatives.
PATIENT: "These ghosts are perched on the tops of fence posts around my garden every night. They sit there and watch me and watch me and watch me. What can I do? What can I do?"
PSYCHIATRIST: "That's easy. Just sharpen the tops of the posts."

JUDGE: "So you want a divorce from your wife? Aren't your relations pleasant?"
HUSBAND: "Mine are . . . but hers are horrible."

FRIEND: "Was your uncle's mind sane and vigorous up to the very last minute?"
HEIR: "I don't know . . . they're not reading the will until tomorrow."

They were identical twins: he was twenty-nine, she was twenty-three.

I didn't mind when my wife and my mother-in-law both said, "I do," but when I had to carry them both over the threshold—that was too much.

Max Asnas always likes to take his wife with him to the race track because, as he says, "When I go there I always lose everything I have with me."

He has his wife, three daughters, and his mother-in-law living with him. The only time he gets a chance to open his mouth at home—is to yawn.

The rich never have to seek out their relatives.

Only a friend can become an enemy—a relative is one from the start.

Religion
(look under Resticted, Ethnic Humor, Churches, Bible Humor)

The grocery clerk overheard two nuns debating as to which should drive back to the convent. One said: "You drive, Sister Luke, and I'll pray."

"What's the matter?" Sister Luke countered. "Don't you trust my praying?"

The pretty Catholic girl wanted to marry a nice Jewish boy. The mother of the girl told her daughter, "If he loves you, he'll become a good Catholic. Talk to him, convince him of the great things about the Catholic religion. You're a good talker, honey, you can do it." So she talked and talked to her boyfriend and finally everything was going right. They had even set a wedding date, until one day the girl came home crying and said, "We're not getting married." "But why?" said the mother. "I thought he was convinced of our faith after you talked to him." Her daughter tearfully replied, "That's just it, mom. I talked to him, but I talked too good—now he's going to become a priest."

A Jewish boy and a Catholic boy were arguing. "My priest knows more than your rabbi," the Catholic boy challenged.
"Why not? You tell him everything."

The two youngsters saw the Protestant minister walking down the street. "Who's that Father?" one kid asked. "He's no Father," said the other. "He's got four kids."

The woman was bragging about her son Mark. "He's a lawyer—and making a lot of money."
"How about your son Max? What happened to him?"
"He became a rabbi."
"A rabbi, how nice. How is he doing?"
"By me—that's not a business for a Jew."

The one about the rabbi, the Protestant minister, the Catholic priest and the Baptist minister. They're always meeting to discuss religion. Finally the rabbi says, "Look, we've been meeting for years and all we talk about is religion; why don't we discuss something else? For instance, I'd like to know your vices and I think you'd like to know

mine. For example, I'm a rabbi and I'm not supposed to eat ham or pork; but I'll be honest. I love it. But naturally in my neighborhood I couldn't do it. So once a year I take a little place in the country and I stock up with twenty pounds of ham, ten pounds of pork, and for a week I just lock the door and eat myself into shock. That's my vice."
The Protestant minister says, "Well, ham or pork doesn't interest me, but I do have a vice—I like to take a drink. I'm no Dean Martin, but I like to get loaded once in a while; but of course around my parish, it's impossible. So once a year I take this little place and I stock up with ten cases of booze and for a week I'm fractured. I just lie there stoned—that's my vice."
The Catholic priest says, "Those vices are mild compared to mine. I'll be honest, I like girls, so once a year I take this place in the country and I have this girl, and for a week I'm flyin'. That's my vice."
The three of them looked at the Baptist minister, who hadn't said anything. "Haven't you got any vices?" they asked him. "Well, only one," he said. "I like to gossip!"

Yom Kippur—Instant Lent.

A young man recently quit rabbinical school to become a Catholic priest. Now his mother introduces him as, "My son, the Father."

The Bishop's files were marked "Sacred" and "Top Sacred."

Billy Graham was lecturing to his audience that "Elizabeth Taylor is more to be pitied than censured—we should pray for her."
"I've been praying for her for years," one listener spoke up, "but I never get her."

410

He's so religious—on the Holy days he wears stained glass in his eyeglasses.

A very religious Quaker heard a noise in his house and when he investigated he found a robber. He went for his gun and stood quietly in the doorway pointing at the burglar. "Friend," he said softly, "I would do thee no harm—but thee standest where I am about to shoot."

Republicans
(*see Democrats, Politics, etc.*)

One day Franklin D. Roosevelt gleefully told this story:
An American Marine, ordered home from Guadalcanal, was disconsolate because he hadn't killed even one of the enemy. He stated his case to his superior officer, who said, "Go up on that hill over there and shout: 'To hell with Emperor Hirohito'! That will bring the Japs out of hiding." The Marine did as he was bidden. Immediately a Jap soldier came out of the jungle shouting, "To hell with Roosevelt!"
"And of course," said the Marine, "I couldn't kill a Republican."

I made so much money betting on the Democrats—I became a Republican.

I came from a long line of waiters—Republicans.

FDR met an old neighbor when he was running for a third term as President. "I'm voting Republican," the man insisted. "How come?" F.D.R. asked. "Do you object to my third term?"
"No, Franklin," the neighbor explained. "It's just that I voted Republican the first time you ran, and I voted Republican the second time, and I'm gonna vote Republican again—because I never had it so good."

"You're my second choice," the little old lady said to the Republican candidate. "Thank you," the politician gushed, "and who is your first?"
"Anybody who is running against you," she said.

A Maine farmer had twelve children —all boys, and when they came of age they all voted Republican, just like the father. That is, all except one boy. He was ashamed for the neighbors. One asked, "How come?"
"Well," he explained, "I always bring my boys up to fear the Lord and vote Republican, but this youngest son of mine—the little devil—he learned to read."

One young lawyer from the North wrote to a friend in the South asking about the prospects in his state for an attorney who is honest and Republican.
"As a good lawyer you have a chance," his friend answered, "and as a Republican, the game law will protect you."

The Republicans couldn't carry the South if they came out for slavery.

As a child I never knew what a Republican was. Every time the subject came up they made me leave the room.

Restaurants
(*see Bars, Night Clubs, etc.*)

For one dollar you eat like a horse. If you want to eat like a human being —it costs eight dollars.

CUSTOMER: "There's a fly in my soup."
WAITER: "It's possible—the chef used to be a tailor."

They serve wonderful dishes. The food is lousy—but the dishes are great.

411

A terrible thing just happened to me. I stopped off to grab a bite to eat before the show. I ordered steak, and when I got it I couldn't even cut it. I called the waiter over, and said, "This steak tastes like rubber!" He said, "That's funny, all the other steaks taste like leather!"

A gal ordered a filet mignon, the most expensive dish on the menu. The waiter looked at her escort and said, "What do you wish, sir?" "I wish I hadn't brought her," moaned the guy.

Two men wandered into Chez Vito for dinner and ordered the most expensive dishes and the finest champagne. They looked well groomed but they didn't have a penny between them. When the check arrived, one said to the other, "Let's split the check—you wash and I'll dry."

That restaurant is so high class, they even pick up the check with a fork.

The food is so bad there, instead of a check, the waiter gives you a citation.

When a customer complained to the waiter that the chicken he served him had one leg shorter than the other, the waiter said, "Look, are you gonna eat it or rhumba with it?"

The chef told Jack E. Leonard: "I put my heart into this clam chowder." Jack snapped, "Never mind your heart —put a few clams into it."

I told the waiter I didn't like the looks of the codfish and he said, "If it's looks you want, why don't you order goldfish?"

I said, "Hey, waiter, how long did these eggs boil?" He said, "Five seconds." I said, "Five seconds? But I want three-minute eggs." He said, "I'm sorry, the chef can't hold them in the water for three minutes—burns his hand!"

The restaurant is so swanky, before you use the finger bowls you have to wash your hands.

I asked Max Asnas why he doesn't have a parking lot for his Stage Delicatessen. "If I had a parking lot," he explained, "I wouldn't need a restaurant."

"Fire that waiter—he's a spy!"
"Yes, but the next spy maybe wouldn't be such a good waiter."

HOLDUP MAN TO CASHIER IN CHINESE RESTAURANT: "Give me all your money!"
"To take out?"

Comedian Alan Gale was once about to leave Max's Stage Delicatessen to visit his niece. Max said, "Listen, let me get you some cookies to take her." Gale said, "Forget it, Max, she's only three months old," Max said. "So are the cookies!"

When the restaurant had a big fire, almost twenty-five comics sent the same wire: "The first time the food's been hot in your place in twenty years."

DINER: "Have you any wild duck?"
WAITER: "No sir, but we can take a tame one and irritate it for you."

Those topless waitresses—and I used to complain when the waitress got her *finger* in my soup.

"What's that in my soup?"
"I better call the manager—I can't tell one insect from the other."

The food is untouched by human hands—the chef is a monkey.

The waiters went on a slow-down strike. After one week they had to give it up—nobody noticed the difference.

Restricted
(also look under Integration, Religion, Ethnic Humor)

Groucho Marx was with his wife and daughter when they passed a beautiful swimming pool. It was a very hot Sunday afternoon and they decided to take a dip. The manager was sorry, "but this place is restricted."
"That's okay," Groucho flattened him, "I'm Jewish and my wife is Gentile. That makes my daughter half-Jewish. Do you mind if she goes in the water up to her waist?"

A friend of mine was in Toronto and found himself at a United Jewish Appeal Dinner. The man sitting next to him was a rabbi. "What is your name?" the cleric wanted to know. "Joe Cohen," was the answer.
"Mr. Cohen," the rabbi said, "you're a Jew. You should be proud you're a Jew. There are 80,000 Jews here in Toronto—and not one Jew is in jail."
"Why?" asked Joe. "Is it restricted?"

Dick Gregory walked into a restaurant in the South and sat down at the front table. "I'm sorry," the waitress said, "we don't serve Negroes." "That's okay," he answered, "I don't eat 'em. I'll have some fried chicken."

Dick Gregory says: "I spent six months once, sitting at an Alabama lunch counter waiting to be served. And when they finally served me they didn't have what I wanted."

Sammy Davis jokes about his background: "My mother is Puerto Rican, my father is colored, my wife is Swed-ish, and I'm Jewish. Man, there ain't too many neighborhoods I can move into."

Rich
(see Money, Banks, Business, etc.)

I know a girl who is so wealthy, she has four automobiles. One for each direction. Her car is so low that you don't come in through the side door, you have to come up through a manhole cover.

This man was so rich the finance company owed him money. He had a diamond stomach pump, silver walls and mink garbage. In his house, if you wanted a salad of mixed greens, they served you shredded tens and twenties.

Rockefeller treats his children like any normal kids. They play with blocks like all children: 51st Street, 52nd Street, 53rd Street.

He's so rich, his friend couldn't understand why he didn't trade his car in this year.
"I like this car," he said. "I'm just going to redecorate it a little—take out the swimming pool and put in a bowling alley."

He had a car 100 feet long so he could play tennis on his way to work every afternoon.

His eyes were so bad even his car had a prescription windshield.

They say Rockefeller has a ranch in Venezuela. His ranch *is* Venezuela.

He's so rich—he has bookends for his bank books.

A Hollywood producer is so rich—he's got an unlisted wife.

He was rich but lazy. When his wife wanted to go to the Riviera for the winter he said, "Oh, honey, I don't feel like packing—let's send for it."

Bob Hope evaluating Bing Crosby's wealth: "He's so rich—he sends Care Packages to Nelson Rockefeller."

For a birthday present Rockefeller gave his son a valuable miniature—Rhode Island.

London Lee, the rich comic, says his father is so wealthy that, "When my mother was pregnant with me, he had her morning sickness changed to the afternoon."

I was raised in a home that was so big that when it was 3 P.M. in the kitchen—it was noon in the bathroom.

I once asked my father to buy me what the poor kids had. He said, "What do you want?" I said, "Buy me a slum." He then asked my mother for her okay. She said, "Okay with me—just make sure it's in a nice neighborhood."

He's so rich he has wall-to-wall carpeting in his swimming pool.

He's so rich he has wall-to-wall bank books.

This town is so rich—the station wagons are bigger than the station.

He's so rich he's got monogrammed garbage.

He's so wealthy—he has his garbage gift-wrapped.

He's got so much money he has to pay storage on it.

414

Don Rickles

The murderer with an actor's union card packs them in. Some of the biggest stars pay the minimum wherever he works, just to get killed by him.

TO FRANK SINATRA: "Make yourself at home—hit somebody."

TO ERNEST BORGNINE: "Oh! My gosh! Look at you! Anyone else hurt in the accident?"

TO EDDIE FISHER: "For gosh sakes, next time marry someone famous and keep your name alive."

TO BOB HOPE: "You've got no right to be in this city. The government has no troops stationed here."

TO JACK BENNY: "Before Jack made his reservation here tonight—he called the maitre d' to make sure the tips were included in the minimum."

TO GEORGE MURPHY: "Senator, I'd go into politics too—but I'm already working."

TO MAURY WILLS: "I've watched you play shortstop this season. Take my advice. Improve on the banjo—fast."

TO GEORGE BURNS: "Here's a guy who came to California for arthritis forty years ago—and he's finally got it."

TO LIBERACE: "There's Liberace, folks —he's trying to look inconspicuous with a sequined jacket and a candelabra in his mouth."

TO THE AUDIENCE: "Thanks for the applause, folks. My maid gets a bigger hand when she runs a rag over the piano keys."

Riddles
(*see "Games" chapter*)

How can a girl keep a boy's love?
  By not returning it.

What do you call a church on fire?
  Holy smoke.

What smells like lox, looks like a box, and flies?
  A flying lox-box.

When the clock strikes 13, what time is it?
  Time to have the clock fixed.

What goes farther the slower it goes?
  Money.

Who was the most popular actor in the Bible?
  Sampson. He brought down the house.

To whom does every man take off his hat?
  The barber.

Why is a rabbit's nose always shiny?
  Because he has the powder puff on the wrong end.

How can you make money fast?
  Don't feed it.

What kind of a nut is the guy who goes to see the topless girls?
  A chestnut.

If two is company and three is a crowd, what are four and five?
  Nine.

Why is it useless to send letters to Washington?
  Because he's dead.

What is worse than finding a worm in an apple?
  Finding half a worm.

If you threw a black stone in the Red Sea, what would it become?
  Wet.

What do you get when you lean a corpse against a doorbell?
  A dead ringer.

What do you get if you drop limburger cheese in the toaster?
  You get out of the kitchen fast.

Describe a cow that jumped over a barbed wire fence.
  An utter catastrophe.

Rock 'n' Roll
(*see Music*)

This rock 'n' roller wore a hearing aid for three years—and then found he only needed a haircut.

The waiter dropped a tray of dishes and six couples got up to dance.

Her father threw him out of the window. He came home and saw his daughter doing the frug with her boy friend but he was deaf and didn't hear the music.

The reason most of those rock 'n' roll music combos are so young is that if they were older—they would be embarrassed.

There's a new rock 'n' roll group in Israel called, "The Rolling Cohens."

"You're darn right that music sends you, son—and don't slam the door!"

A rock 'n' roll dancer has no future, it's such a shaky business.

The dance floor was so crowded we had to rock 'n' roll up and down instead of sideways.

415

Will Rogers

Will Rogers had a friendly feud with all film-writing men. His regular greeting to any scenario writer always was: "Hi, boy. What you spoilin' now?"

Yep. The United States never lost a war or won a conference.

Spinnin' a rope is fun—if your neck ain't in it.

Communism to me is one-third practice and two-thirds explanation.

We call Rome the seat of culture—but somebody stole the chair.

Grammar and I get along like a Russian and a bathtub.

We are a nation that runs in spite of and not account of our Government.

I might have gone to West Point but I was too proud to talk to a Congressman.

A bunch of American tourists were hissed and stoned yesterday in France, but not until they had finished buying.

When someone called his attention to his using the word "ain't" he said, "Maybe ain't ain't correct, but I notice that lots of folks who ain't usin' ain't—ain't eatin'!"

Anyone can be a Republican when the market is up, but when stocks is selling for no more than they're worth, I'll tell you—being a Republican is a sacrifice.

Some of the things he said still hold true today:
On foreign policy: "Our dealings are an open book—a check book."

With Congress, every time they make a joke it's a law. And every time they make a law it's a joke.

ON THE AUTOMOBILE: "The only way to solve the traffic problem is to pass a law that only paid-for cars are allowed to use the highways."

Romance
(*see Love, Dates, Engaged, Prostitutes, etc.*)

"What makes you suspect she loves another?"
"Last night she said that I'd have to leave before the milkman came."

He's very romantic and sentimental. He always carries that five-dollar bill in his wallet. It's a keepsake—Lincoln looks like his wife.

I'm looking for a man who will treat me like I was a vote and he was a candidate.

Girls, don't go looking for the ideal man—a husband is easier to find.

Any girl can be had for a song—trouble is, most of them want the wedding march.

She didn't want to get married for money—but she couldn't find any other way to get it.

She broke off the engagement with the rich fella: "I saw him in his bathing suit and he looked so different without his wallet."

The fourth drink and he said, "You know, one more drink and I'll feel it."
And she said, "You know, one more drink and I'll let you."

The devoted fiancé ordered two dozen roses sent to his loved one on her twenty-fourth birthday, with a card: "A rose for every precious year of your life." The florist who was filling the order threw in an extra dozen flowers because the man was one of his best customers. The wedding hasn't taken place yet.

He and I like the same things—we like the same food, the same entertainment, the same sports. The trouble is—we don't like each other.

The wife came home to her husband packing. "Where are you going?" she asked.
"To Australia—there's a shortage of men. The women are paying fifty dollars a night for a romance."
"Unpack," she snarled. "How can you live on fifty dollars a month?"

It's the little things that I like about him—he has a small racing stable, a small yacht and a small mansion.

"Why do you keep refusing to marry me? Is there somebody else?"
"There must be!"

The only way I could really be happy is to combine their qualities—Joey is charming, rich, handsome, witty and brilliant, and Sam wants to marry me.

He fell in love with her at second sight—the first time he met her he didn't know she was rich.

She won't marry him while he's drunk and he won't marry her when he's sober.

The Wit of
Franklin Delano Roosevelt

As a young man with a large family, FDR cracked to a friend: "It's hard nowadays for a man with five children and eleven servants to make a living."

When you get to the end of your rope—tie a knot and hang on.

We all know the story of the unfortunate chameleon which turned brown when placed on a brown rug, and turned red when placed on a red rug, but who died a tragic death when they put him on a Scotch plaid.

I am as busy as a one-armed paperhanger with the itch.

REPORTER: "Will reporters be allowed to use the new swimming pool and play tennis on the White House courts?"
FDR: "Of course, and the children will have a sandpile. You boys can play in it, if you like."

In 1938, Roosevelt was asked to address the Daughters of the American Revolution. He opened his speech: "Fellow immigrants . . . "

FDR's advice to son James on speechmaking:
"Be sincere, be brief, be seated."

FDR commenting on a much needed haircut:
"It got to the point where I had to get a haircut or a violin."

FDR once boasted that he sliced his turkey so thin that: "You can almost read through it."

A radical is a man with both feet planted—in the air. A conservative is a man with two perfectly good legs who, however, has never learned to walk forward. A liberal is a man who uses his legs and his hands at the behest of his head.

Commenting on his affliction, President Roosevelt said:

"I can't move around my office, but what advantage is there in moving around an office anyway? I used to walk the rug in the old days, and what did I accomplish? I wore a hole in the rug."

Royalty
(*see Goofs*)

1ST MAN: "I was presented to the Queen of England."
2ND MAN: "Really? What happened?"
1ST MAN: "She refused me."

My family is so blue-blooded, we never use fountain pens when we write —we just cut our fingers.

Everybody is so impressed with the Queen of England. What's the big deal? She got her job through relatives.

I was invited to the Royal Palace in England. I didn't know what kind of a present to bring—so I brought cash.

When Churchill visited Lord Beaverbrook he was told by one of the servants, "The Lord is walking in the Park."
Churchill replied, "Oh? On the lake, I presume?"

If you're traveling for the government, the first thing they warn you is never touch royalty—especially in Thailand.
There was a time Siamese commoners hid their faces and were forced to bolt their doors so as not to behold their monarch when he passed through the streets. There was a time Thai custom forbade touching royalty under any circumstances. The rule was so strong that many years ago a group of able-bodied swimmers stood around and watched their Queen drown rather than touch her.

When I took a troupe of entertainers with me to Thailand on behalf of the President, we did a command performance for the King and Queen of Siam. After the show their Majesties received us. When one of our dancers came before the Queen she put out her hand. He grabbed it and embraced her, saying, "You're a hell of a gal, Queen."

One of our camera bugs said to the King, "Hey, King—stand over here, will yuh? So I can get you and the missus in the picture."

Russia
(*see "International Humor" chapter, International, Communists*)

Russia is where you are allowed to go anywhere they please.

A traveler came back this year from Stalingrad and claimed he saw a sign in a secret church, warning: "IN PRAYING HERE, YOU KEEP YOUR EYES CLOSED AT YOUR OWN RISK."

The newspaper *Pravda* is running a contest for the best political joke. First prize—twenty years.

The story is told of the Communist who died and went to hell. Upon his arrival, he told Satan, "Boy, am I happy to be in heaven."
"But you're mistaken," the devil told him. "This isn't heaven."
"That's what you think," sighed the comrade. "I just came from Siberia."

The Russians expect to reach the moon this year, Mars next year, and by 1975 they expect every Russian will own a pair of shoes.

A Muscovite was convicted of having called the Minister of Culture a fool. He got a twenty-year sentence. Five years for slander and fifteen for revealing a state secret.

One thing about living in Russia. You'd never lose an election bet.

A man walking down a street in Kiev spit on the sidewalk. The voice behind him warned, "Do not talk politics, comrade."

In Leningrad an old man sat on a park bench and dozed. When he awoke he noticed two uniformed policemen sitting on either side of him. "My God!" he mumbled. "What did I dream?"

My secret underground joke spy informs me there's a sign in every government official's office which carries this legend: "HEAD UP AS LONG AS YOU HAVE ONE."

An American visitor was trying out his transistor radio on a Soviet train. Seated nearby was a Russian unable to contain his curiosity. But, patriotically, he phrased it this way: "We have those too," he said, and added, "What is it?"

The Chinese man asked, "How do you handle intellectuals in the Russian Communist party?" The Russian replied: "Very carefully. We handle them just like eggs." The Chinese nodded appreciatively: "Very good. We, too, handle intellectuals just like eggs. We bury them for sixty years until they are good and rotten."

A student asked in class, "Why is the Kremlin so high?"
"To keep the scoundrels from crossing it," his teacher explained.
"From the Kremlin?" asked the student.

"What money gives you the most pleasure to travel with?"
"Russian money—everybody laughs when they see it."

A worker came home and found his wife in the arms of another man. "What kind of wife are you, idling around the house and amusing yourself on Lenin's birthday—and he isn't even a party member."

The Russians' big joke these days is about the Chinese.
Have you heard that the Chinese finally launched a Sputnik of their own? Yes, they did, and you've got to give them credit. True, it took six million coolies to pull the slingshot, but they did it.

In time, not only the Chinese development of an atomic bomb but also China's great mass of humans began to dismay the Russians. A Soviet story now has it that in the first day of a Sino-Soviet war one million Chinese are captured by the Russians. The second day, three million Chinese surrender. The third day, five million are trapped and disarmed. The Russians are awed by the ease of their victory, then stunned—for now they must feed their captives. The fourth day brings ten million more Chinese prisoners—and a telephone call from Mao Tse-tung to Brezhnev and Kosygin: "Had enough? Give up?"

A boy and girl were sitting on a bench in a Leningrad park. They were holding hands and listening to the nightingale sing his song. She was all romance: "Do you like the song of the nightingale?"
"Until I know who wrote the melody," he answered, "I can say nothing."

The Russian peasant reported to the police that his parrot was missing.

419

"Does the parrot talk, comrade?" the policeman asked.

"Yes—but believe me, any opinions he expresses are strictly his own."

There was a knock on the door in the middle of the night. The comrade jumped out of bed. "Don't be upset," said a voice, "it's only the janitor. Don't worry. It's only a fire in the building."

The Muscovite waited a half hour at the famous subway station in Moscow—but no train. He finally approached another patient subwayite: "Where are those wonderful automated trains of ours that we hear so much about? They are supposed to be so clean, light, airy, and especially prompt."

"You can't believe that capitalist propaganda," was his answer.

Sadist

A sadist is a doctor who keeps his stethoscope in the refrigerator.

Safari
(*see Hunting*)

Hunter misses, lion leaps, hunter ducks, lion runs away. Hunter goes back to camp and practices shooting. Goes after lion. Finds him in a small clearing, practicing short leaps.

SUE: "Last week when that bear got out you ran away and left me, and once you told me you would face death for me."
DICK: "Yes, I would—but that bear wasn't dead."

The explorer was telling the boys at the club about the tribe of wild women he found in the wilds of South America. "They had no tongues," he added.

"How did they talk?" one non-believer asked.

They couldn't," he explained. "That's what made them so wild."

The hunter was captured by the African tribe. Just as they were about to boil him in soupgreens he exclaimed, "Look here—I make fire." With that he flicked his lighter and it burst into flame. The savages fell back in amazement.

"Magic," cried the hunter in triumph.

"It sure is," the chief replied. "It's the first time I ever saw a lighter work the first shot."

Mort Sahl

I like Governor Wallace although I wouldn't marry his sister.

I think I'm a pacifist except in wartime when I think you should be sensible and get a commission.

During his campaign Governor Rockefeller was promising the kids little league polo.

If we're lucky Russians will steal some of our secrets and then they'll be two years behind us.

In regard to Shelley Berman—his search for the perfect telephone call is like my search for the perfect woman, and I know I've looked from one end of the bar to the other.

Did you date an airline stewardess? You know, they wear flats in the car and when they get out of the car they put on their heels.

Savings
(*see Banks, Money, etc.*)

My wife saves Green Stamps like they were money and spends money like they were Green Stamps.

420

We're saving money now that my wife does all the cooking—I don't eat a thing.

She found a new way to save money —she uses mine.

Save your money—some day it may be worth something.

I found a new way to save money. I buy traveler's checks and I stay home.

If I continue to save at the present rate, I'll retire owing $100,000.

Sayings
(*look under Quotations, Punch Lines, Proverbs*)

The Broadway phony: even when he says hello you know he's lying.

In America, the rich people live good and the poor people suffer. In Russia, there's equality. Everybody suffers.

A woman will never become President. She would never be able to say, "No comment."

It's funny how a showdown will show up a show-off.

It's a good thing Sophia Loren is a woman. A build like that would be wasted on a man.

The most dangerous thing in an automobile is the nut behind the wheel.

If you're drinking, don't drive to work. In fact, if you're drinking, don't come to work at all—stay home and have a ball.

If horseshoes are lucky, what good are the four on the horse that comes in last?

When you're right, no one remembers. When you're wrong—no one forgets.

A girl in the hand is worth two on the phone.

Two can live as cheaply as one— but now it takes both to earn enough money to do it.

Never send a boy on a man's job, or you'll have the unions on your back.

No man goes before his time—unless the boss leaves early.

Ability is what will help you get to the top if the boss has no daughter.

Diamonds are a girl's best friend and dogs are a man's best friend. Now you know which sex has more sense.

Eat, drink and be merry—for tomorrow ye diet.

Woman would be more charming if one could fall into her arms without falling into her hands.

People say you mustn't love your friend's wife—but how can you love your enemy's wife?

"The old believe everything, the middle-aged suspect everything, the young know everything."—Oscar Wilde

Schools
(*see also Education, Juvenile Delinquents, Colleges, Universities, etc.*)

Some school boards are unprogressive. One group fought to keep out a teacher with a long black beard—but finally they had to take her.

One progressive public school was very strict. They had signs posted in all the little boy and little girl rooms: "Absolutely NO smoking permitted—but if you insist, make sure they are filter tips."

The woman went to night school and asked to be enrolled immediately: "I want to learn French as fast as possible."
"Very well," the teacher replied, "but what's the rush?"
"We just adopted a six-month-old French baby and we want to be able to understand him when he talks."

It was a very tough neighborhood—any kid with a clean shirt was hissed. If you didn't have cauliflower ears you were considered a sissy. In that neighborhood, you became a judge or a killer. But the school was very strict. You had to raise your hand—before you hit the teacher.

The teacher was talking about her class of delinquents. "I got one kid," she complained, "who lies, cheats, spits, kicks, swears, takes marijuana—and what bothers me the most, he's the only kid in my class with a 100 per cent attendance record."

"The teacher said I must learn to write more legibly," the kid told his mother, "but if I do, she'll find out I can't spell."

It was a pretty progressive school. Even the kid's father, one of the original playboys, was startled when he saw his kid's books on sex. He was reading it himself and then decided to talk it over with his son. He went looking for him and found him in a clinch with the maid. "Son," he said, "when you're finished with your homework, I'd like to talk to you."

Science
(*see Atomic Energy, Outer Space, Martians, etc.*)

Scientists say we now live twenty years longer than the generation before us. Big deal. We have to—to pay our taxes.

Isn't science wonderful! It couldn't open a Pullman window—so they air-conditioned the trains.

The scientist looked over the toy missiles on sale at Macy's and said, "They're still ahead of our Defense Department but a little behind the Russians."

The State Department is trying to get one of our greatest scientists to take over our missile program—but he refuses to leave his toy company.

One embarrassing thing about science is that it is gradually filling our homes with appliances smarter than we are.

Scotland
(*see International Humor*)

Sandy found a box of corn plasters —so he went out and bought a pair of tight shoes.

The Scotsman built his own home but left the roof off one room. "That's the shower," he explained.

The doctor told McTavish that his wife was run-down and needed salt air —so he fanned her with a herring.

He's a true Scotsman—he saved all his toys for his second childhood.

I never knew until now that the Scotsmen resent these stories of penny-

422

pinching that are credited to them. As one Scot friend explained, "They are all told at our expense."

ANGUS: "How much whiskey ken ye drink?"
SANDY: "Any given quantity."

FRONT PAGE NEWS: A Scotsman gave a waiter a tip—the horse came in last.

SANDY: "Ye ken I'm a thrifty mon. Ken ye tell me wot to bring to the Golden Wedding of ma parents?"
ANGUS: "Ay, mon—bring a goldfish."

Secrets
(*see Gossip*)

No, I didn't tell anybody—I didn't know it was a secret.

The man who has no secrets from his wife—either has no secrets or no wife.

The FBI agent interviewed the man about his friend who was looking for a government job. "Do you think he is suited for this kind of position?"
"It all depends on the job," the friend said honestly. "What is it?"
"Sorry, I can't tell you—it's top secret."

Sex
(*see Love, Romance, Prostitutes, Mistress, etc.*)

St. Peter was interviewing a pretty girl at the Pearly Gates. "While you were on earth," he asked, "did you indulge in necking, petting, smoking or dancing?" "Never! Never!" she roared emphatically. "Then why haven't you reported sooner?" asked St. Peter. "You've been dead a long time."

A smart female is one who quits playing ball when she makes a good catch.

The young man was making love to the starlet and said, "I don't have a lot of money like Aly Khan. I don't have expensive houses like Aly Khan and I can't afford a big diamond like Aly Khan, but I love you."
"I love you too," the starlet replied, "but tell me more about Aly Khan."

The new secretary was telling her employer about her last job. "If you must know," she explained, "my last boss fired me because of the mistake I wouldn't make."

A debutante is a girl whose life is one mad whirl of activity—day in and night out.

Guys who pinch pennies will never pinch chorus girls.

Sex is the most fun you can have without laughing.

If sex is such a driving force as them scientists say—how come so much of it is always parked?

FIRST STARLET: "How would you act if the producer made a pass at you?"
SECOND STARLET: "In all the future pictures he'd make."

The patient was thrilled because the psychiatrist had helped her. Leaning over, she cooed to the headman, "Oh, doctor, you've made me so happy I could hug you."
The psychiatrist cautioned her, "You'd better not. Actually, we shouldn't even be lying on the couch together."

The traveling salesman had to write his report to the company but he had no writing paper, so he popped by the town's greeting card store. "Greetings," said the salesman to the saleslady, whose neckline was sliced to her hemline. "Do you keep stationery?"

"Yes I do, right up until the last second—then I go simply wild."

All her dresses had labels on them: "Made in Hollywood—by almost everybody."

She was willing to do anything to get in pictures—and she finally made bad.

They say sex is overrated. If it is, can you imagine where everything else stands?

She is so sexy that the birds and the bees study *her*.

Her hourglass figure can show you a good time.

"The thing that takes up the least amount of time and causes the most amount of trouble is sex."—John Barrymore

George Bernard Shaw

Mr. Shaw was at a benefit affair and gallantly asked a dowager to dance. "Oh, Mr. Shaw," she gushed, "what made you ask poor little me?" Shaw answered, "This is a charity ball, isn't it?"

From the picture—don't fool around with Gene Autry or George Bernard Shaw. He answered William Douglas Hume: "Go on writing plays, my boy. One of these days a London producer will go into his office and say to his secretary, 'Is there a play from Shaw this morning?' and when she says 'No,' he will say, 'Well, then we'll have to start on the rubbish'! And that's your chance, my boy."

The modest Shaw announced humbly to his admirers: "The writer I despise the most is Shakespeare, when I measure my mind against his."

A youthful anthologist wanted to include a Shaw story in his forthcoming collection. "However," he explained, "I cannot afford to pay your usual fee as I am a very young man."

"I'll wait till you grow up," Shaw answered.

Allan Sherman

Dick Gehman says, "Allan Sherman has a voice like a strangling mynah bird."

Allan says he sings like anyone in a bathtub—not good—but with enthusiasm. That's why he needs good musical background for his sings. "The effect is like this—you're looking into Tiffany's most elegant show window, and in the window is a black velvet pillow, and right in the middle of the pillow is an onion—that's me!"

Our family motto is: "Eat first—later we'll talk."

Allan's first literary success was copying Ogden Nash's satiric quatrain and sending it to a newspaper for publication:

"I think that I shall never see
A billboard lovely as a tree
In fact unless the billboards fall—
I'll never see a tree at all."

That's the first and last bit of burglary by the man with a "Gift for Laughter," whose satire is aimed at a sick world with laughter as the only real remedy.

George Washington may have never told a lie—but don't forget: in those days no one had to fill out an income tax form.

It's been verified that girlie pictures in magazines increase circulation—mine.

Nobody ever told me anything about sex. I was a nice Jewish boy so I knew you shouldn't *do it,* whatever *it* was, to nice girls. All my life I have been attracted to nice girls—the kind you aren't supposed to *do it* to. And they, too, have been brought up, at least in my generation, that they shouldn't *do it* either. How *it* ever gets done between nice people is a mystery to me. What I think happens is, nice people do it, but their hearts aren't in it.

Sarah Jackman, Sarah Jackman
How's by you? How's by you?
How's your cousin Seymour?
Seymour joined the Peace Corps,
He's nice too,
He's nice too.

He knows Seymour doesn't rhyme too good with Peace Corps, but go fool around with Gene Autry. His albums and verses have sold more copies than Shakespeare, and besides, the Bard couldn't sing a note—and Allan sounds like a mynah bird in heat.

Any man whose actions leave his wife speechless has hit on a gold mine.

Shopping

When she goes shopping she comes home with everything but money.

If she used her library card the way she uses her credit cards—she'd be the most brillant woman in America.

She went into the supermarket and bought a radio, two pairs of shoes, a dozen pairs of nylon hose, six books and two cartons of cigarettes. When the clerk added up the bill she complained, "The food bills are getting higher all the time."

I spent the day with the biggest spender in town—my wife.

Sign In La Maternity Shop: "We supply the accessories after the fact."

Woman shopping for hat, to clerk: "Now we're getting someplace—that's the exact opposite of what I want."

Never mind the large economy size —I'll take the small expensive box we can afford.

I'm sorry I can't remember the brand —but I can hum a few bars of the commercial.

Why does Christmas always come when the stores are most crowded?

A man went into a store to do some holiday shopping. It was so crowded that when he scratched his back three girls slapped him.

The way some women shop you would think they were taking inventory.

My wife is just crazy about Macy's. She spent some of the happiest pages of my checkbook on the third floor.

The store was so busy I put my handbag on the table and three girls bought it.

A supermarket in the Midwest advertised that it had come up with quite a unique idea. It put in a counter and a clerk stands behind it and waits on you.

425

Short

She was so short—she used a mini-skirt as a full-length evening gown.

He's so short—when he stands up and sits down he's the same size.

He looks like he's standing in a manhole.

I had an argument with him and he stood on his toes to bite me in the knee.

He kissed her on the lips—but somebody put him up to it.

Show Business
(see Vaudeville, Show People, Actors; names of comics, under their name)

She was the wife of a third-rate comic. When she announced she was going to have a baby, her agent said, "I hope you have a better delivery than your husband."

"Give me a break," the actor said to his landlord, "just carry me a little while longer until a job sets in."
"Are you kidding?" the landlord answered. "I've carried you longer than your mother did."

I signed with the biggest booking agency in the world. Now I'm not only out of work in this country, but in Europe and Asia as well.

Eddie Cantor and Georgie Jessel were on the same bill on a vaudeville unit. When they arrived in town Jessel saw the billing which read: "Eddie Cantor *with* Georgie Jessel."
"What kind of conjunction is that?" he berated manager Irving Mansfield.
Irving promised to fix it. The next day the marquee sign read, "Eddie Cantor *but* Georgie Jessel."

The actress was being divorced for the fifth time. "It's the same old story," said the agent, "she can't hold an audience."

My brother-in-law was a sad case. He used to mumble all the time. Finally we enrolled him in the actor's studio where nobody noticed him at all.

He had a bad cold and wanted some sympathy. When his agent called he hollered, "Where were you when I was dying?"
"In the audience, watching your act."

Young comic Jackie Clarke said he was finally getting his big break. He was offered a job at a night club in England. "I told the good news to my mother last night," said Jackie, "that I was going to work in London. And Mom said, "I don't mind where you work as long as you come home to sleep every night!"

At Danny's, one crowded dinner time, he was bothered by a new-rich star who insisted he didn't want to be annoyed by autograph seekers. "I hate to disturb you," said Danny, "but if you'll just sign your name we can get rid of them."
All right," sighed the ham, "as a personal favor to you. But just ten. No more.
"But," butted Danny, "there are only two."

Show People
(see also Actors, names in alphabetical listing, and Show Business)

Georgie Jessel and I were laughing and talking on a flight once from Cleveland to New York's La Guardia airport. He was talking and I was laughing. Due to the low ceiling over the field, we couldn't land and kept circling for more than an hour. Tension mounted and all sounds in the plane ceased. Soon all that could be heard was the steady drone of the motors. "My luck," I blurted out to Georgie. "We'll get killed and the papers will give you top billing."

Not a sound, not a word, not even a nod from Georgie. I didn't even think he had heard me. Twenty minutes later when we were safe on the ground, Jessel laughed. "That was very funny what you said up there—about me getting top billing."

Julius Tannen was one of the great vaudeville stars for many years, but with vaudeville's demise, Tannen, too, passed out of the picture. After much intrigue and many calls to many friends, Tannen finally was to enact the role of an editor in a newspaper drama subject to the producer's approval. Tannen dressed for the part, donned his toupee and read for the producer.

"I'm sorry, Mr. Tannen, but I don't think you'll do for the part."

Julius asked if he was too tall, too thin, too old, or too young.

"Neither," said the producer. "Your capabilities are fine, but I've always visualized a bald-headed man in the part."

Julius smiled and slowly removed his toupee. The producer stared at Tannen's shiny pate, shook his head again and pronounced, "I'm sorry, Mr. Tannen, but I simply cannot visualize you as a bald-headed man."

Many people in our business shorten their names even more than they do their noses because it's easier to get on a marquee. Red buttons was Aaron Chwatt, Vic Damone was Vito Farinola, Milton Berle was Milton Berlinger, Robert Alda was Al D'Abruzzio, and Irving Gray, the producer, was Irving Ginsberg. When a nephew who hadn't seen him in years wanted to communicate with him, he sent him a letter addressed to: Mr. Irving Grey, NBC. Irving finally received the letter after it had been shunted around for a bit, and sent him an answer by return mail. It said: "Dear Nephew, I received your letter. I would have gotten it more quickly except for the way you addressed it. Ginsberg is spelled G-R-A-Y, not G-R-E-Y."

When a civilian's house burns down he calls his insurance man. The actor calls his press agent.

"I've got a new act that will murder 'em," the magician told Ed Sullivan. "I saw a woman in half."

Smiley, who was around when vaudeville was at its height and has never let it die, looked at him like he was a nut. "Are you kidding?" he said. "A new act? Magicians have been sawing people in half for a hundred years."

"Lengthwise?"

This must be followed by the legendary story of the magician who met his old agent. "What ever happened to the girl in your act you used to saw in half?" he asked.

"She's living in New York and California," he said.

Some actors like to change their lines to fatten their parts as the show keeps running. If the producer or the director doesn't cut them, this can go on until the show is completely changed. George M. Cohan once posted a sign backstage, "There will be a rehearsal at 2 P.M. tomorrow to delete all the improvements."

When two performers meet, it's usually an I for an I.

427

Herb Shriner
(*also see "Humorists" chapter, Hick Towns, and Small Towns*)

Herb tells about the surgeon who was arrested in his home town for drunken driving. "They let him go, though. He was already an hour late for an operation."

I spent my youth in an Indiana town so small, it was located between the first and second sign on a Burma Shave poem. I finally left town to find out how the poem came out.

The big excitement in my town was to go down to the railroad station and watch them give haircuts.

It was exciting sitting on the porch and watching the girl's face break out.

The only hotel in my home town wasn't much but at least it had a bridal suite. That was the room with the lock on the door.

Sick Jokes
(*see Hospitals, Doctors, Hypochondriacs, Off-Beat Humor, Crazy Mixed-up Humor*)

Aside from that, Mrs. Lincoln, how did you enjoy the play?

And how much would you care to contribute to the Indian Relief Fund, Mrs. Custer?

Must be getting close to town—we're hitting more people.

"Mom, Pop was hit by a car."
"Don't make me laugh, son, you know my lips are chapped."

"Father, Auntie just fell into the fireplace."
"Well, poke her up—it's chilly in here."

"I hate to tell you this, but your wife has fallen in the well."
"That's okay—we use city water now."

I don't care who you are, Fatso. Get them reindeer off my roof.

Mother, where are the marshmallows? Marvin is on fire.

A doctor is the only man who does not have a guaranteed cure for a cold.

Mamma Cannibal: "How many times have I told you not to talk with someone in your mouth?"

Death is just nature's way of telling you to slow down.

"Mommy, the teacher says I look like a monkey."
"Shut up and comb your face."

"But Henry, that isn't our baby."
"Shut up—it's a better carriage."

Want Ad: "Man to work as garbage collector. $50 a week and all he can eat."

"You've helped me a lot," he said to his psychiatrist as he pointed the gun at him, "but now you know too much."

The deaf and dumb kid was shaping dirty words with his hands, so his parents washed his hands with soap.

"What do you mean your wooden leg hurts you? You can't feel pain in a wooden leg."

"You don't understand. During the fight with this man—he hit me over the head with it."

Signs

Sign on a Midtown Bar Ceiling: "What the hell are you looking up here for?"

Sign on a Tailor Shop: "We'll clean for you. We'll press for you—we'll even dye for you."

Sign on Cleaning Store Specializing in Gloves: "We clean your dirty kids."

Sign in Doctor's Office:
"The three stages of man are:
20-30—tri weekly
30-40—try weekly
40-50—try weakly."

Sign in a Brassiere Shop: "What God has forgotten—we stuff with cotton."

Sign in Restaurant: "One of the two most overrated things in the world is home cooking."

Sign in Discotheque:
"At 5, baby wants a doll, she gets it. At 15, baby wants a coat, she gets it. At 20, baby wants a man—*he* gets it."

Sign in Agent's Office: "Wanted, Understudy for Human Cannonball Act—must be willing to travel."

Sign in Restuarant: "We do not serve women at the bar—you have to bring your own."

Sign in a Hollywood Charm School: "THINK MINK."

Sign in a Brassiere Shop: "We fix flats."

Sign in French Shop: "English and French spoken—cash understood."

Sign at Reducing Salon: "A word to the wide—is sufficient."

A Fortune Teller's Sign: "Your problem solved or your mania cheerfully refunded."

Debutante Dress Shop: "Convertible sun dresses—very sporty with the tops down."

Mortician: "Must you be going? Try us."

Bar Sign: "If you drive your husband to drink—drive him here."

Hollywood Bar: "Not responsible for ladies left over 30 seconds."

Dallas Jewelry Store: "Diamond rings $85,000, three for a quarter of a million."

Sign in Vermont Above the Cracker Barrel: "Smokers and chewers will please spit on each other—and not on the stove or floor."

Dress Shoppe: "Maternity Dresses—for the Modern Miss."

In a New Haven Hospital: "No children allowed in the maternity wards."

Sign at Hertz: "If you don't see what you want—it was towed away."

Sign on Electric Chair: "You can be sure if it's Westinghouse."

Sign in Reducing Salon: "Rear today —gone tomorrow."

Sign in Front of Department Store: "5 Santa Clauses—no waiting."

429

Sign at Race Track: "Keep off the grass—it may be your supper."

Sign in Store: "No use shoplifting at our prices."

Sign in Bar: "We don't have TV but we do have fights every night."

Sign at Delicatessen: "If you don't smell it—we ain't got it."

Sign in Antique Shop: "Come in and buy what your Grandma threw out."

Sign in Bar: "If you drink to forget—please pay in advance."

Sign at Entrance of Women's Club: "Enter and knock."

Sign in Store Window: "In compliance with the President's order to eliminate poverty—we are raising our prices."

In Maternity Shop: "Way-out dresses—you should have danced all night."

Sign on Fire Hydrant: "Park now—pay later."

On Mail Box: "Post No Bills."

Sign on Minnesota Billboard: "Help beautify our junkyards—throw something lovely away."

Sign on Girdle Shop: "This world is in bad shape—must you be too?"

On Fortune Teller's Door:—"Medium prices."

"What's the hurry—we can foul things up just as well later."

"Money isn't everything—but it's sure ahead of whatever is in second place."

"Looking for someone with a little authority?—I have as little as anyone."

"I'd like to help you out—which way did you come in?"

"Be original—at least make a different mistake each time."

"Be reasonable—do it my way."

"This is a non-profit organization—we didn't plan it that way—but that's the way it turned out."

"Do it tomorrow—we've made enough mistakes today."

"Use your head—it's the little things that count."

"Keep your eye on the ball, your shoulder to the wheel and your ear to the ground—now try to work in that position."

"It's better to give than to receive—so what have you brought me?"

"I love my job—it's the work I hate."

"In case of nuclear attack—run like hell."

"Use our easy credit plan—100 per cent down—no payments."

"PLEASE don't ask for credit—what little we have is not so hot."

"PLEASE don't do anything for me—I can't afford it."

"I can't be bought—but make me an offer."

"Knowledge is power—if you know the right things about the right people."

"Quiet, please—I like to listen to what I have to say."

"I'm a pacifist—and I'll kill anybody who says I'm not."

"Fools rush in—and get the best seats."

"You have a perfect right to express your opinion here—as long as it agrees with mine."

"Help a man in trouble and he'll never forget you—especially the next time he's in trouble."

"A penny saved—isn't worth the effort."

"A fool and his money—are invited everywhere."

"For that rundown feeling—try jay-walking."

"Love thy neighbor—but don't let it get around."

"Don't feel useless—you can always be used as a bad example."

"If you have a minute to spare—tell me all you know."

"I'm not prejudiced—I hate everybody regardless of race, creed or color."

"Join the campaign to end poverty—send me money."

"Who says nothing is impossible?—I've been doing nothing for years."

"Please don't wake me while I'm working."

A Houston plumber named Carr uses this slogan: "HONEST CARR THE USED JOHN DEALER."

In Front of the Road Block: "Road closed—Do not enter." On the back of the same sign was another message: "Welcome back—STUPID."

On Be-Bop Music Firm Door: "Real Gone—to lunch."

On Gas Service Station: "Easy credit plan—100% down—nothing to pay each month."

In Greenwich Village Apartment House: "Room for rent—one room efficiency—no bath—suitable for beatnik."

In Night Club: "Welcome, sucker—if you don't see what you want by now —maybe it's time to go back to your wife."

Night Club: "Customers wanted – no experience necessary—just money."

Under an Office Clock: "It's earlier than you think."

Gandhi had this sign on the wall in his home: "When you are in the right, you can afford to keep your temper, and when you are in the wrong, you cannot afford to lose it."

Similes

As relaxed as spaghetti.

As happy as an untipped waiter.

As satisfying as an income tax refund.

As phony as an undertaker's get-well card.

As useless as a movie at the drive-in theatre.

431

As sexy as an unblown-up football bladder.

As tight as a Scotsman's wallet.

As much personality as the inside of a fountain pen.

As vivacious as a shoe box.

As welcome as a mother-in-law on a honeymoon.

As desirable as Phyllis Diller in tights.

As exciting as a dunked tea bag.

As much personality as warmed-over farina.

As pretty a face as an alligator handbag.

As charming as a loose sneaker.

As solid as the lint on your trouser cuff.

As crisp as a sweaty sock.

As smart as a grammar school dropout.

As much personality as an enema bag.

As beautiful as a throbbing blackhead.

As enjoyable as an infected hangnail.

As welcome as poison ivy in a nudist camp.

As tough to shake as an advanced case of dandruff.

As shapely as a camel in heat.

As welcome as Nasser in Tel Aviv.

Red Skelton

I used to catch sparrows in the park, color them with iodine and sell them as canaries.

Two pigeons were flying over a parking lot and one said to the other, "Let's make a deposit on that Cadillac."

Red ran into an old friend from Vincennes, Indiana, where he was born. "Red," he exclaimed, "you sure have put on a lot of weight."
"Yeah," Red agreed, "I only weighed seven pounds when I was born."

Two nuts were walking along late at night and they came to a big wall.
One said, "How are we gonna get over it?"
Other guy said, "Well, I'll shine this searchlight up there and you climb up the searchlight beam."
First guy said, "Oh, no. I'll get halfway up and you'll turn it off!"

Beautiful girl walked by and I said, "Are you a model?" She said, "No, I'm full-scale."

A drunk was lying in the gutter with one arm on the curb, yelling, "I'll get over this wall if it takes me all night."

A woman brought her husband into court for physical cruelty. "He beats me in the morning, bats me around in the afternoon, and clobbers me every night," she cried to the judge.
"Is this true?" the judge asked the husband.
"You can't believe a word she says, your honor," the husband answered. "She's punch-drunk."

432

Sleep

WIFE: "Do you know you were saying nasty things to me in your sleep last night?"
HUSBAND: "Who was sleeping?"

He's so lazy—he takes naps even when he's sleeping.

He really has a bad case of insomnia —he can't sleep even when it's time to get up.

He's so lazy—the first thing he does when he wakes up—is take a sleeping pill.

"I haven't been able to sleep—my wife is always nagging and nagging."
"Here," the doctor said, "this pill will do you good."
"When do I take it?"
"You don't—you give it to your wife."

The only time the wife listens to what I say—is when I'm asleep.

The trouble with Italian coffee is that a week later you are sleepy again.

Small Towns
(*see Hick Towns, Herb Shriner*)

The town is so dead, they don't even ring the curfew at 8 P.M. anymore. It kept waking everybody up.

COLLEGE BOY: "Excuse me, sir, I'm taking a survey and I found that people live longer in small towns— what is the death rate here?"

"One to a person."

You know how big our town is? Well, our town crier has to whisper.

I once lived in a town so small that one alarm clock woke everybody up.

Definition of a small town: a place in which there is no place to go that you shouldn't.

The old-fashioned girl spent her time hanging around the village square. Then she married him.

Smith and Dale's
Ethiopian National Bank

DALE: (Enters) "Pardon me, is this the Ethiopian National Bank?"
SMITH: "Yes. I'm the president."
DALE: "Are you Ethiopian?"
SMITH: "If I were to do business under the name of the Eagle Pants Company, I don't have to be an eagle."
DALE: "Well, with your beak you could be."
SMITH: "Thanks—the feeling is optional. You came here for some purpose?"
DALE: "Yes, I'm thinking of becoming a depositor."
SMITH: "Welcome. Now, how much do you want to deposit?"
DALE: "Don't rush me, first I want to examine you."
SMITH: "Examine me? I'm the president."
DALE: "I'm leary."
SMITH: "Mr. Leary, you're wasting my time. My time is money, and not my money either."
DALE: "I came here to deposit money and money talks."
SMITH: "Let's hear it."
DALE: "Good-bye" (about to leave).
SMITH: "Sit down—this is a friendly bank. Do you smoke?"
DALE: "No, but I chew."
SMITH: "Fine." (hands him an apple)
DALE: (About to take a bite)
SMITH: "Ten cents, please!"
DALE: "What are you doing? Selling apples?"
SMITH: "Just a sideline. Now. How much do you want to deposit?"

433

DALE: "First, where do you keep your money?"

SMITH: "I keep it in escrow."

DALE: "Escrow? Where's that?"

SMITH: "Some place near Boston. Now. How much do you want to deposit?"

DALE: "If I was to deposit my money right now—how do I get it out, by gas?"

SMITH: "You give twenty-four hours notice."

DALE: "I see you want to leave town."

SMITH: "Don't you trust me, haven't I got an honest face?"

DALE: "I'm not putting my money in your face. By the way, who's the treasurer?"

SMITH: "He went away for a rest, but he'll be out soon. Now how much do you want to deposit?"

DALE: "I want to deposit six dollars in quarters, a quarter at a time." (throws coins on desk)

SMITH: "This is a bank, not a slot machine."

DALE: "You don't get me."

SMITH: "I don't want you."

DALE: "I want to start a trust fund."

SMITH: "A trust fund with a quarter? Why don't you deposit a nickel and start a collection?"

DALE: "In case I need money during the night, what's your phone number?"

SMITH: "007-4321."

DALE: "Is that your home phone?"

SMITH: "No. That's a candy store downstairs, but they'll call me."

**Smith and Dale's
"The Boss and the Chef"**

Scene: The kitchen of a Hungarian restaurant.

DALE AS BOSS: (Enters looking for the chef) "I'll bet he's out playing the horses."

WAITER: (Enters) "Oh boss, the mailman just gave me this letter for you."

BOSS: "Sam, read it, I left my glasses home."

WAITER: (Reads) "From the law office of Kaiser, Peyser, Nizer and McGonigill. To the proprietor of the Hungarian Restaurant. Dear Sir: We understand you have in your employ a chef by the name of Bernard Shnapps. If this is true, kindly have him get in touch with us as his Uncle Morris died and left him a legacy of ten thousand dollars cash."

BOSS: "Thank you. Let me have the letter."

CHEF: (Enters)

BOSS: "Where were you?"

SMITH AS CHEF: "I just had a good meal across the street, you expect me to eat here too?"

WAITER: "Say, chef. Irving Caesar wants to know if he's good for a meal."

BOSS: "Did he just order it?"

WAITER: "No. He just ate it."

CHEF: "He's good for it."

WAITER: "I'll tell him."

BOSS: "What do you mean he's good for it?"

CHEF: "Caesar is an honest man."

BOSS: "That's Julius Caesar, but not his brother Irving."

CHEF: "He'll pay you, his word is as good as yours."

BOSS: "Then I'll never get paid."

WAITER: "Boss? Mister Adamavitch is kicking about his steak."

CHEF: "It's his steak, let him kick it about!"

WAITER: "He said it's tough."

CHEF: "It's the same steak he had yesterday."

WAITER: "That's what he's kicking about. He said if you give him another tough steak you're gonna lose him."

BOSS: "You tell him. I lost my grandmother, the chef lost his mother-in-law and we can lose him too. Hey chef, give the orders for tomorrow, I wanna make up the menu."

434

CHEF: "Put down six ounces of noodles, a half a pound of rice, three drams of oatmeal."

BOSS: "Wait a minute, what is this, an order or a prescription?"

CHEF: "Put down important sardines and a half a dozen chissels."

BOSS: "Chissels? What do we want with chissels?"

CHEF: "Cream chissels!" (starts to eat a banana)

BOSS: "Hey! Don't eat up the profits!"

CHEF: "This ain't profits, it's all overhead."

BOSS: "Put it away!"

CHEF: "I am putting it away." (still eating)

BOSS: "If you want to eat something, eat onions."

CHEF: "I can eat bananas if I like it, and I like it."

BOSS: "But I don't like it."

CHEF: "Do I ask you to eat it?"

BOSS: "Do I ask you to ask me do you? Do you hear me?"

CHEF: "I hear you calling me. But I don't see you."

BOSS: "I'll grab you by the neck . . ."

CHEF: "If you lose your temper, hold your tongue."

BOSS: "I should hold my tongue?"

CHEF: "Then choke!"

BOSS: "Is this the way to insult the boss?"

CHEF: "If you know a better way, tell me."

BOSS: "I'm the boss!"

CHEF: "Boss, outside."

BOSS: "I'm the boss inside out."

CHEF: "You talk like a shoe shine."

BOSS: "You'll get a shine in your eye if you don't behave."

CHEF: "And you'll get two in one. Y'know you are cooking on a chef, also a baker over a good baker."

BOSS: "A common loafer. You look like a Siberian snuff-chewer."

CHEF: "Thank you. You look good too."

BOSS: "You're jealous how I look?"

CHEF: "I wouldn't look like you even if I looked like you and then I wouldn't look like you."

BOSS: "I should worry what you say. By golly my wife likes me!"

CHEF: "I know a lot of women that likes monkeys."

BOSS: "Insulting me again? Apologize y'hear?"

CHEF: "All right. I didn't know what I said, but I meant it."

WAITER: "Boss? Mister Adamavitch is going to sue you. He just broke a tooth eating that tough steak."

BOSS: "Chef! You cooked the steak. Let him sue you."

CHEF: "And you bought it, so according to the law you are an accessory before, behind and after the fact. That's the law."

BOSS: "What do you know about the law?"

CHEF: "My brother-in-law is a notary public."

BOSS: "What does he do?"

CHEF: "He takes oaths."

BOSS: "He takes oats? He's a horse!"

CHEF: "One more word from you and I quit."

BOSS: "You!"

CHEF: "That's the word. I'm through."

BOSS: "Don't be foolish, I was only fooling. In fact I want to make you a partner in the business."

CHEF: "You know I ain't got any money."

BOSS: "You don't need to, only if some of your relatives die and leave you some money you are to put it in the business."

CHEF: "That's O.K. with me."

BOSS: "Shake hands, partner."

CHEF: "Wait a minute. I'll call the waiter to be a witness. Hey Sam?"

WAITER: "Chef, did you call me?"

CHEF: "I want you to be a witness that the boss is making me a partner."

WAITER: "Congratulations, chef."

CHEF: "Well, partner, let me have ten dollars. I wanna celebrate."

BOSS: "Sure. Here is ten dollars, enjoy the new partnership."

CHEF: "Come on, Sam, let's go."

BOSS: "Oh, chef. I almost forgot. I got a letter here concerning you it says your Uncle Morris died and left you ten thousand dollars cash. Here, read it, see what it says."

CHEF: "I know what it says. I wrote it myself."

Smog
(*see Air Pollution, Fog, etc.*)

Mayor Lindsay did something constructive about the New York City fog —he's putting up street signs in braille.

A visitor arrived in Los Angeles during the fog—he felt the sights— and went home.

Smog is caused by the exhaust from the cars—only one solution—put the exhaust *inside* the cars.

Smog martini—two drinks and you can't see the bartender.

The L. A. smog is the greatest. Where else can you see night baseball in the afternoon?

Smoking
(*see Cigarettes*)

Cigar anonymous is a new organization—when you feel like smoking, you dial a number and hear a lot of coughing.

Winston tastes good like a cigarette should—unless you prefer to smoke a herring.

He walked down the street with a pipe in his mouth, a girl on his arm and a hole in his pocket.

The way-out hypochondriac smokes only filter-tip marijuana.

He got a double hernia trying to inhale one of those double filter tip cigarettes through the charcoal.

People who give up smoking have the same problem as the newcomer in the nudist camp—they don't know what to do with their hands.

Snobs
(*see Society*)

A snobbish Park Avenue matron walked into a pet shop and ordered the proprietor to give her the finest dog he had in the store. He showed her several of his prize animals but she was dissatisfied. Finally, he picked up an adorable little pup and handed it to her. "Is he pedigreed?" she asked haughtily. "Pedigreed?" smiled the dealer. "If this dog could talk, he wouldn't speak to either of us."

A haughty socialite died and arrived at the gates of heaven. "Welcome," St. Peter greeted him, "come right in." "I will not," sneered the snob. "Any place where a perfect stranger can get in without a reservation is not my idea of heaven."

She should go to a plastic surgeon to have her nose lowered.

It was an exclusive country club— the men were stuffed shirts and the women stuffed shorts.

He wears a riding habit—just to pitch horseshoes.

436

Her nose is so high—every time she sneezes—she blows her hat off.

They insist they belong to the upper crust—a bunch of crumbs.

Mrs. Snooty was showing off as usual. "I have all my diamonds cleaned with caviar juice, my rubies with imported wine, my emeralds with the finest brandy from Spain, and my sapphires with fresh milk from baby goats."
"When my jewels get dirty," Mrs. Snob topped her, "I throw them away."

"Are you looking for a grand piano, madam?"
"Grand?—I want one that is magnificent."

He's such a snob—he won't ride in the same car with his chauffeur.

They were such big snobs they refused to come over on the Mayflower—they took their own boat.

Society
(*see Snobs*)

Two older society gals, poor but snobbish, were talking about a matrimonial prospect.
"He's got plenty of money," one said, "but isn't he too old to be termed eligible?"
"Dahling," the other answered, "he's too eligible to be termed old."

Whoever she is, she has certainly never moved in great society—she shakes hands like she means it.

He's such a blue-blood he doesn't need a fountain pen—when he wants to write he just cuts his finger.

She's so fashionable—if she was going to shoot her husband—she'd wear a hunting outfit.

The only thing he ever did for a living was read his father's will.

The best part of his family tree is underground.

This group of society nudists were so snobbish—they insisted you wear a tie when you enter.

The Bostonian looked down at Mr. Cohen. "One of my ancestors signed the Declaration of Independence."
"Big deal," Cohen answered, "one of mine signed the Ten Commandments."

She had a coming-out party—but they made her go back in again.

She's such a snob—she has monogrammed tea bags.

When his son went into the army—he demanded an unlisted serial number for him.

They live in a restricted area—nobody in their neighborhood has a home they can afford.

He thought it would be chic to take a job—but he insisted on an unlisted Social Security number.

Soldier
(*look under Army, Draft, etc.*)

"Twenty years ago I asked Santa for a soldier suit—*now* I get it!"

Song Titles

"I'll be seizing you in all the old familiar places."

"I want a girl, just like the girl, that Dad had on the side."

"Hello young lovers, wherever you are —watch out for the house detective."

"If you knew Suzie like I know Suzie— you'd go out with Margie."

"Everyone has someone—but all I have is you."

"Don't go in the stable, Grandma— you're too old to be horsing around."

"She used to go with the landlord, but now she just goes with the lease."

"You must have been a beautiful baby, but baby look at you now."

"She must be philanthropic—she keeps giving things away."

"Drink to me only with thine eyes— somebody stole the scotch."

"Mother, buy some liniment—I'm getting stiff tonight."

"Every time I wash my hair—I dye a little."

"Grandma dear, don't worry that I'm sitting in front of the electric fan with a B-B gun, I just came in to shoot the breeze."

"Since Grandma shot a hole in Grandpa's head—it sure cleared up his sinus."

"There is no R in my mother-in-law's name—but she looks like an oyster just the same."

"A hero unsung—is Mr. Lum Fung— he fed his chicken a rice cake—and it laid an egg foo young."

"Twenty-five children has Mrs. O'Brien —she feels fine but the stork is dyin."

"I'm glad I made you cry, baby, your face is cleaner now."

"I'm dancing with tears in my eyes— 'cause the shoes on my feet are too tight."

"Her boy friend stole her only brassiere and then he left her flat."

"The shades of night were falling fast —but I got a good look just the same."

"I'll wear my Easter bonnet—with all the bills upon it."

"If there's a woman for every man, baby, how come I got you?"

"I guess you have to be somebody— but why do you have to be you?"

"I'm walking behind you—because I've seen your face."

"How can I miss you—if you won't go away?"

"Her heart belongs to Daddy but the rest she's renting out."

"She was only a bearded lady but she certainly gave me the brush."

"I had an apartment in front and she had a flat behind."

"Don't elope with a pilot, Grandma, you're too old to take a flier."

"She was only a loose woman—but she always liked to get tight."

"She was only a cannibal's daughter but she liked her men stewed."

Speakers
(see Dais, Roast of the Town, etc.)

TOASTMASTER: "I'm not going to stand up here and tell you a lot of old jokes —but I'll introduce speakers who will."

I don't care if you walk out on me— it's when you walk toward me that I worry.

Speaker who doesn't strike oil in the first few minutes—should stop boring.

Speeches are like babies—easy to conceive—but hard to deliver.

And now before I start—I want to say something.

"A toastmaster is a man who eats a meal he doesn't want so he can get up and tell a lot of stories he doesn't remember to people who've already heard them."—George Jessel

A long-horn speech: That's two widely separated points with a lot of bull between.

If a thing goes without saying—let it.

The greatest after-dinner speaker I ever heard is the fellow that said: "Waiter—bring me the check."

Adlai Stevenson explained to the lady that he didn't go in for sports. "I got this tan making speeches—outdoors— in Florida."
"Well," the woman heckled, "if you got so brown—you talked too long."

I was so surprised in getting the nomination—I almost dropped my acceptance speech.

He can always rise to the occasion— but he never knows when to sit down.

To many speakers a speech seems to be something that makes you feel numb on one end and dumb on the other.

A proverb for all banquet speakers: "The mind cannot accept what the seat cannot endure."

Winston Churchill offered this advice to speakers on a dais: "Say what you have to say, and the first time you come to a sentence with a grammatical ending, sit down!"

The lion ate a bull and he roared and roared—a hunter heard him roaring and killed him with one shot. The moral of the story is: "When you're full of bull—keep your mouth shut."

The human brain is a wonderful thing. It starts working the moment you are born—and never stops until you stand up to speak in public.

Spinsters
(see Old Maid, Age, Old Age)

A spinster saw a handsome fellow's picture in a wanted poster and is offering $100 more than the FBI.

She could have married anyone she pleased. She just didn't please anyone.

"I just read where Mrs. Davidson had her husband cremated," one spinster said to the other.
"Isn't that always the way?" her friend answered. "Some of us can't get one, and others have husbands to burn."

SPINSTER: A red hot mamma—whose fire has gone out.

Spiritualism

"Ah, I hear the spirit of your late wife knocking."
"Who is she knocking now?"

"I want to speak to my dear departed husband."
"Why?"
"He died before I finished telling him what I thought of him."

The woman sitting at the seance said: "Tell my husband I'll talk with him— if he'll keep his big mouth shut."

Sports
(*see Golf, etc.*)

"What did you think of the fight last night?"
"Big fight! If my wife and I had a fight like that—the kids would boo us."

I sure was lucky at the races yesterday—I found a quarter and I didn't have to walk home.

The coach walked into the dressing room between halves to bawl out his highly touted college team: "You guys are playing like a bunch of amateurs."

The basketball star was in danger of flunking out of school. A special test was given him orally by the dean as a last attempt to pass. His coach accompanied him to the test to help.
The dean asked, "How much is eight times seven?"
"Fifty," replied the star.
"Wrong," said the dean. "I'm afraid I can't pass you."
"Aw, dean," said the coach, "c'mon, he only missed by two."

The conceited new rookie was pitching his first game. He walked the first five men he faced, and the manager took him out of the game. The rookie slammed his glove on the ground as he walked off and yelled, "Damn it, the jerk takes me out when I have a no-hitter going."

The third baseman had one of those bad days. He made three errors and struck out four times in a row. Then he went down to the dressing room and cut himself doing the TV razor commercial—and it was an electric razor.

The horse was so slow—the jockey carried a change of saddle.

I have a system to beat the first four races at the track every day—don't show up till the fifth.

The Russians are becoming great track stars—the starters are using real bullets in their starting guns.

Shivering wife in rowboat to husband who is fishing, "Tell me again how much fun we're having—I keep forgetting."

Do you know why mountain climbers rope themselves together? To keep the sensible ones from going home.

Golf is a game in which a little white ball is chased by men too old to chase anything else.

I feel great—played thirty-two holes today—on my harmonica.

I want tickets for the fight—but I want to sit so close, I'll have to defend myself.

The fighter was getting the beating of his life. Both eyes were cut and bleeding and his nose was broken. His ribs were the color of catsup as he returned to his corner at the end of the fifth round

His manager consoled him as he applied medication to his busted face and body. "You're going great on the radio —the announcer is a friend of mine."

The fighter had been taking a beating for eight rounds. When he came back to his corner his second cautioned, "As it stands now, you gotta knock that guy out to get a draw."

He finally figured out a way to leave the track with money—he gave up picking horses—and started picking pockets.

WIFE: "John, what becomes of a ball player when his eyesight starts to fail?"
HUSBAND: "They make an umpire of him."

He broke the underwater record by staying under for three hours and twenty-five minutes. Funeral services will be held tomorrow.

1ST MAN: "I used to play hockey."
2ND MAN: "Why did you quit?"
1ST MAN: "I ran out of things to hock."

At baseball game:
SHE: "What's the man running for?"
HE: "He hit the ball."
SHE: "I know. But does he have to chase it too?"

WIFE: "Remember the salmon you went fishing for last year?"
HUSBAND: "Yes, dear?"
WIFE: "Well, one of them called you this afternoon!"

The Attorney General's office was after him as a monopoly. He was operating six ski lodges and two hospitals.

Girls who are good sports—go out more often than anybody.

The only wrestling matches that aren't fixed are those in back of a car.

Bowling is the second most popular indoor sport.

The wrestler couldn't understand why he lost the bout—he won the rehearsal.

FISHING: A thoughtful wife is one who has the steak ready when her husband comes home from a fishing trip.

A man who will sit on a pier fishing all day waiting for a bite—will lose his temper if dinner is late five minutes.

He was carrying the biggest fish he ever caught—twice his size. When he met his friend carrying a few tiny ones on a string, he dropped his big catch and grinned, "Huh?"
His friend stared, then said sadly, "Just caught the one, huh?"

BASEBALL: I'm all for the little leaguers —but those Mets are ridiculous.

If Japan is so crazy about baseball— let's give 'em the Mets—it'll be the first thing in Japan made in America— and they can have it.

The Mets feel they are on TV and doing good 'cause they're in the first ten—that's right—they're tenth.

The Mets aren't lost yet by any means—they can still win it if they get on a little winning streak—like about a hundred games.

Vince Lombardi, the coach of the Green Bay Packers, is known as something of a tyrant. The inside information is that he remains aloof in order to instill a certain fear and respect in his players. Others say that's the way

441

Vince really is. At any rate, there's a story going around that one evening he returned home from a workout in below-zero weather. He got into bed and his wife complained, "God! Your feet are cold."

"Look," Lombardi said, "when we're in bed, it's O.K. for you to call me Vince."

Clerk at ski lodge to registering guest: "Just your name, address and Blue Cross number."

Square

My idea of a square is a guy who goes to a Brigitte Bardot movie and complains because the picture doesn't have a plot.

SQUARE: He takes a girl to a drive-in theatre—and watches the movie.

He would marry Sophia Loren for her money.

Squelchers
(see Hecklers and Insults)

Stay with me. I want to be alone.

Why don't you send your wits out to be sharpened?

Are you a self-made man, or do you want to blame someone else?

Why don't you go on a diet and quit eating my heart out?

There was something I always liked about him—but he spent it.

His idea of an exciting night is to turn up his electric blanket.

Most of our top-drawer actors are amiable folks, approachable, tolerant, often eager to help newcomers. The old-timers held themselves more aloof. Perhaps the most irascible, sharp-spoken was the late Wilton Lackaye— a great performer but not the most amiable gentleman. Once, after his opening night in The Pit, he came into the Lambs Club and was approached by an eager young hopeful who exclaimed enthusiastically, "How does it feel, Mr. Lackaye, to receive all that wild acclaim for your great acting?" Lackaye stared at him coldly and snapped: "You'll never know!"

The sort of man with whom to eat, drink and be wary.

Oscar Levant, after listening to George Gershwin talk about himself: "George, if you had it to do over, would you fall in love with yourself again?"

They're about as compatible as ham and matzos.

ACTOR: "I hear he's changing his faith."
ACTRESS: "You mean he no longer believes he's God?"

It was the day after their wedding. He took her in his arms and said, "Darling, now that we're married, I must tell you a few little defects I've noticed about you."
"Well," she answered, "it was those little defects that kept me from getting a better husband!"

You're the sort of guy who talks penthouses and takes subways.

He's the kind of guy who picks his friends—to pieces.

He's an intellectual. He can bore you on every subject.

You're snappy on the comeback—like your checks.

Don't you ever get tired of having yourself around?

"Do you believe it possible to communicate with the dead?"
"Sure—I can hear you distinctly!"

The next time you pass me by—I'll be very grateful.

"When I was sixteen I was chosen Miss America."
"In those days there were very few Americans."

"Why aren't you in the army?" the lady heckled Will Rogers while he was on stage at the Ziegfeld Follies. "For the same reason, madam," he answered, "that you aren't in the Follies—physical disabilities."

A Bostonian visited San Antonio, Texas, and asked a native, "What is that dilapidated-looking ruin over there?" "That, suh, is the Alamo. In that building, suh, 136 immortal Texans held off an army of 15,000 of Santa Anna's regulars for four days."
"Um-m-m," said the Bostonian, "and who was that man on horseback on that hill over there?"
"That, suh, is a statue of a Texas ranger. He killed 46 Apaches in single-handed combat and broke up 47 riots in his lifetime. Where you from, stranger?"
"I'm from Boston. We have our heroes there, too. Paul Revere, for instance."
"Paul Revere!" snorted the Texan. "You mean that man who had to ride for help?"

George Bernard Shaw received an invitation from a celebrity hunter with this legend, "Lady Martin will be at home between 7 and 10 P.M." The vitriolic author returned the card with his own notation: "Mr. Bernard Shaw likewise."

Adlai Stevenson

Eggheads, unite! You have nothing to lose but your yolks.

In my very brief political career I've sometimes wondered if I had any friends left. And then they suddenly nominated me for President, and I wondered if I hadn't too many friends.

The Republicans have a "me too" candidate running on a "yes but" platform, advised by a "has been" staff.

I like a lot of Republicans. Indeed there are some I would trust with anything—anything, that is, except public office.

If the Republicans stop telling lies about us, we will stop telling the truth about them.

In an election they pick a President —and then for four years they pick *on* him.

Speaking to a television audience after his defeat in the Presidential campaign of 1952 Stevenson said: "A funny thing happened to me on the way to the White House."

When Adlai Stevenson conceded the election, he made his most moving speech of all:
"I am reminded of a story that a fellow townsman of ours used to tell—Abraham Lincoln. They asked him how he felt once after an unsuccessful election. He said he felt like a boy who had stubbed his toe in the dark; that he was too old to cry, but it hurt too much to laugh."

443

Mr. Stevenson was introduced at a theatrical dinner where he followed the great Fred Allen, who was only hilarious for twenty minutes. "Ladies and gentlemen," he started, "I met Mr. Allen in the corridor before the dinner and he told me he didn't have a speech for tonight, so I gave him mine, which you just heard—thank you." And he sat down.

Stock Market
(*see Wall Street*)

Hildegarde commenting about the stock market said: "To be preferred— a girl must be very common."

He had an inside tip and bought 1,000 shares at 10. When it went to twenty he asked his advisor what to do. "It's a better buy at 20 than it was at 10," he was told.
"Gee," he said, "if only I had waited."

He bought some Canadian Uranium at ten cents a share on a can't-lose tip. When it went to twenty he called his broker and ordered another 5,000 shares. When it went to fifty cents he called again and said to his broker anxiously, "Get me another 10,000 shares." When it went to a dollar he called for 20,000 more. When it finally hit five dollars he called his broker gleefully. "Sell," he shouted, "it's time to take my profit—sell everything."
"To who?" asked the broker.

I dropped plenty in the market—my shopping bag broke.

I made a killing in the market—I shot my broker.

BROKER: What you become when you continue to play the stock market.

I don't want to talk about my stock market exploits this year but I've got five new dependents: Merrill, Lynch, Pierce, Fenner and Smith.

The difference between playing the market and the horses is that one of the horses must win.

This stock market is creating a whole new class of people in the U. S.—the nouveau poor.

My family wasn't affected by the stock market crash of 1929—they went broke in 1928.

The stockbroker called his lady customer to tell her that Bell and Howell split. "What a shame," she said, "and they've been together such a long time."

The stock market is like a Sultan— it's been touching new bottoms too often.

"Don't gamble. Take all your savings and buy some good stock and hold it till it goes up—then sell it. If it don't go up—don't buy it."—Will Rogers

Stripper
(*see Burlesque*)

A stripper is a girl who has everything—and shows it.

I wouldn't say she had a bad body —but when she started to strip, one voice in the back hollered—"Put it on!"

I guess that's what they mean by a community chest.

One stripper bills herself as "The Treasure Chest."

A STRIPPER: She spends the best years of her life being seen in the right places.

She drove her doctor crazy trying to vaccinate her in a place where it wouldn't show.

She is barefoot—up to her chin.

A STRIPPER: A girl on whom nothing looks good.

The only thing on her is the spotlight.

A STRIPPER: No matter how good she is—has to leave the audience wanting less.

STRIPPER: One who makes a bare living.

She does a modernistic fan dance—she uses an electric fan.

STRIPPER: Good to the last drop.

Strong

He's so strong—he bends the spoon stirring coffee.

He gets out of breath when I ask him to pass the salt.

He needs help with his toothbrush.

He calls the super when he wants to open the window.

The only thing strong about him is his breath.

Strong men are my weakness.

I like my coffee strong and my women weak.

He looks strong but he isn't that solid—he's got starch in his underwear.

Stunt Man
(*see Hollywood*)

Roger Moore doesn't have any stand-ins. He prefers to do his own fighting and stunts in pictures. His favorite story concerns Victor Mature who, he says, would want a stunt man if it involved sitting down in a rocking chair.

This was a jungle scene. In the water. Janet Leigh is already in the water so it can't be too bad.

They tell Victor Mature, "Ready, now, Vic, would you get in the water?"

He says, "How deep is it?" They say it's just to his knees. He says to Janet Leigh, "Yeah, but you're standing on a rock." She says she isn't. Victor says, "Yeah, but this water is full of alligators." They say there aren't any alligators around. He says there are. So they say they're going to go out with guns and fire blank cartridges and scare all the alligators out of the water.

Victor says, "But how do you know if one of them mothers isn't deaf?"

Suburbs
(*also see Alan King, Neighbors, Apartment Houses*)

An American city is a place where by the time you've finished paying for your home in the suburbs, the suburbs have moved twenty miles farther out.

SUBURBAN HUSBAND: Gardener with sex privileges.

When you're a suburbanite, you must listen to the radio guys that give you the traffic picture. I love those helicopters that give traffic statistics. They say, "Traffic on the highway is moderate." Well, up there it's moderate. Down here it's jammed like hell.

Every house in the suburbs has wall-to-wall carpeting. When I was a kid in

445

the tenements, we were lucky if we had wall-to-wall floors.

A fellow walked into a suburban bar and ordered a martini. Before drinking it, he removed the olive and carefully put it into a small glass jar. Then he ordered another martini and did the same thing. After an hour, when he was full of martinis and the jar was full of olives, he staggered out. "Well," said a customer, "I never saw anything as peculiar as that."
"What's so peculiar about that?" the bartender said. "His wife sent him out for a jar of olives."

SUBURBIA: Where the houses are farther apart—and the payments are closer together.

A suburbanite believes in these inalienable rights: life, liberty, and the pursuit of his neighbor's wife.

I knew it would happen sooner or later. One of the suburban stores opened a downtown branch.

A fellow who reads a lot about the wild life of suburbia says he hears about the orgies, but he only gets invited to the PTA.

Suicide

Statistics prove that marriage is a preventative of suicide—statistics also prove that suicide prevents marriage.

Superstitions

"Do you think it's unlucky to postpone a wedding?"
"Not if you keep on doing it!"

I don't believe in that seven years' hard luck baloney if you break a mirror. My uncle broke one and he

didn't have seven years' hard luck at all—he died the day he broke it.

Black cats are unlucky? This one isn't—he just ate your dinner.

SHE: "That's my husband—better go out the window."
HE: "But it's thirteen stories up!"
SHE: "This is no time to be superstitious."

"I knew I would have bad luck—thirteen people at dinner!"
"You don't believe in that junk about thirteen being unlucky?"
"It was for me—I paid the check!"

The madam was instructing the new maid, "Remember, always serve from the left and take the plates from the right."
"Whatsa matter, ma'am, you superstitious?"

Tall

He was so tall—when he fell down he was out of town.

He rents out in May as a totem pole.

You got to climb her to kiss her.

He doesn't peek through keyholes—strictly transoms.

When he is on the road—the telephone company keeps wiring him for sound.

Taxes
(*see Income Tax*)

If you do wrong you get fired. If you do right you get taxed.

A merchant got into trouble with the income taxers, so he went to the office to explain his records, which were full of shorthand and mysterious markings. They told him they only wanted to know how much he spent, how much he took in, and how much he profited. He said, "That's all? I wouldn't even tell that to my partner."

"Gentlemen," begged the Republican chairman of a bipartisan Congressional committee, "permit me to tax your memories for a moment." "Golly," muttered a Democrat member to a crony, "why haven't we thought of that?"

By the way, have you seen the new tax forms? They're printing them on Kleenex. That's to keep you comfortable while you pay through the nose!

"Pay your taxes with a smile." I'd like to, but they insist on cash.

Nowadays we don't make money, we just hold it for the government between tax collections.

The difference between death and taxes is that death doesn't get worse every time Congress meets!

The tax collector mus ove ocr people he' crea ing so many of hem

AD N NEWSPAPER 'Man with nccme ax olank would ike o neet ady with income '

I wrote the income Tax Bureau o have a heart, and they wrote back and said, WE'LL TAKE IT!

With taxes taking everything, you work like a dog all your life so you can live like a dog.

I found out that it's the Ways and Means Committee that takes care of your taxes—if you have Means they'll find Ways to get it!

The income tax is the government's version of instant poverty.

Maybe the President can't cure poverty, but the way taxes are going— they're sure gonna cure wealth.

I feel wonderful. I went down to the Internal Revenue Bureau and gave them all the cash I had—now I'm paid up to 1932.

Those government boys are pretty clever. They figured out a way, with that withholding tax, to get to my salary before my wife does.

If St. Patrick's Day is the wearing of the green, April 15th is when you get rid of your green.

The income tax has created more liars in America than golf.

I have no trouble filling out my income tax—I have trouble paying it.

Pretty clever. First they put a big ax on liquor. Then they raise all other axes—to drive people to drink.

The axpaye was furious because he tax boys had ruled that a baby born in January was not deductible on last year's income 'I can't understand it, ' he reasoned 'it was last year's business!"

I'm putting all my money in taxes— it's the only thing sure to go up.

Arthur Godfrey says: "I'm proud t pay taxes in the U.S.A. But the only thing is—I could be just as proud for half the money."

The current take-home pay is hardly worth the trip.

There's a new way to beat the inheritance tax—leave everything to the government.

Build a better mousetrap—and the Internal Revenue boys will beat a path to your door.

Taxicab Drivers

Two stuffy old dowagers were sitting in a cab. One turned to the other and said, "These cab drivers make so much money they all have homes on Long Island." The two women went on talking about how wealthy the driver should be. He remained silent. Finally one of the matrons said to the other, "Some service. There's not even an ashtray back here."

At this point the driver turned and said, "Oh, just throw it on the floor, I have a woman who comes in once a week."

I know a guy who is so rich he takes taxicabs to go to the drive-in movies.

The taxi went out of control and was screaming through the middle of town. "Stop it this instant," said the lady passenger.

"I can't," the cabbie shouted frantically.

"Well, at least turn off the meter."

This is a Hy Gardner classic: It all started in front of the Waldorf-Astoria. A mink-befurred, lorgnette-dangling dowager, with trunks and suitcases stacked up like planes over Kennedy, was helped into a cab while a second taxi took care of her excess. "Mrs. Whittlestick," the uniformed doorman said, "wishes to be driven to Pier 8.

She's sailing on the S.S. *United States*." The hackie nodded, dropped the flag and beckoned with his little finger to have the baggage car follow.

In no longer than it takes to read a union contract, the cabs arrived at the pier, the baggage was checked into staterooms A through X, and the passenger spoke to the cabby. "If you're single and want to double your income, I'd like to offer you a proposition to see the world through your own windshield. I simply loathe hailing strange cabs in strange places. How would you like to drive me around Europe, all expenses paid?"

The hackie's mouth opened, but no words came out. Finally he nodded. In a few minutes, arrangements were made to have the cab hoisted into the hold of the ship where it remained till the ship berthed in Le Havre. From there they drove to Paris, then Nice, then Monte Carlo, then back to Paris for the Channel crossing to England, then to Rome, Berlin, and through the Scandinavian countries. Like the cab's two occupants, the meter never stopped running. Eventually, the party retraced its tire treads, and the *United States* docked again at the point of origination, Pier 8. The cab was hoisted out of the hold and plunked on terra firma.

"Well, my good man," the fatigued dowager sighed, paying the $12,457 clicked on the clock, "we're on native soil again, thank goodness. Now will you please drive me home?" "Where is home, ma'am?" the hackie smiled. "It's near Prospect Park, in Brooklyn," his benefactor replied. "Brooklyn!" the hackie snorted, slamming the door. "Are you nuts? You'll have to take another cab. Every time I go to Brooklyn I have to come back to Manhattan empty!"

The taxi driver was having such a bad day, his flag was at half-mast.

There's still a bit of risk in aviation. The taxi ride from the city to the airport.

What most people would like to save for a rainy day is a taxi.

TAXI DRIVER: A man who drives away customers.

Teenagers
(see Youth, Juvenile Delinquents, Children, Kids, Colleges, Universities and Hippies)

"How did you get your broken leg?"
"My girl's father threw me out of the window."
"Why?"
"We were doing the frug when her old man came in—he's deaf and he couldn't hear the music."

The aunt suggested to the fifteen-year-old girl to tell her mother everything.
"I can't," she answered. "Mother is so innocent, really, I haven't got the heart."

"My teenage son obeys me to the letter."
"How do you do it?"
"Easy—I tell him to do as he pleases!"

The two teeners, fifteen years old, were refused a marriage license. "How about a learning permit?" one of them asked the clerk.

"Mother, what's the name of that boy I met on my vacation?" the teener asked.
"Which one?"
"You know, the one I couldn't live without?"

She took her teenage son to the doctor because he couldn't see. "He doesn't need a doctor," the medic said, "he needs a haircut."

"Let's cool it tonight," the teener said to her boyfriend. "Dad and I are in outsville—he found out we used his car last night."
"How did he find out?"
"It wasn't hard. We hit him!"

I wonder if Mr. Bell would have bothered to invent the telephone if he had a teenage daughter of his own?

In the old days a boy gave a girl his class ring when they were going steady. Nowadays he lets her use his hair curlers.

The teen at school was bragging about her roommate, "I should be so lucky—she's going with a Thunderbird, two Lincolns and a Chris-Craft."

The mother was trying to get her daughter to wear her hair a little shorter. "But mother," the teenager pleaded, "my boy friend wears his hair longer than mine now."

"I got 10,000 or more men who work for me and jump at my slightest whim," the big business tycoon told his psychiatrist, "but I can't persuade my one teenage son to get a haircut."

She would run away from home if she could figure a way to take the phone with her.

A young lady of seventeen started her search for summer employment a few days ago by putting on her most adult clothes and making the rounds of department stores. In one of them she favorably impressed the personnel chief, who showed her around the store

449

and said: "You know, it certainly is refreshing to see a teenager who believes in dressing properly." At that moment, one of the young lady's school chums, dressed in torn jeans, dirty sneakers and a sloppy sweat shirt, came by and yelled out:

"Hey, Cindy, how come you're wearing those funny clothes?"

The hardest part of telling young people about the facts of life is finding something that they don't already know.

I know a teenage boy who's clean-cut, neatly dressed and a dedicated student. His parents have been advised that with a year in analysis he can be completely straightened out.

The teen phoned her mother and said: "Mom, I got a surprise for you. I'm here in Irving's apartment—and we're engaged."

"My God," mamma yelled, "in what?"

No wonder today's teenager is confused. Half the adults are telling him to find himself and the other half are telling him to get lost.

Television

Movies on TV are cut so much for commercials—one of these days we are going to see "The Five Commandments."

He didn't have a TV set, so he bored a hole into his neighbor's apartment and watched wrestling every night—until he found his neighbors didn't have a TV set either.

TV is a wonderful thing. You meet so many new people—mostly repairmen.

He'd be the most popular man on TV if he were as well known as his jokes.

TV is proof that people would rather look at anything—than each other.

There was a TV producer who was doing fine with a summer replacement—until his wife found out about her.

We owe a lot to daytime TV. Think of all the women who might otherwise be out driving.

I believe in pay TV—we should definitely be paid for seeing some of those shows.

Television is very educational. My nephew has learned three ways to mug a woman, four ways to avoid leaving fingerprints, and five ways to ambush a cop.

The husband was complaining: TV not only replaced radio—it also replaced housework.

In Russia, television watches you.

Russians like our Westerns. There is only one difference. They are rooting for the Indians.

Television is really getting to be murder. You turn on the set and you see the worst kind of violence, crime, degeneracy, murder, and rape—and that's only the *news*.

Television has been so bad lately—the children are doing their homework again.

Remember when your children used to be exposed to all that violence, vulgarity, temptations, drugs, and evil on the streets of New York? Now with TV they can see the same thing but in the safety of their own home.

Television will never replace the newspaper—you can't wrap a herring in a television set.

"Television is called a medium because anything good on it is rare."— Fred Allen

A movie on TV is just like a wife— it's home and it's free.

I'm enjoying TV more than ever. I have a six-foot screen—it's Chinese and I have it in front of my TV set.

Before television, nobody ever knew what a headache looked like.

Summer reruns on TV had one thing in their favor. You actually enjoyed having them interrupted by commercials.

They say one star of a TV series took his role so seriously that his signature became illegible.

Texas
(*see Rich; Texas in the Monologues*)

The El Paso merchant was helping his son with his homework on astronomy. "Some day, daddy," said the boy, "I'd like to go to the moon."
"Don't worry, son," the father reassured him, "we'll send for it tomorrow."

A Fort Worth resident wanted Louis Armstrong to fly his thirty-piece orchestra down to his ranch. The price was right but the King of the Trumpet wanted to know how many guests would be at the party. "It ain't no party," said the Texan. "My doorbell chimes is busted and I feel neighbors who visit me like to hear music when they ring."

A Texan visiting Niagara Falls was told, "Look at that beautiful sight. I bet you don't have anything like that in your country."
"Nope," answered the man, "but we got a plumber in Dallas who could stop that leak in ten minutes."

A rich Waco kid wanted a new playpen, so his father bought him Alcatraz.

An oil man from Houston is dickering to buy Hollywood 'cause his kid would like to study the stars.

A Texan was dictating his will to his lawyer: "To my son I leave three million dollars—and he's lucky I didn't cut him off entirely."

I know a Texan who only carries $300 in cash with him—but that's not too bad for a three-year-old.

Theatres
(*see Actors, Hollywood, Show Business, etc.*)

My brother is practicing to be an actor—so far he's learned to sleep until noon.

Business was pretty bad. A woman called the box office and asked, "What time does the show start?"
The manager replied, "What time can you get here?"

The fat lady showed her two tickets to the usher. "Where's the other party?" the usher asked. "They're both for me," she said. "I'm a big woman and I like to be comfortable."
"Well," the usher said, "it ain't gonna be easy—your seats are A10 and G102."

451

Theatres are like brothels—one never knows what he will find inside, or whom.

Danny Thomas

The women of today really have it easy. They have automatic stoves, automatic mixers, automatic dishwashers, and automatic driers. When the bride pokes her finger at the groom for the wedding ring—that's the last thing she does by hand!

And how about the kids? They really have it made! Their mothers drive them everywhere. They drive them to school, to their friends' houses, to the movies, to the bowling alley, and to dancing lessons. I know one kid who wanted to run away from home and his mother said, "Wait—I'll drive you."

And each kid nowadays has his own TV set, hi-fi and air-conditioning. Why, when I was a boy, the only time we had air-conditioning was when my mother blew on the minestrone.

One of my pet peeves is that Beverly Hills doctors charge such outrageous prices for doing nothing. One particular visit to my doctor, for which he charged me fifty dollars, was the straw that broke the camel's back. I went into his office, raised my arm, and said, "It hurts when I do this. What's your advice?"
His answer: "Don't do that."

My youngest boy, Tony, came to me one day with the inevitable question which I had been expecting for some time. "Daddy, where do I come from?"
After a gulp or two, I went into the age-old business about the birds and the bees, after which I asked him why he wanted to know.

"Well," said Tony, "my friend Bobby came from Toledo and I just wondered where I came from."

The firing squad was lined up. They put the blindfold on the political prisoner. The head of the firing squad raised his hand for the men to shoot, when all of a sudden the prisoner started to shout, "Fidel Castro is a bum." The captain of the firing squad stopped everything, walked over to the prisoner and said, "Listen you wanna get yourself in trouble?"

There was a long line waiting in the early morning in front of a clothing store that advertised a special sale. A man walked to the front of the line. The people grabbed him and pushed him to the end. Again he walked to the front and they beat him up and shoved him to the back. Once more he headed for the front of the line and they kicked him and pushed him into the gutter. Finally, he got up, brushed himself off, and said to a man at the end of the line, "If they do that once more—I'm not opening the store."

Guy saw a sign on a restaurant that said, "Elephant Ear on a Bun." Guy went in to try it. Ordered from the waiter. Five minutes later the waiter came back and said, "I'm sorry, we can't serve you the sandwich." Guy said, "Aha! It's a lie. You really don't have elephant ears here. You're out of them. Fake!" Waiter said, "No, sir, we have the elephant ears—but we're out of buns."

Thin
(*see Fat, Twiggy, Diet, etc.*)

Be true to your figure or they'll be falsies to you.

If a girl doesn't watch her form—a boy won't.

When a girl says she's got a boyish figure, it's usually straight from the shoulder.

She's so skinny that without her Adam's apple she'd have no shape at all.

This chick was so thin—I have seen more meat on a busboy's vest.

You could find better bodies in a used car lot.

She was so flat chested—she wore Band-Aids instead of a bra.

She was so skinny—she could creep through a piccolo without hitting a single note.

The only thing a sweater does for her is keep her warm.

A man on the beach was throwing sticks out into the ocean so his dog could bring them back. She was so skinny that the dog brought her back three times instead.

She's so thin—she wears suspenders to hold up her girdle.

She is so thin that she looks like six o'clock—up and down.

She was so thin she could look through a keyhole with both eyes.

She's so thin she can take a bath in a fountain pen.

She's so skinny she swayed in the breeze of an electric fan.

She's so skinny, she can walk through a harp without hitting a note.

She was so thin she once swallowed a black olive and eight men left town.

She was so thin that every time she yawned her dress fell down.

He's so thin that if he stood on a dime you could still read "In God We Trust."

Tipping
(*see Restaurants*)

My garage man sent me a Christmas card three weeks in advance. When it got closer to the holiday and he hadn't heard from me cash-wise, I received a second Christmas card with the notation, "HAPPY HOLIDAYS—second notice."

"I eat in a different restaurant every day."
"Why don't you try tipping the waiter?"

The rich manufacturer was drowning in a Miami Beach pool. The lifeguards pulled him out and brought him back to life. When he came to he asked his friend, "What do you tip for a thing like that?"

The waiter described one of his customers. "He reminds me of a couple of entertainers—Dean Martin when he drinks and Jack Benny when he tips."

The swank country club car attendant was in shock when the guest asked him to change a dollar. "Around here," the doorman said, "a dollar *is* change."

Helpful hints on how to tip a topless waitress—add up her measurements and give her 20 per cent.

Tombstones
(*see Cemeteries, Death, etc.*)

FOR A WAITER: God finally caught his eye.

453

Rest in peace, dear husband, until we meet again.

Here lies my wife—here let her lie! Now she is at rest—and so am I.

My uncle died while playing a pinball machine—so they tilted his tombstone.

He was always a polite man. Even his tombstone reads, "Pardon me for not rising."

He was the roughest guy to do business with. He always insisted on dating his checks ahead. When he finally died his tombstone read, "Here lies Frank Tanker. Died January 9th as of February 15th."

If men could see the epitaphs their family write on their tombstones—they would think they got in the wrong grave.

FOR THE OLD MAID: Who said you can't take it with you?

This is all over my head.—Robert Benchley

Involved in a plot.—Dorothy Parker

Here lies Walter Winchell in the dirt he loved so well.—Walter Winchell

This one's on me!—Milton Berle

I had a hunch something like this would happen.—Fontaine Fox

On the whole I'd rather be in Philadelphia.—W. C. Fields

Topless Waitresses

Until now, the only thing I had to worry about was the waitress getting her *finger* in the soup.

I don't go for topless waitresses, bar maids, shoeshine girls, or topless any-thing—the best part of getting a present is unwrapping it.

Some of these topless waitresses are so dumb, they have to be topless to count to two.

My ambition is to see a topless accordion player.

I liked the topless waitresses. I could have glanced all night.

One of the topless waitresses was being tried for indecent exposure. "Were you covered by anything at all?" the district attorney asked her. "I certainly was," the young woman answered. "What, specifically?" the D. A. asked. "Workmen's compensation."

TOPLESS WAITRESS: A wild waist show.

A topless waitress is a girl you look up to—very, very slowly.

All topless waitresses are unsuited for their job.

Misery is being a topless waitress and having a customer call you mister.

CUSTOMER TO TOPLESS WAITRESS: "A dozen oysters, please—one at a time."

Helpful hints on how to tip a topless waitress—add up her measurements and give her 20 per cent.

The topless waitress walked over to a customer and snapped, "Sir, please stop staring at me—this isn't my table."

Tough

He's so tough that every time he sticks his tongue out—he breaks a tooth.

He is so tough he eats sardines without removing the can.

She's so tough she uses barbed wire for a hairnet.

I came from a neighborhood that was so tough, if you didn't have at least one cauliflower ear—you were considered a sissy.

If you wore a clean shirt you got hissed.

In my neighborhood you became a judge or a killer.

"I didn't know you started using sawdust on the floor?"
"That's not sawdust—that's last night's furniture."

"My kid brother was so tough he once slapped Al Capone right in the kisser."
"I'd like to shake hands with your kid brother."
"I'm not gonna dig him up just for you."

"What steps would you take if somebody was coming at you with a knife?"
"Long ones."

He talked through the side of his mouth so much—he could spit around corners.

He's not afraid to face the music—except Lohengrin.

My neighborhood was so tough—any cat with a tail was a tourist.

Tourists
(*see Travel, International Humor, etc.*)

A tourist in France was eating at one of those outside restaurants. He couldn't pay his check—so they throw him *in!*

The Indian in Arizona asked the tourist from New York fifty dollars for the blanket. "I'll give you ten," he counter-offered.
"Oh no," said the Indian. "Don't start that Manhattan bit again."

An American tourist was telling his pals about his auto trip in Russia. "How do you know you're violating the traffic laws?" one listener asked.
"Easy—you go to prison."

The tourist from New York stopped at a small boite on the French Riviera. He ordered an ordinary ham sandwich. The bill was six dollars.
"Is ham so scarce?" the tourist asked in amazement.
"No, but American tourists are."

There were so many tourists they were getting into each other's snapshots.

Traffic
(*see Parking, etc.*)

The main reason for traffic congestion in New York is—automobiles!

It's not as easy as you think to get a parking ticket in New York. First you have to find a place to park.

The traffic situation has changed since last year. Last year it took me an hour and a half to get from the airport to midtown, no more. That's all changed. Today it took two hours —and I was coming by helicopter.

Solve the problem by making all the streets one-way going west—then it will be New Jersey's problem.

There is only one way to solve the traffic problem in New York. We got 8 million people in New York City. That's too many people. My idea is to take 5 million and move them to Hoboken. That will cause a traffic congestion in Hoboken—but that's *their* problem.

A policeman arrested me for running over a button—it was on *his* coat.

There are more cars in New York than England and France combined. There are more cars in California than Italy, Germany, and Belgium put together. There is only one solution—we will have to park overseas.

Alleviate traffic in one way: make every two-way street—a dead end.

The traffic was so bad that rescue planes had to drop supplies and food to the Good Humor man.

I read where a man is knocked down by a car every five minutes, in traffic. That guy must be made of iron.

The only time a pedestrian has the right of way is in an ambulance on the way to the hospital.

A rookie cop was asked by his sergeant what he was doing away from his corner where he was supposed to be directing traffic. He said, "I want another corner, Sarge. The traffic at my corner is always getting balled up."

I love those helicopters that give traffic statistics. They say, "Traffic on the highway is moderate." Well, up there it's moderate. Down here it's jammed.

The best way to kill an hour in New York City—is to drive around the block.

There are only two types of pedestrians in Los Angeles—the quick and the dead.

While driving crosstown—I got a ticket for parking.

What we need is drive-in streets.

Mayor Lindsay quotes Traffic Commissioner Barnes on our crowded streets: "The only way to get to the West Side is to be born there."

Travel
(*see also International and chapter on "International Humor," Tourists, alphabetical listing of countries, Airplanes, Railroads, Automobiles, etc.*)

1ST WOMAN: "This year I went to Majorca."
2ND WOMAN: "Where's Majorca?"
1ST WOMAN: "I don't know—we flew."

The Eiffel Tower looks likes an erector set that made good.

The Eiffel Tower looks like the Empire State Building after taxes.

The Colosseum is nice, but I think they ought to fix it up a little—it could use a good paint job.

But after seeing those backward broken-down countries it's good to be back in New York and see those broken-down streets.

I was amazed what they did to one street just a few blocks from here . . . they fixed it!

I dunno if Edison invented the electric light or the sledge-hammer.

When my wife packs for a trip, the only thing she leaves behind is a note for the milkman.

After looking at a prospective tourist's passport photo, a fellow at a travel bureau commented, "If the owner really looks like that, he's too sick to travel."

I tried traveling by boat but I wound up on the rails. I was so seasick, for six days after I was on land I was afraid to yawn. I'll never forget my last boat trip—and, it was! During a terrific storm, one middle of the night, the captain called us together and asked, "Is there anyone here who can pray?"

"I can," I shouted.

"Well," he warned, "better get started; we're one life preserver short."

Traveling to Europe has become fashionable. These days you can get to Paris sooner than you can go cross-town. My pal Morey Amsterdam, his wife Kay, and son Gregory made a trip to Europe between commercials on his TV show and returned gleeful about his exploits in Scotland and jolly old England. Says Mo: "It sure got foggy in London. I've only been in one city that was more foggy, but it was so foggy at the time, I couldn't see what city it was. So, my wife and I took a walk around the bank of the river. Suddenly, we were enveloped in a heavy fog. We couldn't see where we were going and got panicky. I called out in the fog, 'Hello!' Soon a voice came back through the fog, 'Hello!' I called, 'Can you tell us where we're going?' The voice came back through the fog: 'Into the Thames—I just came out.' "

You can always tell a backward country—kids there still listen to their parents.

I was in Europe for three weeks and had twenty-one days of uninterrupted diarrhea.

PASSENGER: "What makes this train go so slow?"
IRATE CONDUCTOR: "If you don't like it, get off and walk."
PASSENGER: "I would, only I'm not expected until train time."

Road maps tell a motorist everything he wants to know—except how to fold them up again.

AIRPLANE TRAVEL: Seeing less and less of more and more.

In Indonesia I couldn't find anybody in at the government offices in the afternoons. I finally found a clerk and asked, "Don't they work in government offices in the afternoon?"

"It's in the mornings they don't work," he explained; "in the afternoons they don't come."

Traveling Salesmen

This traveling salesman was stuck in a small town and went to the only available farm house for a place to sleep. "Can you put me up for the night?" he asked the farmer.

"I reckon I can," he answered, "if you don't mind sharing a room with my young son."

"My God," said the salesman, "I'm in the wrong joke!"

The traveling salesman gave his route over to a new man. He also gave him his little black book. "You've got to look up this girl in Cleveland. She takes to good-hearted men—also *from*."

She has a good head on her shoulders—each night it's a different one.

"Where you been?" one salesman asked the other.

"In the phone booth talking to my girl, but someone wanted to use the phone—so we got out."

"Treat your husband with more consideration and kindness," the psychiatrist advised the wife of the traveling salesman, "if you want him to come home more often. Instead of insulting him be loving."

When her husband came home the next night she followed the doctor's advice. The traveling man staggered home and plopped down on the couch and fell asleep. The wife gently stroked his head, kissed him on the ear and attempted to rouse him from his drunken stupor. "Honey," she said sweetly, "it's late. Let's go upstairs and go to bed."

"Might as well," he blubbered, "I'll get hell when I get home anyway."

A farmer's daughter in Virginny
Met a salesman one night and he
Felt a gun at his head.
"Have no fear, sir," she said,
"As long as you feel givinny."

"Did I have trouble with that farmer's daughter. She wanted me to sit in the back seat—while she was driving."

The traveling salesman held the farmer's daughter in the moonlight. Their lips and bodies met in complete harmony.

She looked up at him ecstatically: "My paw is the best pistol shot in the country," she gushed.

"And what does that make you?" he asked.

"Your bride!" she blushed.

The beautiful lady answered the door to the salesman. "Is your husband in?" he asked.

"He won't be back for a week," the stacked one said.

"Can I come in and wait?" he leered

TRAVELING SALESMAN: "I knew I would have hard luck. We had dinner on the train and there were thirteen in the party."

FRIEND: "That's only superstition. What makes you think thirteen at dinner is unlucky?"

TRAVELING SALESMAN: "I had to pay the check."

Troubles

Men's troubles are due to three things—women, money, and both.

If you want to forget all your troubles—wear tight shoes.

"I want to share all your troubles," she said lovingly to her fiancé.

"I have no troubles," he said sweetly. "We're not married yet."

You've heard of cigarette lighters that won't work? Mine won't go out.

I owe the federal government $10,000, the state $5,000, the city $1,000, and I'm 20 cents overdue on my library card.

You think you got trouble? I know a harmonica player with chapped lips.

He sent for a Sears Roebuck haircut and they sent back the wrong head.

The Wit of Harry S Truman

Commenting on the praise heaped on him by the toastmaster, Truman cracked, "I am really overcome. You don't know how difficult it is to be present at your own funeral and still be able to walk around."

President Truman wasn't too happy constantly making speeches. He used to tell a story to illustrate the point. "When I have to make a speech I feel like the fellow who was at the funeral of his wife, and the undertaker had asked him if he would ride to the cemetery in the same car with his mother-in-law. He said. 'Well, I can do it, but it's just going to spoil the whole day for me!' "

When he accepted the Democratic Presidential nomination, Truman immediately started swinging at the Republicans:

"Herbert Hoover once ran on the slogan: 'Two cars in every garage!' Apparently the Republican candidate this year is running on the slogan 'Two families in every garage!' "

In 1940, the Republicans had a poll that told them they had the edge. Well, it was a mighty sharp edge. They got cut to ribbons on election day.

I am trying to fix it so that the middle income bracket can live as long as the very rich and the very poor.

When President Truman vetoed a bill after waiting till the end of the ten-day grace period, a Congressman asked if it had been difficult for him to make up his mind.

"I intended to veto it all along," he answered. "In fact, I feel like the blacksmith on the Missouri jury. The judge asked if he was prejudiced against the defendant.

" 'Oh, no, judge. I think we ought to give him a fair trial. Then I think we ought to take the S.O.B. out and string him up.' "

The remark that the President's father, John Anderson Truman, had been a failure in life caused the President to crack, "My father was not a failure. After all, he was the father of the President of the United States."

Lee Tully

My doctor was writing a prescription with a thermometer. I said: "How can you write with a thermometer?"

"Oops!" he said. "One of my patients must be walking around with my fountain pen stuck in him!"

A man rushed into a drugstore and asked the man behind the counter: "Do you do urinanalyses here?"

"Yes," was the reply.

"Then wash your hands and make me a malted."

I went to my psychiatrist and told him that my wife and I are slowly drifting apart—so he showed me how to speed it up.

I took my dog to a psychiatrist. Now I got the only dog that barks with a lisp.

Hospitals are so expensive that people can't afford to get sick today. The President said he was against Medicare —he didn't want the hospital too crowded when he came for his free visit.

Whenever I go to my doctor, he always gives me a prescription written in Latin. I had a friend read it and it said, "I got my ten—now you get yours."

This fellow was sitting in a hospital and he called over the nurse.

"How is the fella in 379 doing?"

"Much better, sir, he'll be released tomorrow."

"That's fine. My doctor never tells me anything."

This man and woman were walking around the Museum of Modern History when they noticed a mummy all wrapped up in bandages in a case. The woman asked her husband: "What's that number on the case?"

"Must be the guy who hit him," replied her husband.

They're talking about making men's pants out of wood. Then they won't have zippers—they'll have revolving doors.

Imagine a woman's pajamas made of newspaper—and the man says, "Turn over, I want to read the sports page."

TWIGGY: I haven't seen a figure like that since I left day camp.

She gets $300 an hour to pose—it takes 45 minutes just to find her body.

If she didn't have goosebumps, she'd have no figure at all.

Lee Tully to hostile audience: "Now let's understand each other. I'm a professional comedian—and you're an amateur audience."

California is the only place in the country where if you bite into an orange—it bites back!

Everything in California is drive-ins: drive-in theatres, drive-in movies, drive-in restaurants, etc. The only time you get out of your car is to make a trade.

At the drive-in restaurants they have hamburgers in all sizes: tiny size, mini size, small, medium, regular, large, jumbo, and super. Now they have a special large economy size—they open the back of your trunk and slide a whole steer into your fanbelt.

In California everything nowadays is hi-rise: Forest Lawn is putting in a special hi-rise where they bury you standing up with an I.D. card in your hand.

The freeways are unbelievable. The traffic is so bad, if you push in your cigarette lighter the driver in front of you says whoops!!

1ST MAN: "Do you have any nude pictures of your wife?"
2ND MAN: "No, I don't."
1ST MAN: "Would you like to buy some?"

Two women were talking. The first woman said, "I just bought a condominium."

"Aren't you better off with birth control pills?" asked the other.

Turkey

They must have a girls' ball team in the Sultan's harem. One day one of the girls asked the Sultan if she was in tomorrow's line-up.

Don't *any* of your wives understand you?

When the lad came of age, his father presented him with fifty concubines as a sort of Bar-Mitzvah present. The youngster was bewildered. "It's not that I don't know what to do," he mumbled, "but where do I begin?"

Twiggy
(see Figures, Mini-Skirts, Thin, etc.)

Twiggy could put her bra on backwards and it would fit.

Twiggy came here to pose for hosiery ads—she posed for a hose.

When she drinks tomato juice—she looks like a thermometer.

She's well-reared—and looks good in the front, too.

She'd make a good model—for slip-covers.

Description of Raquel Welch: the thinking man's Twiggy.

Joey Bishop: "I'll send you a picture of Twiggy—a 1 x 12 glossy."

You have to look at the bottom of her feet to find out which way she's facing.

Ugly

There was one gal named Judy Schwartz who had a beautiful face except for her nose. She had to lift it up to eat. But a girl's face isn't everything. Listen to this: Judy's measurements were 38-23-38—those were her leg measurements.

An acquaintance tells of a wise-guy husband saying to a visiting friend, "Yes, that was my wife who opened the door for you—do you think I would hire a maid that homely?"

Her head sticking out of a cellar door would start a hockey game in anybody's neighborhood.

She's so ugly she rents herself out for Halloween parties.

She was too ugly to have her face lifted so they lowered her body instead.

She used to do scarecrow work by appointment only.

If all girls are sisters under the skin—I wish she'd go back under there and send out her sister.

She had everything a man desires—muscles and a beard.

She used to model bicycle pumps.

When she came into the room—the mice jumped on the chairs.

She had a real shady background. Why not? She had hips like a beach umbrella.

I asked the girl in front of me at the movies to remove her hat. She became very angry. She wasn't wearing any. I liked her face. It reminded me of my home—especially the front stoop. I began talking to her and commented favorably about her wavy hair. Later, I found out that her hair was straight, but her head was wavy.

His second wife is so ugly that two weeks before he took her home he told his children ghost stories so they wouldn't be frightened when they saw her.

She sent her picture to the lonely hearts club and they sent it back—they said they weren't *that* lonely.

Has she got buck teeth? We haven't used a bottle opener in years.

I'm not saying she has buck teeth—but her nose looks like it's playing the piano.

She was a neat girl—not a wrinkle out of place.

461

She's got a very unusual figure. Her seams are straight—but her legs are crooked.

Her mouth is so big she can sing duets by herself.

She's got more wrinkles than a road map.

I've seen better legs on kitchen tables.

She certainly has what it takes. Only she had it so long—nobody wants it.

She's the only girl I know who parts her teeth in the center.

She's so ugly that I had to buy her back from the dog catcher eight times.

She is so ugly that even starvation wouldn't look her in the face.

She went to the zoo. She had to buy two tickets—one to get in and one to get out.

She looked like a dunked tea bag.

She has a winning smile—but a losing face.

He is knock-kneed, cross-eyed, fat and stupid—and those are his good points.

Her photographs do her an injustice —they look like her.

If he were a building—he'd be condemned.

When she passes the waterfront— even the tugboats don't whistle.

She had a coming-out party—but they made her go back in again.

The only time she passes as normal —is Halloween.

After my first TV show I got three offers—from plastic surgeons.

She looks like a million—every year of it.

It's easy for her to avoid peeping toms. All she has do to is leave her shades up.

Undertakers
(see Death, Tombstones, etc.)

I visited a friend of mine at his funeral parlor and noticed two of the corpses suddenly sit up. "What's that?" I exclaimed hysterically.
"My partners," he soothed. "They just wanted the place to look busy."

This guy made millions, but was the unhappiest man in the world. "Everyplace," he told the psychiatrist, "I am a big man, but at home I'm nothing."
"Go home and be the boss," the doctor told him. He went home, banged the door shut, grabbed his wife and shouted, "I want dinner on the table, and draw my bath, and lay out my evening clothes. I'm going out with a beautiful blonde tonight and you know who's going to tie my black bow tie."
"Yes," she said. "Park West Memorial Chapel."

He's such an ambitious mortician— he keeps bringing his work home with him.

He works for an undertaker—and keeps bringing samples home.

One mortician in L.A. spent a fortune advertising the slogan: "Go now —pay later."

Unions
(*see Pickets, Work, Employment*)

The little girl's father was a union organizer. "Daddy," she asked him one evening, "I can't sleep—tell me a bedtime story!"

Daddy nodded, "Once upon a time and a half . . ."

The unions are pressing for a four-day week. One stenographer complained, "Who is going to pay for the two coffee breaks and the lunch hour I'll be missing?"

Bernard Baruch walked into a classy restaurant with two men dressed in sweat shirts. When the owner protested, Mr. Baruch explained, "I can't help it. I bought a hearing aid, and the union makes me carry two electricians."

I joined an international union—now I can be out of work all over the world.

Some people are still willing to do an honest day's work—but they want a week's pay for it.

It's no surprise to see the Russians trying to make up with us now. We've got more workers on strike than they've got working.

A very red-hot labor leader walked into a matchmaker's joint looking for a bride. "Before we decide on anything," he said, "I must tell you I'll only do business with a union shop."

"You came to the right place. This is a strictly union establishment."

Then he picked out a gorgeous twenty-year-old redhead. "I'll take her," he said happily.

"No," said the head matchmaker, "you have to take this one." She was the picture of a professional ugg—strictly a Social Security reject.

"Why do I have to take this early Salvador Dali?' the labor leader asked.

"She has seniority."

A New York sign painter who made a specialty of lettering signs for union strikers was picketed by men who wore signs saying, "These signs were not painted by the firm we are picketing."

The organizer for the union was negotiating with the head of the firm. "That's all well and good," he said, "a minimum basic wage, a guaranteed annual bonus, a pension plan, hospitalization, guaranteed vacation with pay—*now*, my men want a guarantee that you won't go broke!"

One group of Australian dock workers demanded what they called "temptation money" in their union contract. If they loaded or unloaded anything that would tempt them to steal—like perfume, cameras, jewelry or liquor, they reasoned they should be compensated by extra money against the temptation to steal.

United Nations
(*see International Humor*)

I say do not let China in the U.N. You know the Chinese—once they vote—an hour later they want to vote again.

The U.N. is trying to get all the countries in the world to live as one big family. If you want to take my family as an example—they've succeeded.

The trouble with the U.N. is—there are too many foreigners in it.

Universities
(*see Colleges, Teenagers, Juvenile Delinquents, etc.*)

Pop was complaining about his son. "I sent my son to college and he spent

463

fours years going to parties, having fun, and necking. It's not that I'm sorry I sent him, I should have gone myself."

Anyone who watches a student demonstration long enough will realize that youth is stranger than fiction.

The beatniks carried signs at a university when Vice-President Humphrey appeared to speak. The signs read, "Stop U.S. aggression in Vietnam." Another group of students picketed the disheveled beatniks with signs that said, "Bathing can be fun."

When Pop went to see his daughter graduate, she took him aside and confessed, "Pop, I need your help—I ain't a good girl any more."

"After sacrificing for you for four years, killing and denying myself to send you through college, I came up here to see you graduate—and you're still using the word *ain't?*"

They tried an experiment at the university. All the dates for the dance were arranged by a computer. After a rough evening, one student remarked, "What a frightening experience—to find out just what you deserve."

He is well-informed about anything he doesn't have to study.

Then there was the faint-hearted college student who was afraid to burn his draft card—so he boiled it.

The President of Harvard explained why universities have so much learning: "The freshmen bring a little in and the seniors take none out—so it accumulates through the years."

The President of the University of Oklahoma: "We're working to develop a university the football team can be proud of."

The President of Indiana University: "A college education is one thing a person is willing to pay for and not get."

They have a new course at Columbia U.—Reading, Writing, and Rioting.

Used Car Dealers

Pity the minister who bought a used car and then didn't have the vocabulary to run it.

USED CAR DEALER TO CAR OWNER: "Let me put it this way. If your car were a horse, it would have to be shot. Come to think of it, your car *is* shot."

USED CAR DEALER MAKING SPIEL: "And in this car, you never get car sickness. We give you a supply of pills to take before each payment is due."

A man just out of the army bought a used car. As the deal was not aboveboard, the dealer refused to give the young man a bill of sale. However, the young man was insistent and finally the dealer said wearily, "Look here, you've got the car, I've got the money, everybody's satisfied—why on earth do you insist upon a bill of sale?"

"Well," explained the young man, "when I die, Saint Peter won't let me into heaven when I tell him what I've paid because he'll think I'm lying. And I don't want to look all over hell for you to prove that I'm not."

A used car dealer who switched to TV sales, pitched this line to a customer: "This set's hardly been used. It belonged to an old lady in Westchester with weak eyes."

"You the guy that sold me this car two weeks ago?"

"Yes sir."

"Will you tell me again what you

said about it then—I'm getting discouraged."

"Mamma, what happens to a car when it gets too old to run?"
"Somebody sells it to your father as a used car—good as new."

"How did you have an accident with that used car I sold you?"
"I couldn't put my hand out when I was pushing it around the corner."

The person who has a second-hand car knows how hard it is to drive a bargain.

"My advice, sir," said the mechanic to the car owner, "is that you keep the oil and change the car."

Vacations
(*see Borscht Belt Laughs, Travel, Tourists, Hotels*)

The only book that really tells you where to go on your vacation is your check book.

"Does your vacation start soon?'
"Yes, my wife is leaving tomorrow."

A honeymoon is a vacation a man takes before going to work for a new boss.

I was having the time of my life—until my husband found out.

He gets two vacations a year. When his son goes to camp—and when his wife goes to Florida.

Those who say you can't take it with you—never saw the way my wife packs our car for a vacation trip.

On their vacations—people drive thousands of miles to have their pictures taken in front of their cars.

Vacations are easy to plan. The boss tells you when and the wife tells you where.

Vacation at Sing Sing for good behavior: they now give you two weeks at Dannemora.

The bachelor was exasperated at his unsuccessful attempt to rush the girl on the dance floor. "Look, honey," he leered, with that 'let's get out of here and up to my room' look, "I'm only going to be here for the weekend."
"Okay, okay," she snapped back, "I'm dancing as fast as I can."

VACATION TIME: That's when the highway departments close up all the regular roads and open up all the detours.

Vacation is that time of year when you spend two weeks trying to get away from everybody who is trying to get away from you.

The first time I went to Paris, I took my wife with me. You know how it is—you always pack a lot of things you don't need.

Vacation is a system whereby people who are merely tired become exhausted.

VACATION: Three weeks on the sands—the rest of the year on the rocks.

A girl met a boy on a European holiday but they've agreed not to marry until they both finish paying for their trips.

Vaudeville
(*see Show Business, Show People, Actors, Theatres, Hollywood, etc.*)

A small-time vaudeville comic was in a plane crash and awoke to find himself in a strange place. "Where am I?" he asked a fellow beside him. "You're in hell," he was informed. "That's my agent for you," sighed the comic, "he's never booked me in a good spot yet."

A TV salesman was trying to convince a vaudevillian to buy a portable model. "Just imagine,'" he said, "when you're on tour, sitting in a lonely hotel room, all you have to do is press a button and suddenly a gorgeous, scantily dressed girl will be standing in front of you." "The hotels I stop at," said the ham, "I can get the same thing without television."

"I've been out of work four years," one vaudevillian was telling another.

"I've been out of work eight years," the second topped him.

"Oh," said the first, "if only I could get out of this business."

The vaudeville comic opened in Boston and only six people showed up in the audience. When he returned to New York he was at the Friars and "on" as usual. "You wouldn't believe it," he bragged. "It was the worst opening of my life—only seven people showed up."

Fred Allen was playing to an audience that sat on its hands throughout his act.

When he returned to his dressing room, a fellow performer asked, "How did it go, Fred? Did you kill them?"

"No," said Allen. "They were dead when I got there."

Jackie Vernon

To show you the kind of guy I am I must tell you I'm the only person Dale Carnegie ever punched in the mouth.

The other night I was in the White House. President Johnson took me aside—and left me there.

Things happen to me that never happened to anybody else. I bought a set of snow tires—and they melted. I had a nose job and my nose grew back. I was adopted by a Korean family.

To really understand me, you have to know a bit of my philosophy. Here's the bit: There are two sides to every broken window. A bird in the hand is a dead duck. A sieve may not hold water, but it will hold another sieve. Horse sense is what keeps a woman from becoming a nag. It usually takes more than three weeks to prepare a good impromptu speech. Overeating reduces the life span—a word to the wide should be sufficient.

I invented a square bathtub which cannot leave a ring.

Volkswagen Jokes

Half-car, will travel.

The Texan paid for his Cadillac with a $10,000 bill and asked for his change in Volkswagens.

SIGN ON REAR BUMPER: "Don't hit me —I have a big brother in the garage."

Actually, you don't get into it—you put it on.

I got two of them. I use them for cuff links—they also make good bookends.

Oh, I admit it's cheap to buy, inexpensive to operate, easy to handle—but what good is it otherwise?

It has a fourth speed—just for passing through Jewish neighborhoods.

ONE CAR WASH ATTENDANT TO THE OTHER: "Here comes one of them spit jobs."

"I'm only going fifty miles. Don't fill her up—just spray the tank."

"My brother got so thin. Remember that Mack truck he had tattooed on his chest? It's now a Volkswagen!"

My Volkswagen gets a car wash in a laundromat.

SIGN IN APARTMENT HOUSE: "No baby carriages or Volkswagens allowed in the lobby."

I didn't believe that there was a recession until I heard about the Texan that bought a Volkswagen—on time.

WOMAN: "You've got to help me reduce. My husband just gave me a present and I can't get into it."
VIC TANNY: "Don't worry, madam, in two weeks you'll be able to get into that dress."
WOMAN: "What dress? It's a Volkswagen!"

A cop was chasing me when I was driving my Volkswagen this afternoon. I knew it was impossible to outrun him —so I drove up on the sidewalk and got lost in the crowd.

He had twenty-one parking tickets on his Volkswagen. They put him in jail and deported the car.

AD IN PAPER: "Boy with Volkswagen anxious to meet girl with MG. Object: Share parking meter."

Volkswagen is putting out a new six-pack carton.

Wall Street
(*see Stock Market*)

"What's the latest dope on Wall Street?"
"My son!"

He was a bear on Wall Street—and that's how he wound up.

She complained to her broker, "I can't understand it. Every time they talk about panic—my stocks go down."

The only thing I've learned about the stock market is that you have to be patient—and the way it's going lately, I'm going to become one.

Bob Hope says he still remembers that Blue Monday on Wall Street. "Even the holders of the gilt-edged AT&T were ready for the big jump. I remember I put a dime in a coin telephone and a voice said, 'God bless you, sir.'"

War
(*see Army, Soldier, Air Force, etc.*)

A Norwegian, during the last war, was talking to the village quisling and asked him what he was going to do when the Allies won the war. The quisling said, "Oh, I'll just put my hat on and leave." The loyalist said, "Yah, but what are you going to put your hat on?"

I don't know what the silly talk is about us being involved in World War III—we just can't afford to win one more war.

It's like Will Rogers said—and it still holds good—we never lost a war or won a conference.

The Prime Minister of a tiny little country suggested at his cabinet meeting that they start a war with the U.S. "Then," he said, "when we lose, America will give us roads, and food, and money—we'll be rich."

"But," said a sad-faced minister, "suppose we win?"

During a blackout in London, the girl yelled, "Take your hands off me—not you—*you!*"

LIEUTENANT: "When you see the whites of their eyes—shoot. Being color blind, I better stay out of this."

CAPTAIN: "When the enemy gets within 100 yards of us I want you to retreat. Being a little lame, I better start now."

This uniform fits me perfectly. Tell me, am I deformed?

This kid wrote to his mom from a foxhole, "As I write this, there are planes fighting overhead, bombs are bursting all around, bullets are whizzing by and all around me there is hand-to-hand fighting." His mother answered, *"DON'T BUTT IN."*

The private was running away from the front lines a mile a minute when a captain jumped out from behind a tree and commanded, "Why are you running?"

"Because," said the private, "I can't fly."

He was so ugly he looked as if a plastic surgeon had started to lift his face but was interrupted. He was the ugliest soldier in the army. He won the French Medal of Honor for bravery, but never got it because they couldn't find a French general who would kiss him.

They threw me out of the submarine service. They caught me sleeping with the windows open.

OFFICER: "What were you in civilian life?"

PRIVATE: "Happy, sir."

A Marine in Vietnam said to Bob Hope after one of his shows there, "You look tired, Bob. Next time stay home and send for us."

Washington, D. C.
(*see Politics, Republicans, Democrats, etc.*)

"Rome had Senators. Now I know why it declined."—Will Rogers

Congress is anxious to adjourn—I'd imagine they'd be scared to go home.

Adam Clayton Powell was reprimanded for putting his family on the payroll and taking Congressional junkets. Now what's new about that. I know one Congressman who pays his nephew $10,000 a year as his correspondence secretary—and the kid is only eight months old.

And about the junkets—that's why we can't get in a war with any of those countries. If we dropped a bomb anyplace—we're bound to hit a few of our own Congressmen.

They say George Washington was first in war and first in peace—but if he really never lied like I've been told—he'd never make it in politics today.

Two Senators in Washington were talking about the Bobby Baker case. "Do you think he got what he deserved?" asked the first Senator.

"Who cares?" said the other. "I gave already from the office."

Vice-President Hubert Humphrey tags the nation's capital so well with the story of his first election to the Senate in 1948. The night before the

Humphreys left Minneapolis, the new Senator heard his little girl's bedtime prayers. At the end she said, "And now, good-bye, God—we're going to Washington."

Wealth
(*see Rich, Texas*)

Max Asnas, the lox and bagel Confucius, said of wealth, "I was born poor, and I will die poor. But in between, I'd like to be rich."

With the value of the dollar today, it's just as well money doesn't grow on trees—it would cheapen the neighborhood.

He's so rich—but he doesn't like those air-conditioned cars—so he keeps a dozen Cadillacs in his refrigerator at home.

The tycoon landed on the roof of a Florida hotel with "his" and "her" helicopters. It took eleven bellhops to unload his baggage, which included sleds, skis, and six Alaskan huskies.
"I beg your pardon, your excellency," said the startled room clerk, "are you sure you landed in the right place? This is Florida. We never have snow here."
"Young man," the billionaire said matter-of-factly, "the snow is coming with the rest of my luggage in the next plane."

Wealthy? He doesn't count his money—he weighs it.

Oh, he's wealthy all right, but a three-room Rolls Royce is putting it on a bit thick—and a split level Cad?

He was so rich, his kids walked up to every Santa in town and asked, "What can I do for you?"

Weather
(*see Hot, Cold, Smog, Air Pollution*)

In Hawaii where the weather is the same all year round, how do they start conversation?

WEATHERMAN: "My corns hurt too, lady, but I still say it will be clear and sunny."

My room was so cold I had to use an ice pick to take off my clothes.

You're perfect for hot weather—you leave me cold.

Chicago is so windy—I spit in my own eye.

The temperature was 80 in Florida— 40 in the daytime and 40 at night.

She likes the cold weather. If it weren't for goose pimples she wouldn't have any figure at all.

It was so hot we had to feed the chickens cracked ice to keep them from laying hard-boiled eggs.

California is great—on a clear day when the fog lifts—you can see the smog.

I can make it rain any time I want to. All I have to do is wash my car.

Don't despair if all your dreams come out wrong. It may mean you have a future in weather forecasting.

The only thing good about rain is that you don't have to shovel it.

California weather is perfect. The last time I was there the sun came down in torrents for weeks.

469

Not that it rains a lot in California—but one day I got a ticket for going through a red light—and I was in my house at the time.

Spring is when the farmer and the golfer start their plowing together.

One of the most annoying things about the weather reports—they're not always wrong, either.

"It was so cold—I almost got married."—Shelley Winters

Weddings
(*see Brides, Marriage, Engaged, Husbands, Wives, etc.*)

"Hey, you're wearing your wedding ring on the wrong hand."
"I know—I married the wrong man."

I just found out why they rope off the aisles at a wedding—it's so the groom can't get away.

They got a 250-piece dinner set for their wedding—a box of matches.

"But," her mother cried as she watched her daughter walk down the aisle, "they have only known each other for a week."
A friend replied, "Do you know a better way to get acquainted?"

Westerns
(*see Movies, Television, Hollywood, etc.*)

I saw a Western on TV last night so adult that they didn't let Billy the Kid in the saloon because he was under twenty-one.

I saw a Western on TV last night so modern the Indians couldn't burn down the settlement because their lighters weren't working.

If Horace Greeley were alive in this TV age, he'd probably advise, "Go Western, young man . . . "

I saw a Western on TV so modern that the hero chewed filter-tipped tobacco.

I saw a Western on TV last night so old that Gabby Hayes had five o'clock shadow.

An adult Western is where a man still loves his horse, but now he's worried about it.

I don't care how modern those TV Westerns get, but:
A corner saloon that's a member of the Diner's Club?

There are so many Westerns on TV that the Indians are demanding equal time.

He used to be called "tall in the saddle" until his blisters broke.

Here's my favorite Western scene. 80,000 irritated Iroquois Indians have Shlepalong Cassiday tied to the stake—which will become their steak. They're dancing around him as he burns. He is steaming, because Indians like their food well done, and are burning him to a crisp.
Don't get excited—Shlepalong does not come to a bad end. He goes down a one-way street and comes to a dead end! You expect the villain to come to a bad end, but he dies a natural death. Shlep throws him off a 10,000 foot cliff, so death comes to him naturally.

I've seen so many Westerns on TV I think I hate cowboys more than the Indians do.

Widows
(*see Husbands, Wives, Marriage, Death, Tombstones, etc.*)

WIDOW: "I've had so much trouble collecting the money from my husband's estate—sometimes I wish he hadn't died."

I'd certainly rather be the second husband of a widow than the first.

She was sobbing her heart out when he died even though she abused him every moment of their married life. "Don't worry," her friend tried to console her, "you'll find another man some day."
"I know," she sobbed, "but what will I do tonight?"

She never gave him one day of peace. When he finally died and was laid to rest, she put on his tombstone: "AT PEACE—UNTIL WE MEET AGAIN."

Wills
(*see Death, Cemeteries, Tombstones, etc.*)

Having been of *sound mind*—I spent all my money.

An art collector spotted an ad in the paper for a Van Gogh for $250. Although he was positive it was a misprint, he rushed over to the address listed in the ad. "It's no mistake," said the lady who had placed the ad, "it's a genuine Van Gogh." The collector quickly made out a check and bought the painting. "I don't get it, lady," he questioned after the sale; "you could get at least 100 times as much for this picture." "Well," explained the woman, "my husband died two weeks ago and stipulated in his will that the picture was to be sold and the money given to his secretary. And I," she added triumphantly, "am the executrix of his will!"

The old man was dictating his will. "To my son," he said, "I leave one hundred thousand. To my daughter, one hundred thousand. To my grandson, ten thousand."
The lawyer interrupted. "But sir, you only have three thousand dollars."
The old man growled, "Let them go out and work for a living like I did."

I leave to my beloved nephew—all the money he owes me.

In his will he left a loudspeaker to the church—in memory of his wife.

"They say he married her because her uncle left her a lot of money."
"That's not true. He would have married her no matter who left her the money."

And to my nephew who always kept telling me that health is more important than all the money in the world I leave the entire contents of my second-floor closet—my sun lamp.

He didn't leave any money in his will—he was separated from it.

When she married the billionaire forty-five years older than herself, all her friends sent "Get Will" cards.

Many a girl is looking for a man with a strong will—made out to her.

"Did your grandfather remember you when he made his will?"
"He sure did—he left me out."

"To my nephew Charlie, who always said I'd never remember him in my will—hello, Charlie."

471

Wisdom
(*see Sayings, Proverbs, Quotations*)

Every man should have a wife—preferably his own.

People who throw kisses are lazy.

People who live in glass houses—should use their neighbor's bathroom.

He who marries for money—earns it.

The best way to hold a man—is in your arms.

A good girl is good—but a bad girl is better.

An old maid is a lemon that has never been squeezed.

A dollar goes very fast nowadays—but not very far.

Pity the man who marries for love and then finds his wife has no money.

Nothing holds liquor like a bottle.

The bigger a man's head gets—the easier to fill his shoes.

Kissing your own wife is like scratching a place that doesn't itch.

Never pet a polar bear until he's a rug.

A bird in the hand is worthless when you want to blow your nose.

Nothing improves your driving like having a police car follow you.

Never hit a man when he's down—he might get up and hit you.

Never slap a man in the face when he's chewing tobacco.

It's better to give than receive—especially a punch in the mouth.

Wives
(*see Husbands, Marriage, Divorce, etc.*)

How can I tell my wife her hair looks like a mop? She doesn't know what a mop is.

My wife and I have a joint account—I deposit and she draws out.

My wife has been affected by the latest fads. Every time I ask her to do something she says, "Do it yourself!"

Research has told us that 50 per cent of all the couples in the world today are wives, and the other 50 per cent says that they are glad to live in a free country where a man can still do as his wife pleases!

The average woman worries about the future until she gets a husband. The average man never worries about it until he gets a wife. Don't misunderstand, marriage is a wonderful institution, my wife tells me . . . and anyway, this would be a pretty scarce world without women.

When "the boys" get together, the target is always "the little woman." "My wife leads a double life," complained one sufferer, "hers and mine." Another husband moaned, "One way to get along with your wife is to let her think she has her own way and then let her have it." "When my wife goes shopping," wailed another, "she comes home with everything but money."

Sad Sam was complaining that his wife was spending too much money in the department stores. "I may as well shop," she reasoned. "You'll only throw your money away on the government anyhow."

A certain local character is so henpecked, he'd need his wife's permission to kill himself.

"I can't work," complained the husband. "My wife broke a leg."
"What's that got to do with you?"
"It was my leg she broke."

"We had a child last week and was I disappointed!"
"Why? What'd you want, a boy or a girl?"
"Neither. I wanted a divorce."

"My wife dresses to kill and cooks the same way," said one miserable man. "How could anybody louse up cornflakes?"
"Well," consoled his friend, "she must have some redeeming features."
"Yeah, she does my washing and ironing," he admitted.
"What's bad about that?"
"Yeah, but what a price to pay for laundry."

He was a great linguist. He mastered every tongue—but his wife's!

He didn't care how much she spent on clothes, because, as he put it, "She takes excellent care of her wardrobe." In fact, to press his point he explained, "The other day I came home and found a guy in the closet watching them."

There's nothing a wife loves more than a double chin—on her husband's old girl friend.

My wife will put on almost anything for dinner except an apron.

Whoever called women the fair sex —didn't know about justice.

"Bertha," bellowed Herman on his office phone, "I'm bringing my assistant home to dinner."
"What?" screamed Bertha. "You got a nerve. You know the maid left without notice, both kids are sick, the house is a wreck, I have a bad cold and the butcher won't let us have any more meat until you pay the bill. And you want to bring home that guy to dinner? Drop dead!"
"Nevertheless, I'm bringing him home to dinner," Herman announced firmly. "That dumbbell is thinking seriously of getting married and I just want him to see for himself."

Cheating wife gets up in the morning and says: "I feel like a new man."

Henny Youngman says his wife is so neat, that if he gets up at four in the morning for a glass of water—when he gets back, the bed is made.

"The way to fight a woman is with your hat—grab it and run."—John Barrymore

I finally discovered the perfect way to get rid of dishpan hands—I let my husband do the dishes.

He acquired a large vocabulary—he married it.

She keeps her husband—in debt.

For every man there's a woman— and he's lucky if his wife doesn't know about her.

One sure way for a woman to find out the kind of husband she doesn't want—is to marry him.

"There is nothing in the world like the devotion of a married woman— something no married man knows anything about."—Oscar Wilde

473

She didn't want to marry him for his money—but it was the only way she could get it.

My wife meets me halfway on everything. It's my home—she lives in it. It's my car—she drives it. It's my money—she spends it. Now she's waiting for me to get a nervous breakdown —so she can go to Miami.

He was so distrustful of his wife, that when she presented him with twins, he insisted only *one* bore any resemblance to him.

"My wife can talk for hours on any subject."
"My wife don't need a subject."

FRIEND: "Was that your wife who let me in?"
HOST: "Do you think I'd hire a maid that ugly?"

You can't win. My first wife could cook but wouldn't. My second wife can't cook but does.

HUSBAND: "A neighbor just told me that the milkman who delivers here makes love to every woman in this building but one."
WIFE: "Yeah, it's that snooty Mrs. Lerner on the third floor."

She leads a double life—hers and his.

She's brought more bills into the house than any Congressman.

The best way to keep your wife in the kitchen—is to put a phone there.

HUSBAND: "That couple across the street certainly are in love. Every morning Mr. Green kisses Mrs. Green on the steps of their house."
WIFE: "Why don't you ever do that?"
HUSBAND: "How can I? I don't even know her."

The husband asked his wife angrily, "Another new hat! Where will I get the money to pay for it?" She answered, "Whatever my faults, dear, I'm not inquisitive."

There's buried treasure in this country. If you don't think so, listen to some women talk about their first husbands.

"My wife has a terrible habit—I can't break her of it—she stays up every night until two or three in the morning."
"What the hell is she doing up that late?"
"Waiting for me to come home."

She stuck with him through all the troubles he never would have gotten in —if he didn't marry her in the first place.

Second wives always work out better. Like it says in the ads, when you're number two—you try harder.

They call our language the mother tongue because father seldom gets a chance to use it.

WIFE: "My husband was so disappointed when I gave birth to girls. He was hoping for a boy to help him with the housework."

"How's your wife?"
"Compared to who?"

BUTCHER: "Mr. Levy, your wife sent you out on a stormy night like this for fifty cents' worth of chopped meat?"
LEVY: "Who then? My mother?"

Wolves
(see Playboys, Playgirls, etc.)

The poor wolf didn't have an etching to his name—so he brought her up to see the handwriting on the wall.

The wolf at the bar was trying to make time with a gorgeous creature whose dress was bursting at the seams, which is as good a place as any. "Oh," said the babe, who had been around more than a carousel, "I bet your wife doesn't understand you." "She understands me all right," said the gent, "it's just that she's fat and ugly."

A wolf is always in there pinching.

He's just what the doctor ordered—a pill.

He's a wow—a worn out wolf.

"Where have you been all my life?" the old wolf said to the young girl as he leered.
"Well," she squelched, "for the first half of it—I wasn't born."

I'll never be able to figure out the female of the species. She jumps on a chair if she sees the tiniest mouse—but she drives anywhere with the biggest wolf.

He asked the little redhead to come to his house because he promised his wife he wouldn't go out with other women while she was gone.

One wolf to another: "Who was that girl I saw you outwit last night?"

All his life he worked like a dog to keep the wolf from the door. Then his daughter grew up—and brought him right into the living room.

I know a former wolf who is reforming and going into charity work. He's starting by helping the chorus girls home!

He stopped chasing girls ever since he lost his hair. "But now he's thinking of getting a toupee—will that start him wolfing again?" the wife asked.
"What are you worrying about? You can change the top of the convertible—but if the engine is lousy—nothing will help."

There is some co-operation between wild creatures—the stork and the wolf usually work the same neighborhood.

NOVICE: "What's the first thing you notice about a girl?"
WOLF: "That depends on which direction she's facing."

Elderly wolf: a fellow who's not going to lust much longer.

"My husband could never be a wolf. He could never chase after young girls. He's too decent, too fine, too old."

A new approach is the style of the aging wolf. He sent a note to the pretty young redhead sitting in the restaurant by herself, "Would you mind joining my expense account?"

He's got a good head on his shoulders—but it's a different one every night.

Women
(see Girls, Wives, Mothers, Playgirls, etc.)

Two women were talking and one said to the other, "Did I tell you about Mildred?"
"What happened?"
"You know Mildred got mixed up with what's-his-name and she and what-do-you-call-him got stuck with you-know-who. I told you the story before, didn't I?"
"Yes, but this is the first time I've heard all the details."

One woman said to the other, "I've already told you more about it than I actually know myself."

A woman could never be President. A candidate must be thirty-five or over —and where are you going to find a woman who will admit she's over thirty-five?

Never underestimate a woman—unless you are talking about her weight or her age.

She's so sensitive about her age—her Social Security number is registered with a Swiss bank.

She's a pretty shrewd woman. She's not one of these gullible women who believe everything they hear. But that doesn't stop her from repeating it.

A woman's brain is divided in two parts—dollars and cents.

Diamonds are tranquilizers for women.

The quickest way to change a woman's viewpoint is to agree with her.

Two women were talking. "That Ruth is always knocking her husband. I never saw anything like it in my entire life. She's always complaining about her better half. Look at my husband, he's such a louse he should drop dead, but do I ever say anything to anybody?"

Sir Winston Churchill was once asked about the notion that in the 21st Century women will rule the world. He said—"They still will."

WOMAN BUYING FERTILIZER: "Is that the only scent it comes in?"

Revenge is when a woman gets even with a man for what she's done to him.

Women are fools to marry—but what else can men marry?

Women's styles may change—but their designs remain the same.

Women have a tough life. They have to clean, cook and sew. That's hard to do without getting out of bed.

I don't get the bit about women always yelling about equal rights—it would be a reduction for them.

There's no man so bad—that a woman can't make him worse.

"American women expect to find in their husbands a perfection that English women only hope to find in their butlers!"—Somerset Maugham

Men who try to understand women usually succeed only in marrying them.

Nobody wants to hear your troubles —unless a woman is involved.

The hardest job of a girl's life is to prove to a man that his intentions are honorable.

A well-adjusted woman is one who not only knows now what she wants for her birthday, but what she's going to exchange it for.

Work
(see Business, Bosses, Employment, Executives)

BOSS: "I wish you wouldn't whistle while you work."
CLERK: "I'm not working—I'm just whistling, boss."

"Guess how much I made this year?" the braggart was showing off.
"Half."

476

BOSS: "You should have been here at 8 o'clock."
STENO: "Why, what happened?"

He's one of the big guns of the industry—he's been fired six times.

My secretary quit—she caught me kissing my wife.

He's an independent salesman—he takes orders from no one.

There's a guy who joined five unions —so he's always on strike.

BOSS: "We are giving you a raise because we want your last week to be a happy one."

Works as a meatpacker—he sells girdles.

He takes a taxi to work every day— he's a taxi-driver.

He's got an unusual job—goes door to door selling falsies—sort of a Fuller Bust Man.

Remember the song, "Heaven Protects the Working Girl"? Now it takes a union, unemployment insurance, health insurance, Medicare, pensions, vacations, coffee breaks and the National Labor Relations Act.

Hard work is the soundest investment. It provides a neat security for your wife's next husband.

I'm so underpaid—I can't cash my own check.

He's the Head Adjuster—drop in any time and he'll adjust your head.

Workers are still willing to do an honest day's work—only they want a week's pay for it.

He puts in a full day's work—in a week.

Writers
(*see Books, Book Titles, Records, etc.*)

She explained why she became a writer. "It's the only respectable profession where a woman can do her work in bed."

"It took me twenty years to realize I have no talent for writing."
"You mean you're quitting?"
"How could I? I'm too famous now."

I once saw an ad in some village paper offering to show me how to make a fortune as a writer. It was a picture of a man who looked like a Presbyterian minister and he was pointing right at me saying, "How do you know you can't write?" So I sent him all my stories, anecdotes, gags, and manuscripts. Three months later I received a reply, "Now you know you can't write."

He comes from a family of writers: his sister writes poems nobody will recite, his brother writes songs nobody will sing, and he writes checks nobody will cash.

If you want to write something that will live forever—sign a mortgage.

"When I first started in show business I went to a writer for material. What do you think he wrote me for $300? A receipt!"

I wrote for magazines. I wrote something accepted by a magazine—a check for a year's subscription.

Ed Wynn

Mr. Wynn played one of his great comedy scenes as a hunter going out

477

to stalk a moose. Just before he leaves, he sees himself in the mirror, "Thank God I'm out of season."

Ed introduced one of the chorus girls at a night club he worked: "Miss Soft Drink—she'll go out with anybody from 7-Up."

A TV salesman tried to sell a set to Mr. Wynn. He really put it on: "Imagine, you can sit in your hotel room, press a button on your TV set and a gorgeous, sexy girl is suddenly in front of you."
"Big deal—in the hotels I stay in I get the same thing without television."

Ed wrote this joke in 1910 and it's still making the rounds. A young man walked into a saloon and was reprimanded by a man standing next to him. "Young man, you shouldn't drink, it's very bad for you." He flexed his muscles and continued, "Look at me. I'm 45 years old—never drank—never smoked—never chewed in my whole life."
The young man answered, "Sir—my great-grandfather started drinking moonshine when he was 10. He smoked at 11, chewed tobacco at 12. At 22 he was drinking 3 quarts of rum a day and he died at 103. We dug him up the other day. And I'll be darned, sir, if he didn't look better than you do right now."

Ed Wynn once said there was only one difference between himself and Pat Boone. "We're both extremely popular," he explained. "But when my fans swoon it takes them longer to get up."

Xmas
(*see Gifts, Holidays, Children*)

I'll spend a typical American Christmas: My tree comes from Canada. The ornaments come from Italy. The lights from Japan. The idea comes from Bethlehem.

A young soldier was depressed. In the spirit of the holidays I asked him, "Wasn't Santa Claus good to you?" "Good to me?" he said sadly. "Twenty years ago I asked Santa Claus for a soldier suit—and now I get it!"

I love to shop at Gimbel's around Christmas because everybody is so polite and helpful. One woman broke her leg while shopping and they gift-wrapped it.

The burglars' and pickpockets' association of Madison Avenue have asked me to announce that there are just thirty-six more shoplifting days till Christmas.

You can tell that Christmas is approaching. Macy's has just captured Gimbel's first comparison shopper. And Gimbel's retaliated by capturing a Macy's Santa Claus. A prisoner exchange is being worked out now.

Christmas is the time of the year to get the kids something for the old man to play with.

I'm writing to Santa Claus early this Christmas to tell him what I want—how do you spell Brigitte Bardot?

I'm getting my girl a fountain pen for Christmas as a surprise, and wotta surprise it's gonna be—she expects a Cadillac.

My uncle did his Christmas shopping early and what do you think he got? Thirty days!

"What shall we get dad for Christmas?"

"I hear he's buying us a car—let's get him a chauffeur's outfit."

On Christmas we used to stand my uncle in the window because no tree in the neighborhood was lit up as much as he was.

The department stores are so crowded yuletide that one girl I know walked in and they threw a lampshade on her head, a bulb in her mouth, and I bought her for $1.98.

Just as the store was closing for Christmas Eve, a salesman walked over to me and said, "All right, buddy, if you wanna buy something you'd better do it now and take advantage of our special Christmas price, because at 6 P.M. we close the doors and start marking the stuff down."

We were so poor when I was a kid that instead of stockings, we hung up empty salami casings.

Christmas is the time of the year when the wife gives the husband things he can't afford.

Christmas: when you buy this year's presents with next year's money.

He didn't know what to give a wife who had everything—so he decided to get her a husband who could pay for it.

I got a Christmas card from my garage man about three weeks before the holidays. I didn't get around to giving him his annual yule gift when I got another card the day before Christmas: "Seasons greetings from the man in your garage—second notice."

The old gentleman was cautioning the little girl, "Never hesitate about giving presents on Christmas. Don't you know that for every Christmas present you give away, two will come back?"

"I'll say," said the kid. "Last Christmas my father gave my sister away in marriage and this Christmas she and her husband came back."

When my wife says she's dreaming of a white Christmas she means ermine or white mink.

I always give my wife her Christmas presents before the 15th of December. That way she can exchange them in time for Christmas.

X Ray
(see Hospitals, Doctors, Nurses, etc.)

She married an X-ray specialist but I still don't see what he sees in her.

This guy is so skinny, the doctor looked at his X ray and the report came back, "No man."

"How much are you going to charge me for the operation?"
"Five hundred."
"Listen, maybe for fifty dollars you could touch up my X rays."

A woman used to go to the doctor to see if she could have children—now she goes to the landlord.

Henny Youngman

A drunk walked up to a parking meter and put in a dime. The dial went to 60. He said, "How do you like that —I weigh an hour."

A rich guy in Dallas bought his kid a chemistry outfit—Du Pont.

Want to drive somebody crazy? Send him a wire saying, "IGNORE FIRST WIRE."

479

You know what's embarrassing? When you look through a keyhole and see another eye.

A man went to Las Vegas with a seven thousand dollar Cadillac and came home in a seventy-five thousand dollar bus.

Valentine's Day she gave me the usual gift—she ate my heart out.

Some people play a horse to win, some to place. I should have bet this horse to live.

I never had a penny to my name—so I changed my name.

I just solved the parking problem—I bought a parked car.

My wife puts so much mud on her face before going to bed at night I say, "Good night, swamp."

I bought her a mink outfit—a rifle and a trap.

A woman called up the Police Department and said, "I have a sex maniac in my apartment. Pick him up in the morning."

I saved a girl from being attacked last night—I controlled myself.

Two guys were talking. One said, "Hey, got a match?"
The other guy said, "No, but I got a lighter."
The first guy said, "How can I pick my teeth with a lighter?"

My wife went to the beauty parlor. Every woman who comes out of a beauty parlor looks like Jacqueline Kennedy. Not my wife—she looks like Lyndon B. Johnson.

A guy fell off a ten story building and landed on the sidewalk. A big crowd gathered around him and a cop came over to the guy and said, "What happened?"
The guy said, "I don't know—I just got here."

A guy called up the drugstore and said: "Do you have Prince Albert in a can?"
The clerk said, "Yeah."
The guy said, "Well let him out—he's suffocating."

Youth
(*see Kids, Juvenile Delinquents, Children, Teenagers*)

The best way for a girl to keep her youth is not to introduce him to anyone.

I think that every woman should hold on to her youth. But not while he's driving.

You know a boy is growing up when he stops wanting to go out with girls and wants to stay home with them.

I wasn't exactly a bad boy—but when I was six my parents left home.

"Now, Junior, be a good boy and say *ahhh* so the doctor can get his finger out of your mouth."

SON: "I don't get the best marks in school, dad. Do you get the best salary at your office?"

DAD: "Junior, mother is not going to give you any more martinis if all you do is eat the olives."

"Mamma, that bill collector is here again. Do you have the money or do you want me to go out and play for a while?"

480

And what are you going to be—if your parents let you grow up?

Children have become so expensive that only the poor can afford them.

"Get pop to tell you about the birds and the bees—it's a riot."

Today children of six know all the questions and at sixteen they know all the answers.

Zoo
(*see Animal Stories, Kids, etc.*)

A father took his son to the zoo and pointed out the lions to him, and said, "Son, there is the most ferocious of all animals. If he should ever get out of that cage, he would tear me to pieces." The kid said, "Papa, if he should, what number bus should I take to get home?"

She's so dumb she went to the zoo to see what a Christmas Seal looks like.

She's always attracted to the zoo because she heard that all men are beasts and she just loves animals.

The new lion in the zoo was fed a few bananas, while the old lion in the adjoining cage was fed big chunks of red meat. The new lion finally asked the older lion, "How come I only get bananas while you get steak?" "This zoo," explained the old lion, "works on a low budget and they've got you registered as a monkey."

An absent-minded professor was conducting a class in zoology and addressing the students. He said, "Now students, this morning we will take this frog apart and see what makes him croak." And he took a paper bag out of his pocket, then emptied the contents on his desk. Out rolled a ham sandwich. He scratched his head and said, "Mmm, now that's funny. I distinctly remember eating my lunch!"

Broadway chorus girl is like a zoo: she comes in meek as a lamb—meets a wolf—gets sly as a fox—and winds up with a mink.

A zebra escaped from the circus and ran into a pasture of a nearby farm. He approached a bull and asked, "Are you a strong bull?"
The bull replied, "Take off those silly pajamas and I'll show you!"

Jerry Lewis tells it on himself: "When I was a kid I said to my father one afternoon, 'Daddy, will you take me to the zoo?"
" 'If the zoo wants you,' he answered, 'let them come and get you.' "

A

A.A., 68, 386
Abbott and Costello, 12, 94
ability, 227
absent-mindedness, 191, 231, 361, 378, 481
Academy Awards, 45, 57, 62, 80
accidents, 41, 157, 191-192, 264, 343, 354, 376, 381, 387, 414, 428, 448, 449, 460, 465, 466, 480
accordion, 372, 454
actors, 58, 66, 67, 68, 70, 72, 84, 91, 192-194, 198, 199, 202, 258, 261, 356, 426, 427, 451
Actor's Studio, 55
Adam and Eve, 40, 45, 107, 220, 232, 308, 404
Adams, Cindy, 59, 165, 177, 224, 301
Adams, Joey, 21, 56, 58, 59, 76, 83, 84, 94-97, 98, 99, 100, 101, 176, 244
Adler, Bill, 182
ad libs, 4, 5, 6, 9
adultery, 250, 404, 419
advertising, 80, 165, 194-195, 202, 215, 225, 340, 378, 408, 428, 447, 452, 462, 467, 471, 474, 477
advice, 195, 212, 294, 295, 383, 452, 465
Aesop, 395
affairs, 196, 208, 250, 256, 385-386
Afghanistan, 148, 300, 302, 326
Africa, 148, 196, 204, 420
age, 20, 25, 40, 68, 149, 170, 196-199, 222, 406, 476
agent, 192, 198-199, 387, 426, 466
AGVA, 54
AGVA Youth Fund, 55
air conditioning, 51, 199, 225, 297, 316, 422, 452, 469
Air Force, 199-200
airplanes, 9, 15, 32, 35, 38, 74, 79, 167, 211, 289, 295, 315, 327, 341, 426-427, 445, 455, 457
air pollution, 201
air raid, 165
Alaska, 43, 44, 201, 242, 374
Alda, Robert, 56, 183, 427
Aleichem, Sholem, 406
Alexander, Nicholas Marie, 112
alimony, 201-202, 254, 259, 406
Allen, Fred, 3, 5, 6, 27, 28, 73, 94, 106, 181, 202-203, 218, 342, 406, 466
Allen, Gracie, 94
Allen, Kelcey, 66
Allen, Marty, 23, 55, 56
Allen, Steve, 3, 59, 346
Allen, Woody, 203, 275

alligators, 37, 71, 107, 216, 309, 387, 406, 445
amateur, 347, 440
ambassador, 254
Amos and Andy, 94, 406
Amsterdam, Gregory, 457
Amsterdam, Kathy, 317
Amsterdam, Kay, 176, 317, 457
Amsterdam, Morey, 54, 58, 65, 77, 78, 106, 176, 178, 203, 204, 307, 317, 329, 330, 405, 457
analysis, 14, 204, 293, 450, 459
anemic, 202
angel, 304
animals, 204, 296, 391, 481
Animals, the (Eric Burdon), 184
anniversary, 8, 122, 206, 227, 287, 358, 423
Anti-Defamation League, 73
antiques, 206, 254, 340, 430
Antoine, Tex, 178
apartment, 206, 207, 251, 288, 331, 340, 343, 368, 431, 445-446, 450, 467, 479
applause, 70, 87, 89, 216, 275-276, 336, 414, 466
Arabs, 165, 166, 278, 328
Arlen, Richard, 315
Armstrong, Louis, 171, 451
Army, 207, 208, 267-268, 312, 328, 443, 467
art, 20, 208, 209, 471
artist, 208, 209, 257
Asia, 149, 288
Asnas, Max, 65, 68, 409, 412, 469
assassins, 192
Astor, Lady, 239
astronauts, 130, 171, 172, 210, 232
atheist, 254
atomic energy, 210-211, 322
Attlee, Clement, 239
auction, 211, 234
Australia, 132, 149, 278-279, 463
Austria, 151
autographs, 176-185, 426, 451
automation, 211, 247
automobiles, 31, 211-212, 258, 259, 267, 271-272, 286, 318, 324, 326, 333, 342, 353, 356, 367, 374, 391, 413, 416, 421, 449, 455, 456, 464, 465, 467, 469
Autry, Gene, 57, 63, 346
Avon, 326

B

baby (babies), 104, 212, 236, 291, 295, 307, 310, 321, 338, 373, 377, 387, 390, 392, 393, 422, 429, 439

I

Mc

M

N

Q

R

U

V